THE COLLECTED WORKS
OF W. B. YEATS

VOLUME IX

THE COLLECTED WORKS OF W. B. YEATS

Richard J. Finneran and George Mills Harper, General Editors

VOLUME I THE POEMS
ed. Richard J. Finneran

VOLUME II THE PLAYS
ed. David R. Clark and Rosalind E. Clark

VOLUME III AUTOBIOGRAPHIES
ed. William H. O'Donnell and Douglas Archibald

VOLUME IV EARLY ESSAYS
ed. Warwick Gould and Dierdre Toomey

VOLUME V LATER ESSAYS
ed. William H. O'Donnell

VOLUME VI PREFACES AND INTRODUCTIONS
ed. William H. O'Donnell

VOLUME VII LETTERS TO THE NEW ISLAND
ed. George Bornstein and Hugh Witemeyer

VOLUME VIII THE IRISH DRAMATIC MOVEMENT
ed. Mary FitzGerald and Richard J. Finneran

VOLUME IX EARLY ARTICLES AND REVIEWS
ed. John P. Frayne and Madeleine Marchaterre

VOLUME X LATER ARTICLES AND REVIEWS
ed. Colton Johnson

VOLUME XI MYTHOLOGIES
ed. Warwick Gould and Dierdre Toomey

VOLUME XII JOHN SHERMAN AND DHOYA
ed. Richard J. Finneran

VOLUME XIII A VISION (1925)
ed. Margaret Mills Harper and Catherine Paul

VOLUME XIV A VISION (1937)
ed. Margaret Mills Harper and Catherine Paul

W. B. YEATS

Early Articles and Reviews

UNCOLLECTED ARTICLES AND REVIEWS WRITTEN BETWEEN 1886 AND 1900

EDITED BY

John P. Frayne and Madeleine Marchaterre

Scribner

NEW YORK   LONDON   TORONTO   SYDNEY

SCRIBNER
1230 Avenue of the Americas
New York, NY 10020

SCRIBNER and design are trademarks of Macmillan Library Reference USA, Inc.,
used under license by Simon & Schuster, the publisher of this work.

For information about special discounts for bulk purchases,
please contact Simon & Schuster Special Sales:
1-800-456-6798 or business@simonandschuster.com

Text set in Sabon

Manufactured in the United States of America

1   3   5   7   9   10   8   6   4   2

Library of Congress Cataloging-in-Publication Data
Yeats, W. B. (William Butler), 1865–1939.
Early articles and reviews : uncollected articles and reviews
written between 1886 and 1900 / W. B. Yeats ;
edited by John P. Frayne and Madeleine Marchaterre.
p. cm.—(The collected works of W. B. Yeats ; v. 9)
Includes bibliographical references (p.) and index.
I. Frayne, John P. II. Marchaterre, Madeleine. III. Title.
PR5900.A2 F56 1989 vol. 9
[PR5902]
824'.8—dc22   2003063312

ISBN 0-684-80730-0

CONTENTS

Articles and Reviews by W. B. Yeats

Copy Texts, Emendations, and Notes

PREFACE AND
ACKNOWLEDGMENTS

This volume collects those articles and reviews which Yeats did not publish in book form, nor were they collected and published by Mrs. Yeats after Yeats's death. The chronological scope of this volume goes from 1886, the year of the appearance of Yeats's first prose pieces, to the end of 1899. Articles which appeared after 1899 are collected in the companion volume, *Later Articles and Reviews*, edited by Colton Johnson.

Most of the material in this volume was published in *Uncollected Prose*, vol. 1 (1971), and *Uncollected Prose*, vol. 2 (1975). Added to the pieces already in print are early articles written for *The Gael* as well as more recently identified reviews such as those for G. E. Leland's *Gypsy Sorcery* and George Sigerson's anthology *Bards of the Gael and Gall*.

Pruned from *UP1* and *UP2* were a number of pieces which went into other, more appropriate, volumes of *The Collected Works of W. B. Yeats*. Two pieces for *The Providence Sunday Journal* went into *Letters to the New Island*, a few short stories will appear in *The Celtic Twilight* and *The Secret Rose*, letters to newspapers went into *The Collected Letters*, and some accounts of lectures await their fate.

Yeats expressed great fascination, even enthusiasm when Horace Reynolds collected his American newspaper pieces for publication in 1934. In a letter to Reynolds on 24 December 1932, Yeats expressed some reservations about his early propaganda for the Irish Literary Movement. However, there is evidence that Yeats wished to collect some prose pieces into more permanent form. "Irish Rakes and Duelists" was to be part of a book on the Irish past in the Adventurers series. His four articles on Irish National Literature for *The Bookman* were intended to become a pamphlet, but the plan came to nothing. His six articles on Irish folklore (four of which are in this volume, the last two in *Later Articles and Reviews*) were intended to be part of a collaboration with Lady Gregory which just did not work out. Lady Gregory did publish two volumes, *Visions and Beliefs in the West of Ireland*, based on the material which she had collected with Yeats, and Yeats contributed two essays and notes to that volume.

In these articles and reviews, we can trace the development of some of Yeats's leading ideas on Irish nationalism and literature, on the occult, on folklore, and also on the place where Yeats saw himself and his contemporaries in the evolution of English and European literature as well as in the revival of Irish literature. Yeats's judgments sometimes bear the marks of youthful rashness and daring. From these qualities comes a certain charm which might have been softened or toned down by revisions had Yeats edited his work later in life.

In his reviews, we have primary evidence of Yeats's interaction with his Irish and English contemporaries: Katharine Tynan, AE, Douglas Hyde, John Todhunter, as well as Oscar Wilde, Arthur Symons, Lionel Johnson, and Ernest Rhys. To the daily or weekly reviewer does not fall the privilege of the leisurely appraisal of the great literature of the age. He or she must shoot from the hip at whatever targets are offered. Of some of Yeats's reviews it could be said that what ideas the book inspired in Yeats are of greatly more importance than the original volumes under review.

The immediate inspiration for these pieces was financial, and there is ample evidence in Yeats's letters to show how much he needed the money that magazines could pay. Yet at the same time Yeats seemed to have thoroughly enjoyed himself. He loved sounding boards for his idées fixes, and anything having to do with Ireland, Irish literature, or William Blake brought out the evangelist in him. To say that this was hack work obscures the whole truth. To be sure, there were deadlines, odd assignments, restrictions in length and perhaps treatment, but Yeats seemed to welcome occasions which could induce inspiration, rather than the opposite.

The conventional wisdom is that financial help from Lady Gregory rescued Yeats from the drudgery of journalism. If the purpose of this rescue was to return Yeats's energies to poetry, the help had a somewhat ironic effect. With Lady Gregory's collaboration, Yeats's energies went more and more into the Abbey Theatre, an activity (among others) of which Yeats spoke with exasperation, "All things can tempt me from this craft of verse."

One by-product of these occasional articles and reviews was Yeats's relationships with his editors. John Kelly has written eloquently of Yeats's dealings with the short-lived *Gael*. W. E. Henley, and *The Scots Observer*, also had an important role in shaping Yeats's career. It was Yeats's relationship with *The Bookman*, however, which was to be the most fruitful in the long run. Of the ninety-eight pieces in this collection, forty-three were written for *The Bookman*; this line of reviews began with Yeats's review of Michael Field's *Sight and Song* in July 1892 and ended with his review of Lady Gregory's collection *Poets and Dreamers* in *The Bookman* of May 1903.

Preparing a new edition of *UP1* and part of *UP2* published in the

1970s had its difficulties and opportunities. Yeats scholarship had massively moved on. As a result, such efforts as *The Collected Letters,* edited by John Kelly and others, offer treasure troves of information about Yeats and his contemporaries. At the same time, the guidelines for the Collected Edition series have called for a wider range of footnoted information, the listing of emendations, and a consistency in editorial format. We have been able to hunt down many more of Yeats's literary references, but there remains game to be hunted. We have tried systematically to compare Yeats's copious quotations of the poetry he was reviewing with the edition under criticism. Yeats's or his editors' verbal changes were frequent, the punctuational changes almost automatic.

We have tried to regularize the spelling of names, particularly Irish ones. As an example, the spelling of "Cuchulain" is our standard, and the variety of alternate spellings in the original printings may be found in the list of emendations. Regularization has its limits. If Standish O'Grady entitled his book *The Coming of Cuculain,* then it is left such in the text and in references to it.

Some of the pieces collected here were not signed by Yeats. In the headnotes for such we have discussed the arguments for Yeats's authorship to be found in his letters, also from internal evidence, and from the attributions of Alan Wade, Yeats's bibliographer.

The copy texts used were from the newspapers or magazines themselves. Two exceptions to this rule are number 91, "John Eglinton and Spiritual Art," and number 98, "The Literary Movement in Ireland." Yeats later revised these articles when they were published in book form, and we have printed the revised versions. While there are few manuscript versions of these pieces, one exception is MS 122148 in the National Library of Ireland, which contains clippings of some reviews, corrected in Yeats's hand. We have noted instances when we have incorporated Yeats's changes into the text.

The following typographical and format conventions have been adopted for Yeats's texts, in accord with the general policy for the prose volumes of *The Collected Works of W. B. Yeats.*

1. The presentation of headings is standardized. In this volume, the main headings are set in full capitals (capitals and small capitals for subtitles). Section numbers are in roman capitals. All headings are centered and have no concluding full point.
2. The opening line of each new paragraph is indented, except following a displayed heading or section break.
3. All sentences open with a capital letter followed by lowercase letters.

4. A colon that introduces a quotation does not have a dash following the colon.

5. Quotations that are set off from the text and indented have not been placed within quotation marks.

6. Titles of stories, essays, and poems have been placed within quotation marks; titles of books, plays, long poems, periodicals, operas, paintings, statues, and drawings have been set in italics.

7. Abbreviations such as "i.e." have been set in roman type.

8. A dash, regardless of its length in the copy text, has been set as an em dash when used as punctuation. When a dash indicates an omission, as in "Miss S——," a two-em rule is used.

9. Ampersands have been expanded to "and."

10. When present, the author's signature is indented from the left margin, set in upper- and lowercase letters, and ends without punctuation (except where the signature appears as initials followed by points).

11. When present, the place and date are indented from the left margin, set in italics in upper- and lowercase letters, and end without punctuation.

12. British punctuation conventions are observed in the Yeats text, but American conventions are used in the preface, headnotes, and notes.

First and foremost, the editors would like to thank the University of Illinois Department of English for its assistance in helping to prepare this edition. Also, the University of Illinois Library and its staff have been of incalculable help over many years. Lately, Kathleen Kluegel has been most helpful, and in recent years William Brockman has offered invaluable assistance, especially in acquiring and introducing us to the Chadwyck-Healy CD-ROM edition of Yeats's works. Our gratitude also goes to Richard J. Finneran for his unstinting help and encouragement over this long haul. Our fellow editors, especially George Mills Harper and William H. O'Donnell, have given helpful advice in answering lists of queries about untraced quotations and other problems. During a research trip to the British Library during 1989, Warwick Gould gave invaluable assistance in tracing down arcane references in the collections there, even to rare manuscript sources. Also, the staff at the National Library of Ireland was enormously helpful in guiding us to Irish sources unique to that collection.

John Kelly was most generous in allowing us to use the text and his notes for Yeats's articles for the *Gael* newspaper as well as his text and notes for the review "Gypsy Sorcery and Fortune Telling." Also, Deirdre Toomey kindly allowed us to use the text and notes from her reprinting in *Yeats Annual 5*, 1987, of Yeats's review of Sigerson's *Bards of the Gael and Gall*. We also thank Colton Johnson for the use of notes that he contributed to *Uncollected Prose by W. B. Yeats*, vol. 2, 1976, for the articles and reviews of the years 1897–99.

We would like to thank Michael Yeats for encouraging the preparation of this edition. Anne Yeats in 1989 was very hospitable in allowing John Frayne to examine Yeats's private collection of books, a privilege that resulted in solving a number of untraced allusions.

At an earlier stage of research, much valuable work was done by Edward Jacobs, whose efforts as a graduate assistant were financially supported by the Research Board of the University of Illinois. At a later stage of preparation, Madeleine Marchaterre joined the task of completing the necessary revisions and preparing the manuscript for publication.

Among our English Department colleagues, James Hurt has been most helpful in sharing his extensive knowledge of Irish literature, as well as Julia Saville, Charles Wright, Leon Waldoff, Brian Ó Broin, and August Gering. To Klaus Peter Jochum of the University of Bamberg we owe thanks for the help and advice gained from his years of indefatigable work on the bibliography of the criticism of the works of Yeats. And our special thanks go to Roger Boulter for his help at the National Library of Ireland.

Lastly, our thanks go to our students, whose enthusiasm for Yeats's poetry has helped to stoke our enthusiasm for Yeats's work as a whole, and to our families, who afforded patient support as one more source was tracked down, as one more footnote was revised.

THE EDITORS

ABBREVIATIONS

Au   *Autobiographies.* Edited by William O'Donnell and Douglas N. Archibald. New York: Scribner, 1999.

*BIV*1, 2   *A Book of Irish Verse.* London: Methuen, 1895; 1900 and later editions.

CL1   *The Collected Letters of W. B. Yeats: Volume One, 1865–1895.* Edited by John Kelly and Eric Domville. Oxford: Clarendon Press, 1986.

CL2   *The Collected Letters of W. B. Yeats: Volume Two, 1896–1900.* Edited by Warwick Gould, John Kelly, and Deirdre Toomey. Oxford: Clarendon Press, 1997.

CL3   *The Collected Letters of W. B. Yeats: Volume Three, 1901–1904.* Edited by John Kelly and Ronald Schuchard. Oxford: Clarendon Press, 1994.

E&I   *Essays and Introductions.* London and New York: Macmillan, 1961.

L   *The Letters of W. B. Yeats.* Edited by Allan Wade. London: Rupert Hart-Davis, 1954; New York: Macmillan, 1955.

LAR   *Later Articles and Reviews.* Edited by Colton Johnson. New York: Scribner, 2000.

LE   *Later Essays.* Edited by William H. O'Donnell, with assistance from Elizabeth Bergmann Loizeaux. New York: Scribner, 1994.

LNI   *Letters to the New Island: A New Edition.* Edited by George Bornstein and Hugh Witemeyer. London: Macmillan, 1989.

LTWBY   *Letters to W. B. Yeats.* Edited by Richard J. Finneran, George Mills Harper, and William M. Murphy, with the assistance of Alan B. Himber. London: Macmillan; New York: Columbia University Press, 1977.

Myth   *Mythologies.* London and New York: Macmillan, 1959.

NLI   Manuscripts in the National Library of Ireland.

P&I   *Prefaces and Introductions: Uncollected Prefaces and Introductions by Yeats to Works by Other Authors and to Anthologies Edited by Yeats.* Edited by William H. O'Donnell. London: Macmillan, 1988.

P   *The Poems.* Revised edition. Edited by Richard J. Finneran. New York: Macmillan, 1989.

P2   *The Poems.* 2nd edition. Edited by Richard J. Finneran. New York: Scribner, 1997.

UP1   *Uncollected Prose by W. B. Yeats—I: First Reviews and Articles, 1886–1896.* Edited by John P. Frayne. London: Macmillan; New York: Columbia University Press, 1970.

UP2   *Uncollected Prose by W. B. Yeats—2: Reviews, Articles, and Other Miscellaneous Prose, 1897–1939.* Edited by John P. Frayne and Colton Johnson. London: Macmillan, 1975; New York: Columbia University Press, 1976).

VP   *The Variorum Edition of the Poems of W. B. Yeats.* Edited by Peter Allt and Russell K. Alspach. New York: Macmillan, 1957.

VPl   *The Variorum Edition of the Plays of W. B. Yeats.* Edited by Russell K. Alspach, assisted by Catherine C. Alspach. London and New York: Macmillan, 1966.

YA   *Yeats Annual.* London: Macmillan, 1982–2000; Palgrave, 2001–. Cited by no.

YL   *A Descriptive Catalog of W. B. Yeats's Library.* Edward O'Shea. New York and London: Garland Publishing, 1985.

THE COLLECTED WORKS
OF W. B. YEATS

VOLUME IX

Articles
and Reviews
by W. B. Yeats

THE POETRY
OF SIR SAMUEL FERGUSON—I

This article appeared in The Irish Fireside *of 9 October 1886, under
the heading "Irish Poets and Irish Poetry." Sir Samuel Ferguson had
died on 9 August 1886, and the present article was one of two pieces
written by Yeats to sum up the achievement of Ferguson. This article
may have been written after the longer, more detailed one that appeared
in* The Dublin University Review *of November 1886, pp. 10–27 in
this collection. In the present article Yeats writes about Ferguson's*
Conary, *from* Poems *(Dublin: W. McGee, 1880), "Of this poem's
splendid plot, which I have no space to describe here, I have written
somewhat copiously elsewhere."*

*Sir Samuel Ferguson (1810–86), Belfast-born poet and antiquary,
most heavily influenced Yeats by his attempt to use ancient Irish legends and heroic sagas as subjects for his poems. What Ferguson's
work meant to Yeats is writ large in this and the following article.*

> Of old, unhappy, far-off things,
> And battles long ago.[1]

In the garden of the world's imagination there are seven great foun-
tains. The seven great cycles of legends—the Indian; the Homeric; the
Charlemagnic; the Spanish, circling round the Cid; the Arthurian;
the Scandinavian; and the Irish[2]—all differing one from the other, as
the peoples differed who created them. Every one of these cycles is the
voice of some race celebrating itself, embalming for ever what it hated
and loved. Back to their old legends go, year after year, the poets of
the earth, seeking the truth about nature and man, that they may not
be lost in a world of mere shadow and dream.

Sir Samuel Ferguson's special claim to our attention is that he went
back to the Irish cycle, finding it, in truth, a fountain that, in the pas-

sage of centuries, was overgrown with weeds and grass, so that the very way to it was forgotten of the poets; but now that his feet have worn the pathway, many others will follow, and bring thence living waters for the healing of our nation, helping us to live the larger life of the Spirit, and lifting our souls away from their selfish joys and sorrows to be the companions of those who lived greatly among the woods and hills when the world was young.

It was in Ferguson's later poems that he restored to us the old heroes themselves; in his first work, *Lays of the Western Gael*,[3] he gave us rather instants of heroic passion, as in 'Owen Bawn', and 'Deirdre's[†] Lament for the Sons of Usnach', or poems in which character is subordinated to some dominant idea or event, as in the 'Welshmen of Tirawley', and 'Willy Gilliland', or tales round which is shed the soft lustre of idyllic thought, as the 'Fairy Thorn'.

In other words, he was more lyrical and romantic than dramatic in this first and best known of his books. 'The Fairy Thorn', does[†] the whole range of our rich ballad literature contain a more beautiful ballad of 'the good people' than this? I will quote almost the whole of it:

'Get up, our Anna dear, from the weary spinning-wheel,
    For your father's on the hill, and your mother's asleep;
Come up above the crags, and we'll dance a highland-reel
    Around the fairy thorn on the steep'.

At Anna Grace's door 'twas thus the maidens cried—
    Three merry maidens fair, in kirtles of the green;
And Anna laid the sock and weary wheel aside,
    The fairest of the four, I ween.

They're glancing through the glimmer of the quiet eve,
    Away, in milky wavings of neck and ankle bare;
The heavy sliding stream in its sleepy song they leave,
    And the crags in the ghostly air;

And linking hand in hand, and singing as they go,
    The maids along the hillside have ta'en their fearless way,
Till they come to where the rowen trees in lonely beauty grow
    Beside the fairy hawthorne grey.[4]
    . . . . .
But solemn is the silence of the silvery haze
    That drinks away their voices echoless repose,
And dreamily the evening has still'd the haunted braes,
    And dreamier the gloaming grows.

And sinking one by one, like lark-notes from the sky
    When the falcon's shadow saileth across the open shaw,
Are hushed the maidens' voices, as cowering down they lie
    In the flutter of their sudden awe.

For from the air above, and the grassy ground beneath,
    And from the mountain ashes, and the old whitethorn between,
A power of faint enchantment doth through their beings breathe,
    And they sink down together on the green.[5]
. . . . .
Thus clasped and prostrate all, with their heads together bow'd,
    Soft on their bosoms beating—the only human sound—
They hear the silky footsteps of the silent fairy crowd,
    Like a river in the air, gliding round.

No scream can they raise, nor prayer can they say,
    But wild, wild, the terror of the speechless three—
For they feel fair Anna Grace drawn silently away—
    By whom they dare not look to see.

They feel their tresses twine with her parting locks of gold,
    And the curls elastic falling, as her head withdraws;
They feel her sliding arms from their tranced arms unfold,
    But they may not look to see the cause.

For heavy on their senses the faint enchantment lies
    Through all that night of anguish and perilous amaze;
And neither fear nor wonder can ope their quivering eyes,
    Or their limbs from the cold ground raise.

Till out of night the earth has rolled her dewy side,
    With every haunted mountain and streamy vale below;
When, as the mist dissolves in the yellow morning tide,
    The maidens' trance dissolveth so.

Then fly the ghastly three as swiftly as they may,
    And tell their tale of sorrow to anxious friends in vain—
They pined away,[6] and died within the year and day;
    And ne'er was Anna Grace seen again.

You must go to the book itself for that ringing ballad, 'Willy
Gilliland', or that other, 'The Welshmen of Tirawley', which I am told
the English poet Swinburne[7] considers the best Irish poem, for I can-

not do them justice by short quotations. I could give no idea of a fine building by showing a carved flower from a cornice.

His well-known poem, the 'Lament of Deirdre',[†] is a version from the Irish. It is one of 'the things of the old time before'.[8] The name of him who wrote it has perished, his grave is unknown; and she in whose mouth it is put beheld the dawn from her tent door, and heard the long oars smiting the grey sea, and beheld the hills and the forest, and had her good things long ago, and departed. Well then, perhaps, some one will say, if it has come from so far off, what good can it do us moderns, with our complex life? Assuredly it will not help you to make a fortune, or even live respectably that little life of yours. Great poetry does not teach us anything—it changes us. Man is like a musical instrument of many strings, of which only a few are sounded by the narrow interests of his daily life; and the others, for want of use, are continually becoming tuneless and forgotten. Heroic poetry is a phantom finger swept over all the strings, arousing from man's whole nature a song of answering harmony. It is the poetry of action, for such alone can arouse the whole nature of man. It touches all the strings—those of wonder and pity, of fear and joy. It ignores morals, for its business is not in any way to make us rules for life, but to make character. It is not, as a great English writer has said, 'a criticism of life',[9] but rather a fire in the spirit, burning away what is mean and deepening what is shallow.

Sir S. Ferguson's longest poem, *Congal,* appeared in 1872. Many critics held this to be his greatest work. I myself rather prefer his *Deirdre,*[†] of which more presently.[10] *Deirdre*[†] is in blank verse, which, I think, sustains better the dignity of its subject than the somewhat ballad metre of *Congal.* Nevertheless, *Congal* is a poem of lyric strength and panther-like speed.

It is the story of the death in the seventh century, at the battle of Moyra (or Moira) of Congal Claen. Congal was a heathen; his enemy, the arch-King Ardrigh,[11] was a Christian. This war was the sunset of Irish heathendom. Across Ireland, eager for the battle, march Congal and his warriors. The demons of field and flood appear to them and prophesy their destruction. Defying heaven and hell, on march the heathen hosts. One morning, in the midst of the ford of Ullarvu, they behold that gruesomest of Celtic demons, 'the Washer of the Ford'— a grey hag, to her knees in the river, washing the heads and the bodies of men. Congal fearlessly questions her.

'I am the Washer of the Ford', she answered; 'and my race
Is of the Tuath de Danaan line of Magi; and my place
For toil is in the running streams of Erin; and my cave

For sleep is in the middle of the shell-heaped Cairn of Maev,
High up on haunted Knocknarea,[†][12] and this fine carnage-heap
Before me, in these silken vests and mantles which I steep
Thus in the running water, are the severed heads and hands,
And spear-torn scarfs and tunics of these gay-dressed[13] gallant
    bands
Whom thou, O Congal, leadest to death. And this', the Fury
    said,
Uplifting by the clotted locks what seemed a dead man's head,
'Is thine head, O Congal!'

Still on they go, these indomitable pagans. Surely nothing will resist their onset. Will they not even shake the throne of God in their sublime audacity? No; Congal when he has accomplished deeds of marvellous valour is slain by the hand of an idiot boy who carries a sickle for sword, and the lid of a cauldron for shield. Ah, strange irony of the Celt.

Notice throughout this poem the continual introduction of the supernatural. I once heard a great English poet,[14] in comparing two existing descriptions of the battle of Clontarf, the Irish and the Danish, say that the Irish narrator turns continually aside to discuss some great problem, or describe some supernatural event, while the Dane records only what affects the result of the battle. This was so, he said, because the Celtic nature is mainly lyrical, and the Danish, mainly dramatic.

The lyrical nature loves to linger on what is strange and fantastic.

In 1880, was published Ferguson's last volume, *Poems*.

In England it received no manner of recognition.[15] Anti-Irish feeling ran too high. 'Can any good thing come out of Galilee', they thought.[16] How could these enlightened critics be expected to praise a book that entered their world with no homage of imitation towards things Anglican?

Sir Samuel Ferguson himself, declares the true cause of this want of recognition in English critical centres in a letter published the other day in the *Irish Monthly*.[17] He sought to lay the foundation of a literature for Ireland that should be in every way characteristic and national, hence the critics were against him.

In this last book of his are his two greatest poems, *Conary*, which de Vere[†][18] considers the best Irish poem, and *Deirdre*.[†]

In *Conary*, thus is the king of Ireland described by a pirate's spy—[19]

One I saw
Seated apart: before his couch there hung
A silver broidered curtain; grey he was,

Of aspect mild, benevolent, composed.
A cloak he wore, of colour like the haze
Of a May morning, when the sun shines warm
On dewy meads and fresh-ploughed tillage land;
Variously beautiful, with border broad
Of golden woof that glittered to his knee
A stream of light. Before him, on the floor,
A juggler played his feats;[20] nine balls he had,
And flung them upward, eight in air at once,
And one in hand: like swarm of summer bees
They danced and circled, till his eye met mine;
Then he could catch no more; but down they fell
And rolled upon the floor. 'An evil eye
Has seen me', said the juggler.

Of this poem's splendid plot, which I have no space to describe here, I have written somewhat copiously elsewhere.[21]

Deirdre[†] is the noblest woman in Irish romance. Pursued by the love of King Conor,[†] she flies with her lover and his brethren and his tribe. Who has not heard of their famous wanderings? At last peace is made; but she who has been like a wise elder sister to the sons of Usnach[†] knows that it is treacherous, and warns Naoise,[†] her lover. He will not believe her. Sadly she sings upon her harp, as they leave their refuge in Glen Etive—

Harp, take my bosom's burthen on thy string,
And, turning it to sad, sweet melody,
Waste and disperse it on the careless air.

Air, take the harp-string's burthen on thy breast,
And, softly thrilling soul-ward[22] through the sense,
Bring my love's heart again in tune with mine.

Alba,[†] farewell! Farewell, fair Etive bank!
Sun kiss thee; moon caress thee; dewy stars
Refresh thee long, dear scene of quiet days!

Slowly they are meshed about and entrapped; the sons of Usnach[†] are slain, and she kills herself that she may escape the power of King Conor.[†]

Sir Samuel Ferguson, I contend, is the greatest Irish poet, because in his poems and the legends, they embody more completely than in any other man's writings, the Irish character. Its unflinching devotion to some single aim. Its passion. 'The food of the passions is bitter, the food of the spirit is sweet', say the wise Indians.[23] And this faithfulness to things tragic and bitter, to thoughts that wear one's life out and scatter one's joy, the Celt has above all others. Those who have it, alone are worthy of great causes. Those who have it not, have in them some vein of hopeless levity, the harlequins of the earth.[24]

One thing more before I cease; if I were asked to characterize, as shortly as may be, these poems, I should do so by applying to them the words of Spenser,[†] 'barbarous truth.'[25]

THE POETRY
OF SIR SAMUEL FERGUSON—II

This article appeared in The Dublin University Review *of November
1886. The death of Sir Samuel Ferguson, the Ulster-born poet and antiquary, on 9 August 1886, called forth a number of appreciations of the
man's life and work. The two principal articles, one by John Pentland
Mahaffy in* The Athenaeum *of 14 August 1886 and the other by Margaret Stokes in* The Academy and Literature *(London) of 21 August
1886, had both stressed Ferguson's loyalty to the British crown.
Yeats's article was a reply that Ferguson, whether he meant to be or
not, was a "true member of that company / That sang to sweeten Ireland's wrong . . ." and hence was a nationalist whether he wanted to
be or not. Although this article is one of Yeats's earliest published pieces,
it is his first major statement of his literary philosophy. In choosing a
national literature embodying the ideals of "fatherland and song,"
Yeats declared war on the Anglo-Irish ("West-Briton," as he called it)
literary establishment in its chief institution—Trinity College—and its
chief spokesman, Professor Edward Dowden.*

*Yeats declared for an epic literature, one based on ancient Irish
sagas, which would enable him to escape what he called the "sad
soliloquies of a nineteenth-century egoism." Here Yeats expresses one
of the central forces of his long career: his love of convictions rather
than intellectual reservations, his primitivism, and even a foreshadowing of his self-image in old age. The "aged sea-king" he admired in
Ferguson, he was to aspire to himself.*

*One may doubt whether Yeats's enthusiasm for Ferguson is sup-
ported by the passages he quotes from Ferguson's poems. The appeal
to national loyalties is more powerful than the reasons offered to the
literary judgment. The arrogant and defiant opening to this essay and
its concluding clarion call to a rebirth of the Gael are magnificent and
a fitting opening for a man who would sing the "indomitable Irishry."*

In the literature of every country there are two classes, the creative and the critical. In Scotland all the poets have been Scotch in feeling, or, as we would call it, national, and the cultured and critical public read their books, and applauded, for the nation was homogeneous. Over here things have gone according to an altogether different fashion.

It has not paid to praise things Irish, or write on Irish subjects; but the poet, who is, as far as he is a poet at all, by the very nature of his calling a man of convictions and principle, has gone on remaining true to himself and his country, singing for those who cannot reward him with wealth or fame, who cannot even understand what he loves most in his work. This he has done while the Irish critic, who should be a man of convictions, but generally becomes, by the force of circumstances a man of tact, industry, and judgment; who studies the *convenances*[1] of the literary world and praises what it is conformable to praise, has remained with his ears to the ground listening for the faintest echo of English thought. Meanwhile the poet has become silent or careless, for everywhere the supply ultimately depends on the demand. If Ireland has produced no great poet, it is not that her poetic impulse has run dry, but because her critics have failed her, for every community is a solidarity, all depending upon each, and each upon all. Heaven and earth have not seen the man who could go on producing great work without a sensitive and exacting audience. Why did a writer like Sir Samuel Ferguson publish in a long life so little poetry, and after he had given evidences of such new and vivid power, become no longer vocal, and busy himself mainly with matters of research?

The greatest of his faculties was killed long ago by indifference.

It is a question whether the most distinguished of our critics, Professor Dowden, would not only have more consulted the interests of his country, but more also, in the long run, his own dignity and reputation, which are dear to all Irishmen, if he had devoted some of those elaborate pages which he has spent on the much bewritten George Eliot, to a man like the subject of this article.[2] A few pages from him would have made it impossible for a journal like the *Academy* to write in 1880, that Sir Samuel Ferguson should have published his poetry only for his intimate friends, and that it did not even 'rise to the low watermark of poetry'.[3] Remember this was not said of a young man, but one old, who had finished his life's labour. If Sir Samuel Ferguson had written to the glory of that, from a moral point of view, more than dubious achievement, British civilization, the critics, probably including Professor Dowden, would have taken care of his reputation.

Lately another professor of Trinity appears to have taken most pleasure in writing, not that the author of *Congal* was a fine poet, nor that he was a profound antiquarian, but in assuring us that he was an 'orderly citizen'; which, if it means anything, means, I suppose, that unlike Socrates, he never felt the weight of the law for his opinions.[4]

'I would', said one of the most famous of living English poets to the author of this article, 'gladly lecture in Dublin on Irish literature, but the people know too little about it.'[5]

The most cultivated of Irish readers are only anxious to be academic, and to be servile to English notions. If Sir Samuel Ferguson had written of Arthur and of Guinevere, they would have received him gladly;[6] that he chose rather to tell of Congal and of desolate and queenly Deirdre, we give him full-hearted thanks; he has restored to our hills and rivers their epic interest.[7] The nation has found in Davis a battle call, as in Mangan its cry of despair; but he only, the one Homeric poet of our time, could give us immortal companions still wet with the dew of their primal world.[8]

To know the meaning and mission of any poet we must study his works as a whole. Sir Samuel Ferguson has himself pointed out how this may best be done in his own case. He tells us that the main poems in his first volume and his last should be read in the following order: 'Twins of Macha' (*Poems,*) 'The Naming of Cuchullin' (*Poems,*) 'Abdication of Fergus' (*Lays of the Western Gael,*) 'Mesgedra' (*Poems,*) *Deirdre* (*Poems,*) *Conary* (*Poems,*) 'Healing of Conall Carnach' (*Lays,*) 'The Tain† Quest' (*Lays.*)[9]

'The Twins of Macha' and 'The Naming of Cuchullin' give us the keynote of his work—that simplicity, which is force. He is never florid, never for a moment rhetorical. We see at once that he has the supreme gifts of the story-teller—imagination enough to make history read like romance, and simplicity enough to make romance read like history.

The boy Setanta approaching at night the house of the great smith, Cullan, is attacked by the smith's gigantic watch dog and kills it. The old man laments the loss of his faithful hound:

> Boy, for his sake who bid thee to my board
> I give thee welcome: for thine own sake, no.
> For thou hast slain my servant and my friend,
> The hound I loved, that, fierce, intractable
> To all men else, was ever mild to me.
> He knew me; and he knew my uttered words,
> All my commandments, as a man might know;
> More than a man he knew my looks and tones
> And turns of gesture, and discerned my mind[10]
> Unspoken, if in grief or if in joy.
> He was my pride, my strength, my company,

For I am childless; and that hand of thine
Has left an old man lonely in the world.

The boy declares that till he has trained the watchdog's whelp to take
the place of the dead hound, he himself will guard the house, remaining at his post by day and by night. Those who are standing by cry out
that henceforth his name shall be Cuchulain,[†] the 'Hound of Cullan'.
All this is told with such simplicity and sincerity that we seem to be no
longer in this modern decade, but listening to some simple and savage
old chief telling his companions round a forest fire, of something his
own eyes have seen.[11] There is not much fancy, little of the subtler forms
of music. Many a minor English poet whom the world will make
haste to forget, has more of these; but here are the very things which
he has not, the germinal thoughts of poetry.

The 'Abdication of Fergus' follows next in the cycle. The poet-king,
who loves hunting and the freedom of the great wood, far better than
the councils is delighted by the wisdom with which his stepson who
sits beside him on the judgment seat, arrays in some most tangled case
argument against argument—

> As a sheep-dog sorts his cattle,
> As a king arrays his battle.[12]

He takes from his head the crown and lays it beside him on the
bench. Let Fergus tell his own tale.

> And I rose, and on my feet
> Standing by the judgment-seat,
> Took the circlet from my head,
> Laid it on the bench and said:[13]

> 'Men of Uladh,[14] I resign
> That which is not rightly mine,
> That a worthier than I
> May your judge's place supply.

> Lo, it is no easy thing
> For a man to be a king,[15]
> Judging well, as should behove
> One who claims a people's love.

> Uladh's judgment-seat to fill
> I have neither wit nor will.

One is here may justly claim
Both the function and the name.

Conor is of royal blood:[16]
Fair he is; I trust him good;
Wise he is we all may say
Who have heard his words to-day.

Take him therefore in my room,
Letting me the place assume—
Office but with life to end—
Of his councillor[†][17] and friend.'

So young Conor gained[18] the crown;
So I laid the kingship down;
Laying with it as I went
All I knew of discontent.

In 'Mesgedra', Conall Carnach, after Cuchulain[†] the greatest of the Red-Branch chieftains, finds his enemy, Mesgedra, with one arm disabled, taking sanctuary under a sacred tree, and, in order that they may fight on equal terms, binds one of his own arms to his side, and when a chance blow releases it, binds it again.

We now come to *Deirdre*, which I hold to be the greatest of Sir Samuel Ferguson's poems. It is in no manner possible to do it justice by quotation. There is an admirable, but altogether trivial, English poet called Edmund Gosse.[19] If fate compelled me to review his work, and to review also some princely ancient Homer or Aeschylus,[20] and to do this by the method of short quotations, the admirable Londoner, in the minds of many readers, would rule the roost. For in his works grow luxuriantly those forms of fancy and of verbal felicity that are above all things *portable;* while the mighty heathen sought rather after breadth and golden severity, knowing well that the merely pretty is contraband of art. With him beauty lies in great masses—thought woven with thought—each line, the sustainer of his fellow. Take a beauty from that which surrounds it—its colour is faded, its plumage is ruffled—it is dead.

In this Sir Samuel Ferguson was like the ancients; not that he was an imitator, as Matthew Arnold in *Sohrab and Rustum*,[21] but for a much better reason; he was *like* them—like them in nature, for his spirit had sat with the old heroes of his country. In *Deirdre* he has restored to us a fragment of the buried Odyssey of Ireland.

In Scotch Glen Etive, Naoise,[†] Son of Usnach, lives in exile with his two brothers and his bride—his Deirdre, for he has carried her off from a little lonely island in a lake where the king, Conor, had hidden her away in charge of her nurse and an old Druid, that he might make her his mistress when her beauty had grown to full flower. Deirdre is entirely happy, for love is all sufficient for her; not so her lover—he longs for war, and to sit once more in council with his peers. Suddenly is heard through Glen Etive the hunting-call of ex-king Fergus. He brings a pardon.

Of all those who return with him Deirdre alone is sad, she knows the peace is treacherous, that Conor is only seeking to bring her once more into his power. None believes her. Are they not safe under the protection of Fergus? But no; she will not place trust in one who gave up his kingdom so lightly. They reach land. Fergus is enticed away by a ruse of King Conor. Their protectors now are the two young sons of Fergus. How beautiful, as they ride across the country, is that talk between Deirdre and the youngest of the two, who afterwards dies for her.[22] He does not love the company of warriors:

> I would rather, if I might,[23]
> Frequent the open country, and converse
> With shepherds, hunters, and such innocents.

Then they talk of love, these two, so young, and yet so different; the one on the threshold of life, the other, who has known wandering and weariness. He loves all the world, for in her whom he loves are all the world's perfections. There is something maternal in her reply:

> Long be thou happy in believing so.

Then turning to the other son, who afterwards betrays her, she seeks to sound his nature also. He is one of those who apply to all the moral obligations of life the corrosive power of the intellect, and she, who knows only how to feel and believe, murmurs sadly, half to herself:

> Oh yonder see the lake in prospect fair,
> It lies beneath us, like a polished shield.
> Ah, me! methinks I could imagine it
> Cast down by some despairing deity
> Flying before the unbelief of men.[24]

Close by this lake is the 'Red-Branch' house,[25] where their journey ends.

I have not space to tell how, point by point, she sees fate drawing near them—how to the very end Naoise,[†] the simple soldier, sits calmly playing chess[26] even when they are surrounded—how Conor comes with his magic shield that was hammered in the sea by fairy smiths, and how there was between it and the seas of Ireland a strange sympathy, so that when it is smitten they all surge. I have not space to tell how the sons of Usnach are slain, but I cannot resist quoting in full the beautiful lament of Deirdre:

> The lions of the hill are gone[27]
> And I am left alone—alone—
> Dig the grave both wide and deep,
> For I am sick, and fain would sleep!
>
> The falcons of the wood are flown,
> And I am left alone—alone—
> Dig the grave both deep and wide,
> And let us slumber side by side.
>
> The dragons of the rock are sleeping,
> Sleep that wakes not for our weeping;
> Dig the grave and make it ready;
> Lay me on my true love's body.
>
> Lay their spears and bucklers bright
> By the warriors' sides aright;
> Many a day the three before me
> On their linkèd bucklers bore me.[28]
>
> Lay upon the low grave floor,
> 'Neath each head, the blue claymore;
> Many a time the noble three
> Redden'd these blue blades for me.
>
> Lay the collars, as is meet,
> Of their greyhounds at their feet;
> Many a time for me have they
> Brought the tall red deer to bay.
>
> Sweet companions ye were ever—
> Harsh to me, your sister, never;
> Woods and wilds and misty valleys
> Were, with you, as good's a palace.[29]

Oh! to hear my true-love[30] singing,
Sweet as sound of trumpet ringing;[31]
Like the sway of ocean swelling
Roll'd his deep voice round our dwelling.

Oh! to hear the echoes pealing
Round our green and fairy sheeling,
When the three, with soaring chorus[32]
Pass'd the silent skylark o'er us.

Echo, now sleep,[33] morn and even—
Lark alone enchant the heaven!—
Ardan's lips are scant of breath,
Naoise's[†] tongue is cold in death.[34]

Stag exult on glen and mountain—
Salmon leap from loch to fountain—
Herons[35] in the free air warm ye—
Usnach's sons no more will harm ye!

Erin's stay no more you are,
Rulers of the ridge of war;
Never more 'twill be your fate
To keep the beam of battle straight.[36]

Woe is me! By fraud and wrong,
Traitors false and tyrants strong,
Fell Clan[37] Usnach, bought and sold,
For Barach's feast and Conor's gold!

Woe to Emain, roof and wall!—
Woe to Red Branch, hearth and hall!—
Tenfold woe and black dishonour
To the foul and false Clan Conor![38]

Dig the grave both wide and deep,
Sick I am, and fain would sleep!
Dig the grave and make it ready,
Lay me on my true-love's body!

This is not the version in the text but an earlier and more beautiful
one—a version from the Irish, which I have followed Judge O'Hagan's[39]

lead in quoting from the *Lays of the Western Gael*. I know not any lament so piercing.

No one will deny excellence to the *Idylls of the King*; no one will say that Lord Tennyson's Girton[40] girls do not look well in those old costumes of dead chivalry. No one will deny that he has thrown over everything a glamour of radiant words—that the candelabras shine brightly on the fancy ball. Yet here is that which the *Idylls* do not at any time contain, beauty at once feminine and heroic. But as Lord Tennyson's ideal women will never find a flawless sympathy outside the upper English middle class, so this Deirdre will never, maybe, win entire credence outside the limits—wide enough they are—of the Irish race.

There is a great gap that Sir Samuel Ferguson never filled up between this poem and the next. Here should have come the record of the foiled vengeance of Fergus.[41]

In *Conary*, a pirate fleet is shown us, lying off Howth, commanded by the banished foster brothers of King Conary and the British pirate Ingcel. Spies have been sent on shore. They return. 'What saw ye?' They have seen a line of seventeen chariots—in the first, reverend men, judges or poets; in the second heralds; in the third an aged man, 'full-grey, majestical, of face serene';[42] in the others a numerous household. 'What heard ye?' They have heard one within a guest-house lighting a fire for the reception of a king. The pirates land; a spy is sent before them—he approaches the guest-house and hears within—

> A hum as of a crowd of feasting men.
> Princely the murmur, as when voices strong
> Of far-heard captains on the front of war,[43]
> Sink low and sweet in company of queens.

On his return he describes one by one the great chiefs of Ireland that he saw within, and Ferragon, foster brother of Conary, declares their names. There is Cormac Condlongas, son of Conor, who in rage for the betrayal of the sons of Usnach, made war on his father and his kin.

> The nine he sat among,
> Were men of steadfast looks, that at his word,
> So seemed it me, would stay not to inquire
> Whose kindred were they he might bid them slay.

> 'I knew them also,' answered Ferragon.
> 'Of them 'tis said they never slew a man
> For evil deed, and never spared a man

For good deed; but as ordered, duteous slew
Or slew not. Shun that nine, unless your heads
Be cased in caskets[44] made of adamant.'

There too is Conall Carnach:

> Fair-haired he is,[45]
> And yellow-bearded, with an eye of blue.
> He sits apart and wears a wistful look,
> As if he missed some friend's companionship.
> Then Ferragon, not waiting question, cried:[46]
> Gods! all the foremost, all the valiantest
> Of Erin's champions, gathered in one place
> For our destruction, are assembled here!
> That man is Conall Carnach; and the friend
> He looks for vainly with a wistful eye
> Is great Cuchulain[†]: he no more shall share
> The upper bench with Conall; since the tomb
> Holds him, by hand of Conall well avenged.

One by one the great chieftains are re-created for us in words like
the clang of hammer on anvil in fashioning a sword. The arch-king
Conary is there.

> One I saw[47]
> Seated apart: before his couch there hung
> A silver broidered curtain; grey he was,
> Of aspect mild, benevolent, composed.
> A cloak he wore of colour like the haze
> Of a May morning when the sun shines warm
> On dewy meads and fresh ploughed tillage land
> Variously beautiful, with border broad
> Of golden woof that glittered to his knee
> A stream of light. Before him on the floor
> A juggler played his feats; nine balls he had
> And flung them upward, eight in air at once,
> And one in hand! Like[48] swarm of summer bees
> They danced and circled, till his eye met mine;
> Then he could catch no more; but down they fell
> And rolled upon the floor. 'An evil eye
> Has seen me,' said the juggler.

The spy has observed others who were not warriors:

I saw three slender, three face-shaven men
Robed in red mantles and with caps of red.
No swords had they, nor bore they spear or shield,
But each man on his knee a bag-pipe held
With jewelled chanter flashing as he moved,
And mouthpiece[49] ready to supply the wind.

'What pipers these?'

These pipers of a truth
If so it be that I mistake them not,
Appear not often in men's halls of glee:
Men of the Sidhe[†] they are.
. . . . .
To-night their pipes will play[50] us to our ships
With strains of triumph; or their fingers' ends
Shall never close the stops of music more.

The attack is sounded. Conary sends one troop of his warriors
against them, bidding one of the strange pipers sound a pibroch for
the onset:

'Yea, mighty king,' said one,
'The strain I play ye shall remember long,'
And put the mouthpiece to his lips. At once[51]
It seemed as earth and sky were sound alone,
And every sound a maddening battle-call,
So spread desire of fight through breast and brain.

They drive all before them and force a way through the enemy, but
fainter and fainter to the ears of Conary comes the sound of the music
and the swords. For the treacherous piping has led them far away into
the darkness by an irresistible spell; and now the king bids another
troop go out against the pirates:

And let another piper play you on.

Again the sound of the music and the swords comes fainter and
fainter. Conall Carnach must seek them with a third troop, and to these
is appointed the third piper:

'Trust not these pipers, I am but a child,'
Said Ferflath; 'but I know they are not men

Of mankind, and will pipe you all to harm,'
'Peace, little prince,' said Conall, 'trust in me.[52]
I shall but make one circuit of the house.'

They sally out, and those within first hear the sound of 'legions overthrown', but soon 'clamour and scream'[53] grow fainter in the distance. Now that it is too late they see the truth:

> The gods
> Have given us over to the spirits who dwell
> Beneath the earth.

The great arch-king himself prepares for 'battle long disused',[54] and
with his household, 'steward and butler, cup-bearer[55] and groom',
goes out against his besiegers.

In the moment of victory he is attacked by a terrible thirst, and cries
out for water. Cecht, the only great warrior who remains with him, sets
out with the child Ferflath to find it in a distant well. Twice it is spilt,
and when at last in the grey of the morning they return, the arch-king
is slain, and the three strayed troops stand round him:

> As men who doubted did they dream or wake,
> Or were they honest, to be judged, or base.[56]

These things are supposed to have happened near the spot where
Donnybrook[57] bridge now stands, and there, a few years ago, some
workmen found a sword and spear-head of immense antiquity, and a
mass of headless skeletons.

I have not space to do much more than mention the next two
poems. Though lucid and beautiful, they are of much less importance
than *Deirdre* or *Conary*. In these latter the wave of song reaches its
greatest volume of sound and strength. In the 'Healing of Conall Carnach' it ebbs with soft notes that are almost idyllic, and with a half
regretful prophecy of change.

'The Tain Quest' tells how in the course of ages the poem in which
Fergus had recorded the previous stories is lost, and the bards have
sought it everywhere in vain. At last Murgen, the chief bard's son,
resting in a lonely valley finds† written on the stone on which he
leaned, that there Fergus was buried. He calls upon the ghost of the
dead warrior to rise and give the Tain once more to the world. Vainly
he conjures him by the name of Love, by his Nessa's eyes, by the
heroic deeds of his son. At last he conjures him by the sacred name of
Song:

> In dark days near[58] at hand
> Song shall be the only treasure left them in their native land.

Fergus rises:

> .... A mist and a flush
> Of brazen sandals blended with a mantle's wafture green.[59]

So the song is recovered, but Murgen has to give his life in exchange.

There is a wonderful incident full of Celtic irony in the epic of *Congal*. The great chief, from whom the poem takes its name, having driven all his enemies before him, finds himself suddenly face to face with an idiot boy with a bill-hook for sword and the head of a cauldron for a shield. Congal turns away half in scorn and half in pity, but as he turns the idiot wounds him mortally with the bill-hook, and seeking out his king, reports what he has done. The king, in gratitude, promises him great gifts:

> ''Tis good,' said Cuanna, and sat down, and from the gravelly
> soil
> Picking the pebbles smooth, began to toss with patient toil[60]
> The little stones from hand to hand, alternate back and palm,
> Regardless of the presence round, and lapsed in childish calm.

Meanwhile a notorious coward[61] seeing Congal faint from loss of blood, resolves to win the glory of having killed him. He severs Congal's wrist with a sword-cut, and the hand is driven far over the ground grasping, but he who gave the sword-cut has fled without waiting to see the effect of his blow. So the most famous warrior of his time bleeds to death, slain by the hands of an idiot boy and a coward.

In thus describing these poems I have not sought to convey to my readers, for it were hopeless, their fine momentum, the sign manual of the great writers. I am in every way satisfied if I have made plain the personality of the work.

I must now speak of the slighter poems. To these it is more possible to do justice by quotation.

It is a long cry from the days of Congal to those of Davis:

> I walked through Ballinderry in the springtime,
>   When the bud was on the tree;
> And I said, in every fresh-ploughed field beholding
>   The sowers striding free,

Scattering broadcast forth the corn in golden plenty
  On the quick seed-clasping soil,
Even such, this day, among the fresh-stirred hearts of Erin,
  Thomas Davis is thy toil.
  . . . . .
O brave young men, my love, my pride, my promise,
  'Tis on you my hopes are set
In manliness, in kindliness, in justice,
  To make Erin a nation yet;
Self-respecting, self-relying, self-advancing,
  In union or in severance, free and strong—
And if God grant this, then, under God, to Thomas Davis
  Let the greater praise belong.[62]

Thus wrote Sir Samuel Ferguson at the time of his friend's death. Of the sincerity of the national feeling running through this and all his other poems he gave earnest by being at one time an ardent politician. Towards the last, however, when he had exchanged poetry for antiquarian studies, his Nationalism (in the political sense), though not his patriotism, became less ardent, 'Years robbed him of courage',[63] as Wordsworth said of himself in a moment of melancholy insight.[64]

Beautiful with their desire for some stronger life, one with the rapture of the sea and the stars, are those opening lines from 'Grace O'Maly'—[65]

  She left the close-air'd land of trees
    And Proud MacWilliam's palace,
  For clear, bare Clare's health-salted breeze,
    Her oarsmen and her galleys:
  And where, beside the bending strand
    The rock and billow wrestle,
  Between the deep sea and the land
    She built her Island Castle.

  The Spanish captains, sailing by
    For Newport, with amazement
  Behold the cannon'd longship lie
    Moored to the lady's casement;
  And, covering coin and cup of gold
    In haste their hatches under,
  They whispered, ''Tis a pirate's hold;
    She sails the seas for plunder!'

But no; 'twas not for sordid spoil
    Of barque or sea-board borough
She plough'd, with unfatiguing toil,
    The fluent-rolling furrow;
Delighting, on the broad-back'd deep,
    To feel the quivering galley
Strain up the opposing hill, and sweep
    Down the withdrawing valley[66]

Or, sped before a driving blast,
    By following seas uplifted,
Catch, from the huge heaps heaving past,
    And from the spray they drifted,
And from the winds that toss'd the crest
    Of each wide-shouldering giant,
The smack of freedom and the zest
    Of rapturous life defiant.

Almost all the poetry of this age is written by students, for students. But Ferguson's is truly bardic, appealing to all natures alike, to the great concourse of the people, for it has gone deeper than knowledge or fancy, deeper than the intelligence which knows of difference—of the good and the evil, of the foolish and the wise, of this one and of that— to the universal emotions that have not heard of aristocracies, down to where Brahman and Sudra[67] are not even names.

The following lines from the poem to Brittany, are very different, with their love of peace and their regret for the past. Those who remember that last year's address of Renan's[68] on the same subject will notice how like it they are in temper and substance:

Leave to him—to the vehement man
    Of the Loire, of the Seine, of the Rhone,—
In the Idea's high pathways to march in the van,
    To o'erthrow, and set up the o'erthrown:
Be it thine in the broad beaten ways
    That the world's simple seniors have trod,
To walk with soft steps, living peaceable days,
    And on earth not forgetful of God.
Nor repine that thy lot has been cast
    With the things of the old time before,
For to thee are committed the keys of the past,
    Oh grey monumental Arvôr![69]

Of all the lesser poems of Sir Samuel Ferguson there is none more beautiful than that on the burial of Aideen,[70] who died of grief for the death of Oscar, and whose grave is the cromlech at Howth:

> They heaved the stone; they heap'd the cairn,
>   Said Ossian. 'In a queenly grave[71]
> We leave her, 'mong the fields of fern,
>   Between the cliff and wave.
>
> 'The cliff behind stands clear and bare,
>   And bare, above, the heathery steep
> Scales the clear heaven's expanse, to where
>   The Danaan[72] Druids sleep.
>
> 'And all the sands that, left and right,
>   The grassy isthmus-ridge confine,
> In yellow bars lie bare and bright
>   Among the sparkling brine.
>
> 'A clear pure air pervades the scene,
>   In loneliness and awe secure;
> Meet spot to sepulchre a queen
>   Who in her life was pure.
>
> 'Here, far from camp and chase removed,
>   Apart in Nature's quiet room,
> The music that alive she loved
>   Shall cheer her in the tomb.
>
> 'The humming of the noontide bees,
>   The larks loud carol all day long,
> And borne on evening's salted breeze,
>   The clanking sea-bird's song
>
> 'Shall round her airy chamber float,
>   And with the whispering winds and streams,
> Attune to Nature's tenderest note
>   The tenor of her dreams.
>
> 'And oft, at tranquil eve's decline,[73]
>   When full tides lip the old Green Plain,[74]
> The lowing of Moynalty's kine
>   Shall round her breathe again.

'In sweet remembrance of the days
    When, duteous, in the lowly vale,
Unconscious of my Oscar's gaze,
    She filled the fragrant pail.
. . . . .

'Farewell! the strength of men is worn;
    The night approaches dark and chill;
Sleep, till perchance an endless morn
    Descend the glittering hill.'

Of Oscar and Aideen bereft,
    So Ossian sang. The Fenians sped
Three mighty shouts to heaven; and left
    Ben-Edar[75] to the dead.

At once the fault and the beauty of the nature-description of most modern poets is that for them the stars, and streams, the leaves, and the animals, are only masks behind which go on the sad soliloquies of a nineteenth century egoism. When the world was fresh they gave us a clear glass to see the world through, but slowly, as nature lost her newness, or they began more and more to live in cities or for some other cause, the glass was dyed with ever deepening colours, and now we scarcely see what lies beyond because of the pictures that are painted all over it. But here is one who brings us a clear glass once more.

The author of these poems is the greatest poet Ireland has produced, because the most central and most Celtic. Whatever the future may bring forth in the way of a truly great and national literature—and now that the race is so large, so widely spread, and so conscious of its unity, the years are ripe—will find its morning in these three volumes of one who was made by the purifying flame of National sentiment the one man of his time who wrote heroic poetry—one who, among the somewhat sybaritic singers of his day, was like some aged sea-king sitting among the inland wheat and poppies—the savour of the sea about him, and its strength.

In these poems and the legends they contain lies the refutation of the calumnies of England and those amongst us who are false to their country. We are often told that we are men of infirm will and lavish lips, planning one thing and doing another, seeking this to-day and that tomorrow. But a widely different story do these legends tell. The mind of the Celt loves to linger on images of persistence[†]; implacable hate, implacable love, on Conor and Deirdre, and Setanta watching by the door of Cullan, and the long waiting of the blind Lynott.[76]

Of all the many things the past bequeaths to the future, the greatest are great legends; they are the mothers of nations. I hold it the duty of every Irish reader to study those of his own country till they are familiar as his own hands, for in them is the Celtic heart.

If you will do this you will perhaps be saved in their high companionship from that leprosy of the modern—tepid emotions and many aims. Many aims, when the greatest of the earth often owned but two—two linked and arduous thoughts—fatherland and song. For them the personal perplexities of life grew dim and there alone remained its noble sorrows and its noble joys.

I do not appeal to the professorial classes, who, in Ireland, at least, appear at no time to have thought of the affairs of their country till they first feared for their emoluments—nor do I appeal to the shoddy society of 'West Britonism',[77]—but to those young men clustered here and there throughout our land, whom the emotion of Patriotism has lifted into that world of selfless passion in which heroic deeds are possible and heroic poetry credible.

THE POETRY OF R. D. JOYCE

This article on Robert Dwyer Joyce (1830–83) appeared in The Irish Fireside *in two installments, part one on 27 November and part two on 4 December 1886, under the heading "Irish Poets and Irish Poetry." R. D. Joyce was the brother of Patrick Weston Joyce, the Gaelic scholar and compiler of* Old Celtic Romances *(London: C. Kegan Paul and Co., 1879). There is no known family relationship between these men and James Joyce. R. D., a doctor, had gone to Boston to practice medicine. After his stay in America, he returned to Ireland and he died in Dublin on 24 October 1883.*

Unlike some of Yeats's early enthusiasms—Mangan, Ferguson, Allingham—R. D. Joyce was seldom recommended by Yeats to Irish readers. He is mentioned again in Yeats's review of Tynan's Shamrocks *in* The Gael *of 11 June 1887, where Yeats speaks of him as "a gallant storyteller lacking the poetic intensity of either [Ferguson or de Vere]." He is also mentioned in "Popular Ballad Poetry of Ireland" (pp. 93–108 in this collection), where Yeats notes that Joyce's* Deirdre *(Boston: Roberts Brothers, 1876) reputedly sold ten thousand copies "mainly among Irish Americans." Joyce is missing from Yeats's longest reading list, compiled for* The Bookman *in October 1895, entitled "Irish National Literature, IV: A List of the Best Irish Books," pp. 288–92 in this volume.*

PART ONE

Poets may be divided roughly into two classes. First, those who—like Coleridge, Shelley, and Wordsworth[1]—investigate what is obscure in emotion, and appeal to what is abnormal in man, or become the healers of some particular disease of the spirit. During their lifetime they write for a clique, and leave after them a school. And second, the

28

bardic class—the Homers and Hugos, the Burnses and Scotts[2]—who sing of the universal emotions, our loves and angers, our delight in stories and heroes, our delight in things beautiful and gallant. They do not write for a clique, or leave after them a school, for they sing for all men.

Both classes are necessary; yet these, though they have not, as the first often have, a definite teaching intention, are perhaps more valuable to mankind, for they speak to the manhood in us, not to the scholar or the philosopher. They are better for a nation than savans or moralists, or philosophers. Such may teach us to know the good from the evil, the true from the false, the beautiful from the ugly and the coarse; but only the poets can make us love what they please—and that which makes men differ is not what they know, but what they love.

To this latter class belongs Joyce, and, indeed, almost all our Irish poets. He is essentially a bard. He sought to give us whole men, apart from all that limits; therefore he went for his subjects to that simple and legendary past, whither every hill in his own many-fabled Limerick[3] must have appeared to beckon him.

What an effect they must have had on a sensitive boy—those hills and valleys, with their memories of heroic wars—those ruined castles, where lovers had pined for each other's footsteps, and been befooled of fate—that cave, wherein men thought if you wandered far enough you crossed a stream, and came to the flowers and the fields of fairyland, when you might wed a fairy princess, and never return to your native village.

In this book, *Ballads, Romances, and Songs,* published in '61, as I turn over the leaves I see legend after legend of Limerick, and the counties most immediately about it, embodied in verse—not great, yet such as will sweeten the hills and streams for many a long day with memories; and without memories, the most wonderful scenery is like a beautiful and soulless face. The aim of a ballad writer is not character or passion—the story is everything with him. He chooses simple words that, when they have served their purpose, step aside and efface themselves. The old Fenian story of the Black Robber[4] is a beautiful instance:

I

By Mumhan's mountain,[5] airy and stern,
A well lies circled by rock and fern,
And fiercely over a precipice near
Rusheth a waterfall brown and clear.

II

In a hollow rent by that bright well's fount,
A mighty robber once made his home;—
A man he was full sullen and dark
As ever brooded on murder stark.

III

A mighty man of a fearful name,
Who took their treasures from all who came,
Who hated mankind, who murdered for greed,
With an iron heart for each bloody deed.

IV

As he went[6] by the torrent ford one day,
A weird-like beldame came down the way:
Red was her mantle, and rich and fine,
But toil and travel had dimmed its shine.

V

A war axe in his red hand he took,
And he killed the beldame beside the brook,
And when on the greensward in death she rolled,
In her arms, lo! a babe, clad in pearls and gold!

VI

He buried the beldame beside the wave,
And he took the child to his mountain cave,
And the first jewel his red hand met,
A Fern and a Hound on its gem were set.

VII

Yet darkly he raised his hand to kill,
But his fierce heart smote him such blood to spill;
Oh! the rage for murder was then delayed
By the innocent smile of that infant maid!

VIII

He made it a bed of the fern leaves green
And he nursed it well from that evening sheen,
And day by day, as the sweet child grew,
The heart of the robber grew softer too.

IX

Ten long years were past and gone,
And the robber sat by the ford's grey stone,
And there on the eve of a Springtide day
A lordly pageant came down the way.

X

Before them a banner of green and gold[7]
With a Fern and a Hound on its glittering fold,
Behind it a prince with a sad pale face,—
A mighty prince of a mighty race.

XI

The robber looked on the Fern and Hound,
Then sprang towards the prince with an eager bound,
And 'Why art thou sad, O King?' said he,
'In the midst of that lordly companie!'[†]

XII

His kindly purpose they all mistook,
For though wan and worn yet fierce his look,
And sudden a noble drew out his glaive,
And cleft his skull on the beldame's grave!

XIII

'Sad,' said the pale prince 'my fate has been,
Since the dark enchanters have ta'en my queen,
Since they bore my child from the nurse's hand
And keep her away in th'enchanted land.'

XIV

The dying robber half rose by the wave,
'Oh! enter,' he cried, 'you lonely cave!'
They entered,—the pale prince[8] found his child,
And all was joy in that mountain wild.

Altogether too long for quotation are some of the best ballads, such as the 'Baron and the Miller', or 'Murgal and Garmon',[9] that story of a lover who, touching on the phantom shores of Hy Brasil, returns for his betrothed, that they may dwell together where the birds are like 'the children of the rainbow'.[10] Legend dear to the Celtic heart, sung of in a thousand ways—surely this love of shadowy Hy Brasil is very characteristic of the Celtic race, ever desiring the things that lie beyond the actual; dreamy and fanciful things, unreal if you will, as are all the belongings of the spirit from the point of view of the body, that loves to cry 'dreamer, dreamer', to its hard task-master the spirit.

Of songs and ballads of the homely type, such as 'The Spalpeen', there are several fine examples, reminding us that though we have perhaps no poet equal to the best of the English, we have a poetry of the people, altogether different to those vulgar ballads of modern England, that I sometimes fear will invade us; those stories of impossible street boys sentimentalising about heaven, those half Police News half didactic poems so popular as penny readings, or those still lower songs of the London streets.[11] When we have touched pathos we have redeemed it with beauty, when we have touched the familiar we have set it to music.

We now come to the songs, altogether inferior to the ballads.

I

The cock and the sparrow[12]
One morn, at the sack of Cragnour,[13]
A cock and a sparrow were speaking,
While neath where they sat on the tower
The crop-ears their fury were wreaking—
Were wreaking in blood, fire and smoke.
'Ah! the castle is ta'en, bone and marrow,
And my poor Irish heart it is broke,'
Said the brave jolly cock to the sparrow.

II

'For the crop-ears will have us full soon,
And our bed will be no bed of roses;
They will starve us right dead to the tune
Of a psalm that they'll twang thro' their noses.
Never more shall I crow in the hall,
For the gloom there my bosom would harrow,
May the fiend whip them off, psalm and all',
Said the brave jolly cock to the sparrow.

III

' 'Tis certain the castle they've got,
And 'tis sure that they'll slay all that's in it;
But as victory's theirs and what not,
You're expected to crow like a linnet',
Cried the sparrow with voice sad low.
'But I'd[14] rather my grave cold and narrow,
Than at Puritan triumph[15] to crow,'
Said the brave jolly cock to the sparrow.

We must say farewell to the songs and ballads, their virtues are simplicity and strength, the faults occasional baldness and a lack of finish in the style—a besetting sin of the Irish poets; though indeed the poets of what I have called the bardic class are often less careful than the others about finish; not heeding, I suppose, so sensitive an instrument of expression, having to deal with things large and simple rather than subtle. In a later edition were added other poems, including the 'Blacksmith of Limerick', a fine ballad, far too well known for me to quote it. It is in nearly all the 'collections'.[16]

PART TWO

In 1866 Joyce settled in Boston, U.S.A., as a doctor, and, in 1876, appeared *Deirdre,*† by far his finest work, written, as his brother, Professor Joyce, tells us, in his carriage, going from patient to patient.

Founded on one of those romances, called by the old Celtic bards 'The Three Sorrows of Song',[17] it has all the essentials for a popular poem—a fine story, swiftness of narration, richness of colouring, typical character, a hero for its centre—that is to say, it was, before all things, bardic. In three or four days ten thousand copies were sold.

In the first canto warriors are feasting at the house of the king's story-teller, Feilimid,[†] who, finding himself sad—he knew not why—had given a great feast, and invited the king, his master; and now—

> Full soon the old man felt his soul restored,
> As laugh and jest were bandied round the board,
> As the king smiled upon him, kind and gay,
> As songs were sung, and harps began to play,
> And cups were kissed by many a bearded lip.[18]

In the midst of the feast comes the news that a daughter has been born to Feilimid. The feasters are all silent—

> As from the door, in solemn slow array,
> A bevy of old beldames, two by two,
> Paced rustling up the hall.
> . . . . .
> First of all there came
> Old Levarcam,[†] the conversation dame
> Of the great king, who told him all the sport,
> And loves, and plots, and scandals of the court.
> A pace before them walked she mincingly,
> And to each great lord bent the pliant knee;
> Sharp eyes she had, each speck and fault that saw,
> And face as yellow as an osprey's claw,
> And wrinkled, like tough vellum, by the heat,
> As moved she toward the monarch's golden seat,
> Smirking and smiling on the baby bright.[19]

Caffa,[†20] the Druid, rises, and prophesies that in times to come this child shall be a woman so beautiful that mighty queens shall long for her destruction, and kings fall down before her, and her face shall kindle war through the whole land,

> Led by one aged lord
> Now unto all things callous grown.[21]

The warriors agree that the child shall be slain at once.

> As when, mid Allen's bogs, some sunny day
> The wild geese with their offspring are at play,
> And as they gambol by the lakelet's edge,
> The hunter's arrow shears the rustling sedge

And splashes in the shallow marsh there by,
At once the wild fowl raise their signal cry
Of danger, and, loud cackling in their fear,
Some hide in reeds, some seek the middle mere;
So at the grisly warriors' words of doom,
The aged dames 'gan rustling round the room,
Some fled the hall, some gathered round the child,
And shrieking, clapped their hands with clamour[22] wild.

But the king decides that the child shall be hidden in a lonely palace, in the charge of Levarcam,[†] and when old enough, he will make her his wife.

The second book, dealing with the childhood of Deirdre, is perhaps the most beautiful in the poem. At first she is happy, but gradually a sadness, a foreshadowing, falls on her, and she begins to ask questions about everything in a beautiful child-like way.

Oh, Levarcam,[†]
Come, tell me!—oh, come tell me what I am!
Did I come here just like the summer fly
To sparkle in the sun, and then to die?
I've asked the flies full oft, but murmuringly
They said they were too full of present glee
To give me answer, and they passed away;
And once unto the streamlet did I say
'What am I?' for in grove or garden walk,
I oft feel lonely and perforce must talk
To all things round that creep, or walk, or fly,
And well I know their speech. And 'what am I?'
I asked the stream; and it is curlish too,
And would not speak, but from its weeds upthrew
A great brown frog puffed up with too much pride,
And ugly! ugly! ugly! hoarse he cried;
And then from off the streamlet's grassy brim
He made great mouths at me, and I at him.[23]

At first she knows nothing of the world but the palace garden. Years go by, and at last one day she climbs a tree, and sees over the high walls

The great world spread out.[24]

One day, as I sat neath the beechen bough,
I saw a little squirrel climb the tree,

Sit on a branch and eye me roguishly.
These were my glad times, and the squirrel gay,
Amid the branches did it seem to say,
With wild bright eyes, and bushy tail upcurled,
Come up! Come up! come up, and see the world!
And up I clomb the green tree after him,
Higher and higher still, from limb to limb.[25]

From this tree she sees the young warrior and is seen by him; hence all the trouble.

They escape, and then begin their wanderings, their odyssey of love, the beauty of Deirdre[†] kindling war everywhere. By land and sea they go, flying the wrath of the king. When they reach the shores of Alba,[26] they have been so long at sea that 'many an old dame's tongue wagged voluble' with joy, and the warriors 'shook their spears with gladness'.

They are enticed home to Eman[27] by treacherous promises from the king, from a beautiful island in the sea, where at last they had found peace. For a time the tent of Deirdre[†] is guarded by Manannan,[†] the sea god. He stands by the door, unseen by any but Deirdre[†] and her child. There is a beautiful passage where the child—with all the fearlessness of infancy—asks the giant phantom for his jewelled dagger. Soon their death is planned. Naoise[†] and all his tribe are treacherously slain, and Deirdre[†] falls dead on the body of her lover.

What gives the poem its especial excellence, after its unlingering narrative, are the descriptions and the little touches of character. There is no vapour of the study about them; they come direct from nature— earth touches.

In 1879 appeared his last work, *Blanid*. The dedication is lovely, and sad with that Celtic sadness that is half tenderness.

O Thou, to come, though yet perchance unborn,
    My country's poet, prince of bards, sublime
'Mongst those who in the future's gleaming morn
    Will make great music, in thy manhood's prime
And day of fame, remember me, and climb
    My hill of rest, and take thy musing way
Unto the place of tombs, and with sweet rhyme
    Stand thou beside my headstone lone and gray,
And strike thy sounding harp and sing no little lay!

For I am of the race of those longsyne,
The maker of heroic minstrelsy.[28]

But the poem itself is much inferior to Deirdre.[†] It is more literary; there is more of the study, less of the earth in it. It has less of that barbaric simplicity that makes *Deirdre*[†] so delightful. The characters have lingered in the vestibules of modern thought, and have learned to talk like this:

> Where the vapours thicken
> Through the city's ways,
> And the people sicken
> In the poisoned blaze
> Of the sun that rots the swamp,
> There beside the failing lamp
> Of the lowly and the stricken,
> He hath stood to cheer and quicken,
> With his harp life's dying rays.[29]

And so on. This is modern, with its cities and its philanthropy. The old heroes were as simple as children who had never been to school.

There is a slight hint of Swinburne[30] in the rhythm of one or two of the lyrics that is startling after the originality of all the rest of Joyce's work. Not that the poem does not contain many original things, such as this description of how a harper finds his fairy sweetheart:

> And now he touched his harp, and soft and low
> The strings spoke to his fingers, and anear
> The kine drew in the ever-brightening glow
> Of the calm dawn, while one, unknown to fear,
> The infant of the herd, with footsteps slow
> Came nigher still, and stood with raptured ear,
> As if she ne'er again cared to behold
> The buttercups that turned her teeth to gold.
>
> And still the sweet strings spoke, and nearer yet
> To the green tree the large-eyed listener drew,
> With dainty footsteps that scarce seemed to fret
> From the young flowers and grass the diamond dew.
> Then stooped the player; down his harp he set
> Beside the tree, and from his ambush flew
> And grasped the bright-backed offspring of the morn
> By one pink ear, and by one budding horn.
>
> A hurrying by the lakelet, and a cry,
> A sparkle in his eyes—no more, no more

He held his little captive; with a sigh
He turned, and on the meadow's blossomed floor,
His love stood near the stream-bank,[31] bright and shy
As a young seagull on some sunny shore.[†]

In this poem Joyce kept much less close to the original story than in *Deirdre*.[†] I think this was a mistake, for no one knew better than an old bard what moved men, for he was taught in a bitter school—the school of fierce dissent and applause. He was like a great orator, who only when he feels all hearts beat in unison with his, rises to his best, and becomes alone with the universe and his own voice. Therefore, the bardic work ever human and living.

I hold Joyce to be the poet of all the external things that appertain to the barbaric earth—the earth of hunters and riders, and all young people; the poet of armour and hunting, of hounds and horses. That he was in no way a singer, also, of man's inner nature, of the vague *desires*, though it takes from his stature as a poet, makes him so much the dearer to many worn with modern unrest. In seeking to restore the young world, long faded, he has restored to us for an instant our childhood.

CLARENCE MANGAN

(1803 1849)

*This article on Clarence Mangan appeared on 12 March 1887, as part
of the series entitled "Irish Poets and Irish Poetry" that Yeats contributed
to* The Irish Fireside *during 1886 and 1887. Yeats's first article on Sir
Samuel Ferguson (pp. 3–9 in this collection) and his review "The
Poetry of R. D. Joyce" (pp. 28–38 in this collection) were both published in* The Irish Fireside *under this heading. In the issue that contains this article, the series title has been changed to "Irish Authors and
Poets," but clearly Yeats's article is of a piece with his reviews of Ferguson and Joyce.*

*During these years, Yeats seems to have carried out much research
into Mangan's life. As his italicized notice of copyright under his title
indicates, Yeats was quite proud of announcing in print for the first
time the name of Mangan's love, Miss Stackpoole. Much of the information and opinions of this piece were repeated in an article entitled
"Clarence Mangan's Love Affair," which appeared in* United Ireland
*on 22 August 1891 (pp. 134–38 in this collection). It is apparent from
this second article that Yeats's identification of Mangan's beloved had
not gone unchallenged. By 1891, however, Yeats had the corrobora-
tion of Sir Charles Gavan Duffy, who knew both Mangan and Miss
Stackpoole.*

*Of the three poets—Thomas Davis, Sir Samuel Ferguson, and
Mangan—whom Yeats claimed as his literary forebears in his poem "To
Ireland in the Coming Times," Mangan was admired the most for his
literary, non-nationalistic qualities. James Joyce "discovered" Mangan
again about 1900 without being aware of, or perhaps not caring
about, Yeats's and others' efforts on Mangan's behalf during the previous decades. It has been Mangan's fate to be often discovered.*

All my Divinities have died of grief,
And left me wedded to the Rude and Real.[1]
MANGAN

One thing is to be remembered concerning Mangan. Unlike most poets, his childhood was not spent among woods and fields, with Nature's primitive peace and ancient happiness. He had no early dream—no treasure-house of innocent recollection: his birthplace sooty Fishamble-street—his father a grocer, who boasted that his children would run into a mouse-hole to escape him. His school, round the corner in Saul's-court, in those days given over to clothes-lines and children and sparrows, and now abolished to make room for Lord Edward-street. From here he was transferred to a scrivener's office, his family having come down in life and now depending in the main on him. Concerning his office companions, he himself has left something on record in that strange fragment of autobiography prefixed to the Poets of Munster:[2]

My nervous and hypochondriacal feelings almost verged on[3] insanity. I seemed to myself to be shut up in a cavern with serpents and scorpions, and all hideous and monstrous things, which writhed and hissed around me, and discharged their slime and venom upon my person.

Yet, likely enough, these office companions were by no means bad fellows. From time immemorial the children of genius have got on ill with the children of men. King Alfred let the cakes burn, and the housewife did her best to lead him a life of it; for her the smoke and smother of her burnt cakes, for him the fiery dream and the tremendous vision.[4] Seven years Mangan spent in this office, three more as an attorney's clerk; yet acquired, after his day's work, much polyglot knowledge of foreign tongues, loving especially to read about the strange and mysterious—contributed largely to the Dublin Penny Journal and other papers poems, acrostics, &c. Meanwhile the cloud had drawn closer and closer about him; already he had written 'The Dying Enthusiast' and 'The One Mystery', all but the saddest of his songs. His style was fully developed, with its energy and old-fashioned directness. Of late the muse has left her ancient ways, and is now a lady of fashion, learned in refined insincerities and graceful affections, smiling behind her fan—ça ira.
Whatever fragment of inbred happiness remained to his spirit, that had asked all things and was given routine and ill health, was lost now;

he loved and was jilted; concerning the object of his love, rumour has contradictory voices, beautiful and *spirituelle,* says Mitchel,[5] by no means so, says my informant. One thing alone seems pretty certain, she was a Miss Stackpoole (now for the first time named) of Mount Pleasant Square,[†] one of three sisters.

A short dream this love affair of Mangan's. Before long between him and his Eden was the flaming cherub and the closed gate. I have heard a curious story, which I give for what it is worth, of his rushing with drawn knife at one who had spoken ill of his faithless 'Frances;' now, if not before, he sought the comfort of rum, and some say also, opium—

> And when the inanity of all things human,
> And when the dark ingratitude of man,
> And when the hollower perfidy of woman
> Comes down like night upon the feelings—[6]

What cure for this? Why, rum and water. So writes he in one of his strange latter poems.[7]

About this time he is described as follows, by Mitchel, who saw him in the library of Trinity College, when Mangan was employed compiling a catalogue—[8]

An acquaintance pointed out to me a man perched on the top of a ladder, with the whispered information that the figure was Clarence Mangan. It was an unearthly and ghostly figure, in a brown garment, the same garment (to all appearance) which lasted till the day of his death. The blanched hair was totally unkempt; the corpse-like features still as marble; a large book was in his arms, and all his soul was in the book. I had never heard of Clarence Mangan before, and knew not for what he was celebrated,[9] whether as a magician, a poet, or a murderer; yet took a volume and spread it on a table, not to read, but with pretence of reading, to gaze on the spectral creature upon the ladder.

Towards the last Mangan commenced his autobiography, or 'confession', as he called it. But, haunted by apparitions, as he believed, and overpowered by his ever-growing misery, he could no longer at all do that which was so difficult to calm Goethe—distinguish between fact and illusion.[10] When this was pointed out to him he bid them destroy what he had written. Fortunately this was not done, and it remains not so much a record of his early life as a wonderful piece of the sorrow of his latter, that had stained even memory its own colour.

For days he would disappear, living in a barn or some such place, drinking and brooding. His haunts were ever the lowest taverns. I read in Mrs. Atkinson's '*Biography of Mary Aikenhead*,'[11] that once he was brought to St. Vincent's Hospital. 'Oh! the luxury of clean sheets!' he exclaimed. The man with the 'face handsome in outline, bloodless, and wrinkled, though not with age', and the 'blue eyes, distraught with the opium eater's dreams', and the 'heavy lids', appears to have proved a somewhat troublesome patient. Said one of the sisters—'These poets have nerves in every pore'.[12] Yet, withal, he does not seem to have been so much a weak character as a man fated. He had powerful convictions, political and other; and convictions bear the same relation to the character as thoughts do to the intellect. In all he wrote there was a sort of intensity, not merely of the intellectual or of the aesthetic nature, but of the whole man; and supreme misery, like supreme happiness, or supreme anything, seems only given to the world's supreme spirits.

At last death released him from his misery. He died of cholera in the Meath Hospital. I have it from one who had it from the doctor in attendance, that when he was dead his face became beautiful and calm. When the contorted soul had gone, the muscles relaxed, and the clay returned to its primal innocence.

Other poets have found refuge from their unhappiness in philosophic subtleties and aerial turnings and pirouettings of the spirit. But this man, Mangan, born in torpid days in a torpid city, could only write in diverse fashions, 'I am Miserable'. No hopes! No philosophy! No illusions! A brute cry from the gutters of the earth! and for solace or rather for a drug—this—

No more, no more, with aching brow,
    And restless heart, and burning brain,
We ask the When, the Where, the How,
    And ask in vain.
And all philosophy, all faith,
    All earthly—all celestial lore,
Have but one voice, which only saith—
    Endure—adore.[13]

His work is divided into translations from the German, the Irish, and poems from apocryphal Persian or other sources, and original poems in the main personal. Pages there are abundantly wearying and hollow, but whenever there are thoughts on the littleness of life or the short time its good things stay with us, or the vanity of all subtile and sad longings, or if there be any fragment of ghostly pageantry, then from beneath the pen of this haunted (for so he believed) and prematurely aged man, the words flowed like electric flashes. I do not find as much beauty in his oriental poems as others do, though they, like his Irish poems, have a certain radiant energy. Of these last, 'My Dark Rosaleen', is quite wonderful with the passionate self-abandonment of its latter stanzas. But powerful and moving more than anything else that he has done are his few personal poems 'Twenty Golden Years Ago', with its beautiful ending—

> Soon thou sleepest where the thistles blow,
>   Curious anti-climax to thy dreams,
> Twenty golden years ago.[†14]

'Nameless',[15] and, may[16] say 'Siberia', for that Siberia where the White Tzar[17] sends so many of his wisest and best, seems a sort of type of that Siberia within, where his thoughts wandered and murmured, like outlaws cast from the world's soft places for some unknown offence—

> Pain as in a dream,
>   When years go by,
> Funeral paced yet fugitive,
> When man lives and doth not live,[18]
>   Doth not live nor die.

But far the strongest of all his poems is 'Nameless'. He who has once learnt this poem will never forget it; it will stay with him with something of the eternity of painful things. Many poems as delicate and fragrant as rose-leaves we soon forget—they vanish with the coquetry of joy. All the great poems of the world have their foundations fixed in agony—not that this is, in the highest sense, a great poem; it is a great lyric, an altogether different thing.

I know not whether I may not seem to have over-valued Clarence Mangan. No, I am not impartial—who is? Under even the most philosophic utterance is a good dose of personal bias. There is no impartial critic save Time, and he only seems so, maybe, because there is no one to accuse him.

Plainly, this scrivener's clerk brought one thing into the world that was not there before, one new thing into letters—his misery—a misery peculiar in quality. He never lost belief in happiness because he was miserable, or faith in goodness because his life was spent among the taverns. He had not that solace.

He can never be popular like Davis, for he did not embody in clear verse the thoughts of normal mankind.[19] He never startles us by saying beautifully things we have long felt. He does not say look at yourself in this mirror; but, rather, 'Look at me—I am so strange, so exotic, so different'.

FINN MACCOOL

This article was presumably Yeats's first contribution to The Gael, *a weekly newspaper mainly devoted to Gaelic sports news, published by the Gaelic Athletic Association. The literary editor was Yeats's mentor John O'Leary. The first issue of this paper appeared on 9 April 1887. The issue in which this article came out was dated 23 April 1887.*

Long thought to be lost, this article, in fragmentary form, was found in the Crone Papers of Belfast Public Library. A very full account of Yeats's involvement with The Gael, *and the circumstances surrounding the composition of this Finn MacCool article as well as the review of Katharine Tynan's* Shamrocks, *which follows in this collection, may be found in John S. Kelly's article "Aesthete among the Athletes: Yeats's Contributions to* The Gael, *" in* Yeats: An Annual of Critical and Textual Studies *2 (1984), pp. 75–143 (edited by Richard J. Finneran; Ithaca: Cornell University Press, 1984).*

John S. Kelly has kindly allowed the use of his notes in this edition and they are so identified in brackets. Before the reprinting of the Finn article in Yeats: Annual, *Kelly explained the source of Yeats's narrative and also conjectured what words were missing in this following passage from his article:*

> *The original Irish narrative that Yeats summarizes in this essay is, as he points out, awkward and poorly constructed. It was transcribed into the Psalter of Cashel in 1453 by John Boy O'Clery and others from a twelfth-century original at Potterlath in Kilkenny for Edmond Butler, head of the sept of Mac Richard, later Earls of Ormonde. It was this Edmond, and not a "brother Edmund," that the scribe wished home earlier from the meeting. In planning his article, Yeats probably would have begun by discussing the place of Finn in Irish mythology, before turning to an account of the early adventures paraphrased from O'Donovan's translation. This translation, and also presumably Yeats's version,*

begins with an account of the Battle of Cnucha fought between Cumhall (Finn's father) and Uirgrenn for the chieftainship of the Fianna, in which Cumhall is slain by Goll, a son of Morna, a killing that is to lead to a continuous feud between the two clans. At his death, Cumhall's wife Muirenn is with child, and upon the birth of her son, whom she names Deimne but who is subsequently to be known as Finn, she asks two aged druidesses to rear him secretly, as she fears for his safety at the hands of the sons of Morna. The two wise women sequester him in the woods of Sli- abh Bladma (Slieve Bloom), and after six years his mother, now pregnant by her second husband, makes a clandestine and per- ilous journey to see him. Finding him asleep in a forest hut, she composes a tender lullaby over him, and before leaving, she asks the women if they will continue to foster him until he is of age and able to hunt. They evidently agree to this, for the narrative moves on to his first hunting kill: "The boy came forth alone on a certain day, and saw the ducks upon the lake. He made a shot at them, and cut off her feathers and wings, so that she died, and afterwards took her to the hunting booth: and this was Finn's first chase" [Fenian Poems, ed. John O'Daly, Transactions of the Ossianic Society 4 (1859), 295 (Kelly's note)]. It is at this point that the preserved fragment of Yeats's article in The Gael begins, and by reference to the translation it is possible to guess at the words missing because of a tear in the page. These appear in brack- ets below. (Yeats Annual 2 (1984), 85–86)

——nt to return to the boy in his forest. [His] first exploit is the killing of a wild [duck] with an arrow; later on he aston[ishes] his two old nurses by dragging a [wil]d deer to them by the horns; but the budding hero does not long use so innocently his boyish strength. While roving about, he had made the acquaintance of a large party of boys, and played hurley against them, and beaten them. Then he played singlehanded against a fourth, then a third, then all of their number, and won. All this they told to the master of a neighbouring fort, who answered "kill him." They tried, and failed. Some time afterwards, while wandering in the forest, he came upon a place where the boys were bathing, and being full of rage, he sprang in and drowned nine of them. Now, hav- ing come to his strength, it was needful that he should acquire the sec- ond power of an ancient warrior, that of poetry. Accordingly, we find him living seven years on the banks of the Boyne, with an old bard called Finn-eges[11] who sought the salmon of wisdom. At last the famous salmon is taken. 'Have you eaten of it?' says the bard. 'No, but it's burnt my finger, and I put my finger in my mouth'. 'Then you have tasted it, and you are the Finn[†] of whom they prophesied and not I'. Ever after, if Finn[†] wished to know anything that was going on in the world, he had only to put his finger in his mouth. He was now admitted into the order of Fenians—the Irish 'Table Round'—and to prove his mastery of verse, composed a poem to May Day, the day, perhaps, of his initiation, which has come down to us. I give here a somewhat hasty, though fairly literal version of it, in rhyme:

> How beautiful thy colours are, oh marvellous morn of May,
> The black-birds pour their copious lays; would Leigha were
>   here,
> The cuckoos sing unceasingly; how welcome day by day
> The gay and noble seasons; the summer swallows shear
> The streams beside the branchy wood, the horses seek the
>   pool,
> The heather spreads her long loose hair; the frail marsh-
>   cottons grow,
> The far bewildered planets pour on all an influence cool,
> And seas are lulled in quietness, and lavish blossoms blow.[2]

The book, translated by the Ossianic Society, from which the early adventures of Finn[†] are taken, was copied by some medieval monk from an older MS., and being much wearied by it all, he probably shortened and marred it. Ah, poor monk, what a bore you found; ah, this heathen world! 'Oh, Virgin Mary, what a long time till brother Edmund comes home from the meeting,' he wrote in Gaelic on the margin, and there it is still.[3]

Finn[†] was now a member of the Fenians or Fiani. Hard trials had each competitor for membership to undergo. He was first chased through a wood, with the odds of a single tree, by men with spears, and he failed if they reached him, if his arms trembled in his hands, if his plaited hair was unloosed by the boughs, if his feet broke a withered branch. He had to leap as high as his forehead, stoop under a branch as high as his knees, and pluck a thorn out of his heel without stopping in his course. When this trial was over, standing in a trench to his knees, a willow wand in one hand, a shield in the other, he defended himself against nine of the Fenians, casting their spears all together. If they touched him he failed. Succeeding in all these, he had to prove his proficiency in the many sorts of poetry. This over, he swore many things; never to receive a portion with a wife, but choose her only for herself; never to refuse anything to him who has asked; never to fly from less than nine champions. Henceforth he shall have no home, his food he shall cook by laying it, wrapt in rushes, in a hole dug in the earth, and strewing red hot stones above.[4]

These Fenians, of whom before long Finn[†] became the chief, having around him Ossian, Oscar, Dermot, Caoilte,[†] and many more, were the Militia[†] of Ireland; their duties, the defence of the country against Alban[†] and African Pirates, the protection of the Ardrigh,[5] at this time the famous *Cormac Mac Art,* in whose reign Tara was at its greatest splendour; but far from this luxury in the vast forests, the Fenians lived rudely and simply as Cuchulain[†] of old; while those around them sought to be architects of kingdoms, of armies, of splendour, they longed only to be the architects of themselves, to be braver than any, and generous beyond dreams. Homeless, in winter they were quartered on the people; in summer they slept on the earth they loved—that earth they were ever wont to kneel down and kiss before they entered the battle.

They sought to be that which Cuchulain[†] and his followers were without seeking—men of nature. They were chivalrous; the primeval men were heroic. History knows of nothing more important than this brotherhood, for the wave of their influence swept on through Wales with her Arthurian[†] Knights, on over Britain, over Europe, till joining with the worship of the Virgin, surging in from the east, it became mediaeval chivalry, that dim seeking for a light departed in the morning of the world.

Not till he is old, with his sons, and his sons' sons about him, does Finn[†] do his greatest deeds. First he challenges the demons. It is a fine scene from the epic of those times,[6] the now old Finn[†] on the grey peak of Slieve Cullin[†] defying the demons of the earth. Henceforth he has dealings without end with men and phantoms; at Ventry he repels the invasion of the 'King of the world'. For a year the battle rages with such frenzy, that a young prince who has done most brave deeds, goes mad in the battle, and rushing away, screams and chatters in a far off valley, where, says the old story, all the madmen of Ireland would congregate if loose.[7]

Like Conor, the pursuer of Deirdre in the previous cycle, this old man, full of the solitude and weariness of age, has an implacable love. He pursues the wise and beautiful Grania and her lover Dermot, over the whole of Ireland; they escape through the friendship of the Fenians; at last Dermot is wounded mortally by a boar. Finn[†] can cure him by giving him a drink from his enchanted hands; he will not, and the lover dies foretelling the battle in which shall fall the hosts of Finn.[†] The Fenians are gathered apart, muttering and planning, yet still obedient. Suddenly they see Finn[†] and Grania approaching. Yes, even she, fascinated by that imperious, fatal, and scarce human existence on which she leant. Strangest of love stories. Mysterious tragedy of a soul. From the whole ranks of the Fini there goes a single shout of laughter.[8]

Scorning everyone who was not daring as themselves; imposing on the whole country such terrible game laws, that no one, according to Mr. O'Grady, would venture to pick up a hare even if he found it dead on his path;[9] they had raised up innumerable enemies, who, under Cairby of the Liffy, gave them battle at Gabra. They kill Cairby, and his people they scatter to the winds. But their power is broken; three alone of the heroes remain: Finn,† Caoilte,† and Ossian. In the battle they find Oscar dying, the blood pouring from his mail. He dies. They sit on the ground beside him heeding nothing, says the old tale, till, through the dim air of morning shone his masterless banner, and the red berries of the quicken trees. They make him a great Tomb. Soon after, his wife, Aideen, dies, and they bury her under the cromlech at Howth:

> They heaved the stone; they heaped the cairn;
>   Said Ossian, in a queenly grave
> We leave her 'mong the fields of fern,
>   Between the cliff and wave.
>
> The cliff behind stands clear and bare,
>   And bare, above the heathery steep,
> Scales the clear heaven's expanse, to where
>   The Danaan Druids sleep.[10]

Finn† is killed. How? Rumour has confused voices; and now he sleeps in the centre of a mountain in Donegal, his hound and his steed beside him, awaiting, like another Barbarossa,[11] the time of his country's greatest need, when he will awake and sound his dreadful horn. And Ossian? He passed away to the island of Hy-Brasil,† till longing after three hundred years to see Finn† once more, he returned; but the moment his feet touched an earthly shore, his three hundred years fell on him, and his beard swept the ground, and his form bent double, and his eyes became blind. Patrick and his saints kept him with them, and tried hard to make him think of heaven, but the burthen of his cry was ever, 'better Hell with the Fini, than Heaven without them'. And, what of the unconquerable Caoilte†? He stormed the palaces of the Gods at Ossory; and lives there in immortal youth.[12]

Under all these old legends there is, without doubt, much fact, though, I confess, I care but little whether there be or not. A nation's history is not in what it does, this invader or that other; the elements or destiny decides all that; but what a nation imagines that is its history, there is its heart; than its legends, a nation owns nothing more precious. Without her possible mythical siege of Troy,[13] perhaps, Greece would never have had her real Thermopylæ. Learn those of your own country, let the young love them. I wish I could recommend you some poem concerning these events, but there is none of any importance. About the previous cycle there are plenty, by Ferguson, and Joyce, and de Vere.[†]

Miss Tynan, however, will soon publish a 'Dermot and Grania'. A fragment descriptive of the peace that followed the long flight, and preceded the death of Dermot, appeared in the last GAEL.

THE CELTIC ROMANCES
IN MISS TYNAN'S NEW BOOK

This review of Katharine Tynan's Shamrocks *(London, 1887) appeared in* The Gael *on 11 June 1887. The circumstances of its composition were discussed in full in John S. Kelly's comprehensive article on Yeats's contributions to* The Gael, *the newspaper of the Gaelic Athletic Association. Kelly's article is entitled "Aesthete among the Athletes: Yeats's Contributions to* The Gael," *and it appeared in* Yeats: An Annual of Critical and Textual Studies 2 *(1984), pp. 75–143 (ed. Richard J. Finneran; Ithaca: Cornell University Press, 1984). Kelly notes in his article that "An extract from this review was discovered in* The Irish Monthly 16 *(February 1888), 110–15, by Taketosh Furmoto [probably a misspelling of Taketoshi Fumoto], and was printed as 'W. B. Yeats's Missing Review,'* Times Literary Supplement, 4 January 1974, p. 12 (98)." *The text reprinted in this volume is that which appeared in Kelly's article. John S. Kelly has kindly permitted his notes to be used in this edition, identified by his name in brackets.*

Tynan (1861–1931), Irish poet and novelist, was the first of a long series of women writers from whom Yeats sought advice and sympathy. Yeats first met her in 1885, and when he went to London in 1887 they wrote to each other regularly. Their correspondence during the period of their warmest friendship, 1887–92, contains, in the letters of Yeats that have survived, the most accurate account of this period of his life. Since Tynan had published a volume of poems in 1885, four years before Yeats's The Wanderings of Oisin *appeared in 1889, Yeats treated her as his superior in literary experience. He told her how important it was to stress the Irish qualities in her writing, and, it is clear from her memoirs, she treated Yeats, who was in his late Romantic phase, with affectionate indulgence. In his unpublished autobiography,* Memoirs *(1972), Yeats discusses the possibility of marrying Katharine Tynan (32). There are signs in the correspondence that she reacted with jealousy to Yeats's account of his first meeting with Maud Gonne (McHugh, ed.,* W. B. Yeats: Letters to Katharine Tynan, *89–90). No mat-*

ter what their feelings toward one another, the rules of Victorian propriety were adhered to in their letters. They had corresponded for about two and a half years before Yeats presumed to ask to address her by her Christian name; thereafter she was "My dear Katey."

After Tynan married Henry Hinkson in 1893, she and Yeats corresponded less frequently, and rarely wrote to each other after 1895. Yeats's spiritualism had always been repugnant to her deep Catholic convictions, and with his widening intellectual interests Yeats soon had less and less in common with his old friend. To earn money, Tynan had to turn her attention away from the Irish Literary Movement to the writing of novels, an activity in which she was prolific, producing more than one hundred romances for the circulating libraries.

In her 1913 volume of memoirs, Twenty-five Years: Reminiscences, *she quoted extensively and haphazardly from Yeats's early letters to her. Yeats was angry, partly because she had been indiscreet and partly because she had not given him an opportunity to "improve" the letters. Perhaps because of this difference of opinion, Yeats mentions Tynan only once by name in the published version of his* Autobiographies, *p. 101.*

Tynan's first volume of poems, Louise de la Vallière *(London, 1885), was heavily influenced by Christina Rossetti. Her second volume,* Shamrocks *(London, 1887), although dedicated to William Michael and Christina Rossetti, showed the effect of Yeats's injunctions to be as Irish as possible. Her mild-mannered cheerfulness is well summed up in her epigraph to* Shamrocks: *"'Tis always Morning somewhere in the world."*

*In Carolyn Holdsworth's full account of the relationship of Yeats and Katharine Tynan in the article "'Shelly Plain': Yeats and Katharine Tynan" (*Yeats Annual 2, *ed. Richard J. Finneran [London: Macmillan, 1983], pp. 59–92), she explains the circumstances of the appearance of the one-paragraph notice of* Shamrocks *which appeared in the London weekly* Truth, *11 August 1887. Barry O'Brien signed the column, but Roger McHugh, editor of Yeats's letters to Tynan, thinks that this paragraph was by Yeats. The paragraph reads as follows:*

> *Have you read any of Miss Katherine [sic] Tynan's poetry? I have just been reading "Shamrocks," which seems to me full of gorgeous colour and rich music. Miss Tynan is an Irish Jean Ingelow, neither very subtle nor very thoughtful, but, what is perhaps better, fervid and passionately direct. Her longest poems deal with wild and pathetic Irish legends; but, probably, such half-religious poetry as "The Heart of a Mother" and "St. Fran-*

*cis and [sic: "to"] the Birds" will be most popular. I should like
you to read "Shamrocks," and to let me know if you think with
me, that the author is at the beginning of a long and famous
career.*

Frankly, in what follows I write somewhat uncritically—as fellow-worker of fellow-worker—having my hands on the same plough—lacking altogether the needful aloofness of the critic. The leaders of the Irish legendary and barbaric school have long been Ferguson, de Vere,[†] and Joyce.[1] Ferguson easily best. De Vere, though not surpassed in the notes of minor passion—witness the bard, Ethell[†]—withall somewhat monkish; like the old nobleman in the play 'no thronging presence but a ceremonious chapel filled with music,'[2] and Joyce, a gallant story teller, lacking the poetic intensity of either. To this band Miss Tynan joins herself with the story of Dermot and Grainne (ancient), with the story of Fergus (half her own), and the story of Aibric (her own). 'Dermot and Grainne', the biggest argosy[†] she has yet sent forth on the troubled waters of song, I shall do my best to describe, letting Miss Tynan, as often as may be, speak for herself.

At Tara, in the halls of Cormac Mac Art, there was much feasting, for his daughter, Grainne, was to wed with Finn MacCool[†]—'June's red rose with snow'.

> This was the bridegroom, Finn,[†] the king of Eire:
> Gnarled like an oak, his face like lichened stone;[3]
> Sullen and fierce, his red eyes sunk and weary,
> Towered o'er all men that giant frame alone.
>
> Like an old tiger that hath lonely lasted
> Years after all his kin be turned to clay;
> Like a huge tree, the thunderbolt hath blasted,
> Black and accurst it stains the face of day.
>
> Yet a great hero—famed in many a story,
> Victor on many a bloody field of fight;
> But drunk with blood and war, and blind with glory,
> And as men deemed, too old for lovers delight.[4]

In Grainne there are no smiles, though her maidens laugh around her, nor does she care that her name be named among the toasts. Little does she prosper among these rubies and silks and ambers, these diamonds that lighten 'like the sea's floor when summer moons are white'.[5] Ah! how evade this old man, whom armies follow, whom omens encircle?

To her side comes Daire, the high priest, and commences naming and describing all that assembled bright host. Little does she heed him. Oh! that she were beyond the 'pleasant plains' and 'wide grey seas,' afar in *Tír na nÓg*.[†] There are no old men there.

> Then she woke up from dreams, and sighed full drear,
> And heard the old voice crooning in her ear[6]
> Of this and that fair deed of many a one;
> And so she turned her weary sense to hear.

He over there is Ossian 'whose song might wake dead world's again.'[7] Beside him his son, Oscar, but who, she asks, is that bronzed warrior 'freckled with many a noon sun's heat.'[8]

> The stateliest man of all the world of men,
> Yon with the great hound's head upon his knee.[9]

Ah, that is Diarmuid.

> Oh! the warm flash rose up from chin to hair;
> And down amid the great feasts song and glare[10]
> All in a stillness and a sudden pause,
> Diarmuid, the knight, looked up and found her fair.

She whispers to one of her maidens, who goes, and returns with a silver goblet studded with gems, lurid like a serpent's eyes. From feaster to feaster it is sent; all sink into a deep drugged slumber save Oscar, Ossian and Diarmuid, to whom the wine was not given. Unto the three, passing among the sleepers, with drooping head, goes Grainne. Unto the fated Diarmuid she tells her love, and places him under Gesa, those mysterious bonds no Fenian might break.

> 'One golden summer hour,
> Through the blue windows of my maiden bower,
> At the great games, I saw thee victor crowned,
> And my heart gave to thee its rose-red flower.[11]

> Who knew thee not, nor how they named thy name,
> Until this night; now by thy knightly fame
> Take me.' Her heavy hair was on the ground,[12]
> And o'er his hands and feet. His eyes 'gan flame,

And flamed and lightened all his dusky face,
Who leaned to her, and for a minutes space
Looked on her, thinking how all loss were gain,[13]
To kiss the lovely eyelids in their place;

Yet forced his gaze from her, and loyally
Urged his allegiance to the king, but she,
'Your bonds—your bonds, my knight,' like silver rain,
Rang through her tears, her laughter, suddenly[14]

Then he bent down and swung her from her knee,
And kissed her long, and kissed her passionately,
Held to his heart her face so still and chill;
'Sweet thou and I together till death,' said he.[15]

They fly. Omens are about the palace of Tara. The corpse lights dance on the heath—all night the banshee cries.

Away they go, into the forests, the faithful Oscar and Ossian speeding them on their way. Out into the entangled forest, no more for him the battle Standard—the Council of his Peers no more, only the entangled forests. No more for her the dance and the brightening of eyes, nor dear companionships for ever; but year after year, life shall wax and wane in flight and in hiding below the interlacing boughs. They have no illusions; Finn[†] never forgives, alike implacable in hatred and in love. Youth, with all its weakness, with all its generosity has long gone by and left him steel and fire. His sons and his sons' sons have many a day been warriors about him. On this supernatural existence even time fawns.

Before the morning, the great hound, Bran—sent by Oscar and Ossian—warns them by thrusting his head against the breast of Diarmuid.

Then Diarmuid woke, and kissed his love in her sleeping,
    'Waken, heart of my heart, for the king is here,[16]
And his wrath is only for me; thou art safe in his keeping.'
    'With thee I live or I die,' was her answer clear.
She bathed her face in a brooklet, singing and sunny;
    She plaited her wealth of hair to a crown for her head;
            She cheered the gloom from his heart with her
            words like honey,
And fed his lips with the wine and the good white bread.

With the gathering of the followers of Finn[†] about them, finish the first three parts. Heretofore the manner has been passionate and lyrical, now it becomes, as is needful for the rendering of an intricate story more purely narrative, though still changing the metre every canto to the end. A Druid, from whose fingers flows the mist, befriends them, and would carry them away beneath his cloak, but Diarmuid sending Grainne, remains himself, for he will not fly from the face of his enemy in secret now or at any time.

'Silken-foot as a thief that flieth by night'[17]

He has built a fort of wattles, with seven doors; at every door are the Fenians; from door to door he passes; they tell him they are friends, he may go free and they will not harm him.

'Not he, for all his hundred fights shall hurt a single hair.'[18]

Well he knows how terrible for them would be the rage of Finn,[†] and passes on; at the seventh door is Finn himself, to[†] him blithely—

> By the door at which thou keepeth watch,[19]
> I win my way to freedom.

And through them he escapes and comes where Grainne waits him by the Lower Shannon, in a cave, where a boar hangs roasting before a wood fire. There that night they slept, and in the grey of the morning, while the old moon waned in the air, the Druid Angus roused them and sent them on their way, warning—

> 'Before I go, my lovers, this warning take from me—
> Seek refuge not, nor shelter in, a single trunked tree,
> With but a single opening, or a cave with but one door,
> Or an island of the sea with single channel;
> Wherever you shall cook your meal you shall not stay to eat,
> Nor sleep where you have eaten, but still with tireless feet,
> Lie down afar and rise afar from the place you slept before.'[20]

Nay, not all the forests of the world piled above their heads would hide them secure from Finn.[†] They visited in their flight, says the old tradition, every corner of Ireland. Of the quaint old narrative which Miss Tynan had to draw upon, I will give one fragment. For a time, a great, gentle giant, called Muadhan, became their servant, and their fisher; and thus is his fishing described:

'He betook himself to a neighbouring wood, and, plucking the straight, long rod of a quicken tree, made fast upon the rod a hair and a hook, and put a holly berry upon the hook, and went and stood over the stream, and took a fish that cast. He put up the second berry, and killed the third fish. Then, putting the hook and the hair under his girdle, and the rod into the earth, he took his three fish with him where Diarmuid and Grainne waited, and laid the fish upon spits. When it was broiled, Muadhan said—'I give the dividing of this fish to thee, Diarmuid.' 'I had rather that thou shouldst divide it thyself,' said Diarmuid. 'Then,' said Muadhan, 'I give the dividing of this fish to thee, O Grainne.' 'It suffices me that thou divide it,' said Grainne. 'Now, hadst thou divided the fish, O Diarmuid,' said Muadhan, 'thou wouldst have given the largest share to Grainne; and had it been Grainne that divided it, it is to thee she would have given the largest share; and since it is I that am dividing it, have thou the largest fish, O Diarmuid, and let Grainne have the second largest fish, and let me have the smallest fish.'[21]

It would take me a long while to tell their other adventures with sufficient detail for interest. Suffice it to say, they are narrated in this poem with full and picturesque utterance. Peace at last is made with Finn;[†] for many years they are happy. The beautiful lines descriptive of their life, you read, doubtless, in the initial GAEL. When was sumptuous leisure and victorious love more beautifully described?—

> They loved as in that hour's surprise,
>   When, with a sudden flush and quiver,
> Each looked to meet the other's eyes,
>   And knew they loved for ever![22]

> They loved as in those days of old
>   When death was with them night and morning;
> Upon their eyes his breathings cold—
>   Within their ears, his warning![23]

Diarmuid was killed at last by the enchanted boar of Ben Bulben,[†] roused from his lair treacherously for this slaying, by Finn.[†] Finn[†] might have saved him, but he would not and Angus, the Druid, came on the wind,

> 'And shrieked three times, so that the shriek did fill
>   The waste world of the clouds, and the wild heaven,
> And the sea islands, and the greenwood seas;
>   And valley and forest, and the highest hill
> Reeled at that sound that rung from morn to even,
>   Blown on all airs, and borne on every breeze.[24]

'I cannot give thee life, son, whispered he;
    But I will heal thy gaping wounds, and bear thee
To my bright house, and on a golden bed
Thou'lt lie, and every day I'll breathe on thee,
    Life for an hour; thou'lt speak, and I shall hear thee,[25]
We two together till the world is dead.'

Through the dusk glooming came a golden bier
    Borne by four eagles whose wide wings were golden,
And hovering, lit the startled evening grey,
And took the good knight with crossed sword and spear,
    And sailed away, and never of man beholden[26]
Was Angus or my Diarmuid from that day.

Here Miss Tynan's poem ends, and few, I fear,[27] will miss that laugh from
the assembled Feni that greeted Grainne leaning on the neck of Finn.†
Grainne whose lamentations once were heard 'in the clouds of the
heaven and the wastes of the firmament.' Ideal love! Long years of devotion! Failure and laughter inextinguishable! A vast and bitter poem, no
dreamy operatic idyl this; we pause, remembering this little deed and
that other. Were they only as they seemed a pretty wilfulness or rather
some inbred frailty of the nature subtly portrayed. Mystery—sea at all
times flowing beneath great books. Our spirits float forth like footless
frigate birds, nor long to plunge there in. The luxury of the great deep
is upon them.

    This is a digression; but then, quoth Sir Walter Raleigh. 'We digress
all the days of our life'.[28] In not treating this latter episode, Miss
Tynan was right. It would need a longer and more subtly dramatic
method, and her genius is, in the main, lyrical and passionate, rather
than dramatic. Limitations are as needful as aught else; they are the
dam that contains the stream. I notice in this poem its luxuriant life,
like the greater number of Miss Tynan's poems it is very positive. You
will not read it with indifference; At once you will either like or dislike. And yet, it were advisable to begin with the *story of Aibhric*,[29] if
it be for those greenwood adventures of the lovers ye lack some needful sympathy, say a fountain of childlike wonder, since from the win-
ning melancholy and delicate word finesse of Aibhric, ye cannot turn.
Aibhric, the king, rode a hunting through the reeds of the river bed.

    We had been hunting since out of, in the eastern skies,
        The dawn fires began;
    The stag was king of the head—he was fearless and wise,[30]
        Thrice the age of a man.

On rode Aibhric until evening, when he looked round him, and he was alone.

> Lord and lady were gone.
> Back to the lighted board in the palace huts—
> I was riding alone.[31]

> The stag had vanished;—a long gold gleam in the West;
>   The grey pools mirrored all chill,
> And the shrieking water-fowl flew up from the nest;
>   The wind in the reeds sobbed shrill.[32]

> Dreary, dreary seemed the place and strange;
>   The moon was barred with drifts,
> And great cloud-mountains rose stormily, range after range,
>   And broke into rifts;
> An eagle sailed overhead with a flapping wing,[33]
>   And a wild, long cry.
> I stayed my horse, and I mused with much questioning,
>   In what strange country was I.

> The hounds looked up in my face, and shivered with dread,
>   Then cowered, and were still;
> Only the moon's wild face, like the face of the dead,
>   Looked up from each marsh-pool chill.[34]

From the air falls a 'strange song, subtle and slow'. The voice of one of the children of Lir changed into a swan, with still a human voice, by evil enchantment, long ago. Year after year he follows; a hundred winters go by; she sang his manhood away—

> I am old and weary—the lost years vanished apace while I
>   wandered alone,
> Forgotten of men, and another reigned in my place on my
>   father's throne.[35]

At the sound of the first saint's bell, they fall, with broken wings, those nurselings of heathendom.

> Then he to whom God had spoken bent in his place, and
>   laid on each brow[36]
> The life-giving waters;

and they lay there, four dying, human creatures; and she whom
Aibhric loved, died at his feet, wrapt in her bright hair, turning on
him her eyes for a moment—

> Oh! sweet is her sleep in the earth that the saint
>   hath blest,
>   there she shall not hear
>   The cruel waves; but the birds will sing her to
>   rest, and the
>   voices of children dear;
> And the wind will chant overhead, and the grasses wave, all
>   for her sake.
> When I die—I am old—I shall sleep by her side in the
>   grave, and I shall not desire to wake.[37]

Complimenting this poem of 'Aibhric', I have received a note from
a hand not altogether unknown in Irish literature—complimenting this,
and, in appearance, blaming Dermot and Grainne, because it is not
'Fergusonish'[†].[38] Surely imitation is ever barren? They are all individual, these legendary poems; a new voice—a strong voice—a passionate voice.

In a book rich in stories, the most fantastically dreamy and beautiful, is the tale of 'Fergus'.[39] Heretofore it was treated by Ferguson with
that Homeric definiteness of his, and hardness of outline that seem to
the conventional or the sophisticated, baldness.[40] Altogether too delicate a flower for that mountain atmosphere. It needed a more lyrical
mind. Indeed the story is well nigh Miss Tynan's own, so much has she
added to the ancient hints in the introductory portion of the Brehon
laws.

Once reigned, as she tells the tale, a wise and in every way desirable king; well, one fine day his enemies abolished him. After his
death there was born unto him a son with a most foul face, some witch's
power had marred the whole of his body. But through his eye there
looked a soul uncorrupted by all witch spells whatsoever. In that
beauty worshipping land there was a law that all its kings should be
of stateliest make. Surely he cannot reign, this boy. The Druid High
Priest has a vision, this deformed one is the gift of the high Gods, there
should be none like him in wisdom.

> As he ceased his, face grew shadowed, for
>   some pain he groaned aloud,
>   Unheard of all the crowd;

> And thrice he touched the piteous babe and
> shook his hoary head,
> To his own heart whispered—[41]

He has seen another vision dimly, one of sadness beyond measure. Thereafter is proclamation made, maugre his marred beauty and the law he shall be king. Twenty years go by. Never in this land was there so wise a king. The father of his people; 'a brother to his knights in arms'.

> And well the people loved him—on sea shore or the street
> Would fall to kiss his feet;
> And the women sang his praises to the children on their knees,
> For their babies lullabies.[42]

But all these years he knows not of his own foul face. The great High Priest, fearing that in his justice he would obey the law and reign not, had issued an edict, and the secret slept.

> Would a damsel busk her bravely then for feasting in the hall,
> For the dearest knight of all,
> She might out unto the lake side, and when no ripples are,
> See her own face like a star.[43]

> These were no days of mirrors, and the king was guarded well,
> From knowledge of the secret no mortal tongue dare tell;
> So he took his youth's day brightly, chased the deer and cast
> the ball.[44]

But sometimes when he rides along the woodland path, turning with cheerful[†] words to some peasant mother at the wayside, he saddens vaguely, seeing her baby weep and spring away from him. At last he falls in love, as even the gift of the high Gods will do, and she whom he loved,

> She shrank as sore afraid,[45]
> When he would urge his wooing, and she fled him with a cry
> Whenever he came nigh.

Finally, one evil day he sees in her eyes a shrinking hate,[46] and turning away his head goes forth in silence, and taking his steed from stall, rides furiously—

By dead forest paths unknown to men, by many a tangled
    brook
And haunted mound, and fairy rath, and eerie pool and lake.[47]

At the setting of the sun he finds a little mere. He will slake his
thirst and rest his weary limbs. The water mirrors his stooping form.
With a cry he casts himself 'down to meet the face that was his own'.

'His steed came home at day-break, and they sought him far
    and near,
Through many a hopeless year;
Though the birds sang out his story, and the wood sprite cried
    in vain,
And the spirit of the rain;
And the maids of mist and mountain knew the grey pool
    where he lay,
And sometimes was his wild cry heard at dawn or close of
    day,
But they never knew his people, who in war and famine drear,
Prayed the gods to give them back their king again.'[48]

The story is beautifully told. I do not believe the choice of the peculiar Gaelic stanza was equally fortunate—a stanza whose ultimate
line is so far from its rhyming[†] fellow is surely more fitted for poems
with a resonant burden, like 'the fair hills of holy Ireland', than flowing narrative.[49]

I have now fulfilled my bond, which was the reviewing of the
Celtic romances only, but cannot finish without concerning myself
somewhat with the shorter poems that in future anthologies will,
many of them, delight thousands of simple people, whom the longer
poems, in their more expensive form, may never reach. In the earlier
volume *Louise de la Vallière*,[†][50] there was much youthful ardour—some
garish colour, and a somewhat over display of lyrical vehemence. In
the best of these is the old fervour subdued into a far nobler music—
for do not 'the gods approve the depth and not the tumult of the soul'.[51]
In the romances there are things I would gladly see changed, for no one
spends a week with the best of friends, or the best of books, without
sometimes differing, but all in 'A Child's Day'[†], and 'The Heart of a
Mother', and 'St. Francis to the Birds' seems very right.[52] Truly in their
sadness there are tears and[†] in their happiness a brightening of the eye
and a jubilant step. Miss Tynan's very highest note is a religious one,
as in 'the Heart of a Mother' and some few lines in 'Death and the
Man', and here and there in other places, but besides these dealing with

the here and the hereafter there are others of the hereafter and the spiritual world, more exclusively such as 'Sanctuary'.[53] Poems full of the passionate and sensuous religion of Italy and the South. In caring less for these I do so diffidently, know how much in the matter of one of them, I differ thereby from possibly the highest judge of sacred verse now living.[54] Other good things are there I have found no space to mention. Verses that already have gone hither and thither solacing many a weary heart. I have heard of a peasant woman from the west crying over one of them as she read it to her gossip. Here is a lyric that I find most solemn and musical.[55]

> In September,
> The land grows gold with miles of waving wheat;
>   Sad heart! dost thou remember
> How tall and fair the green spears stood in May?
> Alack! the merry morn that might not stay;
>   'Tis sunset now, and night comes grey and fleet.[56]

> In September,
> Droopeth the red fruit in the orchard close;
>   Sad heart! dost thou remember
> How the boughs bloomed auroral in the May;
> Waxed paler, flushed rose-redder day by day?
>   For these, we shall have winter, with his snows.[57]

> In September,
> Chirps the bright robin, with his breast afire;
>   Sad heart! dost thou remember
> How the thrush trilled his love-song in the May,[58]
> And the bold blackbird sang when eve was grey?
>   Silence hath fallen on all the tuneful choir.

> In September,
> Redly the trees, like wind-blown cressets, burn;[59]
>   Sad heart! dost thou remember
> How the leaves gleamed transparent in the May,
> And danced against the sky in happy play?
>   The hearth grows cold, the fires to ashes turn.

> In September,
> The green, young world is waxen old and sere;[60]
>   Sad heart! dost thou remember
> The golden breath the cowslips had in May;

> How the breeze waved each scented hawthorn spray?
> Our year goes out, and we go with the year.

I find this book a garden, where here and there a bough needs pruning, and here and there a blossom has grown astray; and yet with all,
boscage and verdure enough for many a score of common gardens—
a book, in every way, an advance on all hitherto coming from the same
hand. I find, also, no imitation—a rare spontaneity, once or twice
marred by an over-weighting of picturesque detail, an originality
without caprice or any pride of strangeness—a delight in whatever
man's heart has dwelt on from the beginning, in birds and fields, in the
reaping of the reapers, in hounds and horses. Grainne stroked their
raven-dark necks; and

> They knew the hands that every day to the manger
> Brought them the ruddy apples, so crisp and sweet;
> In their true-hearts they guessed at her need and her danger,[61]
> And whinnied low, and stamped with their eager feet.

A delight in those things that are common to all classes and all ages.
Wishing for an external standard I open the volume of another
deservedly noted poetess of our days, and find a sequestered nature of
abnormal likings, singing for the leisured and the well read.[62] Besides
an ever increasing number of leisurely and well read people, Miss Tynan
has, for hearers many simple folk in many lands, and provided the mind
of an author be too watchful to grow careless, there is no better audience, year after year it will draw forth whatever belongs to humanity,
and leave to wither whatever belongs to a coterie.

MISS TYNAN'S NEW BOOK

This review of Katharine Tynan's Shamrocks *(London: K. Paul, Trench, 1887) appeared in* The Irish Fireside *on 9 July 1887. It is Yeats's second and much shorter review of this book. His first review has appeared in* The Gael *of 11 June 1887 (see pp. 51–64 above). For a third, one-paragraph notice of this book, attributed to Yeats, from the 11 August 1887 issue of the magazine* Truth, *see the headnote to* The Gael *review, pp. 52–53 above.*

Yeats reviewed more of Tynan's work later. In The Evening Herald *(Dublin) for 2 January 1892, Yeats published "Poems by Miss Tynan," a review of* Ballads and Lyrics *(London, 1891) (see pp. 153–56).*

Verses mainly simple, always sensuous and passionate—the year will hardly see a pleasanter book. The pre-Raphaelite[†] mannerism and alien methods of thought that obscured the nationality of Miss Tynan's first volume[1] are here almost entirely absent; and in the finding of[†] her nationality she has found also herself, and written many pages of great truthfulness and simplicity. Considering the small space allowed me, it is only possible to say concerning 'Dermot and Grania— The Fate of King Fergus and the Story of Aibhric',[2] that there can be no better companions these summer afternoons than those ancient warriors and star-crossed lovers, and pass on with less regret—having given several columns elsewhere to the longer[3]—to the shorter poems.

'I now', said the youthful Goethe, 'write of the metaphors of things; some day I shall write of the things themselves'.[4] This, in its most verbal sense, is true of the difference between Miss Tynan's first book and her second. In the first we have 'The sun and his good knights' riding 'Up the eastern field of the cloth of gold', and the dead spring 'Like Elaine, with small dead hands on her resting heart',[5] and many more such lines—the mind drawn off from the thing to the metaphor; while in the second the things themselves are often painted

65

with passionate and careful fidelity, as in these lines from 'The Sick Princess':

> Outside, the peacocks on the terraces
>   Flash to the sun their green and purple eyes,
>   And doves are wheeling, and the dragon-flies;
> The garden all one bower of beauty is—
> So still, so still, the sun dreams in the blue,
>   A midday silence brooding over all;
>   The city's bells sound faint and musical—
> The leaves thirst for the dew.[†6]

> The Roman de la Rose lies on the ground,
>   Face downward, as she cast it yesterday;
>   Her palfrey calls with far, impatient neigh—
> Her hawk goes with his jesses still unbound—
> Though kites fly low, and trembling doves are mute.
>   Her needle rusts in her embroidery—
>   Her half-done missal fades, her paints run dry;
> The string snaps of[7] her lute.

Not that the first method is not beautiful in its degree, but the second must ever be the main thing. This I say dogmatically, believing there are no two sides to the question; but the next criticism is a mere personal predilection possibly. I wish the sick princess ended differently, even though she were to die of some common sickness—of something, at any rate, not operatic and literary.[8] I object to the motive, not because it is fanciful, but because it is a kind of motive becoming more and more conventional.

'The metaphors of things' and 'The things themselves!' There is I imagine, this same difference in the religious poems, 'the things themselves' becoming more numerous as time goes on. In the first, the religion of symbol and metaphor, as in 'A Tired Heart', 'The Two Way-farers', and 'Faint Hearted'; in the second book, besides many poems in the first manner, like that rich and beautiful 'Angel of the Annunciation':

> None saw as he passed their way;
> But the children paused in their play,
>   And smiled as his feet went by;
> A bird sang clear from the nest,
> And a babe on its mother's breast
>   Stretched hands with an eager cry.

The women stood at the well,
Most grave, and the laughter fell,
	The chatter and gossip grew mute;
They raised their hands to their eyes—
Had the gold sun waxed in the skies?
	Was that the voice of a lute?

All in the stillness and heat,
The angel passed in the street,
	Nor pausing nor looking behind,
God's finger-touch on his lips;
His great wings fire at the tips,[9]
	His gold hair flame in the wind.

may be found such mingling of earthly love and unearthly resignation as in the 'Heart of a Mother', and such naive and ancient piety as 'St. Francis to the Birds'—as I take it, the most faultless poem in the book. Be sure they will do more to give the mind a holy and temperate thought than a great number of poems of the symbols and metaphors of religion—of the 'viols and lutes', and the 'harp playing', and the 'jasper gates'.

THE PROSE AND POETRY
OF WILFRED BLUNT

This review of Wilfred Scawen Blunt's Love Sonnets of Proteus
(London, 1885) appeared in United Ireland, *28 January 1888. Wilfred Scawen Blunt (1840–1922), poet, horseman, and traveler, was a champion at various times in his life of the causes of nationalism in Egypt, India, and Ireland. In 1887 he became involved in that peasant agitation against absentee landlordism which he was later to call the "Land War in Ireland." As a result of holding a forbidden meeting in the West of Ireland, Blunt was arrested, tried, and sentenced to two months' imprisonment in Galway. While in prison, he wrote the sonnets which made up his volume* In Vinculis *(1889). His journal of this period served as the basis for his* Land War in Ireland *(1912).*

To the nationalist journal United Ireland, *Blunt was a martyr, and to the young Yeats he served as a model of heroic manhood rather than an exemplar of poetic craftsmanship. The reprinting of Blunt's* Love Sonnets of Proteus *served as a probable pretext for an article of more political than literary inspiration.*

Yeats does not seem to have known Blunt at the time of this article. Lady Gregory, a lifelong friend of Blunt, introduced Yeats to Blunt on 1 April 1898. On that occasion, they talked of "the coming doom of England," and Yeats experimented magically on Blunt, a performance which Blunt called "imperfect, not to say dull" (Blunt, My Diaries *[London, 1919], part one, pp. 358–59). Although Yeats included some poems of Blunt in his* Oxford Book of Modern Verse, *he implied in his introduction that he was not, in his youth, very familiar with Blunt's work (pp. v—vi).*

Yeats and Blunt became well acquainted after 1900. Blunt attended meetings of the Irish Literary Society in London as well as performances of Irish plays. In 1902 he finished a drama on an episode of the Cuchulain legend, Fand of the Fair Cheek. *Yeats and Lady Gre-*

gory were enthusiastic about the play, but the performance they promised did not take place until 1907, when the play was staged without Blunt's knowledge.

Mr. Wilfred Blunt has asked for pen and paper that he may edit a volume of his poems[1]—believed to be the *Love Sonnets of Proteus* (1880), now out of print—a book as daring and unconventional as his own life of adventure; not with the self-conscious originality of so many modern books, but with the barbaric sincerity of one who has not time for conventions.

A Brahman philosopher[2] said once to the author of this—'I see in Europe members of society and members of professions, but no men'. But here, in these Proteus sonnets at any rate are the poems of one who is man first, not even poet or thinker or artist first—scarcely artist at all unhappily. He writes always like a man of action—like one who is intent on living his life out.

They are so frank and personal—these sonnets—that the reader thinks more of the writer than the writing. The book was anonymous for three editions, but to the fourth[3] was added this preface—'No life is perfect that has not been lived—youth in feeling—manhood in battle—old age in meditation. Again, no life is perfect that is not sincere. For these reasons I have decided to add my name to the title-page'.

Many of his best poems are not love poems at all, but lookings forward into that manhood to be spent in battle, and protests against that life of domestic ease and public indifference most men wish for, and against love itself.

> If I could live without the thought of death,
>   Forgetful to Time's waste, the soul's decay,
> I would not ask for other joy than breath,
>   With light and sound of birds and the sun's ray.
> I could sit on untroubled day by day
>   Watching the grass grow and the wild flowers range
> From blue to yellow and from red to gray[4]
>   In natural sequence as the seasons change.
> I could afford to wait, but for the hurt
>   Of this dull tick of time which chides my ear.
> But now I dare not sit with loins ungirt
>   And staff unlifted, for Death stands too near.
> I must be up and doing—ay, each minute.
> The grave gives time for rest when we are in it.

As in the writings of all strong natures, whether men of thought or men of action—of men of action more than any, perhaps—there is much melancholy, very different from the ignoble, self-pitying wretched-ness—with a whimper in it—of feeble natures.

'Laughter and Death' is a fine contemplative sonnet without the false rhymes that mar so many of the others:

> There is no laughter in the natural world
> Of beast or fish or bird, though no sad doubt
> Of their futility to them unfurled
> Has dared to check the mirth-compelling shout.
> The lion roars his solemn thunder out
> To the sleeping woods. The eagle screams her cry.
> Even the lark must strain a serious throat
> To hurl his blest defiance at the sky.
> Fear, anger, jealousy has found a voice—
> Love's pain or rapture the brute bosoms swell.
> Nature has symbols for her nobler joys,
> Her nobler sorrows. Who had dared fortell
> That only man, by some sad mockery,
> Should learn to laugh who learns that he must die.[5]

In 1874 was made the first of his many Arabian journeys. I know not to which these lines on the oasis of Sidikhaled[6] must be referred:

> How the earth burns! Each pebble under foot
>   Is as a living thing with power to wound.
> The white sand quivers, and the footfall mute
>   Of the slow camels strikes but gives no sound,
> As though they walked on flame, not solid ground.
>   'Tis noon, and the beasts' shadows even have fled
> Back to their feet, and there is fire around.
>   And fire beneath, and overhead the sun.
> Pitiful heaven! what is this we view?
>   Tall trees, a river, pools, where swallows fly,
> Thickets of oleander where doves coo,
>   Shades, deep as midnight, greenness for tired eyes—
> Hark, how the light winds in the palm-tops sigh—[7]
>   Oh, this is rest. Oh, this is paradise.

On his third Arabian journey he was accompanied by Lady Blunt, who chronicled it in her *Bedouins of the Euphrates*,[8] a most interesting book, wherein may be learned many things concerning the life and religion, or non-religion, of the Bedouins. How they do not believe in the immortality of the soul, because they never think of death, being always busy with matters of the moment. How they believe in God, and do not pray. How as a race they are brave, but do not reprove the coward. 'God has not made me courageous', one will say.[9] How they are virtuous without law;[10] and acquire in old age a look of fierceness from contracting their eyebrows, because of the sun as they look out over the desert. Children of nature who age rapidly, but live their short lives without care or regret—taking everything in the day's work. In the *Sonnets of Proteus* they are addressed thus:

> Children of Shem.[11] First born of Noah's race,
>   But still for ever children; at the door
> Of Eden found, unconscious of disgrace,
>   And loitering on, while all are gone before;
> Too proud to dig; too careless to be poor;
>   Taking the gifts of God in thanklessness,
> Not rendering aught, nor supplicating more,
>   Nor arguing with Him when He hides His face.
> Yours is the rain and sunshine, and the way
>   Of an old wisdom by our world forgot,
> The courage of a day which knew not death.
>   Well may we sons of Japhet in dismay
> Pause in our vain mad fight for life and breath,
>   Beholding you I bow and reason not.[12]

1878–1879 were the years of the notable '*Pilgrimage to Nejd,*' recorded in Lady Blunt's second book of travels.[13] The motive was romantic. Mohammed, son to the chief of Palmyra—Solomon's[†] 'Tadmour in the Wilderness'[14]—had been their guide in the Euphrates expedition. On their return Mr. Blunt gave him his choice between a large sum of money or becoming, according to Bedouin custom, his brother. He chose the last. Now, this young Bedouin was the descendant of one of three brothers who fled, during a time of political trouble a hundred years before, on one camel from Nejd. The event was still preserved in a popular Arabian ballad, the three brothers having been great men in their day. One settled in the oasis of Jôf. The other two quarrelled—one going one way, one the other. Mohammed's forefather settled in Palmyra and in the end became its chief. Then he married a woman not of the noble or Bedouin blood like himself, but one of the townspeople. Thereupon his descendants were looked down upon. Bedouin fathers would not give them their daughters. They had ceased to be thought of as nobles. This was a secret trouble to the young

Mohammed. Mr. Blunt offered in his capacity of brother to go with him to Nejd and find a wife for him from his own relations if any remained, and so redeem the race. After a long journey through places unknown to Europe they reached Nejd, with its shepherd kings as in Bible days. But word reaching them of a rising in Palmyra, the young chief hurried home, where he was imprisoned by the Turkish authorities on some charge or other. Mr. Blunt succeeded[†] in getting him released, however, and so acted out his part of brother.

After this journey the well-known Arabian articles began in the *Nineteenth Century,* and *The Fortnightly Review*—'The Sultan's Heirs in Asia', 'Recent Events in Arabia', and the notable series, 'The Future of Islam',[15] with their continual cry against the Turk and their showing how England put him on his legs again once upon a time, and filled his wallet and sent him on his way with a blessing to tyrannise and brutalise. But according to Mr. Blunt he is not to last always. Cairo or Mecca is to be the Islamitish capital, and the Arab the heir of the Tartar.[16] Neither is Mahomedism[17] a decaying power, but the most living and growing thing in Asia. In 'The Egyptian Revolution'[18] he described the diplomacy that led up to the Egyptian War. This is what he said of Arabi:[19]

It was evident that he believed he had a mission to restore good Mussulman government in his country. On the other hand, he was as evidently the reverse of a fanatic. When informed that my wife, Lady Anne Blunt, who was with me, was a granddaughter of Lord Byron the poet[20] 'who had fought for the Greeks', he showed great interest and satisfaction, a sign by which I judged him more than all else to have a true love of Liberty. Indeed, the universal sympathy we have received from Mussulmans in Egypt, because we are connected with one who died in arms against the Turks, seems to me a most convincing proof of the national and liberal character of the movement.

And again:

He understands that broader Islam which existed before Mohammed, and the bond of a common worship of the one true God, which unites his own faith with that of Judaism and Christianity. I have but once heard this idea more clearly expressed. He disclaims all personal ambition, and there is no kind of doubt the army and the country are devoted to him. . . . Of his own position he speaks with modesty. 'I am,' he says, 'the representative of the army, because circumstances have made the army trust me; but the army is but the representative of the people, its guardian, till such time as the people shall no longer need it. At present, we are the sole National force standing between Egypt and its Turkish rulers. . . . We have won for the people their right to speak in the assembly of notables, and we keep the ground to prevent their being cajoled or frightened out of it. In this we work not for ourselves, but for our children and those who trust us.'[21] 'We soldiers,' he once said to me, 'are for the moment in the position of those Arabs who answered the Caliph Omar,'[22] when in old age he asked the people whether they were satisfied with his rule, and whether he had walked straightly in the path of justice. 'Oh, son of El Khattab,' said they, 'thou hast, indeed,[23] walked straightly, and we love thee; but thou knewest that we were at hand and ready, if thou hadst walked crookedly, to straighten thee with our swords.'

It is still fresh in men's memory how he saved Arabi from probable shooting or hanging, paying £5,000 for his defence, if I remember rightly. Terrible disastrous wars, in which once more God was on the side of the big battalions—for a time. Meanwhile, the Right can but register its protest and its prophecy. He did both in an impassioned poem, 'The Wind and the Whirlwind'.[24]

In 1884 were printed in the '*Fortnightly*' his articles, 'Ideas about India',[25] being his statement of the grievances he found most complained against in that country, where it is officially stated that 40 per cent of the natives go through life on insufficient food, and where, according to his calculations, the peasant of the Deccan pays 40 per cent off the produce in taxation, and where, to quote the 'Ideas',

It is a perpetual astonishment to travellers to note the scale of living of every Englishman employed in India, in however mean a capacity. The enormous palaces of governors and lieutenant-governors, their country houses, their residences in the hills, their banquets and entertainments, their retinues of servants, their carriages and horses, their special trains on their journeyings, their tents, their armies of retainers and camp followers—these are only samples of the universal profusion; an equally noble hospitality reigns in every bungalow on the plains; and endless dinners of imported delicacies, with libations of imported wines, tempt, night after night, the inhabitants of the most solitary stations to forget the dismal fact that they are in Asia, and far from their own land.[26]

The Viceroy during Mr. Blunt's visit was Lord Ripon;[27] in the light of whose Irish action it is interesting to know how they thought of him in that perhaps other Ireland:

No Viceroy, [says Mr. Blunt,] Lord Canning possibly excepted, ever enjoyed such popularity as Lord Ripon did in the early part of last winter. Wherever I went in India I heard the same story—from the poor peasants of the South, who for the first time, perhaps, had learned the individual name of the ruler; from the high caste Brahamans of Madras and Bombay; the Calcutta students; from the Mohammedan divines of Lucknow; from the noblemen of Delhi and Hyderabad; everywhere his praise was in all men's mouths, and moved the people to surprise and gratitude. 'He is an honest man,' one said, 'and one who fears God.'[28]

But from the officials, it seems, he earned a hatred in equal measure. In Hyderabad, a protected State, there had been going on among the English officials, to quote the 'Ideas' again, a general scramble at the expense of the Treasury. Lord Ripon announced his intention of investigating the matter in person.

There was a scare of cholera raised and the Viceroy's camp was fixed twelve miles from the city. It was given out that the Viceroy wished to see no one, and a kind of quarantine cordon was established. The camp itself was put in the enemy's keeping, and intimidation was to my knowledge used to prevent the Nizam speaking all his mind, and a huge body of officials surrounded the Viceroy day and night.[29]

Nevertheless the Viceroy did get to the bottom of the matter, and made that part of the Empire a little cleaner any way—washed that particular sucker of the octopus somewhat.

IRISH FAIRIES,
GHOSTS, WITCHES, ETC.

This article is a relic of Yeats's association with Madame Blavatsky's London Theosophical Society. It appeared in the theosophical magazine Lucifer *in the issue dated 15 January 1889. The work was unpaid and the sequel promised at the end of this article never appeared. By the end of 1890, Yeats was asked to resign from the inner circle of the Theosophical Society because of his criticisms of it. In a letter to Katharine Tynan, dated 4 December 1890, Yeats wrote, "I too have had a quarrel with the follower & withdrawn from all active work in the society. I wrote some articles they objected to about 'Lucifer'" (CL1, 238).*

This discussion is the closest Yeats ever came to "explaining" the Irish fairies. The explanation here is theosophical, not scientific in the skeptical, rationalizing sense. The information Yeats gave in this article parallels closely the introductory material in Yeats's compilation, Irish Fairy and Folk Tales *(London, 1892).*

It has occurred to me that it would be interesting if some spiritualist or occultist would try to explain the various curious and intricate spiritualistic beliefs of peasants. When reading Irish folk-lore, or listening to Irish peasants telling their tales of magic and fairyism and witchcraft, more and more is one convinced that some clue there must be. Even if it is all dreaming, why have they dreamed this particular dream? Clearly the occultist should have his say as well as the folk-lorist. The history of a belief is not enough, one would gladly hear about its cause.

Here and there an occult clue is visible plainly. Some of the beliefs about ghosts are theosophical; the Irish ghost or *thivish*, for instance, is merely an earth-bound shell, fading and whimpering in the places it loved. And many writers, from Paracelsus to d'Assier,[1] have shed a somewhat smoky light on witches and their works, and Irish witches do not differ much from their tribe elsewhere, except in being rather more harmless. Perhaps never being burnt or persecuted has lessened the bitterness of their war against mankind, for in Ireland they have had on the whole, a very peaceable and quiet time, disappearing altogether from public life since the 'loyal minority' pilloried and imprisoned three and knocked out the eye of one with a cabbage stump, in 1711, in the town of Carrickfergus.[2] For many a long year now have they contented themselves with going out in the grey of the morning, in the shape of hares, and sucking dry their neighbour's cows, or muttering spells while they skimmed with the severed hand of a corpse the surface of a well gathering thereon a neighbour's butter.

It is when we come to the fairies and 'fairy doctors', we feel most the want of some clue—some light, no matter how smoky. These 'fairy doctors', are they mediums or clairvoyants? Why do they fear the hazel tree, or hold an ash tree in their hands when they pray? Why do they say that if you knock once at their doors they will not open, for you may be a spirit, but if you knock three times they will open. What are these figures, now little, now great, now kindly, now fierce, now ugly, now beautiful, who are said to surround them—these fairies, whom they never confuse with spirits, but describe as fighting with the spirits though generally having the worst of it, for their enemies are more Godfearing? Can any spiritualist or occultist tell us of these things? Hoping they can, I set down here this classification of Irish fairyism and demonology. The mediaeval divisions of sylphs, gnomes, undines and salamanders will not be found to help us. This is a different dynasty.

FAIRY DOCTORS

Unlike the witch, who deals with ghosts and spirits, the fairy doctor is never malignant; at worst, he is mischievous like his masters and servants the fairies. Croker,[3] in the 'Confessions of Tom Bourke', said by Keightly,[4] of the *Fairy Mythology,* to be the most valuable chapter in all his writings, describes the sayings and doings of such a man. Each family has its particular adherent among the 'good people', as the fairies are called, and sometimes when a man died the factions of his father and mother would fight as to the grave-yard he was to be buried in, the relations delaying the funeral until Tom Bourke told them one party or other had won. If they buried in the wrong grave-yard all kinds of ill luck would follow, for fairies know how to kill cattle with their fairy darts, and do all kinds of mischief.

The fairy doctor is great with herbs and spells. He can make the fairies give up people they have carried off, and is in every way the opposite of the witch.

Lady Wilde,[5] in her *Ancient Legends,* thus describes one who lived in the Island of Innis-Sark: 'He can heal diseases by a word, even at a distance, and his glance sees into the very heart and reads the secret thoughts of men. He never touched beer, spirits or meat in all his life, but has lived entirely on bread, fruit, and vegetables. A man who knew him thus describes him: Winter and summer his dress is the same, merely a flannel shirt and coat. He will pay his share at a feast, but neither eats nor drinks of the food and drink set before him. He speaks no English, and never could be made to learn the English tongue, though he says it might be used with great effect to curse one's enemy. He holds a burial-ground sacred, and would not carry away so much as a leaf of ivy from a grave; and he maintains that the people are right in keeping to their ancient usages—such as never to dig a grave on a Monday, and to carry the coffin three times round the grave, following the course of the sun, for then the dead rest in peace. Like the people, also, he holds suicides accursed;[6] for they believe that all the dead who have been recently buried turn over on their faces if a suicide is laid amongst them.

'Though well off, he never, even in his youth, thought of taking a wife, nor was he ever known to love a woman. He stands quite apart from life, and by this means holds his power over the mysteries. No money will tempt him to impart this knowledge to another, for if he did he would be struck dead, so he believes. He would not touch a hazel stick, but carries an ash wand, which he holds in his hand when he prays, laid across his knees, and the whole of his life is given to works of grace and charity.[7]

'Though an old man, he has never had a day's sickness; no one has ever seen him in a rage, nor heard an angry word from his lips but once, and then, being under great irritation, he recited the Lord's Prayer backwards as an imprecation on his enemy.[8] Before his death he will reveal the mystery of his power, but not till the hand of death is on him for certain', and then we may be sure he will reveal it only to his successor.

THE SOCIABLE FAIRIES

These are the Sheogues[†] (Ir. *Sidheog,* 'a little fairy'), and are usually of small size when first seen, though seeming of common human height when you are once glamoured. It sometimes appears as if they could take any shape according to their whim. Commonly, they go about in troops, and are kind to the kindly and mischievous to the evil and ill-tempered, being like beautiful children, having every charm but that of conscience—consistency.

Their divisions are sheogue, a land fairy, and merrow (Ir. *moruadh,*[19] or 'sea maid')[†] (the masculine is unknown), a water fairy. The merrow is said not to be uncommon. I asked a peasant woman once whether the fishermen of her village ever saw one. 'Indeed, they don't like to see them at all', she answered, 'for they always bring bad weather'. Sometimes the merrows come out of the sea in the shape of little, hornless cows. When in their own shape, they have fish tails and wear a red cap usually covered with feathers, called a *cohullen druith*. The men among them have green teeth, green hair, pigs' eyes and red noses, but their women are beautiful, and sometimes prefer handsome fishermen to their green-haired lovers. Near Bantry,[10] in the last century, lived a woman covered with scales like a fish, who was descended from such a marriage.

All over Ireland are little fields circled by ditches, and supposed to be ancient fortifications and sheep folds. These are the raths or forts. Here, marrying and giving in marriage, live the land fairies. Many a mortal have they enticed down into their dim world. Many more have listened to their fairy music, till all human cares and joys drifted from their hearts, and they became great fairy doctors, or great musicians, or poets like Carolan,[11] who gathered his tunes while sleeping on a fairy rath; or else they died in a year and a day, to live ever after among the fairies.

These sociable fairies are in the main good, but one most malicious habit have they—a habit worthy of a witch. They steal children, and leave a withered fairy a thousand, or may be two thousand years old, for the matter of that, instead. Two or three years ago a man wrote to one of the Irish papers, telling of a case in his own village, and how the parish priest made the fairies deliver up again the stolen child.

At times full grown men and women have been carried off. Near the village of Ballisodare, Sligo, I have been told, lives an old woman who was taken in her youth. When she came home, at the end of seven years, she had no toes, for she had danced them off.

Especially do they steal men, women and children on May eve, Midsummer eve, and November eve, for these are their festivities.

On May eve,[12] every seventh year, they fight for the harvest, for the best ears of corn belong to them. An old man told me he saw them fighting once. They tore the thatch off a house in the battle. Had you or I been there we had merely felt a great wind blowing; the peasantry know better than to mistake the fairies for the wind. When a little whirlwind passes, lifting the straws, they take off their hats and say: 'God bless them', for the fairies are going by.

On Midsummer eve, Bonfire Night, as we call it, the sheogues[†] are very gay, and on this night more than any other do they steal beautiful mortals to be their brides.

On November eve, according to the old Gaelic reckoning the first night of winter, the fairies are very gloomy, and in their green raths dance with the ghosts, while abroad in the world witches make their spells, and a solitary and wicked fairy, called the Pooka, has power, and girls set tables with food in the name of the devil, that the fetch of their future lovers may come through the window and eat.

The sociable fairies are very quarrelsome.

Lady Wilde tells about one battle in which, no stones being at hand, they stole butter and flung it at each other. A quantity stuck in the branches of an alder-tree. A man in the neighbourhood mended the handle of the dash of his churn with a branch of this tree. As soon as he began churning, the butter, until now hanging invisible in the alder branches, flowed into his churn. The same happened every churning-day, until he told the matter to a fairy doctor, which telling broke the spell, for all these things have to be kept secret.[13]

Kennedy describes a battle heard by a peasant of his acquaintance. The sheogues[†] were in the air over a river. He heard shots and light bodies falling into the water, and a faint sound of shouting, but could see nothing. Old Patrick Kennedy,[14] who records this, was a secondhand bookseller in Dublin, and claimed in one of his works to know spells for making the fairies visible, but would not tell them for fear they might set dangerous forces in action—forces that might destroy the user of the spell.[15] These battles are often described by Irish fairy seers. Sometimes the sociable sheogues,[†] dressed in green coats, fight with the solitary red-coated fairies.

THE SOLITARY FAIRIES

The best known of these is the Leprechaun[†] (Ir. *Leith bhrogan, i.e.,* the 'one shoe maker').[†] He is seen sitting under a hedge mending a shoe, and one who catches him and keeps his eyes on him can make him deliver up his crocks of gold, for he is a rich miser; but if he takes his eyes off him, the creature vanishes like smoke. He is said to be the child of a spirit and a debased fairy, and, according to McAnally,[†16] wears a red coat with seven rows of buttons, seven buttons in each row, and a cocked hat, on the point of which he sometimes spins like a top.

Some writers have supposed the Cluricaun to be another name of the same fairy, given him when he has laid aside his shoe-making at night and goes on the spree. The Cluricaun's one occupation is robbing wine-cellars.[17]

The Gonconer or Gancanagh (Ir. *Gean-canagh, i.e.,* 'Love talker')[18] is a little creature of the Leprechaun[†] type, unlike him, however, in being an idler. He always appears with a pipe in his mouth in lonely valleys, where he makes love to shepherdesses and milkmaids.

The Far Darrig (Ir. *Fear-Dearg, i.e.,* red man) plays practical jokes continually. A favourite trick is to make some poor mortal tramp over hedges and ditches, carrying a corpse on his back, or to make him turn it on a spit. Of all these solitary, and mainly evil, fairies there is no more lubberly wretch than this same Far Darrig. Like the next phantom, he presides over evil dreams.

The Pooka seems to be of the family of the nightmare. He has most likely never appeared in human form, the one or two recorded instances being probably mistakes, he being mixed up with the Far Darrig. His shape is that of a horse, a bull, goat, eagle, ass and perhaps of a black dog, though this last may be a separate spirit. The Pooka's delight is to get a rider, whom he rushes with through ditches and rivers and over mountains, and shakes off in the grey of the morning. Especially does he love to plague a drunkard—a drunkard's sleep is his kingdom.

The Dullahan is another gruesome phantom. He has no head, or carries it under his arm. Often he is seen driving a black coach, called the coach-a-bower (Ir. *Coise-bodhar*), drawn by headless horses. It will rumble to your door, and if you open to it, a basin of blood is thrown in your face. To the houses where it pauses it is an omen of death. Such a coach, not very long ago, went through Sligo in the grey of the morning (the spirit hour). A seaman saw it, with many shudderings. In some villages its rumbling is heard many times in the year.

The Leanhaun Shee (fairy mistress) seeks the love of men. If they refuse, she is their slave; if they consent, they are hers, and can only escape by finding one to take their place. Her lovers waste away, for she lives on their life. Most of the Gaelic poets, down to quite recent times, have had a Leanhaun Shee, for she gives inspiration to her slaves. She is the Gaelic muse, this malignant fairy. Her lovers, the Gaelic poets, died young. She grew restless, and carried them away to other worlds, for death does not destroy her power.

Besides these, we have other solitary fairies, such as the House Spirit and Water Sheerie, a kind of Will-o'-the-Wisp, and various animal spirits, such as the Anghiska, the water-horse, and the Pastha (*Piast bestea*)[119] the lake dragon, a guardian of hidden treasure, and two fairies, the Far-gorta and the Banshee, who are technically solitary fairies, though quite unlike their fellows in disposition.

The Far-gorta (man of hunger) is an emaciated fairy that goes through the land in famine time, begging, and bringing good luck to the giver of alms.

The Banshee (*Bean-sidhe*) seems to be one of the sociable fairies grown solitary through the sorrow or the triumph of the moment; her name merely means woman-fairy, answering to the less common word Farshee [*Fear-sidhe*], man-fairy. She wails, as most people know, over the death of some member of an old Irish family. Sometimes she is an enemy of the house, and wails with triumph; sometimes a friend, and wails with sorrow. When more than one Banshee comes to cry, the man or woman who is dying must have been very holy or very brave. Occasionally she is undoubtedly believed to be one of the sociable fairies. Cleena, once an ancient Irish goddess, is now a Munster sheogue.

O'Donovan,[20] one of the very greatest of the Irish antiquarians, wrote in 1849 to a friend, who quoted his words in the *Dublin University Magazine:* 'When my grandfather died in Leinster, in 1798, Cleena came all the way from Tonn Cleena, at Glandore, to lament him; but she has not been heard ever since lamenting any of our race, though I believe she still weeps in the mountains of Drumaleague[†] in her own country, where so many of the race of Eoghan More are dying of starvation.'[21]

The Banshee who cries with triumph is often believed to be no fairy, but the ghost of one wronged by an ancestor of the dying. Besides these are various fairies who fall into none of the regular groups, such as 'Dark Joan of the Boyne'. This fairy visits houses in the form of a hen with a lot of chickens, or a pig with a litter of banyans. Several now living say thay have fought with this fairy pig. This taking the appearance of several animals at one time is curious, and brings to mind how completely a matter of whim, or symbolism the form of an enchanted being must be thought. Indeed, the shape of Irish fairies seems to change with their moods—symbolizing or following the feelings of the moment.

When we look for the source of this spirit rabble, we get many different answers. The peasants say they are fallen angels who were too good to be lost, too bad to be saved, and have to work out their time in barren places of the earth. An old Irish authority—the *Book of Armagh*[22]—calls them gods of the earth, and quite beyond any kind of doubt many of them were long ago gods in Ireland.

Once upon a time the Celtic nations worshipped gods of the light, called in Ireland Tuatha dé Danaan[†] and corresponding to Jupiter and his fellows, and gods of the great darkness corresponding to the Saturnian Titans.[23] Among the sociable fairies are many of the light gods; perhaps, some day, we may learn to look for the dark gods among the solitary fairies. The Pooka we can trace, a mysterious deity of decay, to earliest times. Certainly, he is no bright Tuatha dé Danaan.[†] Around him hangs the dark vapour of Domnian Titanism.[24]

(To be continued.)[25]

IRISH WONDERS

David Rice McAnally Jr.'s book Irish Wonders: The Ghosts, Giants, Pookas, Demons, Leprechawns, Banshees, Fairies, Witches, Widows, Old Maids and Other Marvels of the Emerald Isle *(Boston and New York: Houghton Mifflin, 1888) was reviewed by Yeats in two journals. Aside from the review below, printed in* The Scots Observer *of 30 March 1889 (not 1890, as stated by Allan Wade in his Yeats bibliography), Yeats wrote an article on McAnally's book for* The Providence Sunday Journal *of 7 July 1889 (initially reprinted in* Letters to the New Island, *edited by Horace Reynolds in 1934, now in LNI, 91–97). Yeats's American review was rather more severe on McAnally's "stage-Irish" language than his* Scots Observer *one. Both reviews repeat the same stories from McAnally—the fairy ball and Darby O'Hoolighan, whose wife returns to the land of fairy. The two reviews, however, are by no means identical.*

The previous summer, during Yeats's compilation of his own Fairy and Folk Tales of the Irish Peasantry, *he had gone to considerable trouble to locate* Irish Wonders *in the hope of using some of its material. Some of the severity of Yeats's review may have stemmed from his disappointment when he finally located the book. McAnally was clearly not a professional collector of folklore. His book was aimed at an audience attracted to what Yeats called the "Harps and Pepperpots" school of Irish verse. Whatever Yeats's reservations about McAnally's methods, the author of* Irish Wonders *was included in Yeats's list of authorities on Irish folklore at the end of* Fairy and Folk Tales of the Irish Peasantry.

A clipping of this anonymous review is contained in MS 12147 (National Library of Ireland) along with other Yeats articles, some of them corrected in the author's hand. It was reprinted by Horace Reynolds in January 1942 in The Tuftonian, *magazine of Tufts College, Medford, Massachusetts, with a note explaining why Reynolds then thought it to be Yeats's work.*

In the matter of folk-tales, the scientific-minded wish for the very words they are told in. Others would allow some equivalent for the lost gesture, local allusions, and quaint manners of the story-tellers— some concentrating of humour and dialect. They consider that a folk-tale told by Carleton[1] gives a truer impression of what it sounds like when some old voice is reciting in the turf smoke, than any word-for-word version. Carleton has never added anything untrue, anything incongruous: no other man ever knew the Irish peasantry as he did; none other ever touched Irish folk-lore with like genius. But because genius is justified of all her children, that does not prove Mr. McAnally[†] right in leaving the accurate, reverent way, to dress up his fine tales in a poor slatternly patchwork of inaccurate dialect and sham picturesqueness. Had he told them word for word, or even in common literary English, he might have produced a book that students would turn to for years to come. Instead, he has made his whole work smack of the tourist's car. The dialects of north and south, and east and west, are all rolled into one ridiculous mixture. Why, the village children in Ireland laugh at the speech of the next county, almost at that of the next village. Mr. McAnally[†] is an Irish-American. In his feelings for the old country there is a touch of genuine poetry. But the Ireland he loves is not the real Ireland: it is the false Ireland of sentiment. He strains to make everything humorous, according to the old convention, pretty according to the old prepossession. From his desperate search for the pretty and humorous, he has brought home some strange baggage. He fathers, or rather mothers, the following on a 'knowledgable woman' of Coloney, Sligo. The matter discussed is a fairy ball, 'seen by her grandmother's aunt': 'It was the 'cutest sight alive. There was a place for thim to shtand on, an' a wondherful big fiddle av the size ye cud slape in it, that was played be a monsthrous frog, an' two little fiddles that two kittens fiddled on, an' two big drums baten be cats, an' two trumpets, played be fat pigs. All round the fairies were dancin' like angels, the fire-flies givin' thim light to see by, an' the moon-bames shinin' on the lake, for it was be the shore it was; an' if ye don't belave it, the glen's still there, that they call the Fairy Glen to this blessed day'.[2]

The writer of this article, though he has not gathered folk-tales in Coloney, has done so within two miles of it, as well as reading most, if not all, recorded Irish fairy tales, but never has he heard anything like this. Even if the fire-fly were forgiven, this would remain the worst-invented piece of folk-lore on record. These fiddling and trumpeting beasts are quite alien to Celtic myth; for Celtic fairies are much like common men and women. Often the fairy-seer meets with them on some lonely road, and joins in their dance, and listens to their music; and does not know what people they are till the whole company melts away into shadow and night. On those occasions when it pleases them to take on diminutive size, and so be known at once, they are still, in well-nigh all their works and ways, like human beings. This fiddling fancy may be German; good Celtic it cannot be. The whole surroundings of the *deenee shee*³ (fairy people) are simple and matter-of-fact. The peasant credits them with what he himself admires. 'They have', said one old peasant to the writer, 'the most beautiful parlours and drawing-rooms'.⁴ By saying it was the poor 'knowledgable woman's' grand-mother's aunt that saw the fiddling, Mr. McAnally† means, we suppose, to suggest the old calumny that nobody but somebody's dis-tant relation ever saw a spirit. There is probably not a village in Ire-land where a fairy-seer or two may not be found. As to the last sentence of Mr. McAnally's† amusing nine lines, there is, of course, not a peasant in Ireland who would use such an argument.

It is sincerely to be regretted that Mr. McAnally† has not the con-vincing art: one often really wishes to believe him, as in the lep-rechauns† chapter—the most full of detail of anything ever written about that goblin shoemaker.⁵ It sounds for the most part like honest folk-lore; but then that fire-fly! There is one tale in the chapter too good, however, to have been changed in any essential. There was a child who was stolen at birth by the fairies of Lough Erne.⁶ When she began to grow up, they gave her a dance every night down under the lake. The queen meant to find her a good husband among the fairies, but she fell in love with an old leprechaun†. Thereupon the queen, 'to circumvent her',⁷ gave her leave to walk on the shore of the lake, where she met Darby O'Hoolighan, and loved him. They married, and the queen gave them cattle and household things, but told her to tell her husband she would return to the fairies if he struck her three blows. For seventeen years they lived happily, and had two big sons. At last, one day they were going to a wedding, and she was very slow. Darby struck her on the shoulder with his hand, and she began to cry, and said it was the first of the three blows. A year later he was teaching his boy to use a shillaly, and she got behind and was struck. That was the second blow. 'Divil take the stick',⁸ he cried, and flung it against the wall. The stick bounced back and struck her, and made the third blow. She kissed her sons, and went and called the cows in the fields, and they quit grazing and followed her; and the oxen in the stalls heard her, and stopped eating and followed. She spoke to the calf they had killed that morning, and it came down from where it was hanging in the yard and followed her. The lamb that was killed the day before, and the pigs that were salted and hung up to dry, went after her in a string. Next she called the things in the house. The chairs and tables, and the chest of drawers, and the boxes, and the pots and pans and grid-irons, and buckets, and noggins, all put out legs 'like bastes', and walked after her; and the house was left bare and empty. They came to the edge of the lake, and all went under, down again to fairy-land. After this she used sometimes to come close to the shore to see her two sons. One day there was seen 'a little atomy of a man along wid her, that was a leprechaun';[19] therefore it got about that the real reason she left her husband was to get back to the old leprechaun[†] she was in love with before she married Darby.

Mr. McAnally's[†] stories are nearly all good in themselves. His sentences, too, have often an Irish turn in them, though the pronunciation is written anyhow. It is mainly his isolated assertions that trouble. He says the most momentous things in the most jaunty, careless way. He tells us, for instance, that, of the spirits of the bad, 'some are chained at the bottom of the lakes, others buried under ground, others confined in mountain gorges; some hang on the sides of precipices, others are transfixed on the tree-tops, while others haunt the houses[10] of their ancestors: all waiting till the penance has been endured, and the hour of release arrives'. There is a fine gloomy suggestion about the ghosts swinging on the tree-tops which we feel sure that Mr. McAnally[†] has honestly reported. But why is there not some authority reverently given for so strange a thing? In what part of Ireland was it said, this saying recalling *Mahabharata* and *Divine Comedy*?[11] We believe it to be honest folk-lore and defy that shining insect circling and flickering before us, anxious to remind us of another name for the God of Flies.[12]

JOHN TODHUNTER

This biographical sketch of John Todhunter was written for The Magazine of Poetry, *edited by C. W. Moulton in Buffalo, New York, from 1889 to 1895. It appeared in the April 1889 issue. For further information on Yeats's opinions of Todhunter, see "Plays by an Irish Poet," pp. 131–33 below, and "Dr. Todhunter's Irish Poems," pp. 160–62.*

John Todhunter was born in Dublin, Dec. 30th, 1839. His father was a timber merchant; his grandfather a Cumberland man who had settled in Dublin as a merchant; his great-grandfather a ship-owner in a small way, who sailed his own ships as officer, trading as a coaster along the Irish Sea. His mother and immediate relations were Irish, and all good Quakers[1]; and he still remembers the wearisomeness of the silent Quaker meetings.

At twelve years old we find him at a Quaker boarding school learning some French and Greek, among other things, and telling stories, remembered or invented, to his school-fellows before going to sleep at night. At sixteen he was apprenticed to a Quaker firm of tea and sugar importers, where, as collector, he made acquaintance with well-nigh all the streets of dear, dirty Dublin, and something of the life that went on in them.

So far he had been almost shut out from literary and artistic influences, except that his father sketched a little, and now and then whistled an Irish air, though music was regarded by the Quakers, as the most diabolical of arts, all evil in their way. But now he got hold of Scott, Moore, above all, Byron,[2] whom he used to carry in his pocket when going to pay duties at the Custom House, and read in some quiet corner while the sugar-hogsheads were a-weighing. After Byron came Spenser, Milton, Tennyson, Browning, Coleridge, Keats and Shelley.[3] At about eighteen he began to write verses, a skit containing imitations of some of his favorite poets gaining him an introduction to Archbishop

Whatley.[4] In 1860 a performance of Handel's *Messiah*[5] in Christ-Church Cathedral came as a great awakening to his imagination. It was the first great music he had heard. Here was music not in any way a thing of the devil, but certainly a divine revelation. After this he began timidly to go to the opera instead of prayer-meetings; heard the great singers, and became music mad.

At last, finding it impossible to settle down to business, Mr. Todhunter entered Trinity College in 1862, with the object of studying medicine. He soon became a member of the 'Undergraduate Philosophical Society' (really a literary society) and made the acquaintance of Edmund and George Armstrong,[6] the poets, and of Edward Dowden,[7] now the well-known professor of English literature. In college he tried to combine literature with science, and began his hospital work where he won the marked confidence of Dr. Hudson, the famous Dr. Stokes,[8] whose clinical clerk he was. The poet in him, however, asserted itself in the fact of his taking a much deeper interest in the patients as human beings than as 'cases.' They in turn liked him, for he would always listen to their stories sympathetically. In spite of much ill-health consequent upon a bad fever, he obtained several medical prizes, and after a trip to Switzerland for his health took his medical degree in 1867. While in college he three times won the Vice-Chancellor's prize for English verse, and in 1866 his first published poem appeared in the *Cornhill Magazine,* then edited by Thackeray.[9]

In 1869 Mr. Todhunter went to Vienna and there completed his medical studies. Returning in the spring of 1870, he married Miss Ball, sister of the present Astronomer Royal for Ireland, Sir Robert Ball,[10] and settled in Dublin as president physician to Cork St. Fever Hospital. In the autumn of 1870 he succeeded Professors Ingram[11] and Dowden to the chair of English Literature at Alexandra College, Dublin, where he lectured twice a week for four years. In 1871 his wife died, leaving one child who died in 1874. After this Mr. Todhunter finding he had taken no root in Dublin, determined to abandon medicine for literature. In 1876 his first volume of poems, *Laurella and Other Poems,* appeared; in 1878, *Alcestis;* and in 1879 he married Miss Digby,[12] of Dublin, and finally settled in London. Since then he has published *A Study of Shelley, The True Tragedy of Rienzi, Forest Songs, Helena in Troas,* and *The Banshee and Other Poems,* the last a volume containing some fine Irish poems.[13] *Helena in Troas* is a drama, Greek in form. It was acted with great success in 1886, under the direction of Mr. E. W. Godwin,[14] F. S. A.

WILLIAM CARLETON

This review of Yeats's compilation Stories from Carleton *(London, 1889) and* The Red-Haired Man's Wife *appeared in* The Scots Observer, *19 October 1889.*

Although this review was printed anonymously, the style and opinions of the reviewer mark it as Yeats's as well as does the evidence of a letter of Yeats to Katharine Tynan on 21 April 1889: "The Scots Observer *people have asked me to write an article on him [Carleton] apropos of the 'Red-Haired Man's Wife', the posthumous tale of his discovered somewhere and printed the other day by Sealy, Bryers & Walker" (CL1, 159; see also a letter to Fr. Matthew Russell of 13 July 1889 in the same volume, pp. 171–72).*

Somewhat incoherent as a review, this article was more a product of Yeats's current interests than a critical examination of the works at hand. Yeats was then in the midst of an extensive reading of Carleton's works, an effort which was to supply him with short excerpts for his Fairy and Folk Tales *book as well as his two volumes of* Representative Irish Tales, *and all the materials for his* Stories from Carleton *(1889).*

The few sentences noticing his Stories from Carleton *at the beginning of the review were probably not by Yeats. Even if they were, their tone is too perfunctory to consist of self-praise. The body of the article consists of opinions which closely parallel his introduction to his Carleton selection. To save his editor from embarrassment, he had rushed through his introduction to his* Stories from Carleton. *He therefore must have welcomed the opportunity for a more leisurely exposition of his ideas.*

His advocacy of Carleton, who had turned from Catholicism to the Church of Ireland, got Yeats into difficulties in Ireland. As in so many other instances in his life, Yeats's universalist notions about religion led him to underestimate the force of Irish sectarian prejudice. Yeats had to defend Carleton's religion even to the liberal Fr. Matthew Russell, S.J., the editor of The Catholic Monthly *(CL1, 174–75). The Nation of Dublin, in reviewing Yeats's selection, called Carleton a "rene-gade" to be placed in the "literary pillory" for his stories attacking Catholic rites and practices. Yeats replied in a strongly worded letter of 11 January 1890 that in his works taken as a whole Carleton showed a predominant affection for the church of his fathers (CL1, 205–7). When Carleton's autobiography was published in 1896, Yeats reviewed it for* The Bookman *in March 1896 (see pp. 298–301).*

Like many other of Yeats's early passions, his admiration for Carleton waned quickly. In a copy of Stories from Carleton, *presented to John Quinn in 1904, he wrote, "I had thought no end of Carleton in those days & would still I dare say if I had not forgotten him" (Wade, 220).*

Of Mr. Yeats's selection from Carleton's *Traits and Stories* it will be enough to say that it is good and representative, and that the prefatory matter is judicious and well written. Of the second number on our list, it is proper to note that, the last of Carleton's novels, it was published a few years ago—(do the publishers know this?)—in the *Carlow College Magazine,* under the editorship of that Father Kavanagh[1] who was killed by the fall of an image while celebrating mass, after a series of incidents that made the awe-struck peasantry see in his death an event unearthly and tremendous. It is at last re-issued in a flaring red cover. From the preface about a 'serious mishap' and 'a literary friend', and from internal evidence, we gather that only a portion is by Carleton; the first two-thirds are his any way.[2] It is not possible to determine the line of cleavage, for never was Carleton so little like himself and so like a score of others, and the *Carlow College Magazine* is long dead and vanished even from the book-stalls; and when he wrote he was old and feeble. Once he apologises for his many repetitions by saying he has passed his seventieth year, and that old men love to be repeating. The manner is all the more pathetic in its feebleness from the whimsical Carletonian matter. There was a family of peasants who never could make up their minds; they decided everything by a toss-up. The head[†] of the family had[†] settled the amount of dowry he got with his wife by 'heads or harps', and when he died he left his land to be tossed for by his two sons. His strong-souled wife, who always knew her own mind, had made him very miserable; so his son was to avenge his father on all women-kind. This son became a haunter of fairs on the look-out for hearts to trouble; and, being good-looking and supposed to be rich, found many. He was nicknamed 'Sthagan Varagy', or 'The Market Stroller',[3] and a Gaelic song was made about him. It goes in English:

As I was one day going through the town,[4]
Whom did I meet but Sthagan Varagy?—
Sthagan Varagy, the beloved of the girls,[5]
Horo! fare you well.[6]

He had a merry time, till one day the people drove him from the fair with sticks.

There are three distinct periods in the life of Carleton. First, the period that followed his conversion to Protestantism: a time of short stories, beginning with *Lough Derg,* and ending with the *Traits and Stories* and *Irish Life and Character.* Then, after his heart at any rate had returned to Catholicism, he wrote a series of long stories of peasant life, beginning with *Fardorougha* and ending with *The Black Prophet.*[7] And last of all there was his twenty years' decadence: a time mainly of bad historical novels. When, about 1820, his short stories began appearing, there was no Irish public taking Irish things seriously, and the general reading world had agreed to find certain attributes of Irish peasant life more marketable than others. They wanted to laugh a great deal, and they did not mind weeping a little, but they wished all through to retain their sense of superiority. Carleton could not help being a little conscious of this; and hence these short stories, full as they are of abundant youthful vigour, are less perfect as works of art or as social history than the best of the long stories—as *Fardorougha* and *The Black Prophet,* written when a true Irish public had gathered for a brief while round the *University Magazine.*[8]

In *Fardorougha* there is none of the fierce political feeling that degraded some of Carleton's later novels into caricature. The book has a perfect unity: the scene is filled by a single character, the miser Fardorougha, and by the battle between his love for his money and his love for his son. That son is falsely charged with murder. Though half-dead of a broken heart, the old man tries to cheapen the defence. He is robbed of his money by a fraudulent county treasurer; and having delivered himself of one of those superb Irish curses, he falls sick and dies of sorrow. Before his death he turns to his son—having been commanded by his priest to warn him against miserliness—and bids him to be careful not to give the Church as much as it asks for the masses. He himself, he says, saved enough to buy a new pair of boots by beating it down over the masses for his father's soul; and with these words he passes away. He is one of the strangest figures in literature, and yet there is no caricature. The wrinkle of almost any old Irish farmer might harbour an identical soul. Miserliness, according to Carleton, is more often than people think an Irish peasant sin. They who take their notions from Lever's descriptions of his own very different class think of him rather as a spendthrift. As for *The Black Prophet*, it describes a local famine in one of the early decades of the century: the gradual perishing of the crops, the long period of rain, the supernatural terror of the people, the slow decay of well-to-do folk, the bargaining with a thieving meal-seller, the fever slaying what the famine has spared. From the first to last it is full of a mournful fervour strange to those who know Carleton merely as a humourist; and through all its mournfulness there runs a kind of unhuman fatalism that makes one think of barren moors at moonlight and leaden sunsets over sea.[9] He has never used the dialect to such purpose elsewhere. It serves him for everything, from grotesque humour to intense lyricism.

Carleton would have been strangely puzzled had he known that the Irish public, which loves tales of nobles and rapparees and beautiful women, would finally take most of all to one of the novels of his decadence and read forty editions of such rubbish as *Willy Reilly;* for he knew well he had written himself out. He would have been a little comforted to learn that his humourous tales contributed to the 'National Library'—that series of blue-covered sixpennies which has done so much for Ireland[10]—his *Paddy go Easy,* and the three volumes of extracts from *Traits and Stories* and *Irish Life and Character,* are on the counter of every little stationer's shop in the island. The stories that won him the name of the 'Prose Burns of Ireland' are popular as ever, but his two best novels can only be had from the second-hand book-stalls. Only one novel of his good period, *Valentine M'Clutchy,* is still published; but the artist has passed, and only the politician remains. Carleton had every passion of the peasant; to him a bad landlord, a process server, an agent or a gauger were persons of demoniac wickedness. It is the same feeling that starts the stories, so common in Ireland, of squires and squireens carried off by the devil in person. 'How fast they are going,' said an onlooker at a funeral a while since, 'the Devil is dragging at him.' *Valentine M'Clutchy,* where half the characters are devils, would be intolerable but for its wild humour and the presence of the village madman, in whose half-inspired and crazy oratory Carleton seems to pour himself out. Among the things that have helped the book to its great popularity is perhaps the satire on a rich proselytising vicar of the Established Church[11]—a satire coming strangely from a new convert like Carleton. He wrote against the Scarlet Woman[12] in the *Christian Examiner,* but his whole heart was northern Catholic—was Catholic made stubborn by the near neighbourhood of Orangeism.[13] At no time could he refrain from commending his heroines for their devotion to their creed; and when the father of one of them dies he wills that his body be laid in a certain graveyard where a Protestant was laid but once, and then a thorn-bush sprang from his body. Perhaps he was thinking of himself when he makes two converts fight about their new creeds, and before it is over unconsciously return to their old ones: the new-made Catholic 'bloody-ending' the Pope, the new-made Protestant abusing the Hero of the Boyne.[14]

The great thing about Carleton was that he always remained a peas-ant, hating and loving with his class. On one point he was ever con-sistent, was always a peasant moralist; that is the land question. Almost every story he wrote deals with it; and in *The Red-Haired Man's Wife*, written just before his death in 1870,[15] he makes a curious prophecy. Then Fenianism[16] was everywhere; but this, he said, was not the movement to be dreaded, but a new one that was coming—a land war that would prove the greatest movement Ireland had seen. He says this several times in different parts of the book. A few years later a now famous agitator called on an old Fenian (since dead) and asked him, Would the people take up a land cry? 'I am only afraid', was the answer, 'they would go to the gates of hell for it,' and the event has shown how far he was right.[17]

POPULAR BALLAD POETRY
OF IRELAND

Although this article first appeared in The Leisure Hour *(London) in November 1889, it was written long before. Yeats first mentioned it in a letter to Katharine Tynan on 11 July 1887: "I am writing on Irish poets for* Leisure Hour—*also on Irish faeries" (CL1, 25). On 14 March 1888, he told Tynan of two long articles awaiting the decision of editors. Finally, in a letter dated 6 November 1889, he told Tynan that he was sending along a copy of* The Leisure Hour *with the article in it, and he added: "It is very incomplete—you are not mentioned at all—the reason is that when I wrote I intended to deal with contemporary writers in a separate article. The Leisure Hour* people, however, having an Irish story and other Irish things running, were afraid of so much Ireland" (CL1, 195).*

Behind Ireland fierce and militant, is Ireland poetic, passionate, remembering, idyllic, fanciful, and always patriotic. With this second Ireland only have I to do in this article, and what it writes and reads. I have here a row of little blue-paper-poem books[1]—a whole ballad literature as foreign from all modern English ways as though it were of farthest Iceland and not of neighbouring Ireland, and unknown in name even to most Anglo-Saxon households.[2]

Every now and then the world may read in the accredited organs of enlightenment that the ballad or dramatic poem, or something else, is obsolete. The writers of these little blue books wrote on regardless; but then, perhaps, the accredited organs of enlightenment never reached them or their barbarous mountains, or their readers, who read and sang, and delighted in what they wrote, as men delighted in poetry of old before organs of enlightenment were even heard of. It is centuries since England has written ballads. Many beautiful poems in ballad verse have been written; but the true ballad—the poem of the populace—she has let die; commercialism and other matters have driven it away: she has no longer the conditions.

For a popular ballad literature to arise, firstly are needful national traditions not hidden in libraries, but living in the minds of the populace. These Ireland has. Every ivy-matted tower carries its legend of stormy feud or love-lorn lady; every little round rath earth-piled its story of leprechaun[+] and pooka;[3] and over all broods the one great dominant thought, love of country, while around that thought gather the long-remembered names of exiles.

Secondly, it is needful that the populace and the poets shall have one heart—that there shall be no literary class with its own way of seeing things and its own conventions. This condition Ireland has long had—whatever the people were the poets have been more intensely; were the people poor, they were poorer; did the people suffer, they suffered also. Did the people love their country, did not the poets keep alive that love through years of misfortune? They were one with the people in their faults and their virtues—in their aims and their passions.

Hence, long before the days of these little blue-paper-poem books, in the more Gaelic-speaking days, was a copious ballad literature going from mouth to mouth, for few could read. Since the time of Elizabeth[4] (when English ballad literature began to die) have arisen in Ireland twenty-six Gaelic-speaking poets of fame,[5] no less; and many a fameless one-song man, like the author of that old seventeenth-century song so popular in Galway and Mayo, with its pathetic ending, as it goes in a translation now old itself:

> 'Tis my grief that Patrick Loughlin is not Earl of Irrul still,
> And that Brian Duff no longer rules as lord upon the hill;[6]
> And that Colonel Hugh McGrady[7] should be lying dead and
>   low,
> And I sailing, sailing swiftly from the county of Mayo.

In the last century there gathered in Munster a most notable group of Gaelic poets, some of them strolling ne'er-do-weels of genius, like that O'Tuomy,[8] who wrote over the door of his inn, when he had a door to write over, much to the indignation of his wife—

> Should one of the stock of the noble Gael—
>   A brother bard who is fond of good cheer—
> Be short of the price of a tankard of ale,
>   He's welcome to O'Tuomy a thousand times here.[9]

Others were hedge schoolmasters, who, when to educate was penal, taught for a living in the hedges and ditches, and while the thing was forbidden seem to have aroused among the ploughboys of whole country-sides quite a furore for Latin, ay, and even Greek. Men like that Macnamarah,[10] who, banished by poverty brought on by his own love of frolic and imprudent satire, wandered away into foreign lands far from mirth and boon companions, and composed the 'Fair Hills of Eire[†], O'; or like him who, exiled at Hamburg,[†] wrote the more famous 'Hills of Holy Ireland'. Thus beautifully has Ferguson[†] translated this exile song of a nation of farmers:

A plenteous place is Ireland for hospitable cheer,
  Uileacan dubh O![11]
Where the wholesome fruit is bursting from the yellow barley
 ear,
  Uileacan dubh O!
There is honey in the trees where her misty vales expand,
And her forest paths in summer are by falling waters fanned;
There is dew at high noontide there, and springs i' the yellow
 sand,[12]
  On the fair hills of Holy Ireland.
Curled he is, and ringleted,[13] and plaided to the knee,
  Uileacan dubh O!
Each captain who comes sailing across the Irish Sea,
  Uileacan dubh O!
And I will make my journey, if life and health but stand,
Unto that pleasant country, that fresh and fragrant strand,
And leave your boasted braveries, your wealth and high
 command,
  For the fair hills of Holy Ireland.

Large and profitable are the stacks upon the ground,[14]
  Uileacan dubh O!
The butter and the cream do wondrously abound,
  Uileacan dubh O!
The cresses on the water and the sorrels are at hand,
And the cuckoo's calling daily his note of music bland,
And the bold thrush sings bravely his song i' the forests grand,
  On the fair hills of Holy Ireland.

Beautiful as some of their poems were, the hedge schoolmaster's work was often pedantic in manner and tepid in matter, far inferior to the

mere peasant poetry. The hedge schoolmaster indeed, with his zeal for
learning, and his efforts, not often successful, to do creative work, was
a not uninteresting forerunner of the modern man of letters.

The poets of those days would make a long list—Andrew Macgrath,
surnamed 'The Merry Pedlar'; O'Sullivan the Red, pious and profligate; John MacDonnell, of vision-seeing memory; John O'Cullen,
who lamented in such famous words over the Abbey of Timoleague;[†]
and Heffernan,[†] the blind, who in his old age loved to stand listening
while the ploughboys in the hedge school droned out some Greek poet;
and many another.[15]

Twice a year, in the earlier portion of last century, they held what
were called sessions of the bards.[16] Young poets used to recite their verse
against each other, the victors being crowned. These meetings were
finally suppressed by the penal laws.

The political poetry of these men was no light matter in its day.
Because of it they were hated and pursued by the powerful and the rich,
and loved by the poor. They disguised their meaning in metaphor and
symbol. The poet goes out in the morning and meets a beautiful spirit
weeping and lamenting, a 'banshee' with 'a mien of unearthly mildness'.
On her he lavishes all his power of description, and then calls her Ireland. Or else he evades the law by hiding his sedition under the guise
of a love-song. Then Ireland becomes his Kathleen, Ny-Houlahan, or
else his Roisin Dubh,[17] or some other name of Gaelic endearment. To
her he sings:[18]

> Oh! the Erne shall run red
>   With redundance of blood,
> The earth shall rock beneath our tread,
>   And flames wrap hill and wood,
> And gun-peal and slogan cry
>   Wake many a glen serene,
> Ere you shall fade, ere you shall die,
>   My dark Rosaleen!
>   My own Rosaleen!
> The judgment hour must first be nigh,
> Ere you can fade, ere you can die,
>   My dark Rosaleen!

As it goes in Mangan's version.

So things went on, until some two or three decades before the
printing of these little blue books men began to look for a national poetry
printed in English. A new literature commenced. The stock of originals
at first was scanty; the new movement depended for a time mainly on

translations. At the beginning of this new movement were Walsh and Callanan.[19]

Callanan crowded much capricious incident into his short life, beginning in 1795 and ending at Lisbon[20]—whither he had gone as a tutor, in hopes of recovering his health—in 1829. After training for the priesthood he enlisted as a solider, and was bought out by his friends as his regiment was on the point of sailing for Malta.[21] Subsequently he wandered through the country collecting old legends to dress up in verse or prose for magazine or newspaper, and translating old Gaelic peasant songs.

It is interesting to know that shortly before his death the old passion came uppermost, and he began collecting songs and legends among the Spanish peasantry.

His friends found him, I fear, a great ne'er-do-weel, and yet he asked not much—no man's wealth—only food to eat and a little leisure to hunt out and meditate on the stories he loved. Maybe in some distant time the poets will no longer gather together in cities, but stay, as he did, in their own country-sides, content to write of the people about them, and so shall poetry sweeten the lives of even the simplest of folk, for assuredly the legends of the hills that we see in childhood and age from our own doors, so far as we are simple and natural, are more to us than the legends of any other place on earth. Such a poetry would go deeper into men's lives than any verses of the cities, no matter how full these be of the passion of intellectual attainment.

Callanan, like his successor, Edward Walsh, has left a few original poems—passionate, sincere, and simple verses, celebrating the scenes and legends of his native Munster.[22]

Edward Walsh, born in Londonderry in 1805, a militiaman's son, had all along a hard time of it—first overworked schoolmaster of Cork, afterwards overworked schoolmaster of Spike Island.[23] Nevertheless, he did manage to bring out two small collections of translated popular songs, Gaelic and English side by side. 'We remember,'[24] writes his latest editor, '(though now forty years since),[25] following Walsh in the twilight of an autumn evening, drinking in the odd chords that came from the little harp that lay on his left arm as he wandered, lonely and unknown, by the then desert Jones's Road, or reposed himself on one of the seats that at the time were outside the walls of Conliffe House.'[26] Passionate, wild songs were they, well-nigh Oriental in their ardour, that he loved to sing to the little harp on his left arm.

A simple and spontaneous thing was this peasant poet-craft. The man who wrote love-songs really was in love. The man who wrote laments really was unhappy. Poor dead Gaelic men, how many centuries ago did they sing the funeral song above you, and here are your passions and sorrows crying from Edward Walsh's little harp!

The troubled year of '48 found him still schoolmaster to the convicts at Spike Island. When John Mitchel[†27] was sent there on the way to his Bermuda hulk, Walsh approached him reverently, and stooping, kissed the famous rebel journalist's hand, and said, 'You are now the man in all Ireland most to be envied'.[28] That night John Mitchel[†] meditated over it all in his journal, thus: 'Poor Walsh, he has a family of young children; he seems broken in health and spirits. Ruin has him in the wind at last; there are more contented galley-slaves toiling at Spike than the schoolmaster. Perhaps this man does really envy me, and most assuredly I do not envy him.'[29]

His death was not so far off now, for the schoolmaster, having got little good of his five-and-forty years, died in 1850; but lived long enough to see in his last decade the rise of a literary movement that gathered his and his fellow-workers' poems from old newspapers and magazines or readerless volumes, and printed them in thousands with new and worthy companions.

This movement began with the founding in 1842 of the *Nation,* a powerful and seditious sheet in those days. Everything was considered Irish that embodied Irish passion and thought. In the ballad collections that began in 1845 with Gavan Duffy's[30] *Ballad Poetry of Ireland*—a volume with a larger circulation than any other published in Ireland—and the first of these little blue books—a few Orange ballads even found place.

An Irish poet[31] was to write on his title-page later on:

> We are one at heart if you be Ireland's friend,
> Though leagues asunder our opinions tend;
> There are but two great parties in the end.

In Duffy's ballad book what was to grow plainer as years went on was already plain—that three men, Davis, Ferguson,[†] and Mangan, stood above all other Irish writers of that day.

Not one of those I have heretofore discussed could have been called a prosperous or happy man, and Clarence Mangan, the greatest, it will be seen, was also the most miserable. The others were poets of the farm and the hills. The lover in the old ballad laments because he has no riches for his beloved, no cattle 'to drive through the long twilight.'[32] In the earliest poems of seven hundred years ago,[33] as in the latest, the singer's sweetheart has lips the colour of the berries of the quicken-tree (the mountain ash). In his more sentimental moods he sings like the lover in the Munster peasant song, whereof I make this version:[34]

My love, we will go, we will go, I and you.
And away in the woods we will scatter the dew,
And the salmon behold and the ousel too.
My love, I and you, we will hear, we will hear,
The calling afar of the doe and the deer,
And the bird in the branches will cry for us clear,
And the cuckoo unseen in his festival mood.
And death, O my fair one! will never come near
In the bosom afar of the fragrant wood.

Than which same pastoral aspiration I know nothing more impossibly romantic and Celtic. Nature with these men was a passion, but in the poetry of Mangan are no beautiful descriptions.[35] Outer things were only to him mere symbols to express his own inmost and desperate heart. Nurtured and schooled in grimy back streets of Dublin, woods and rivers were not for him. His father boasted that his children would run into a mousehole to escape him; afterwards shut up in a scrivener's office, the amenity and beauty of human intercourse was not for him. Sensitive in an extreme degree, persecuted and solitary, in this scrivener's office he spent seven years; three more years he laboured as an attorney's clerk to support father, brother, and sisters, then wholly depending on him; for the father, when Mangan was quite a young lad, finding him of working age, appears to have struck work. Hard drudging it was year in year out. No wonder he wrote—

All my divinities have died of grief,
And left me wedded to the rude and real.[36]

And yet he found time to read many an out-of-the-way book and to teach himself German, Spanish, Italian, French, Latin, and maybe some smattering of Oriental tongues, though this is not certain, and to write several strange and pessimistic poems.

But already from his ever-growing misery he seems to have sought solace in opium and gin. In Mount Pleasant Square, Dublin, lived three sisters, of higher social position than he. With Frances,[37] the youngest of these, he fell in love madly, hopelessly. She encouraged him; and then, when the novelty wore off, sent him about his business. Whatever of brittle happiness had staid with him was quite gone now. More and more did he seek to blot out memory with gin and opium.

His father was dead, but his ghost, as he believed, with other phantoms, haunted him day and night. In his latter days some one found him a post in the Library of Trinity College, more congenial then scrivening. 'An acquaintance pointed out to me', wrote Mitchel[†], 'a man perched on the top of a ladder, with the whispered information that the figure was Clarence Mangan. It was an unearthly and ghostly figure, in a brown garment (the same garment to all appearance which lasted to the day of his death).[38] The blanched hair was totally unkempt; the corpse-like features still as marble; a large book was in his arms, and all his soul was in the book. I had never heard of Clarence Mangan before, and knew not for what he was celebrated, whether as a magician, a poet, or a murderer, yet took a volume and spread it on the table, not to read, but with pretence of reading, to gaze at the spectral creature upon the ladder.'[39]

Many of his earlier poems had been printed in the *Nation;* but now he transferred his allegiance to Mitchel's[†] *United Irishman,* contributing thereto much verse, original or translated, from Gaelic song or German ballad. But gradually he became useless for any good purpose. For days together he would disappear. A priest, I have heard said, brought him once before a looking-glass, and pointed to his haggard face and tattered clothes therein reflected. 'Ah!' cried Mangan, 'it is nothing to the state of the inner man.'

In the end he fell a victim to cholera (he always believed he would die of cholera), at the Meath Hospital, in 1849, he being in his forty-seventh year.[40] After death his face was sketched by the present head of the National Gallery of London, and the sketch hangs now in the Irish National Gallery.[41] In the beautiful profile there is visible no mark of his life's struggle. The poor crazed soul, as it seemed, had left the clay to the ancient innocence of dead things. Few more pitiful stories are on record. But who will say anything about his life, momentous as he himself has said, under the symbol of Siberia:[42]

> In Siberia's wastes
>   The ice-wind's breath
> Woundeth like the toothèd steel;
> Lost Siberia doth reveal
>   Only blight and death.
>
> Blight and death alone—
>   No summer shines.
> Night is interblent with day.
> In Siberia's wastes alway
>   The blood blackens, the heart pines.
>
> In Siberia's wastes
>   No tears are shed,

For they freeze within the brain.
Nought is felt but dullest pain—
  Pain acute, yet dead;

Pain as in a dream,
  When years go by
Funeral-paced, yet fugitive;
When man lives and doth not live—
  Doth not live—nor die.

In Siberia's wastes
  Are sands and rocks;
Nothing blooms of green or soft,
But the snow-peaks rise aloft,
  And the gaunt ice-blocks.

And the exile there
  Is one with those;
They are part and he is part—
For the sands are in his heart,
  And the killing snows.

Therefore in those wastes
  None curse the Czar.
Each man's tongue is cloven by
The north blast, who[43] heweth nigh
  With sharp scymitar.

And such doom he drees
  Till, hunger-gnawn
And cold-slain, he at length sinks there;
Yet scarce more a corpse than ere
  His last breath was drawn.

Where among your drawing-room bards of fashionable pessimism are any verses regal and terrible as these? Be it noted they do not arraign Heaven; nor here nor elsewhere does he excuse or luxuriously pity and fondle himself, this poet of the depths.

Of his translations the most often printed in the ballad books are those from the Gaelic: The 'Testament of Catheir Mor', 'Dark Rosaleen', 'Lament for the Princess of Tyrone and Tyrconnell', and 'The Woman of Three Cows'.

Oh! think of Donnell of the ships, the chief whom nothing
    daunted;[44]
See how he fell in distant Spain, unchronicled, unchanted!
He sleeps the great O'Sullivan, where thunder cannot rouse;
They ask yourself, should you be proud, good woman of three
    cows?[45]

And many more. Instead of giving any of his ballads—for to quote
at length is not possible, and to quote piecemeal is scant justice to any
poem with a story—I give a few stanzas of his version of those curious rhymes by King Alfred of Northumberland descriptive of Ireland,
whither he had gone in youth to be educated:[46]

> I found in Innisfail the Fair,
> In Ireland, while in exile there,
> Women of worth, both grave and gay men—
> Many clerics and many laymen.
> . . . . .
> Gold and silver I found, and money,
> Plenty of wheat and plenty of honey;
> I found God's people rich in pity,
> Found many a feast and many a city.
> . . . . .
> I found the good lay monks and brothers
> Ever beseeching help for others;
> And in their keeping the Holy Word
> Pure as it came from Jesus the Lord.
>
> I found in Munster, unfettered of any,
> Kings, and queens, and poets a many—
> Poets were skilled in music and measure—
> Prosperous doings, mirth, and pleasure.
> . . . . .
> I found in Ulster, from hill to glen,
> Hardy warriors, resolute men—
> Beauty that bloomed when youth was gone,
> And strength transmitted from sire to son.
> . . . . .
> I found in Leinster, the smooth and sleek,
> From Dublin to Slewmargy's peak,[47]
> Flourishing pastures, valour, health,
> Long-living worthies, commerce, wealth.
> . . . . .

> I found strict morals in age and youth,
> I found historians recording truth.
> The things I sing of in verse unsmooth
> I found them all; I have written sooth.

A very different ancient Ireland from the barbarous place some have imagined. To almost everything he[48] gave a rueful and visionary tinge. You must not go to his work for delicate grace or tender pity, for such are the expressions of the happy moments of usually happy men, but for desolation and sympathy with whatever is barbaric in men's hearts.

It is not possible to imagine two men more different than Clarence Mangan and Thomas Davis[49]—the one absorbed, moody, and morbid, in penury, one of the people, wilful and self-taught, wasted by routine; the other, university trained, a man of action, patient and gay, one of the gentry, surrounded by friends. The one wrote because he was miserable, the other wrote because he was happy and noble and wished to make others so. Thomas Osborne[†] Davis, Ireland has no name more widely loved, no more potent maker of opinion. At college in no way different from his fellows save in his contempt for the oratorical honours of the Debating Society, few would have imagined him destined to lead a rebel party.[50] He was twenty-seven before he made a single verse, and then only because his 'young Irelanders' felt the need of ballads for the *Nation* newspaper, started in 1842; and all he wrote was done within the limits of a year and a half. In 1845 he died. Diverse parties—the O'Connellites[51] whose power he had broken, and they to whom his ideals were a veritable fire-pillar, and they who held them the merest Jack-o'-lantern flickerings—all trooped to his funeral. Ferguson[†] wrote his burial ode:[52]

> I walked through Ballinderry[53] in the spring-time,
>   When the bud was on the tree;
> And I said, in every fresh-ploughed field beholding
>   The sowers striding free,
> Scattering broadcast forth the corn in golden plenty[54]
>   On the quick seed-clasping soil,
> 'Even such, this day, among the fresh-stirred hearts of Erin,
>   Thomas Davis, is thy toil!'[†55]

> I sat by Ballyshannon in the summer,[56]
>   And saw the salmon leap;
> And I said, as I beheld the gallant creatures
>   Spring glittering from the deep,

Through the spray, and through the prone heaps striving onward
   To the calm clear streams above,[57]
'So seekest thou thy native founts of freedom, Thomas Davis,
   In thy brightness of strength and love!'[†]
     . . . . .
Young husbandmen of Erin's fruitful seed-time,
   In the fresh track of danger's plough!
Who will walk the heavy, toilsome, perilous furrow,
   Girt with freedom's seed-sheets now?[58]

Many a fine war-ballad has he left us, many a fine war-song. Of the first, the most notable being 'The Sack of Baltimore', a history of a descent by Algerian pirates on the Irish shore, written just before his death; of the last, the song, 'Oh, for a sword and a rushing steed'.[59] Yes, Ireland has no name more beloved. Often have I heard the children of the people singing his songs, putting their whole soul therein. There are concerts where all the singers are children and all the songs are his— their beloved. Here is one I have heard well rendered:

Oh! the marriage, the marriage![60]
   With love and *mo bhuachaill* for me;[61]
The ladies that ride in a carriage
   Might envy my marriage to me.
For Eoghan is straight as a tower,
   And tender and loving and true;[62]
He told me more love in an hour
   Than the squires of the county could do.
         Then, oh! the marriage! etc.

His hair is a shower of soft gold,
   His eye is as clear as the day,
His conscience and vote were unsold
   When others were carried away.[63]
His word is as good as an oath,
   And freely 'twas given to me;
Oh! sure 'twill be happy for both
   The day of our marriage to see.
         Then, oh! the marriage! etc.

His kinsmen are honest and kind,
   The neighbours think much of his skill,
And Eoghan's the lad to my mind,
   Though he owns neither castle nor mill.

But he has a tilloch of land,
　A horse, and a stocking of coin,
A foot for a dance, and a hand
　In cause of his country to join.
　　　　　Then, oh! the marriage! etc.

We meet in the market and fair,
　We meet in the morning and night;
He sits on the half of my chair,
　And my people are wild with delight.
Yet I long through the winter to skim—
　Though Eoghan longs more, I can see—
When I will be married to him,
　And he will be married to me.
　　　　　Then, oh! the marriage, the marriage![64]
　　　　　With love and *mo bhuachaill* for me;
　　　　　The ladies that ride in a carriage
　　　　　Might envy my marriage to me.

Of his political poetry I cannot speak; suffice it to say it still goes on, whether for good or evil, serving its purpose, making opinion.

Perhaps reading and reasonable Irishmen should put Ferguson[†65] where they put Mangan, at the head of their poets. He has not the other's lyrical intensity, but his power is more serene and lofty. His ballad, 'The Vengeance of the Welshmen of Tirawley',[66] is admittedly the best of Irish ballads, and in some ways the most Homeric poem of the century. His *Conary* is the most perfect equivalent for the manner of the ancient Celtic bards in modern literature. The very breadth and serenity of Ferguson[†] has robbed him of popularity—there is an antique coldness about him. I heard him discussing a few months before his death some recent decorative architecture. To him it seemed florid and unimpressive. He preferred the plain buildings of earlier times. This severity of mind is in all he wrote. When reading the 'Welshmen of Tirawley', or his more recent *Conary,* one seems to be listening to some old half-savage bard chanting to his companions at a forest fire. If we long, while listening, for the more elaborate music of modern days, the fault is in us and in our time. The lives of Mangan and Davis were short and crowded with incident. The life of Ferguson[†] was long and uneventful. He died some three years since, full of years and honours. A collected edition of his poems and prose writings—he was a noted antiquarian and old-fashioned romance writer—has been coming out in shilling volumes since his death.

In the little blue ballad books there is many another name dear wher-

ever the Irish are—Griffin with his 'Gille Machree', and Banim, truer
to peasant nature and mother earth, with his famous and typical 'Soggarth aroon' (priest dear).[67]

Am I the slave they say,
   Soggarth aroon?
Since you did show the way,
   Soggarth aroon,
Their slave no more to be,
While they would work with me
Ould Ireland's slavery,
   Soggarth aroon?

Why not her poorest man,
   Soggarth aroon,
Try and do all he can,
   Soggarth aroon,
Her commands to fulfil
Of his own heart and will,
Side by side with you still,
   Soggarth aroon?

Loyal and brave to you,
   Soggarth aroon,
Yet be not slave to you,
   Soggarth aroon.
Nor out of fear to you—[68]
Stand up so near to you—
Och! out of fear to you!
   Soggarth aroon!

Who in the winter's night,
   Soggarth aroon,
When the cold blast did bite,
   Soggarth aroon,
Came to my cabin door,
And, on my earthen-flure,[69]
Knelt by me, sick and poor,
   Soggarth aroon?

Who on the marriage day,
   Soggarth aroon,
Made the poor cabin gay,

Soggarth aroon—
And did both laugh and sing,
Making our hearts to ring,
At the poor Christening,[70]
Soggarth aroon?

Who as a friend only met,[71]
Soggarth aroon,
Never did flout me yet,
Soggarth aroon?
And when my hearth was dim[72]
Gave, while his eye did brim,
What I should give to him,
Soggarth aroon?

Och! you, and only you,
Soggarth aroon!
And for this I was true to you,
Soggarth aroon.[73]
In love they'll never shake
When for ould Ireland's sake
We a true part did take,
Soggarth aroon!

And Keegan, the farm-labourer, and Frazer, the weaver, and Florence
McCarthy, whose work was more of the fancy than the heart, and
D'Arcy[†] Magee, afterwards assassinated, and rebel Doheny, with his
one memorable song, written as he lay in hiding, and Gavan Duffy, and
Ingram with his famous 'Memory of the Dead'; and later on in Fenian times, Casey, with his 'Rising of the Moon', and Kickham, Fenian
leader and convict, most rambling and yet withal most vivid, humorous, and most sincere of Irish novelists, with his ballad of 'Blind Shee-
han', and his 'Irish Peasant-girl'; and Joyce, with his many ballads, also
author of a national epic, that reached, it is said, a sale of ten thousand copies in a few days, mainly among Irish Americans; and in our
own times Alfred Percival Graves, with his

Little red lark
Like a rosy spark,

and his 'Father O'Flynn'; and many more besides these, anonymous
and named. Others again whose work is in the main written for the
few, have yet occasionally reached the people, like Allingham, with his

'Fair Maid of Ballyshannon', by the help of music, or, like de Vere,[†] through the ballad books.[74]

The English reader may be surprised to find no mention of Moore, or the verses of Lever and Lover.[75] They were never poets of the people. Moore lived in the drawing-rooms, and still finds his audience therein. Lever and Lover, kept apart by opinion from the body of the nation, wrote ever with one eye on London. They never wrote for the people, and neither have they ever, therefore, in prose or verse, written faithfully of the people. Ireland was a metaphor to Moore, to Lever and Lover a merry harlequin, sometimes even pathetic, to be patted and pitied and laughed at so long as he said 'your honour', and presumed in nowise to be considered a serious or tragic person. Yet the poetry of the men I write of is above all things tragic and melancholy. We must not seek, however, from these, or any other makers of popular song and ballad, the same things we love in more studious writers. The grass is merely green to them and the sea merely blue, and their very spontaneity has made them unequal. But a wonderful freshness and sweetness they have, like the smell of newly-ploughed earth. They are always honest companions; no one of them wrote out of mere vanity or mere ambition, but ever from a full heart.

BARDIC IRELAND

Yeats reviewed Sophie Bryant's Celtic Ireland *(London: Kegan Paul, 1889) in* The Scots Observer *of 4 January 1890. Mrs. Bryant (1850–1922), Irish-born educator, wrote on biblical and historical subjects. She made another contribution to the background literature of the Irish Literary Revival in 1913 with her* Genius of the Gael, A Study in Celtic Psychology and Its Manifestations *(London: T. Fisher Unwin, 1913), in which she praised the dramas of Synge and Yeats as masterpieces of Gaelic psychology.*

A good deal has been written about the first few centuries of Irish history both for the specialist and the general reader. He who cannot be persuaded to dip into the *Senchus Mor* and *The Book of the Dun Cow*[1] for himself, can turn to the histories of Mr. Standish O'Grady, or to Lady Ferguson's[†] *Irish Before the Conquest,* or to Mrs. Bryant's *Celtic Ireland* (London: Kegan Paul).[2] Sir Samuel Ferguson's[†] ballads and Mr. Aubrey de Vere's *Legends of St. Patrick,* and the retrospective poems in his *Inisfail*[†]—these more than the *Legends*—are full, too, of the spirit of these stormy centuries.[3] Mrs. Bryant runs over what is known of the eleven hundred years from the Nativity to the landing of Strongbow.[4] She does not take it king by king and saint by saint like Lady Ferguson,[†] but picks out facts that seem to her of moment and comments on these. Thus, she has chapters on the influence of ancient Ireland and England on each other, on the bardic order, on St. Patrick[5] and his clerics, on the working in precious metals and the missal-painting of the Irish, and so forth; and the general effect is good.

In those ages the genius of the Gael seems to have found its most complete expression. From the monasteries of Ireland Europe learned to illuminate its bibles and psalters, and therewith the manner of working beautifully in metals. Irish music, also, was widely heard of; and some believe that the modern harp came thus from Ireland. Celtic

conquest poured out too, one Irish *ard-reigh*[6] meeting his death by lightning as he crossed the Alps; and when St. Patrick had Christianised the
country another kind of conquest began, and England, Scotland, Iceland, Germany, and France owed their Christianity mainly to the Irish
missions. In these first centuries the Celt made himself: later on Fate
made him. It is in his early history and literature that you must look
for his character: above all in his literature. The bards, kept by the rules
of their order apart from war and the common affairs of men, rode
hither and thither gathering up the dim feelings of the time, and making them conscious. In the history one sees Ireland ever struggling vainly
to attain some kind of unity. In the bardic tales it is ever one, warring
within itself, indeed, but always obedient, unless under some great
provocation, to its high king. The *Tain Bo*,[7] the greatest of all these
epics, is full of this devotion. Later, when things were less plastic, men
rose against their *ard-reigh* for any and everything: one because at dinner he was given a hen's egg instead of a duck's.[8]

The bards were the most powerful influence in the land, and all manner of superstitious reverence environed them round. No gift they
demanded might be refused them. One king being asked for his eye by
a bard in quest of an excuse for rousing the people against him
plucked it out and gave it. Their rule was one of fear as much as love.
A poem and an incantation were almost the same. A satire could fill a
whole country-side with famine. Something of the same feeling still sur-
vives, perhaps, in the extreme dread of being 'rhymed up' by some local
maker of unkindly verses. This power of the bards was responsible,
it may be, for one curious thing in ancient Celtic history: its self-
consciousness. The warriors were not simply warriors, the kings simply kings, the smiths simply smiths: they all seem striving to bring
something out of the world of thoughts into the world of deeds—a
something that always eluded them. When the Fenian militia[9] were
established in the second century they were no mere defenders of
coast-line or quellers of popular tumult. They wanted to revive the kind
of life lived in old days when the Chiefs of the Red Branch[10] gathered
round Cuchulain.[†] They found themselves in an age when men began
to love rich draperies and well-wrought swords, to exult in dominion
and the lordship of many flocks. They resolved to live away from these
things in the forest, cooking their food by burying it under a fire; and
passing such laws as that none of their order should take a dowry with
his wife, but marry her for love alone. Nor would they have among
them any man who did not understand all the several kinds of poetry.
In the end they grew proud and tyrannical, and the people rose and
killed them at Gavra.[11] Old Celtic Ireland was full of these conscious
strivings—unless[12] her whole history be fiction. Indeed Cuchulain,[†]

Finn, Oisin,[13] St. Patrick, the whole ancient world of Erin may well have been sung out of the void by the harps of the great bardic order. Almost certainly a number of things taken most literally by Mrs. Bryant are in no sense history. She supposes it a matter proven and indisputable that the primeval races, Fomorians, Tuatha dé Danaans,[†] Milesians and the rest mentioned in *The Book of Invasions,* were historic peoples; and Rhys, Jubainville,[†] and others have made it certain that they were merely bardic myths.[14] Their present was not their ancient shape. The monks amused themselves by humanising these old gods, turning them into pious early colonisers, and tracing their descent to Noah.[15] It has been found possible, however, to pick out something of their old significance, and discern in them the gods of light warring on the spirits of darkness—on the Fomorians who had but one leg under them and one arm in the middle of their breasts, and lived under the sea: creatures who turned under the monkish touch into common two-armed and two-legged pirates. Some few of the divine races, indeed—the Tuatha dé Danaan[†] chiefly—preserved a parcel of their ancient dignity, and, becoming the fairies, dwell happily near their deserted altars. The monks were sad spoilers of things pagan. The old warlike centuries bored them. On the margin of a Latin history of the early days of Finn MacCool,[†] the scribe has written in Gaelic: 'Holy Virgin, when will brother Edmund come home from the meeting?'[16]

Mrs. Bryant takes this hurly-burly of gods quite seriously, and tries to identify them with Iberian, Ugrian, Belgae,[17] and other races. She does not seem to have heard even of the mythologic view. Other portions of her book are excellent. Her chapter on the Brehon Laws[18] could scarce be better. She shows how Ireland was above all things democratic and communistic—all lands belonging to the tribe. It was just such a system that a sociable people full of restless energies would make themselves; and, as might be said of Greece, it turned out good for the world, bad for the nation. When other countries were bowed under military despotism, missions poured forth over Europe from the schools of Ireland, but when the day of battle came she could not combine against the invader. Each province had its own assembly and its own king. There was no focus to draw the tribes into one. The national order perished at the moment when other countries like Germany and Iceland were beginning to write out their sagas and epics in deliberate form. The trappings of the warrior ages had not yet passed away, yet modern thought was near enough to give them a certain remoteness, so that the artist could detach himself from his material. The moment had come to write out old tales in *Nibelungenlieds* and *Eddas;*[19] but Ireland was doomed to have no rest, no peace, no leisure for students to labour in: the bees were too hard pressed by the wasps to make any honey. Her passionate bardic inspiration died away, leaving nothing but seeds that never bore stems, stems that never wore flowers, flowers that knew no fruitage. The literature of ancient Ireland is a literature of vast, half-dumb conceptions. The moment when the two worlds, ours and theirs, drew near to speak with each other was wasted in flight. No sooner were the Danes expelled than Strongbow came in.[20] The shaping of bardic tales, the adornment of missals, the working in precious metals, all came to an end. The last-wrought gold shrine was done in 1166, three years before the landing of the Norman.[21] Instead of the well-made poems we might have had, there remains but a wild anarchy of legends—a vast pell-mell of monstrous shapes: huge demons driving swine on the hill-tops; beautiful shadows whose hair has a peculiar life and moves responsive to their thought; and here and there some great hero like Cuchulain,[†] some epic needing only deliberate craft to be scarce less than Homer. There behind the Ireland of to-day, lost in the ages, this chaos murmurs like a dark and stormy sea full of the sounds of lamentation. And through all these throbs one impulse—the persistence of Celtic passion: a man loves or hates until he falls into the grave. Years pass over the head of Conchobar[22] and Finn: they forget nothing. Quinet has traced the influence of the desert on the Israelitish people.[23] As they were children of the earth, and as the Parsees[24] are of the fire, so do the Celtic Irish seem of the fellowship of the sea: ever changing, ever the same.

TALES FROM THE TWILIGHT

This review of Lady Wilde's Ancient Cures, Charms, and Usages of Ireland *(London: Ward and Downey, 1890) appeared in* The Scots Observer, 1 March 1890. *Jane Francesca, Lady Wilde (1826–96), the mother of Oscar Wilde, enjoyed considerable fame of her own as poet, propagandist, translator from German and French, and a folk-lorist. Under the pseudonym "Speranza," she was an important contributor to* The Nation *magazine between 1845 and 1848. Lady Wilde also published a two-volume set of folktales in 1887,* Ancient Legends, Mystic Charms, and Superstitions of Ireland *(London: Ward and Downey).*

This new book of Lady Wilde's—*Ancient Cures, Charms, and Usages of Ireland* (London: Ward and Downey)—is a collection of folk-lore mainly from the western islands,[1] the most unpuritan places in Europe. Around and northward of Dublin no small amount of gloom has blown from overseas, though not more than a few miles from Dublin—at Howth,[2] for instance—the old life goes on but little changed. But westward the second century is nearer than the nineteenth, and a pagan memory is more of a power than any modern feeling. On Innismurray,[3] an island near my own district, the people look reverently on the seals as they lie in the warm, shallow water near the shore; for may they not be the spirits of their forebears? Even in their social customs they do not recognise our century; for two peasants, hereditary king and queen of the island, control disputes and deal out laws as occasion demands. From these remote parts Sir William Wilde[4] collected a vast bulk of tales and spells and proverbs. In addition to the peasants he regularly employed to glean the stubble of tradition for him, he got many things from patients at his Dublin hospital; for when grateful patients would offer to send him geese or eggs or butter, he would bargain for a fragment of folk-lore instead. He threw all his gatherings into a big box, and thence it is that Lady Wilde has quarried the materials of her new book: a farrago of spells, cures, fairy-tales, and proverbs—these last beyond price—the districts seldom specified and the dates of discovery never. I heartily wish they had been better and more scientifically treated, but I scarce know whom to blame: Lady Wilde, Sir William Wilde, his collectors, or the big box. However that may be, and in spite of these defects, my author's two volumes of *Ancient Legends* and this new collection are the fullest and most beautiful gathering of Irish folk-lore in existence. Mr. Douglas Hyde[5] may some day surpass it—no one else can. In the 'Spells and Cures'[6] section Lady Wilde has lighted on a subject which, so far as Ireland is concerned, has hitherto been almost ignored. Well-nigh all prove with how little gloom the Irish peasant looks on death and decay, but rather turns them to favour and to prettiness. For madness he would give you 'three things not made by the hand of man'—salt and honey and milk, to be drunk out of a sea-shell before sunrise; for the falling sickness he would hang about your neck three hairs of a milk-white greyhound; for almost any minor evil he would prescribe an ointment made of cowslip roots or red berries of rowan, unless indeed you have chanced on one of those desperate ailments that require a plaster of spiders or a draught of water from the skull of a man.[7]

For we too have our horrors, but all are so fancifully self-conscious that they are in no wise burdensome. For instance, if you love and love in vain, all you have to do is to go to a grave-yard at midnight, dig up a corpse, and take a strip of skin off it from head to heel, watch until you catch your mistress sleeping and tie it round her waist, and thereafter she will love you for ever.[8] Even our witches are not so horrible as other peoples'. Sometimes they do things wicked as weird:[9] such, for instance, as burying a sheaf of corn and leaving it to rot away while some hated life rots with it.[10] But the witches themselves are country-women of ours, and so we try to forget and forgive. Mostly, too, they are guilty of nothing worse than stealing corn or milk, or making their own fields flourish in unnatural abundance. We have not soured their temper with faggot and stake. Once, it is true, we knocked out a witch's eye with a cabbage-stump, but that was long ago and in the north.[11] Lady Wilde gives a good witch-tale of one of the western islands.[12] There was a man, one Flaherty, who was greatly suspected by his neighbours of foregathering with the Evil One, because with little land he had always much corn. Turns and turns about they watched by night, until one morning a watcher saw something black moving in the field and carrying a grain of corn. That grain the something planted. Then it brought another and did the same, and then another, and yet another, and many hundreds of others; and the man drew near and found it a hideous insect. So he stooped and caught it, and put it in a horn snuff-box, and shut down the lid, and went off home; and presently there was great commotion and excitement, for Flaherty's wife had disappeared. The man happened to mention the black thing in the snuff-box; and 'How do you know', said his friend, 'but it may be Flaherty's wife?' Flaherty heard the tale, and begged the man to go with him, and carry the snuff-box into the house, and open it in his presence. The man went home with him, and some neighbours likewise; and when the box was opened out crawled a great black insect, and made straight into Mrs. Flaherty's room as hard as it could go; and after a little Mrs. Flaherty came out, and she was very pale and one finger was bleeding. 'What means the blood?' asked the man of the snuff-box; and says Flaherty: 'When you shut down the lid you snapped off a little bit of the beetle's claw, and so my wife suffers.' After this Flaherty was shunned, and one day he and his wife sailed for another island. There was no trial, no punishing, no 'swimming'. The people did not even throw stones.

Not only witches but the whole demoniac nation is surrounded with fancies that show almost an affection for its terrors: an affection made possible, perhaps, by a sense that he that pays his chapel-dues and has a good heart and does not pull up a sacred hawthorn may get through the world secure, nor find a need for hate. One evil spirit of very murderous habits was accustomed to take the shape of a bag of wool and go rolling along the road;[13] and Death himself at Innisshark comes down and stands by the dying in the form of a black cock, and has been pleased into harmlessness by the blood of a crowing hen.[14] Once by mischance a woman caught not a common barn-door bird but the son of the King of the Cats, who was taking the air in that shape. Then two huge black cats came in and tore her face until they were tired; but her sick child got well, for Death had leave to take but one life, and the son of the King of the Cats was dead.[15] Lady Wilde thinks these stories may be relied on, because the western islanders are an accurate people, who never exaggerate but tell only the simple truth, and are too homely to invent. At Hollandtide[16] they are much troubled by the dead from their graves, who return to ride the sea's white horses, so that no wise fisherman will push out that night. A man once did so, and just as he reached the shore he heard the noise of the breakers behind him, and turning round saw a dead man upon every wave. One came close to him, and he recognised a neighbour drowned the year before; and the neighbour leaned over and bade him hasten home, for the dead were seeking him. He left boat and cargo and fled, and never again put out at Hollandtide.

[17]In Ireland this world and the other are not widely sundered; sometimes, indeed, it seems almost as if our earthly chattels were no more than the shadows of things beyond. A lady I knew once saw a village

child running about with a long trailing petticoat upon her, and asked the creature why she did not have it cut short. 'It was my grand-mother's', said the child; 'would you have her going about yonder with her petticoat up to her knees, and she dead but four days?' Lady Wilde tells a story of a woman whose ghost haunted her people because they had made her grave-clothes so short that the fires of purgatory burned her knees.[18] And to them the truth is that beyond the grave they will have houses much like their earthly homes, only there the thatch will never grow leaky, nor the white walls lose their lustre, nor shall the dairy be at any time empty of good milk and butter. But now and then a land-lord or an agent or a gauger will go by begging his bread, to show how God divides the righteous from the unrighteous.

Irish legends and Irish peasant minds, however, have no lack of melancholy. The accidents of Nature supply good store of it to all men, and in their hearts, too, there dwells a sadness still unfathomed. Yet in that sadness there is no gloom, no darkness, no love of the ugly, no mop-ing. The sadness of a people who hold that 'contention is better than loneliness',[19] it is half a visionary fatalism, a belief that all things rest with God and with His angels or with the demons that beset man's for-tunes. 'God is nearer than the door', they say; 'He waits long; He strikes at last.'[20] They say too that 'Misfortune follows fortune inch by inch'; and again, 'It is better to be lucky than wise'; or, 'Every web as it is woven, every nursling as it is nursed.'[21] Shakespeare's witches are born of the Teuton gloom;[22] our Irish sadness grows visible in other shapes. Somewhere I have read a tale[23] that is touched with its very essence. At the grey of dawn an Irish peasant went out to the hills, to shoot curlew or what not. He saw a deer drinking at a pool, and levelled his gun. Now iron dissolves every manner of spell, and the moment he looked along the barrel he saw that the deer was really an old man changed by wizardry; then, knowing him for something wicked, he fired, and the thing fell, and there upon the grass, quite dead, lay the oldest man he ever set eyes on; and while he stood watching a light wind rose, and the appearance crumbled away before his eyes, and not a wrack was left to tell of what had been. The grey of the morning is the Irish witches' hour, when they gather in the shapes of large hares and suck the cattle dry; and the grey morning melancholy runs through all the legends of my people. Then it is that this world and the other draw near, and not at midnight upon Brockens[24] amidst the foul revelry of evil souls and in the light of the torches of hell. At the dawning the wizards come and go and fairy nations play their games of hurley and make their sudden journeys. Nations of gay creatures, having no souls; nothing in their bright bodies but a mouthful of sweet air.

IRISH FAIRIES

"Irish Fairies" first appeared in the October 1890 issue of The Leisure Hour *(London). This article is probably the one on Irish fairies which, along with an article on Irish popular ballad poetry, Yeats told Katharine Tynan he was working on all the way back in July 1887. The article on ballads finally reached print in November 1889, after Yeats's first book of poems,* The Wanderings of Oisin, *gave him some reputation. This article had to wait another year, perhaps because, as Yeats told Miss Tynan (CL1, 195),* The Leisure Hour *people were afraid of too much Ireland.*

Soon after the composition of this article Yeats became busy with his compilation of Fairy and Folk Tales of the Irish Peasantry *(London, 1888). Three of the stories in "Irish Fairies," those of the Sligo servant girl who disappeared, of the three O'Byrnes, and of Michael Hart and the corpse, also appeared in* The Celtic Twilight *(London, 1893). In telling fairy and ghost stories, Yeats was successful in avoiding a bogus stage-Irish charm on the one hand and a ponderous scientific air on the other. Oscar Wilde described this quality well (allowing for the exaggerations) in his review of* The Wanderings of Oisin: *"He is very naive and very primitive and speaks of his giants with the air of a child"* (A Critic in Pall Mall, *London, 1919).*

When I tell people that the Irish peasantry still believe in fairies, I am often doubted. They think that I am merely trying to weave a forlorn piece of gilt thread into the dull grey worsted of this century. They do not imagine it possible that our highly thought of philosophies so soon grow silent outside the walls of the lecture room, or that any kind of ghost or goblin can live within the range of our daily papers. If the papers and the lectures have not done it, they think, surely at any rate the steam-whistle has scared the whole tribe out of the world. They are quite wrong. The ghosts and goblins do still live and rule in the imaginations of innumerable Irish men and women, and not merely in remote places, but close even to big cities.

At Howth, for instance, ten miles from Dublin, there is a 'fairies' path', whereon a great colony of other-world creatures travel nightly from the hill to the sea and home again. There is also a field that ever since a cholera shed[1] stood there for a few months, has broken out in fairies and evil spirits. The last man I have heard of as seeing anything in it is an industrious fisherman of great strength. He is a teetotaler; his sister indeed has told me that his wife and wife's sister often sit and talk of him and wonder 'what he would do if he drank'. They half regret that sobriety should make so strong a man hide his light under a bushel. One night he was coming home through the field, when he saw in front of him a small white cat. While he looked at it the creature began to swell bigger and bigger, and as it grew in size he lost in strength, as though it sucked out his vitality. He stood for a time motionless with terror, but at last turned and fled, and as he got further away his strength came back. It was, a peasant would tell you, a fairy animal, for not all the fairies have human shapes.[2]

Everyone has heard of changelings, how a baby will be taken away and a miserable goblin left in its stead. But animals, it is not generally known, run the same risk. A fine fat calf may be carried off, and one of the fairies of animal shape left in its stead, and no one be the wiser until the butcher tries to kill it; then it will rush away and vanish into some green hillside. The fairy kingdom has everything we have, cats, dogs, horses, carriages, and even firearms, for the sounds of unearthly volleys fired by troops of spirits embattled on the winds have been heard by a Munster[3] seer who lived about twenty years ago.

It is, however, further afield than Howth, down westward among the deep bays and mountain valleys of Sligo,[4] that I have heard the best tales and found the most ardent belief. There, many a peasant dreams of growing rich by finding a fairy's crock of gold, and many a peasant's daughter trembles as she passes some famous haunted hillside, and goes over in her mind the names of men and women carried off, as tradition will have it, to the dim kingdom. Only very recently one of these fabled robberies is reported to have been attempted. A little girl, who is at service with a farmer in the village of Grange, suddenly disappeared.[5] There was at once great excitement in the neighbourhood, because it was rumoured that the fairies had taken her. A villager was said to have long struggled to hold her from them, but at last they prevailed, and he found nothing in his hands but a broomstick. The local constable was applied to, and he at once instituted a house-to-house search, and at the same time advised the people to burn all the *bucalauns* (ragweed) on the field she vanished from, because *bucalauns* are sacred to the fairies. They spent the whole night burning them, the constable repeating spells the while. In the morning the little girl was found, the story goes, wandering in the field. She said the fairies had taken her away a great distance, riding on a fairy horse. At last she saw a big river, and the man who had tried to keep her from being carried off was drifting down it—such are the topsy-turvydoms of fairy glamour—in a cockle-shell. On the way her companions had mentioned the names of several people who were about to die shortly in the village. Such is the story. I will not pretend to find out what really did happen. I at any rate have not the heart to break upon the wheel so quaint a butterfly.

Sligo is, indeed, a great place for fairy pillaging of this kind. In the side of Ben Bulben is a white square in the limestone.[6] It is said to be the door of fairyland. There is no more inaccessible place in existence than this white square door; no human foot has ever gone near it, not even the mountain goats can browse the saxifrage beside its mysterious whiteness. Tradition says that it swings open at nightfall and lets pour through an unearthly troop of hurrying spirits. To those gifted to hear their voices the air will be full at such a moment with a sound like whistling. Many have been carried away out of the neighbouring villages by this troop of riders. I have quite a number of records beside me, picked up at odd times from the faithful memories of old peasants. Brides and new-born children are especially in danger. Peasant mothers, too, are sometimes carried off to nurse the children of the fairies. At the end of seven years they have a chance of returning, and if they do not escape then are always prisoners. A woman, said still to be living, was taken from near a village called Ballisodare,[7] and when she came home after seven years she had no toes—she had danced them off. It is not possible to find out whether the stolen people are happy among 'the gentry', as the fairies are called for politeness. Accounts differ. Some say they are happy enough, but lose their souls, because, perhaps, the soul cannot live without sorrow. Others will have it that they are always wretched, longing for their friends, and that the splendour of the fairy kingdom is merely a magical delusion, woven to deceive the minds of men by poor little withered apparitions who live in caves and barren places. But this is, I suspect, a theological opinion, invented because all goblins are pagans. Many things about fairies, indeed, are most uncertain. We do not even know whether they die. An old Gaelic poem says, 'Death is even among the fairies',[8] but then many stories represent them as hundreds of years old.

There are a number of Gaelic songs and ballads about them, and about the people they have stolen. Some modern Irishmen also have written beautifully on the same matter. An Irish village schoolmaster,

named Walsh, wrote the following.[9] It is supposed to be sung by a
fairy over a child she has stolen:

> Sweet babe! a golden cradle holds thee,
> And soft the snow-white fleece enfolds thee;
> In airy bower I'll watch thy sleeping,
> Where branchy trees to the breeze are sweeping.
>   Shuheen, sho, lulo, lo!
>
> When mothers languish, broken-hearted,
> When young wives are from husbands parted,
> Ah, little think the keeners[10] lonely,
> They weep some time-worn fairy only.
>   Shuheen, sho, lulo, lo!
>
> Within our magic halls of brightness
> Trips many a foot of snowy whiteness;
> Stolen maidens, queens of fairy,
> And kings and chiefs a sluagh shee[11] airy.
>   Shuheen, sho, lulo, lo!
>
> Rest thee, babe! I love thee dearly,
> And as thy mortal mother, nearly;
> Ours is the swiftest steed and proudest,
> That moves where the tramp of the host is loudest.
>   Shuheen, sho, lulo, lo!
>
> Rest thee, babe! for soon thy slumbers
> Shall flee at the magic koel shee's[12] numbers;
> In airy bower I'll watch thy sleeping,
> When[13] branchy trees to the breeze are sweeping.
>   Shuheen, sho, lulo, lo!

   The poor schoolmaster has perfectly given the fascination of the
mysterious kingdom where the fairies live—a kingdom that has been
imagined and endowed with all they know of splendour and riches by
a poor peasantry amid their rags. As heaven is the home of their spiritual desires, so fairyland has been for ages the refuge of their earthly
ideals. In its shadow kingdom they have piled up all they know of
magnificence. Sometimes there is a quaint modernness in the finery.
One old man said to me, 'It is full of beautiful drawing-rooms and
parlours'.[14]
   The fairies are of course not merely feared as robbers, they are

looked up to and respected for their great wealth. If a man always speaks respectfully of them, and never digs up one of their sacred thorn bushes, there is no knowing but he may some day dream of a crock of gold and the next day go and find it, and be rich for ever. A man once confessed to me that he had gone at midnight into my uncle's garden and dug for a treasure he had dreamed of, but there was 'a power of earth' in the place, and so he gave up the search and went home.

The finest treasure tale[15] I have, however, comes from Donegal. A friend was once at a village near Slieve† League.[16] One day he was straying about a rath called 'Cashel Nore'.[17] (Raths are small fields encircled by earth fences; they were inhabited by the ancient races, and are now great haunts of fairies.) A man with a haggard face and unkempt hair, and clothes falling in pieces, came into the rath and began digging. My friend turned to a peasant who was working near and asked who the man was. 'That is the third O'Byrne', was the answer. A few days after he learned this story: A great quantity of treasure had been buried in the rath in pagan times, and a number of evil fairies set to guard it; but some day it was to be found and belong to the family of the O'Byrnes. Before that day three O'Byrnes must first find it and die. Two had already done so. The first had dug and dug until at last he got a glimpse of the stone coffin[18] that contained it, but immediately a thing like a huge hairy dog came down the mountain and tore him to pieces. The next morning the treasure had again vanished deep into the earth. The second O'Byrne came and dug and dug until he found the coffer, and lifted the lid and saw the gold shining within. He saw some horrible sight the next moment, and went raving mad and soon died. The treasure again sank out of sight. The third O'Byrne is now digging. He believes that he will die in some horrible way the moment he finds the treasure, but that the spell will be broken, and the O'Byrne family made rich for ever, and become again a great people, as they were of old. A peasant of the neighbourhood once saw the treasure. He found the shin-bones of a hare lying on the grass. He took it up; there was a hole in it; he looked through the hole, and saw the gold heaped up under the ground. He hurried home to bring a spade, but when he got to the rath again he could not find the spot where he had seen it through the spell-dissolving bone.

This tale of the O'Byrnes is right full of Celtic intensity. The third O'Byrne, at this moment in all likelihood digging, digging, with ragged hair blown in the wind, and growing old amid his resolve, deserves some more permanent record than this ephemeral article and will perhaps find it some day. Some poet looking for tales in Donegal, long decades hence, may hear the story of the life and death of the third O'Byrne. Tradition is sure to make him find the treasure.

There is one well-known Cork[19] family, all of whose riches are traced back by the people to the days when an old henwife dreamed of a certain field where an iron pot full of gold lay hidden. She is well remembered, because a Celtic poet of the last century, who had come down in the world through the great quantities of whisky he had given away to other Celtic poets, was employed in minding her hens and chickens. He wrote a well-known Gaelic song about her, called 'The Dame of the Slender Wattle'.[20]

I have spoken, so far, entirely of the malice or kindness of the fairies, and said nothing of their mere wantonness. They are as little to be trusted as monkeys and jackdaws. The worst among them may be known, however, by their going about singly or in twos and threes, instead of in tumultuous troops like the more harmless kinds. The best known among the solitary fairies is the Leprechaun.[†] He is something of a dandy, and dresses in a red coat with seven rows of buttons, seven buttons on each row, and wears a cocked-hat, upon whose pointed end he is wont in the north-eastern counties, according to McAnally,[†21] to spin like a top when the fit seizes him. His most common pursuit, as everyone knows, is cobbling. The fairies are always wearing out their shoes and setting him to mend them. At night he sometimes rides shepherds' dogs through the country, leaving them muddy and panting at the dawn. He is constantly described as peevish and ill-natured. His mischief, for all that, is much less gruesome than that of the Fir Darrig[22] or Red Man, the most unpleasant joker of all the race. I heard a grim story from a one-armed Sligo man that is probably a chronicle of one of his practical jokes.[23] It is a type of story always told in the first person:

'In the times when we used to travel by canal',[24] said the one-armed man, 'I was coming down from Dublin. When we came to Mullingar[25] the canal ended, and I began to walk, and stiff and fatigued I was after the slowness. I had some friends with me, and now and then we walked, now and then we rode in a cart. So on till we saw some girls milking a cow, and stopped to joke with them. After a while we asked them for a drink of milk. "We have nothing to put it in here", they said; "but come to the house with us". We went home with them and sat round the fire talking.

'After a while the others went, and left me, loth to stir from the good fire. I asked the girls for something to eat. There was a pot on the fire and they took the meat out and put it on a plate and told me to eat only the meat that came from the head. When I had eaten, the girls went out and I did not see them again.

'It grew darker and darker, and there I still sat, loth as ever to leave the good fire; and after a while two men came in, carrying between them a corpse. When I saw them I hid behind a door. Says one to the other, "Who'll turn the spit?" Says the other, "Michael Hart, come out of that and turn the meat!" I came out in a tremble, and began turning the spit. "Michael Hart", says the one who spoke first, "if you let it burn we'll have to put you on the spit instead!" and on that they went out. I sat there trembling and turning the corpse until midnight. The men came again, and the one said it was burnt, and the other said it was done right. But having fallen out over it, they both said they would do me no harm that time; and, sitting by the fire, one of them cried out, "Michael Hart, can you tell us a story?" "Never a one!" said I, on which he caught me by the shoulders and put me out like a shot.

'It was a wild, blowing night; never in all my born days did I see such a night—the darkest night that ever came out of the heavens. I did not know where I was for the life of me. So when one of the men came after me and touched me on the shoulder, with a "Michael Hart, can you tell a story now?" "I can", says I. In he brought me, and, putting me by the fire, says, "Begin!" "I have no story but the one", says I, "that I was sitting here, and that you two men brought in a corpse and put it on the spit and set me turning it." "That will do", says he; "you may go in there and lie down on the bed." And in I went, nothing loth, and in the morning where was I but in the middle of a green field!'

In spite of such horrible doings as this, the fairies are in the main innocent and graceful and kindly. The English peasantry have forgotten their fairies. The Irish peasant remembers and believes—and the Scotch, too, for the matter of that.

We will not too severely judge these creatures of the imagination. There are worse things after all than to believe some pretty piece of unreason, if by so doing you keep yourself from thinking that the earth under your feet is the only god, and that the soul is a little whiff of gas, or some such thing.

The world is, I believe, more full of significance to the Irish peasant than to the English. The fairy populace of hill and lake and woodland have helped to keep it so. It gives a fanciful life to the dead hillsides, and surrounds the peasant, as he ploughs and digs,[26] with tender shadows of poetry. No wonder that he is gay, and can take man and his destiny without gloom and make up proverbs like this from the old Gaelic—'The lake is not burdened by its swan, the steed by its bridle, or a man by the soul that is in him.'[27]

IRISH FOLK TALES

Beside the Fire: A Collection of Irish Gaelic Folk Stories with English translations by Douglas Hyde (London: David Nutt, 1890) was reviewed by Yeats in The National Observer of 28 February 1891. This review was included in the 1893 The Celtic Twilight under the title "The Four Winds of Desire," but it was omitted from the 1901 edition and never after reprinted. Douglas Hyde (1860–1949) was born in Co. Roscommon in the province of Connacht. He was responsible as much as any single man for the revival of the Gaelic League in Ireland. In an 1892 speech that led to the founding of the Gaelic League in 1893, Hyde called for "the de-Anglicizing of Ireland." In a letter to United Ireland (17 December 1892) Yeats replied to Hyde that the language in which a culture was expressed was not so important as the great ideas and myths of that culture (CL1, 338–40).

In the notes at the end of *Beside the Fire* (London: Nutt) Dr. Hyde contrasts with certain tales of Indian jugglery[1] an old Gaelic account of a magician who threw a rope-ladder into the air and then sent climbing up it all manner of men and beasts. It reads like an allegory to explain the charms of folk-and fairy-tales: a parable to show how man mounts to the infinite by the ladder of the impossible. When our narrow rooms, our short lives, our soon-ended passions and emotions, put us out of conceit with sooty and finite reality, we have only to read some story like Dr. Hyde's 'Paudyeen† O'Kelly and the Weasel', and listen to the witch complaining to the robber, 'Why did you bring away my gold that I was for five hundred years gathering through[2] the hills and hollows of the world?' Here at last is a universe where all is large and intense enough to almost satisfy the emotions of man. Certainly such stories are not a criticism of life[3] but rather an extension, thereby much more closely resembling Homer than that last phase of 'the improving book',[4] a social drama by Henrik Ibsen.[5] They are an existence and not a thought, and make our world of tea-tables seem but a shabby penumbra.

It is perhaps, therefore, by no means strange that the age of 'realism' should be also the harvest-time of folk-lore. We grow tired of tuning our fiddles to the clank of this our heavy chain, and lay them down to listen gladly to one who tells us of men hundreds of years old and endlessly mirthful. Our new-wakened interest in the impossible has been of the greatest service to Irish folk-literature. Until about three years ago the only writers who had dealt with the subject at any length were Crofton Croker, a second-hand bookseller named Kennedy and an anonymous writer in *The Dublin and London Magazine* for 1825 and 1828.[6] Others, it is true, had incorporated (like Gerald Griffin) odd folk-tales in the pages of long novels, or based on them (like Carleton and Lover) stories of peasant-life.[7] Croker was certainly no ideal collector. He altered his materials without word of warning, and could never resist the chance of turning some naïve fairy tale into a drunken peasant's dream. With all his buoyant humour and imagination he was continually guilty of that great sin against art—the sin of rationalism. He tried to take away from his stories the impossibility that makes them dear to us. Nor could he quite desist from dressing his personages in the dirty rags of the stage Irishman. Kennedy, an incomparably worse writer, had one great advantage: he believed in his goblins as sincerely as any peasant. He has explained in his *Legendary Fictions* that he could tell a number of spells for raising the fairies, but he will not—for fear of putting his readers up to mischief.[8] Years went by, and it seemed that we should never have another gathering. Then about three years ago came Lady Wilde's two volumes and David Fitzgerald's contributions to the *Revue Celtique;* with McAnally's[†] inaccurate and ill-written *Irish Wonders* and Curtin's[9] fine collections a little later; and now appears Dr. Hyde's incomparable little book. There has been published in three years as much Irish folk-lore as in the foregoing fifty. Its quality, too, is higher. Dr. Hyde's volume is the best written of any. He has caught and faithfully reproduced the peasant idiom and phrase. In becoming scientifically accurate, he has not ceased to be a man of letters. His fifteen translations from traditional Gaelic originals are models of what such translations should be. Unlike Campbell of Islay,[10] he has not been content merely to turn the Gaelic into English; but where the idiom is radically different he has searched out colloquial equivalents from among the English-speaking peasants. The Gaelic is printed side by side with the English, so that the substantial accuracy of his versions can always be tested. The result is many pages in which you can hear in imagination the very voice of the sennachie,[11] and almost smell the smoke of his turf fire.

Now and then Dr. Hyde has collected stories which he was compelled to write out in his own Irish through the impossibility, he tells us, of taking them down word for word at the time. He has only printed a half of one story of this kind on the present occasion. One wishes he had not been so rigorous in the matter, especially as it is for this reason, I conclude, that 'Teig O'Kane',[12] still the weirdest of Irish folk-tales, has been omitted. He has printed it elsewhere, but one would gladly have had all his stories under one cover. He is so completely a Gael, alike in thought and literary idiom, that I do not think he could falsify a folk-tale if he tried. At the most he would change it as a few years' passing from sennachie to sennachie must do perforce. Two villages a mile apart will have different versions of the same story; why, then, should Dr. Hyde exclude his own reverent adaptions? We cannot all read them in the Gaelic of his *Leabhar Sgeuluigheachta*.† Is it the evil communications of that very scientific person, Mr. Alfred Nutt[13] (he contributes learned notes), which have robbed us of the latter pages of 'Guleesh na Guss Dhu'?[14] We might at least have had some outline of the final adventures of the young fairy seer and the French princess. After all, imaginative impulse—the quintessence of life—is our great need from folk-lore. When we have banqueted let Learning gather the crumbs into her larder, and welcome. She will serve them up again in time of famine.

Dr. Hyde has four tales of hidden treasure, five stories of adventure with a princess or a fortune at the end, a legend of a haunted forest, and a tale of a man who grew very thin and weakly through swallowing a hungry newt, which was only dislodged when made wildly a-thirst by a heavy dinner of salt pork and the allurement of a running stream. Love, fortune, adventure, wonder—the four winds of desire! There is also a chapter of quaint riddles in rhyme. The whole book is full of charming expressions. The French princess is described as 'the loveliest woman on the ridge of the world. The rose and the lily were fighting together in her face, and one could not tell which would get the victory'.[15] Here and there, too, is a piece of delicate observation, as when Guleesh na Guss Dhu waits for the fairies listening to 'the cronawn (hum) of the insects,' and watching 'the fadogues† and flibeens† (golden and green clover) rising and lying, lying and rising, as they do on a fine night'.[16] The riddles also have no lack of poetry. Here is a description of a boreen or little country lane:

> From house to house he goes,
> A messenger small and slight,
> And whether it rains or snows
> He sleeps outside in the night.

And here is one of the lintel on a wet day:

There's a poor man at rest[17]
With a stick beneath his breast,
And he breaking his heart a-crying.

These riddles are the possession of children, and have the simple fan-
cifulness of childhood.

It is small wonder that this book should be beautiful, for it is the
chronicle of that world of glory and surprise imagined in the unknown
by the peasant as he leant painfully over his spade. His spiritual
desires ascended into heaven, but all he could dream of material well-
being and freedom was lavished upon this world of kings and goblins.
We who have less terrible a need dream less splendidly. Mr. Hyde bids
us know that all this exultant world of fancies is passing away, soon
to exist for none but stray scholars and the gentlemen of the sun-myth.[18]
He has written on his title-page this motto from an old Gaelic poem:
'They are like a mist on the coming of night that[19] is scattered away by
a light breath of wind'. I know that this is the common belief of folk-
lorists, but I do not feel certain that it is altogether true. Much, no doubt,
will perish—perhaps the whole tribe of folk-tales proper; but the fairy
and ghost kingdom is more stubborn than men dream of. It will perhaps, in Ireland at any rate, be always going and never gone. I have
talked with men who believe they have seen it. And why should Swedenborg[20] monopolise all the visions? Surely the mantle of Coleridge's
'man of ten centuries'[21] is large enough to cover the witch-doctors also.
There is not so much difference between them. Swedenborg's assertion,
in the *Spiritual Diary*,[22] that 'the angels do not like butter', would make
admirable folk-lore. Dr. Hyde finds a sun-myth in one of his most ancient
stories. The sun and the revolving seasons have not done helping to draw
legends from the right minds. Some time ago a friend of mine[23] talked
with an old Irish peasant who had seen a vision of a great tree amid
whose branches two animals, one white and one black, pursued each
other continually; and wherever the white beast came the branches burst
into foliage, and wherever the black one, then all withered away. The
changing of the seasons, among the rest, is here very palpable. Only let
it be quite plain that the peasant's vision meant much more than the
mere atmospheric allegory of the learned. He saw within his tree the
birth and death of all things. It cast a light of imagination on his own
dull cattle-minding and earth-turning destiny, and gave him heart to
repeat the Gaelic proverb: 'The lake is not burdened by its swan, the
steed by its bridle, nor a man by the soul that is in him'.[24]

GYPSY SORCERY
AND FORTUNE TELLING

This review of Charles Leland's Gypsy Sorcery and Fortune Telling
Illustrated by Numerous Incantations, Specimens of Medical Magic,
Anecdotes and Tales *(London: T. Fisher Unwin, 1891) appeared,
unsigned, in the* The National Observer, *18 April 1891. Charles
Leland (1824–1903) studied and wrote about folklore and Gypsies
throughout his life; his other works include* The Breitmann Ballads
(1871), The English Gypsies *(1873), and* The Gypsies *(1882). A main
source for the footnotes for this article is John S. Kelly's "Yeatsian Magic
and Rational Magic: An Uncollected Review of W. B. Yeats," Yeats*
Annual 3, *ed. Warwick Gould, pp. 182–89.*

When young Hartley Coleridge, aged four, was asked why he was
named Hartley, he replied: 'Which Hartley? there's a deal of Hartleys.
There's Picture Hartley and Shadow Hartley and there's Looking-
glass Hartley and Echo Hartley', and then, catching his arm with his
hand, 'there is Catch-me-fast Hartley'.[1] Mr. Leland in his *Gypsy Sorcery* has adopted this theory without acknowledgment, and decided
there is a Dream Mr. Leland and also a Waking Mr. Leland who is perpetually aghast at the amount of things that Dream Mr. Leland must
know, and the quantity of sweetness and light[2] he must possess.
Magic, it appears, is the power of getting this knowledge out of the all-
remembering dreamer into the soon-forgetting Philistine of common
life. 'We visit a sick man, and the dream spirit out of the inexhaustible
hoards of memory, aided by association, which results in subtle,
occult *reasoning,* perceives that the patient will die in a certain time,
and this result is served up in a dramatic dream.'[3] Mr. Leland is so
delighted with his theory that he insults every witch, warlock, and fairy
doctor in creation. He should not do so, because though a good folk-
lorist he is a very bad occultist, and remains a trophy to the enemy when
he writes such sentences as: 'In the whole range of occult literature,

from *Hermes Trismegistus* down to Mme. Blavatsky, there is not a shade of a suspicion that all the absolutely authentic marvels of magic began and ended with man himself'.[4] This statement must have been made by Waking Mr. Leland, because the other who knows all things would have known better. Then, again, when he asserts that 'outside of us was always somebody else to be invoked, conciliated, met in vision or trance, united to in spiritual union or syncope',[5] he forgets the salutation of the Rosicrucian Fratres of Germany: 'Man is God and son of God, and there is no God but man'.[6] Nor is the notion of a dream personality from which come visions, omens, and such strange gear a discovery, as Mr. Leland imagines, of 'Murriker'[7] and science, but it has been perfectly familiar to all students of magic worth their salt from the days when the great shoemaker of Altseidenburg[†] saw the sun glitter on a tin pot hung on his wall, and fell into a three days' walking trance in which, in his own phrase, 'truth fell upon him like a bursting shower.'[8] It does not belong to Mr. Leland, even though he has given in proof of it a quite new story told him by a lady 'of excellent family'.[9] No: nor is it made any more his by knowledge of a system of education founded upon it which can make any child 'exceptionally clever in *all* studies' (italics his own).[10]

It is really a pity that 'Hans Breitmann'[11] wrote this book when he was awake, for it is full of interesting material: of such pleasant sayings as that the bones of wizards turn into black hens and chickens;[12] such charming and temperate incantations as this against the toothache:

> My mouth is not thy house:
> I love thee not at all:
> Stay thou away from me.
> When this straw is in the brook
> Go away into the water.[13]

But no sooner has the mind set forth voyaging on the seas of faëry lands forlorn[14] than the ship goes to pieces on some irrelevant truism, flattery of our time, or discussion worthy a school debating society or a Secularist lecturer as to the merits of the Church of Rome. How gladly one would welcome, too, his tales of Nivasis and Pchuvuse, spirits of wind and flood,[15] if he were not so fond of telling us that all this old magic, whose ideal was after all spiritual power and spiritual insight, was, even if true, wholly less beautiful than a telephone with a stockbroker thoroughly awake at each end. Let us think if we must that space is empty of spiritual beings, or even put the word 'spirit' itself in inverted commas like Mr. Leland, or go if needs be as far as the learned German scientist who considers the soul of man 'a volatile liq-

uid capable of solution in glycerine';[16] but let us be honest with ourselves, and by no means pretend that this new creed is beautiful and
ourselves are happy to live in its day. Let us frankly admit that the body
and pressure of time has brought us the last degradation and mingled
us with the dust. Because we hurry over the ground at sixty miles an
hour, and may some day do so at a hundred and sixty, with a penny
comic paper in our hands and our nerves awry from the crush at the
ticket-office, we are not proved, in spite of Mr. Leland, wholly to
over-top Merlin, or to be wise as Faustus or the Centaur Chiron or he
that met his image walking in a garden.[17] We are made great not by the
things we do or have done to us but by the thing we are in ourselves.

PLAYS BY AN IRISH POET

This review of performances of John Todhunter's plays A Sicilian Idyll: A Pastoral Play in Two Scenes *(London: Elkin Mathews, 1890) and* The Poison Flower *appeared in the Parnellite weekly,* United Ireland, *on 11 July 1891. In Yeats's 1934 prefatory remarks to the collection of his American newspaper articles,* Letters to the New Island, *he admitted to having overpraised Todhunter, a neighbor of the Yeats family in London and an old friend of Yeats's father. Yeats claimed that he praised Todhunter not out of friendship but because such poetic dramas as* A Sicilian Idyll *were worthy reactions to oratorical, rhetorical dramas such as Tennyson's* Becket *and realistic plays. In all,* A Sicilian Idyll *received four notices from Yeats. He had mentioned this play in his* Boston Pilot *article of 14 June 1890 (LNI, 36–39). The same production as the one reviewed in the present* United Ireland *article was noticed by Yeats in another* Boston Pilot *piece of 1 August 1891 (LNI, 50–52), and in* The Providence Sunday Journal *of 26 July 1891 (LNI, 98–101).*

Irish readers know Dr. Todhunter's name from the modern versions of old legends he published two years ago in a volume called 'The Banshee', and from his contributions to *The Poems and Ballads of Young Ireland.*[1] The Londoner knows him, however, from a series of dramatic experiments, beginning with *Helena in Troas,* some five years ago, and ending for the time being in the reproduction of *A Sicilian Idyll* and *The Poison Flower* at the Vaudeville[2] a few days ago. He has also published two long dramas that as yet have not been tried upon the stage. *Helena,* the most ambitious of his acted plays, was performed on the only exact reproduction of an old Greek theatre the modern world has seen. Many of the audience afterwards said that the whole gave them a curious religious feeling, singularly unlike the impression made by the modern stage. The sonorous, if somewhat elaborate, verse, with its continuous burden of imminent Fate, was well suited to prolong the feeling, and stamp it with the rhythmical form needed to give it permanence in the memory. Day after day the theatre was crowded with all that was most fashionable or most cultured in London society. The first matinee alone produced, I believe, three hundred pounds. The success of *A Sicilian Idyll* at the little playhouse in Bedford Park[3] last year was more clearly a triumph of drama; for much of the vogue of *Helena* was undoubtedly due to the curiosity aroused by its strange surroundings. *The Idyll,* a much more dramatic play than its forerunner, was beautifully staged, and, as far as one of the performers was concerned,[4] beautifully acted it is true; but still there was nothing in either to bring people for its own sake. We see good acting and good scene-painting every day. The play itself was the main thing this time at any rate. The little theatre was crowded from end to end during the whole of the short run. Twice the number of performances originally intended were given, and almost everyone who loved poetry managed to put in an appearance. The play, charmingly printed by the Chiswick Press and introduced by a frontispiece by Walter Crane, is now to be had in the distinctive white and grey of Mr. Elkin Matthews's[†] publications. It is a pastoral romance suggested by Theocritus and written in the elaborate verse which we expect to find in plays of Arcadia ever since Fletcher sang of the grove's 'pale passion lover.'[5] There is one scene of incantation which was delivered the other day at the Vaudeville by Miss Florence Farr with astonishing power and effect—a scene that has the very stateliest qualities of dramatic verse. When the poem was revived a week ago it was preluded by a new drama called *The Poison Flower,* founded on a story by Hawthorne. In it Dr. Todhunter again went to magic for his strangest effects, but laid the scene of the story in mediaeval Italy instead of classical Sicily. He has off and on seen a good deal of Italian life, and has laid the scene of no small number of his poems in the land so loved by Browning.[6]

This gives him a certain advantage over Hawthorne, who had never been there.[7] Hawthorne's story, 'Rappaccini's[†] Daughter', as he called it, is exquisite, but I have always felt that it is a little over fanciful. It seems to have no meaning of sufficient weight to justify its great sadness. Even the folk-tale, when it becomes sad, grows full of some spiritual significance like our Irish story, 'The Countess Kathleen'.[8] Hawthorne's beautiful story is fantastic, and a little arbitrary. A great writer should have shown more lofty intention than to make your flesh creep. Dr. Todhunter's play, on the other hand, seems to me to improve on Hawthorne in this matter. He has given an allegorical significance to the garden of poisonous flowers, in which the magician's daughter lives, until she, too, has grown as deadly for all her gentleness and beauty as the dreadful flowers she tends. The magician is seeking, by his mysterious art, to change her into the Eve of a new race, to whom the poison of the world—its sins and diseases—shall be harmless; for this new race will have in its blood the essences of every poison all tempered into harmlessness and health. Just such a dream for the physical redemption of the world was dreamed the other day by that new Italian Rappaccini[†] who thought he had discovered the *bacillus* of old age, and that it was only necessary to inoculate people with it to bring about for all men an eternal youth. A happy dream that would, if fulfilled, have made unnecessary the prayers of the heroine in the French play, 'Oh, Lord, confine my wrinkles to my heels'.[9] Dr. Todhunter, too, in making the magician a Kabalist[10] has given him historical reality and made it much more easy to believe in him. The copy of the Kabala, here in front of me on my own table, pleads for him, and tells me that such men have lived and dreamed such dreams for the bettering of the world. They dreamed them even in Dublin itself, as a certain record I have close to my hand sets forth.[11] He has brought Hawthorne's beautiful story down from no man's land and set it on the common earth of Italy, and realised all the characters until it moves before one with that vivid life of noble drama which makes faint as mist the poor crippled existence we all live. It is a very long time since any play has given me the same kind of pleasure, and I here record my gratitude. What can the prose drama do at its very best compared to that elevation of the whole mind caused by dramatic poetry?

When our political passions have died out in the fulfillment of their aim[12] shall we, I wonder, have a fine native drama of our own? It is very likely. A very great number of the best playwrights who have written for the English stage, from Sheridan and Goldsmith[13] to our own day, have been Irishmen. We are a young country, and still care, I think, for the high thoughts and high feelings of poetry, if in a somewhat uncultivated fashion. We love the dramatic side of events and have too much imagination to think plays which advertise 'a real locomotive engine' or 'a real fire engine'[14] as the chief attraction to be a better form of drama than the heroic passions and noble diction of the great ages of the theatre. We have never yet been fairly tested. Our playwrights have been poor men who were forced to write for an English public in the very last stages of dramatic decadence. I should very much like to see what Dr. Todhunter could do with an Irish theme written for and acted before an Irish audience. Surely, they would not find the mere fact of its being poetry the very great difficulty English audiences seem to find it. We have had the only popular ballad literature of recent days. Does not that prove the poetic capacities of our uneducated masses? Or has English influence and 'the union of hearts'[15] made us as prosaic as our neighbours?

CLARENCE MANGAN'S
LOVE AFFAIR

This article, Yeats's second piece on Mangan, appeared in United Ireland *on 22 August 1891. Much of the biographical information is repeated from Yeats's earlier piece, which appeared in* The Irish Fireside *on 12 March 1888. The first article included a discussion of Mangan's poetry as well as his miserable life. In the years between 1888 and 1891, Yeats added Blake and Swedenborg to his list of authorities.*

In the 1888 piece, Yeats had claimed to have named a Miss Stackpoole for the first time as Mangan's beloved. Some admirers of Mangan had objected to this identification, but by 1891 Yeats thought that he had stronger evidence in the testimony of Sir Charles Gavan Duffy. In her 1897 edition of Mangan's works, Louise Imogen Guiney said that Miss Susan Gavan Duffy, the daughter of Yeats's expert, told her that Mangan's beloved was Margaret, not Frances, Stacpoole [sic] (p. 16).

I do not now busy myself with the poetry of Clarence Mangan, but with the making and marring[†] of the man, and with the kind of soul he had, and with the fashion in which he lived. I write mainly to put on record one or two new facts that have come to my knowledge with the thought that they may interest the biographer who at some time, near or distant, must gather up all the threads and weave them into a coherent life.

Mangan was born in Fishamble-street,[1] then somewhat less shabby and smoke-discoloured than it has been for many a day now. His father was a grocer, who did well in business, retired, spent what he had made to the last halfpenny in extravagant living, went bankrupt, and died of a broken heart. Apart from this we know little of his character except that, according to Mangan himself, he boasted that his children would run into a mouse-hole to escape him. He seems to have possessed that curious but not unknown combination—the flint heart and the open hand. The shadow of his thriftless gaiety was Clarence Mangan's life-long agony. Upon his death the poet, full of endless desire for a life of joy and freedom, found himself in a scrivener's office, left thus to drudge on, the sole support of a penniless family of young brothers and sisters. Life seemed to promise him nothing except that he might cover with his pen numberless sheets of paper, as the Wandering Jew covers the earth with his feet.[2] He asked 'more than any understood',[3] and was given routines, the saddest of things upon this old, dirty planet. Nor was he happy with his office companions. 'My nervous and hypochondriacal feelings almost verged on insanity', he wrote in later life. 'I seemed to myself to be shut up in a cavern with serpents and scorpions and all hideous and monstrous things, which writhed and hissed around me, and discharged their slime and venom on my person'.[4] I have been told that Mangan could not have been unhappy with these fellow-clerks, because one of them afterwards became a bishop. When you have a flaming heart, and it has been plunged down into commonplace, it does not redeem everything to have a future bishop among your companions. Yet these clerks were probably no worse than others. The children of genius have got on badly in all ages with the children of men. The old woman in the story saw nothing more in King Alfred than a careless, good-for-nothing loon, who let her cakes burn, and accordingly did her best to lead him a life of it.[5] Shelley was so tortured at school that he thrust a knife through the hand of a schoolfellow.[6] The great mysterious poet and artist, William Blake, was when a boy so ill-treated by the Westminster students that he flung one of them from a scaffolding where he was at work copying cornices or inscriptions.[7] The abstracted ways and unusual opinions of the man of thought are deadly offenses to commonplace people. The exceptional is ever persecuted. If you tie a red ribbon to the leg of a sea-gull the other gulls will pick it to death. To the soul of Clarence Mangan was tied the burning ribbon of genius.

Mangan had now reached manhood. He had grown up amid penury, cut off from education and refinement. The few poems written during these years, acrostics and other dismal puzzles with words, have no value whatever. They are as sordid as his life. The man needed one thing before he should be ready to deliver his message. He had to love hopelessly—to look out of his 'cavern' to a brighter and more beautiful world and then turn his eyes upon the darkness and keep them there for the rest of his life. This love affair is the first of my new facts. Mangan met—between his twentieth and twenty-fifth year apparently—a Miss Stackpoole, one of three sisters, who lived in Mount Pleasant Square.[†] She was a fascinating coquette, who encouraged him, amused herself with his devotion, and then 'whistled him down the wind'.[8] Mitchel knew of her, but did not know her name, with the result that many, Father Meehan for instance, have since doubted her existence and set the whole story down to Mangan's imagination.[9] She was real enough—a handsome girl, with a tint of red in her hair, a very fashionable colour in our day, whatever it was then. When I first published her name some time ago[10] I received a letter from a well-known Mangan enthusiast denying the whole story point blank. I had then no proof except the word of an eccentric Protestant clergyman who remembered both her and Mangan. He might readily have been mistaken. Sir Charles Gavan Duffy has since, however, corroborated the story, and stated to me that he lent a dozen or more unpublished letters of Mangan's, giving, I understand, Mangan's own account of it, to the Irish Exhibition at Earl's Court, but has never been able to recover them, owing to the scandalous neglect of the committee. My old clergyman also told me an anecdote, which Sir Charles Gavan Duffy had never heard, of Mangan's rushing with knife or dagger at one who spoke ill of his faithless 'Frances'. This, then, is the truth, and I fear all the truth we are ever likely to know, about that mysterious beauty whom Mangan saw 'a little while—and then no more'.[11] His world had flamed up and then died down into grey ashes—and ashes henceforth it remained. When a man's love affair goes bankrupt, romance-makers assure us, a little devil gets into the soles of his feet and drives him hither and thither, on into his heart and makes him seek out some exciting activity, but for Clarence Mangan there was nothing but scrivening—scrivening; he could only watch his labouring quill travelling over ream after ream of paper.

It was after this that we begin to hear of Mangan's rum-loving and, if Mitchel speaks truth, opium-eating habits. He became a member of 'The Comet Club', a gathering of journalists and writers of whom the most important was Samuel Lover. He there[†] seems to have first drunk deeply. In 'The Nameless One'[12] he certainly implies that misery drove him to it. He yet found time to learn several foreign tongues, and to begin the long series of translations from the German, published in 1845, as the *Germanica Anthologia*.[13] He contributed much to the *Dublin Penny Journal, The Comet,* the newspaper from which the club took its name, *The Dublin University Review*[14] and finally to the *Nation* and *United Irishman*. As times went on he passed from scrivening to an attorney's office, and from that through a period of irregular employment on the *Nation* to a small post in the College Library, where he was employed compiling a catalogue. Here Mitchel[†] saw him for the first time: 'An acquaintance pointed out to me a man perched on the top of a ladder, with the whispered information that the figure was Clarence Mangan. It was an unearthly and ghostly figure in a brown garment (to all appearances) which lasted till the day of his death.[15] The blanched hair was totally unkempt, the corpse-like features still as marble; a large book was in his arms, and all his soul was in the book. I had never heard of Clarence Mangan before, and knew not for what he was celebrated, whether as a magician, a poet, or a murderer; yet took a volume and spread it on a table, not to read, but with pretence of reading, to glare on the spectral creature on this ladder'.[16]

The unearthly something that made Mitchel compare him to a magician had its justification in a strong visionary bent that lay deep in the man. He describes himself as 'one whom some have called a seer',[17] and seer he was if visions can make man such. One who remembers him has told me of his devotion to Swedenborg's *Heaven and Hell,* and another how he would see, like the great Swede, a sphere of light about men's souls. He himself has asserted that he was continually haunted by this persecuting phantom of his follies. It sometimes happens to a man that when this outer world has grown utterly blank there exists within a spiritual illumination. Such seems to have come to Mangan, but only dimly and fitfully, and bearing with it visions of terrible things more often than of joyous and beautiful. One good thing it brought him—an infinite faith in man's destiny. He never denied happiness because he was miserable, or goodness because his own life was in the gutter.

When the internal eye grows bright the outward gaze sometimes is bleared and uncertain, and we confuse the real and the unreal, and see men as trees walking.[18] It was thus with Mangan. He wrote at this latter end of his life an autobiography called a *Confession,* full of terrible, untrue things that he believed. Thus he asserts that he was brought to an hospital when a boy for some broken bones or other, and put into a bed with a leper, from whom he caught leprosy, but as an inward, spiritual disease, invisible to all, but none the less eating his soul away. Once (before he came there to die) he really was brought to an hospital, but in late life. It was St. Vincent's, and his visit is described in Mrs. Atkinson's biography of Mary Aikenhead.[19] 'Oh, the luxury of clean sheets', he exclaimed. His face is described in this book from the words of an eye-witness as 'handsome in outline, bloodless and wrinkled', with 'heavy lids' and 'blue eyes, distraught with the opium-eater's dreams'. Clean sheets may well have been a wonder to him, for he had long now been haunting the lowest taverns, disappearing often for days to live in some barn, drinking and brooding, turning over in his mind, perhaps, some one of those wild songs of his 'The Nameless One', 'Siberia', 'The Dying Enthusiast', or some other; or watching phantoms coming and going amid the straw, or listening to unearthly voices whispering in the air. Once after one of these disappearances, the late Father Meehan, I have been told, brought him before a looking-glass and made him look at his own worn and ragged form. 'Ah, but the state of the outer man is nothing to the state of the inner', was the answer.[20]

At last he died, and journeyed elsewhere. He died in the Meath Hospital of cholera. Some say he had foretold his own death from the epidemic some time before. I have it from one who had it from the doctor in attendance, that when he was dead his face became beautiful and calm. When the contorted soul had gone the muscles relapsed, and the clay returned to its primal innocence; or, if you prefer it, when life had fallen away the departing soul shed some of the light of its new peace upon the body. The dawn touched it, and the lustre of the dawn was reflected into the valley of the shadow it had fled from.

A RECKLESS CENTURY
IRISH RAKES AND DUELLISTS

This article appeared in United Ireland *on 12 September 1891. Yeats's researches into Irish rakes of the eighteenth century were part of his preparation of a volume for the "Adventurers Series" published by T. Fisher Unwin.*

In a letter dated 17 October 1892, Yeats told Edward Garnett, a reader for Unwin, that he had finished the introduction of the "Adventurers" volume (CL1, 323). For some reason or other, the volume never appeared and this article is the only relic of that research. In Yeats's letters of the early nineties there is some talk of a projected romance on eighteenth-century Ireland, but that project never came to fruition.

Many of the anecdotes in this article are taken, as Yeats admitted, from Ireland Sixty Years Ago *(Dublin: McGlashan, 1847), a volume attributed to John Edward Walsh. A few stories came from Sir Jonah Barrington's* Personal Sketches of His Own Times, 3 vols. *(London: Colburn, 1827–32).*

Yeats mentions this article in a piece on Oscar Wilde for United Ireland *(26 September 1891). The ferocious energy of the old rakes had been channeled, in Yeats's opinion, into the intellectual wit of such Irishmen as Oscar Wilde and Bernard Shaw.*

On the top of Mount Pelier, one of the Dublin hills, stands the building of the Hellfire Club,[1] upon its stone roof a few tufts of grass resembling hair, and in its front dark openings reminding one of sightless eyes—the whole like a grinning skull, hideous symbol of an age without ideals, without responsibility, without order, without peace. About it the winds howl unceasing, as though they keened for a violence that was as theirs is, for an age in whose unbridled life there was something elemental, something of the winds and floods. The neighbourhood still mutters with tales of deeds done within their grey walls. Here the devil came often, the story is, and feasted among these eighteenth-century worshippers of his,[2] leaving on one notable night his hoof-mark on the hearthstone; here a number of the gentry of Ireland were wont to drink to the toast 'May we be all damned', and to go through the ceremony of the Mass with obscene accompaniments; and here, to show their contempt for that eternal flame thought to be their lot, did they set fire to the building in a drunken spree, and sit on mocking the flames until they were driven out half stifled. Murders too, the peasants will have it, were not unknown; and now a hundred years after the last of its frequenters has brawled himself into the grave it is haunted, the tale goes, by drunken phantoms, who feast and gamble, with their master in the midst of them. For all this copious tradition not much is known for certainty of this Hellfire Club. There is something in Walsh[3]—the anonymous author of *Ireland Sixty Years Ago*— something in Barrington,[4] something in old magazines, and something in popular tradition; but it is not much at best, and little reliable. We know more of the 'Cherokees', whose iniquitous rules and regulations have been preserved by a contemporary writer.[5] No man was eligible for membership unless he gave clear evidence of a debauched life, and no man could be president until he could swear to having killed his man in a duel. This club became a terror in Dublin, and had many encounters with the authorities, beating them on every occasion. It was wont to march through the streets dressed as a military corps, and no power was found to cope with it.

There were also the 'Hawkabites', the 'Sweaters', and 'Pinkindindies',[6] who took an inch or so off the point of their scabbards, and went about prodding people out of sheer high spirits, and now and then killing a barber or two who had made them late for ball or dinner party by not turning up in time to powder and pomatum their empty heads. Sometimes they would stand at cross roads, notably at the College end of Dame-street, and prod the passers-by.

The wild passion for duelling that past through the country in that age is somewhat more worthy of sympathy. The destruction of the national forces at the battle of the Boyne[7] had filled the land with Catholic gentlemen who had no defence against insult but their own unaided swords, and from their contests with their supplanters spread through the country a habit of fighting for anything and everything. Men lived for it, and pistol practice became a consuming passion. Swaggering swashbucklers though they were, they did after all hold their lives lightly and risk them for a song. A little conviction would have made them good rebels. We hear of a certain Fitzgerald fighting a duel across a table, and when his opponent's pistol missed fire going over and priming it himself, and then returning to his place to receive the shot; nor can one help giving sympathy to Power of Daragle, when two Englishmen at an English inn bribed the waiters to give him for dinner, in mockery of his nationality, a dish of potatoes, and he replied by eating the potatoes, and then having served two dishes, one for himself and one for the Englishmen, which proved when the covers were lifted to contain pistols. Nor do we sympathize less because the Englishmen, much shocked at the notion of anything so foolish and Irish as a duel, fled hurriedly from the room leaving an unsettled bill which Power of Daragle paid charitably. The bragadoccio[†] of Brian Maguire—huge, whiskered bully that he was—standing at a narrow crossing and daring the passerby to jostle him, is not so pleasant an object even though his skill was so great that he always rang his bell with a bullet and could snuff a candle held in his wife's hand with a pistol shot; nor does the statement of a certain contemporary pamphleteer that his ancestors were once kings in Ireland, but that 'the infamous invader had been impoverishing Mr. Maguire for centuries',[8] make us feel any the more anxious to see his like again.

This reckless and turbulent spirit was by no means confined to the upper classes, but spread to the shopkeepers and artisans to a considerable extent. Poor men, when condemned to death, would spend the night before their hanging gambling upon the lids of their own coffins, making amends for a life without dignity by a death without fear. During all the early part of the eighteenth century the nation had little or no sense of national duty and public responsibility, the proper chiefs of the people were dead or exiled with foreign armies, the bards had passed away—the last bardic college came to an end in 1680[9]—and the ballad-makers had only just begun to take their place. The Anglo-Irish gentry who had succeeded to the defeated chiefs held allegiance only to England, and were responsible to no man. They had not yet awakened to the temporary patriotism of the Volunteer movement, nor listened as yet to the terrible raillery of Swift.[10] The contemporary life of England was reckless enough, but its recklessness, never at all equal to that of Ireland, was tempered by some sense of public welfare. The gentry of Ireland thought only to eat, drink, and be merry, for tomorrow might come rebellion and confiscation. Almost the only sense of national duty was, for long, among the poor. They were driven to their excesses often enough by patriotic hope. With what different feelings do we look back at the irresponsible turbulence of the gentry and at that storm of popular indignation when the mob attacked the Parliament House[11] and made the members swear truth to Ireland one after another, and then, to show their contempt of England, set an old woman with a pipe in her mouth upon the throne of the Viceroy.

Such were the thoughts and stories brought to my mind the other day by that grinning skull at Mount Pelier. All the four winds of heaven seemed to be howling at once upon the green hilltop, and telling to each other tales of forgotten violence and dead recklessness. What message of hope did they bring me? What judgment are we to pronounce upon that eighteenth century? What should it make us expect from the future? I find nothing but fortunate prophesies in that dead century. I see there the Celtic intensity, the Celtic fire, the Celtic daring wasting themselves, it is true in all kinds of evil, but needing only the responsibility of self-government and the restraint of a trained public opinion to have laboured devotedly for the public weal. The vast energy that filled Ireland with bullies and swashbucklers will some day give us great poets and thinkers. It is better to be violent and irresponsible than full of body-worship and money-grubbing. The duellist Whaley going off for a bet to play ball against the ramparts of Jerusalem is a nobler sight than the railway king putting his millions together. Those eighteenth-century duellists, at any rate, tried to really live, and not merely exist. They took their lives into their hands and went through the world with a song upon their lips; and if a curse was mingled with the song they are none the less better to think of than had they grown rich and much-esteemed, and yet lasted on no more than half alive, toadstools upon the state. The energy that filled them is still in our veins, but working now for public good. If a man or a people have energy all is well with them, and if they use it for ill to-day they will turn it to good to-morrow. When the devil is converted, goes the old proverb, he will be the first of the sons of God.[12] If the sword be strong it will make so much the better ploughshare when the day of peace is at hand.[13] Their swords were strong, at any rate, though they were not turned often enough, or persistently enough, towards the enemies of their country.

OSCAR WILDE'S LAST BOOK

This review of Oscar Wilde's Lord Arthur Savile's Crime and Other Stories (London, 1891) appeared in United Ireland, 26 September 1891. From the beginning of their acquaintance, Yeats regarded Oscar Wilde more highly as a wit and figure of legend than as an author. He met Wilde at the soirées of William Ernest Henley, one of the first magazine editors to print Yeats's poetry.

Before their meeting, Wilde had reviewed Yeats's book of fairy tales for Woman's World *(February 1889), and he had helped the reception of Yeats's first volume,* The Wanderings of Oisin, *with two reviews* (Woman's World, *March 1889, and* Pall Mall Gazette, *12 July 1891).*

We have the irresponsible Irishman in life, and would gladly get rid of him. We have him now in literature and in the things of the mind, and are compelled perforce to see that there is a good deal to be said for him. The men I described to you the other day under the heading, 'A Reckless Century',[1] thought they might drink, dice, and shoot each other to their hearts' content, if they did but do it gaily and gallantly, and here now is Mr. Oscar Wilde, who does not care what strange opinions he defends or what time-honoured virtue he makes laughter of, provided he does it cleverly. Many were injured by the escapades of the rakes and duellists, but no man is likely to be the worse for Mr. Wilde's shower of paradox. We are not likely to poison any one because he writes with appreciation of Wainewright[+2]—art critic and poisoner—nor have I heard that there has been any increased mortality among deans because the good young hero of his last book tries to blow up one with an infernal machine; but upon the other hand we are likely enough to gain something of brightness and refinement from the deft and witty pages in which he sets forth these matters.

'Beer, bible, and the seven deadly virtues have made England what she is', wrote Mr. Wilde once;[3] and a part of the Nemesis that has fallen upon her is a complete inability to understand anything he says. *We* should not find him so unintelligible—for much about him is Irish of the Irish. I see in his life and works an extravagant Celtic crusade against Anglo-Saxon stupidity. 'I labour under a perpetual fear of not being misunderstood',[4] he wrote, a short time since, and from behind this barrier of misunderstanding he peppers John Bull[5] with his pea-shooter of wit, content to know there are some few who laugh with him. There is scarcely an eminent man in London who has not one of those little peas sticking somewhere about him. 'Providence and Mr. Walter Besant have exhausted the obvious', he wrote once, to the deep indignation of Mr. Walter Besant; and of a certain notorious and clever, but coldblooded Socialist, he said, 'he has no enemies, but is intensely disliked by all his friends'.[6] Gradually people have begun to notice what a very great number of those little peas are lying about, and from this reckoning has sprung up a great respect for so deft a shooter, for John Bull, though he does not understand wit, respects everything that he can count up and number and prove to have bulk. He now sees beyond question that the witty sayings of this man whom he has so long despised are as plenty as the wood blocks in the pavement of Cheapside.[7] As a last resource he has raised the cry that his tormentor is most insincere, and Mr. Wilde replies in various ways that it is quite an error to suppose that a thing is true because John Bull sincerely believes it. Upon the other hand, if he did not believe it, it might have some chance of being true. This controversy is carried on upon the part of John by the newspapers; therefore, those who only read them have as low an opinion of Mr. Wilde as those who read books have a high one. *Dorian Gray*[†] with all its faults of method, is a wonderful book. *The Happy Prince* is a volume of as pretty fairy tales as our generation has seen; and *Intentions* hides within its immense paradox some of the most subtle literary criticism we are likely to see for many a long day. To this list has now been added *Lord Arthur Savile's Crime and other Stories* (James R. Osgood, McIlvaine[†], and Co.). It disappoints me a little, I must confess. The story it takes its name from is amusing enough in all conscience. 'The Sphinx without a Secret' has a quaint if rather meagre charm; but 'The Canterville Ghost' with its supernatural horseplay, and 'The Model Millionaire', with its conventional motive, are quite unworthy of more than a passing interest.

In *Lord Arthur Savile's Crime: A Study of Duty,* a young aristocrat is told by a cheiromantist[8] that he is fated to commit a murder. At first he is very miserable, because he is engaged to be married, for he considers it would be a great crime to marry with such a doom hanging over him. Presently he sees his duty. He does not hesitate a moment, being a young man of principle. He must commit the murder at once, and get it over. He postpones his engagement, and picks out an old aunt to be the victim. She had no money to leave him, so there would be no sordid motives. He gives her a box containing a piece of aconite which she is to take when she next gets an attack of heartburn she is subject to. It is an American cure he assures her. Presently he hears of her death, and grows quite happy making preparations for his wedding. Alas, one day, he finds the aconite untasted among her papers. She died of the heartburn, not of the poison. Again he postpones his marriage and chooses a victim—the Dean of Chichester.[9] He sends him an infernal machine in the form of a clock. The clock, however, goes off with a whizz and a puff of smoke, and the dean thinks it must be a kind of alarm clock sent him by an admirer of his sermons, and gives it to his children, who take it to the nursery, and make explosions all day long by putting a little powder under a clapper they find among the works. The good young aristocrat is in despair. He had tried to do his duty in vain. Fate, however, is kind to him; and as he is pacing up and down the Thames Embankment he comes upon the cheiromantist leaning against the parapet, and with a vigorous shove sends him into the river, and watches him drown with satisfaction at this accomplishment of his duty. 'Did you drop anything, sir?' says a policeman.[10] 'Nothing of importance, sergeant', he answers, as he hailed a hansom. After this he marries and lives out his life in perfect happiness, and with a proud sense of duty done against much temptation to have done otherwise.

Surely we have in this story something of the same spirit that filled Ireland once with gallant, irresponsible ill-doing, but now it is in its right place making merry among the things of the mind, and laughing gaily at our most firm fixed convictions. In one other Londoner, the socialist, Mr. Bernard Shaw, I recognize the same spirit. His account of how the old Adam gradually changed into the great political economist Adam Smith is like Oscar Wilde in every way.[11] These two men, together with Mr. Whistler,[12] the painter—half an Irishman also, I believe—keep literary London continually agog to know what they will say next.

THE YOUNG IRELAND LEAGUE

This article was printed in United Ireland *on 3 October 1891, three days before the death of Charles Stewart Parnell. Yeats had then high hopes for the passage of a Home Rule bill, but the scandal over Parnell's affair with Kitty O'Shea and the sudden death of "the Chief" had doomed such hopes. The occasion for the article was the banding together of local Young Ireland societies into a literary society. Such a project was for Yeats only a prelude to a larger undertaking. At the end of December 1891, he founded with T. W. Rolleston the Irish Literary Society in London, and on 24 May 1892 he helped to found the National Literary Society in Dublin. Maud Gonne helped Yeats in the attempt to establish local libraries.*

The newspapers have not been able to make out the meaning of this League of ours. That a number of literary societies should wish to band themselves together and sing Irish ballads instead of the songs of the music halls, and recite Irish poems at their meetings, and help each other to the possession of good books seems the last thing likely to the great wisdom of the Press. Anything else seems more worthy of belief. We are coming forth, the English papers tell us, trying to trouble the peace of nations with our pikes. We are Fenians coming to take care of Mr. Parnell.[1] Nor is the wisdom of our Irish Press much more equal to the occasion, for no matter how they vary the minor notes the old hurdy-gurdy can play but one tune—the wickedness of Mr. Parnell. It really seems needful to say that our aim is to help to train up a nation of worthy men and women who shall be able to work for public good, whether we are about to win an Irish Parliament or whether the old war against English dominion is still to go on. The general election, or the coming of Home Rule itself, will not do away with the need for our work, for our enemies are ignorance and bigotry and fanaticism, the eternal foes of the human race which may not be abolished in any way by Acts of Parliament.[2]

To do this work of ours we seek to revive certain educational instruments—the young Ireland societies—that proved effective in the past and at the same time to do away with various defects which we have learned to remedy by experience. The old societies were started in 1880, and spread all over the country, setting everywhere groups of young men working and thinking. For six years there were twenty or thirty branches in active existence, and there might be as many still if the central body in Dublin had not come to an end in 1885, but had gone on feeding them from its central life. We now seek to pour new life into those branches which are still living, to revive those which have died, and to make new societies where there were none before, and to bring all under the influence of an elective council of fifty members. These members are to be elected yearly and will be independent of any particular branch and its varying fortunes. The old branches and members are promising their support. In Dublin the Leinster Literary Society, the Rathmines National League Literary Society, the Arran-quay National League Literary Society, the National Club Literary Society, and probably the Ninety Club Literary Society will join with us; and in the country the Passage West, Maryborough, and Thurles Young Ireland Societies will shortly affiliate.[3] Groups of young men in Cork, Belfast, Clonmel, Macroom, Kingstown, Kilmailock, Waterford, Glasgow, Bray, Middleton, Limerick, Tralee, Cavan, and Bruff,[4] promise to form branches; and there is[†] also some hope of help from the Irishmen in England. The Belfast and Cork Young Ireland Societies still hold aloof from us, but they will be drawn in when they find that we are really neutral in the present political dispute, that we welcome Parnellite and M'Carthyite[5] equally, that our League holds out the flag of truce to all Nationalists, and that, perhaps, in ours alone of national organizations may they find the peace that comes from working for distant purposes. We desire to make the fanatic, on which side soever he be found, less fanatical, and to make the rancorous[†] heart, wheresoever it be, less bitter. In no other sense have we to do with parties.

The actual work before the League is definite enough. Classes will be organized to teach the history and language of Ireland, lectures will be given upon Irish subjects, and most important of all, reading-rooms will be started in connection with the various branches. They need not cost much. It has been calculated that a reading-room, where the papers of all sides and the best magazines are taken, can be kept going in a country village for 4s. or 5s. a week. This includes the rent of a room. No caretaker would be required, for each member might have his own key. For four or five pounds additional such a room could be stocked with a library containing, not only the best Irish books, but the masterpieces of other countries as well. It is proposed that the council draw up a list for the guidance of the local members, and that the organization as a whole bear a portion of the cost. The Irish books in these reading-rooms should be before all else (though by no means excluding all else) the books that feed the imagination. They should include Mitchel, Mangan, Davis, both prose and verse, all the Irish ballad collections, the radiant and romantic histories of Standish O'Grady, the *Celtic Romances* of Joyce, the poems of Sir Samuel Ferguson, the poems of William Allingham, the best novels of Carleton, Banim, Griffin, and Lever, three or four of the Irish stories of Miss Edgeworth, the folk-lore writings of Hyde, Croker, and Lady Wilde, Moore's Melodies, and some of the best translations from the old Celtic epics.[6] Most of these books are very cheap, and when they are at all dear they can be got secondhand. The best hundred Irish books, as set forth in the *Freeman* some time ago,[7] would be both far too many and quite of the wrong kind. Imagination, and not learning, is the centre of life, and from the direction it takes spring thought and conduct, and in books like those I have mentioned dwells the best imagination of National Ireland. Irish writers of equal or greater merit there have been whom I have not mentioned, because they did not make Ireland their subject matter, but united with the main stream of English literature. They have no special claim upon us, but must be read when, like Goldsmith, they are important enough to make a needful part of general knowledge. But those writers who have made Ireland their study have a peculiar claim on our affections. An article in the *National Press,* in which I recognise a hand worthy of a better cause, has assured us that we have no literature except a few songs and stories, and that the sooner we of the Young Ireland League find it out the better.[8] I, at any rate, found it out long ago, and was well pleased, for songs and stories are no inconsiderable things when the men who wrote them loved the grass under their feet and the flying Irish clouds over their heads, and the blue mountains, and the bowed forms of the ploughing and reaping people among whom they lived, and when they know how to fill others with the same love.

A POET WE HAVE NEGLECTED

Yeats reviewed the six-volume collected edition of the poems of William Allingham (London: Reeves and Turner, 1887–91) in the 12 December 1891 issue of United Ireland. *The six volumes published by Reeves and Turner were:* Irish Songs and Poems *(1887);* Flower Pieces and Other Poems *(1888);* Life and Phantasy *(1889);* Laurence Bloomfield *(1890);* Thought and Word *and* Ashby Manor *(1890), and* Blackberries *(1884, reissued 1890).*

Although not included by Yeats before this article in the holy trinity of "Davis, Mangan, and Ferguson," William Allingham (1824–89) was a powerful influence upon the early fairy and peasant ballad poems of Yeats.

Three years before the present article, Yeats had written as his first prose contribution to an American newspaper the account of Allingham that was printed in The Providence Sunday Journal *of 2 September 1888 (LNI, 71–78). The critical judgments are similar in both articles, even the phrasing at times, although in 1888 Yeats had been more severe on Allingham's lack of a strong Irish nationalism.*

In 1892 Yeats contributed a sketch on Allingham to Miles's anthology The Poets and the Poetry of the Century, *and in 1905 he prepared for the Dun Emer Press an edition of* Sixteen Poems *by William Allingham.*

Of all recognised Irish poets, William Allingham is at once the most delicate and the least read on this side of the water. To most Irishmen and women he is merely the author of 'Fairies', or of some other stray lyric which has drifted into our ballad collections. In England he is becoming better known, and now, two years after his death, Messrs. Reeves and Turner have completed the collected edition of his works by the addition of *Thought and Word* and *Blackberries*. These six little books, with their vellum backs and illustrations by Dante Rossetti, and Millais,[1] and their advertisement of more expensive editions on luxe paper, have all the signs of being addressed to an assured public, who will both read their Allingham and pay for him too. It is time for us over here to claim him as our own, and give him his due place among our sacred poets; to range his books beside Davis and Mangan, and Ferguson;[2] for he, too, sang of Irish scenes and Irish faces.

He was the poet of Ballyshannon,[3] though not of Ireland; perhaps that is the reason why we have not known more of him. His feeling was local and not national, and we have now[4] such dire need for all our national fire that we have had but little time or thought for any narrower inspiration. Yet, certainly, we have been wrong to neglect this man. *Irish Songs and Poems,* the first volume of his collected works, should be on all Irish bookshelves. In it is enshrined that passionate devotion that so many Irishmen feel for the little town where they were born, and for the mountains they saw from the doors they passed through in childhood. It should be dear to our exiles, and grow a new link in the chain that binds them to their native land. Some day, when copyrights have lapsed, it will be reprinted for a few pence, I doubt not, and grow dear and familiar to many of our sea-wandering and land-traversing people. Its author will take his place among that band of poets whose swift shuttles weave about us a web of tender affection and spirited dreams. He will always, however, be best loved by those who, like the present writer, have spent their childhood in some small Western seaboard town,[5] and who remember how it was for years the centre of their world, and how its enclosing mountains and its quiet rivers became a portion of their life for ever. How kindly in their ears will ever sound Allingham's lines—

> A wild west coast, a little town
> Where little folk go up and down,
> Tides flow and winds blow.
> Human wile and human fate,
> Night and tempest and the sea,
> What is little, what is great?
> Howsoe'er the answer be
> Let me sing of what I know.[6]

The greater part of his life was spent there 'where little folk go up and down', and for them he printed many of his poems on broad sheets that had so wide a circulation that the Government gave him a small pension on the ground of their value as education for the people.[7] It is well to remember these broad sheets, for they prove his genuine wish to be considered an Irish poet, and not a mere cosmopolitan choosing his themes from Ireland, as he might choose them in another way from

Kamchatka.[8] One song of his, 'Kate O' Bellyshanny',[†] was often sung by the peasantry. It is one of the deftest of Irish mock serious songs—

One summer's day, the banks were gay,
    The Erne[9] in sunshine glancin' there,
The big cascade its music play'd
    And set the salmon dancin' there.
Along the green my joy was seen;
    Some goddess bright I thought her there;
The fishes, too, swam close to view
    Her image in the water there.
From top to toe, where'er you go,
    The loveliest girl of any, O,
Ochone! your mind I find unkind,
    Sweet Kate O' Bellyshanny,[†] O![10]

My dear, give ear!—the river's near,
    And if you think I'm shammin' now,
To end my grief I'll seek relief
    Among the trout and salmon now;
For shrimps and sharks to make their marks,
    And other watery vermin there;
Unless a mermaid saves my life,
    My wife and me her merman there.
From top to toe, etc.[11]

The Ballyshannon poems contain many much more serious and beautiful things than these dancing verses, such as the well-known 'Fairies' and 'The Winding Banks of Erne' which is known through being included in Sparling's *Irish Minstrelsy*[†12] and 'Lovely Mary Donnelly', which has found its way into the ballad books. Two hundred years hence those songs of his may have turned Ballyshannon into one of the spots held sacred by literary history, and travelling Germans and Americans will think it would 'discredit their travel' to have come to Ireland and not gone there. A mild light of imagination will shine upon its streets such as shines where a Herbert, or a Crashaw, or a Herrick lived and laboured.[13]

When I wrote a while since that Allingham's poems should be included in the books[†] recommended by the Council of the Young Ireland League to the projected village libraries, I had the first volume, *Irish Poems,* in my mind.[14] Those who care to know his genius more perfectly should add to it the third volume, *Flower Fancies,* for the sake of the poems called *Day and Night Songs.*[15] A few of them have to do with Ireland, but most are expressions of personal feeling, like that most exquisite of all his lyrics, 'Twilight Voices', wherein he sings of the coming of old age, and of the mysterious voices that call to him 'out of the dimness, vague and vast', of the unknown world beyond the tomb.[16] They need not concern themselves—unless they be very ardent readers—with the other volumes; for, though they contain one or two fine things, they were written for the most part either after Allingham had left Ballyshannon for London, and lost his inspiration, or before he had found it, or are merely reprints of long poems like *Laurence Bloomfield*,[17] and for long poems he had no faculty. When he had to deal with a large subject, the inherent limitation of his mind marred all. He is essentially a poet of the accidental and fleeting—of passing artistic moments. The pilot's daughter in her Sunday frock, the sound of a clarionet[18] through the ruddy window of a forge, the fishers drawing in their nets with a silver wave of salmon—these are his true subject matter. He had no sense of the great unities—the relations of man to man, and all to the serious life of the world. It was this that kept him from feeling Ireland as a whole; from writing of the joys and sorrows of the Irish people, as Davis, and Ferguson, and Mangan have done, and from stirring our blood with great emotions. Had he felt the unity of life, he, with his marvellous artistic faculty, could have given us long poems that would be really alive; but, not feeling it, the best he could do was *Laurence Bloomfield*, with its fine pictures of detached things, and its total failure as an Irish epic of the land troubles. But let us be grateful for what he has given us. If he was no national poet, he was, at any rate, no thin-blooded cosmopolitan, but loved the hills about him and the land under his feet.

POEMS BY MISS TYNAN

This review of Katharine Tynan's Ballads and Lyrics *appeared in* The
Evening Herald *(Dublin) for Saturday, 2 January 1892. A shortened
version of the review was reprinted in Roger McHugh's edition of
W. B. Yeats's* Letters to Katharine Tynan *(New York: McMullen
Books, 1953). For information on Yeats's literary relationship with
Katharine Tynan, see the headnote to "The Celtic Romances in Miss
Tynan's New Book," pp. 51–64.*

A great change has come over our Irish writers in recent years. In '48
they made songs and ballads from some passionate impulse of the
moment.[1] Often the same song would contain poetry of the most
moving power, side by side with flaccid and commonplace lines. Men
like Doheny,[2] under the stress of strong excitement, would strike off a
ringing ballad and then sink into tuneless silence. We can reproduce
now neither the merits nor defects of that poetry, in which all was done
from sudden emotion, nothing from deliberate art. It was like the days
of the Arabs before Mahometanism, when the same man led the tribe
to war and wrote its songs of love and battle. Such periods cannot last.
If literatures are to go on they must add art to impulse and temper their
fire with knowledge. Literary Ireland is going through such a training.
The days of Davis were followed by those of Allingham's Ballyshannon songs and de Vere's[†] *Inisfail*[†] and his *Legends of St. Patrick,* and
Ferguson's[†] later and greater work, his *Deirdre* and *Conary.*[3] These men
were all experimenters, trying to find out a literary style that would be
polished and yet Irish of the Irish. Those who follow them have their
work made more easy through their experiments.

In reading this new book of Miss Tynan's, *Legends and Lyrics*[4] (Kegan
Paul, Trench, Trubner and Co), I feel constantly how greatly she has
benefited by study both of the old Irish ballads and of the modern writers I have named. Her first book, *Louise de La Vallière,* was too full of
English influences to be quite Irish, and too laden with garish colour

to be quite true to the austere Celtic spirit. *Shamrocks*[5] was better, and now *Ballads and Lyrics* is well nigh in all things a thoroughly Irish book, springing straight from the Celtic mind, and pouring itself out in soft Celtic music. Though perfectly original, I can yet feel in it the influence of more than one master of Celtic speech, and in thus gaining nationality of style Miss Tynan has found herself and found the world about her. The landscapes are no more taken from the tapestry-like[†] scenery of Rossetti and his imitators,[6] but from her own Clondalkin[†7] fields, and from the grey Dublin hills. She apologises for this charming provincialism in an 'Apologia' as exquisite as Allingham at his best, but with an added richness—

> Here in my book there will be found
> No gleanings from a foreign ground:
> The quiet thoughts of one whose feet
> Have scarcely left her green retreat;
> A little dew, a little scent,
> A little measure of content,
> A robin's song, perchance to stir
> Some heart-untravelled traveller.
>
> A low horizon hems me in,
> Low hills, with fields of gold between,
> Woods that are waving, veiled with grey,
> A little river far away,
> Birds on the boughs and on the sward,
> Daisies that dancing praise the Lord.[8]
> . . . . .
> And in my garden, all in white
> The Mary-lilies take the light,
> And southern wood and lavender
> Welcome the bee in golden fur,
> A splendid lover, and on high
> Hovers the spangled butterfly,
> Where roses old and sweet, dream on,
> Fading to rich oblivion.[9]
> . . . . .
> So in my book there will be found
> No gleanings from a foreign ground,[10]
> If such you seek, go buy, go buy
> Of some more travelled folk than I.
> Kind Master Critic, say not, please,
> How that her world so narrow is,

Since here she warns expectant eyes
That homely is her merchandise.†

In Miss Tynan's earlier books colour was too often sought for its own sake, as if an artist were to rest satisfied with the strange and striking combinations of the colours spread upon his palettes, instead of using them to make manifest the beautiful things about him. In this book, however, is many a fine landscape† and much fine portraiture of noble woods. How well suggested is the gloomy landscape in 'The Children of Lir†', and how subtly† expressed are their wistful human souls wrapped round with the birds' bodies.

How rare a thing is good religious poetry is known to all reviewers, and yet some of the most successful poems in this book are on the most hackneyed symbols of Christianity. Miss Tynan draws from them even some new and quaint beauty. Some of† her religious poems have the *naïveté*† of mediaeval song; nor is their simplicity any the less genuine for being conscious—for being a product quite as much of art as of impulse. Some fourteenth century monk† might have murmured, as he bent over an illuminated missal, lines like these:[11]

The sheep with their little lambs
    Passed by me[12] on the road;
All in the April evening
    I thought on the Lamb of God.

The lambs were weary, and crying
    With a weak, human cry,[13]
I thought on the Lamb of God
    Going meekly to die.

Up in the blue, blue mountains
    Dewy pastures are sweet;
Rest for the little bodies,
    Rest for the little feet.[14]

But for the Lamb of God,
    Up on the hill-top green,
Only a cross[15] of shame
    Two stark crosses between.

All in the April evening,
    April airs were abroad;
I saw the sheep with their lambs,
    And thought on the Lamb of God.[16]

Good, too, is 'Rose in Heaven', a memorial song for the late Miss Rose Kavanagh;[17] but best of all is, perhaps, 'In a Cathedral', the story of a wood-carver who lived all his life unknown and solitary amid the cathedral shadows, content to serve God by the beauty of art, by the grace of the carven roof where 'he fashioned many a singing bird,[18] whose lovely silence praised the Lord'.

> The patient carver toiled apart;
>   The world roared on—a world away.
> No earthly ties were round his heart,
>   No passion stirred his quiet day;
> His carvings in the cloisters dim
> Made home, and wife, and child for him.[19]

> He was so young when he began—
>   A fair-haired boy, whose wistful eyes
> Saw earth and heaven, and scarcely man,
>   But weighed large issues and was wise:
> The years that all unheeded[†] sped
> Shook their grey dust upon his head.[20]

Here and there is a poem that leaves me cold, a song, that does not seem to me to sing, a ballad where art has become artificial and stifled impulse instead of guiding it; but what need is there to single them out, when there is so much beauty, so many verses that may well be dear to the hearts of our people, when I[†] who write and you who read are under the green grass or 'where[†] the thistles grow'.

THE NEW 'SPERANZA'

This article, from United Ireland, *16 January 1892, was the first of two pieces which Yeats wrote during that month in support of Maud Gonne's nationalistic activities in Paris. Gonne served as the inspiration for his drama* The Countess Cathleen *and for most of his early love poems. What Yeats did not know at this time was that Gonne was in love with a French journalist, Lucien Millevoye. Part of her influence upon the French may have been Millevoye's work. She bore Millevoye two children: George (born 11 January 1890 and died 29 July 1891) and Iseult (born 6 August 1894), who was publicly acknowledged as Maud's niece (see CL1, 248, 289–90).*

Millevoye became editor of the newspaper La Patrie *in 1896 and Maud Gonne founded a small paper for Irish propaganda called* L'Irlande Libre *in 1897. Later in this decade, Yeats contributed two pieces to this paper, one on Fiona Macleod and one on John O'Leary.*

By the title of this article Yeats intended to draw a parallel between the new "Speranza" (Maud Gonne) and Lady Wilde, who had signed the name "Speranza" to her fiery pieces for The Nation *in the 1840s. The word* speranza *means "hope" in Italian.*

An article very similar to this one appeared in The Boston Pilot *on 30 July 1892 and was included in the collection of Yeats's American newspaper pieces,* Letters to the New Island, *pp. 61–63.*

The quotations Yeats provides below are from a speech Gonne gave in 1891 at the Dîner de Saint Patrice, an annual banquet of L'Association du Saint Patrice.

One little colony of Irishmen and women has ever stood outside the National organization. No Irish leader of recent days has ever given a thought to the little community of Irish people living in Paris, and yet the good will of Europe is of moment to us, and they might help to answer that ceaseless stream of calumny England has sent forth against us through continental nations. To have the ear of Paris would be to have the ear of Europe, and no oppressed nation can well spare any friend. Miss Maud Gonne has set herself the task of organizing this community and has founded an *'Association Irlandais'* to bring the Irish of Paris into touch with one another, and to keep France informed of the true state of the Irish Question. She began her work by presiding at a dinner given by French sympathizers with the cause of Ireland, and made a great stir by her eloquent statement of the case for Ireland. The French papers are loud in her praise; the *Figaro* has interviewed her, and described her speech as having made a sensation.[1] *L'Etendard National*† cannot find words strong enough to describe its effect. 'Pathetic and persuasive, sweet and passionate, full of truth and indignation', it writes; 'now dwelling on the past and now prophetic, she was soon absolute mistress of her audience. While speaking, the Celtic Druidess looked at no one, her great black eyes, full of flame, gazed out into the future full of hope of better days. In a kind of wild ecstasy this Irish patricienne† seemed to address legions of adherents visible on the horizon to her mystical foreknowledge†; and one knew that upon that mysterious horizon she could divine her defenders—her avengers, also, perhaps.

'Before her speech had closed the women were all in tears and the men seeking in vain to hide their emotion. Colonel Chareton, the Marquis de Castellane, Jean Dupuis, the Prince de Lusignan, the Baron de Chambourg, Charles Joller, the Comte of Susini d'Ariscia, the Duc de Chartres,† and the Marquis of Villeneuve were the first to furtively brush away their tears. The example was contagious, and I affirm that I have never seen an audience of the elite of Paris so moved.'[2] *Le Bien Public* is no less enthusiastic. 'Very singular', it says, 'Was the emotion that seized upon that audience of politicians', and then goes on to describe the great beauty and the marvellous voice of the young orator.

The speech itself is given by one paper[3] in its entirety, to the complete exclusion of the speeches of Clovis Hugues†[4] and the other eminent politicians who were present. Shorn of the marvellous delivery of the speaker, it has yet many beautiful passages, and has throughout the wild sweetness of an Aeolian Harp[5] upon which the winds play, a little fitfully perhaps, but ever musically. 'I have given all my heart to Ireland', she began, 'and I will give her my life also if events permit me. If I could tell to France, the great country of noble and generous ideas, all that I have seen in Ireland of heroism and patriotism, of misery that never flinched, and of invincible national faith, and if I can make pass into your hearts and consciences the indignation which fills my soul against the oppressors of my country, I shall have fulfilled my mission as a patriot and a woman.

'Ah, how can I make you see, how can I make you feel, the marvellous past which lives eternally in the heart and in the memory of my race? Our illustrious dead, our heroes, our martyrs, all that world of memories, of examples, of glories, of immortal actions which England would bury in the tomb, but which shall rise one day against her!

'Gentlemen, the tyranny of England towards Ireland for many centuries has been a crime against God and against the whole of humanity. She made us first a vassal and then a slave. We cannot tread upon any sod of our country without passing above the trace of a crime. Your great poet, Victor Hugo, has called hunger 'a public crime,' and that crime England has carried out against Ireland by cold premeditation and calculation. For centuries she has reached forth her arms to seize Ireland and to strangle her, but she has forgotten that the blood of martyrs is the eternal seed of liberty.

'Do you ask us what we are seeking for? I will tell you. We are three things—a race, a country, and a democracy—and we wish to make of these three a nation.'

Miss Gonne then went on to describe the ancient civilization of Ireland, and how England came to destroy it. She ran swiftly through the history of Ireland, and told how in modern days we had shrunk from twelve millions to nine, and then from nine to four, with the rare tact of the orator. She dwelt much on the brigades[6] and on the battles they won for France—'always dying, always living'—and told them that if Ireland was to be separated from France 'twenty pages of our common history would have to be torn out', and then concluded amid great enthusiasm.

What a singular scene—this young girl of twenty-five addressing that audience of politicians, and moving them more than all their famous speakers although she spoke in a language not her own. What does it mean for Ireland? Surely, that here is the new 'Speranza' who shall do with the voice all, or more than all, the old 'Speranza' did with her pen. Surely there is here a new orator who adds the power of beauty to the power of the golden tongue, and who shall be a marvellous standard-bearer for that better Future that is dawning for our race.

DR. TODHUNTER'S
IRISH POEMS

This review of The Banshee and Other Poems *by John Todhunter (1839–1916) appeared in* United Ireland, 23 January 1892. *Yeats had reviewed the first edition of* The Banshee *for* The Providence Sunday Journal *on 10 February 1889 (LNI, 79–90). For the American newspaper Yeats had concentrated on Todhunter's translations of Irish bardic tales.*

The alliance of politics and literature that marked the "'48 movement"[1] resulted in so great a popularity for the poets and prose writers who taught the doctrine of nationality that we are accustomed ever since to think of those years as our one period of literary activity. The writers who came after, lacking the great wind of politics to fill their sails, have lived and wrought almost forgotten of the nation. Allingham found English audiences, but won few listeners this side of the Channel, and de Vere[†] is to-day more noted as a poet of the English Catholics than as an Irish writer, despite his *Inisfail,*[†] and his 'Children of Lir', and 'Fardiar', and *Legends of St. Patrick.*[2] When time has removed this century into the dimness of the past it will be seen that Ireland, like England, has had a literary development of her own, and that "'48' was not a mere isolated outburst. 'The king is dead; long live the king'. Davis, and Carleton, and Mangan passed away, but Allingham, and de Vere,[†] and O'Grady and the Ferguson of *Conary*[†] and *Deirdre,*[3] came to take their places, and to find, alas! the ear of the people closed. Among these later writers who took up the golden chain of Irish literature, we should, I think, place Dr. Todhunter, by right of his book of Irish legendary verse, called *The Banshee and other Poems.* It has just been republished at 1s. by Seeley, Bryers, and Walker, of Dublin, and Dr. Todhunter promises a 'Deirdre' as its successor. *The Library of Ireland* when first issued was more expensive, and yet I wonder will this artistically bound shilling's worth win half the success of the least able volume in the famous *Library*.[4] The time he lives in, and not Dr. Todhunter, is to blame if this be so, for it should be incumbent on all good Irishmen to know something of their old legends, and it has been well said that a better idea of what that renowned old legend of the *caoine* of Lir must have sounded like to the folk who gathered about the old bards who chanted it can be got from the version in this *Banshee and other Poems* than from any translation. The name-poem, too, should be widely known. It is a noble chant over the sorrows of Ireland. How well the wild, irregular verses—something between Walt Whitman and the Scotch Ossian[5]—would go in recitation:

Green in the wizard arms
Of the foam-bearded Atlantic,
An isle of old enchantment,
A melancholy isle,
Enchanted and dreaming lies;
And thou, by Shannon's[6] flowing,
In the moonlight, spectre-thin
The spectre Erin sits.[7]

An aged desolation,
She sits by old Shannon's flowing,
A mother of many children,
Of children exiled and dead,
In her home, with bent head, homeless,
Clasping her knees she sits,
Keening, keening!
. . . . .
How[8] the nations hear in the void and quaking time of night,
Sad unto dawning, dirges,
Solemn dirges,
And snatches of bardic song;
Their souls quake in the void and quaking time of night,
And they dream of the weird of kings,
And tyrannies moulting, sick
In the dreadful wind of change.

Wail no more, lonely one, mother of exiles, wail no more,
Banshee of the world—no more!
Thy sorrows are the world's, thou art no more alone;
Thy wrongs the world's.[9]

'The Sons of Turann' is a fine version of another of 'The Three Sorrows of Story-Telling', as the bards called 'Deirdre', 'The Children of Lir', and 'The Sons of Turann', and 'Aghadoe'† must be well known to many through its inclusion in *Poems and Ballads of Young Ireland.*[10] All the poems are extremely simple and almost rough in their strain for primeval utterance. They are so far removed from conventional poetic diction as to be at times too matter-of-fact and bald, like the old stories themselves.

The twenty pages of poems on other than Irish subjects bound up with them are, I cannot help thinking, a mistake. They are in quite a different manner, and as full of poetic diction as the others are free of it. 'Methinks I saw these sixteen things of storm'[11]—the opening of one of the sonnets—is a strong line, and little the worse for its conventional 'methinks', but certainly it is in a very different style to the clear utterance of the Celtic poems. These 'other poems' were, I believe, added to please an English publisher who seemed sceptical of his chance of making English readers take to anything with an Irish subject. They might have been left out of the present Irish edition with advantage to the unity of the book.

Gradually as Irish readers begin to understand that they have a literature which is racy of the soil,[12] and that it goes on decade by decade, and was not a strange spirit of a unique period, they will begin to look for and study books like this. Miss Tynan's new volume, *Poems and Lyrics,* Dr. Hyde's stories, the humor of F. J. Allan,[13] and volumes like the one here noticed, will gradually, I believe, convince them that it is a literature various enough for many tastes. Gavan Duffy's projected new *Library of Ireland*[14] also, if it be not too exclusively a basket to gather up the fragments that remained after the feast of the old *Library,* may do much to foster a reading public in Ireland.

CLOVIS HUGUES† ON IRELAND

This piece, from United Ireland, *30 January 1892, was a sequel to Yeats's article of two weeks before, "The New 'Speranza,'" and a continuation of his efforts to support Maud Gonne's nationalistic agitation in Paris.*

The French papers have not yet ceased to celebrate both the beauty and eloquence of our new 'Speranza', and divers English papers have followed suit, notably Mr. Stead's *Review of Reviews,*[1] which gives a bad portrait of Miss Maud Gonne, and explains that she is a Parnellite, or Separatist[2]—a luminous definition very suggestive of the kind of Home Rule Mr. Stead believes the seceders to be looking for—and that her mission to Paris is to win armed help for Ireland, in which, it adds, although 'one of the most beautiful women in the world', she will hardly succeed. Now, in spite of the *Review of Reviews,* Miss Maud Gonne is not only no Separatist under present conditions, but is succeeding beyond all expectations in her perfectly practical businesslike, and unsensational project of organising the Irish people of Paris and the Parisians of Irish descent into a society which will be able to serve Ireland by bringing politicians at home into touch with distinguished continental statesmen, should the need arise, by helping the home organization with funds in the event of the society spreading widely; by keeping the continental Press well posted in the matter of our Irish wrongs; and by generally cultivating good relations between Ireland and her old ally, France. The most charming of the many marks of the sympathy it has already awakened, is a poem which the distinguished poet and politician, Clovis Hugues,†[3] has dedicated to Miss Maud Gonne. My friend, Mr. Edwin J. Ellis,[4] himself a poet, whom the world will receive gladly some day, has made for me a translation no less charming than the original poem. I do not think that any thought or any beauty has been missed:

A Toast to Ireland[5]

(Dedicated to Miss Maud Gonne.)

The Masters, in derisive laurel crowned,
With Death for President, are sitting round
At a most monstrous banquet: see them here,
Decked out with crimes, ready to drink a tear,
Or blood, or wine unto the brim high poured!
Yet while they toast the horror of the sword,
Insult the vanquished, mock the sad ones more,
I, in the waves name and the long, low shore,
Drink to the form of dreaming Ireland, where
Along the salt wind blows her level hair.

From bearded Celts the shipmen from afar
Have stolen their fields, and stolen their guiding star;
Yet, though these go, the tempest in their shrouds
Planting their poles and canvas home like clouds
Around the marshes where the rushes bend,
A dawn will clear the coast from end to end.
A star will flower again in heaven more bright,
Oh, ancient bards, leap up with new delight!
I drink to Ireland, kissing the earth green,
Where sleep in peace her great ones that have been.

The peaks were looking far beyond the hills:
'What sight is this that your sad seeing fills?'
Cried all the waves. 'Murder and rape,' they said,
'And storm-wind on the rafterless homestead,
And Women vainly weeping as they go.'
I, too, have seen and known a land in woe,
And heard sad secrets from the burial place.
Up on thy feet! Up, up, oh! thou lost race!
I drink to Ireland, bidding her prepare,
While on the stones they drag her by the hair.

'What see you now?' Again the blue wave speaks.
'All-powerful Evil!' answered the high peaks.
'Youth and sweet love have no more time to flower,
But fortune-gilded thieves are gods in power—

Gilded with gold of barley ripe, and rye,
And wheat-ears pillaged as they wandered by.'
The thunder growls behind the reddening cloud,
Those whom the darkness knows I name aloud;
I drink to Ireland, Ireland hungry grown,
Amid the yellow corn herself has sown.

By her dead hearths and troubled soul, where through
The winged hopes were song-birds in the blue,
Green Erin is made now in all her space
Like one great tear, sad on the heaven's face,
Where palely shine reflected woods and shore.
Do nations die, and is a race no more
Because her torn and ragged cloak is sold?
The days go by. Right keeps her dwelling old.
I drink to Ireland, while I see outpour
Tears on the doorstep of a tomb's white door.

At moments, tired of the scythe, so vain
When held by her, she arms herself again,
Starting with joy, a people's king to hear,
When some O'Connell⁶ rises without fear.
Oh, bid your flute-players guard you on the moor,
Landlords, who make men poor and gibe the poor!
Beware, for those who rise more high shall see
A greater fall in the near days to be.
I drink to Ireland, who wrestles now
Even with the thorns bound close around her brow.

Ah, though a hideous blank be the grave's word,
Let us be Ireland's brother. Never heard
From our lips, by her, be this sad news.
That never more the branch with heavenly dews
The holy dove shall now be seen to bring.
For fallen is our dream with broken wing.
Faith smiles on her, to whom St. Patrick brought
This treasure, therefore now in reverent thought
I drink to Ireland, praying with bent head,
For prayer is still the strong man's daily bread.

She, too, but lately saw her hopeful day
When France, my mother, cast her kings away,
And sent her sons to render Ireland free.

But destiny betrayed us, and the sea
More bitter proved than ills endured or tears.
But bronze is reddened e'er the statue rears—
Who thinks on all those evil days again?
For life gone past is even with the slain.
I drink to Ireland, who disaster knew
On the same day when we were conquered, too.

The poem is a little vague, perhaps, as is indeed inevitable in the work of a man writing of a country he has never seen, and of history of which he has but a very general knowledge; but there is a great beauty, especially in the later stanzas. It was an improvization made at the dinner of the *Union Méditerranéenne*[17] after Miss Maud Gonne's speech, and I think the slightly conventional opening, with its banquet, when the masters of Ireland's destiny drink blood and tears, is evidence that the *improvisar* took time—a very short time certainly—before he got into the full stream of inspiration with the winds of poetry in his sails. The last stanza, with its allusion to the day when France, no less than Ireland, was conquered, is very touching in the mouth of a Frenchman. The poem when published in a French newspaper was marked with the French equivalent for 'please copy', and has, no doubt, been widely quoted throughout France; and even if it were less fine as a poem it would be still of importance both as an evidence, and, in some slight degree, as a cause even, of sympathy between Ireland and her ancient ally. The stars of destiny shall have to bring several things about before we can finally say that such sympathy is no longer needed, and that a movement to bring the men at home into bonds of friendship with their fellow-countrymen in Paris and with the descendants[†] of the old brigade,[8] is a movement without good right to exist.

SIGHT AND SONG

Yeats's review of Michael Field's book of poems, Sight and Song *(London, 1892), appeared in* The Bookman *in July 1892. It was the first of a long series of reviews by Yeats for this magazine. The early dramas of Michael Field, the composite pseudonym of Katherine Harris Bradley (1860–1914) and Edith Emma Cooper (1862–1913), had been a youthful passion of Yeats's.*

By the time of this review, Yeats's enthusiasm had evidently waned. Yeats's disillusionment with Michael Field was not permanent, however, for he included nine poems by them in his Oxford Book of Modern Verse *(Oxford, 1936). Nor was Yeats always so dogmatically opposed to works of art serving as inspiration for poetry, at least for his own later poems.*

There is a long, rather unsympathetic reminiscence of Yeats in Works and Days, From the Journal of Michael Field *(London, 1933). "Michael Field" found Yeats to be ". . . not one of us—he is a preacher. He preaches some excellent things and some foolish things." In 1903 Yeats refused their play* Deirdre *for production at the Abbey Theatre.*

According to Allan Wade, among Yeats's papers there are parts of a manuscript review of Michael Field's plays The Father's Tragedy, William Rufus, *and* Loyalty in Love *(1885), but the place of publication of the review, if any, is unknown.*

This interesting, suggestive and thoroughly unsatisfactory book is a new instance of the growing tendency to make the critical faculty do the work of the creative. 'The aim of this little volume is, as far as may be', says the preface, 'to translate into verse what the lines and colours of certain chosen pictures sing in themselves; to express not so much what these pictures are to the poet, but rather what poetry they objectively incarnate.'[1] That is to say, the two ladies[2] who hide themselves behind the pen-name of Michael Field have set to work to observe and interpret a number of pictures, instead of singing out of their own hearts and setting to music their own souls. They have poetic feeling and imagination in abundance, and yet they have preferred to work with the studious and interpretive side of the mind and write a guidebook to the picture galleries of Europe, instead of giving us a book full of the emotions and fancies which must be crowding in upon their minds perpetually. They seem to have thought it incumbent upon them to do something serious, something worthy of an age of text-books, something that would have uniformity and deliberate intention, and be in no wise given over to that unprincipled daughter of whim and desire whom we call imagination.

We open the book at a venture, and come to a poem on Benozzo Gozzoli's 'Treading the Press'.[3]

> From the trellis hang the grapes
>   Purple deep;[4]
> Maidens with white, curving napes
>   And coiled hair backward leap,
> As they catch the fruit, mid laughter,
> Cut from every silvan rafter.
>
> Baskets, over-filled with fruit,
>   From their heads
> Down into the press they shoot
>   A white-clad peasant treads,
> Firmly crimson circles smashing
> Into must with his feet's thrashing.
>
> Wild and rich the oozings pour
>   From the press;
> Leaner grows the tangled store
>   Of vintage, ever less:
> Wine that kindles and entrances
> Thus is made by one who dances.

The last couplet has some faint shadow of poetry, perhaps, but as for the rest—well, it is neither more nor less than *The Spanish Gypsy*[†] again.[5] It is impossible not to respect it, impossible not to admire the careful massing of detail, but no man will ever feel his eyes suffuse with tears or his heart leap with joy when he reads it. There are scores of other verses in the book which are as like it as one pea is to another. None of them have any sustained music, for music is the garment of emotion and passion, but all are well put together with carefully chosen rhymes, out of the way adjectives and phrases full of minute observation. Having looked in vain for anything conspicuously better or worse than the lines we have quoted, we open the book again at a venture, and find a poem on Cosimo Tura's 'St. Jerome'.[6] We quote the first two stanzas:

> Saint Jerome kneels within the wilderness;
> Along the cavern's sandy channels press
> The flowings of deep water. On one knee,
> On one foot he rests his weight—
> A foot that rather seems to be
> The clawed base of a pillar past all date
> Than prop of flesh and bone;
> About his sallow, osseous frame
> A cinder-coloured clock is thrown
> For ample emblem of his shame.
>
> Grey are the hollowed rocks, grey is his head
> And grey his beard, formal and as dread[7]
> As some Assyrian's on a monument,
> From the chin is sloping down.
> O'er his tonsure heaven has bent
> A solid disc of unillumined brown;
> His scarlet hat is flung
> Low on the pebbles by a shoot
> Of tiny nightshade that among
> The pebbles has maintained a root.

These stanzas do not contain a single commonplace simile or trite adjective, the authors even prefer 'osseous' to 'bony' in their search for the unexpected. There is intellectual agility in every sentence, and yet of what account are these verses, or any number like them? They are simply unmitigated guide-book.

One regrets the faults of this book the more because they are faults which have for some time been growing on 'Michael Field'. *Callirrhoë*[8] had imagination and fancy in plenty, and we hoped its authors would in time get more music and less crudity and at last create a poem of genius. A few years later *Brutus Ultor* came and almost crowned our hopes, but now we have watched and waited for a long time in vain. *Sight and Song*, following as it does *The Tragic Mary*, is enough to make us turn our eyes for ever from the 'false dawn' we believed to be the coming day.

SOME NEW IRISH BOOKS

This review of the collected works of George Savage-Armstrong (9 vols., London, 1891–92); Fand by William Larminie (Dublin, 1892); and Songs of Arcady by Robert J. Reilly (Dublin, 1892) appeared in United Ireland, 23 July 1892.

This review was printed anonymously. However, Yeats admitted the authorship of the Armstrong and Larminie portion in a letter to John O'Leary dated by Kelly and Domville as the week of 23 July 1892. Yeats told O'Leary, "I have Armstrong's collected works—nine volumes—to review for The Bookman, and have given them a preliminary notice, mainly hostile, in this week's United Ireland, also like treatment to Larminie" (CL1, 302–4). For Savage-Armstrong's response to Yeats's hostile review in The Bookman, September 1892, see note 7 in CL1, 303–4.

It seems evident that the Reilly review was written by the author of the Armstrong and Larminie portion. Some miscellaneous historical volumes were included in the same column, but Wade thought them not the work of Yeats.

George Francis Savage-Armstrong (1845–1906) was professor of history and English at Queen's College, Cork. His English loyalties are evident in his "Victoria Regina et Imperatrix, a Jubilee Song from Ireland," 1887. In his Bookman review of September 1892 ("'Noetry' and Poetry," see pp. 180–81), Yeats was less caustic and even quoted a part of Armstrong's dialogue atop Lugnaquilla. He had made an enemy, however, and in 1898 Yeats recounted to Lady Gregory a public quarrel with Armstrong. The latter had denounced the Irish Literary Movement in a public lecture and had claimed that the work of dissenters from Gaeldom like himself was boycotted. Yeats replied with the charge that Armstrong, a West Briton, was ignorant of contemporary Ireland in and out of literature (CL2, 231–32).

We have here before us, bound in solid blue covers and printed on thick paper, the most substantial edition of the collected works of any Irish poet which has appeared for many years. Mr. Allingham's slim vellum-backed volumes, and Aubrey de Vere's three or four big green ones, cannot compete with Mr. Armstrong's nine, some of which have more than four hundred pages apiece. What public they are intended for it is hard to imagine, for there is little, indeed, in *The Tragedy of Israel,* or *Ugone,* or in the prolonged rhetoric of *Poems: Lyrical* and *Dramatic,* to stir the soul of man. Mr. Armstrong has cut himself off from the life of the nation in which his days are passed, and has suffered the inevitable penalty. He has tried to be an Englishman and to write as an Englishman, instead of reflecting the life that is about him, the history of which every hillside must remind him, and the legends the women murmur over the fire in the cabins by the roadside. An Irishman might possibly succeed in writing and thinking as the best Englishmen do if he left Ireland in his childhood and threw himself wholly into the life of his adopted country; but if he lives here he must choose between expressing in noble forms the life and passion of this nation, or being the beater of the air all his days. Despite his very genuine poetic feeling and obvious intellectual forces Mr. Armstrong has, we believe, written but one volume with which the future will feel any concern whatever, and that is his one book upon an Irish theme—*Stories of Wicklow.*[1] Despite an obvious unfamiliarity with the Celtic feeling and the Celtic traditions of this country he has written in this one book many pages for which we feel heartily grateful. Even at his best in blank verse he has made the dialogue on the top of Lugnaquilla[2] entirely moving, glowing, and beautiful. The more humorous parts of the book are a little touched with that conventionality of feeling which seems inseparable from West Britonism.

Mr. Larminie[3] is, on the other hand, Irish enough, and, so far as his metres go, quite unconventional, but then he does not show at present the same innate poetic faculty as that which Mr. Armstrong has thrown away through a false philosophy of life. At the same time Mr. Larminie may do better when he has either abandoned or perfected the experimental rhythmic metres he has invented. He will probably find they are a mistake, for a metre is the slow growth of time and is evolved as blank verse was evolved in the last two or three centuries, to meet some practical need. That he can do fairly well now and then, despite his metres, is plain enough from the following:

'Ghosts of day's thoughts are dreams,
Beautiful shapes benign,

Or hateful, hideous, and evil;
Phantom growth of the seeds
That are sown in the hours of our waking;
Blossoms of brightest hue and scent most sweet—
Or airs—odorous, poison-laden.
Therefore, if death be night and life be day,
Take heed unto day's thoughts that they be fair,
And fair shall be the shapes that haunt thy sleep:
A garden of sweet flowers thy soul shall be:
Let thy dreams come!
Thou shalt have fear of none.'4

The thought in these lines is poetical; but it loses rather than gains from the metre into which it is thrown. There are plenty of passages of equal or greater interest in the two long legendary poems, 'Fand' and 'Moytura',15 which make up the bulk of the volume.

Mr. O'Reilly's6 *Songs of Arcady*† are anything but experimental in their metres. He prefers the oldest and the simplest forms of verse, and for the most part uses them with admirable effect. Simple, sincere, and lucid, his poetry will delight its little class of readers and delight them all the more because it is wholly without ambition and as quiet and unobtrusive as the tasteful brown paper cover in which Messrs. Sealy, Bryers, and Walker have bound it up. If we were writing at any other time than now, when election news and election gossip treads into even smaller compass the narrow space a newspaper can allow to the reviews of verse, we would gladly quote a poem or two, but can do no more as things are than dismiss the little book with a hearty God-speed.

DUBLIN SCHOLASTICISM
AND TRINITY COLLEGE

This article appeared in United Ireland, *30 July 1892. Yeats had not attended Trinity College, Dublin, although his father was a graduate and had wanted his son to go there. Yeats's lifelong hostility to learned institutions was particularly intense in his youth, although in old age he lamented his lack of knowledge of the Greek language.*

Yeats's disdain for Trinity in 1892 was partly caused by the hostility of English literature professor Edward Dowden toward the Irish Literary Movement. More specifically, though, on 2 June 1892, The Dublin Daily Express had printed a letter by Yeats about the ongoing scheme for the publication of a series of Irish books. Therein Yeats said, "These books and lectures will be national but not political in any narrow sense of the word. They will endeavour to make the patriotism of the people who read them both deeper and more enlightened, and will set before them the national and legendary heroes as they present themselves to the minds of scholars and thinkers" (CL1, 299–300). In a 3 June leader, the Express spoke of the literary talent in the Trinity College Senior Common Room. The suggestion drew from Yeats this article (Foster I, 120).

In 1910, when Edward Dowden fell ill, Yeats was considered for his position. See Foster I, pp. 429–31.

I am writing in the National Library,[1] and as I look around me I see a great number of young men reading medical, mathematical, and other text-books, many of them with their note-books open before them. Opposite me is a student deep in medical diagrams, and on my right is another with an algebraical work on the bookrest in front of him. And as the readers are to-day, so were they yesterday, and the day before, and the day before that again, and back as far as the memory of any frequenter of the library can carry him. The glacial weight of scholasticism[2] is over the room and over all the would-be intellectual life of

Dublin. Nobody in this great library is doing any disinterested reading, nobody is poring over any book for the sake of the beauty of its
words, for the glory of its thought, but all are reading that they may
pass an examination; no one is trying to develop his personal taste, but
all are endeavoring to force their minds into the mould made for them
by professors and examiners. What wonder is it that publishers complain that no book is bought in Dublin unless it be the text-book for
some examination, that alone among the great cities of the United Kingdom Dublin is deaf to the voice of genius—deafened by the roar of politics on the one hand and lulled into the deadly sleep of scholasticism
upon the other.

Let it be admitted that we are a poor nation, and must seize upon
every chance of making 'an honest penny' out of intermediate examinations and college scholarships, even at the expense of much travail
of the soul, much blinding and deafening of the personal inspiration
that is or should be in every one of us, and of most dire dilution[†] of the
whole man. Let this be admitted, and yet the explanation does not lie
here, for half the energy we have given to covering the roads with bicy-
cles and to all manner of muscular occupations would have made us
both a reading and reasonable people. I know poor clerks in London
who read the best books with entire delight and devotion, while here
in Dublin countless numbers of fairly-leisured and well-to-do men and
women hardly know the very names of the great writers of the day. Nay,
further, they do not know the commonest legends or the most famous
poems of their own land. Here in this very library, called National, there
are Greek grammars in profusion and an entire wilderness of text-books
of every genera and species, and but the meagrest sprinkling of books
of Irish poetry and Irish legends. The library authorities are little if at
all to blame, for they would get them if they were asked for. The blame
is upon the teaching institutions which have given us scholasticism for
our god.

I was four or five years at an English school and then four or five
years at an Irish one,[3] and I found in the contrast much to ponder and
remember. In England every clever boy had his hobby—literature,
entomology, or what not. In Ireland every energy of the kind was discouraged and trampled upon, for the shadow of scholasticism was over
all and the great god of examinations ruled supreme. But the worst
blame does not lie at the door of the schools, but rather at the door of
the university which gives them their tone and is the very centre of their
life. As Dublin Castle[4] with the help of the police keeps Ireland for England, so Trinity College with the help of the schoolmasters keeps the
mind of Ireland for scholasticism with its accompanying weight of
mediocrity. All noble life, all noble thought, depends primarily upon

enthusiasm, and Trinity College, in abject fear of the National enthusiasm which is at her gates, has shut itself off from every kind of ardour, from every kind of fiery and exultant life. She has gone over body and soul to scholasticism, and scholasticism is but an aspect of the great god, Dagon of the Philistines. 'She has given herself to many causes that have not been my causes, but never to the Philistines', Matthew Arnold wrote once of Oxford.[5] Alas, that we can but invert the sentences when we speak of our own University—'Never to any cause, but always to the Philistines', is written over her chimneys. She has piped to us, and we have danced at her bidding, and flung our caps into the air; but let us not refrain from saying, even with the Tercentenary uproar[6] still in our ears, that she has no great part in the higher life of the people. Let us not sentimentalize over her, but let us grant her all that she has, her mathematics, and her metaphysics, and then acknowledge that a tractarian movement, or a single poet of the rank of Arnold or of Clough even,[7] were more than all these things, for not out of any logic mill, but out of prolonged and fiery ardour and an ever present consciousness of the overshadowing mysteries of life, emerges the soul of man and the heroic heart.

In that attempt to bring a true cultivation into the minds of the people of Ireland, which was sketched out by Sir Charles Gavan Duffy in his speech last Saturday, we will have to reckon with the apathy of all the Trinity College personages, and with the certain apathy and the probable hostility of all scholastic persons outside its walls, and with the antagonism of the shallow persiflage which passes for wit among those who have not even the perverted convictions of which Blake speaks when he says that the foolish man has been compelled by God 'to defend a lie that enthusiasm and life may not cease'.[8] We have more to expect from the Orangemen of the North who 'defend' their 'lie' than from the West Britons of the South who have not fire enough to defend even a falsehood.[9]

A NEW POET

Yeats reviewed Edwin J. Ellis's Fate in Arcadia *(London, 1892) in* The Bookman *of September 1892.*

Ellis (1848–1916) was an old friend of John Butler Yeats, and from 1889 he had been collaborating with W. B. on their edition of Blake. *With all this, Yeats could hardly play the objective critic—as he himself admitted.*

Ellis contributed to The Bookman *an article on Bernard Quaritch (July 1893), the publisher of the Yeats-Ellis edition of Blake, and an article on Blake by Ellis appeared in February 1893. For Yeats's private opinion of Ellis as a poet, see Au 143–44. Yeats also reviewed Ellis's* Seen in Three Days *in* The Bookman *of February 1894 (see pp. 229–32), and he was then less successful in concealing his inability to follow Ellis's symbolism.*

The majority of books of verse impress the reader with the conviction that the feeling and thoughts they contain have been invented for the sake of the poems. It is rare to come across a book where the poems have all been written obviously for the sake of the feelings and thoughts, where the verses seem to come out of a great depth of emotion which exists for itself alone, where every beautiful image and simile is but, as it were, the embroidered hem of the garment of reverie which wraps its author's life about. When we do meet with such books we make them our continual companions, and admit them into the secret fellowship of the soul. Such a book is Mr. Edwin Ellis's *Fate in Arcadia*.[1] Exquisite as the verse constantly is, it is almost impossible to criticise it as verse alone, 'for he who touches this book touches a man', as Whitman puts it,[2] and one is tempted to write rather of the beliefs and fancies and moods that are in it as one would of the spoken words of some deep thinking and much experienced person. Most books of poetry are collections of isolated poems which gain little from each other, but here every verse seems the deeper because of the all-pervading personality of the writer. The very defects of the book, its occasional obscurity, and the careless way in which the stanzas are built every now and then, come from excess, and not, as is commonly the case, from lack of personality—everything is vitalised, though often vitalised awry. In drawing attention to such a book for the first time, however, it is the duty of the reviewer to praise its excellences, and leave the discussion of its defects to those coming years whose more considerate judgment it is destined to challenge.

The name-poem, an Arcadian drama of about thirty pages, though full of beautiful things, is not, I think, so good as several of the lyrics, notably, 'The Hermit Answered', 'The Maid Well Loved',[3] 'The Maid's Confession', 'Thrice Lost', 'Outcast', and that strange poem, perhaps the most powerful in the book, 'Himself'. 'Himself' is the lament of the selfhood of Christ, the outcry of that portion of humanity which is perpetually sacrificed for great causes and great faiths. The poet comes to Golgotha, and sees there a phantom Christ upon a phantom cross, and listens to the terrible cry, 'Eli, Eli, thou hast forsaken me'.[4] Thus the phantom complains in the night:

> Where is the life I might have known
> If God had never lit on me?
> I might have loved one heart alone,
> A woman white as chastity.
>
> I might have hated devils, and fled
> Whene'er they came. I might have turned
> From sinners, and I might have led
> A life where no sin-knowledge burned.
>
> But between voice and voice I chose,
> Of these two selves, and clave to this—
> Who left me here, where no man knows,
> And fled to dwell with light in bliss.
>
> Oh, you who still have voice and deed,
> Call Eli! Eli call, my soul;
> But if He comes to thee and plead
> That thou shalt let him have the whole
>
> Of all thy will and life, and be
> Christ come again by flesh of thine;
> Thou, too, shalt know what came to me
> Then, when I bound my selfhood fine,

And called it Satan for His sake,
    And lived, and saved the world, and died
Only for Him, my Light, to make
    His joy, who floated from my side,

And left me here with wound of spears,
    A cast-off ghostly shade, to rave
And haunt the place for endless years,
    Crying, 'Himself He cannot save.'

So spake the ghost of Joseph's son,[5]
    Haunting the place where Christ was slain:
I pray that e'er this world be done,
    Christ may relieve his piteous pain.

Is not this poem one of those startling imaginations which illuminate thought and emotion with their strange light, and which, when
once known, can never be forgotten? I find something of the same
curious depth of feeling in the little lyric called 'Outcast'—

When God, the ever-living, makes
    His home in deathly winter frost,
And God, the ever-loving, wakes
    In hardening eyes of women lost,
Then through the midnight moves a wraith:
Open the door, for this is Faith.

Open the door, and bring her in,
    And stir thy heart's poor fires that shrink.
Ah, fear to see her pale and thin.
    Give love and dreams to eat and drink;
For Faith may faint in wandering by—[6]
In that day thou shalt surely die.

The lyrics on lighter themes and in lighter manner are a great contrast to those I have just quoted. Could anything be prettier and
brighter than the following poem, called 'Thrice Lost'?—

First his parents said they lost him,
No one knew where to accost him,
    Though his loss had made no showing,
    He was there, and yet no knowing
    Where he was—he was but growing.

Yet his parents said they lost him
And the secret to accost him.

Then his friends found out they missed him
It was since a maid had kissed him.
  And with no great outward seeming
  He went through the world of dreaming,
  And this loss had no redeeming.
No one knew the maid had kissed him;
Quite in vain they said they missed him.

Now the world of busy men
Cannot find him once again,
  While he seeks in vain to nerve them
  To high duty, and to serve them.
  He can make, not break, nor curve them;
For, outgrowing busy men,
Like a child, he's lost again.[7]

I have quoted enough from this book to prove its varied power and its constant possession of that greater beauty which, according to the Elizabethan, cannot be without strangeness.[8] He who buys it will have obtained a wise comrade and an ever-fascinated friend.

'NOETRY' AND POETRY

Yeats's review of the nine volumes of George Savage-Armstrong's (1845–1906) verse and drama appeared in The Bookman *of September 1892. Yeats had reviewed these volumes previously in* United Ireland *of 23 July 1892, and there he had accused Savage-Armstrong of the literary treason of "West Britonism." The Bookman review finds fault on purely literary grounds.*

A friend of mine[1] is accustomed to say that there is poetry and there is prose, and a something which, though often most interesting, and even moving, is yet neither one nor the other. To this he applies the curious term 'noetry'; a word ingenious persons derive from the Greek word nous, and consider descriptive of verse which though full of intellectual faculty, is lacking in imaginative impulse. I do not know my friend's own derivation of his word, but find 'noetry', whatever its derivation be, a term of most constant utility. Mr. Savage-†Armstrong[2] has published nine volumes, of which seven are 'noetry' pure and simple, and the remainder a compound of 'noetry' and authentic poetry itself, and these nine volumes he has just gathered into 'a collected edition' (Longmans† and Co.). There are first his early verses, *Poems Lyrical and Dramatic*, which are rhetoric and nothing better; and then there are *Ugone* in one, and the *Tragedy of Israel* in three volumes, and of these plays be it said that they are of the kind that neither gods nor men nor booksellers can tolerate,[3] and after these come *A Garland from Greece*† and *Stories of Wicklow*, two very readable and pleasant works, especially in their blank verse parts, and *Mephistopheles in Broadcloth*, a rather crude satire; and last of all, *One in the Infinite*, a work more or less religious, in not very musical lyric stanzas.

When one has flung by the board the seven volumes of 'noetry', one finds that after all there does remain in the Greek and Irish poems a very fairly bulky collection of more or less interesting verse—all the more interesting because Mr. Armstrong takes the world and his own mission very seriously. The trifler is too much with us, and it is a pleasure to find a poet who is best when writing of the most weighty themes and in the most lofty metrical forms. In an age of lyrical poets, it is good, by way of change, to meet with one who is most at home in the full dress of blank verse, and evidently uncomfortable in the *deshabille* of lighter measures. 'The Oracle' in the Greek book and 'Lugnaquillia'[†] in the Wicklow book, are typical of his power over great themes and great metres. In the first, three old priests of Apollo lament together the decay of the old faith and the coming in of the new, and in the second a circle of Irish students, who have climbed to the top of Lugnaquilla[†] to see the sunrise, discourse of faith and immortality in cadences not wholly unworthy of the beauty of the scene and of the solemn hour. One talks of doubt, and one of earth and its pleasures in which he finds sufficient joy without seeking a life beyond. A third bursts forth in lofty affirmation of immortality:

> "And if you ask me what the vision is
> That lures my heart I answer, 'Tis a dream
> Of life unending and invulnerable;
> A life of tranquil joy; communion close
> With Godlike spirits in untroubled love;
> Glad operance in the labours infinite
> Of the dread Mind that shapes the infinite worlds;
> Of ever-widening knowledge of the cause,
> And birth and growth of the innumerable,
> Immeasurable products of that Mind;
> A life of motion and of rapturous toil
> That fevers not nor strains; of ministering help
> In angel-errands on from orb to orb;
> Of painless conflict with the powers confused
> Of Chaos and of Darkness; and the shaping
> Of Light, of Beauty, Order, Peace and Law."[4]

We have here Mr. Armstrong at his best, and it is a best more than once reached in other parts of the volume. The whole book is full of Wicklow scenes and Wicklow memories, and may well prove a companionable friend to many a Wicklow scholar, and stand on his shelves side by side with the local history, and commemorate for a generation or two Mr. Armstrong's name and keep him a king among his own people. Some may even grow curious enough to turn over the pages of the Greek book, and they shall have their reward. As for the other volumes—well, time takes heavy toll from the best, and for 'noetry' in all its shapes and fashions, has neither mercy nor tolerance.

INVOKING THE IRISH FAIRIES

This article appeared in the first issue (October 1892) of The Irish Theosophist. *The initials signed at the end, "D.E.D.I.," represent the Latin phrase "Demon est deus inversus," or in English, "A demon is an inverted god." These initials are known to have been those assumed by Yeats when he joined the Order of the Golden Dawn in March 1890, a short time before he was expelled from the Esoteric Section of Madame Blavatsky's Theosophical Society in London. John Kelly notes that he took it from "the chapter-title of Section IX, Part II, Book I, of Madame Blavatsky's* The Secret Doctrine *(1888)" (CL3, 27).*

This account of a trance is filled with learning that Yeats would have been acquiring as he passed through the first stages of initiation in the Golden Dawn. His companion, "D.D.," was probably Florence Farr ("S.S.D.D." in the Golden Dawn). According to Kelly, "S.S.D.D." stood for "Sapientia Sapienti Dona Data (Wisdom is Given to the Wise as a Gift)" (CL3, 25).

The Irish Theosophist *was the magazine of the Dublin Theosophical Society. AE was the guiding spirit of this branch of the society, and the magazine was edited by David M. Dunlop. Yeats, though never formally a member, took part in some of the group's activities. For another account of a trance attended by Yeats, see "The Sorcerers" in* The Celtic Twilight.

The Occultist and student of Alchemy whom I shall call D. D. and myself sat at opposite sides of the fire one morning, wearied with symbolism and magic. D. D. had put down a kettle to boil. We were accustomed to meet every now and then, that we might summon the invisible powers and gaze into the astral light; for we had learned to see with the internal eyes. But this morning we knew not what to summon, for we had already on other mornings invoked that personal vision of impersonal good which men name Heaven, and that personal vision of impersonal evil, which men name Hell. We had called up likewise, the trees of knowledge and of life, and we had studied the hidden meaning of the Zodiac,[1] and enquired under what groups of stars, the various events of the bible story were classified by those dead Occultists who held all things, from the firmament above to the waters under the Earth, to be but symbol and again symbol. We had gone to ancient Egypt, seen the burial of her dead and heard mysterious talk of Isis and Osiris.[2] We had made the invisible powers interpret for us the mystic tablet of Cardinal Bembo,[3] and we had asked of the future and heard words of dread and hope. We had called up the Klippoth[4] and in terror seen them rush by like great black rams, and now we were a little weary of shining colours and sweeping forms. 'We have seen the great and they have tired us', I said; 'let us call the little for a change. The Irish fairies may be worth the seeing; there is time for them to come and go before the water is boiled.'

I used a lunar invocation and left the seeing mainly to D. D. She saw first a thin cloud as though with the ordinary eyes and then with the interior sight, a barren mountain crest with one ragged tree. The leaves and branches of the tree were all upon one side, as though it had been blighted by the sea winds. The Moon shone through the branches and a white woman stood beneath them. We commanded this woman to show us the fairies of Ireland marshalled in order. Immediately a great multitude of little creatures appeared, with green hair like sea-weed and after them another multitude dragging a car containing an enormous bubble. The white woman, who appeared to be their queen, said the first were the water fairies and the second the fairies of the air. The first were called the Gelki and the second the Gieri (I have mislaid my notes and am not quite certain if I give their names correctly). They passed on and a troop who were like living flames followed and after them a singular multitude whose bodies were like the stems of flowers and their dresses like the petals. These latter fairies after a while, stood still under a green bush from which dropped honey like dew and thrust out their tongues, which were so long, that they were able to lick the honey-covered ground without stooping. These two troops were the fairies of the fire and the fairies of the earth.

The white woman told us that these were the good fairies and that she would now bring D. D. to the fairies of evil. Soon a great abyss appeared and in the midst was a fat serpent, with forms, half animal, half human, polishing his heavy scales. The name of this serpent was Grew-grew and he was the chief of the wicked goblins. About him moved quantities of things like pigs, only with shorter legs, and above him in the air flew vast flocks of cherubs and bats. The bats, however, flew with their heads down and the cherubs with their foreheads lower than their winged chins.—I was at the time studying a mystic system that makes this inversion of the form a mark of certain types of evil spirits, giving it much the same significance as is usually given to the inverted pentagram.[15] This system was unknown to D. D. whose mind was possibly, however, overshadowed for the moment by mine; the invoking mind being always more positive than the mind of the seer.— Had she been invoking the conditions would have been reversed.

Presently the bats and cherubs and the forms that a moment before had been polishing the scales of Grew-grew, rushed high up into the air and from an opposite direction appeared the troops of the good fairies, and the two kingdoms began a most terrible warfare. The evil fairies hurled burning darts but were unable to approach very near to the good fairies, for they seemed unable to bear the neighbourhood of pure spirits. The contest seemed to fill the whole heavens, for as far as the sight could go the clouds of embattled goblins went also. It is that contest of the minor forces of good and evil which knows no hour of peace but goes on everywhere and always. The fairies are the lesser spiritual moods of that universal mind, wherein every mood is a soul and every thought a body.[6] Their world is very different from ours, and they can but appear in forms borrowed from our limited consciousness, but nevertheless, every form they take and every action they go through, has its significance and can be read by the mind trained in the correspondence of sensuous form and supersensuous meaning.

D.E.D.I.

HOPES AND FEARS
FOR IRISH LITERATURE

This article, from United Ireland, *15 October 1892, presents with great clarity the dilemma that faced Yeats in the early 1890s. In London he was a founder and active member in the "Rhymers' Club," a group of aesthetes notably indifferent to politics, which met at the "Cheshire Cheese," to read and discuss each other's poems. In Dublin his Rhymers' aestheticism was exchanged for the patriotic fervor of a man committed to the expression of Irish culture in literary form.*

He tried to combine the best of both cities and thus pleased neither. His London literary friends thought that he was wasting his poetic gifts on Irish literary politics. In Dublin his view of life was considered too remote and delicate for nationalistic struggles. Though he did not succeed in uniting such extreme views, he was successful in mitigating the faults of both. He lured the aesthete Lionel Johnson into supporting the Irish cause, and in Dublin he made it increasingly difficult for patriotic fervor alone to pass for poetic genius.

When I come over here from London or cross over to London I am always struck afresh by the difference between the cultivated people in England and the cultivated people—alas! too few—here in Ireland. They could not differ more if they were divided from each other by a half score of centuries. I am thinking especially of the men of my own age, though not entirely of them. In England amongst the best minds art and poetry are becoming every day more entirely ends in themselves, and all life is made more and more but so much fuel to feed their fire. It is partly the influence of France that is bringing this about. In France a man may do anything he pleases, he may spend years in prison even, like Verlaine,[1] and the more advanced of the young men will speak well of him if he have but loved his art sincerely, and they will worship his name as they worship Verlaine's if he have but made beautiful things and added a little to the world's store of memorable experiences. The influence of France is every year pervading more completely English literary life. The influence of that school which calls itself, in the words of its leader, Verlaine, a school of the sunset, or by the term which was flung at it 'as a reproach, and caught up as a battle cry', Decadents[12] is now the dominating thing in many lives. Poetry is an end in itself; it has nothing to do with thought, nothing to do with philosophy, nothing to do with life, nothing to do with anything but the music of cadence, and beauty of phrase. This is the new doctrine of letters. I well remember the irritated silence that fell upon a noted gathering[3] of the younger English imaginative writers once, when I tried to explain a philosophy of poetry in which I was profoundly interested, and to show the dependence, as I conceived it, of all great art and literature upon conviction and upon heroic life. To them literature had ceased to be the handmaid of humanity, and become instead a terrible queen, in whose services the stars rose and set, and for whose pleasure life stumbles along in the darkness. There is a good deal to be said in favour of all this. Never before, perhaps, were men so anxious to write their best—as they conceive that best—and so entirely loth to bow to the prejudices of the multitude. There is much to be said even for Verlaine, for he who writes well and lives badly is usually of more service to the world at large than he who writes badly and lives well, and he is always better than the crowd who do both indifferently. But one thing cannot be said. It is not possible to call a literature produced in this way the literature of energy and youth. The age which has produced it is getting old and feeble, and sits in the chimney-corner carving all manner of curious and even beautiful things upon the staff that can no longer guide its steps. Here in Ireland we are living in a young age, full of hope and promise—a young age which has only just begun to make its literature. It was only yesterday that it cut from the green hillside the staff which is to help its steps upon the long road. There is no carving upon the staff, the rough bark is still there, and the knots are many upon its side.

When I talk to people of literary ambition here in Ireland, I find them holding that literature must be the expression of conviction, and be the garment of noble emotion and not an end in itself. I found them most interested in the literary forms that give most opportunity for the display of great characters and great passions. Turning to our literature I find that such forms are plenty, often absolutely crude and uninteresting, as in the case of MacCarthy's[†] 'Ferdiah',[†] and Joyce's *Blanid;* occasionally crude and interesting, like Joyce's *Deirdre,* and Ferguson's *Congal;* and once or twice beyond all praise and all imitation like Ferguson's *Conary,* and his better known 'Vengeance of the Welshmen of Tirawley.'[4] But side by side with this robustness and rough energy of ours there goes most utter indifference to art, the most dire carelessness, the most dreadful intermixture of the commonplace. I have before me a letter from a young man in a remote part of Ireland asking an opinion about some verses and telling me, as if it was a special merit, that he did them at great speed, two columns in an hour, I think. I have not yet read his poems; but it is obvious that good poetry cannot be done in this fashion. There is a printed letter of John Francis O'Donnell's,[5] in which he claims to have written I know not how many columns of verse and prose in two or three days. Yet, he who would write a memorable song must be ready to give often days to a few lines, and be ready, perhaps, to pay for it afterwards with certain other days of dire exhaustion and depression, and, if he would be remembered when he is in his grave, he must give to his art the devotion the Crusaders of old gave to their cause and be content to be alone among men, apart alike from their joys and their sorrows, having for companions the multitude of his dreams and for reward the kingdom of his pride. He who would belong to things eternal must for the most part renounce his allotted place amid the things of time. Here in Ireland the art of living interests us greatly, and the art of writing but little. We seek effectiveness rather than depth. We produce good correspondents, good journalists, and good talkers, and few profound and solitary students. 'You Irish people', said a witty woman to me once, 'will never have a future because you have a present.' 'We are', said a famous Irishman[6] to me, 'too poetical to be poets, we are the greatest talkers since the Greeks, we are a nation of brilliant failures.' I no more complain of this absorption in mere living than I complain of the narrow devotion to mere verbal beauty of the newest generation of literary men in France and England. We have the limitations of dawn. They have the limitations of sunset. We also in the coming centuries will grow into the broad noon and pass on at last into twilight and darkness.

Can we but learn a little of their skill, and a little of their devotion to form, a little of their hatred of the commonplace and the banal, we may make all these restless energies of ours alike the inspiration and the theme of a new and wonderful literature. We have behind us in the past the most moving legends and a history full of lofty passions. If we can but take that history and those legends and turn them into dramas, poems, and stories full of the living soul of the present, and make them massive with conviction and profound with reverie, we may deliver that new great utterance for which the world is waiting. Men are growing tired of mere subtleties of form, self-conscious art and no less self-conscious simplicity. But if we are to do this we must study all things Irish, until we know the peculiar glamour that belongs to this nation, and how to distinguish it from the glamour of other countries and other races. 'Know thyself'[7] is a true advice for nations as well as for individuals. We must know and feel our national faults and limitations no less than our national virtues, and care for things Gaelic and Irish, not because we hold them better than things Saxon and English, but because they belong to us, and because our lives are to be spent among them, whether they be good or evil. Whether the power that lies latent in this nation is but the seed of some meagre shrub or the seed from which shall rise the vast and spreading tree[8] is not for us to consider. It is our duty to care for that seed and tend it until it has grown to perfection after its kind.

THE DEATH OF OENONE

Yeats's review of The Death of Oenone, Akbar's Dream, and Other Poems (London, 1892) appeared in The Bookman of December 1892. Alfred, Lord Tennyson had died on 6 October 1892. The Bookman, along with many other literary journals of the English-speaking world, was full of retrospective notices and appreciations. This magazine held a symposium of four letters from poets on the question of Tennyson's successor in the laureateship. The second letter was from Yeats, as he admitted in a letter to John O'Leary (CL1, 327–28). In his statement (CL1, 324–26), he pleaded for a broader interpretation of the office of the laureate, and he put forward the names of William Morris and Algernon Charles Swinburne, although he admitted that neither poet could accept the office as it was then defined.

This review could hardly give Yeats's whole mind on the subject of the great Victorians. In the introduction to his Oxford Book of Modern Verse (1936) he offered a catalog of Victorian faults, which included, ". . . irrelevant descriptions of nature, the scientific and moral discursiveness of In Memoriam . . . , the political eloquence of Swinburne, the psychological curiosity of Browning, and the poetical diction of everybody" (p. ix). At a banquet honoring Wilfred Blunt in January 1914, Yeats said, "We are now at the end of Victorian romance—completely at an end. One may admire Tennyson, but one can not read him . . ." (quoted in A Poet's Life by Harriet Monroe [New York, 1938]). How complete an end of Victorianism Yeats and his friends had reached in January 1914, they had no way of knowing.

Modern writers, the great no less than the small among them, have been heavily handicapped by being born in a lyrical age, and thereby compelled for the most part to break up their inspiration into many glints and glimmers, instead of letting it burn in one steady flame. A hundred years hence their work will seem to lack largeness and simplicity when compared with the work of an earlier time. It is true that they have their compensations, for the glints and glimmers find their way into many a corner and cranny that never could be reached by the great light of a *Divine Comedy* or an *Iliad*,[1] for lyrics are very easy to read and remember when compared to the long masterpieces into which men put their whole lives and their whole beings. It is true also that while a writer lives men are too near him to judge him as a whole, and that it takes generations before he sinks far enough into the distance for his palace of art to stand clear against the heavens. Let the lyric poet eat, drink, and be merry for some to-morrow his work in its totality will be compared with those great buildings of the past which were built out of so great stones and upon so magnificently simple a plan, and beside them it may seem like a phantastic and flimsy pagoda. Lord Tennyson seems to have felt this with ever-increasing intensity, for despite the discouragement of critics, who long would have it that he was a lyrist and nothing else, and the disappointment of the public, who cried out for ever-new lyrics, he attempted great work after great work, now triumphing with *The Idylls of the King,* and now failing dismally with *Queen Mary* and *Harold,* and battling between failure and victory with *Becket.*[12] For long it seemed as though his latter years were to be given wholly to such experiment and the lyrical outburst of the volume called *Tiresias*[3] was a distinct surprise. It is well, perhaps, that this last book of his, his farewell volume, should contain a little fleet of the lyrics that the people love, and no great argosy of drama or epic, built expressly for the high seas of Time. It is well, too, that it should contain, as it does, an epitome of his latest manner, alike in its faults and its virtues, and so bring him the nearer to us. The new Oenone is, indeed, but a feeble ghost of the old, and the account of his refusal to cure Paris but mere scene-painting beside the haunting rhythms and lofty melancholy of Mr. Morris' account thereof in *The Earthly Paradise;*[4] but then 'Churchwarden and Curate' is no less a masterpiece than the 'Northern Farmer', and the verse of 'Akbar's Dream', 'Telemachus', 'The Wanderer', and 'Silent Voices'[5] is shining with that vivid personal exaltation which only attained complete development long after he had reached his prime; while 'The Dawn', 'The Making of Man', 'God and the Universe', are charged with that sense of the travail of the world which came to him in its full imaginative significance only when he had dulled with gathering years the too comfortable optimism of the first 'Locksley Hall', and cast angrily away in the second his once great faith in material progress and in that coming day when 'the heavens' would 'fill with commerce, argosies of magic sails, pilots of the purple twilight',[6] and learned to base his dreams alone upon the regeneration of the heart of man. As years passed over him the poet grew not less and the man grew incomparably greater, and this growth was accompanied ever by a shedding off of hopes based upon mere mechanical change and mere scientific or political inventiveness, until at the last his soul came near to standing, as the soul of the poet should, naked under the heavens. In early days a too great sense of the mere corporeal bigness of the universe and of the infinity of its transformations had interfered with his sense of spiritual vastness and of the momentousness of spiritual change, but in his latter days he seems to have grown conscious of this interference. In 'God and the Universe' in the present book, he asks—

> 'Will my tiny spark of being wholly vanish
>   in your deeps and heights?
> Must my day be dark by reason, O ye Heavens,
>   of your boundless nights,
> Rush of suns,[7] and roll of systems, and your
>   fiery clash of meteorites?'—

and then bids himself be of good cheer, for God is in all. Tennyson's attitude towards material things reminds one of the astronomical person with whom Blake quarrelled. The astronomical person bored Blake by talking of the immense distance of the fixed stars until Blake would hear no more, but burst out with, 'I tell you that it is not so, for I touched the heavens with my stick at the end of a dark lane the other night.'[8] To Blake the only real world was the mental world, and the rest was of the stuff that dreams are made of.[9] The heavens were to him merely the limit of the world of thought and feeling, which limit is now near, now far. That they should have seemed so very different, so very real, to Lord Tennyson is made the more strange by his being scarce less of a visionary in some ways than Blake himself, for has he not told us of visions and trances obtained by meditating on the letters of his own name, and how in these visions and trances the spiritual world became 'the clearest of the clear, the surest of the sure'?[10] And has not Mr. Stead just made known to us the startling fact that Lord Tennyson believed himself, like Blake, to be in constant communication with unseen intelligences?[11]

This observation on outer things has its good side, for in it lies the secret of that marvellous picturesque power, that wonderful gift of sight into the world about him. Had he been more Blake-like, or even more Shelley-like, he could never have turned from work so subjective as 'The Silent Voices', 'The Wanderer', 'The God and the Universe', to the miraculous observation and penetrating satire of 'The Churchwarden and the Curate.'[12]

From his penetration into outer things, and his never-ceasing interest in every movement of his age, came too, I doubt not, that exalted reason and inspired temperance which made him kin to Plato. 'Victor Hugo', said Carlyle once to an acquaintance of mine, 'is the greatest poet of the day, for he has most music'—he meant by music, I take it, no mere verbal harmony—'but Tennyson has the most reason'.[13] 'Akbar's Dream' is a supreme instance of this reason, and even Tennyson has written nothing wiser than Akbar's remonstrance with the warring sects:

> He knows Himself, men nor themselves nor Him,
> For every splinter'd fraction of a sect
> Will clamour, 'I am on the Perfect Way,
> All else is to perdition.'
>   Shall the rose
> Cry to the lotus, "No flower thou"? the palm
> Call to the cypress, "I alone am fair"?
> The mango spurn the melon at his foot?
> "Mine is the one fruit Alla† made for man."[14]

THE VISION
OF MACCONGLINNE

The Vision of MacConglinne *or* Aislinge Meic Conglinne, *edited by Kuno Meyer, was reviewed by Yeats for* The Bookman *of February 1893. Yeats borrowed the plot of the "Vision" for his story "The Cru-cifixion of the Outcast" included in* The Secret Rose *(1897). The suc-cessful and victorious medieval bard of the legend is replaced in Yeats's modern version by the outcast artist who is crucified at the end of the story. Yeats gave no indication in his review that Meyer's book was a formidable, scholarly, facing-page translation of this Middle Irish wonder tale, with copious notes.*

This certainly is one of the most singular and suggestive Irish books I have ever come across. It brings before one with very startling vivid-ness that strange mixture of extravagant asceticism and extravagant indulgence, mystical aspiration and gross materialism which we call the Middle Ages. It is a romance, in prose and verse, written down first, according to the surmise of its editor and translator, about the end of the twelfth century. It is the work of a gleeman, or strolling story-teller and juggler, and gets its greatest interest from the fierce attacks upon the monks, and upon the very symbols of religion itself, in which the author avenges the sufferings of his persecuted tribe. The law made the gleemen outlaws, and the Church denied them salvation, and against this double persecution they had but one weapon—satire. *The Vision of MacConglinne* exists to prove that the weapon was both sharp and glittering. The gleeman MacConglinne is described upon the one hand as wise and learned, and such beautiful phrases are put in his mouth as 'my treasure is only in heaven or on earth, in wisdom or in poetry';[1] while the best that can be said of the monks is, 'Ye curs, and ye robbers, and dunghounds, and unlettered brutes, ye shifting, blun-dering, hang-head monks of Cork.'[2] The whole story, too, is but a description of the gradual rout of the monks and the slow triumph of the gleeman, until it leaves him sitting at the right hand of the king.

The plot is a masterpiece. MacConglinne arrives one night at the Guest House of Cork, and finds the fire out and the blanket alive with vermin, 'numerous as the sands of the sea, as sparks of fire, or dew on a May morning, or the stars of heaven.'[3] He makes a great noise singing hymns that he may attract attention, and succeeds at last in awaking the bishop himself, who sends his servant to bring him his 'rations.' These rations are but two lumps of turf and a little straw to make a fire, and some whey water for his supper. MacConglinne is so filled with wrath that he indites a satire upon the bishop and the monks. The bishop, when he hears this, is filled with a great rage, and declares that 'little boys will sing those verses, unless the words are avenged on him who made them.'[4] Accordingly he bids them strip the clothes off the gleeman, beat him almost to death, and dip him in the river Lee,[5] and then put him back into the guest house, naked as he was, and leave him thus until the morning, and in the morning he must be crucified for reviling the Church. He is beaten and dipped in the river accordingly, and in the morning taken to be crucified. He is made to cut down his 'passion-tree' himself, but manages to delay his execution by various ruses, until it is so late that the monks plead with the bishop to postpone it until the next day, for they are hungry and tired. MacConglinne is accordingly tied to a pillar-stone and left there for the night, when he has a vision of a land of plenty, where the lakes are of milk and the houses built of various kinds of food. This vision is told in such a way as to parody those religious visions of monks and saints which were so common at the time. In the morning he tells his tormentors of his vision, reminds them that Cathal,[†] the King of Munster, is tormented by a devouring demon so that he is eating up the whole produce of the land, and declares that it has been revealed to him that the revelation of this vision will cure him. The bishop also, it appears, has had a revelation telling him that MacConglinne can deliver the king. MacConglinne is accordingly released, and sent to the court of Cathal.[†] He explains his mission to Pichan,[†] a great nobleman with whom the king was staying, and begins work by inducing the king to fast for two days by trapping him into an oath to grant him what he will. At the end of the two days he induces Pichan[†] to have the king seized and tied to a pillar. He then spreads great quantities of food before him, and tantalizes Cathal[†] and the demon that possesses him by holding pieces of meat just in front of his mouth, but beyond his reach, and by repeating his vision of plenty the while. At last the demon can bear it no longer, but rushes out to seize a piece of meat, and is caught under an inverted cauldron. Every one then leaves the house, and it is set fire to, and the demon rushes out of it, and after sitting for a while upon the roof of the next house, flies 'into the air among the people of Hell'.[6] The king is now cured and full of gratitude, but the bishop and the monks of Cork still seek to take their prey. The king bids them lodge in court a large sum of money, and he himself will lodge an equal sum in the name of the gleeman, and when the judges have tried the case the money shall go to the winner. The judges decide for the gleeman, and the monks beget them to their monastery discomfited, while their victim remains at court as the guest and friend of the king, and receives for reward 'a cow out of every close in Munsterland, and an ounce for every householder, and a cloak for every church, and a sheep for every house from Carn to Cork.'[7]

Besides the interest of its curious story, the work is crowded with picturesque details of medieval manners and customs, and will be a treasure to the writer of historical romance and to the student of history.

THE WANDERING JEW

Yeats reviewed Robert Buchanan's poem The Wandering Jew: A Christmas Carol *(London: Chatto & Windus, 1893) in* The Bookman *of April 1893.*

The literary controversy involving this book was three months old by the time Yeats's review appeared. The book had been reviewed adversely by Richard Le Gallienne in The Daily Chronicle *of 11 January and in* The Star *of 12 January 1893. Buchanan replied by letter to* The Daily Chronicle, *and a long public controversy followed, largely on the question of whether Christianity was "played out." Le Gallienne capitalized on his position of* defensor fidei *by publishing that same year his* Religion of a Literary Man.

Buchanan was a seasoned literary gladiator. In 1871, under the name of Thomas Maitland, he had provoked a storm of abuse by his article in The Contemporary Review, *"The Fleshly School of Poetry: Mr. D. G. Rossetti." Oddly enough, Buchanan and Yeats had in common a contempt for the poetry of Thomas Moore. In an article in his* Look Round Literature *(1887) on "The Irish 'National' Poet," Buchanan had rejected Moore because Moore "lacked simplicity, that one unmistakable gift of all great national poets."*

It may also seem odd to hear Yeats invoking "precision of thought and phrase" and lamenting that "the intellect had nothing to ponder over." Yeats's ideas on intellect, borrowed from Blake, involved precision and accuracy of imagination, not the analysis of ideas. In his last paragraph, Yeats repeated what he had been preaching unsuccessfully to the Rhymers' Club—that literature and philosophy cannot be separated.

De la Motte Fouqué in one of his romances describes the Father of Evil as having a face that no man could remember and a name that sounded 'Greek and noble', but passed out of men's minds as soon as it was uttered.[1] I find Mr. Buchanan's new poem well-nigh as hard to remember now that I take it up a month after first reading it. I have a vague recollection of something vehement, insistent, eloquent, and chaotic, with here and there a touch or two of serener beauty. I recollect also that while I was reading it Mr. Buchanan was hurling no less vehement, insistent, eloquent, and chaotic expostulations at the head of one who liked him not, and that he was explaining—I remember no more—that the bulk of English literature, from the *Faerie Queene*† and *Paradise Lost* to our own day, was quite ineffective because 'mere literature'.[2] Poem and expostulations alike were no doubt 'Greek and noble', or some modern equivalent for these things, but they are, so far as I am concerned, with the snows of yester year. But I must try and bring this *Wandering Jew* back into memory again.

The poet meets in the streets of the city, late one night, an old man, weak and forlorn. This old man reveals himself to be the Wandering Jew.[3] Then by various signs, the control of the elements, the stigmata on his hands, the Wandering Jew makes himself known as Christ. Finally the poet sees a vision of a vast Golgotha amid a sea of human souls, and upon this Golgotha 'the Spirit of Humanity' sits as judge.[4] Christ is brought before him and is accused by a skeleton-like figure, who is apparently Death, and by a cloud of witnesses from all periods and nations. Among these witnesses are Buddha, Nero, Galileo, Bruno, Montezuma, Petrarch, da† Gama, Columbus and countless others.[5] Christ, they say, was a noble but self-deluded enthusiast who misled the world and cheated it of present happiness by fatal dreams of happiness hereafter, by the persecution of his clergy, and by a feverish asceticism. They talk, no matter what their period or nation, as though they came fresh from a study of the *National Reformer*, and the publication of a certain Fleet Street house,[6] and all agree with Mr. Buchanan that Christianity 'is played out'.[7] In despair of getting anything but 'mere literature' from the witnesses, we turn to the symbolism itself, and find a very well-arranged 'grand valley' of the Last Judgment, and nothing more.[8] I do not wish to be flippant, or to be guilty of that easiest of shallow things, 'smart writing', but I can find no other phrase. This 'valley' affects the nerves and the senses certainly, but the heart and the intellect—no. Blake painted a Last Judgment, but how different his method was can be seen by his own description. 'I entreat that the spectator', he wrote, 'will attend to the hands and feet, to the lineaments of the countenance. They are all descriptive of character, and not a line is drawn without intention, and that most discriminate and particular. As poetry admits not a letter that is insignificant, so painting admits not a grain of sand or a blade of grass insignificant, much less an insignificant blur or blot.'[9] Let us look to the 'lineaments' of Mr. Buchanan's personages. Here is his 'Spirit of Humanity':

> Then my soul was 'ware
> Of One who silent sat in judgment there,
> Shrouded and spectral; lonely as a cloud
> He loomed above the surging and shrieking crowd.
> Human he seemed, and yet his eye-balls shone
> From fleshless sockets of a skeleton,
> And from the shroud around him darkly roll'd
> He pointed with a fleshless hand and cold
> At those who came.[10]

Compare this admirable fragment of rhetoric with the no less admirably rhetorical description of the accuser, Death or whatever he be:

> Then calmly amid the shadows of the throne
> Another awful shrouded skeleton,
> Human, yet more than human, rose his height,
> With baleful eyes of wild and wistful light.[11]

There is surely no 'discriminate and particular' intention in these vague and commonplace affrightments. Does Mr. Buchanan think that 'the Spirit of Humanity' and 'Death' have no distinct identity? If he thinks that they have not, then why not make this plain? and if he thinks they have—and surely even Mr. Buchanan would not make them different personages unless he saw a difference—why not give some outer sign of opposing function and nature, for 'poetry admits not a letter that is insignificant'? He seems anxious alone to make a vague impression of sublimity by piling up indefinite words and pictures, veritable offspring of the void, and by uttering sonorous words that, howsoever 'Greek and noble', have made† them stick in the heart and the memory. He fails, as most moderns fail when they attempt long poems; he has no real sublimity because no precision of thought and phrase. When once the vague shock to the nerves has gone by, the intellect has nothing to ponder over and to recall the impression by.

   Mr. Buchanan is perhaps hardly to blame except in his choice of subject, for he is neither mystic, metaphysician, or theologian, and you cannot write to any purpose about human hope and human fate—Christ and Golgotha—without being one or other of these three things. He has in fact given us 'mere literature', when we had a right to expect not only high literature, but high philosophy. I say this with the more regret because I am heartily at one with much of Mr. Buchanan's disgust at the worship of 'mere literature'. Great literature is always great because the writer was thinking of truth and life and beauty more than of literary form and literary fame. The belief of the typical literary man of the time, that you can separate poetry from philosophy and from belief, is but the phantasy of an empty day. Dante, who revealed God, and Shakespeare, who revealed man, must have spent their days in brooding upon God and upon man, and not upon the technique of style and the gossip of literary history.[12] When philosophy and belief have gone out of life, then, and then only, shall they be gone out of literature. Let us certainly, if we will, hold with Mr. Buchanan that 'mere literature' is accursed; but do not let us trumpet, as Mr. Buchanan does, 'mere literature', which is also 'mere journalism' set to rhyme, as never-to-be-forgotten revelation, but let us remember always that Providence has provided a place for it and a use in the journals of the day. So long as it keeps to that place and that use we should give thanks for whatever of 'Greek and noble' it may have, but let us not encourage it to revolt like him who fell into pride of old time.[13]

A BUNDLE OF POETS

This is an anonymous review from the 22 July 1893 Speaker *of the following books:* The Poems of Arthur Henry Hallam, Together with His Essay on the Lyrical Poems of Alfred Tennyson *(London: E. Mathews, 1893); Francis A. H. Terrell's* Anne Boleyn: A Historical Drama in Five Acts *(London: A. P. Marsden, 1893); Charles Sayle's* Musa Consolatrix *(London: David Nutt, 1893); and Sarah Piatt's* An Enchanted Castle, and Other Poems *(London/New York; Longmans, Green and Co., 1893).*

The evidence for Yeats's authorship of this review is a clipping of it, corrected in the author's hand, in MS 12148 (National Library of Ireland), which contains other reviews written by Yeats. From other sources, we know that Yeats was acquainted with Hallam's essay on Tennyson, and the author of the present review was familiar with Hallam's essay. A month after this review, in a notice of Laurence Housman's selection of Blake, Yeats was echoing Hallam's statement that the sensitivity of the artist precluded easy public acceptance of true poetry, and the banality of bad poetry assured its acceptance by a public that adores images of itself. Yeats quoted Hallam frequently thereafter (see Yeats's review of Sir C. G. Duffy's Young Ireland, The Bookman, *January 1897, pp. 326–28 below).*

Of the other authors in this review, Charles Sayle (1864–1924) was a librarian at Cambridge University and also an editor of Sir Thomas Browne; and Sarah Morgan Bryan Piatt (1836–1919) was acquainted through her husband, John James Piatt (1835–1917), the American consul at Queenstown (now Cobh), with the circle of young Irish writers.

Yeats was active on the liberal weekly The Speaker *at this time. Barry O'Brien, an editor of this magazine, was a friend of Yeats, and John Davidson, a fellow Rhymer, not always on good terms with Yeats, was in charge of a column of short notices of new books. Most of the book reviews in* The Speaker *were, like the present one, unsigned.*

Messrs. Mathews and Lane have done altogether well in re-issuing some of the prose and poetry of Arthur Hallam, and in getting Mr. Le Gallienne to write the introduction, but by no means well in omitting a portrait of the author.[1] We do not get such a great deal for our five shillings in their slender volume that we can pardon the lack of any visible presentment of one who was so much more remarkable than his work. We turn over page after page of fluid and graceful if cloudy verse, of subtle and serene if academical prose, and come to nothing to bring visibly before us the inspirer of the most famous friendship of the century.[2] Arthur Hallam seems to have been ever deliberate, conscious, and reasonable, with nothing of that wilful and incalculable temperament out of which comes self-portraiture. The very things, perhaps, which made him a loyal and valuable friend made him of no account as an artistic personality. He seems, if one can judge by this book, to have been so preoccupied with excellent reasons and laudable purposes that he had no time for those unconscious feelings and bitter protests through which men express themselves, and out of which they create beautiful things. Since time out of mind the world has looked to its Lancelots and not to its King Arthurs to sing it songs and tell it stories.[3] It expects obviously deliberate, conscious, and reasonable natures to give it critical rather than creative work, and will find, in the present book at any rate, criticism which is of the best and rarest sort. If one set aside Shelley's essay on poetry and Browning's essay on Shelley,[4] one does not know where to turn in modern English criticism for anything so philosophic—anything so fundamental and radical—as the first half of Arthur Hallam's essay 'On some of the Characteristics of Modern Poetry and on the Lyrical Poems of Alfred Tennyson'.[5] We have plenty of criticism in which a stray passage out of one poet is compared with a stray passage out of another, but all mere impressionism of this kind is easy and superficial in comparison to such an exposition of the first principles of a school—and that the least philosophically articulate because the most entirely instinctive of all schools—as is contained in this essay. Writing long before the days of Rossetti and Swinburne,[6] Arthur Hallam explained the principles of the aesthetic movement,[7] claimed Tennyson as its living representative, and traced its origin to Keats and Shelley, who, like Wordsworth, made beauty the beginning and end of all things in art. Any who adopt their principles, he explained, share their unpopularity, and 'How should they be popular whose senses told them a richer and ampler tale than most men could understand; and who constantly expressed, because they constantly felt, sentiments of exquisite pleasure or pain which most men were not permitted to experience?'[8] 'And yet', he went on, 'every bosom contains the elements of those complex emotions which the artist feels, and every

head can, to a certain extent, go over in itself the process of their combination, so as to understand his expressions and sympathise with his
state. But this requires exertion. . . . Since then the demand on the reader
for activity, when he wants to peruse his author in a luxurious pas-
siveness, is the very thing that moves his bile: it is obvious that those
writers will be always most popular who require the least degree of exertion.[9] *Hence, whatever is mixed up with art, and appears under its
semblance, is always more favourably regarded than art free and
unalloyed.* Hence, half the fashionable poems in the world are mere
rhetoric, and half the remainder are perhaps not liked by the general-
ity for their substantial merits.' The passage we have put in italics is
the best explanation we have seen of the popularity of the didactic poets
and our[†] one complaint against Mr. Le Gallienne is that he does not give
us some other of those essays of which he speaks in his graceful introduction.[10] The poetry is of little account, and many pages might well
have been spared to make room for them.

The writer of *Anne Boleyn,* who is an evident Roman Catholic, with
a brief against Henry and Cranmer,[11] has precision of thought and phrase
and some facility for writing dignified blank verse, and with more developed sense of character might write a readable if not an actable play.
The present writer has read every word of *Anne Boleyn,* and got pleasure out of it; but then he can read almost anything which is written
in dramatic form.

Mr. Charles Sayle quotes Verlaine,[12] and has sent forth his book, after
the Parisian fashion, in a paper cover. One reads it with a vague sense
of instruction, as though one were reading a foreign language; and yet
the thing is naught. Mr. Sayle has, however, humility, and in a poem—
'To Modern Rhymers'[13]—puts it into verse not without a touch of
music—

> I have no strength to blow a blast to fill
> This England glutted with the healthy bread
> Of Liberty and Equal Right. I tread
> A lowlier, silent, older path alone,
> And, challenged, hardly dare to raise my head.
> I sit apart and watch you.

Both Mr. Sayle and the author of *Anne Boleyn* have not a little of
Arthur Hallam's fatal love for the laudable and the excellent, and
show as yet no clear mastery over that art which resembles the sun in
smiling alike upon the just and the unjust,[14] the excellent and the inferior, the laudable and the blameworthy. Turning from them with pleasure to one who has a pure aesthetic ideal, and is a master in her sphere,

we take up with relief Mrs. Piatt's delicate, if somewhat mannered, reveries over old buildings and dead celebrities.[15] They are all perhaps a little obviously American, a little too plainly the tribute of a new nation to an old, a pleasant and comely expression of that instinct which impels a certain Boston gentleman[16] to spend all his days at the British Museum, working up old English genealogies. But, after all, is not our complaint against America's self-assertiveness upon the one hand, and her profound interest in ourselves upon the other, a trifle contradictory. Mrs. Piatt has sung only of this latter feeling, and we have no cause to complain of our flatterer. She is neither profuse nor grudging, and, but for a too copious use of epithets like 'Old World', would pay her homage with admirable skill. 'In the Round Tower at Cloyne'[17] is surely perfect after its kind—

> They shivered lest the child should fall;
>   He did not heed a whit.
> They knew it were as well to call
>   To those who builded it.
>
> 'I want to climb it any way
>   And find out what is there;
> There may be things—you know there may—
>   Lost in the dark somewhere.'[18]
>
> He made a ladder of their fears
>   For his light, eager feet;
> It never, in its thousand years,
>   Held anything so sweet.
>
> The blue eyes peeped through dust and doubt,
>   The small heads[19] shook the Past;
> 'He'll find the Round Tower's secret out,'
>   They, laughing, said at last.
>
> The enchanted ivy that[20] had grown,
>   As usual, in a night
> Out of a legend, round the stone,
>   He parted left and right.
>
> And what the little climber heard
>   And saw there, say who will,
> Where Time sits brooding like a bird
>   In that grey nest and still.

> . . . About the Round Tower tears may fall;
> He does not heed a whit.
> They know it were as well to call
> To those who builded it.

Mrs. Piatt has not written many pages altogether, and even the present little book is not all new. She seems anxious to constantly remind us, by making the best of her old poems a large part of each new book, of how light a burden she has fashioned for the wallet of Father Time. She knows him to be a lazy porter who loves best the lightest load.

THE WRITINGS
OF WILLIAM BLAKE

This review of Laurence Housman's Selections from the Writings of William Blake (London: K. Paul, Trench, Trübner, 1893) appeared in The Bookman of August 1893. Usually scornful of scholarship, Yeats is here seen in a rare guise of a defender of scholarly accuracy. After he finished his collaboration with Edwin J. Ellis (1848–1916) on an edition of William Blake in 1893, Yeats took a proprietary interest in the text of Blake. After all, his and Ellis's edition was designed to fore-stall such hasty compilations as the one by Housman (1865–1959). The Yeats-Ellis edition had run into heavy fire from critics who found their interpretation of Blake's prophetic writing unconvincing, if not useless.

The attitude of Blake's editors towards his text and his thought has long been a cause of blaspheming to the few earnest students of his work. These editors appear to hold him to have had so much either of the spoilt child or of the crazy enthusiast in him, that it was their veritable duty to improve his text and warn the unwary not to take his deepest con-victions seriously. At first the 'improvement' and warning alike were intelligible, and perhaps excusable, for the first editors, Messrs. Dante Gabriel and William Rossetti,[1] had to introduce him for the first time to a public which hates the unusual and the obscure with a bitter per-sonal hatred based largely upon the notion that he who is either unusual or obscure claims to be more distinguished in some way than it is itself, perhaps even to have senses and faculties which it does not possess. The public loves writers that are magnified reflections of itself, but abhors all who claim to belong to some special community, some special cult, some special tribe which is not of its kin. What won-der, then, that Blake's first editors said in substance to their readers, 'Do tolerate this strange friend of ours; he is really very nice, though he does talk nonsense at times about inspiration and about seeing visions, and that kind of thing. If you will be civil to him we will smooth his hair, and put him into a coat as like your own as possible, and hide quite out of sight his own outlandish one.' It is, however, wonderful and again wonderful, and no less inexcusable than wonderful, that any later editor should accept this dressed and brushed Blake for the real man, and do this without any word about the men who did the brushing and the tailoring, or without even mention that such a thing had been done. Yet Mr. Dante Rossetti was frank enough. In printing from Blake's MS. he found it necessary, he said, 'to omit, transpose, or combine' in order to lessen 'obscurity' or to 'avoid redundance.'[2] He also made many corrections of metre and grammar in poems which had been printed before, and avowed doing so, and against this little can be said, for the originals were in print and posterity could judge. Nor would even his doctoring of the poems from MS. have been a very serious falsification had he but taken care to preserve the originals from the vicissitudes of an already fading manuscript. He was wise in his generation, and to his wisdom perhaps Blake owes something of his popularity.

But what excuse can be offered for a publisher, for I do Mr. Housman the credit of supposing that publishers' reasons prevailed over the dictates of scholarship, who, months after the correct text has been printed in *The Works of William Blake* (B. Quaritch),[3] re-issues the old doctored text not only without a word of explanation or excuse, but without a single sentence to warn the reader that this is not Blake's own text? Would that the fiery mystic who taught that 'The tigers of wrath are wiser than the horses of instruction', could shake the dust of Bunhill[+] Fields from his old bones, and, dropping in upon editor and publishers, explain in person that 'improvement makes straight roads, but the crooked roads without improvement are roads of genius.'[4]

Mr. Housman's book is only a book of selections, and some among the most 'improved' verses are therefore left out, but certainly enough of them are included in all conscience. A comparison of 'Broken Love', to use the misleading title which Mr. Housman adopts from Gilchrist, as given here with Blake's own manuscript, shows not only that there are five stanzas of great importance left out without a word, but that certain other stanzas which Blake put separately, with no clue to their proper place are inserted at the places chosen by Mr. Rossetti, and that the remaining stanzas are put into an order not Blake's. The version of 'The Grey Monk' is quite as arbitrary, for Mr. Housman has simply reprinted Rossetti's text in which Blake's second stanza is made the third, his third the fourth, his fourth the fifth, his fifth the seventh, his seventh the ninth, and in which one whole stanza of his, the ninth, is left out altogether, and a stanza which he wrote for a different poem imported to go second. Then, too, Mr. Housman reproduces Mr. W. M. Rossetti's version of 'The Garden of Love' in all its formlessness, and has not a word to tell us that the first two stanzas were never printed by Blake in any known copy of *The Songs of Experience,* but left in manuscript and as an entirely different poem. Again, we have 'The Vision of the Last Judgment' in the arbitrary order and incomplete form in which it appears in Gilchrist's *Life of Blake.* And all the while there is not a single word to show that the editor is even aware that he is uttering other people's false coin.

I turn from the text to the introduction, and I find it equally typical of the kind of thing which has been accepted these last twenty years for Blake scholarship. It is fairly well written, it is highly intelligent, and it is now and then eloquent, but besides one or two old errors of no great importance, such as the statement that the Peckham Rye vision was Blake's first,[5] and one new error, the statement that 'The Island of the Moon' has hitherto remained wholly in manuscript—it treats 'the prophetic books' with the amused patronage, and dismisses them with the shallow remark about their formlessness, which we all know so well, and chatters about their unintelligibility. 'They are too large and too sad a ground to be searched for any sound result',[6] Mr. Housman explains; though how 'sadness' and 'largeness' can cause obscurity is a statement more obscure to my ears than anything in 'the prophetic books' themselves. 'It matters little', however he assures us, 'whether the meaning can ever be wrung out that is there; the process must always be unlovely and[7] partial and artificial in its results', though he omits to tell us how he can possibly know until he has given the books a much deeper study than this introduction gives evidence of. A man has a perfect right, even before he has read them, to think 'the prophetic books' nonsense, but if he think this, then let him, in the name of the nine gods, keep from editing Blake; or if an importunate publisher or his own enthusiasm for song or picture drive him on to do so, let him, having apologised for his lack of knowledge, write with all diffidence upon even the painter and the poet, and keep from commenting at all upon the mystic. Even if he have read 'the prophetic books', and have no sympathy for mysticism of any kind, he should turn aside from all comment upon them, or confine himself to those moments in which, in Mr. Housman's words, 'clean fury[8] of temperament' and several other strange things comes through 'in some recall of lyric thought, when[9] prophecy is relinquished and the decorative hand with its sense of gold restored.'

Blake was a great poet and a great painter, but he was a great mystic also, and cast his mysticism into a form which, however chaotic when compared with his lyrics and his painting, was in every way more beautiful than the form chosen by Swedenborg or Boehme.[10] It was even less chaotic in many ways than the *Mysterium Magnum* and *Aurora*.[11] And what would we think of an editor who had no more to say of Swedenborg or of Boehme than that their literary style was objectionable?

I say these hard things about Mr. Housman's *Blake* with deep regret, for I have the most profound respect, or rather admiration, for his work as a book illustrator, and would gladly have left him alone were it not necessary for the sake of the great causes of poetic mysticism and of good scholarship to speak the truth about the way Blake has been treated by his editors. Mr. Housman is less to blame than the tradition, and would be ashamed, if left to his own devices, to dismiss in a few patronising words books which he has never pretended to understand, and probably never read more than a few lines of, and to reprint an 'improved' text without warning or explanation. I have done my best to put the tradition in the pillory, and would let him go free. It is time that Blake should cease to be a theme of endless eloquence without knowledge, and for the board, with the inscription 'fine sentences may be shot here', to be taken down from the doorway to his House Beautiful.[12]

THE MESSAGE
OF THE FOLK-LORIST

This article, printed in The Speaker *issue of 19 August 1893, under the title "A Literary Causerie," is actually an enlarged review of T. F. Thiselton-Dyer's* The Ghost World *(London: Ward and Downey, 1893).*

Yeats had been long waiting to write this "causerie." In a letter to John O'Leary, dated July 1892, Yeats asked, "When am I to do that 'Causerie' for the Speaker? *I have waited to hear from Barry O'Brien but have not done so" (CL1, 302). If this dating is correct, Yeats waited a full year or more before O'Brien, a fellow member of the London Irish Literary Society, printed this piece. The* Speaker's *steadiest writer of "causeries" was Arthur Quiller-Couch. The usual causerie was not an expanded review as Yeats's piece is but informal literary chatter.*

In his earlier pieces on folklore, Yeats advised Irish writers to produce a simple ballad literature. By 1893 Yeats wanted a sophisticated poetry in the manner of Keats, based upon folklore. This article contains one of the earliest uses of the term "the moods," which Yeats was later to develop into an aesthetic doctrine to account for divine inspiration of poetry. His allusion to "the poetry of cigarettes and black coffee, of absinthe, and the skirt dance . . ." reflects his difficulty in convincing his fellow Rhymers—Symons, Dowson, Davidson—that every grass blade asserted the existence of God.

There exists in MS 12148 (National Library of Ireland) a galley proof of this article, corrected in Yeats's hand. Some of the corrections were incorporated in the printed version in The Speaker, *but others were not. The text reflects Yeats's corrections, and the version from* The Speaker *is given in the notes. Since Yeats waited for a year for this article to appear, it is possible that he corrected two sets of page proof, the copies in MS 12148 and another copy, whose changes were reflected in* The Speaker *printing.*

In one of his unpublished watercolour illustrations to Young's *Night Thoughts*,[1] William Blake has drawn a numberless host of spirits and fairies affirming the existence of God. Out of every flower and every grass-blade comes a little creature lifting its right hand above its head. It is possible that the books of folk-lore, coming in these later days from almost every country in the world, are bringing the fairies and the spirits to our study tables that we may witness a like affirmation, and see innumerable hands lifted testifying to the ancient supremacy of imagination. Imagination is God in the world of art, and may well desire to have us come to an issue with the atheists who would make us naught but 'realists', 'naturalists',[2] or the like.

Folk-lore is at once the Bible, the Thirty-nine Articles, and the *Book of Common Prayer*,[3] and well-nigh all the great poets have lived by its light. Homer, Aeschylus, Sophocles, Shakespeare, and even Dante, Goethe, and Keats,[4] were little more than folk-lorists with musical tongues. The root-stories of the Greek poets are told to-day at the cabin fires of Donegal;[5] the Slavonian[6] peasants tell their children now, as they did a thousand years before Shakespeare was born, of the spirit prisoned in the cloven pine; the Swedes had need neither of Dante nor Spenser to tell them of the living trees that cry or bleed if you break off a bough;[7] and through all the long backward and abysm of time, Faust, under many names, has signed the infernal compact, and girls at St. Agnes' Eve have waited for visions of their lovers to come to them 'upon the honeyed middle of the night'.[8] It is only in these latter decades that we have refused to learn of the poor and the simple, and turned atheists in our pride. The folk-lore of Greece and Rome lasted us a long time; but having ceased to be a living tradition, it became both worn out and unmanageable, like an old servant. We can now no more get up a great[9] interest in the gods of Olympus[10] than we can in the stories told by the showman of a travelling waxwork company. And[11] for lack of those great typical personages who flung the thunderbolts or had serpents in their hair,[12] we have betaken ourselves in a hurry to the poetry of cigarettes and black coffee, of absinthe, and the skirt dance, or are trying to persuade the lecture and the scientific book to look, at least to the eye, like the old poems and dramas and stories that were in the ages of faith long ago. But the countless little hands are lifted and the affirmation has begun.

There is no passion, no vague desire, no tender longing that cannot find fit type or symbol in the legends of the peasantry or in the traditions of the scalds and the gleemen. And these traditions are now being gathered up or translated by a multitude of writers.[13] The most recent of books upon the subject—*The Ghost World* (Ward & Downey)—is neither a translation nor a collection of tales gathered among the people by its author, but one of those classifications and reviews of already collected facts of which we stand in great need. Its author, Mr. T. F. Thiselton† Dyer,[14] treats as exhaustively as his four hundred odd pages permit him with the beliefs about ghosts held in every part of the world. The outside of the book is far from comely to look at, and the inside is that mixture of ancient beauty and modern commonplace one has got used to in books by scientific folk-lorists. Mr. Dyer collects numbers of the most entirely lovely and sacred, or tragic and terrible, beliefs in the world, and sets them side by side, transfixed with diverse irrelevancies—in much the same fashion that boys stick moths and butterflies side by side upon a door, with long pins in their bodies. At other times he irritates by being hopelessly inadequate, as when he follows a story of priceless beauty with the remark that 'these folktales are interesting as embodying the superstitions of the people among whom they are current.'[15] But then no one expects the scientific folk-lorist to have a tongue of music, and this one gives us a great deal less of himself than the bulk of his tribe, and has the good taste to gird at no man—not even the poor spiritualist.

He deals in thirty-one chapters with such subjects as 'The Soul's Exit', 'The Temporary Exit of the Soul', 'The Nature of the Soul', 'Why Ghosts Wander', 'Phantom Birds', 'Animal Ghosts', 'Phantom Music', and the like. The pages upon the state of the soul after death are particularly interesting and have as much of the heart's blood of poetry as had ever Dis or Hades.[16] Jacob Boehme held that every man was represented by a symbolic beast or bird,[17] and that these beasts and birds varied with the characters of men, and in the folk-lore of almost every country, the ghosts revisit the earth as moths[18] or butterflies, as doves or ravens, or in some other representative shape. Sometimes only voices are heard. The Zulu sorcerer, Mr. Dyer says, 'hears the spirits, who speak by whistlings, speaking to him',[19] while the Algonquin Indians of North America 'could hear the shadow souls of the dead chirp like crickets.'[20] In Denmark, he adds, the night ravens are held to be exorcised evil spirits who are for ever flying towards the East, for if they can reach the Holy Sepulchre they will be at rest;[21] and 'In the *Saemund Edda*[22] it is said that in the nether world singed souls fly about like swarms of flies.' He might have quoted here the account in the old Irish romance called 'The Voyage of Maeldune' of that[23] great saint who dwelt upon the wooded island among the flocks of holy birds who were the souls of his relations, awaiting the blare of the last trumpet. Folk-lore often[24] makes the souls of the blessed take upon themselves every evening the shape of white birds, and whether it put them into such charming shape or not, is ever anxious to keep us from troubling their happiness with our grief. Mr. Dyer tells, for instance, the story of a girl who heard a voice speaking from the grass-plot of her lover, and saying, 'Every time a tear falls from thine eyes, my shroud is full of blood. Every time thy heart is gay, my shroud is full of rose leaves.'[25]

All these stories are such as to unite man more closely to the woods and hills and waters about him, and to the birds and animals that live in them, and to give him types and symbols for those feelings and passions which find no adequate expression in common life. Could there be any expression of Nature-worship more tender and lovely than that tale of the Indians who lived once by the river Pascagoula,† which Mr. Dyer tells in his chapter on 'Phantom Music'?[26] Strange musical sounds were said to come out of the river at one place, and close to this place the Indians had set up an idol representing the water spirit who made the music. Every night they gathered about the image and played to it sweet tunes upon many stringed instruments, for they held it to love all music. One day a priest came and tried to convert them from the worship of this spirit, and might have succeeded; but one night the water was convulsed, and the convulsion drew the whole tribe to the edge of the river to hear music more lovely than the spirit ever sang before. They listened until one plunged into the river in his ecstasy and sank for ever, and then men, women and children—the whole tribe— plunged after him, and left a world that had begun to turn from the ancient ways.

The greatest poets of every nation have drawn from stories like this, symbols and events to express the most lyrical, the most subjective moods. In modern days there has been one great poet who tried to express such moods without adequate[27] folk-lore. Most of us feel, I think, no matter how greatly we admire him, that there is something of over-much cloud and rainbow in the poetry of Shelley, and is not this simply because he lacked the true symbols and types and stories to express his intense subjective inspiration?[28] Could he have been as full of folk-lore as was Shakespeare, or even Keats, he might have delivered his message and yet kept as close to our hearthstone as did the one in *Midsummer†* *Night's Dream* or as did the other in 'The Eve of St. Agnes'; but as it is, there is a world of difference between Puck,†[29] Peasblossom and the lady who waited for 'The honeyed middle of the night' upon the one hand and the spirit of the hour and the voices of *Prometheus the Unbound* upon the other.[30] Shakespeare and Keats had the folk-lore of their own day, while Shelley had but mythology; and a mythology which had been passing for long through literary minds without any new inflow from living tradition loses all the incalculable instinctive and convincing quality of the popular traditions. No conscious invention can take the place of tradition, for he who would write a folk tale, and thereby bring a new life into literature, must have the fatigue of the spade in his hands and the stupor of the fields in his heart. Let us listen humbly to the old people telling their stories, and perhaps God will send the primitive excellent imagination into the midst of us again. Why should we be either 'naturalists' or 'realists' alone? Are not those little right hands lifted everywhere in affirmation?

TWO MINOR LYRISTS

This review of Verses by the Way *(London: Methuen and Co., 1893) by James Dryden Hosken and* The Questions at the Well *(London: Digby, Long and Co., 1893) by Fenil Haig (Ford Madox Ford's earliest pseudonym) appeared anonymously in* The Speaker, 26 August *1892. A clipping of this article, corrected in Yeats's hand, may be found in MS 12148, a manuscript volume of press clippings in the National Library of Ireland.*

The praise given to a slim volume by the then unknown Ford Madox Ford attests to Yeats's critical powers. Ford said that despite praise from The Times, The Daily News, *and* The Academy, *the public bought only fourteen copies of his first book of poems (in his* Collected Poems *[London, 1914]).*

'Q' introduces *Verses by the Way* with an admirable account of how their author was driven from pillar to post through a good ten years, being now an 'extra outdoor' Customs officer at the Albert Docks—whither 'half the wild adventures and floating wickedness of this planet find their way at one time or other'—now a 'super' at a theatre, and now a postman at a little town in West Cornwall, besides several other things between-whiles.[1] One reads these matters and thinks what strange impressions, what unique experiences, what a salient turn of thought, must needs have come to Mr. Hosken amid the obscure places of the earth; and when, on first turning over the pages of the poems themselves one finds that he really does know how to write, hope grows ardent indeed. He must have found new symbols of emotion, new forms of thought! He has been down in the waters above the pearl-beds, and must needs have his hands loaded with the glimmering merchandise. 'The indolent reviewer'[2] thinks these things for a moment and is happy; but, alas! here is no new Burns, but one who makes sonnet sequences, and sings 'In vain my teardrops flow for thee, dead Imogene'[3] in the way we all know so well. How gladly one would have heard of those 'wild adventures' and of that 'floating wickedness';[4] for in such things human energy finds ever new expression for itself, and the record could not be other than radical and original also. The present indolent reviewer, at any rate, is ever a-thirst for a new sensation, and forgives but slowly one who sells a unique experience for a mess of Elizabethan phrases, however pretty and musical. For a single noble or beautiful reflection wedded to the incidents and symbols of the docks or the postman's beat he would gladly let all Mr. Hosken's Imogenes[†] go pack. He still keeps alive a smouldering fit of anger against the late Mr. Allingham for having in his latter days renounced Ballyshannon[†] and Ballyshannon[†] songs, and thereby watered his good grain until it became a kind of cosmopolitan water-gruel.[5] Emerson's admirable saying—

> To thine orchard's edge belong
> All the brass and plume of song—

should be writ over the mantelpiece of every poet.[6] The spirits in Blake's *Milton* are shut up within eggs of light, that they may be forced 'to live within their own energy'.[7] Till Mr. Hosken has got such an egg of light, either from the events of his own life or from some other and less likely quarter, one can but say of him that he has done better than Capern the Devon postman, and not so well as Mr. Skipsey, the northern miner, despite a better mastery over metre and rhythm; for Mr. Skipsey has sung the blackness of the pit and the loves and tragedies of the pit-mouth.[8] Mr. Hosken writes often, however, with real force and beauty, and all would be well but for the great masters who have sung of like things before him. He is quite at his best in 'Robin Hood,' and to take it apart by itself is almost to forget one's desire for a more personal song:

> I read 'A Lytell Geste of Robyn Hode'[9]
>   Within an ancient forest far withdrawn:
> The story rapt me in a wondrous mood,
>   And I outread the dawn.
> There was a trembling light upon the page,
>   The meeting of the morning and the day;
>   The dewdrops[†] shook not on the silent spray;
> The world forgot its age—
>   The silent golden world that[10] morn in May.
>
> The fever and the dust of this worn time
>   Passed like a dream from me, and left me free

Musing on that antique dramatic rime
   Beneath an old-world tree.
I looked and saw a merry company
   Down a green avenue with laugh and song[11]
   And little joyful noises come along;
Then died the tyranny
   Of this grey world in me, with hoary wrong.

There saw I—Robin, with his fearless brow
   And eye of frolic love; Maid Marian;
The moon-faced Tuck; and, sporting 'neath a bough,
   John, Robin's master man.
Scarlet, and Much, and all the outlaw clan,
   With polished horn and bow, in Lincoln green,
   Moved ceaselessly between the leafy screen.
A natural freedom ran
   Through every spirit on that sylvan green.[12]

The two remaining verses are well nigh as good.

The temptation to preach 'thine orchard's edge' to Mr. Fenil Haig is not quite so strong, though strong withal. His *Questions at the Well* is one of the few first[13] books of promise which come to a reviewer in a season; nor is the promise the less evident because one does not quite know what it promises. It would be a work of remarkable achievement as well if Mr. Fenil Haig had only staked and hedged his orchard about and been careful never to stray beyond the boundary. His apples of knowledge are of his own growing, but he has let them get mixed up with sticks and stones from over the way. In other words, he is yet but little of an artist, for art is before all other things the finding and cleaving to one's own. The best of his longer poems[14] is a queer realistic idyll beginning—

Down there near the Gare du Nord,
   At the corner of the street,
   Where the double tram-lines meet,
Bonhomme Simon Pierreauford,
   And his nagging wife, Lisette,
Kept their café, he and she;[15]
He lets life slip carelessly,
   She a sleepless martinet.

He in posing, portly rest,
   Stands for ever at the door,

Glancing at his waiters four,
Or chatting with a well-known guest;[16]
She, with tongue that never stops,
Scolds the sweating cooks for waste,
Makes the panting waiters haste,
Wipes the marble table-tops.

There is a right lyrical vehemence in most of his shorter verses too—notably in 'The Wind's Quest'[†17]

'O where shall I find rest?'
Sighed the Wind from the West,
'I've sought in vale, o'er dale and down,
Through tangled woodland, tarn and town,
But found no rest.'

'Rest, thou ne'er shalt find,'
Answered Love to the Wind;
'For thou and I, and the great grey sea,
May never rest til eternity[18]
Its end shall find.'

But really he must hedge and stake that orchard with more care. No man is an artist until he has made his orchard, even though it be but an orchard in Cloud-Cuckoo-Land.[19] This hedging and staking by no means involves any narrow specialism; for there is all the difference in the world between the man who finds one thing in everything and him who finds everything in one thing—between the pedant and the artist.

OLD GAELIC LOVE SONGS

Yeats reviewed Douglas Hyde's translation of Love Songs of Connacht *(in Gaelic and English) (London: T. Fisher Unwin/Dublin: Gill
and Son, 1893) in* The Bookman *of October 1893.*

*This review marks the apex of Yeats's opinion of Douglas Hyde
(1860–1949) as a translator and folklorist. Never again did he find
Hyde's work to be quite so flawless. Yeats had always suspected that
the scholar in Hyde would overcome the artist. As events turned out,
Hyde's Gaelic League drew him from both books and poems into
the center of Irish nationalistic politics. Lady Gregory eventually
replaced Hyde as Yeats's guide through the Gaelic past and present.*

*A version of Yeats's story "Costello the Proud, Oona Macder-
mott and the Bitter Tongue," first printed in* The Pageant, *1896, and
included in* The Secret Rose *(London: Lawrence & Bullen, 1897), may
be found on pp. 51–59 of Hyde's book.*

Connacht is a province in the west of the Republic of Ireland.

Dr. Hyde's volume of translations, *Love Songs of Connacht* (T. Fisher
Unwin), is one of those rare books in which art and life are so completely blended that praise or blame become well-nigh impossible. It
is so entirely a fragment of the life of Ireland in the past that if we praise
it we but praise Him who made man and woman, love and fear, and
if we blame it we but waste our breath upon the Eternal Adversary[1]
who has marred all with incompleteness and imperfection. The men
and women who made these love songs were hardly in any sense conscious artists, but merely people very desperately in love, who put their
hopes and fears into simple and musical words, or went over and over
for their own pleasure the deeds of kindness or the good looks of their
sweethearts. One girl praises her lover, who is a tailor, because he tells
her such pretty lies, and because he cuts his cloth as prettily as he tells
them, and another cannot forget that hers promised her shoes with high
heels.[2] Nor is any little incident too slight to be recorded if only it be

connected in some way with the sorrow or the hope of the singer. One poor girl remembers how she tossed upon her bed of rushes, and threw the rushes about because of the great heat.[3]

These poems are pieced together by a critical account, which is almost as much a fragment of life as are the poems themselves. Dr. Hyde wrote it first in Gaelic, of that simple kind which the writers of the poems must have thought, and talked, and then translated poems and prose together, and now we have both English and Gaelic side by side. Sheer hope and fear, joy and sorrow, made the poems, and not any mortal man or woman, and the veritable genius of Ireland dictated the quaint and lovely prose. The book is but the fourth chapter of a great work called *The Songs of Connacht*.[4] The preceding chapters are still buried in Irish newspapers. The third chapter was about drinking songs, and the present one begins: 'After reading these wild, careless, sporting, airy drinking songs, it is right that a chapter entirely contrary should follow. Not careless and light-hearted alone is the Gaelic nature, there is also beneath the loudest mirth a melancholy spirit, and if they let on (pretend) to be without heed for anything but sport and revelry, there is nothing in it but letting on (pretence). The same man who will today be dancing, sporting, drinking, and shouting, will be soliloquising by himself to-morrow, heavy and sick and sad in his poor lonely little hut, making a croon over departed hopes, lost life, the vanity of this world, and the coming of death. There is for you the Gaelic nature, and that person who would think that they are not the same sort of people who made those loud-tongued, sporting, devil-may-care songs that we have been reading in the last chapter, and who made the truly gentle, smooth, fair, loving poems which we will see in this part, is very much astray. The life of the Gael is so pitiable, so dark and sad and sorrowful, and they are so broken, bruised, and beaten down in their own land and country that their talents and ingenuity find no place for themselves, and no way to let themselves out but in excessive, foolish mirth or in keening and lamentation. We shall see in these poems that follow, more grief and trouble, more melancholy and contrition of heart, than of gaiety or hope. But despite that, it is probably the same men, or the same class of men, who composed the poems which follow and the songs which we have read. We shall not prove that, and we shall not try to prove it, but where is the person who knows the Gaeldom of Erin and will say against (or contradict) us in this? They were men who composed many of the songs in the last chapter, but it is women who made many of the love-songs, and melodious and sorrowful they made them',[5] and in like fashion the critical account flows on, a mountain stream of sweet waters. Here and there is some quaint or potent verse, like a moss-covered stone or jutting angle of rushes. Thus, for instance, lamented some girl long ago.[6] 'My heart is as black as a sloe, or as a black coal that would be burnt in a forge, as the sole of a shoe upon white halls, and there is great melancholy over my laugh. My heart is bruised, broken, like ice upon the top of water, as it were a cluster of nuts after their breaking, or a young maiden after her marrying. My love is of the colour of the raspberry on a fine sunny day, of the colour of the darkest heath berries of the mountain; and often has there been a black head upon a bright body. Time it is for me to leave this town. The stone is sharp in it, and the mould is cold; it was in it I got a voice (blame) without riches and a heavy word from the band who back-bite. I denounce love; woe is she who gave it to the son of yon woman, who never understood it. My heart in my middle, sure he has left it black, and I do not see him on the street or in any place.'

As the mournful sentences accumulate in our ears, we seem to see a heart dissolving away in clouds of sorrow. The whole thing is one of those 'thrusts of power' which Flaubert has declared to be beyond the reach of conscious art.[7] Dr. Hyde is wise in giving it to us in prose, and in giving, as he does, prose versions of all the poems, but one would gladly have had a verse version also.[8] He has shown us how well he can write verse by his versions of some of the more elaborate poems, especially of the wonderful 'My love, O, she is my love':

> She casts a spell, O, casts a spell,
>   Which haunts me more than I can tell,[9]
>   Dearer, because she makes me ill,
>   Than who would will to make me well.
>
> She is my store, O, she my store,
>   Whose grey eye wounded me so sore,
>   Who will not place in mine her palm,
>   Who will not calm me any more.
>
> She is my pet, O, she my pet,
>   Whom I can never more forget;
>   Who would not lose by me one moan,
>   Nor stone upon my cairn set.
>
> She is my roon, O, she my roon,
>   Who tells me nothing, leaves me soon;
>   Who would not lose by me one sigh,
>   Were death and I within one room.

> She is my dear, O, she my dear,
> Who cares not whether I be here,[10]
> Who would not weep when I am dead,
> Who makes me shed the silent tear.

This translation, which is in the curious metre of the original, is, without being exactly a good English poem, very much better than the bulk of Walsh's and beyond all measure better than any of Mangan's in *The Munster Poets*.[11]

I have now given examples of Dr. Hyde's critical prose, and of his prose and verse translations, and must leave him to do the rest himself. As for me, I close the book with much sadness. Those poor peasants lived in a beautiful if somewhat inhospitable world, where little had changed since Adam delved and Eve span.[12] Everything was so old that it was steeped in the heart, and every powerful emotion found at once noble types and symbols[13] for its expression. But we—we live in a world of whirling change, where nothing becomes old and sacred, and our powerful emotions, unless we be highly-trained artists, express themselves in vulgar types and symbols. The soul then had but to stretch out its arms to fill them with beauty, but now all manner of heterogeneous ugliness has beset us. A peasant had then but to stand in his own door and think of his sweetheart and of his sorrow, and take from the scene about him and from the common events of his life types and symbols, and behold, if chance was a little kind, he had made a poem to humble generations of the proud. And we—we labour and labour, and spend days over a stanza or a paragraph, and at the end of it have made, likely as not, a mere bundle of phrases. Yet perhaps this very stubborn uncomeliness of life, divorced from hill and field, has made us feel the beauty of these songs in a way the people who made them did not, despite their proverb:

> A tune is more lasting than the song of the birds,[14]
> A word is more lasting than the riches of the world.

We stand outside the wall of Eden and hear the trees talking together within, and their talk is sweet in our ears.

THE AINU

This review of Life with Trans-Siberian Savages *by B. Douglas Howard (London and New York: Longmans, 1893) appeared unsigned in* The Speaker, 7 October 1893. *A clipping of it, corrected in Yeats's hand, is in the National Library of Ireland, MS 12148. This book was certainly Yeats's strangest reviewing assignment. Yet, despite the exoticism of the topic, Yeats seems to have been informed about the Ainu of Japan as, indeed, he was interested in all primitive myth and religion. The last paragraph has the true "Celtic Twilight" ring.*

It is likely that the readers of this book will find themselves as utterly ignorant of the Sakhalin[†1] savages it describes as of the traveller who has written it. Yet both are memorable, for the first have preserved more perfectly than any other Asiatic race their primitive habits and beliefs, and the second can talk quietly of 'leisurely meanderings'[2] in Russia, Northern India, Thibet, Korea,[†] and Siberia. Mr. Howard appears to be an English sportsman with a turn for religion and primitive life, and a double portion of that disposition which brings adventures. He travelled, he tells us, through Siberia bent on getting to the bottom of the Russian exile system, and on seeing how it worked in even the most out-of-the-way places. He came in this way to Vladivostock, the only Russian port upon the east coast of Siberia, and there heard shuddering mention of a terrible island where intractable exiles, great criminals, and recaptured fugitives were imprisoned. The name was rarely if ever mentioned but the description was plainly that of the long woody island Sakhalin.[†] He now met by good luck the governor of the island, and was invited to be his guest; and while with him saw in the hospital his first Ainu,[3] a black, hairy creature tattooed and hideous, and had his curiosity so excited that he set out, with a convict for guide, to see the Ainus in their own forests. As soon as he found an Ainu village, he sent his convict home and threw himself upon the hospitality of its inhabitants, and was received with that courtesy which seems common to all ancient and primitive peoples. Though he could only talk to them in signs, he soon learnt to enter into their life, and to take part in their hunting and their fishing, in their ceremonies and their festivals. In time he was even made one of the two chiefs of the village, and taught the carefully-guarded secret of their arrow-poison. In this way he learnt more of the simple and kindly Ainus of Sakhalin than any other traveller has learnt even of the far better known Ainus of Japan. Miss Bird[4] has done more than anybody else to make us know these latter, but her description is avowedly and obviously from without—the stray notes of a passer-by. Mr. Howard, on the other hand, needed little but some tattoo marks—and these he avoided, he tells us, with much difficulty—to make him a veritable Ainu; and when we lay down his book, we do so with something of reverent affection for those fishers and hunters, and, above all, for his old fellow-chief; and with no little admiration for that simple and beautiful creed which he holds to be the very crown of all the Ainu life, the very essence of all their being—a creed which would have seemed almost entirely admirable to most of the great European mystics.

The savage looks upon naked eternity, while we unhappy triflers have built about us a wall of odds and ends. Mr. Howard's friends affirm one supreme god the maker of gods and men, but hold that he has under him innumerable minor divinities, such as the god of running waters, the god of lakes, the god of the sea, the god of the waters as a whole, and as the great goddess of the sun's fire, and the minor and mediatorial goddess of the household flame.[5] There is an ancient Catholic writer who holds that 'The Most High set the borders of the nations after the number of the angels of God.'[6] Are not fire and the waters more unchanging and mightier than any nations? There are, say the Ainu, three heavens—the supreme heaven of outer space where the supreme god lives, the star-bearing heaven, and the heaven of the clouds which is about us.[7] The gods dwell in these heavens, but each has for his contrary an evil spirit, and these evil spirits are ruled over by one supreme evil deity and inhabit six hells. The souls of the dead whether of men or animals,[8] go either among the good or evil spirits after death, but are permitted to return at times, the animals to help and the old women to injure men. The Ainu worshipper has neither priest nor chapel, but whittles the end of a long stick into a kind of fringe and then thrusts the stick into the earth and prays beside it, and according to the place of the god prayed to in the celestial hierarchy is the place of the chip fringe upon the stick.[9] The women are not permitted to pray for fear they might bring to the gods tittle-tattle about the men.[10]

Mr. Howard tells all this so admirably and sympathetically that his concluding appeal[11] to someone to go preach Christianity to his late subjects may excite surprise. If a member of the Women's Liberal Federation would go and talk to them of the rights of her sex they would be better off in the matter of religion than the bulk of us, and would at any rate have a more developed creed than many a captain in the Salvation Army.[12] Should we not rather ask them to send us a tattooed and hairy missionary to help evangelise our own heathen? He cries out, too, for someone to do something for their material well-being. The Russians leave them alone, forbid anybody to sell them drink, and abandon to them the game of the island, and for these things Mr. Howard is fittingly grateful, and yet he calls out for the philanthropists. Has not the Ainu the great woods and the overwhelming mountains? and if the winter be cold and food scarce at times, how is he worse off than his fathers before him? He has his spear and his supple-bow, and the delight of the long-followed trail, and love, and the talk about the fire, and at the end of all the heaven of stars or the heaven of cloud. Is our own life so much the better that we must needs give him of its abundance?

REFLECTIONS AND REFRACTIONS

This review of Reflections and Refractions *by Charles Weekes (London: T. Fisher Unwin, 1893) appeared in* The Academy, *4 November 1893. Weekes was an old Dublin friend of Yeats. He had joined Yeats in 1885 in founding the Dublin Hermetical Society. Among the Yeats manuscripts in the National Library of Ireland is a note to Mr. Cotton, perhaps James Sutherland Cotton (1847–1918), the editor of* The Academy *from 1896 to 1903: "This is a book of poems by a young Dublin man 'Reflections and Refractions by Charles Weekes.' May I review it for you? Yours . . . W. B. Yeats" (see CL1, 361).*

Weekes was dissatisfied with the book or with its reception, for he withdrew it from circulation soon after publication. Copies of it are very rare.

A poem cast into an impersonal artistic shape can be judged by recognised canons. But a poem taking nearly all its interest from the expression of personal idiosyncrasy comes before a very different court, and is liked, or disliked, from reasons as personal as its own inspiration, or as the reasons for which we like or dislike the people we meet in daily life; and if it be not more personal than difficult or rugged, our judgment is likely to be somewhat of the summary kind. A Tennyson, or a Mr. Swinburne, finds his public with a volume or two; while a Browning has for years to publish at his own expense, and a Whitman to be his own bookseller.[1] A rugged, obscure personal book, if it be at all excellent, has, therefore, a double claim upon our hospitality: the claim to be received for its own sake, and the claim to be received because of the dangers and difficulties that beset its future.

Mr. Charles Weekes's uncouthly-named *Refractions and Reflections*[2] is just such a book. It is as interesting as it is rugged and obscure. There is not a poem without some unusual thought or pleasant phrase, and there is scarcely one that can be taken apart from the rest and left to explain itself with security. One of the best and most intelligible is undoubtedly 'Phthisical', as Mr. Weekes has horribly named a very beautiful description of the approach of dawn, supposed to be written by a dying man. I quote the central verses:

> Long before the dawn
>   Yesterday,
> Sleepless thro' the twilights fair,
> I was somehow drawn,
>   Unaware,
> Into love of this old earth—
>   Could I say!
>
> First the stillness; then
>   Round the house
> Flew the owls a moment; and
> Silence once again:
>   All the land
> Lay in perfect twilight; stirred
>   Not a mouse.
>
> Fallen thus on peace,
>   I awoke
> To that speechless thought of her;
> Gave me wondrous ease.
>   Not a stir
> Marked I till the mellow-tongued
>   Blackbird spoke.
>
> Then returned the owls.
>   From the wall
> Dropped the plaster on the walk.
>   Jackdaw-talk.
> In the Herrick Farm the cock
>   Gave a call.
>
> Silence then. In haste
>   O'er the town
> Thatched and steepled, every star,
> By the morning chased,
>   Crowded far
> With the copper-coloured moon
>   Going down.

Shortly barked the fox;
　　And the cart
Rumbled on the market-road;
Then the choir of cocks
　　Hoarsely crowed;
Lastly, pulsed once more the whole
　　Eternal heart.[3]

There is surely notable literary power of some kind in this massing of
significant detail; but whether a prose power or a verse power is not
yet perfectly clear. Most of the other poems halt likewise between the
analytic method of prose, and the synthetic method of poetry; but here
and there is a poem or a stanza which in its fashion and degree is pure
poetry. 'Hesperus', despite its slightness, is such a poem:

Hesperus at milking time,
Is most beautiful of stars
Well he likes our shepherd maids,
Well he likes our lowing herds,
Rumbling wheels and clink and chime,
Of our pails and milking cars.

All our young men are made mild
When they see him in the sky;
And whenever he has smiled,
Simple mortals do not sigh:
Hesperus is friend to all,
Hesperus at milking time.[4]

The bulk of the poems are, however, less expressions of mood and
feeling than definitions or expositions of intricate arguments, subtle
conceptions, detailed observations or obstinate questionings; and if but
seldom these arguments, conceptions, observations, and questionings
are expressed with enough precision of form and boldness of cadence
to be absolutely poetry, they are well-nigh always poetical and stimu-
lating, and here and there put some fine or curious thought into really
memorable shape, as in the little lyric called 'Art'[5]—

Upon the mid-stream rushing hence,[6]
　　To hold those wild hot lips which burn
　　Thy face, but never more return,
Detached from every other sense.

Upon the stream that whirls along
  To hold that wondrous hue alone;
  Or that delightful undertone
Detached from every other song.

At last, upon the flowing stream
  To hold, and with the inward sight,
  That thought within a blaze of light,
Detached from every other dream.

—or reset an ancient question in a new way, as in 'That':[7]

What is that beyond this[8] life,
And beyond all life around,
Which, when this quick brain is still,
Nods to thee from the stars?
Lo, it says, thou hast found
Me, the lonely, lonely one.

Mr. Weekes is least successful in his longer poems, though in all there are fine stanzas and passages; for a big canvas or long discussion seems to absorb too much of his attention and make his style get out of control like a ship in a high wind. These longer poems are full of uncouth ejaculations and abbreviations, no less than of echoes from Browning, Arnold, and Omar Khayyam,[9] strange in so original a writer. The book is, however, marked by daring—and in literature the prize falls to the bold sooner or later—and is, apart from its promise, both moving and interesting.

SEEN IN THREE DAYS

Yeats reviewed Seen in Three Days, *a long poem written, engraved, and illustrated by Edwin J. Ellis (London: Quaritch, 1893), in* The Bookman *of February 1894.*

After spending almost five years with Ellis in puzzling out the symbolism of Blake, Yeats seems to have been unwilling to spend very much time puzzling out the symbolism of E. J. Ellis. Yeats had given Ellis's first book of poems, Fate in Arcadia, *a good review, but* Seen in Three Days *was intractable to all but summary. Yeats and Ellis seem to have drifted apart after completing their edition of Blake. Yeats visited Ellis in 1913, after Ellis was paralyzed by a series of strokes. When Yeats included some of his friend's poems in his* Oxford Book of Modern Verse, *he could not locate Ellis's literary executors. See a summary of his life in CL1, 484–85, and Yeats's Au, 143–47.*

It will ever be a matter of argument how far a poet may be obscure. I myself hold he cannot be obscure from imperfect expression except at his peril, but that obscurity born of subtle and unusual thought must often be inevitable, unless we are to lack a whole class of poetry. No wise man rails at the great Persian poet because he was called the tongue of the secret,[1] for we know his obscurity to have been inherent in his subjects. The average man reads poetry for amusement, or as a mere rest after the day's work, and to him there naturally seems nothing more absurd and abominable than a poem which gave him a great deal of trouble. Yet even the poetry which mingles something of the illegitimate obscurity with the legitimate is often very powerful and desirable, for poetry is not an amusement and a rest, but a fountain of ardour and peace, whither we must force our way even through briar and bramble.

Mr. Ellis's *Seen in Three Days* has a good deal of both obscurities, or this review would not be as belated as it is. The greatest difficulty in the way of a clear comprehension of its strange pages of mingled verse

Gathered and showed their playthings. Mother Night
Put off old age and raised her love-lamp high
And the world saw, and under her dark feet's
Smiled well content, and closed her flowers & slept.

This page of Ellis's *Seen in Three Days* was reproduced in *The Bookman* of February 1894 to accompany Yeats's review.

and picture is the lack of any very visible story or sequence. One is tempted to think that its pages, like the leaf-inscribed oracles of the sybil of old, were tossed hither and thither by the wind, and then bound together in the order in which the wind left them. I have at last, however, puzzled out what is, I imagine, pretty nearly the correct story. Errors I may have made, for Mr. Ellis does not, like Blake, use a technical language in which every word has the same invariable interpretation.

The poem is in blank verse, with the exception of an opening sonnet describing the being of whose wanderings it is the history.

> The great sun laughs in his eternal home
>   At this poor earth, still circling round in pain,
>   Yet in each little drop of rainbow'd rain,
> In each small bublet of the soft sea-foam,
> The same sun in a tiny crystal dome,
>   From milky morning to red evening stain
>   Rises and labours, shines and sets again.
> So, though not now we look to witness come
>   The angel of the Presence Divine to earth,[2]
> Yet in each heart there is a Presence Divine,
>   And in each Presence has an angel birth.
> If mine has wandered, has not also thine?
>   As mine returns, lo, thine returns as well,
>   Interpreting before what we would tell.

This angel of the heart enters the heart of the poet by the doorway of a dream, lifting the moon-shaped knocker.

> Three moons had made her beauty. The sea moon
> Had given the gleam in darkness to her eyes,[3]
> The moon that drives the milky flocks had woven
> Of whiter mist than theirs the slender breast
> Through which her childhood shone. The morning moon
> That looks on sunrise taught her wind-blown hair
> The tender secret of its dewy gold.

She has wandered for three days and two nights, and is shrinking in fear from the third night. 'A chain of strange learning',[4] the memory of what she has seen and heard, encircles her. The poet asks her history, and the chain wraps him round. Every link is an incident and a symbol. After a vision of dumb show and blind words, painting and poetry, he listens to the story of the angel. She first saw a girl dragged from a cave by two men upon one horse, and by this is typified the alternation throughout the poem of certain opposites, love and time, sacrifice and selfishness, innocence and experience, and so on. She then saw a vision of Fate parting lovers, for this first day is to be taken up chiefly with ill-starred love. She next saw a youth dragging a stone to the edge of a precipice. He is chained to the stone, and struggles to end his life and his captivity. This is a symbol of 'sacrificial victory', of life struggling towards death, driven on by some great enthusiasm. Immediately its opposite rises, and she sees a youth driving a spear into the breast of a maiden, because she had asked his eyes, and so releasing himself.

> But with defeat in sacrifice, for now
> He saved himself to die for Death[5] alone,
> Who might have died for her.

Near at hand her sister has asked the eagle for his wing—

> Who dares to blame the red lips of the maid
> For asking gifts? Why did God make the world,
> If not as gift-house for a maid?[6]

The eagle, who is a minor type of sacrificial victory, gave the wing and died. After that she saw the maiden mourning for the death of the eagle, and in a little, amid the coming on of night, descends, like the figure in one of Blake's designs to Blair's *Grave,* into the caverns of the grave, 'love's home in error', and sees therein the upas tree under which are those who have wedded unhappily.[7] The night is now upon her, and in the night she sees Life typified in a young girl wandering, with a panther, her incarnate fear, looking for Death to slay him with a look of abhorrence. The angel sees Death in the shape of four men, who typify human life, one full of pride about to begin the contest of life, another chained to him and crawling feebly towards an open grave, another digging the grave, and another, divine and beautiful, flying in the air. The last is the Death that 'chills the blood', but 'warms the wondering, exultant soul'.[8] The sun rises and the second day begins. The first day was devoted to love, but this is given to Time. Life, the young girl, comes out of the wood, but Fear is now in her arms disguised as a child, who apparently typifies Hope. Presently the angel sees Time changing innocence into experience. He is flinging serpents among a group of young girls who sail in a boat along a stream, which is perhaps the river of dreams. While looking at them the angel finds the child Pity in her arms. She ascends into a world of exalted contemplation, and Pity leaves her, for Pity cannot live there. She sees Beauty, 'the first of all the storms

Eternity let loose', defying time by the right of her immortality. Fate, 'silently parting lovers', brooded over the first day, the day of love, and Beauty broods over the second day, the day of time. The angel asks Beauty for 'the stone of choice'. He who lives for Beauty lives in the free will, choosing and rejecting. Beauty says that 'choice' and 'fear' are one, and will not give the stone.⁹ The angel flies, and sees for a moment a pastoral people at peace with time, and then a youth running along the seashore with a torch. He falls and dies, and another lights a new torch from his, and begins in his turn to run. This is the defeat of Time. Then the night begins to gather, and in the twilight she sees a woman with a child and two men who are friends, and these, with another man and woman and child who join them later, form a group and talk splendidly of love and friendship. This second night is ushered in, not by the vision of the upas tree, but by peace and love. Then the beneficent night comes, and 'Mother Night put off old age and raised her love lamp high'.¹⁰ The two nights are among the opposites typified by the two horsemen, as are also the two days, the day of love and the day of time, the day of that which desires steadfastness and the day of that which is eternal change. The third day now dawns, and combines the nature of the first and second days. The angel sees the unchanging and change typified, respectively, by the wandering Jew, who sees all things pass away, but is himself ever the same, and Pythagoras, who remembers a thousand lives and a thousand deaths.¹¹ They talk together magnificently for many pages.

This abstract and partial interpretation will, in spite of its inadequacy, help the reader, I think, to read with pleasure one of the most singular poems of our time. I feel there are oppositions and correspondences in plenty which I do not understand, for the mystics cannot, or will not, let any quite pluck out the heart of their mystery. Though not equal to Mr. Ellis's *Fate in Arcadia,* it is full of music and beauty, and the illustrations are a considerable advance upon those in the previous book. The method, too, which Mr. Ellis has adopted of writing and then lithographing his verse, instead of printing it in the ordinary way, has reduced the merely mechanical part to a minimum, and helps to make the whole vivid with personality.

The subject of the design given above is Moonrise—¹²

> Laughing stars
> Gathered and showed their playthings. Mother Night
> Put off old age, and raised her love-lamp high,
> And the world saw, and under her dark trees
> Smiled well content, and closed her flowers and slept.¹³

A SYMBOLICAL DRAMA IN PARIS

Yeats reviewed a performance of Axël *by Jean Marie Mathias Phillippe Auguste, comte de Villiers de L'Isle-Adam (1838–89), which appeared in* The Bookman *of April 1894; it was the result of Yeats's trip to Paris in February 1894.*

He had gone to see Axël *with Maud Gonne, who must have been able to translate some of the play for him. About this time he was slowly making his way through the play in French and his difficulties with the language made the philosophy of the play seem more profound (Au, 246).*

During this visit to Paris he lived with his fellow-adept Macgregor Mathers. He called on Verlaine and turned their meeting into a short article for the April 1896 issue of the Savoy.

Axël *was a powerful influence on Yeats in the later nineties. One has only to repeat the lines quoted by Yeats, "Oh, to veil you with my hair, where you will breathe the spirit of dead roses," to evoke many poems from the collection* The Wind Among the Reeds *(the title of this book is even mentioned in the review), as well as the final lines of Dectora in* The Shadowy Waters, *"Bend lower, that I may cover you with my hair, / For we will gaze upon this world no longer."*

Yeats contributed a preface to H. P. R. Finberg's translation of Axël *(Stonebridge, Bristol: John Wright & Sons, 1925) and used three passages from this 1894 review, which I have enclosed in brackets. The preface is reprinted in* P&I, *pp. 156–58.*

The scientific movement which has swept away so many religious and philosophical misunderstandings of ancient truth has entered the English theatres in the shape of realism and Ibsenism,[1] and is now busy playing ducks and drakes with the old theatrical conventions. We no longer believe that the world was made five thousand years ago, and are beginning to suspect that Eve's apple was not the kind of apple you buy at the greengrocer's for a penny, but we have still a little faith in the virtuous hero and the wicked villain of the theatre, and in the world of tricks and puppets which is all that remains of the old romance in its decadence. Outside the theatre, science,[†] having done its work, is beginning to vanish into the obscurity of the schools, but inside there is still so much for it to do that many forget how impermanent must be its influence, and how purely destructive its mission there, and write and talk as if the imaginative method of the great dramatists, of Kalidasa,[12] of Sophocles, of Shakespeare, and of Goethe was to let its house on a lease for ever to the impassioned realisms of M. Zola[3] and of Dr. Ibsen in his later style, or to the would-be realisms of Mr. Pinero or Mr. Jones.[4] The barricades are up, and we have no thought for anything but our weapons—at least here in England. In France they had their Independent Theatre[5] before we had ours, and the movement which must follow the destructive period has come, it seems, to them already. Those among the younger generation whose temperament fits them to receive first the new current, the new force, have grown tired of the photographing of life, and have returned by the path of symbolism to imagination and poetry, the only things which are ever permanent. [The[6] puppet plays of M. Maeterlinck[7] have been followed by a still more remarkable portent. Thirty thousand francs and enthusiastic actors have been found to produce the *Axël*[†] of his master, Villiers de L'Isle-Adam.[†] On February the 26th a crowded audience of artists and men of letters listened, and on the whole with enthusiasm, from two o'clock until ten minutes to seven to this drama, which is written in prose as elevated as poetry, and in which all the characters are symbols and all the events allegories. It is nothing to the point that the general public have since shown that they will have none of *Axël*,[†] and that the critics have denounced it in almost the same words as those in which they denounce in this country the work of Dr. Ibsen, and that they have called the younger generation both morbid and gloomy.] That they would do so was obvious from the first, for to them the new dramatic art is 'like a lawyer serving a writ,' and must be for a good while to come. [One[8] fat old critic who sat near me, so soon as the Magician of the Rosy-Cross,[9] who is the chief person of the third act, began to denounce the life of pleasure and to utter the ancient doctrine of the spirit, turned round with his back to the stage and looked at the pretty girls through his opera-glass. One can well imagine his feelings, at least if they were at all like those which an elderly English critic would feel under like circumstance. Have we not proved, he doubtless thought, that nothing is fit for the stage except the opinions which everybody believes, the feelings which everybody shares, the wit which everybody understands? and yet, in spite of all we have done, they have brought Dr. Ibsen and the intellect onto the boards, and now here comes Villiers de

L'Isle-Adam† and that still more unwholesome thing the soul.] I don't know which of the criticisms that I have read was by my fat old neighbour, but really he might have written any of them, even those by men supposed to be 'advanced'. Revolutions have notoriously eaten their own children, and the imaginative movement can do no other than be the death of the merely analytic and rationalistic critics who have made it possible by clearing away the rubbish and the wreckage of the past.

M. Paul Verlaine says of a type of woman common in the works of Villiers de L'Isle-Adam,† 'Villiers conjures up the spectre of a mysterious woman, a queen of pride, who is mournful and fierce as the night when it still lingers though the dawn is beginning, with reflections of blood and of gold upon her soul and her beauty'.[10] In the play Sara, a woman of this strange Medusa-like type, comes to the castle of a Count Axël,† who lives in the Black Forest studying magic with Janus,[11] a wizard ascetic of the Rosy Cross. When she arrives he has already refused first the life of the world, typified by the advice of a certain 'commander' his cousin, the life of the spiritual intellect labouring in the world but not of it, as symbolized by the teaching and practice of the adept Janus; and she herself has refused the religious life as symbolized by the veil of the nun. In a last great scene they meet in a vault full of treasure—the glory of the world—and avow their mutual love. He first tries to kill her because the knowledge that she is in the world will never let him rest.[12] She throws herself upon his neck and cries, 'Do not kill me; what were the use? I am unforgettable. Think what you refuse. All the favour of other women were not worth my cruelties. I am the most mournful of virgins. I think that I can remember having made angels fall. Alas, flowers and children have died in my shadow. Give way to my love. I will teach you marvellous words which intoxicate like the wine of the East. . . . I know the secrets of infinite joys, of delicious cries, of pleasures beyond all hope . . . , to veil you with my hair, where you will breathe the spirit of dead roses'.[13] The marvellous scene prolongs itself from wonder to wonder till in the height of his joyous love Axël† remembers that this dream must die in the light of the common world, and pronounces the condemnation of all life, of all pleasure, of all hope. The lovers resolve to die. They drink poison, and so complete the fourfold renunciation—of the cloister, of the active life of the world, of the labouring life of the intellect, of the passionate life of love. The infinite is alone worth attaining, and the infinite is the possession of the dead. Such appears to be the moral. Seldom has utmost pessimism found a more magnificent expression.

The final test of the value of any work of art to our particular needs, is when we place it in the hierarchy of those recollections which are our standards and our beacons. At the head of mine are a certain night scene long ago, when I heard the wind blowing in a bed of reeds by the border of a little lake,[14] a Japanese picture of cranes flying through a blue sky, and a line or two out of Homer. I do not place any part of *Axël*[†] with these perfect things, but still there are lines of the adept Janus, of the Medusa Sara, which are near them in my hierarchy. Indeed the play throughout gives a noble utterance to those sad thoughts which come to the most merry of us, and thereby robs them of half their bitterness. We need not fear that it will affect the statistics of suicide, for the personages of great art are for the most part too vast, too remote, too splendid, for imitation. They are merely metaphors in that divine argument which is carried on from age to age, and perhaps from world to world, about the ultimate truths of existence. It is not 'Ecclesiastes,'[15] but the sordid and jangled utterance of daily life which has saddened the world. In literature, moreover, it is seldom the sad book, the sad play which corrupts, but rather the cheap laughter, the trivial motive of books and plays which give the mind no trouble. In a decade when the comic paper and the burlesque are the only things sure to awaken enthusiasm, a grim and difficult play by its mere grimness and difficulty is a return to better traditions, it brings us a little nearer the heroic age.

I hear that there is a chance of *Axël*[†] being performed in London;[16] if so, I would suggest that the second and third acts be [enormously[17] reduced in length. The second act especially dragged greatly. The situation is exceedingly dramatic, and with much of the dialogue left out would be very powerful. The third act, though very interesting, to anyone familiar with the problems and philosophy it deals with, must inevitably as it stands bore and bewilder the natural man, with no sufficient counterbalancing advantage. There was no question of the dramatic power of the other acts. Even the hostile critics have admitted this.] The imaginative drama must inevitably make many mistakes before it is in possession of the stage again, for it is so essentially different to the old melodrama and the new realism, that it must learn its powers and limitations for itself. It must also fail many times before it wins the day, for though we cannot hope to ever again see the public as interested in sheer poetry, as the audiences were who tolerated so great a poet, so poor a dramatist as Chapman,[18] it must make its hearers learn to understand eloquent and beautiful dialogues, and to admire them for their own sake and not as a mere pendent to the action. For this reason its very mistakes when they are of the kind made by the promoters of *Axël*[†] help to change the public mind in the right direction, by reminding it very forcibly that the actor should be also a reverent reciter of majestic words.

THE EVANGEL OF FOLK-LORE

This review of William Larminie's West Irish Folk-Tales *(London: E. Stock, 1893) appeared in* The Bookman, *June 1894. The years 1893–1894 represented the height of Yeats's interest in folklore. His own* Celtic Twilight *had appeared in 1893. In such essays as "The Message of the Folk-lorist" (*The Speaker, *19 August 1893), Yeats had claimed, as he does here, that the greatest writers of the world were dependent upon folklore for their inspiration.*

Larminie (1849–1900) was a poet as well as a folklorist. A book of his poems, Fand and Other Poems *(Dublin: Hodges, Figgis, and Co., 1892), was reviewed by Yeats in* United Ireland, *23 July 1892. Larminie contributed, with Yeats, to the symposium* Literary Ideals in Ireland *(Dublin, 1899).*

———

The recent revival of Irish literature has been very largely a folk-lore revival, an awakening of interest in the wisdom and ways of the poor, and in the poems and legends handed down among the cabins. Past Irish literary movements[1] were given overmuch to argument and oratory; their poems, with beautiful exceptions, were noisy and rhetorical, and their prose, their stories even, ever too ready to flare out in expostulation and exposition. So manifest were these things that many had come to think the Irish nation essentially rhetorical and unpoetical, essentially a nation of public speakers and journalists, for only the careful student could separate the real voice of Ireland, the song which has never been hushed since history began, from all this din and bombast. But now the din and bombast are passing away, or, at any rate, no longer mistaken for serious literature, and life is being studied and passion sung not for what can be proved or disproved, not for what men can be made do or not do, but for the sake of Beauty 'and Time's old daughter Truth'. Let us be just to this din and bombast; they did good in their day, helped many an excellent cause, made the young more patriotic, and set the crooked straight in many ways, but they were of practical and not poetical importance. Compare the method of the older writers with the method of the new, and lay the difference at the door of the folk-lorist, for it is practically with his eyes that Miss Barlow, Miss Lawless, Mr. Standish O'Grady, and Mrs. Hinkson[2] in her later work, look at Irish life and manners, and it is he who has taught them to love the wisdom and ways of the poor, the events which have shaped those ways and that wisdom, and the kings and heroes of the phantasies of the cabin with so simple a love, such a quiet sincerity. There is indeed no school for literary Ireland just now like the school of folk-lore; and, lest the school should lack teachers, every year brings us some new collection. Mr. Curtin, Lady Wilde,[†] Dr. Hyde, Mr. McAnally,[†] Mr. Fitzgerald[3] have already given us a goodly parcel of the ancient romance, and now comes Mr. Larminie with as fine a book as the best that has been.

Is not the evangel of folk-lore needed in England also? For is not England likewise unduly fond of the story and the poem which have a moral in their scorpion tail.[†] These little stories of Mr. Larminie's have no moral, and yet, perhaps, they and their like are the only things really immortal, for they were told in some shape or other, by old men at the fire before Nebuchadnezzar[4] ate grass, and they will still linger in some odd crannie or crevice of the world when the pyramids have crumbled into sand. Their appeal is to the heart and not to the intellect. They take our emotions and fashion them into forms of beauty as a goldsmith fashions gold, as a silversmith fashions silver. Our love for woman's beauty is for ever a little more subtle once we have felt the marvel of that tale of a boy who, finding on the road a little box containing a lock of hair which shone with a light like many candles, travelled through numberless perils to find her from whose head it had been shorn;[5] our sense of pity is ever a little more poignant once we have understood the charm of that tale of the woman who dwelt seven years in hell to save her husband's soul, keeping—for such was her appointed work—the ever-bobbing souls of the lost from getting out of a great boiler, and then another seven years that she might have the right to take all she could carry, and bring the souls away clinging to her dress.[6] Nor can our power of wonder be other than a little more transcendent when we have dreamed that dream of 'the place where were seals, whales, crawling, creeping things, little beasts of the sea with red mouths, rising on the sole and palm of the oar, making faery music and melody for themselves, till the sea, arose in strong waves, hushed with magic, hushed with wondrous voices';[7] or of the magical adventurer who became for a year a grey flagstone covered with heaps of ice and snow, and yet died not wholly, but awoke again and turned to his adventures as before.[8]

And there are a plenty of such things in Mr. Larminie's book, more, perhaps, than in any book of Irish folk-lore since Lady Wilde's† *Ancient Legends*. Dr. Hyde is by far the best Irish folk-lorist by the right of his incomparable skill as a translator from the Gaelic, and among the first of Irish story-tellers by the right of 'Teig O'Kane', well nigh as memorable a masterpiece as 'Wandering Willie's Tale';⁹ but his *Beside the Fire* is no such heaped-up bushel of primeval romance and wisdom as *West Irish Folk Tales*. Mr. Larminie gathered his store in remote parts of Donegal, Roscommon and Galway,¹⁰ and his book has the extravagance and tumultuous movement as of waves in a storm, which Mr. Curtin had already taught us to expect from the folk tale of the extreme west. When such tales are well understood; when the secret of their immortality is mastered; when writers have begun to draw on them as copiously as did Homer, and Dante, and Shakespeare, and Spenser, then will the rhetorician begin to wither and the romance maker awake from a sleep as of a grey flagstone, and shake off the ice and snow and weave immortal woofs again.

A NEW POET

Yeats's first review of AE's Homeward, Songs by the Way *appeared in* The Bookman, *August 1894. The title was first published as* Homeward: Songs by the Way *by Whaley and Co. in 1894, but subsequent editions appeared both with the colon and with no punctuation at all. While AE always used a comma in later life, Yeats most often used a colon when referring to this first volume of AE's poems.*

AE, the first two letters to the Gnostic word AEON, meaning "heavenly spirit," was the pen name of George William Russell (1867–1935), one of Yeats's oldest friends. Their acquaintance began when they studied together at the Dublin School of Art. Yeats took part in the activities of the Dublin lodge of the Theosophical Society in Ely Place, where Russell lived until his marriage. Russell printed an article by Yeats on the Irish fairies in his magazine The Irish Theosophist *(see pp. 182–84 above). This present review was part of a publicity campaign that Yeats told John O'Leary (CL1, 391) he would organize in London for AE's first volume of poems. Yeats was unceasing in his praise of Russell until the end of the century.*

In his autobiography Yeats said of Russell, "We are never satisfied with the maturity of those whom we have admired in boyhood . . ." (Au, 200). Although Yeats and AE remained good friends, their disillusionment was mutual.

Yeats wrote a notice of the American edition of this book in the May 1895 issue of The Bookman.

A young Englishman of literary ambition is usually busy with details of rhythm, the advantages of opposing methods, and the like, and is content to leave problems of government to the journalists, and questions of fate, free-will, foreknowledge absolute,[1] to the professors and the devils. In Ireland we go into the other extreme, and our literature has sprung generally from some movement in public affairs, and, but for the lack of education and the belief that all such matters have been settled out of hand by the Catholic Church, would, I doubt not, have sprung also from philosophical movements, for an Irishman cut adrift from his priest is exceedingly speculative. A little school of transcendental[2] writers has indeed started up in the last year or two, as it is, and made many curious and some beautiful lyrics. I make no excuse for telling its history, for not one moment is trivial among the million ages which Blake says go to the making of a flower.[3] About twelve years ago seven youths[4] began to study European magic and Oriental mysticism, and because, as the Gaelic proverb puts it, contention is better than loneliness,[5] agreed to meet at times in a room in a dirty back street and to call their meetings 'The Dublin Hermetic Society'. They gradually accumulated a set of convictions for themselves, of which a main part was, I think, that the poets were uttering, under the mask of phantasy, the old revelations, and that we should truly look for genii of the evening breeze and hope for the final consummation of the world when two halcyons might sit upon a bough and eat once-poisonous herbs and take no harm.[6] As for the rest, they spent their days in battles about the absolute and the alcahest,[7] and I think that none read the newspapers, and am sure that some could not have told you the name of the viceroy. These periodical meetings started a movement, and the movement has begun to make literature. One of the group[8] published last year a very interesting book of verse which he withdrew from circulation in a moment of caprice, and now AE,† its arch-visionary, has published *Homeward,† Songs by the Way*, a pamphlet of exquisite verse. He introduces it with this quaint preface: 'I moved among men and places and in living I learned the truth at last. I know I am a spirit, and that I went forth from the self-ancestral to labours yet unaccomplished; but, filled ever and again with homesickness, I made these songs by the way.'[9] The pamphlet is in no sense, however, the work of a preacher, but of one who utters, for the sake of beauty alone, the experience of a delicate and subtle temperament. He is a moralist, not because he desires, like the preacher, to coerce our will, but because good and evil are a part of what he splendidly calls 'the multitudinous meditation'[10] of the divine world in whose shadow he seeks to dwell. No one who has an ear for poetry at all can fail to find a new voice and a new music in lines like these:

> What of all the will to do?
>   It has vanished long ago,
> For a dream-shaft pierced it through
>   From the Unknown Archer's bow.

What of all the soul to think?
    Some one offered it a cup
Filled with a diviner drink,
    And the flame has burned it up.

What of all the hope to climb?
    Only in the self we grope
To the misty end of time:
    Truth has put an end to hope.

What of all the heart to love?
    Sadder than for will or soul,
No light lured it on above;
    Love has found itself the whole.[11]

Such poetry is profoundly philosophical in the only way in which poetry can be; it describes the emotions of a soul dwelling in the presence of certain ideas. Some passionate temperaments, amorous of the colour and softness of the world, will refuse the quietism of the idea in a poem like 'Our Thrones† Decay', but they can do no other than feel the pathos of the emotion:

'I said my pleasure shall not move;
    It is not fixed in things apart;
Seeking not love—but yet to love—
    I put my trust in my own heart.

I know the fountain of the deep
    Wells up with living joy, unfed:
Such joys the lonely heart may keep,
    And love grow rich with love unwed.

Still flows the ancient fount sublime;
    But, ah, for my heart, shed tears, shed tears;
Not it but love has scorn of time;
    It turns to dust beneath the years.'[12]

Nor would AE† be angry with one who turned away from his ideas, for he himself knows well that all ideas fade or change in passing from one mind to another, and that what we call 'truth' is but one of our illusions, a perishing embodiment of a bodiless essence:

The hero first taught it:
  To him 'twas a deed;
To those who retaught it
  A chain on their speed.

The fire that we kindled—
  A beacon by night—[13]
When darkness has dwindled
  Grows pale in the light.

For life has no glory
  Stays long in one dwelling,
And time has no story
  That's true twice in telling.

And only the teaching
  That never was spoken
Is worthy the reaching
  The fountain unbroken.

There are everywhere such memorable lines as 'Come earth's little children, pit pat from their burrows in the hill', 'White for Thy whiteness all desires burn', 'Withers once more the old blue flower of day', 'The fiery dust of evening shaken from the feet of light', 'We are but embers wrapped in clay', 'Make of thy gentleness thy might', 'Be thou thyself that goal in which the wars of time shall cease', and 'No image of the proud and morning stars looks at us from their faces'.[14]

The book has faults in plenty, certain rhymes are repeated too often, the longer lines stumble now and again, and here and there a stanza is needlessly obscure; but, taken all in all, it is the most haunting book I have seen these many days. Books published in Ireland are only too often anything but comely to look at, but this little pamphlet makes us hope much from the new house of Whaley,[15] for it is beautifully printed upon excellent paper.

SOME IRISH NATIONAL BOOKS

In this article for The Bookman, *August 1894, Yeats reviewed* The New
Spirit of the Nation, *edited by Martin McDermott (London and
Dublin: T. Fisher Unwin and P. J. Kennedy, 1894); A Parish Providence
by E. M. Lynch (London and Dublin: T. Fisher Unwin, 1894); and* The
Jacobite War in Ireland, 1688–1691 *(Dublin: Sealy, Bryers and
Walker, 1894) by Charles O'Kelly, edited by George Noble Count Plun-
kett and the Reverend Edmund Hogan, S.J.*

*This review was Yeats's sweet revenge for his defeat two years
before by Sir Charles Gavan Duffy in their battle for the editorship of
the New Irish Library series, a publishing venture that grew out of the
inauguration in 1892 of the National Literary Society. Yeats had pre-
dicted that Sir Charles, in his old age, would choose books according
to outmoded taste, and he was not slow in pronouncing the same opinion over the books as they appeared. Some of his reviews of later volumes were more favorable.*

Lord Beaconsfield[1] once said that the way to give a successful supper
party was never to ask anybody who had to be explained, and the
advice is good for more important matters. The members of 'The Irish
Literary Society' of London and 'The National Literary Society' of
Dublin, and the other persons responsible for the present Irish literary
movement, had done well to have taken it to heart and avoided anything so desperately in need of explanation as three out of the four
books already published in this *New Irish Library.* Their first volume,
The Patriot Parliament,[2] was an historical tractate which, if modified
a little, had done well among the transactions of a learned society, but
it bored beyond measure the unfortunate persons who bought some
thousands of copies in a few days, persuaded by the energy of the two
societies, and deluded by the names of Sir Charles Gavan Duffy and
Thomas Davis[3] upon the cover. Pages upon pages of Acts of Parliament
may be popular literature on the planet Neptune, or chillier Uranus,

but our quick-blooded globe has altogether different needs. The admirable and picturesque book by Mr. O'Grady,[4] which followed, did well, I understand, despite the vehement refusal of numbers of the peasantry to take anything from a series which had already beguiled them outrageously; but I cannot believe that the most skilful advertising, the most eloquent appeals to patriotism, the most energetic canvassing will make the Irish people read *The New Spirit of the Nation* or *The Parish Providence.*

The New Spirit of the Nation is a gleaning from the same fields from which the editors of *The Spirit of the Nation*[5] reaped their not too golden sheaves. If, however, one except three or four songs of excellent oratory by D'Arcy McGee,[6] and an interesting fragment by Davis called 'Maurye Nangle', it contains nothing good which cannot be found with better company in several other collections. If one desire to possess 'The Dark Rosaleen', or 'O'Donovan's Daughter'[7]—and this about exhausts the list of desirable things—one had best give nine pence for Mr. Sparling's *Irish Minstrelsy.*[8]

The editor of this series, Sir Charles Gavan Duffy, should have given us a book which, while containing the best work of Callanan, Walsh,[9] and Davis, and the other ballad makers, would have drawn more largely and carefully than Mr. Sparling's from the masters of Irish song—Ferguson, Mangan, Allingham, and de Vere[†10]—and, unlike his, have taken up whatever well-wrought fragments remain of Tom Moore's[11] ruined house. Such a book would have won the enthusiastic admiration of every class in Ireland, and could have been put into the hands of a cultivated man of any country without need of explanation. But what educated person, even when you have explained its political value, its moral earnestness, its practical utility, can take pleasure in

> Come, Liberty, come! we are ripe for thy coming;
>   Come[12] freshen the hearts where thy rival has trod;
> Come, richest and rarest! come, purest and fairest,[13]
>   Come, daughter of science! come, gift of the god!

Such jigging doggerel[†]—I regret I have no gentler word—is in its place upon a broadsheet, or in one of Cameron and Ferguson's little Irish song-books,[14] but how can it do other than hinder a literary movement which must perish, or dwindle into insignificance if it do not draw into its net the educated classes? You may persuade the half-educated country clerk or farmer's son that 'Come richest and rarest, come purest and fairest' is noble rhythm and shining poetry, but the wholly uneducated peasant of the mountains and the wholly educated professional man of the cities will have none of it, for the one has his beautiful Gaelic ballads and his tumultuous world-old legends, while the gleaming city of English literature flings wide its doors to the other.

The truth of the matter is that Sir Charles Gavan Duffy has let that old delusion, didacticism, get the better of his judgment, as Wordsworth did when he wrote the Ecclesiastical Sonnets,[15] and has given us a library which, however pleasing it be to 'the daughter of science, the gift of the god', is, if we except Mr. O'Grady's stories, little but a cause of blaspheming to mere mortals, who would gladly see the Irish reading classes discovering the legends and stories and poems of their own country, instead of following at a laborious distance the fashions of London.

To make it wholly clear that he has some other intention than to gather into one series the best works of the Irish writers of the past and present, Sir Charles Gavan Duffy has made a book out of one of the poorest of Balzac's novels,[16] not improved by having the French names turned into English ones; an introduction on agriculture and local industries forty pages long, and made up mostly out of a fifty-year old article of his own, and an appendix full of quotations from a blue book. We might, it seems, have taken even a bad Balzac for that impracticable thing, 'mere literature', and so must needs suffer the blue books and the agricultural information with what grace we may. Not that Sir Charles Gavan Duffy has compiled this queer piece of 'Irish literature' altogether without wisdom; on the contrary, he has been careful to issue his wares as an innocent 'country tale' by 'E. M. Lynch', and suppresses upon cover and title-page alike all mention either of Balzac or of agriculture; they spring on you together in the introduction. He has been always, the fact is, an influence making for didacticism, rather than literature—for his great qualities are essentially practical. William Carleton,[17] after a succession of masterpieces, contributed three stories to his 'Library of Ireland', and in them departed from his own admirable manner, and, instead of creating new masterpieces of pity and humour, wrote three tracts against intemperance, sloth, and the secret societies, and never after quite got the beam out of his eyes. Yet it is no way clear why it should be held for righteousness in any man to over-balance the right proportions of nature and caricature humanity to make some commonplace moral shine out with artificial distinctness; or that a wiser age would do other than hold all such works for the creation of the Father of Lies.[18]

The first volume of *The Irish Home Library,* the Dublin rival to *The New Irish Library,* is a good book of its kind, being an account of the war of William and James[19] in Ireland by a man who was in the thick of it, but one has some doubt whether it be of a good kind to start a popular library. Surely one needs something more picturesque, more vivid, if one would catch the general taste. For instance, we have famous figures flitting about the pages—Sarsfield, Schomberg, William, James, Tyrconnell[†20]—but not one is ever described or made live as a man before us. O'Kelly[21] wrote for historians who had them already before their eyes, or for comrades who had seen them in the flesh, and did all needful for his purpose. Yet it is a good book, edited carefully by two excellent scholars—Father Hogan and Count Plunkett[22]—and cannot be recommended too strongly to one already interested in the period of which it treats. It is, however, books which can create an interest where there is none which are needed for a series of this kind, and if any publisher would set Mr. O'Grady, Dr. Hyde, Miss Lawless, Miss Barlow, Dr. Todhunter, Mrs. Bryant, and Mrs. Hinkson,[23] to the making of such books, he would probably prosper.

AN IMAGED WORLD

This anonymous review of Edward Garnett's An Imaged World: Poems in Prose (London: J. M. Dent & Co., 1894) appeared in The Speaker of 8 September 1894. Edward Garnett (1868–1937) was the son of Richard Garnett (1835–1906), the Keeper of Printed Books at the British Museum, and the father of David Garnett (1892–1981), the author. As a reader for T. Fisher Unwin, Garnett was influential in having this firm publish some of Yeats's early works.

During the controversy over the management of the New Irish Library, Yeats appealed to Garnett to help save this projected series of books from the editorship of Sir Charles Gavan Duffy (the firm of Unwin was to publish the books in England). Garnett may have used his influence, but the forces combined against Yeats were too strong, and Duffy became the editor of this project.

In October 1892, Yeats asked Garnett: "How does the Imaged World thrive? Please let me know before any work of yours comes out as I am now reviewing on the Bookman and and may be able to be of use" (CL1, 323). An Imaged World: Poems in Prose was given a bad review in The Bookman of August 1894. There is no strong indication that Yeats wrote this review. Although he may have used his influence to get the book reviewed, he could not control the opinion of the reviewer. Yeats previously had solicited reviews for friends only to have the reviews turn out badly.

This Speaker review has many signs of Yeats's authorship, including the references to Vaughan the Silurist, an alchemist named Dr. Rudd, and the quotation from Blake. We know from other reviews that Yeats was familiar with The Bard of the Dimbovitza, referred to in the phrase "the peasant poets of Roumania." He did not like prose poems and this attitude is made plain in this review in spite of the friendliness shown to Garnett. The misquotations, in contrast to the letter-perfect Bookman review, are usual in Yeats's reviews.

When Vaughan the Silurist said that man was a world and had another to attend him,[1] he but expressed the faith of those mediaeval mystics who held the soul to correspond exactly to the universe, and its emotions to the stars and the forest, the seas and the storms. Man had Nature for his friend or foe, they held, and must study her whims and phantasies, or she would pelt him with hail and rain or affright him with choleric meteors, and some of the wisest among them were so privileged as to behold her in human shape, like the alchemist, Dr. Rudd,[2] who met her walking, 'black but comely', in his garden in Devonshire, and when she departed after much wise conversation, noted down that she went, 'half smiling and half sad', in a way that was 'very pretty', for she was loth to fade from him and be disguised in the noisy elements again.

Mr. Garnett has cultivated this ancient intimacy with tact and patience, and the images of his *Imaged World* are but the haphazard shapes and shadows which Nature casts upon the 'glass of imagination';[3] and through his whole work runs a sense of union with her and hers which lacks only the hard touch of philosophy to become mediaeval and mystical. It is supposed to be written by a lover who finds in every change of weather, in every passing face, a symbol of his own joy or trouble, an adherent or an enemy of his hopes. Now it is the path in the wood which shares his longing: 'O Hyld! down there in the woods my feet have bruised a tiny path amid the autumn grass, as I went, thinking of thee; a little path amid nut-bushes winding. It has not led me to an end; O girl, have pity on that poor bruised path, which cannot speak its heart, and come and pass by it'.[4] And now the night holds his love from him, and he calls out to the storms: 'Tear the swart twilight, O rushing white rain-storm; tear the edge of the fast-travelling night, and let my love through to me! Yes, all the sombre horizon is ravelling with a foam edge of light in the dying west—ah, if I could get there, if I could get there, thou and my fate would meet me! Art thou jeering at me, O storm-wind? Ah! wait a little, O lone night, and thou shalt hear us whispering our secrets together! O streaming leaves, when the wind has flung ye dying on earth's cold bosoms, I shall be lying on my love's warm breasts'.[5] And yet, again, it is the faces in the street that keep her from him: 'Faces, faces; everywhere I see fresh faces, yet I could not see her gentle face. Faces, faces; fixed and serious faces all keep passing in long procession, yet I could not find her frightened face. It is you, you thousand secret-hiding faces, that she feared, your curious eyes and sneering looks, if you had guessed her secret'.[6] Sometimes he broods over other things than love, but always as a lover—always as one who seeks to be alone, always as one filled with a consuming idealism which makes every imperfect thing dreadful; and through all his meditations is the recurring thought that men and women have fallen for ever from beauty and happiness. His final word is: 'O young earth, fresh earth, earth of ecstasy, would that we, the grey multitudes with our pale pleasures, had never been born in thy green lap! O grant that memory of us be lost when to the young clear-eyed race shalt pass thy mountains, plains, and forests. Grant then that our cities lie buried deep, and thy heart, O earth, betray us not when the surf-waves break athwart the dance of the twining, laughing girls, at purple eve, on the great sea's windy shore'.[7]

There is enough of poetry in this remarkable book for many poems, and yet it seldom perfectly satisfies the artistic conscience or quite lays asleep the thought that we will forget it when it is thrust into the shelf. It is almost impossible to open it without finding beauty, but in the midst of the most beautiful passages will come a word without precision[8] or a phrase without music, and the impression of the whole is a little vapoury. Here and there, too, Mr. Garnett's own thoughts and methods struggle for mastery with a mannerism from Walt Whitman or Richard Jefferies, or the peasant poets of Roumania.[9] The truth is that Mr. Garnett has discovered a medium which suits him and which, despite the general prejudice against everything called 'a poem in prose,' is as legitimate as any other, but can, as yet, only at times fulfil the ideal of the inevitable words in the inevitable order; and that he has gathered many pathetic and lovely impressions and moods, but has not yet amassed them into a coherent image of the world and marked them round with what Blake called 'the outline of the Almighty.'[10] The more emotional and ideal a writer's manner and material the more firm must be his hand, the more orderly the procession of his moods, if he would have his book draw us out of our common interests and linger in the memory when we have returned to them again. Despite all defects, however, *An Imaged World* is full of delightful things; nor is it other than delightful to look upon, for Mr. William Hyde,[11] who has no equal within his limits, has made for it five illustrations full of the exultation of wind and sea, of the triumph of moon and stars, and two designs of barbed leaves for the cover and margins, which, though less memorable and though one is repeated too often, are comely and pleasant to the fancy.

THE STONE AND THE ELIXIR

Yeats reviewed Ibsen's Brand, *in a verse translation by F. E. Garrett (London, 1894), in* The Bookman *of October 1894.*

Yeats deplored the influence of Ibsen on the English stage. He tells in his autobiography of his dislike for a performance of A Doll's House. Rosmersholm *is described as a play ". . . where there is symbolism and a stale odour of spilt poetry" (Au, 219). Yeats could neither agree with "very clever young journalists" who admired Ibsen's realism nor adopt the views of conventional people who were shocked by Ibsen's themes.*

Yeats liked Brand *and* Peer Gynt, *after his fashion. This review gave him an opportunity to raise poetry above didactic art and the early verse plays of Ibsen over his later problem plays.*

Certain alchemical writers say that the substance left behind in the retort is the philosopher's stone, and the liquid distilled over, the elixir or alkahest; and all are agreed that the stone transmutes everything into gold, while the elixir dissolves everything into nothing, and not a few call them the fixed and the volatile. One might take these contraries as symbols of the minds of Brand and Peer Gynt. Peer Gynt lets sheer phantasy take possession of his life, and fill him with the delusion that he is this or that personage, now a hunter, now a troll, now a merchant, now a prophet, until the true Peer Gynt is well-nigh dissolved. Brand, upon the other hand, seeks to rise into an absolute world where there is neither hunter, nor troll, nor merchant, nor prophet, but only God and his laws, and to transmute by the force of his unchanging ideal everything about him into imperishable gold, only to perish amid ice and snow with the cry in his ears, 'Die! the earth[1] has no use for thee!' His mistake is not less disastrous, though immeasurably nobler, than the mistake of Peer Gynt, for the children of the earth can only live by compromise, by half measures, and by disobedience to his impassioned appeal:

Grant you are slaves to pleasure; well,
Be so, from curfew-bell to bell;
Don't be some special thing one minute
And something else the next, by fits!
Whate'er you are be whole soul in it,
Not only piecemeal and in bits!
There's beauty in a true Bacchante;
But in your toper's headache, scanty.
Silenus still is picturesque;
A tippler is the god's grotesque.
Go round the country, do but fling
A watchful glance at folks; you'll see
That every one has learned to be
A little bit of everything.
A little smug (on holy days);
A little true to old-time ways;
A little sensual when he sups—
(His fathers were so in their cups). [2]

Poetry has ever loved those who are not 'piecemeal,' and has made of them its Timons and its Lears,[3] but Nature, which is all 'piecemeal,' has ever cast them out.

Dr. Jaeger and Mr. Boyesen[4] will have it that *Peer Gynt* is a description of what Ibsen believes his countrymen to be, and *Brand* of what he would have them become, while Mr. Bernard Shaw reads *Brand* as a satire upon ideals of all kinds.[5] These various readings are but so many proofs that the poem is not an argument, but a work of art; not criticism, but the substance of life; not propaganda, but poetry. Ibsen saw two types underlying all others; he saw everywhere the old duality of the alchemist, the fixed and the volatile, and created two characters to embody them, and having carried each character to its moment of perfect expression, the one amid overwhelming and lifeless snow, the other face to face with the button moulder[6] who would melt him down to make new buttons, new personalities, passed on to fresh creations. It is our business and not his to judge and measure and condemn, for the work of the poet is revelation, and the work of the reader is criticism. If he turned aside from his office he would enslave us instead of liberating us, and his work would be as ephemeral as the newspaper, or the last invention.

Ibsen is, however, a man of his age, and to him individual character, instead of being an end in itself, as it was to the Elizabethan dramatist, is but a means for the expression of broad generalisations and classifications, and of the pressure of religion and social life upon the soul; and it is his peculiar glory that he makes us share his interest in these things, and makes them move us as they move him, and yet never sinks the artist in the theorist or the preacher. But because he writes of things of which the theorist makes his theories, the preacher his commandments, he has been caught up by all manner of propagandists, who dream him one of themselves. And because prose is more syllogistic than poetry, and because the theorist and the preacher have devoured the land like the locust, the later and less imaginative though profoundly interesting plays have been acted and expounded to the neglect of the works of his prime, and until two or three years ago neither *Brand* nor *Peer Gynt* had been translated. Now, however, we have one, presumably literal though not over poetical, translation of *Peer Gynt*, and three of *Brand*, one in prose and two in verse, and have seen a pathetic and incomparable fragment of *Brand* upon the stage. This last *Brand* by Mr. Garrett is rather more vigorous than its immediate predecessor by Dr. Herford, and on the whole more satisfactory than Mr. Wilson's prose version.[7] A poem when robbed of its metrical architecture seems vague and rhetorical, just as the best prose if put into rhyme and metre would seem incredibly flat and long drawn out. Prose translations are of infinite use as books of reference, but can never be final. On the other hand, neither Dr. Herford nor Mr. Garrett can claim to have given us a definitive translation, but then definitive translations are even rarer than works of original genius.

BATTLES LONG AGO

This review of Standish James O'Grady's The Coming of Cuculain *(London: Methuen & Co., 1895) is from* The Bookman, *February 1895.*

Every one of the great European legend cycles has inspired the poets and musicians of our time, except, curiously enough, the one which is probably the most copious and ancient. The German and Scandinavian lives again in Wagner and Morris, the Welsh delights thousands in *The Idylls of the King*, and in Mr. Swinburne's *Tristram and Iseult*; but the Irish was until yesterday the exclusive possession of Professor Dryasdust and his pupils.[1] That it is becoming again an imaginative existence is due almost wholly to Mr. Standish O'Grady, whose *History of Ireland, Heroic Period*, published in 1878, was the starting point of what may yet prove a new influence in the literature of the world.[2] A couple of years ago, after a long devotion to mediaeval Ireland, he returned to his old studies, and wrote his delightful *Finn and his Companions*, and now he has just issued *The Coming of Cuculain*,[†] the memorable first part of a kind of prose epic. It is probable that no Englishman can love these books as they are loved by the many Irishmen who date their first interest in Irish legends and literature from the *History*. There is perhaps, too, something in their tumultuous vehemence, in their delight in sheer immensity, in their commingling of the spirit of man with the spirit of the elements, which belongs to the wild Celtic idealism rather than to the careful, practical ways of the Saxon. The heroes of *The Idylls of the King* are always merely brave and excellent men, calculable and measurable in every way; but the powers of Cuchulain[†] are as incalculable and immeasurable as the powers of nature. When he leaps, for instance, into his chariot, after his knighting, the spirits of the glens and the demons of the air roar about him; the gods shout within the armoury, and clash the swords and shields together; the god 'Lu, the[3] Long-handed', 'the maker and decorator of the firmament', whose hound was the sun, thunders; the god of the sea, Mananan Mac

Lir, passes 'through the assembly with a roar of innumerable waters'; and the goddess of Battle, 'the Mor Reega',[†] stands with a foot on each side of the plain, and shouts with 'the voice of a host'.

Mr. O'Grady does not attempt to give the old stories in the form they have come down to us, but passes them through his own imagination. Yet so familiar is he with the old legends, so profound a sympathy has he with their spirit, that he has made the ancient gods and heroes live over again their simple and passionate lives. The Red Branch feasting with Cullan the smith, Cuchulain[†] taming the weird horses, Cuchulain[†] hunting down in his chariot the herd of enchanted deer, whose horns and hoofs are of iron,[4] belong in nothing to our labouring noontide, but wholly to the shadowy morning twilight of time.

AN EXCELLENT TALKER

Yeats's review of A Woman of No Importance, *a comedy by Oscar Wilde (1854–1900), (London, 1894) appeared in* The Bookman *of March 1895.*

After a brief period of friendship in 1888–89, Yeats and Wilde ceased to be close friends. Wilde regarded the Rhymers' Club, especially when it met at the Cheshire Cheese, as too bohemian.

Yeats never reviewed Wilde's early works, which he admired. In his review of Lord Arthur Savile's Crime and Other Stories *(United Ireland, 26 September 1891) Yeats looked, as he did in the present review, to a better Wilde, the author of* The Picture of Dorian Gray *and the essays collected in* Intentions.

This review appeared shortly before the scandal that resulted in Wilde's imprisonment. In his autobiography, Yeats expressed his admiration of Wilde's decision to remain in England and face the vengeance of society (Au, 226).

Mr. Pater once said that Mr. Oscar Wilde wrote like an excellent talker,[1] and the criticism goes to the root. All of *The Woman of No Importance*[†] which might have been spoken by its author, the famous paradoxes, the rapid sketches of men and women of society, the mockery of most things under heaven, are delightful; while, on the other hand, the things which are too deliberate in their development, or too vehement and elaborate for a talker's inspiration, such as the plot, and the more tragic and emotional characters, do not rise above the general level of the stage. The witty or grotesque persons who flit about the hero and heroine, Lord Illingworth, Mrs. Allonby, Canon Daubeny,[†] Lady Stutfield, and Mr. Kelvil, all, in fact, who can be characterised by a sentence or a paragraph, are real men and women; and the most immoral among them have enough of the morality of self-control and self-possession to be pleasant and inspiriting memories. There is something of heroism in being always master enough of oneself to be witty; and therefore the public of to-day feels with Lord Illingworth and Mrs. Allonby much as the public of yesterday felt, in a certain sense, with that traditional villain of melodrama who never laid aside his cigarette and his sardonic smile. The traditional villain had self-control. Lord Illingworth and Mrs. Allonby have self-control and intellect; and to have these things is to have wisdom, whether you obey it or not. 'The soul is born old, but grows young. That is the comedy of life. And the body is born young and grows old. That is life's tragedy.'[2] Women 'worship successes', and 'are the laurels to hide their baldness'.[3] 'Children begin by loving their parents. After a time they judge them. Rarely if ever do they forgive them'.[4] And many another epigram, too well known to quote, rings out like the voice of Lear's fool over a mad age. And yet one puts the book down with disappointment. Despite its qualities, it is not a work of art, it has no central fire, it is not dramatic in any ancient sense of the word. The reason is that the tragic and emotional people, the people who are important to the story, Mrs. Arbuthnot, Gerald Arbuthnot, and Hester Worsley, are conventions of the stage. They win our hearts with no visible virtue, and though intended to be charming and good and natural, are really either heady and undistinguished, or morbid with what Mr. Stevenson has called 'the impure passion of remorse'.[5] The truth is, that whenever Mr. Wilde gets beyond those inspirations of an excellent talker which served him so well in 'The Decay of Lying'[6] and in the best parts of *Dorian Gray*,[†] he falls back upon the popular conventions, the spectres and shadows of the stage.

DUBLIN MYSTICS

This review from The Bookman *of May 1895 deals with the second edition of AE's* Homeward: Songs by the Way, *1895, and an American pirated edition, with additional poems (Portland, Maine: T. B. Mosher, 1895), as well as John Eglinton's* Two Essays on the Remnant *(Dublin: C. Whaley, 1895). See the introduction to "A New Poet," pp. 241–44 above, for more information on the punctuation of the title of AE's book of poems. Yeats had reviewed the first printing of* Homeward: Songs by the Way *in The Bookman of August 1894. To John O'Leary, Yeats had promised to organize a reception for AE's book, and he was faithful to his word.*

John Eglinton (1868–1961) was the pen name of William Kirkpatrick Magee, a member (with AE) of the Dublin Theosophical Society. In 1898 Yeats became involved with Eglinton in a newspaper controversy over the question of whether the ancient Irish myths were suitable subjects for the dramas of the Irish Literary Theatre. The articles of Yeats and Eglinton, as well as contributions of AE and William Larminie, were reprinted in a pamphlet entitled Literary Ideals in Ireland *(see "John Eglinton and Spiritual Art," pp. 418–22 below). Eglinton was for many years assistant librarian of the National Library of Ireland, where one may observe him in the "Scylla and Charybdis" section of James Joyce's* Ulysses, *discussing Shakespeare with AE and Stephen Dedalus.*

Yeats selected passages from Eglinton's prose for a collection printed by the Dun Emer Press in 1905. Eglinton's account of Yeats appeared in Irish Literary Portraits *(London: Macmillan, 1935).*

The success of these little books is certainly one of the significant things in the imaginative awakening of our time. *Homeward,*[†] *Songs by the Way* has been reprinted in America in an edition of 975 copies, as well as running into its second five hundred at home; while *Two Essays on the Remnant,* though published much later, is already in its

second edition.[1] Yet both books bear the imprint of an unknown publisher, and are issued in a city which has long published little but
school-books and prayer-books, and both are full of unfamiliar ideas.
They owe their success to a kind of charm rare in an age when artists
and writers obey only too much the command of the Elizabethan
painter who bade his pupils grind the whole world into paint. One
feels that the thoughts they contain were thought out for their own
sake, and not for the sake of literature; that their writers could become
silent to-morrow without a pang, and that their silence would be no
mere refuge from thought, no mere laying down of a burden. Other
writers may celebrate life and joy and love, or set their hearts on fame,
or in the sheer delight of writing, but these men write to hearten the
pilgrims to the eternal city, and to keep them from forgetting the day
AE[†] sings of:

> When the shepherd of the Ages draws his misty herds away
> Through the glimmering deeps to silence, and within the awful
>   fold
> Life and joy and love for ever vanish as a tale is told.[2]

AE[†] is always the visionary and the poet, and like all purely creative
forces, is unanalysable and incalculable; but John Eglinton[†] is none the
less a theorist and a thinker because he wraps his theories and his
thoughts in sentences which are rich and elaborate as old embroidery.
We live, he tells us, at a period when we must 'perpetuate the onward
impulse in our own individual lives', or 'content ourselves with maintaining a decadent literature, art and science';[†] and his book is a passionate and lofty appeal to the 'idealists' to come out of the modern
world as the children of Israel came out of Egypt.[3] His appeal is no mere
literary method of giving weight and emphasis to his subtle criticisms
of men and books, for it is born of the influence and doctrines of a little group of men and women who have been for years living the life he
preaches, as best they can under modern disabilities, and setting themselves in 'league', as he would have them, 'with the green hosts[†] of trees'
'and the countless[4] horde of grass that springs in the breaches of ruins
and in the interstices of depopulate pavements.'

THE STORY
OF EARLY GAELIC LITERATURE

This review of The Story of Early Gaelic Literature *by Douglas Hyde (London, 1895) from* The Bookman, *June 1895, marks a parting of ways for Yeats and Hyde. Yeats had enthusiastically greeted Hyde's earlier works of folklore, but he had ever been suspicious of the nationalism inherent in Hyde's efforts to revive the Gaelic language. By 1895 Yeats seems to have realized that the scholar and linguist in Hyde had overwhelmed whatever there had been of the imaginative artist in him. Yeats does not mention it, but this volume was from the New Irish Library. Because of his disappointment that Sir Charles Gavan Duffy had been appointed editor of the series, Yeats usually had a negative reaction to its volumes.*

Dr. Douglas Hyde is probably the most successful of all that little group of men of letters who are trying to interest the Irish people in their history and literature. His lectures in English to the National Literary Society and in Gaelic to 'The Gaelic League'[1] have had the most extraordinary effect in awakening interest in the Irish language. In towns where three or four years ago there was not a single Gaelic-speaking person there are now hundreds, and the movement is growing every day. The present book is probably intended as a textbook for these groups of enthusiasts; and though too full of exposition and appeal to have the haunting charm of the *Connacht*[†] *Love Songs,* and too full of crowded facts to touch the imagination like *Beside the Fire,* it is certainly moving and excellently readable.[2] It describes the great legend cycles, the mythological, the Cuchulain,[†] the Fenian, and discusses the views, as to their antiquity and origin, held by Nutt, Rhys, Jubainville[†] and others, in short but sufficient chapters.[3] In the great controversy which divides Irish scholars as to whether Finn and Cuchulain, their friends and their followers, their battles and their huntings, are legend coloured by history or history coloured by legend, Dr. Hyde throws in his lot with those who hold them historical in the main; and this choice seems to an obstinate upholder of the other theory but a part of the one capital defect of his criticism. He is so anxious to convince his little groups of enthusiasts of the historical importance of the early Irish writings, of the value to modern learning of the fragments of ancient customs which are mixed up with their romance, that he occasionally seems to forget the noble phantasy and passionate drama which is their crowning glory. He does not notice at all, for instance, 'The Death of Cuchulain',[†] which is among the greatest things of all legendary literature; and gives an entire chapter to 'The Feast of Brian', which is among the least; and all because 'Posidonius, who was a friend of Cicero, and wrote some hundred years before Christ, mentions that there was a custom in Gaul' which is also in 'The Feast'.[4] This defect is probably caused to some extent by the traditions of Irish learning which are hopelessly dry-as-dust, but if our own profoundly imaginative Irish scholar cannot throw off the ancient chains we are indeed lost.

IRISH NATIONAL LITERATURE, I: FROM CALLANAN TO CARLETON

This article is the first of four pieces on Irish national literature that Yeats contributed to The Bookman *from July to October 1895. They represent the most extended critical exposition of the Irish Literary Movement of which Yeats was the leader, and the most concerted effort on Yeats's part to place that movement in the perspective of past Irish literature.*

Yeats wanted to have these articles preserved in more permanent form. He wrote to the publisher T. Fisher Unwin on 3 November 1895:

> *I have been so busy that I have only just found time to find and tare [sic] out the articles on Irish Literature which I want you to publish in a pamphlet under the title 'What to Read in Irish Literature'. When I have restored certain quotations, cut out by the* Bookman *people for lack of space, and written half a dozen pages or so of introduction on the relation of Irish literature to general literature and culture and to contemporary movents [sic] there should be material enough for a decent shillings worth (CL1, 475).*

The proposal came to nothing. The only subsequent use of these articles was the reprinting of the opening paragraphs of the second and third articles in Ideas of Good and Evil *(1903).*

This first article in the present series molded the Irish literary past by omitting the Anglo-Irish Augustans—Swift, Berkeley, Burke—and by attempting to diminish the importance and influence of the Young Ireland movement of the 1840s. The remaining writers whom Yeats found attractive—Callanan, Carleton, and John Mitchel—he liked for their rude strength, evidence of a creative vitality which Yeats and his co-revivalists wished to match with craftmanship in order to make a high art.

Some of my countrymen include among national writers all writers born in Ireland,[1] but I prefer, though it greatly takes from the importance of our literature, to include only those who have written under Irish influence and of Irish subjects. When once a country has given perfect expression to itself in literature, has carried to maturity its literary tradition, its writers, no matter what they write of, carry its influence about with them, just as Carlyle remained a Scotsman when he wrote of German kings or French revolutionists,[2] and Shakespeare an Elizabethan Englishman when he told of Coriolanus or of Cressida. Englishmen and Scotsmen forget how much they owe to mature traditions of all kinds—traditions of feeling, traditions of thought, traditions of expression—for they have never dreamed of a life without these things. They write or paint or think or feel, and believe they do so to please no taste but their own, while in reality they obey rules and instincts which have been accumulating for centuries; their wine of life has been mellowed in ancient cellars, and they see but the ruby light in the glass. In a new country like Ireland—and English-speaking Ireland is very new—we are continually reminded of this long ripening by the immaturity of the traditions about us; if we are writers, for instance, we find it takes longer to learn to write than it takes an Englishman, and the more resolute we are to express the national character, and the more we understand the impossibility of putting our new wine into old bottles, the longer is our struggle with the trivial, the incoherent, the uncomely. A young Englishman of little knowledge or power may write with considerable skill and perfect good taste before he leaves his university, while an Irishman of greater power and knowledge will go through half his life piling up in the one heap the trivial and the memorable, the incoherent and the beautiful, the commonplace and the simple.

The Irish national writers who have bulked largest in the past have been those who, because they served some political cause which could not wait, or had not enough of patience in themselves, turned away from the unfolding and developing of an Irish tradition, and borrowed the mature English methods of utterance and used them to sing of Irish wrongs or preach of Irish purposes. Their work was never quite satisfactory, for what was Irish in it looked ungainly in an English garb, and what was English was never perfectly mastered, never wholly absorbed into their being. The most famous of these men was Thomas Moore, who quenched an admirable Celtic lyricism in an artificial glitter learned from the eighteenth century; the most noble was Thomas Davis, who borrowed a manner from Macaulay and Scott and Lockhart, and with this strange help sang 'a new soul into Ireland'; and the most inspired was John Mitchel, who thundered from his convict hulk a thunder that was half Carlyle's against England and the gods of his master.[3] These were the most influential Irish voices of the first half of the century, and their influence was not at all the less because they had not a native style, for the one made himself wings out of the ancient Gaelic music, and the other two were passionate orators, expounding opinions which were none the less true because the utterance was alien; and not poets or romance-writers, priests of those Immortal Moods[4] which are the true builders of nations, the secret transformers of the world, and need a subtle, appropriate language or a minute, manifold knowledge for their revelation. John Mitchel, by the right of his powerful nature and his penal solitude, communed indeed with the Great Gods, now as always none other than the Immortal Moods, and set down his communings in that marvellous *Jail Journal,*[5] but he could give them no lengthy or perfect devotion, for he belonged to his cause, to his opinions, to his oratories.

> A dreamer born,
> Who with a mission to fulfil,
> Left the muses' haunts to turn
> The crank of an opinion mill.[6]

Meanwhile Callanan,[7] a wastrel who wandered from place to place, from trade to trade, and was now a schoolmaster, now a common soldier, had begun, or rather had expressed for the first time in English, the traditions which have moulded nearly all of modern Irish literature. While Moore's sentimental trivialities were in their first fame, he printed in Irish periodicals four translations from the Gaelic of great simplicity and charm, 'The Outlaw of Loch Lene', a wild love song like those in Dr. Hyde's *Connacht[†] Love Songs*; 'The Convict of Clonmel', the lament of a peasant condemned to death for some unknown offence; 'The Dirge of O'Sullivan Bear',[†] a fragment of barbaric cursing; and 'Felix M'Carthy', the complaining of an old man whose children have been killed by the fall of a house. It is very difficult to describe the peculiar quality of these verses, for their quality is a new colour, a new symbol, rather than a thing of thought or form. Despite their constant clumsiness and crudity, they brought into the elaborate literature of the modern world the cold vehemence, the arid definiteness, the tumultuous movement, the immeasurable dreaming of the Gaelic literature. Generations may pass by before this tradition is mature enough in the new tongue for any to measure its full importance, but its importance to Ireland needed and needs no measuring.

Callanan was followed immediately by other translators, of whom Edward Walsh,[8] a village schoolmaster, was the best, and these in turn

by countless ballad-writers, who combined a little of Gaelic manner
with a deal of borrowed rhetoric, and created that interesting, unsat-
isfying, pathetic movement which we call in Ireland 'the poetry of
Young Ireland'. This movement, if we leave out one or two patriotic
songs like 'The Memory of the Dead', a few love songs like 'The Marriage', and a single poignant lament over the failure of the rebellion
called 'Cushla Gal Mo Chree',[†] was of little literary importance, but it
helped to build up an audience for four important poets—Mr. Aubrey
de Vere,[†] William Allingham, Clarence Mangan, and Sir Samuel Ferguson.[9] Mr. Aubrey de Vere[†] has more often written under English
than Irish influence, but the most desirable of his poems are those in
which the immature tradition of Callanan and the ancient poets, modified and expanded to express the moods and passions that interest
men to-day, has taken the place of the grave, impersonal Wordsworthian[10] manner in which he tells of English kings and Saxon saints.
William Allingham has written out in verse full of emotional subtlety
and intellectual simplicity the customs and accidents of his native
Ballyshannon.[11]

> A wild West coast, a little town
> Where little folk go up and down,
> Human will and human fate,
> What is little, what is great,
> Howso'er the answer be,
> Let me sing of what I know.[12]

In him for the first time the slowly ripening tradition reached a perfect utterance; and the Immortal Moods, which are so impatient of
rhetoric, so patient of mere immaturity, found in his poetry the one perfect ritual fashioned for their honour by Irish hands. The most perfect,
but not the most passionate or most powerful, for the most passionate was made by Clarence Mangan, that strange visionary, ruined by
drink and narcotics, who wrought some half-dozen lyrics of inde-
scribable, vehement beauty; and the most powerful by Sir Samuel Ferguson, who has retold so many ancient tales of Deirdre, of Conary, of
Conchubar,[†] of the *Táin Bó,*[13] that younger Ireland believes him, and
I think rightly, the most Irish of poets. At his worst he is monotonous
in cadence and clumsy in language; at his best a little like Homer in
his delight in savage strength, in tumultuous action, in overshadowing doom. He had no deliberate art, and the tradition is often very
immature in him, but in his moments of inspiration he is full of massy
strength or tranquil beauty.

A plenteous place is Ireland for hospitable cheer,
  Uileacan dubh O![14]
Where the wholesome fruit is bursting from the yellow barley
    ear;
  Uileacan dubh O!
There is honey in the trees when her misty vales expand,
And her forest paths in summer are by falling waters fanned;
There is dew at high noontide there, and springs i' the yellow
    sand,
On the fair hills of holy Ireland.

The tradition expressed by these poets was that of the bards and the Gaelic ballad-writers, but there was still another tradition, another expression of the same dominant moods, that which was embodied in the customs of the poor, their wakes, their hedge-schools, their factions, their weddings, their habits of thought and feeling, and this could best be described in prose. Miss Edgeworth had called up for a moment this ancient life in the mournful humour of Thady Quirk, but it was not until the brothers Banim and William Carleton[15] began to write that it found adequate historians. Michael Banim[16] was excellent in much of *Father Connell*, and John Banim in the first half of *The Nowlans,*† and in the opening chapters of *Crohoore† of the Billhook,* and at odd moments in all his books; but only Carleton, born and bred a peasant, was able to give us a vast multitude of grotesque, pathetic, humorous persons, misers, pig-drivers, drunkards, schoolmasters, labourers, priests, madmen, and to fill them all with an abounding vitality. He was but half articulate, half emerged from Mother Earth, like one of Milton's lions,[17] but his wild Celtic melancholy gives to whole pages of *Fardarougha*† and of *The Black Prophet* an almost spiritual grandeur. The forms of life he described, like those described with so ebullient a merriment by his contemporary Lever,[18] passed away with the great famine, but the substance which filled those forms is the substance of Irish life, and will flow into new forms which will resemble them as one wave of the sea resembles another. In future times men will recognise that he was at his best a true historian, the peasant Chaucer[19] of a new tradition, and that at his worst he fell into melodrama, more from imperfect criticism than imperfect inspiration. In his time only a little of Irish history, Irish folk-lore, Irish poetry had been got into the English tongue; he had to dig the marble for his statue out of the mountain side with his own hands, and the statue shows not seldom the clumsy chiselling of the quarryman.

THE THREE SORROWS
OF STORY-TELLING

This unsigned review of The Three Sorrows of Story-telling, and Ballads of Columkille, *translated by Douglas Hyde (London: T. Fisher Unwin, 1895), is from* The Bookman, *July 1895. Allan Wade in his bibliography attributed it to Yeats.*

The stories known traditionally by this name are 'Deirdre', 'The Children of Lir', and 'The Fate of the Children of Tuireann'. Dr. Hyde has put them into verse to make them popularly known as they once were in Gaelic-speaking lands. His is by no means the first attempt. Dr. Joyce included two of them in his *Old Celtic Romances,* and his brother wrote a metrical version of *Deirdre.*[1] We can find them also in Mr. Jacobs' *Celtic Fairy Tales.*[2] There is an obvious advantage in setting them, for popular reading, to metre; and of all the popular versions Dr. Hyde's seems to us, on the whole, the best. Our first feeling on reading them was irritation, but second thoughts modified that. Perhaps he knew what he was about in treating them in the style he has done. A failure in any high poetic attempt, or a miss in the endeavour to express more nearly their native Celtic spirit, would have landed him in obscurities or unfamiliarities which the English reader would have laughed or yawned over. Whether or not he was right in thinking such an attempt on his part would have ended in failure, we are not assured. The translator of *Connacht Love-Songs*[3] is a great deal more of a poet than anyone would guess, judging him from the metrical stories before us. But, at least the simplicity he has aimed at and achieved, the very want of ambition in his rendering—one might almost say, were it not gross ingratitude, the laziness that has left them as they are—have ended in their being models of clearness. The English mind, and what is much to the purpose, the English child's mind, will grasp these stories in their present form with easy understanding, may guess little of their mystic glamour, but cannot fail to recognise in the bare outlines the great beauty

and the tragedy. There are passages of fine vigour in Dr. Hyde's version—
it is far less lumbering and prosaic than Dr. Joyce's. The coming home
of Brian and his brothers, all the tasks of the eric[4] accomplished, but
with Death at their hearts as they near the coast of Erin and the hill
of high Ben Edar,[5] is told with much dignity. And to the beauty of
Deirdre's death-song he has done no wrong.

> The cluster all is fallen, and I am left,[6]
> The fibres snap that hold me; thus I shake
> And tremble fast upon the withered stem,
> And quit my hold upon it—see, I fall
> Down from this cold and dismal bough of life.

And where the stories go clumsily along, it is but well to remember
that Dr. Hyde confidingly tells in his preface that two of them were
sent to press in mistake for another manuscript.

With all due allowances, then, let us accept gratefully what we have got,
one more lucid, popular version of these legends. But it stirs a longing for
what we have not. 'Deirdre', 'The Children of Lir', and 'The Children of
Tuireann' are three of the most beautiful stories in the whole world. Interfered with, patched, and mangled as they may have been, they have even
now a central wholeness, and a haunting melancholy loveliness that is their
very own. 'Deirdre' is one of the many legends of princesses shut up in lonely
towers on account of a prophecy that they will bring hurt to those they
consort with. 'The Children of Lir' is of the great family of transformation legends; and the 'Children of Tuireann', with their burden of tasks,
have as numerous a kin in folk-lore. But they keep their own tragic com-
plexion. For the Celtic fairy-story has this distinction, that, removed
as it is far from the region of average human habitation, remote, ethe-
real, and, other peoples say, too often inhuman, yet no other has so
sternly dared to face inexorable human fate—sorrow, decay, and
death. Beauty, valour, pure happiness, are all with Deirdre, but she and
hers are conquered by the strong hand of the wicked. After ages of wandering and suffering, the swan-children of Lir gain back their human shape,
but with it the feebleness and the palsy of old age, and at the touch of the
holy water they drop dead. All the impossible tasks of the eric are fulfilled
by Brian and his brethren; their fulfillment has been bought by death,
and they come home great matchless heroes, but doomed. With Death alone
they cannot fight. Here are high themes for high imaginations. But as yet
they wander lost in unhappy transformation like Lir's children. Where
is the spiritual poet who shall make these Three Sorrows fast in the
world's great treasure-house?

IRISH NATIONAL LITERATURE, II: CONTEMPORARY PROSE WRITERS— MR. O'GRADY, MISS LAWLESS, MISS BARLOW, MISS HOPPER, AND THE FOLK-LORISTS

This is the second of Yeats's articles on Irish national literature; it appeared in The Bookman, *August 1895. Of all the literary genres, Yeats seems to have understood prose fiction least, and he had little success in writing it. As impresario of the literary revival, he had less success in calling forth novelists than poets or playwrights. (The most famous Irish novelist of Yeats's lifetime was notably hostile to this movement.) This article reflects Yeats's discontent and impatience with Irish prose writers of that decade, but, as a good propagandist, Yeats makes the best of his resources.*

In the opening paragraph (later reprinted as "The Moods" in Ideas of Good and Evil*), Yeats sets forth most extensively his doctrine of the immortal moods as the bearers, through literature, of a transcendental revelation. Yet, spiritual as it seems, the imaginative process is material—angels and demons rising and falling in a manner particularly Yeatsian. The doctrine is an amalgam of Yeats's readings in Jacob Boehme (assisted by Coleridge), Swedenborg, William Blake, and his own visions.*

Literature differs from explanatory and scientific writing in being wrought about a mood, or a community of moods, as the body is wrought about an invisible soul; and if it uses argument, theory, erudition, observation, and seems to grow hot in assertion or denial, it does so merely to make us partakers at the banquet of the moods. It seems to me that these moods are the labourers and messengers of the Ruler of All, the gods of ancient days still dwelling on their secret Olympus, the angels of more modern days ascending and descending upon their shining ladder; and that argument, theory, erudition, observation, are merely what Blake called 'little devils who fight for themselves',[1] illusions of our visible passing life, who must be made serve the moods, or we have no part in eternity. Everything that can be seen, touched, measured, explained, understood, argued over, is to the imaginative artist nothing more than a means, for he belongs to the invisible life, and delivers its ever new and ever ancient revelation. We hear much of his need for the restraints of reason, but the only restraint he can obey is the mysterious instinct that has made him an artist, and that teaches him to discover immortal moods in mortal desires, an undecaying hope in our trivial ambitions, a divine love in sexual passion.

The writer of history or very historical romance can never perhaps be wholly an imaginative artist, for he must reason and compare and argue about mere accidents and chances, and so be bound upon the wheel of mortality; but if he reason and compare and argue only, he belongs to those who record and not to those who reveal, to science and not to literature, for none but the Divine Brotherhood[2] can tell him how men loved and sorrowed, and what things are memorable and what things are alms for oblivion.

Ireland has but one historian who is anything of an artist, Mr. Standish O'Grady,[3] and multifarious knowledge of Gaelic legend and Gaelic history and a most Celtic temperament have put him in communion with the moods that have been over Irish purposes from the hour when, in the words put into the mouth of St. Dionysius, 'The Most High set the borders of the Nations according to the angels of God.'[4] His *History of Ireland: Heroic Period,* which was published in 1878, has done more than anything else to create that preoccupation with Irish folk-lore and legend and epic which is called the Irish literary movement. Ferguson had indeed been long busy with Irish folk-lore and legend and epic, but almost wholly in detached ballads, and always with an old-fashioned rigour of style which repels readers accustomed to the deep colour and emotional cadence of modern literature; but this book retold nearly every great legend, and traced the links that bound them one to another in a chaotic but vehement and lyrical prose. Every character was full of passion to the lips, and half a savage and half a god, like those persons whom the ancients celebrated in the stars, Boötes, Arcturus, the hunter Orion, and their innumerable comrades; and Celtic as the heroes of Macpherson's[†] *Ossian,* with the something added that made them Irish also; and love tales and battle tales that had long been the prey of Dr. Dry-as-Dust and his pupils,[5] started up clothed in the colour and music of a temperament which needed only a passion for precision of phrase and for delicacy of cadence to be the temperament of the great poets. Since then he has retold separate legends and groups of legend with more detail in *Finn*[†] *and his Companions,* his masterpiece, and in *The Coming of Cuculain,*[†] the beautiful but unequal opening of an epic in prose.[6] He has also written a most vivid little book of Elizabethan tales and historical fragments called *The Bog of Stars,* which has had a considerable success in Ireland, and among the Irish in England; *Red Hugh's Captivity,* the only historical book about Elizabethan Ireland which is more than dates and dialectics; and *The Story of Ireland,*[7] an impressionist narrative of Irish affairs from the coming of the gods to the death of Parnell,[8] which has aroused acrimonious controversy, and is still something of a byword, for Ireland is hardly ready for impressionism, above all for a whimsical impressionism which respects no traditional hatred or reverence, which exalts Cromwell and denounces the saints, and is almost persuaded that when Parnell was buried, as when Columba died, 'the sky was alight with strange lights and flames'.[9] In Ireland we are accustomed to histories with great parade of facts and dates, of wrongs and precedents, for use in the controversies of the hour; and here was a man who let some all-important Act of Parliament (say) go by without a mention, or with perhaps inaccurate mention, and for no better reason than because it did not interest him, and who recorded with careful vividness some moment of abrupt passion, some fragment of legendary beauty, and for no better reason than because it did interest him profoundly. 'The effect' of his books, as Mill said of Michelet's *History of France,* 'is not acquiescence, but stir and ferment',[10] and I disagree with his conclusions too constantly, and see the armed hand of nationality in too many places where he but sees the clash of ancient with modern institutions, to believe that he has written altogether the true history of Ireland; but I am confident that, despite his breathless generalisations, his slipshod style, his ungovernable likings and dislikings, he is the first man who has tried to write it, for he is the first to have written not mainly of battles and enactments, but of changing institutions and changing beliefs, of the pride of the wealthy and the long endurance 'of the servile tribes of ignoble countenance'.[11]

Miss Lawless[12] is probably, like Mr. Standish O'Grady, on the unpopular side in Irish politics, but, unlike Mr. O'Grady, is in imperfect sympathy with the Celtic nature, and has accepted the commonplace conception of Irish character as a something charming, irresponsible, poetic, dreamy, untrustworthy, voluble, and rather despicable, and the commonplace conception of English character as a something prosaic, hard, trustworthy, silent, and altogether worshipful, and the result is a twofold slander. This bundle of half-truths made her describe the Irish soldiers, throughout *Essex in Ireland,*[13] as a savage, undisciplined, ragged horde, in the very teeth of Raleigh's letters, which prove them among the best armed and best disciplined in Europe; and made her in *Grania* magnify a peasant type which exists here and there in Ireland, and mainly in the extreme west, into a type of the whole nation; and in *Maelcho* set before us for a typical Englishman the absolute genius of exemplary dullness and triumphant boredom; and it fetters her imagination continually, and comes between her and any clear understanding of Irish tradition. Despite her manifest sincerity and her agile intellect, one would perhaps pass her by with but few words, did she not escape from her theory of England and Ireland when she describes visions and visionaries, as in the chapter upon the rise of the dead multitudes in *Essex in Ireland,* and in the description of the chaunting of Cormac Cass in *Maelcho,* though there is nothing of Ireland in the chaunt that he makes; and in the madness of Maelcho and in his last days in the cavern with the monks. There is a kind of greatness in these things, and if she can cast off a habit of mind which would compress a complex, incalculable, indecipherable nation into the mould of a theory invented by political journalists and forensic historians, she should have in her the makings of a great book, full of an arid and half spectral intensity.

The only contemporary Irish novelist who has anything of Miss Lawless's popularity is undoubtedly Miss Barlow,[14] and it were hard to imagine a greater contrast, for *Irish Idylls, Kerrigan's Quality,* and *Maureen's Fairing* are without theory of any kind. She is master over the circumstances of peasant life, and has observed with a delighted care no Irish writer has equalled, the coming and going of hens and chickens on the door-step, the gossiping of old women over their tea, hiding of children under the shadow of the thorn trees, the broken and decaying thatch of the cabins, and the great brown stretches of bogland; but seems to know nothing of the exultant and passionate life Carleton[15] celebrated, or to shrink from its roughness and its tumult. Her labourers and potato diggers and potheen makers and cockle pickers are passive, melancholy, and gentle, while the real labourers and potato diggers and potheen[16] makers and cockle pickers are often as not grim as their limestone walls, or fiery as a shaken torch.

Miss Nora Hopper[17] is the latest of Irish romance writers, and the one absolute dreamer of Irish literature. Mr. O'Grady is interested in heroic and ungovernable men; Miss Lawless in theories about character and in visions elaborated out of character; Miss Barlow in a poor who are half observed, and half fashioned out of her own gentleness and benevolence; but Miss Hopper is only interested in so much of life as you can see in a wizard's glass. She has less strength than those whose interests are more earthy, but more delicacy of cadence and precision of phrase, a more perfect lyric temperament. Her little book, *Ballads in Prose*,[18] has the beauty of a dim twilight, and one praises it with hardly a reservation, except perhaps that here and there is too much of filmy vagueness, as in visions in the wizard's glass, before the mystical sweeper has swept the clouds away with his broom. The poetry is perhaps the better part, but my concern for the present is with the prose, and I have been haunted all the winter by 'Daluan', 'The Gifts of Aodh and Una', 'The Four Kings', and 'Aonan-na-Righ', and more than all by the sacrifice of Aodh[19] in the temple of the heroes, that the land might be delivered from famine. 'Then the door at which he was striving opened wide, and from the dark shrine swept out a cloud of fine grey dust. The door clanged to behind him, and he went up the aisle, walking ankle deep in the fine dust, and straining his eyes to see through the darkness if indeed figures paced beside him, and ghostly groups gave way before him, as he could not help but fancy. At last his outstretched hands touched a twisted horn of smooth cold substance, and he knew that he had reached the end of his journey. With his left hand clinging to the horn he turned towards the dark temple, saying aloud, "Here I stand, Aodh, with gifts to give the Fianna and their gods. In the name of my mother's god, let them who desire my gifts come to me." "Aodh,[20] son of Eochaidh," a shivering voice cried out, "give me thy youth." "I give," Aodh said quietly. "Aodh," said another voice, reedy and thin, but sweet, "give me thy knowledge. I, Grania, loved much and knew little." There was a grey figure at his side, and without a word Aodh turned and laid his forehead on the ghost's cold breast. As he rested thus, another voice said, "I am Oisin; give me thy death, O Aodh." Aodh drew a deep breath, then he lifted his head, and clasped a ghostly figure in his arms, and holding it there, felt it stiffen and grow rigid and colder yet. "Give me thy hope, Aodh." "Give me thy faith, Aodh." "Give me thy courage, Aodh." "Give me thy dreams, Aodh." So the voices called and cried, and to each Aodh gave the desired gift. "Give me thy heart, Aodh," cried another. "I am Maive, who knew much and loved little," and with a shrinking sense of pain Aodh felt slender, cold fingers scratching and tearing their way through flesh and sinew till they grasped his heart, and tore the fluttering thing away. "Give me thy love, Aodh," another implored. "I am Angus, Master of Love, and I have loved none." "Take it," Aodh said faintly, and there was a pause. But soon the shivering voices began again, and the cold fingers clutched at his bare arms and feet, and the breath of ghostly lips played on his cheek as the cloudy figures came and went, and struggled and scrambled about him.'

There are other Irish novelists of note, such as Mrs. Esler,[21] who writes charmingly of Presbyterian life in Ulster, Mr. Frank Mathew, who has done excellent short stories and promises to do better, Mr. William O'Brien, who has written an able but inchoate political novel, Mr. Downey, who has done one piece of excellent fooling, the authors of *The Real Charlotte,* who have described with unexampled grimness our middle-class life, Mrs. Hinkson, who has written a couple of books of kindly and picturesque sketches of Irish life and people, and various pleasant storytellers who are neither literature nor the promise of literature, and one or two young men who have the promise but are not yet pleasant storytellers. We have also a number of men of letters busy with our history and folk-lore. One of these, Mr. Lecky, is so famous that even if his methods were not those of historical science, rather than of historical literature, and wholly apart from any Irish tradition, it were useless to consider him here; another, Dr. Joyce, has written the most satisfactory of short Irish histories that are not in the manner of literature, and a rather unsatisfactory book of *Old Celtic Romances* that is.[22] Dr. Hyde, on the other hand, though at his worst he is shapeless enough, is at his best an admirable artist, and the manner of his *Beside the Fire* is the ideal manner for a book of folk-lore, because it is the manner of the peasants' talk by the glowing turf, and "Teig O'Kane", which he has reshaped and made his own is nearly worthy to be bound up with "Wandering Willie's Tale", while the prose of his *Connacht† Love Songs* is perfect after its kind.[23] Lady Wilde has told inaccurately, but charmingly, innumerable tales which one cannot come by elsewhere; while Mr. Larminie and Mr. Curtin are recording the tales of the western peasantry with the industrious accuracy of Campbell of Islay; and Mr. Standish Hayes† O'Grady, despite a hateful Latin style, has a place in literature because of the magnificence of much he has translated out of the Gaelic in *Silva Gadelica.*[†24] All these scholars are better workmen, have more skill in arrangement and selection, and a more perfect criticism than the most important of their predecessors; just as Mr. O'Grady, Miss Lawless, Miss Barlow, and Miss Hopper outdo in the things that can be learned most of the earlier novelists. Our public, too, is a little more exacting, a little more conscious of excellence and of what is Irish as apart from what is English or Scottish than it was a few years ago; in the main through the tendency of all traditions of thought and feeling to grow less gross and crude through the sheer boredom of grossness and crudeness; but partly because Dr. Hyde, Mr. Larminie, Dr. Sigerson, Mr. Johnson, Mr. Ashe King,[25] and others, whose names would carry no meaning, have been busy denouncing rhetoric, and interpreting Gaelic history or modern romance in lectures and speeches. Whatever be the cause, we have for the first time in Ireland, and among the Irish in England, a school of men of letters united by a common purpose, and a small but increasing public who love literature for her own sake and not as the scullery-maid of politics; and may hope some day, in the maturity of our traditions, to fashion out of the world about us, and the things that our fathers have told us, a new ritual for the builders of peoples, the imperishable moods.

THAT SUBTLE SHADE

Yeats reviewed Arthur Symons's book of poems London Nights *(London: Leonard Smithers, 1895) in the August 1895 issue of* The Bookman. *Yeats had met Symons (1865–1945) in the early 1890s, and he depended much on Symons's knowledge of French to guide him through the French symbolists. When Yeats visited Paris in 1894, Symons may have supplied him with his introduction to Verlaine, which resulted in an article contributed to Symons's magazine,* The Savoy, *two years later (See UP1, 397–99 and Au, 261).*

Yeats's defense of the erotic realism of Symons is so much based on Yeats's spiritual aesthetic that he gives a rather chaste impression of this book. For its day and city, London Nights *was a daring book. A second edition of this book, published in 1897, contained a preface by Symons which began, "The publication of this book was received by the English press with a singular unanimity of abuse." Surely Yeats's review was an exception to that "unanimity." The preface was signed "Rosses Point, Sligo: September 2, 1896." Symons had been touring the west of Ireland with Yeats.*

A famous Hindu philosopher[1] once told me that one day, when he was a very young man, he walked on the bank of a great Indian river, reading a volume of erotic Sanscrit verse. He met a Hindu priest, and showed him the book, with the remark, 'A book like this must be very bad for the world.' 'It is an excellent book, a wonderful book', said the priest, taking it from him, 'but your calling it bad for the world shows it is bad for you', and thereupon dropped the book into the great river. Before the reviewing of Mr. Symons' *London Nights* has come to an end, it is probable that a number of people will, if the Hindu priest spake truth, have borne witness against themselves, for the bulk of it is about musical halls, and what its author names 'Leves Amores', and a little is a degree franker than Mr. Swinburne's *Poems and Ballads;*[2] and yet, though too unequal and experimental to be called 'an excellent book, a wonderful book', it contains certain poems of an 'excellent' and 'wonderful' beauty peculiar to its author's muses. A great many of the poems are dramatic lyrics, and Mr. Symons' muses have not enough of passion, or his rhythms enough of impulse, to fuse into artistic unity the inartistic details which make so great a part of drama; he is at his best when simply contemplative, when expounding not passion, but passion's evanescent beauty, when celebrating not the joys and sorrows of his dancers and light o' loves, but the pathos of their restless days. But in either mood he is honest and sincere, and honesty and sincerity are so excellent, that even when about immoral things, they are better for the world than hectic and insincere writing about moral things. It is sometimes well for poetry to become a judge and pronounce sentence, but it has always done all we have the right to demand, when it has been an honest witness, when it has given the true history of an emotion; and if it do so it serves beneficence not less than beauty, because every emotion is, in its hidden essence, an unfallen angel of God, a being of uncorruptible flame.[3] It may have been some idea of this kind, though more probably it was but the fascination of a delightful phrase, which induced Mr. Symons to put into the mouth of 'an angel of pale desire' verses which at once describe and embody his more admirable inspiration:[4]

> An angel of pale desire
> Whispered me in the ear
>   (Ah me, the white-rose mesh
>   Of the flower-soft, rose-white flesh!)
> 'Love, they say, is a fire,
> Lo, the soft love that is here.
>
> 'Love, they say, is a pain
>   Infinite as the soul,
>   Ever a longing to be
>   Love's to infinity,
>   Ever a longing in vain
>   After a vanishing goal.
>
> 'Lo, the soft joy that I give
>   Here in the garden of earth;
>   Come where the rose-tree grows;
>   Thine is the garden's rose,
>   Pluck thou, eat and live[5]
>   In ease, in indolent mirth.'

At once the charm and defect of the book is that its best moments have no passion stronger than a 'soft joy' and a 'pale desire'; and that their pleasure in the life of sensation is not, as in Mr. Davidson's music-hall poems,[6] the robust pleasure of the man of the world, but the shadowy delight of the artist. When it broods, as it does far too often, upon common accidents and irrelevant details, it is sometimes crude, sometimes not a little clumsy; but it is wholly distinguished and beautiful when it tells of things an artist loves—of faint perfume, of delicate colour, of ornate and elaborate gesture.

> Olivier Metra's Waltz of Roses
> Sheds in a rhythmic shower
> The very petals of the flower;
> And all is roses,
> The rouge of petals in a shower.
> . . . . .
> Alone apart, one dancer watches
> Her mirrored, morbid grace;
> Before the mirror face to face
> Alone she watches
> Her morbid, vague, ambiguous grace.
>
> Before the mirror's dance of shadows
> She dances in a dream,
> And she and they together seem
> A dance of shadows;
> Alike the shadows of a dream.[7]

On the whole, then, Mr. Symons must be congratulated upon having written a book which, though it will arouse against him much prejudice, is the best he has done; and none who have in their memory Shelley's 'Defence of Poetry'[8] will condemn him because he writes of immoral things, even though they may deeply regret that he has not found an ampler beauty than can be discovered under 'that subtle shade.'[9]

IRISH NATIONAL LITERATURE, III: CONTEMPORARY IRISH POETS— DR. HYDE, MR. ROLLESTON, MRS. HINKSON, MISS NORA HOPPER, AE†, MR. AUBREY DE VERE, DR. TODHUNTER, AND MR. LIONEL JOHNSON

This is the third of Yeats's four articles on Irish national literature; it appeared in The Bookman, *September 1895. Here Yeats did better than in the preceding article on prose, for he had many of his talented friends to praise. Yet there is a large distortion in this article, which stems from Yeats's inability to talk about himself. Without the master, the poetry of AE, Lionel Johnson, Katharine Tynan, and T. W. Rolleston seems small beer indeed.*

The first paragraph was reprinted by Yeats under the title "The Body of the Father Christian Rosencrux" in Ideas of Good and Evil.

The followers of the Father Christian Rosencrux,[1] says the old tradition, wrapped his imperishable body in noble raiment and laid it under the house of their order, in a tomb containing the symbols of all things in heaven and earth, and in the waters under the earth, and set about him inextinguishable magical lamps, which burnt on generation after generation, until other students of the order came upon the tomb by chance. It seems to me that the imagination has had no very different history during the last two hundred years, but has been laid in a great tomb of criticism, and had set over it inextinguishable magical lamps of wisdom and romance, and has been altogether so nobly housed and apparelled that we have forgotten that its wizard lips are closed, or but opened for the complaining of some melancholy and ghostly voice. The ancients and the Elizabethans abandoned themselves to imagination as a woman abandons herself to love, and created great beings who made the people of this world seem but shadows, and great passions which made our loves and hatreds appear but ephemeral and trivial phantasies; but now it is not the great persons, or the great passions we imagine, which absorb us, for the persons and passions in our poems are mainly reflections our mirror has caught from older poems or from the life about us, but the wise comments we make upon them, the criticism of life we wring from their fortunes. Arthur and his Court are nothing, but the many-coloured lights that play about them are as beautiful as the lights from cathedral windows; Pompilia and Guido[2] are but little, while the ever-recurring meditations and expositions which climax in the mouth of the Pope are among the wisest of the Christian age. It seems to a perhaps fanciful watcher of the skies[3] like myself that this age of criticism is about to pass, and an age of imagination, of emotion, of moods, of revelation, about to come in its place; for certainly belief in a supersensual world is at hand again; and when the notion that we are 'phantoms of the earth and water'[4] has gone down the wind, we will trust our own being and all it desires to invent; and when the external world is no more the standard of reality, we will learn again that the great Passions are angels of God, and that to embody them 'uncurbed in their eternal glory',[5] even in their labour for the ending of man's peace and prosperity, is more than to comment, ever so wisely, upon the tendencies of our time, or to express the socialistic, or humanitarian, or other forces of our time, or even 'to sum up' our time, as the phrase is; for Art is a revelation, and not a criticism, and the life of the artist is in the old saying, 'The wind bloweth where it listeth, and thou hearest the sound thereof, but canst not tell whence it cometh and whither it goeth; so is every one that is born of the spirit'.[6]

This revolution may be the opportunity of the Irish Celt, for he has an unexhausted and inexhaustible mythology to give him symbols and personages, and his nature has been profoundly emotional from the beginning. An old Gaelic writer describes him as 'celebrated for anger and for amouresness [sic],' and an old English writer tells of his playing 'hastily and swiftly' upon the harp and the timbre, and a chronicler of Queen Elizabeth's time has no better word for wild sorrow than 'to weep Irish',[7] while Dr. Hyde says of him, as he is in our own time, that 'he will to-day be dancing, sporting, drinking, and shouting, and will be soliloquising by himself to-morrow, heavy and sick and sad in his poor lonely little hut, making a croon over departed hopes, lost love, the vanity of this world, and the coming of death';[8] and from such a temperament must come a literature which, whether important or unimportant, will yet be built after the ancient manner. The *Love Songs of Connacht,*[†] translated by Dr. Douglas Hyde, express this emotional nature in its most extreme form, for, though they have nothing of the verbal extravagance of the bards, they seem to be continually straining to express a something which lies beyond the possibility of expression, some vague, immeasurable emotion. One understands this better from the prose than from the verse translations, good as these often are; from such passages as:[9] 'It is happy for thee, O blind man, who dost not see much of women. Och, if thou wert to see what we see, thou wouldst be sick even as I am. It is a pity, O God, that it is not blind I was before I saw her twisted cool (hair) and her snowy body. . . . I always thought the blind pitiable until my calamity waxed beyond the grief of all; then, though it is a pity, my pity I turned into envy. . . . It is woe for whoever saw her, and it is woe for him who sees her not each day. It is woe for him on whom the knot of her love is tied, and it is woe for him who is loosened out of it. It is woe for him who goes to her, and it is woe to him who is not with her constantly. It is woe for a person to be near her, and it is woe for him who is not near her'; or from such a wild outburst as, 'My love,[10] O she is my love, the woman who is most for destroying me; dearer is she for making me ill than the woman who would be for making me well. She is my treasure, O she is my treasure, the woman of the grey eye . . . a woman who would not place a hand beneath my head . . . She is my affection, O she is my affection, the woman who left no strength in me; a woman who would not breathe a sigh after me, a woman who would not raise a stone at my tomb'. Almost all we have had translated out of the Gaelic is as purely lyrical in spirit, though not always as passionate as this. Mr. Rolleston's translation from a very old original, 'The Dead of Clonmacnois',[11] though it[†] does not strain to express anything which lies beyond the possibility of expression, is so purely emotional that it must stand an example of the Gaelic lyric come close to perfection.

> In a quiet watered land, a land of roses,
>   Stands Saint Kieran's city fair;
> And the warriors of Erin[12] in their famous generations
>   Slumber there
>
> There beneath the dewy hillside sleep the noblest
>   Of the clan of Conn,
> Each below his stone with name in branching Ogham,
>   And the sacred knot[13] thereon.

There they laid to rest the seven Kings of Tara,
　　There the sons of Cairbre sleep—
Battle-banners of the Gael, that in Kieran's plain of crosses
　　Now there[14] final hosting keep

And in Clonmacnois they laid the men of Teffia,
　　And right many a lord of Breagh;
Deep the sod above Clan Creide and Clan Conaill,[15]
　　Kind in hall and fierce in fray.

Many and many a son of Conn the Hundred Fighter
　　In the red earth lies at rest;
Many a blue eye of Clan Colman[16] the turf covers,
　　Many a swan-white breast.

No living Irish poet has learned so much from the translators as Mrs. Hinkson,[17] and the great change this knowledge has made in her verse is an example of the necessity for Irish writers to study the native tradition of expression. Her first two books, *Louise de la Vallière†* and *Shamrocks*,[18] contained here and there a moving lyric, but were on the whole merely excellent in promise, for the political turmoil of the time, and perhaps her own work for 'the Ladies' Land League',[19] continually drew her into rhetoric, while her own haste and inexperience kept her in a bondage of imitation of contemporary English poets. The work of the Irish folklorists, and the translations of Dr. Hyde and of an earlier poet, the village schoolmaster, Edward Walsh,[20] began to affect her, however, soon after the publication of *Shamrocks;* and the best of *Ballads and Lyrics* and *Cuckoo Songs†* have the freedom from rhetoric, the simplicity and the tenderness, though not the passion, of the Gaelic poets. Such avowed imitations as 'The Red Haired Man's Wife' and 'Gramachree'[21] are interesting, but scarcely so interesting as the poems in which she has assimilated the spirit, without copying the letter, of folk-song, and of these none are more touching than 'Sheep and Lambs' from *Ballads† and Lyrics.*

　　All in the April evening,
　　　　April airs were abroad,
　　The sheep with their little lambs
　　　　Passed me by on the road.

　　The sheep with their little lambs
　　　　Passed me by on the road;

> All in the April evening
> I thought on the Lamb of God.
>
> The lambs were weary, and crying
> With a weak, human cry.
> I thought on the Lamb of God
> Going meekly to die.
>
> Up in the blue, blue mountains,
> Dewy pastures are sweet,
> Rest for the little bodies,
> Rest for the little feet.
>
> But for the Lamb of God,
> Up on the hill-top green,
> Only a cross of shame,
> Two stark crosses between.
>
> All in the April evening,
> April airs were abroad,
> I saw the sheep with their lambs,
> And thought of[22] the Lamb of God.

Her best and her most popular book will probably be the forthcoming *Miracle Plays*,[23] for her best inspiration has ever come from Catholic belief, and to give an excellent expression to the ancient symbols is to be for a delight and a comfort to many ardent and dutiful spirits.

The work of the two latest of Irish poets, Miss Nora Hopper and AE,[†24] is, upon the other hand, wholly without any exclusively Catholic, or even Christian feeling. The little songs between the stories in Miss Hopper's *Ballads in Prose* sing, with a symbolism drawn from mythology and folklore, of a pagan fairy world where good and evil, denial and affirmation, have never come, are full of a perception of the spirit without any desire for union with the spirit, have at all times a beautiful, alluring, unaspiring peace; and there is no better mood and manner for songs of the fairies, who must sing in a like fashion themselves. AE's[†] *Homeward,[†] Songs by the Way* embody, upon the other hand, a continual desire for union with the spirit, a continual warfare with the world, in a symbolism that would be wholly personal but for an occasional word out of his well-loved *Upanishads*.[25] No voice in modern Ireland is to me as beautiful as his; and this may well be because the thoughts about the visible and invisible, and the passionate sincerity, of the essays and stories, had long held me under their spell when his poems came as a delight and a surprise; but I am nearly convinced that it is because he, more than any, has a subtle rhythm, precision of phrase, an emotional relation to form and colour, and a perfect understanding that the business of poetry is not to enforce an opinion or expound an action, but to bring us into communion with the moods and passions which are the creative powers behind the universe; that though the poet may need to master many opinions, they are but the body and the symbols for his art, the formula of evocation for making the invisible visible. The spirit, he writes in the last number of that little Dublin mystical magazine[26] which publishes his poems and his coloured symbolic pictures, 'cannot be argued over' or spoken 'truly of from report'.[27] 'It will surely come to those who wait in trust, a glow, a heat in the heart announcing the awakening of the fire.[28] And as it blows with its mystic breath into the brain, there is a hurtling of visions, a brilliance of lights, a sound of great waters vibrant and musical in their flowing, and murmurs from a single yet multitudinous being'. He is describing a mystical state, but one which differs in degree, and not in kind, from the state of poetical inspiration. He says also, and this time thinking probably more of poetic utterance in the ordinary sense, 'every word which really inspires is spoken as if the golden age had never passed away', and surely criticism, even criticism of life, is of the fall and the fatal tree; and bids all believers cast away 'the mood of the martyr', and put on 'a mood at once gay and reverent, as beseems those who are immortal'[29]; and his own songs, but for a little sadness, were no other than like his precept. Certainly he often sings of that energy 'which is eternal delight',[30] as in this from among the new poems in the American edition (published by Thomas B. Mosher) of *Homeward,*[†] *Songs by the Way.*

> We must pass like smoke or live within the spirit's fire,
>   For we can no more than smoke unto the flame return,
> If our thought has changed to dream or will unto desire.
>   As smoke we vanish, though the fire may burn.

> Lights of infinite pity star the grey dusk of our days;
>   Surely here is soul; with it we have eternal breath:
> In the fire of love we live or pass by many ways,
>   By unnumbered ways of dream to death.

Dr. Todhunter and Mr. Aubrey de Vere[†31] are but slightly related to the Irish lyrical movement of to-day, for the bulk of their work is of a past time, and but little of it is Irish in subject or temperament, or written under an Irish influence. In the case of the elder man, Mr. Aubrey de Vere,[†] the part that is Irish in subject is often alien in form. His 'Red Branch Heroes' are knights and wear armour, while his telling of 'Naisi's Wooing' and of 'The Children of Lir' is of a Tennysonian-Wordsworthian elaboration which lets most of the old wine flow out. 'The Bard Ethell' and 'The Wedding of the Clans' are, however, a perfect marriage of meaning and form, and here and there a lyric like 'The Little Black Rose' is at once quaint and beautiful.[32]

The alien manner of much of the rest is perhaps due mainly to the small number of the old epics, lyrics, and folk-tales which were translated, and the small amount of old custom which was expounded when Mr. de Vere[†] was forming his style; but something may be due to a defect of genius, for he seems to me, despite his noble placidity, his manifold and moving exposition of Catholic doctrine and emotion, but seldom master of the inevitable words in the inevitable order, and I find myself constantly distinguishing, when I read him, between that calculable, considered, intelligible and pleasant thing we call the poetical, and that incalculable, instinctive, mysterious, and startling thing we call poetry. Dr. Todhunter, writing later than Mr. de Vere,[†] and with plentiful epics and lyrics and folk-tales to inspire him, has thought out a couple of curious metres, and with their help retold 'The Children of Lir' and 'The Sons of Turann,'[†33] with little loss of meaning, but also with little rhythmical impulse. His 'Banshee', a personification of Ireland, in some sixty irregular, rhymeless lines, is still his best.[34]

> An aged desolation,
> She sits by old Shannon's flowing,
> A mother of many children,
> Of children exiled and dead;[35]
> In her home, with bent head, homeless,
> Clasping her knees she sits,
> Keening, keening!
>
> And at her keene the fairy-grass
> Trembles on dun and barrow;
> Around the foot of her ancient crosses
> The grave-grass shakes and the nettle swings;
> In haunted glens the meadow-sweet
> Flings to the night-wind[36]
> Her mystic mournful perfume;
> The sad spearmint by holy wells
> Breathes melancholy balm.

Mr. Lionel Johnson[37] also has written a few Irish poems of distinguished beauty, but, unlike Mr. de Vere[†] and Dr. Todhunter, is best when he writes on subjects, and under influences, which have no connection with Ireland. All these writers, however—for even AE[†] has begun to dig for new symbols in the stories of Finn[†] and Oisin, and in the song of Amergin[38]—are examples of the long continued and resolute purpose of the Irish writers to bring their literary tradition to perfection, to discover fitting symbols for their emotions, or to accentuate what is at once Celtic and excellent in their nature, that they may be at last tongues of fire uttering the evangel of the Celtic peoples.

IRISH NATIONAL LITERATURE, IV:
A LIST OF THE BEST IRISH BOOKS

*This is the fourth and last of Yeats's articles on Irish national litera-
ture; it appeared in* The Bookman, October 1895. *Yeats adopted here
the most combative tone of the series, for several reasons. The article
is an extension of his quarrel the previous winter with Edward Dowden over the quality and validity of the Irish literary revival. During
that controversy Yeats had assembled a list of the thirty best Irish books
(in a letter to* The Dublin Daily Express, *published 27 February 1895;
CL1, 440–45). His defense of his choice of books is reflected in his
comments in this article. And lastly, the fighting stance was intended
to sell books, or to force publishers into reprinting them. The latter purpose was promoted by including four out-of-print volumes in his list.*

Lists of 'the best hundred books'[1] and the like are commonly among
the most futile of things, for they would erect mere personal liking into
a general law, forgetting that 'the same law for the lion and the ox is
oppression'.[2] In a literature like the Irish, however, which is not only
new, but without recognised criticism, any list, no matter how personal,
if it be not wholly foolish, is a good deed in a disordered world. The
most that read Irish national literature read from patriotism and
political enthusiasm, and make no distinction between literature and
rhetoric. Allingham[3] is but a name, while *The Spirit of the Nation* is
on the counter of every country stationer; Carleton's[4] great novel,
Fardorougha, has but now gone to its second edition, and his scarce
less impressive *Black Prophet* is still out of print, while his formless and
unjust *Valentine McClutchy* and his feeble *Willy Reilly* have gone to
numberless editions; for this zealous public loves vehement assertion
better than quiet beauty and partisan caricature better than a revelation of reality and peace. This public is of no disadvantage to Ireland,
for it is mainly drawn from a class who read a worse literature elsewhere, while its enthusiasm has kept Irish literature alive for better for-

tune; but it has none the less persuaded some of our best writers to immense stupidities, as when it set Carleton writing stories now against intemperance, now against landlords, and it has created out of itself, besides, some few of genius, a multitude of bad writers who fare better than the best. It had done no permanent mischief were it not that our educated classes are themselves full of a different, but none the less noisy, political passion, and are, with some admirable exceptions, too anti-Irish to read an Irish book of any kind, other than a book of jokes or partisan argument.

The professor of literature at Trinity College, Dublin, is one of the most placid, industrious, and intelligent of contemporary critics when he writes on an English or a German subject, but the 'introduction' to his last book of essays[5] is a perfect example of this prejudice. It was written twelve years ago, when scarcely a writer, prominent in Irish literature in our time, was before the public, and at a moment of political excitement, and accused Irish writers with great heat of 'raving of Brian Boru,'[†] of 'plastering' themselves 'with shamrocks', and of having neither 'scholarship' nor 'accuracy', and is reprinted to-day with nothing changed, except that the words, 'Irish Literary Movement', are inserted here and there to make it apply to Mr. Rolleston, Mr. Graves, Dr. Hyde, Mr. Larminie, Mr. Lionel Johnson, Mr. King, Mr. O'Grady, Mrs. Hinkson, Miss Barlow, and Miss Lawless,[6] writers of whom some are not less eminent than Prof. Dowden himself. I quote this criticism not because I have any special quarrel with Prof. Dowden, who is less prejudiced than many, but because his offence is new and flagrant, and because like criticism has done and is doing incalculable harm. It is too empty of knowledge and sympathy to influence to any good purpose the ignorant patriotic masses, and it comes with enough of authority to persuade the undergraduates and the educated classes that neither the history, nor the poetry, nor the folklore, nor the stories which are interwoven with their native mountains and valleys are worthy of anything but contempt. This would perhaps be no great matter if it drove them to read Goethe and Shakespeare and Milton the more and the better. It has no such effect, however, but has done much to leave them with no ideal enthusiasm at all by robbing them of the enthusiasm which lay at their own doors. Year after year the graduates and undergraduates of Trinity College compose vacant verses, and how vacant their best are can be seen from a recent anthology;[7] and young ladies from Alexandra College[8] gather in little groups and read Shakespeare, and common-place is the abundant fruit. It is only when some young man or young girl is captured by a despised enthusiasm that the vacancy is peopled and the common made uncommon; and to make such captures and at length overthrow and sack Dublin scholasticism is one half the

business of 'The Irish Literary Movement'. Its methods are at times artificial, for it has to mend an artificial state of things, and this must be
my excuse for making anything so apparently futile as a list of some
forty best Irish books. The list is in a sense an epitome of my preceding articles, and, like them, confines itself to literature and the material for literature, and takes no stock of historical science, even though
it lose thereby Mr. Lecky's great history;[9] and it includes no book not
upon an Irish subject, or written under some obvious Irish influence.
The time has not yet come for Irishmen, as it has for Scotsmen, to carry
about with them a subtle national feeling, no matter when, or of what
they write, because that feeling has yet to be perfectly elaborated and
expounded by men of genius with minds as full of Irish history,
scenery, and character as the minds of Burns and Scott[10] were full of
Scottish history, scenery, and character. For a like reason it contains
many imperfect books, which seem to me to hide under a mound of
melodrama or sheer futility a smouldering and fragrant fire that cannot be had elsewhere in the world; and even some few poems which,
like 'The Lament of Morian† Shehone for Miss Mary Rourke'† in *A Book
of Irish Verse*,†[11] are precious because of a single line that is the signature of an ancient and Celtic emotion.

I will anticipate one other criticism of a more purely personal
nature, and then have done. Some of the Irish papers have been kind
enough to quote and criticise my articles,[12] and one or two have complained that I have 'log-rolled', and to them I would say that, with the
exception of AE†, who was a fellow student of mine,[13] there is no writer
in this list whose work I did not admire before ever I set eyes upon him,
and whose friendship I have sought for any reason but admiration of
his work. I must apologise for mentioning these personal facts, which
are necessary mainly because my praise of Mr. O'Grady,[14] whom I believe
to be the most important of living Irish prose writers, is described as
mere friendship by Irish Nationalists, who dislike his often anti-
national opinions; and I would have my praise, no matter how small
be its intrinsic value, carry at any rate the weight of its sincerity.

NOVELS AND ROMANCES

Castle Rackrent. By Miss Edgeworth.
The Nowlans.† By John Banim. (Out of print.)
John Doe.[15] By John Banim. (Bound up with *Crohoore*† *of the Bill-
    Hook.*†)
Father Connell. By Michael Banim. (Out of print.)
'Barney O'Reirdon,† the Navigator'. By Samuel Lover (in *Legends
    and Stories of Ireland*†).

The Collegians. By Gerald Griffin.[†]
'Father Tom and the Pope'. By Sir Samuel Ferguson (in *Tales from Blackwood's.*[†])
Traits and Stories. By William Carleton.
Fardarougha.[†] By William Carleton.
The Black Prophet. By William Carleton. (Out of print.)
Charles O'Malley. By Charles Lever.
Flitters, Tatters, and the Councillor. By Miss Laffan. (Out of print.)
Maelcho. By Miss Lawless.
Irish Idylls. By Miss Barlow.
The Bog of Stars. By Standish O'Grady. (New Irish Library.)
The Coming of Cuculain.[†] By Standish O'Grady.
Finn and His[†] *Companions.* By Standish O'Grady.
Ballads in Prose. By Miss Hopper.

FOLKLORE AND LEGEND

Old Celtic Romances. By P. W. Joyce.
History of Ireland. Two vols. By Standish O'Grady.
Ancient Legends. By Lady Wilde.
Beside the Fire. By Dr. Douglas Hyde.
West Irish Folk Tales. By William Larminie.
Hero-tales[†] *of Ireland.* By Jeremiah Curtin.
Myths and Folk-lore[†] *of Ireland.* By Jeremiah Curtin.
Tales of the Irish Fairies.[16] By Jeremiah Curtin.
Fairy Legends and Traditions in Ireland.[†] By Crofton Croker.
'Teig O'Kane'. By Dr. Douglas Hyde (in *Fairy and Folk Tales of the Irish Peasantry*).[17]
Silva Gadelica.[†] By Standish Hayes[†] O'Grady. (Two vols. of Translations.)
Lectures on the Manuscript Materials of Ancient Irish History.[†] By Eugene O'Curry.

HISTORY

A Short History of Ireland. By P. W. Joyce.
The Story of Ireland. By Standish O'Grady.
Red Hugh's[†] *Captivity.*[18] By Standish O'Grady. (Out of print.)
The Jail Journal. By John Mitchel.[†]
The Autobiography of Wolfe Tone (in Mr. Barry O'Brien's edition).
The Story of Early Gaelic Literature. By Dr. Douglas Hyde. (New Irish Library.)

POETRY

Irish Songs and Poems.† By William Allingham.
Lays of the Western Gael. By Sir Samuel Ferguson.
Conary. By Sir Samuel Ferguson (in his *Poems*).
Selections from the Poems of Aubrey de Vere.† Edited by G. E.
    Woodberry.[19]
Ballads† *and Lyrics.* By Mrs. Hinkson.
Homeward,† *Songs by the Way.* By AE†
The Love-Songs of Connacht.† By Dr. Douglas Hyde (and to this
    should be added his *The Religious Songs of Connacht,*† as soon
    as it is reprinted from the Irish magazine in which it is now
    appearing).
The Irish Song Book. By A. P. Graves. (New Irish Library.)
Irish Love Songs. Edited by Mrs. Hinkson.
A Book of Irish Verse.

The last book on my list was edited by myself, and my excuse for
including it is that some anthology was necessary; and that I compiled *A Book of Irish Verse* because I disliked those already in existence. If Mr. Graves' and Mr. Stopford Brooke's promised anthology
were out,[20] I would probably escape the necessity of pushing my
own wares. There is one book, *Mythologie Irlandaise,*† by D'Arbois
Jubainville† which could not be included in my list, as it is by a foreign writer, but is so important that no right knowledge of Irish legend is possible without it.[21]

THE LIFE
OF PATRICK SARSFIELD

This is a review of The Life of Patrick Sarsfield *by John Todhunter (London: T. Fisher Unwin, 1895) from* The Bookman, *November 1895. Todhunter's book was one of the few New Irish Library series that Yeats praised. He had wanted to edit that series when it began in 1892, and when he was pushed out by the supporters of Sir Charles Gavan Duffy, he left with many prophecies of publishing disaster.*

Yeats would hardly have treated a book by Todhunter harshly. A doctor and a poet, he had been an old friend of Yeats's father, and Yeats had been praising his books for almost a decade. Todhunter had been a neighbor of the Yeats family in the Bedford Park section of London in the later 1880s, and Yeats had his first contact with the production of plays when Todhunter's A Sicilian Idyll *was put on in the Bedford Park playhouse.*

The subject of Todhunter's book, Patrick Sarsfield (b. ?, d. 1693), was one of James II's generals in the campaign of 1689; he helped negotiate the Treaty of Limerick in 1691. William of Orange's victory over James II at the Battle of the Boyne River had determined Protestant ascendancy over Catholic Ireland for more than two hundred years. The subject was therefore delicate. Yeats, himself, was somewhat uncertain as to how his ancestors had acted at this crisis. An earlier draft of the opening verses to Responsibilities *has Yeats's forebears on the side of James II, but the final draft changes them over to the cause of William. (See* VP, *270.)*

Ireland has always had a literary history quite separate from the literary history of England; and week after week young men gather together in 'Young Ireland', 'Celtic', and 'National Literary' societies, and discuss, often with as much heat as though there were no other literary history in the world, books and movements of which the greater number are not even names out of Ireland. Few of these books and

movements are of great importance, if measured by merely literary standards, but as stages in the development of a national culture, nearly all
are as important as they are interesting. When a few years have frozen
the changing present into a changeless memory that it may be studied
with deliberate care, young men in Dublin and Limerick and Belfast
will be reading essays to each other about the great transformation of
Irish opinion which marked the early nineties; and whether those who
made it or expressed it be forgotten or remembered by the world at large,
it will seem to them a momentous and memorable transformation. A
few years ago Irish history, if written by Irishmen and with Irish sympathies, did not seek to discover neglected truths, or illustrate novel
points of view, but only to blacken some national enemy more perfectly,
or to set a finger glory about some national hero; for a conventional
patriotism had killed honest research and overthrown imaginative
freedom. The result was that one had to go to Englishmen, whose sympathies were naturally with their own country, for any history not wholly
empty of the historical spirit; for no educated Irishman, not even
among the young men in the literary societies, believes in the mystery
play of devils and angels which we call our national history, though
even to-day the Irish press and the penny story papers, despite Mr.
O'Grady[1] and others of a less genius, keep up the pretence with
admirable courage. A few months ago one of the Dublin societies of
Catholic young men failed to organise a debate on the character of
Oliver Cromwell,[2] because all its members who could speak had forgotten 'the curse of Cromwell' in the study of Carlyle;[3] and this was
from no lack of national spirit, for the most were only not Fenians[4]
because the Fenians are not the party of the moment. I labour this point,
because I believe it is most important for the management of 'The New
Irish Library' to understand this transformation and give us more
books like this admirably sincere Life of Patrick Sarsfield, and less books
like some of its rhetorical and conventional predecessors; and help
thereby to set a new national history in place of the old. I doubt if Dr.
Todhunter writes with a sufficiently decided point of view, or general-
izes his conclusions often enough or vividly enough, to be very widely
read, but his careful scholarship is above praise, and can only do good
to our people. His patriotism has found expression not in vehement
assertion or denial, but in care for the exact truth and in love for all
things which counted, whether for good or evil, in the national and
religious quarrel he is describing. Both Macaulay and Froude,[5] for
instance, writing of events which did not concern them very deeply,
accepted with too little examination the French account of the Battle
of the Boyne, and did, the one regretfully, the other gleefully, a deep injus-
tice to the courage of the Irish peasantry who fought there; but here

the whole story is set out for the first time and every statement proved from contemporary writers, and no rhetoric could so well serve Irish self-respect, for 'raw Irish levies, badly disciplined, half armed,[6] without artillery', 'left to face some of the best troops of Europe, by whom they were outnumbered three to one',[7] are proved to have made an 'heroic' defence of their fords. Irish historians and poets and story-makers, on the other hand, have ever declared Sarsfield the immaculate genius of that time, but here we have it on the word of a friend that, the battle over, the great soldier made confusion 'in civil affairs'[8] by giving out 'many orders', and helped on the plundering of the troops by being 'so easy that he would sign any paper that was laid before him.'[9] One only regrets that the countenance he gave in his more youthful days to a certain rather mercenary elopement[10] were recorded also, for the personal facts about his gallant, alluring personality are of the fewest, and it were a good deed besides to drag him even a little forth from the mystery play.

THE CHAIN OF GOLD

This unsigned review of The Chain of Gold: A Tale of Adventure on the West Coast of Ireland *(London: T. Fisher Unwin, 1895) by Standish O'Grady appeared in* The Bookman *of November 1895. Allan Wade listed it in his first bibliography of Yeats's writings, that which appeared in the eighth volume of the 1908 collected edition of Yeats's work, so we may presume that Yeats acknowledged authorship.*

———————

Mr. Standish O'Grady has a habit of returning on his ideas and incidents, and manifestly out of sheer love for them, and not from any poverty of imagination, for the second telling is for the most part the better. He has, for instance, told the story of Cuchulain[†1] twice over, and the second version is the more minute in finish, the more rich in beautiful detail; and now he returns upon the central accident of *Lost on Du Corrig,*[2] and builds out of it the far more potent *Chain of Gold.* *Lost on Du Corrig* was a boy's story of a boy who fell through a crevice in a cliff and found an immense cavern, and being there entrapped, supported himself by many fascinating shifts, and encountered the ghost of an ancient Irish hero; while *The Chain of Gold* is a history of two boys who go out fishing, and are hurled, boat and all, into the mouth of a cave far above the sea level, by one of the best storms raised in modern fiction, and there keep body and soul together by contrivances as excellent as any of Crusoe's,[3] and encounter the phantom of an ancient Irish hermit, or else endure a strange delirium from hardship and thirst—for we are left in doubt—and return at last to common things and safety. Parts of the earlier book were curiously careless and ill-built, despite its general vigour and freshness, but Mr. O'Grady has now learnt to admiration the difficult art of writing for boys, and of doing so not by warping or imprisoning his own mature imagination, but simply by delighting in such things as were a delight

to men and women at the dawn of the world. If Finn and Cuchulain[†]
lived in our day they would be much like these masterful, resourceful
cave-dwellers, and if Oisin[14] came alive to write of them he would write
in no very different spirit from Mr. O'Grady.

WILLIAM CARLETON

This review of The Life of William Carleton *appeared in* The Book-man *in March 1896. The book is Carleton's incomplete autobiogra-phy, completed and edited by D(avid) J(ames) O'Donoghue (London: Downey and Co., 1896, 2 vols.).*

Around 1890, Yeats had shown much interest in William Car-leton's work. He had edited the selection Stories from Carleton *and had included excerpts from Carleton in his* Representative Irish Tales *(New York, 1891). By the later nineties his interest in Carleton had faded somewhat. He wrote in John Quinn's copy of* Stories from Carleton *in 1904, "I thought no end of Carleton in those days and would still I dare say if I had not forgotten him."*

William Blake expounds the history of inspiration by a very curious and obscure symbol. A lark, he says, mounts upward into the heart of the heavens, and there is met by another and descending lark, which touches its wings to its wings; and he would have us understand, if I remember the passage and its context rightly—for I have not the prophetical book *Milton*[1] by me—that man attains spiritual influence in like fashion. He must go on perfecting earthly power and perception until they are so subtilised that divine power and divine perception descend to meet them, and the song of earth and the song of heaven mingle together. Every literary current and tradition goes, I believe, through something like this development, coming only very late to its Shelleys and Wordsworths.[2] Whether Irish prose literature be or be not to-day awaiting the celestial lark, and though no living Irish romance writer, with the exception of Mr. Standish O'Grady,[3] has anything of Carleton's genius, it is certainly much more subtle, much more spiri-tual than before. The author of *The Traits and Stories*[4] was not an artist, as those must needs be who labour with spiritual essences, but he was what only a few men have ever been or can ever be, the creator of a new imaginative world, the demiurge of a new tradition. He had no predecessors, for Miss Edgeworth[5] wrote by preference of that section of Irish society which is, as are the upper classes everywhere, the least national of all, and was, as the upper classes have seldom been anywhere, ashamed of even the little it had of national circumstance and character; and when she did take a man out of the Gaelic world and put into his mouth the immortal *Memoirs of the Rackrent Family,* it was a poor man living in great men's houses, and not a poor man at his hearth and among his children. She could not have done otherwise, for she was born and bred among persons who knew nothing of the land where they were born, and she had no generations of historians, Gaelic scholones,[6] and folk-lorists behind her, from whom to draw the symbols of her art. Carleton, on the other hand, came from the heart of Gaelic Ireland, and found there the symbols of his art. His description of his peasant father and mother in this unique autobiography would alone prove how strange a race had at length found a voice, and how potent and visionary a power had begun in the world's literature. His father, he writes, 'was unrivalled' 'as a narrator of old tales, legends, and historical anecdotes', 'and his stock of them was inexhaustible.[7] He spoke the Irish and English languages with equal fluency. With all kinds of charms, old ranns,[8] or poems, old prophecies, religious superstitions, tales of pilgrims, miracles and pilgrimages, anecdotes of blessed priests and friars, revelations from ghosts and fairies, he was thoroughly acquainted'. In a later part of the book he tells of his father's supernatural terrors, and of his continual praying, often with a 'round rod, about as thick as the upper end of a horsewhip', under his knees for a penance.[9] His mother 'possessed the sweetest and most exquisite of voices, in her early life, I have often been told by those who have heard her sing,[10] that any previous intimation of her presence at a wake, dance, or other festive occasion, was sure to attract crowds of persons, many from a distance of several miles, in order to hear from her lips the touching old airs of the country'. 'Her family had all been imbued with a poetical spirit, and some of her immediate ancestors composed in the Irish tongue several fine old songs and airs, just as Carolan did—that is, some in praise of a patron or a friend and others to celebrate rustic beauties who had been long sleeping in the dust. For this reason she had many old compositions that were peculiar to her family.'[11] 'I think her uncle, and I believe her grandfather, who were long dead before my time, were the authors of several Irish poems and songs'.[12] 'Perhaps there never lived a human being capable of giving the Irish cry or *keen* with such exquisite effect or of pouring into its wild notes a spirit of such irresistible pathos and sorrow. I have often been present when she has '*raised the keen*'—as it is called—over the corpse of some relative or neighbour, and my readers may judge of the melancholy charm which accompanied this expression of her sympathy when I assure them that the general clamour of violent grief was gradually diminished by admiration, until it became ultimately hushed, and no voice was heard but her own wailing, in sorrowful but solitary beauty'.[13]

I have quoted these passages at length because they show more than anything how this strange Gaelic race lives between two worlds, the world of its poverty, and a world of wild memories and of melancholy, beautiful imaginations. Carleton lived only just in time to describe its manners and customs as they had been left by centuries of purely Gaelic influence, for the great famine[14] changed the face of Ireland, and from that day a hundred influences which are not Gaelic began to mould them anew. His autobiography describes the actual wakes and faction fights and conspiracies and hedge schools and pilgrimages out of which he fashioned the half imaginary adventures of the *Traits and Stories,* and describes them not as one who observes with the philosophic indifference of the historian, but with the moving sympathy of one who has himself mourned and conspired and learnt and taught and gone on pilgrimage, and to whom all these things seem natural and inevitable. He also lived between two worlds, and has set down here the story of a love which touched the very height of passion, and which in old age was still the greatest of his memories, though he and his beloved never spoke, but only gazed at each other on the 'chapel green';[15] and to him also this solid world and its laws seemed somewhat of a shadow and a dream; so much so indeed that when more than nineteen years old and able to talk Latin like English, he was so greatly excited by a folk-tale of a priest who saved himself from drowning by walking on the water that he resolved to try and walk on a pool in an old marl pit, and so be ready for any mischance. 'After three days' fasting and praying for the power of not sinking in water, I stepped very quietly down to the pit, and after reconnoitring the premises, to be sure there was no looker-on, I approached the brink. . . . At the edge of the pit grew large waterlilies, with their leaves spread over the surface. . . . I am ashamed even while writing of this of the confidence I put for a moment in a treacherous water-lily, as its leaf lay spread so smoothly and broadly over the surface of the pond. . . .[16] After having stimulated myself afresh with a *pater* and an *ave,* I advanced—my eyes turned up to heaven . . . my soul strong in confidence, I made a tremendous stride, planting my foot exactly in the middle of the treacherous water-lily leaf, and the next moment was up to my neck in the water'.[17]

The autobiography, the discovery of which we owe to its editor, Mr. O'Donoghue,† does not come beyond his youth and early manhood. The rest of his life is told, and told admirably, by Mr. O'Donoghue† with the help of an immense correspondence which Carleton carried on with peasants in the country, and with journalists and men of letters in London and Dublin; but the interest of the book is necessarily in the earlier part. Even had Carleton lived to write it all with his own hand, it had hardly been otherwise, for the further we get from that strange, wild Gaelic life, the further we get from all that made Carleton a great voice in modern romance and the founder of Irish prose literature. The publisher has attached to the book a critical essay by Mrs. Cashel Hoey,[18] which scarcely seems relevant or excellent in any way. Mrs. Cashel Hoey has, I understand, done much useful work, but she is not a critic; and it is only in Irish literature, which has always been at the mercy of the first comer—priest, leisured amateur, town councillor, member of parliament, or casual jack of all trades—that she would be set to so uncongenial a task. To treat in this way, so important a book as this, is to continue the tradition which has allowed much of the best work of Carleton to drop out of print, while absolute rubbish like *The Evil Eye,*† and readable but empty melodrama like *Willy Reilly,* and dull moralising like *Paddy-Go-Easy,*† are reprinted continually.[19]

WILLIAM BLAKE

This review of Richard Garnett's William Blake *(London: Macmillan, 1896) is from* The Bookman, *April 1896. Blake, whom Yeats referred to as "my master," was the author about whom he was best equipped to do scholarly and critical battle. Garnett was lucky to get off as easily as he did; Laurence Housman's edition in 1893 had been treated more roughly. There is a note of resignation at the end of this review as if Yeats had realized that his and Ellis's edition of Blake, published in 1893, had not changed public ignorance of the mystical aspect of his "master."*

If the saying, that to be representative is to be famous, have anything of truth, the fame of William Blake should overspread the world; for, just as Shelley[1] is the example from which most men fashion their conception of the poetic temperament, Blake is, to the bulk of students, the most representative of seers, the one in whom the flame is most pure and most continual. Swedenborg had perhaps as great an original genius, but he commingled Biblical commentary and moral argument with his vision; while Boehme, who had possibly a greater genius, was much of a theologian and something of an alchemist; and neither Swedenborg nor Boehme[2] had an exterior life perfectly dominated and moulded by the interior spirit. I have said that Boehme had possibly a greater original genius, not because he seems to me so important to our time, but because he first taught in the modern world the principles which Blake first expressed in the language of poetry; and of these the most important, and the one from which the others spring, is that the imagination is the means whereby we communicate with God. 'The word image', says *The Way of Christ,* a compilation from Boehme and Law's interpretations of Boehme, published at Bath when Blake was eighteen, 'meaneth not only a creaturely resemblance, in which sense man is said to be the Image of God; but it signifieth also a spiritual substance, a birth or effect of a will, wrought in and by a spiritual being or power. And imagination, which we are apt erroneously to consider an airy, idle, and important faculty of the human mind, dealing in fiction and roving in phantasy or idea without producing any powerful or permanent, is the magia or power of raising and forming such images or substances, and the greatest power in nature.'³ The proud and lonely spirit of Blake was possessed and upheld by this doctrine, and enabled to face the world with the consciousness of a divine mission, for were not the poet and the artist more men of imagination than any others, and therefore more prophets of God? Boehme taught that prayer was the great power which acts upon imagination, and thereby 'forms and transforms' the souls of men 'into everything that its desires reach after'.⁴ But Blake held the creation of beautiful thoughts or forms or acts to be the greater power, and affirmed that 'Christ's apostles were artist', that 'Christianity is art', that 'the whole business of man is the arts',⁵ that the beautiful states of being which the artist in life or thought perceives by his imagination and tries to call up in himself or others 'are the real and eternal world of which this vegetable universe is but a faint shadow', and that 'the Holy Ghost' is 'an intellectual fountain'.⁶ The old mystics had the words 'goodness' and 'holiness' much in their mouths, and strained out of its true meaning the saying that 'the wisdom of this world is foolishness';⁷ but his cry was, 'I care not whether a man is good or bad; all I care is whether he is a wise man or a fool. Go, put off holiness, and put on intellect',⁸ and by intellect he meant his reason, his imagination. He was the first to claim for imagination the freedom which, Mr. Pater has told us, was won for the heart by the Renaissance, and through his unlearned and obscure voice spoke the unborn learning and glory of the modern world.⁹ There are some who hold that he who wrote, 'grandeur of ideas is founded upon precision of ideas',¹⁰ and whose great word was, according to Palmer, 'precision',¹¹ was a mere child delighting in meaningless words out of sheer love of their sound or their momentary charm; and there are others, and these are perhaps the bulk of idle readers, who will have it that it does not matter whether the 'Prophetic Books' had or had not a meaning, for his more charming lyrics are all we need know, as though a philosophy which has blossomed in so many a vivid aphorism had not its separate interest. It is to Dr. Garnett's credit that he does not, like some of his predecessors, definitely commit himself to the first theory, though such sentences as, he 'could manifestly be as transparent as a crystal when he knew exactly what he wished to say—a remark which may not be useless to the student of mystical and prophetical writings',¹² which is as though one should say, 'the songs of Shakespeare are very clear, let us therefore trouble no more over the mystery of Hamlet, for all that was writ at haphazard', is very nearly a committal. He has, however, very definitely pronounced for the second and greater folly by affirming that if Hayley[13] 'thought that one page of the *Poetical Sketches* or the *Songs of Innocence* was worth many pages of *Urizen*,† apart from the illustrations, he had reason for what he thought', as though one could judge of the value of a book without understanding what it is about; and if the truth be told, Mr. Garnett, like Mr. Gilchrist,[14] Mr. Rossetti, and almost every one who has ever written on the subject, does not show evidence of having ever given so much as a day's study to any part of Blake's mystical writing, or of having anything of the knowledge necessary to make even prolonged study fruitful. This very book of *Urizen*† would alone convict commentators, for they have not even discovered the fact lying upon its threshold, that it is page by page a transformation, according to Blake's peculiar illumination, of the doctrines set forth in the opening chapters of the *Mysterium Magnum* of Jacob Boehme; yet none so certain of their opinion as they, none so sweeping in statement.

These follies, for which he has distinguished precedents, apart, Dr. Garnett has worked modestly and carefully, and produced an essay, which pleasantly accompanies some admirable reproductions, of which two are in colour, and which, though it certainly neither throws nor tries to throw new light on anything, yet tells gracefully enough the essential facts of a beautiful life, and enumerates and describes accurately many famous pictures and poems. There is, however, one curious slip which is several times repeated. Dr. Garnett speaks of 'Sampson' as a blank verse poem,[15] and regrets that Blake did not write his 'Prophetic Books' in a like regular metre, instead of in a loose chant, to the fashioning of which he 'may have been influenced by Ossian'.[16] 'Sampson' was written at a time in which Blake was manifestly 'influenced by Ossian', and both written and printed as prose in the *Poetical Sketches*. Mr. Garnett has evidently seen the poem in Mr. Rossetti's edition, where it is printed as a kind of irregular blank verse, to show how the cadence of verse clung to Blake's mind even in prose, and has confused it with the fairly regular verse of 'Edward the Third'; and if he reads it again he will find that it bears no comparison with the beautiful fluid rhythms of *Thel*,† and of the best parts of 'Vala' and of *The Daughters of Albion*. The pity is, not that Blake did not write the 'Prophetic Books' in blank verse, but that he did not sustain the level of their finest passages. Despite these and some misunderstandings beside, Dr. Garnett's book may be cordially recommended to all who would learn a little of one of the most creative minds of modern days, for its futilities are wholly, and its errors almost wholly, in the parts where it touches mysticism, and for mysticism the general reader cares naught, nor is it dreadful that he should.

AN IRISH PATRIOT

Samuel Ferguson was one of the earliest figures Yeats wrote on in his career as a prose writer. In this review of Mary Catherine Guinness, Lady *Ferguson's biography,* Sir Samuel Ferguson in the Ireland of His Day *(Edinburgh and London: Blackwood and Sons, 1896), from* The Bookman, *May 1896, Yeats expressed his afterthoughts of a decade later. He still admired the poems of Ferguson, but this biography aroused his scorn for the society of Unionist bishops to which Ferguson belonged. Yeats, the grandson of a Church of Ireland clergyman, might have entered those same social circles. In the catalog of that church's faults, Yeats gave great emphasis to the charge ". . . and into whose churches no joyous and mystical fervour has ever come." Lady Ferguson in this biography had quoted (in vol. 2, pp. 287–88) Yeats's words of praise for her husband expressed in his* Dublin University Review *article of November 1886 (see "The Poetry of Sir Samuel Ferguson—II," pp. 10–27 above), but she found his remarks on Thomas Moore in his* Book of Irish Verse *to be "caustic" (vol. 2, pp. 251–52).*

One night about twelve years ago I was standing on the doorstep of a man who had spent several years in prison, and more in exile, for Fenianism, and at whose house met from time to time most of the men and women who now make up what is called 'The Irish Literary Movement'.[1] I had prolonged my 'good-night' to ask my host's opinion of Sir Samuel Ferguson, whose verse I was reading for the first time and with boyish enthusiasm. I was so accustomed to find Unionist hating Nationalist, and Nationalist hating Unionist,[2] with the hatreds of Montague[†] and Capulet,[3] that his answer is impressed on my memory with a distinctness which may seem inexplicable to those who live in more placid lands. 'Sir Samuel Ferguson', he replied, 'is, I understand, a Unionist, but he is a better patriot than I am; he has done more for Ireland than I have done or can ever hope to do.' Enthusiasm for the poetry of Sir Samuel Ferguson was indeed the common possession of

the Irish writers and students under whose influence or among whom
I grew out of my teens—I but mention myself as typical of the new literary generation in Ireland. So soon as they found any to listen they
wrote and talked and, I think, lectured on his writing, and with so much
success that a few months ago, when one of the largest of the young
men's societies debated the question, 'Who is the national poet of Ireland?' Ferguson was voted the place long held by Davis or Moore.[4] I
have not read the debate, and so know nothing of the arguments, but
ours would have been that Mangan had a more athletic rhythm, a more
lyrical temperament, Allingham a more delicate ear, a more distinguished
mastery over words, but that the author of 'The Vengeance of the Welshmen of Tirawley'[5] alone had his roots in no personal idiosyncrasy, but
in Irish character and Irish history, and that he alone foreshadowed the
way of the poets who would come after him. We forgave his failures
readily, and, like all Irish poets, his power of self-criticism was small
and his failures many, because his faults were faults of hardness and
heaviness, and not the false coin of a glittering or noisy insincerity which
Moore and the rhetoricians had made current in Ireland. Davis, Mangan, D'Arcy Magee, Kickham, Carleton, Banim[6]—almost every story-
writer or poet who had taken the popular side in Ireland had ruined a
part of his work by didactic writing, and even when they had written
with a purely artistic purpose they had often failed to shake off habits
of carelessness and commonness acquired in thinking of the widest
rather than of the best audience; they had made themselves, and for the
most generous of reasons, a mirror for the passions and the blindness
of the multitude. Lady Ferguson's life of her husband makes one
understand, however, with a new vividness, that Capulet is no better
than Montague[†] for a poet. Sir Samuel Ferguson lived entirely among
dignitaries, professional condemners of the multitude, archbishops
and bishops, deans and archdeacons, professors and members of
learned societies, Lord Chancellors and leaders of the Bar, and he who
will may read in this book of their opinions and their actions, and try
to read their letters, and when he has laid it down it will be as though
he had wandered, and not without a certain curious interest, in that
fabled stony city of Arabia or in that circle of outer space where
Milton saw 'cowls, hoods, and habits with their wearers, tossed and
fluttered into rags' before melancholy winds.[7] Consumed with one
absorbing purpose, the purpose to create an Irish school of literature,
and overshadowed by one masterful enthusiasm, an enthusiasm for all
Gaelic and Irish things, he wrote and talked through a long life; and,
as he wrote and talked, a hardness and heaviness crept into his rhythm
and his language from the dead world about him, marring the barbaric
power of *Conary*, still, with all its defects, the most characteristic of Irish

poems, and making, as I can but think, the Homeric imagination of *Congal* without avail. This, which could not but have been accompanied by some diminution of his delight in beauty, had mattered less to him had he found ready sympathy for his love for the earth and stones of the land, and for his belief in its ultimate welfare; but even this poor sympathy was so rare that when a dignitary, an archbishop of the Irish Church, sent him some incredibly feeble verses inspired by an amiable but conventional patriotism—

> Go point me out on any map
>   A match for green Killarney,
> Or Kevin's bed, or Dunlo's gap,
>   Or mystic shades of Blarney,
> Or Antrim's caves, or Shannon's waves—
>   Ah me! I doubt if ever
> An Isle so fair you'll find elsewhere,
>   Oh! never, never, never—[8]

he hailed them as giving him more 'hope and pleasure than any other expression of cultivated Irish sentiment that he had seen' for many years.[9] He lived in a class which, through a misunderstanding of the necessities of Irish Unionism, hated all Irish things, or felt for them at best a contemptuous and patronising affection, and which through its disgust at the smoky and windy fires of popular movements had extinguished those spiritual flames of enthusiasm that are the substance of a distinguished social and personal life, a class at whose dinner-tables conversation has long perished in the stupor of anecdote and argument, and on whose ears the great names of modern letters fall to awaken no flutter of understanding, or even of recognition, and into whose churches no joyous and mystical fervour has ever come. When the new school of Irish literature and criticism was founded; a school whose declared purpose is to create in Ireland a true, cultivated, patriotic class, and which for the first time unites Montague[†] and Capulet in the one movement; Ferguson, a very old man, was without fame, and, but for the popular ballad books, which had always a few of his verses, without readers. To-day there are hundreds whom the ballad books could never have reached, who have made his 'Fair Hills of Holy Ireland' an expression of their hearts.

> A plenteous place is Ireland for hospitable cheer,
>   *Uileacan dubh O!*
> Where the wholesome fruit is bursting from the yellow barley
>   ear;

   Uileacan dubh O!
There is honey in the trees where her misty vales expand,
And her forest paths in summer are by falling waters fanned;
There is dew at high noontide there, and springs i' the yellow
   sand.[10]
   On the fair hills of holy Ireland.

Curled he is and ringleted,[11] and plaited to the knee,
   Uileacan dubh O!
Each captain who comes sailing across the Irish sea;
   Uileacan dubh O!
And I will make my journey, if life and health but stand,
Unto that pleasant country, that fresh and fragrant strand,
And leave your boasted braveries, your wealth and high com-
   mand,
   For the fair hills of holy Ireland.

THE NEW IRISH LIBRARY

This review of Swift in Ireland *by Richard Ashe King (Dublin and London, 1896);* Owen Roe O'Neill *by John F. Taylor (Dublin and London, 1896); and* Short Life of Thomas Davis *by Sir Charles Gavan Duffy (Dublin, London, and New York, 1895)—all published by T. Fisher Unwin in the New Irish Library series—is from* The Bookman, *June 1896.*

Yeats dealt in this review with one friend and two enemies. He had quarreled with Taylor and Duffy in 1892 over the editorship of the New Irish Library and lost. He had been continually fighting with the orator Taylor over the respective virtues of oratory and literature. His friend in this group of authors was King, whom he had defended three years before after King had maintained that in Ireland partisan oratory had overwhelmed literature.

Yeats treated Duffy here more kindly than he had in the past. And his gentle reminder to Taylor that his work was good but not literature was mild indeed after the insults Yeats had received from Taylor four years before.

Yeats shows here an admiration for Jonathan Swift as a man but a disdain for the eighteenth century. Twenty-five years later, Yeats was to become obsessed with Swift and to make his peace with that century, which he here accused of setting "chop-logic in the place of the mysterious power, obscure as a touch from behind a curtain, that had governed 'the century of poets.'"

The last time I reviewed a bundle of new Irish Library books I had little good to say of them.[1] The series had all the faults of that 'Young Ireland' literature which, like so many things that did excellent service in their own time, has become a difficulty in the way of good literature and good criticism. It had printed a politico-historical pamphlet of some value, and called it a model of historical writing; a mass of political rhymes of nearly no value, and called it great poetry; and it had debased the coinage of imagination by turning a story of Balzac's into a sermon on village industries.[2] The best of the Irish public, however, having outlived the false ideals of Young Ireland, scouted prose and rhyme alike, and the library suddenly transformed itself and became vivid and scholarly. I praised, at the times of their appearance *The Irish Song Book, The Story of Early Gaelic Literature,* and *The Life of Patrick Sarsfield,* and the new volumes keep the same high level.[3] *Swift in Ireland,* certainly one of the most useful and readable books of its kind in contemporary literature, discusses the life of Swift[4] from the point of view of Ireland with unfailing witty and wise comment, and is a beginning of that scholarly criticism of men and things which is needed in Ireland even more perhaps than creative literature, for until it come we are perforce at the mercy of our rhetoricians and our newspaper hacks. Its only serious defect is that it does not contain enough of purely literary criticism, and makes no serious endeavour to consider the value of Swift's writings taken apart from the light they throw upon his actions and opinions, and in opinion-ridden Ireland some such estimate had been useful.

The recognition of the expression of a temperament as an end in itself, and not merely as a means towards a change of opinion, is the first condition of any cultivated life, and there is no better text than Swift for preaching this. He did not become, like the subject of Sir Charles Gavan Duffy's volume, a great light of his time because of the utility of his projects or of any high standard of honest thinking—for some of his most famous projects were mere expressions of a paradoxical anger, while others he defended with arguments which even he could not have believed—but because he revealed in his writings and in his life a more intense nature, a more living temperament, than any of his contemporaries. He was as near a supreme man as that fallen age could produce, and that he did not labour, as Blake says the supreme man should, 'to bring again the golden age'[5] by revealing it in his work and his life, but fought, as with battered and smoke-blackened armour in the mouth of the pit, was the discredit of 'the century of philosophers': a century which had set chop-logic in the place of the mysterious power, obscure as a touch from behind a curtain, that had governed 'the century of poets'.[6] Some pages of Sir Thomas Browne[7] are, one doubts not, of a greater kind, as pure literature, than any he wrote, but he has given the world an unforgettable parable by building an over-powering genius upon the wreckage of the merely human faculties, of all that the Herr Nordaus[8] of ours and other times have acclaimed and preached; and it is because the most ignorant feel this in some instinctive way that his throne is unassailable. Ireland seems to me to especially need this parable, for she is so busy with opinions that she cannot understand that imaginative literature wholly, and all literature in some degree, exists to reveal a more powerful and passionate, a more divine world than ours; and not to make our ploughing and sowing, our spinning and weaving, more easy or more pleasant, or even to give us a good opinion of ourselves by glorifying our past or our future.

Mr. Taylor's and Sir Charles Gavan Duffy's books, though not literature and the interpretation of literature, are excellently useful so long as our Irish readers do not think them one or the other. Mr. Taylor has explored an obscure historical period with an industry above all praise, and with a strong national enthusiasm, but—and I must apologise for judging him by a standard by which he has never desired to be judged—his book is not literature, because he does not, as Mr. King does occasionally, reveal the actions and persons of his story in the mirror of a temperament, because he has not what Matthew Arnold called 'the literary consciousness'.[9] Sir Charles Gavan Duffy is always interesting on the friends of his youth, and there is no book of his so valuable for Irish purposes as his life of Davis, already well known in its more expensive form. One regrets, however, to find that he still persists in calling Davis—the maker of three or four charming songs that were not great, and of much useful political rhyme that was not poetry—a great poet, and in seeking to prove it by quoting 'Fontenoy' and other savourless imitations of Macaulay.[10] No one who does not know literary Ireland can understand the harm done by such criticism, and the barren enthusiasm for the second-hand and the second-rate it prolongs. Let us sing our political songs with ardour, shouldering our pikes while we sing if we be so minded, but do not let us always call them great poetry.

WILLIAM CARLETON

This article on William Carleton appeared in the American Bookman, *August 1896. Much of it had appeared earlier in Yeats's review of* The Life of William Carleton, *which had appeared in* The Bookman *in March 1896 (see pp. 298–301 above, and the notes to that article). George Monteiro posted his discovery of this article in* Notes and Queries, *January 1974, p. 28.*

William Blake expounds the history of inspiration by a very curious and obscure symbol. A lark, he says, mounts upward into the heart of the heavens, and there is met by another and descending lark, which touches its wings to its wings; and he would have us understand, if I remember the passage and its context rightly—for I have not the prophetical book *Milton* by me—that man attains spiritual influence in like fashion. He must go on perfecting earthly power and perception until they are so subtilised that divine power and divine perception descend to meet them, and the song of earth and the song of heaven mingle together. Every literary current and tradition goes, I believe, through something like this development, coming only very late to its Shelleys and Wordsworths. Whether Irish prose literature be or be not to-day awaiting the celestial lark, and though no living Irish romance writer, with the exception of Mr. Standish O'Grady, has anything of Carleton's genius, it is certainly much more subtle, much more spiritual than before. The author of *The Traits and Stories* was not an artist, as those must needs be who labour with spiritual essences; but he was what only a few men have ever been or can ever be—the creator of a new imaginative world, the demiurge of a new tradition. He had no predecessors, for Miss Edgeworth wrote by preference of that section of Irish society which is, as are the upper classes everywhere, the least national of all, and was, as the upper classes have seldom been anywhere, ashamed of even the little it had of national circumstance and character; and when she did take a man out of the Gaelic world and put into his mouth the immortal *Memoirs of the Rackrent Family,* it was a poor man living in great men's houses, and not a poor man at his hearth among his children. She could not have done otherwise, for she was born and bred among persons who knew nothing of the land where they were born, and she had no generations of historians, Gaelic scholones and folk-lorists behind her, from whom to draw the symbols of her art.[1]

William Carleton, on the other hand, came from the heart of Gaelic Ireland, and found there the symbols of his art. This strange Gaelic race lives between two worlds, the world of its poverty and a world of wild memories and of melancholy, beautiful imaginations. Carleton lived only just in time to describe its manners and customs as they had been left by centuries of purely Gaelic influence, for the great famine changed the face of Ireland, and from that day a hundred influences which are not Gaelic began to mould them anew.[2] Miss Edgeworth had called up for a moment this ancient life in the mournful humor of Thady Quirk; but it was not until the brothers Banim and William Carleton began to write that it found adequate historians. Michael Banim was excellent in much of *Father Connell* and John Banim in the first half of *The Nowlans*[†], and in the opening chapters of *Crohoore*[†] *of the Bill-Hook*[†] and at odd moments in all his books; but only Carleton, born and bred a peasant, was able to give us a vast multitude of grotesque, pathetic, humourous persons, misers, pig-drivers, drunkards, schoolmasters, labourers, priests, madmen, and to fill them all with an abounding vitality. He was but half articulate, half emerged from Mother Earth, like one of Milton's lions; but his wild Celtic melancholy gives to whole pages of *Fardarougha*[†] and *The Black Prophet* an almost spiritual grandeur. The forms of life he described, like those described with so ebullient a merriment by his contemporary Lever, passed away with the great famine; but the substance which filled those forms is the substance of Irish life, and will flow into new forms which will resemble them as one wave of the sea resembles another. In future times men will recognise that he was at his best a true historian, the peasant Chaucer of a new tradition, and that at his worst he fell into melodrama more from imperfect criticism than imperfect inspiration. In his time only a little of Irish history, Irish folk-lore, Irish poetry had been got into the English tongue; he had to dig the marble for his statue out of the mountainside with his own hands, and the statue shows not seldom the clumsy chiselling of the quarryman.[3]

GREEK FOLK POESY

This review of New Folklore Researches, Greek Folk Poesy, *translated by Lucy M. J. Garnett, with* Essays on Folklore *by J. S. Stuart-Glennie, in two volumes (Guilford: Billing and Sons, 1896), is from* The Bookman, *October 1896.*

Yeats's exposition of Stuart-Glennie's theory is particularly interesting for the study of his characteristic attitudes on race and class. Glennie said that civilization was born out of the meeting and conflict of a superior race and an inferior one. Such a theory supported Yeats's aristocratic ideals as well as his absorption with folklore.

Yeats thought Miss Garnett's translations without value, yet he seems to have gained something from reading this book. He tells us in a note (VP, 806) that his poem "The Song of Wandering Aengus" was suggested by a Greek folk song. Perhaps it was Miss Garnett's translation of "The Lover's Return" in which the lover is "a wanderer o'er the hills" and there is much gold, silver, and apple imagery. Or perhaps Yeats's inspiration was "The Fruit of the Apple Tree," which ends:

> *Come, gather youth! Come, gather them, the apples of my*
> *   fruit tree;*
> *And gather them again, again, and stoop again and again!*

R. K. Alspach in "Two Songs of Yeats," Modern Language Notes, lxi, 395–400, suggests that Yeats's source was "The Three Fishes" (cited in A. Norman Jeffares, A Commentary on the Collected Poems of W. B. Yeats [London: Macmillan, 1968], pp. 61–62).

Miss Lucy M. J. Garnett has translated in *Greek Folk Poesy* about four hundred pages of Greek folk poetry, a part newly collected, and a part translated from Greek collections; and Mr. J. S. Stuart Glennie has prefaced the book with certain essays on a new theory of the origin of civilisation. Anthologies of Greek folk prose and of Gaelic folk poetry are to follow, and the introductions and notes, etc., of these books are to be Mr. Stuart Glennie's final proof of his theory. One reads him at first with difficulty and reluctance because of the barbarism of his style. He uses the longest and most unmusical words, and, even when he has a simple word like 'records' ready to his hand, delights in such fruit of his own fancy as 'recordations';[1] while his misuse of capitals passes belief. One gradually, however, becomes aware of a certain force of imagination and lucidity of intellect in the midst of this verbiage; and presently one is mastered by a strong curiosity. For the accepted theories of a spontaneous development of civilisation out of savagery he substitutes what he calls 'the general conflict theory,'[2] and suggests that 'civilised' or 'progressive communities' began when a race of superior intellectual power compelled or persuaded a race of lesser intellectual power to feed it and house it, in return for the religion and science which it had thus found the leisure to make,[3] and to pass on from generation to generation in always growing complexity. This contest, the contest of subtlety against force, the subtlety often of a very few against the force of a multitude, gradually changed from a contest between men of different races to a compact between men of different classes, and so created the modern world. He supports this theory with an elaborate array of arguments, which I have not enough of science to apprise, among the rest with arguments based on the existence 'at the very earliest ages of which we have anthropological evidence' of 'at least two different or intellectually unequal Species or Races of Primitive Man,' differing from each other 'in cranial type as well as in stature, even more than whites differ from blacks'.[4] This theory, if established, Mr. Stuart Glennie points out, will reconcile the theories of writers like Professor Max Müller, who believes the great ancient mythologies, to have a profound and complex meaning, with the theories of writers like Mr. Andrew Lang, who believes them a survival of the beliefs of savages;[5] for the men of the higher race could invent no more certain way of prolonging their own rule than to change the childish beliefs about them into a complex mystery of which they were themselves the prophets and guardians: all that was merely instinctive and spontaneous coming from the many and from the dominant few all that was intellectual and deliberate. I find this theory, which affirms the supremacy of the intellect, much more plausible than any of those theories which imply the origin, by a vague process which no one has explained, of the most exquisite inventions of folk-lore and mythology from the imaginations of everybody and nobody; but only scientific folk-lorists and mythologists can say whether it is consistent with the facts. I am, however, convinced that some such theory will be established in the long run; being no democrat in intellectual things, and altogether per-

suaded that elaborate beauty has never come but from the mind of a
deliberate artist writing at leisure and in peace.

Mr. Stuart Glennie gives certain pages to a destructive analysis of
the accepted classifications and definitions of the science of folk-lore,
and suggests classifications and definitions in accordance with his
new theory. All his definitions appear to me to be excellent, except perhaps his definition of religion, which makes religion too exclusively a
matter of conduct;[6] and his classifications would perhaps be as useful
as they are certainly interesting, but for his lack of any instinct for the
right word. 'Zoonist' is not English, and to make an arbitrary distinction between 'tales' and 'stories' in order to distinguish between the
folk-lore of cosmical and the folk-lore of moral ideas is not good
sense.[7] As he is not worse in this matter than certain other folk-lorists,
one had been content perhaps to forget his style out of respect for his
theory had he not taken to himself a collaboratress who writes seven
times worse than himself. A scientific theory can but suffer a temporary injury from the language of its exposition, but a folk song put into
bad verse loses the half of its scientific and nearly all its literary interest. Miss Garnett would perhaps have made a beautiful book had
she been content to write it in prose. Leconte de Lisle's translations
of Homer, Virgil and Aeschylus, Mr. Lang's, Mr. Butcher's, and Mr.
Leaf's translation of Homer, Mr. Lang's translation of Theocritus, and
the recent translations of Roumanian folk songs were surely a sufficient
precedent.[8] There can be no justification of the writing of verse except
the power to write as a poet writes; and such lines as

> I hear my heart a-sighing, a-grieving with its smart,
> And my *nous* which calls in answer, 'Have patience, O dear
>   heart';[9]

and such lines as

> A flower I took thee to my heart, and there a thorn art thou;
> And marvels all the world to see that lost our love is now;

and such lines as

> 'Vlachopoula,[†] thee I love;
> This I've come to tell my dove.'

> '*Goumene,* if thou lov'st true,
> Go and fetch a boat, now do.'

'Handsome let its boatman be,
To pull the oars for thee and me,'[10]

are not written as a poet writes.

Miss Garnett's translations are indeed so lifeless that it is impossible to form any judgment of the poetical value of the originals, or get more than a few rare and faint emotions from all her four hundred pages. Greek folk poetry is apparently a very civilised poetry, with little of the superhuman preoccupations and extravagant beauty of Roumanian and Gaelic folk poetry. It mentions, for instance, a five hundred years old witch, but takes no pleasure in her age such as the Gaelic folk poet took when he made her cry, 'Who has carried away my gold, which I was for five hundred years gathering in the waste places of the earth?'[11] And its expression of love is prudent, temperate, almost calculating, beside the ungovernable passion of more primitive verse. It has nothing of that search for some absolute of emotion, some mysterious infinite of passion which is in so much of Gaelic poetry. There is never anything like that wild lyrical outburst translated by Dr. Hyde: 'She is my treasure, O, she is my treasure, the woman of the gray eyes, a woman who would not place a hand under my head. She is my love, O she is my love, a woman who left no strength in me, a woman who would not breathe a sigh after me, a woman who would not raise a stone at my tomb. She is my secret love, O she is my secret love, a woman who tells me nothing . . . a woman who does not remember when I am out, a woman who would not weep at my death.'[12] Its emotion is weighted and measured with a nice sense of occasions and circumstances; one feels that the poets who wrote it were well aware of a great civilised literature somewhere behind them, and trod carefully in the footsteps of men preoccupied with the state and with the world. Nor has it that marvellous sense of a subtle union between an emotion and outer things which is in such songs as this Roumanian love song: 'Take which ever way thou wilt, for the ways are all alike; but do thou only come—I bade my threshold wait thy coming. From out my window one can see the graves—and on my life the graves too keep a watch.'[13] It is indeed as unlike such a song as possible, being always definite, lucid, reasonable, having the clear light of the day of work and thought, and not the vague magnificence of sunrise or of sunset. It lacks, in other words, those very characteristics which written literature is continually absorbing from unwritten literature, that it may escape the old age of many reasons, the frailty of feet that tread but upon smooth roads; an absorption which is itself an illustration of Mr. Stuart Glennie's theory. It seems less like a folk literature than an imperfect literature of culture, and if one judged it by its literary characteristics alone, one would class it, not with primitive poetry like the poetry of Gaelic Ireland and Scotland, but with such half-cultivated, half-instinctive verse as that written by men like Walsh, Callanan, and the 'Young Ireland' writers, in Ireland in this century.[14]

THE WELL AT THE WORLD'S END

Yeats reviewed William Morris's romance The Well at the World's End *(London: Longmans, Green and Co., 1896) in* The Bookman *of November 1896.*

Yeats had known William Morris and his family well from 1888 to 1890. He attended some meetings of the Socialist League at Morris's home. After a time, he found this group's indifference to religion so annoying that he left the circle for good.

This review appeared shortly after Morris's death. Yeats gave an extended characterization of Morris in the "Four Years: 1887–91" section of his autobiography (Au, 130–39). In another essay on Morris (reprinted in Ideas of Good and Evil*), he admitted that Morris was not one the greatest of poets but that "he was among the greatest of those who prepare the last reconciliation when the Cross shall blossom with roses."*

Yeats met Morris when the latter was visiting Dublin lecturing for the Dublin arm of the Social Democratic Federation. For an account of this meeting (though Morris is unnamed), see "The Poetry of Sir Samuel Ferguson—I," pp. 3–9 above.

That Mr. William Morris was the greatest poet of his time one may doubt, remembering more impassioned numbers than his, but one need not doubt at all that he was the poet of his time who was most perfectly a poet. Certain men impress themselves on the imagination of the world as types, and Shelley,[1] with his wayward desires, his unavailing protest, has become the type of the poet to most men and to all women, and perhaps because he seemed to illustrate that English dream, which holds the poet and the artist unfitted for practical life: laughable and lovable children whose stories and angers one may listen to when the day's work is done. If, however, a time come when the world recognises that the day's work, that practical life, become noble just in so far as they are subordinated to the sense of beauty, the sense of the perfect, just in so far as they approach the dream of the poet and the artist, then Mr. William Morris may become, instead of Shelley, the type of the poet: for he more than any man of modern days tried to change the life of his time into the life of his dream. To others beauty was a solitary vision, a gift coming from God they knew not how; but to him it was always some golden fleece[2] or happy island, some well at the world's end, found after many perils and many labours in the world, and in all his later books, at any rate, found for the world's sake. Almost alone among the dreamers of our time, he accepted life and called it good; and because almost alone among them he saw, amid its incompleteness and triviality, the Earthly Paradise that shall blossom at the end of the ages.

When Ralph, the pilgrim to the well at the world's end, is setting out upon his journey, he meets with a monk who bids him renounce the world. "Now, lord, I can see by thy face that thou art set on beholding the fashion of this world, and most like it will give thee the rue."

Then came a word into Ralph's mouth, and he said: "Wilt thou tell me, father, whose work was the world's fashion?"

The monk reddened, but answered nought, and Ralph spake again: "Forsooth, did the craftsman of it fumble over his work?"

Then the monk scowled, but presently he enforced himself to speak blithely, and said,[3] "Such matters are over high for my speech or thine, lord; but I tell thee, who knoweth, that there are men in this House who have tried the world and found it wanting."

'Ralph smiled and said,[4] stammering: "Father, did the world try them, and find them wanting perchance?"'

And later on it is said to the seekers of the well, 'If you love not the earth and the world with all your souls, and will not strive all ye may to be frank and happy therein, your toil and peril aforesaid shall win you no blessing, but a curse.'[5]

In the literal sense of the word, and in the only high sense, he was a prophet; and it was his vision of that perfect life, which the world is always trying, as Jacob Boehme[†] taught, to bring forth, that awakened every activity of his laborious life—his revival of mediaeval tapestry and stained glass, his archaic printing, his dreams of Sigurd and of Gudrun and of Guinevere,[6] his essays upon the unloveliness of our life and art, his preaching in parks and at the corners of streets, his praise of revolutions, his marchings at the head of crowds, and his fierce anger against most things that we delight to honour. We sometimes call him 'melancholy', and speak of the 'melancholy' of his poems, and I know not well why, unless it be that we mistake the pensiveness of his early verse, a pensiveness for noble things once had and lost, or for noble things too great not to be nearly beyond hope, for his permanent

mood, which was one of delight in the beauty of noon peace, of rest
after labour, of orchards in blossom, of the desire of the body and of
the desire of the spirit. Like Blake, he held nothing that gave joy
unworthy, and might have said with Ruysbroeck, 'I must rejoice without ceasing, even though the world shudder at my joy',[7] except that he
would have had the world share his joy. There is no picture of him more
permanent in my mind than that of him sitting at one of those suppers
at Hammersmith[8] to which he gathered so singular a company of
artists and workmen, and crying out on those who held it unworthy
to be inspired by a cup of wine: for had not wine come out of the sap
and out of the leaves and out of the heat of the sunlight? It was this vision
of happiness that made him hate rhetoric, for rhetoric is the triumph
of the desire to convince over the desire to reveal. His definition of good
writing would have been writing full of pictures of beautiful things
and beautiful moments. 'My masters', he said once, 'are Keats and
Chaucer, because Keats and Chaucer make pictures'. Dante he held for
a like reason to be more a poet than Milton, who, despite his 'great,
earnest mind, expressed himself as a rhetorician'.[9] These pictures were
not, I imagine, to be so much in great masses as in minute detail. 'The
beauty of Dante', he said to me once, 'is in his detail'; and in all his art
one notices nothing more constant than the way in which it heaps up,
and often in the midst of tragedy, little details of happiness. This book
is full of them, and there is scarcely a chapter in which there is not some
moment for which one might almost give one's soul.

MISS FIONA MACLEOD
AS A POET

Yeats reviewed Fiona Macleod's From the Hills of Dream; Mountain Songs and Island Runes *(Edinburgh: P. Geddes, 1896) in the December 1896 issue of* The Bookman.

Scottish Celticism seems to lend itself to literary double identities bordering on the fraudulent. With the example of Macpherson's Ossian to guide him, William Sharp, a successful literary journalist, created a second identity—that of Fiona Macleod—with a separate literary style and handwriting. Yeats had known Sharp since 1888 and then "hated his red British face of flaccid contentment" (CL1, 24). He came to know of Fiona Macleod during the mid-nineties.

Yeats admired Sharp's psychic powers. The two men joined in experiments in vision and trance until Sharp, complaining that his health was injured, resumed his private vision. For a time Yeats believed Fiona Macleod to be a real person, wrote her letters, and received answers in Sharp's special "Macleod" handwriting. He may have discovered the secret before Sharp's death. Yeats believed that the writings of Fiona Macleod were the genuine products of trancelike visions in which a separate personal identity spoke through Sharp.

At first Yeats thought Fiona Macleod was a writer of great promise, especially since her writings seemed a perfect example of the decline of realistic and the coming of symbolic art. Her work was all the more important to Yeats in that she was a Scottish Celt and hence proved the universality of Celtic traits. With Irish, Welsh, Scottish, and —as he hoped—Breton Celticism in full renaissance, the Saxon empire of realism and materialism might be encircled and destroyed. Despite his wish to be pleased, Yeats's three reviews of her work mark an increasing impatience with the careless, overblown verbiage of Sharp in his Macleod phase.

The section of From the Hills of Dream *entitled "Foam of the Past" was dedicated to Yeats as a kindred Celtic seer. Miss Macleod told Yeats in this dedication, "So you, perhaps, may say of some of these lines in 'From the Hills of Dream' and 'Foam of the Past' that they come familiarly to you in other than the sense of mere acquaintance." Sharp meant a community of experience, but these lines from "The Bugles of Dreamland" may have seemed familiar to Yeats for other reasons:*

> Come away from the weary old world of tears,
> Come away, come away to where one never hears
> The slow weary drip of the slow weary years,
> But Peace and deep rest till the white dews are falling
> And the blithe bugle-laughters through Dreamland are calling.

In France, where every change of literary feeling brings with it a change of literary philosophy, the great change of our time is believed to be a return to the subjective. We no longer wish to describe nature like the 'nature poets', or to describe society like the 'realists', but to make our work a mirror, where the passions and desires and ideals of our own minds can cast terrible or beautiful images.[1] If the French are right—and every new book which seems at all of our time is, I think, a proof that they are—we are at the beginning of a franker trust in passion and in beauty than was possible to the poets who put their trust in the external world and its laws. Some of the poems in *From the Hills of Dream* would have been almost impossible ten years ago. For ten years ago Miss Macleod would have asked herself, 'Is this a valuable and a sober criticism upon life?'[2] and we should probably have lost one of the most inspired, one of the most startling, one of the most intense poems of our time, her incomparable 'Prayer of Women.'[3]

> O Spirit that broods upon the hills,
> And moves upon the face of the deep,
> And is heard in the wind,
> Save us from the desire of men's eyes.[4]
> . . . . .
> Ah, hour of the hours,
> When he looks at our hair and sees it is grey;
> And at our eyes and sees they are dim;
> And at our lips, straightened out with long pain;
> And at our breasts, fallen and seared like a barren hill;
> And at our hands, worn with toil!
> Ah, hour of the hours,
> When, seeing, he seeth all the bitter ruin and wreck of us—
> All save the violated womb that curses him—

All save the heart that forbeareth . . . for pity—
All save the living brain that condemneth him.[5]
. . . . .
O spirit and the nine angels who watch us,
And Thy Son and Mary Virgin,
Heal us of the wrong of man:
We whose breasts are weary with milk
Cry, cry to Thee, O Compassionate.[6]

This poem was, I understand, first written in Gaelic, and Miss Macleod is always best when she writes under a Gaelic and legendary and mythological influence. Emotions which seem vague or extravagant when expressed under the influence of modern literature, cease to be vague and extravagant when associated with ancient legend and mythology, for legend and mythology were born out of man's longing for the mysterious and the infinite. When Miss Macleod writes of 'the white Peace' which 'lies not on the sunlit hill', nor 'on the sunlit plain', nor 'on any running stream', but comes sometimes into the soul of man as 'the moonlight of a perfect Peace', I find her thought too vague greatly to move or impress me;[7] but when she writes of 'the four white winds of the world, whose father the golden sun is, whose mother the wheeling moon is, the north and the south and the east and the west', and of 'the three dark winds of the world; the chill breath of the grave, the breath from the depth of the sea', and 'the breath of to-morrow', I am altogether moved and impressed.[8] I feel, indeed, throughout this book two influences—a Gaelic influence, which Miss Macleod has mastered and remoulded, and an influence from modern literature which she has not yet been able to master and mould; and this is, perhaps, why *From the Hills of Dream* seems to me so much more unequal, so much more experimental, than *The Sin Eater* or *The Washer of the Ford*.[9] Many of the poems which have the strongest Gaelic influence, and therefore the most authentic inspiration, are in wild and irregular measures; and this is a pity, because the best critics are not convinced that wild and irregular measures are perfectly legitimate. The poems in rhyme and in regular measures which seem to be latest in date are, however, a great advance upon their fellows, and have occasional passages of a charming phantasy, like the second, third, fourth, and fifth stanzas in 'The Moon Child', or of a beautiful intensity, like this passage, which expresses something almost beyond the range of expression.

She had two men within the palm, the hollow of her hand;
She takes their souls and blows them forth as idle drifted sand;

And one falls back upon her breast that is his quiet home,
And one goes out into the night and is as wind-blown foam,
And when she sees the sleep of one, ofttimes she riseth there,
And looks into the outer dusk and calleth soft and fair.[10]

YOUNG IRELAND

This review of Sir Charles Gavan Duffy's A Final Edition of Young Ireland *(London: T. Fisher Unwin, 1896) appeared in* The Bookman *in January 1897. In 1892, despite Yeats's strenuous objection, Duffy had gained the editorship of the New Irish Library book series, a post that Yeats had very likely wanted for himself. Yeats's revenge was long and leisurely. He reviewed some of the New Irish Library books favorably, but those volumes produced by Duffy and his coterie received slighting reviews, such as this one. With Duffy's appropriation of the library scheme in mind, Yeats criticized Thomas Davis for dragooning his friends into writing plays for the Young Ireland movement. Within a year after this review, Yeats, who was a better hunter than either Davis or Duffy, was beating the bushes for any talents to contribute to the Irish Literary Theatre.*

The period of Irish history most studied in Ireland is the period between the foundation of the *Nation* newspaper in 1842 and the Rebellion of 1848.[1] During this period the national feeling was expressed for the first time in a definite political philosophy, and the writers and speakers through whose minds it was expressed are sacred names in Ireland. *Young Ireland,* of which Sir Charles Gavan Duffy has just issued a final edition,[2] illustrated with many portraits, is the standard history of their writings and speeches, their plans and their hopes, and without it there is no understanding of modern Ireland.

I can only concern myself here with the literary influence of *Young Ireland,* which has been almost as great as its political, and is, though much weakened of late among educated nationalists, still the one powerful literary influence in Ireland. The 'Young Irelanders' very consciously and deliberately endeavoured to create a literature which was to be 'racy of the soil',[3] and they persuaded every man and woman they could lay hands on to join in their big endeavour. 'Have you ever tried dramatic writing?' Thomas Davis, their inspiring spirit,

wrote to the biographer Madden,[†] who was certainly the least dramatic
and perhaps the dullest writer of any note Ireland has produced.[4] 'Do
you know Taylor's *Philip Van Artevelde* and Griffin's *Gisippus*?[†5] I think
them the two best serious dramas written in English since Shakespeare's time. A drama equal to either of them with an Irish subject[6]
would be useful and popular to an extent you can hardly suppose.' It
seemed to them possible for any clever man to write a good song, a
good history, a good drama, if he only would; for literature meant to
them an exposition of certain opinions about which they were agreed
and hoped to make others agreed, and of certain types of character
which all men might be expected to admire, and not a capricious
inspiration coming with an unforeseen message out of the dim places
of the mind. They published in *The Library of Ireland*[7] hastily written
books of Irish history and Irish biography and Irish ballad poetry, and
in the *Nation* articles on the poets and politicians and revolutionists
of many lands; and this writing, which is inspired by a didactic purpose, and is but excellent journalism for the most part, seems to thousands of young men in Ireland a great ideal literature. It is only a
minority of Irishmen who understand that nearly all of it that is not
politics is now in one of those infirmaries of the human mind where,
M. Maeterlinck says, all truths which are not mystic truths, which are
not truths come out of a solitary and mysterious ideal, go at last and
to die.[8]

The 'Young Irelanders' were of necessity buried in those heterogeneous occupations which Arthur Hallam believed more dangerous to
a writer than the most immoral of lives;[9] and they were too preoccupied with public conduct to attend to the persuasions of their own temperaments, and all good literature is made out of temperaments. To be
preoccupied with public conduct is to be preoccupied with the ideas
and emotions which the average man understands or can be made to
understand, and out of the ideas and emotions of the average man you
can make no better thing than good rhetoric. A characteristic fruit of
their moral and practical lives was the blazing rhetoric of *The Spirit
of the Nation*, just as a characteristic fruit of the immoral and unprac-
tical but solitary and individual life of Clarence[†] Mangan was the
impassioned poetry of 'The Dark Rosaleen' and of 'O'Hussey's[†] Ode
for the Maguire'.[†10] Clarence[†] Mangan might doubtless have been a less
unequal poet, and a poet of a more ample and serene inspiration, had
he drunk less whisky and smoked less opium, but had he been buried
in heterogeneous occupations or preoccupied with public conduct, he
would have been no more than a good rhetorician. It is probable, however, that even if public needs had left the 'Young Irelander' free to
make a national literature, the season to make it had not come, for a

national literature can only be painted, as it were, against a background of patient and minute scholarship, and patient and minute scholarship in Irish things had only just begun in their day. They did the one excellent thing, the one seasonable thing, that cried out to be done—they taught fervour, and labour, and religious toleration, and left their memory for an inspiration to the young men of Ireland.

MR. JOHN O'LEARY

John O'Leary (1830–1907) was a member of the Irish Republican Brotherhood founded in Dublin in 1858. Arrested in 1865, he was imprisoned for nine years, and then lived in exile in Paris until 1885 when he returned to Ireland. In his autobiography (Au, 100–107) as well as in "I Became an Author" (LAR, 297–300), Yeats ascribed to the influence of John O'Leary the native force of his entire career. Yeats was severely disappointed when O'Leary's Recollections of Fenians and Fenianism *(London: Downey, 1896), which he had been writing when the two men lived together briefly, was published in 1896: "In the evening, over his coffee, he would write passages for his memoirs ... taking immense trouble with every word and comma, for the great work must be a masterpiece of style. When it was finished, it was unreadable, being dry, abstract, and confused; no picture had ever passed before his mind's eye" (Au, 178). Thus when Yeats, responding to the urging of his father, undertook his review of* Recollections *for the February 1897 issue of* The Bookman *his approach was to praise the author and ignore the work.*

A very close paraphrase of this article appeared in L'Irlande Libre, *the Parisian political journal sponsored by Maud Gonne (1866–1953), on 1 June 1898. See "Le Mouvement Celtique: II. M. John O'Leary," pp. 413–14 below.*

In Ireland we sometimes celebrate the memories of our national heroes by little suppers, at which we sit round a long table and drink coffee and listen to speeches and patriotic songs. I remember talking a couples of years ago to the man who sat next me at a supper in honour, I think, of Thomas Davis,[1] and his saying, 'Our public men, with the exception of Mr. John O'Leary, have been afraid to differ from the people in anything, and now we haven't got a pinsworth of respect for anybody but for Mr. John O'Leary'.[2] This man was, if I remember rightly, a clerk in a big shop, and typical of many of the younger generation in Dublin. He had probably given his adhesion in practical things to some leader who had more eloquence, or a firmer hold on the questions of the hour, or who had shown him some immediate thing to be done, but he had only given his adhesion in practical things. As long as he could remember, Mr. John O'Leary had been denouncing this or that political expedient, this or that popular leader, and affirming, because manhood is greater than nations, that there are things which a man should not do, perhaps even to save a nation.[3] Had anyone who had not suffered, like Mr. John O'Leary, years of imprisonment and of exile, said these things, my neighbour would not have listened; but as things were, Mr. John O'Leary represented to his imagination the national conscience. There were plenty of others, he would perhaps have said, who could give you better advice as to whether a thing was expedient or inexpedient, but there was only Mr. John O'Leary to tell you whether it was right or wrong, and to tell it not only in the quiet light of your fire, but, if it were necessary, before a raging mob out in the street. To me it has always seemed that the passion for abstract right, which has made the letters to press, the occasional speeches, and above all the conversation of Mr. John O'Leary so influential with the younger generation, is the Celtic passion for ideas, intensified by that mistrust of the expedient which comes to men who have seen the failure of many hopes; and that as Irish men and women become educated they will inherit a like passion, if not in a like degree. Certainly the young men I meet in 'Young Ireland'[4] societies, in Irish literary societies, and in the Irish art schools are more like him than like the loose-lipped, emotional, sympathetic, impressionable Irishman, who is the only Irishman of whom many Englishmen have ever heard. The very inhumanity of Irish journalism and of Irish politics comes from a tendency to judge men not by one another, not by experience of the degree of excellence one may hope to meet in life and in politics, but by some abstract standard.

Mr. John O'Leary's detachment from his own enthusiasms has not come to him with old age, but has given his whole life a curious and solitary distinction. His patriotism was first, he tells us, awakened by the verse of Davis, like the patriotism of so many Irishmen, but he has never so far confused literary with moral qualities as to call Davis a great or even a considerable poet.[5] When very young he organised a band of peasants to attempt the rescue of Meagher,[†] but was able to criticise Meagher's[†] speech from the dock as calmly as though indifferent to his fate.[6] He entered the Fenian[7] organisation, and worked for it with energy and devotion, with no great hope for any better success that a renovation of the national spirit, and when his time came suffered imprisonment and exile without complaining. He is of that supreme type, almost unknown in our heady generation, the type that lives like the enthusiasts, and yet has no other light but a little cold intellect. And his book has a strange impartiality, which must make it, ill-arranged, rambling even, as it is, of the utmost importance both to Irish and to English historians. It has called up for me, who am more interested in the history of the soul than in the history of things, the picture of an impressive personality, and is a new example of that sense of abstract ideas, of abstract law, which I believe the Celtic peoples have preserved, together with a capacity for abstract emotion, longer than more successful and practical races.

MR. ARTHUR SYMONS'
NEW BOOK

The second review by Yeats of Arthur Symons's (1865–1945) work
Amoris Victima *(London: Leonard Smithers, 1897), in* The Bookman
for April 1897, contains his most impassioned defense of the decadents,
a group with which Yeats, by his insistence on a literature expressing
a philosophy of life and race, had as many differences as opinions in
common. Symons's identification with the movement dated from his
essay "The Decadent Movement in Literature," which he had published
in 1893, in reply to Richard Le Gallienne, who had declared that "deca-
*dence is merely limited thinking, often insane thinking" (*Retrospective
Reviews, *London, 1896, vol. 1, 25).*

The catalog here of Yeats's contemporaries is his most explicit
attempt to create an anti-Victorian school and demonstrates Yeats's
power of organizing disparate talents under one banner. In the sum-
mer of 1896, Yeats had toured the west of Ireland with Arthur
Symons. The introduction to the second edition of Symons's London
Nights *(London: Leonard Smithers, 1897) was dated "Rosses Point,*
Sligo: September 2, 1896" and there is in Symons's later volume of verses
Images of Good and Evil *a five-poem cycle, "In Ireland."*

Mr. Arthur Symons attempts in his latest book, *Amoris Victima,* 'to
deal imaginatively with what seems' to him 'a typical phase of modern love, as it might affect the emotions and sensations of a typical modern man, to whom emotions and sensations represent the whole of life.'[1]
The book is divided into four sections—'Amoris Victima,' a group of
fourteen sonnets; 'Amoris Exsul', a group of fourteen lyrics; 'Amor Tri-
umphans', a group of sixteen lyrics; 'Mundi Victima',[2] a poem in
heroic couplets divided into eleven sections of irregular length; and all
these poems, though he hopes 'able to stand alone', are related to 'the
general psychology of the imaginary hero'.[3] It is difficult and dangerous to define the movements and epochs of anything so much a part

of oneself as contemporary literature, but when popular criticism, which does not consider anything difficult and dangerous, has given certain names to certain kinds of work, and hated the work for the name's sake, one is compelled to define. Popular criticism having agreed that poetry like that of Mr. Arthur Symons is 'decadent', and therefore 'immoral', 'insincere', and 'shallow', it is necessary to try and find out what distinguishes poetry like that of Mr. Arthur Symons from the poetry popular criticism has learned to honour. It seems to me that the poetry which found its greatest expression in Tennyson and Browning[4] pushed its limits as far as possible, tried to absorb into itself the science and philosophy and morality of its time, and to speak through the mouths of as many as might be of the great persons of history; and that there has been a revolt—a gradual,[†] half-perceptible revolt, as is the fashion of English as contrasted with French revolts— and that poetry has been for two generations slowly contracting its limits and becoming more and more purely personal and lyrical in its spirit. Mr. Lang, and Mr. Dobson, and Mr. Gosse began the change by their delight in the most condensed of lyric forms; while Mr. Bridges, with his reiteration of the most ancient and eternal notes of poetry and of them alone; Mr. Francis Thompson, with his distinguishing catholic ecstasy and his preoccupation with personal circumstance; Mr. Henley, with his noisy, heroic cry; Mr. Lionel Johnson, with his ecstatic stoicism; Mr. Davidson, with his passionate insistence on a few simple ideas, whose main value is in his passionate insistence; Mr. Le Gallienne, with his fanciful attitude towards life and art; Mr. Watson,[5] with his continual pronouncements on public affairs; and Mr. Symons, with his pleasure in 'the typical modern man, to whom emotions and sensations represent the whole of life', and in 'the typical modern man' alone, are but, according to their very various powers, carrying this change to its momentous fulfilment: the calling of what is personal and solitary to the supreme seat of song. Some of these poets embody this change more than others, and popular criticism seems to me to dislike a poet just in so far as he embodies this change, for popular criticism has learned the importance of the science and philosophy and morality of its time, and of the great persons of history; but a poetry which is personal and solitary, and must therefore be judged by the poetical instinct alone, leaves it puzzled and angry. Mr. Symons, who is not only, in his verse, less of a savant, or a philosopher, or a moralist, or an historian than any poet of his time, but has certain very personal preoccupations which popular criticism has never learned to associate with poetry, has endured the whole burden of its indignation.

Though this book may not decrease the indignation of popular criticism, it will set Mr. Symons' name much higher with the dozen or so of men and women to whom poetry is the first interest in life, for it has far less of that occasional aridity which was the shadow of his particular excellence. Mr. Symons in *Silhouettes* and *London Nights*[6] was often too anxious to make his readers feel as his 'typical modern man' felt at some particular moment, let us say, under the leaves in the Luxembourg gardens;[7] and the inspiration that comes, when one is holding the pen, is despotic, and will not share its dominions with any memory of sensation and circumstance. In this book, however, he writes under a far more fiery influence than memory, than even the most moving, exquisite memory, and the lines at their best leap and live with a strange glowing and glimmering life. The blank verse lyric which his 'typical modern man' addresses to 'the wanderers'[8] is as perfect as his 'La Mélinite:[†] Moulin-Rouge',[9] one of the most perfect lyrics of our time, and has greater intensity.

> Theirs is the world and all the glory of it,
> Theirs because[10] they forego it, passing on
> Into the freedom of the elements;
> Wandering, ever wandering,
> Because life holds not anything so good
> As to be free of yesterday, and bound
> Towards a new to-morrow; and they wend
> Into a world of unknown faces, where
> It may be there are faces waiting them,
> Faces of friendly strangers, not the long
> Intolerable monotony of friends.

'La Mélinite'[†] was an exquisite impression, and 'The Javanese Dancers',[11] in an earlier book, was an exquisite impression, but here is the supreme emotion expressed supremely. The whole book is indeed preoccupied with the great issues and the great emotions of life, with the overmastering things, while *Silhouettes* and even *London Nights* were preoccupied with those little issues and little emotions which one can master and forget. This change of substance is most marked in 'Mundi Victima', which, being the last section, and a logical climax for the other sections, is probably the latest written.[12] 'Mundi Victima' is a long ecstasy of sorrow, a long revery of that bitter wisdom which comes only to those who have a certain emotional distinction, and which is much older than philosophies and sciences, and moralities and histories, which can be taught and understood and perhaps believed by the most undistinguished people.

Even in our love our love could not suffice
(Not the rapt silence whose warm wings abound
With all the holy plenitude of sound,
At love's most shadowy and hushed hour of day)
To keep the voices of the world away.
O subtle voices, luring from the dream
The dreamer, till love's very vision seem
The unruffled air that phantom feet have crossed
In the mute march of that processional host
Whose passing is the passing of the wind;
Avenging voices, hurrying behind
The souls that have escaped and yet look back
Reluctantly along the flaming track;
O mighty voices of the world, I have heard
Between our heart-beats your reiterate word,
And I have felt our heart-beats slackening.[13]

One may say of Mr. Symons that he is in no accurate sense of the word a 'decadent', but a writer who has carried further than most of his contemporaries that revolt against the manifold, the impersonal, the luxuriant, and the external, which is perhaps the great movement of our time, and of more even than literary importance. Popular criticism, which prolongs the ideals and standards of a school of literature, which has finished its great work for this epoch of the world, is, on the other hand, in the most accurate sense of the word, 'decadent'.

MISS FIONA MACLEOD

Yeats's review of Fiona Macleod's Spiritual Tales *(Edinburgh: Patrick Geddes & Colleagues, 1897) in* The Sketch *for 28 April 1897, attests to the durability of the feminine guise of his friend, William Sharp (1855–1905), who was a critic and biographer under his own name (see "Miss Fiona Macleod as a Poet," pp. 322–25 above). By 1897 Yeats's hopes for a Celtic revival had become a fervent conviction and, although he was later to mistrust a multinational "Pan-Celticism," in this essay his two major examples of the new Celtic, spiritual art were the Scot Fiona Macleod and the Belgian Maurice Maeterlinck (1862–1949). Yeats was beginning to see all signs pointing in the direction of his desires, and Robert Louis Stevenson (1850–94), and even Rudyard Kipling (1865–1936), seldom praised by Yeats, fit into his vision.*

Criticism is essentially a civilised thing, and the last age of the world, being very civilised, defined literature as a criticism of life, and expressed itself in certain great writers whose work was full of criticism.[1] Its typical writers—perhaps because the criticism of science was all about in them—had no constant and tranquil belief in the divinity of imagination, no matter how great their imaginations, but were vehement with gospels of all kinds. An English literary revolution, unlike a French one, is so gradual that we have hardly yet begun to understand how completely their heavens have been rolled up and how new an earth has come in the place of their earth. Romance-writers like Mr. Stevenson, with his delight in adventurous circumstance for its own sake, and Mr. Kipling, with his delight in the colour and spectacle of barbarous life,[2] and those countless collections of fairy-tales which are so marked a feature of our times, are but among the most obvious of the signs of change. We no longer complicate imagination with criticism, and we have begun to recover the ancient trust in passion and in beauty, and will soon have forgotten that we

ever doubted. I am convinced that this change is bringing new kinds
of temperaments into our literature—temperaments that have been
too wild and hasty for deliberate criticism of life, and that it is this
change which is making countries like Ireland and like the Highlands,[3]
which critical civilisation has forgotten, begin to be full of voices. And
of all these voices none is more typical than the curious, mysterious,
childlike voice that is in these stories of Miss Fiona Macleod. Mr.
Stevenson and Mr. Kipling have written many simple, passionate
tales, but they have written them as men write, who are too conscious
of having been born to write of simple, passionate things to be themselves simple and passionate. They have never forgotten, and in this
lies the very value of their art, that they have observed picturesque and
barbarous things with the keen eyes of the people of a civilised and
critical land; but Miss Macleod sees everything with the eyes of the
personages of her tales, and they have not any dream too extravagant,
any passion too wild, any hope too impossible, for her heart to be in
it as though there had never been any other dream, any other passion,
any other hope in the world. Her very faults—even the faults which
made, as I think, *Pharais* and *The Mountain Lovers*,[14] her earlier
books, no better than books of great promise—come from this
absolute absorption in the dreams and passions and hopes of her personages. She forgets, in following some spectacle of love and battle,
that she is using words and phrases, paragraphs and chapters,
rhythms and cadences; and so 'thou' and 'you' get mixed together, and
words altogether out of the true key mix themselves into her rushing
sentences. She is, however, gradually learning that writing is not all a
spiritual enthusiasm, and these three books, in which she has collected
the best tales out of her *Sin Eater*[†] and *Washer of the Ford,* with certain new tales, are constantly almost perfect of their kind. I have put
them to a hard test, for I read the tales in *The Washer of the Ford,*
which are reprinted here, on the deck of an Aran[†5] fishing-boat and
among the grey stones of Aran[†] Island; among the very people of
whom she writes, for the Irish and Highland Gael are one race;[6] and
when I laid down the book I talked with an Aran[†] fisherman of the
very beliefs and legends that were its warp and woof. I read of St.
Colum and the seal in the hot sun on the deck—[7]

> The holy man had wandered on to where the rocks are, opposite
> to Soa. He was praying and praying, and it is said that whenever he
> prayed aloud the barren egg in the nest would quicken, and the
> blighted bud unfold, and the butterfly cleave its shroud.
> Of a sudden he came upon a great black seal lying silent on the
> rocks with wicked eyes.

'My blessing upon you, O Ròn!' he said, with the good, kind courteousness that was his.

'*Droch spadadh ort*', answered the seal. 'A bad end to you, Colum of the Gown!'[8]

'Sure, now' said Colum angrily, 'I am knowing by that curse that you are no friend of Christ, but of the evil pagan faith out of the North. For here[†] I am known even as Colum the White, or as Colum the Saint, and it is only the Picts and wanton Normen who deride me because of the holy white robe I wear'.[9]

'Well, well', replied the seal, speaking the good Gaelic as though it were the tongue of the deep sea, as, God knows, it may be for all you and I or the blind wind can say; 'well, well, let that thing be; it's a wave-way here or a wave-way there. But now, if it is a Druid[10] you are, whether of Fire or of Christ, be telling me where my woman is, and where my little daughter.'

At this Colum looked at him for a long while; then he knew.

'It is a man you were once, O Ròn?'

'Maybe ay and maybe no.'

'And with that thick Gaelic that you have it will be out of the North isles you come?'

'That is a true thing'.

'Now, I am for knowing at last who and what you are. You are one of the race of Odrum the Pagan.'[11]

And so on, until it is told that the seal is Judas, looking for his wife Lilith[†12] through all the wastes of the sea. When I had done, I talked to an old man of the mystery of the seals, or of the Ròns, for he did not know them by their English name, and of their human-like eyes and human-like voices, and it was plain to me that he was not altogether at all times certain that they were mere beasts of the sea. And then I read 'The Dan-nan-Ròn',[13] which tells of a man that was descended from the seals, and how he rushed into the sea that he might be a seal again; and when I had done, I talked with another old man, who told me that his own family were come of the seals, but it might 'be all talk'. It seemed to me that Miss Macleod had not, like the rest of us, taken a peasant legend and made it the symbol of some personal phantasy, but that she felt about the world, and the creatures of its winds and waters, emotions that were of one kind with the emotions of these grave peasants, the most purely Celtic peasants in Ireland, and that she had become their voice, not from any mere observation of their ways, but out of an absolute identity of nature. The truth is that she, like all who have Celtic minds and have learnt to trust them, has in her hands the keys of those gates of the primeval world, which shut behind more successful races, when they plunged into material progress.

Criticism, and the art which is of criticism, deal with visible and palpable things; but her art belongs in kind, whatever be its excellence in its kind, to a greater art, which is of revelation, and deals with invisible and impalpable things. Its mission is to bring us near to those powers and principalities, which we divine in mortal hopes and passions, although we cannot see them or feel them, and which M. Maeterlinck has told us in his beautiful *Treasure of the Lowly*[14] are pressing in upon us to-day with a patient persistence, perhaps unknown since the founding of Christendom.

THE TREASURE OF THE HUMBLE

One of Yeats's golden books, for a time, was Maurice Maeterlinck's volume of essays The Treasure of the Humble *(Le trésor des humbles, 1896), the English translation of which he reviewed in* The Bookman *for July 1897. Maeterlinck's prophecies of the millennium agreed with Yeats's own announcements of the coming age of antirealistic, symbolic art. Yeats shared with Maeterlinck an admiration for Plotinus, and the Belgian dramatist probably introduced him to the work of the medieval Flemish mystic Jan van Ruysbroeck (1293–1381).*

What Yeats found lacking in Maeterlinck—"the definiteness of the great mystics"—he found in Blake, and he tried to emulate this definiteness later in his own philosophy, in A Vision. *His attack on A. B. Walkley's introduction to Maeterlinck's volume not only reflects his irritation with profane triflers with mysticism but also his experience of almost a decade as an introducer of books.*

A slightly changed version of this review appeared in the American edition of The Bookman *(August 1897, pp. 518–19).*

We are in the midst of a great revolution of thought, which is touching literature and speculation alike; an insurrection against everything which assumes that the external and material are the only fixed things, the only standards of reality. There have indeed been always plenty of men to write and to say that 'thought is the only reality', but since the rise of the scientific philosophers[1] they have said it with a merely academic conviction, and all their criticisms of life[2] and of literature have assumed that the world and nature were alone realities. But this insurrection has come with a generation young enough to have escaped from servitude to the scientific philosophers, and M. Maeterlinck, who took the red bonnet from the hands of Villiers de L'Isle-Adam,[†] is among the most inspired of its leaders.[3] The soul is to-day, he says, 'clearly making a mighty effort. Its manifestations are everywhere, and they are strangely urgent. . . . I will say nothing of the occult powers, of which signs are everywhere. . . . These things are known of all men, and can easily be verified, and truly they may well be the merest bagatelle by the side of the vast upheaval that is actually in progress, for the soul is like a dreamer, enthralled by sleep, who struggles with all his might to move an arm or raise an eyelid. . . . In the work-a-day lives of the humblest of men spiritual phenomena manifest themselves—mysterious direct workings[4] that bring soul nearer to soul; and of all this we can find no record in former times'. His book is an exposition of the 'mysterious direct workings' of which 'we can find no record in former times'; and the wonder of the book is that M. Maeterlinck has dwelled so long with these dim powers, these mysterious principalities, which are the deep below all deeps, that he writes of them, not with the arid vehemence of a combatant or an innovator, but with a beautiful pathos and tenderness. 'What avail to cultivate an *ego*[5] on which we have little influence? It is our star which it *behoves* us to watch. It is good or bad, pallid or puissant, and not by all the might of the sea can it be changed. Some there are who may confidently play with their star as one might play with a glass ball. They may throw it and hazard it where they list; faithfully will it ever return to their hands. They know full well it cannot be broken. But there are many others who dare not even raise their eyes towards their star, without it detach itself from the firmament and fall in dust at their feet'. The book lacks the definiteness of the great mystics, but it has countless passages of this curious pathetic beauty, and shows us common arts and things, with the light of the great mystics, and a new light that was not theirs, beating upon them. It is very tolerably translated by Mr. Alfred Sutro, and had not Mr. A. B. Walkley[6] written an absurd introduction would have been worthy to be a book of those that have few books and turn to them year after year. Mr. A. B. Walkley has done great service to dramatic literature by his analysis of modern drama, but he has no mystical knowledge and no mystical sympathy. He has introduced a book, which would charm that it may persuade, with a story from Dickens about Mr. Squeers and how his pupils spelled w-i-n-d-e-r before they cleaned the windows.[7] Apart from his special subjects Mr. Walkley is but a popular journalist, and would probably think a quotation from Dickens and a quotation from Dr. Johnson, unfailing symptoms of popular journalism, the only necessary prelude to *The Imitation of Christ*.[8] If publishers would frankly recognise that popular journalism has but a trade value, and perforate the inner margins of the pages of its introductions, no man would have a reason to complain. To merely slip the introductions in like circulars would be to go too far, for numbers will always prefer them to the books themselves.

MR. STANDISH O'GRADY'S
FLIGHT OF THE EAGLE

Yeats has given to Standish O'Grady's History of Ireland *(3 vols., London, 1878–80) the credit for starting the Irish Literary Revival. He had cited* The Bog of Stars *(London/Dublin: T. Fisher Unwin, 1893) as one of the "two or three good books" published by the ill-fated New Irish Library, and six books by O'Grady (1846–1928) appeared on Yeats's list of thirty essential Irish books in 1895. Although he was a Unionist and the principal leader writer for* The Daily Express, *"the most conservative paper in Ireland," Yeats admired O'Grady's gentle, implacable reiteration of his Protestant heritage. "All round us people talked or wrote for victory's sake, and were hated for their victories," Yeats recalled (Au, 183), "but here was a man whose rage was a swan-song over all that he held most dear, and to whom for that very reason every Irish imaginative writer owed a portion of his soul." In two of his last essays, the "General Introduction for my Work" and "I Became an Author," as well as in the late poem called "Beautiful Lofty Things," Yeats coupled O'Grady with John O'Leary as the two powerful influences upon him at the time when his commitment to poetry was being formed.*

Yeats's awe of O'Grady as an historian seems, however, to have lessened with the years, and by the time he reviewed The Flight of the Eagle *(London: Lawrence & Bullen, 1897) in* The Bookman *for August 1897, he had his own ideas about the Irish past. Yeats's basic disagreement with O'Grady was that he could not accept an account of Irish noblemen cooperating with their Elizabethan conquerors—whether O'Grady had evidence to support this feeling or not.*

Mr. Standish O'Grady is the first historian who has written Irish history in a philosophic spirit and as an imaginative art. Many have made long lists of kings and battles, and one or two, like Mr. Lecky,[1] have weighed and measured political and economical movements; but

Mr. O'Grady alone has looked for the great tides of passion and thought that are the substance of life. One goes to other historians to support a political argument, and, indeed, for all those things which, to use a phrase of William Blake's, are 'something other than human life';[2] but one goes to him to enlarge one's imagination, and to have the more of that philosophy that comes of imagination, and these things are human life itself. One need not always agree with him, and I certainly do not yet agree with more than half of the theory, that is, in the foundations of much of his writings on the Elizabethan age in Ireland. Roused into hostility by the extreme view of the popular Irish historians, who talk of an Elizabethan Ireland, united, but for a few knaves and dastards, in a last struggle against English rule, Mr. O'Grady sees a feudal Ireland, with feudal ideas of freedom, struggling against a modern Ireland, with modern ideas of freedom, and all, ancient and modern Ireland alike, loyal to the crown. When the great chiefs went into rebellion, they went, he holds, mourning that they had been loyal in vain; and when they were pulled down they were pulled down by modern Ireland with England helping. I do not find it difficult to follow Mr. O'Grady, when he explains that the crown had so long been the most powerful of the clans, that its rule, and all the more because it was hitherto little but a nominal rule, was accepted, or half accepted, by the great chiefs, in place of that strong native rule which, but for it, would have come to silence their disorders; but I find it difficult to follow him when he says, or seems to say, that this loyalty was more than the cold and fitful loyalty born of expediency and necessity, and that Ireland, speaking a different language and having different traditions from England, had, I will not say no national antagonism, for nationality is a modern idea, but no racial antagonism to England. Mr. O'Grady may be right, for I am no historian, and human nature is a nearly incalculable thing, but I will find it difficult to follow him, until the Gaelic tongue has given up its dead and I know what was sung and repeated at the hearths of the people, and how the traditions of hunters and shepherds magnified or diminished policies and battles. Some of the evidence on which he relies does not seem to me as strong as it does to him, though it is all interesting enough to have made its discovery a great service to history. He tells in this book how Perrot,[3] the Viceroy, boasted that there was no man in Ireland that would not come to Dublin if he but bade him; and calls the speech 'not less true than proud';[4] and yet there was one, Feagh MacHugh, also told of in this book, and more vividly than ever before in any Irish history, who lived but a few miles from Dublin, and would not have budged an inch for all the Perrots in the world, and Feagh MacHugh had a son that would not have budged either, although Perrot had long wanted him, and had 'passionately sought him'.[5] Then, too, in *Pacata Hibernica,*[6] of which Mr. O'Grady has given us the best edition, and on which he relies for much of his evidence, there is a saying of a certain 'loyal' man, that if the Spaniards came there would be no more loyal men. I make these criticisms, not because I am weary of praising Mr. O'Grady, but because I do not wish to be misunderstood by my Irish readers, who see nothing in Mr. O'Grady's, or in anybody else's, histories, but help or hindrance to some political argument; and return to my praising.

There is in no Irish book, except in Mr. O'Grady's own *Bog of Stars,*[7] which should be read with this book, so long a procession of great historical persons: Perrot, with his proud and boastful ways, and his fierce hardihood; the noseless married priest who digs Perrot's grave; the Lady O'Donnell, the 'dark daughter', keeping the lands of her imprisoned son at the sword's point; Feagh MacHugh, the masterful feudal dynast among his hills; Sir Felim O'Toole, politic or half-craven; Art O'Toole, living a disorderly drunken life in Dublin taverns, and denouncing and mocking his brother Felim; Viceroy Fitz William with his ailments and his many venoms; and among these, and with all these to hurt or to hinder him, Red Hugh O'Donnell, twice a captive in Dublin Castle and twice a fugitive.[8] The book is of somewhat new a kind in modern days and hard to class. It is not an historical romance, for all of it that is imagination was made for the sake of history; and it is not a history in our modern sense, for much of it is but inference, and Mr. O'Grady does not always check his story to say when it is but inference. It would have met with no complaints in the day of Herodotus,[9] but our timid day will in all likelihood abuse it roundly. It is written with vigour and music, but with less of sustained style than Mr. O'Grady's legendary books, perhaps because he has not the example of the great epics to guide him. Here and there the commentary is a little obvious, but here and there commentary and style alike are lifted up into an almost lyric simplicity and intensity, and never so truly as when he has to tell of that sea of ancient Celtic legend whose flood-gates he was the first to lift. Red Hugh O'Donnell rides into the North to begin his war upon the Government, 'the last great secular champion of the Gaelic tradition—the foiled champion too—such[10] is the power of the weaving stars'; and as he rides comes upon Slieve[†] Fuad,[11] most legendary of hills, and Slieve[†] Fuad becomes a person of the history, a symbol of 'the Gaelic tradition'. 'Here Ossian's sire slew the enchanter Almain,[†] son of Midna, who once a year, to the sound of unearthly music, consumed Tara[†] with magic flames. On this mountain Cuculain seized the wild faery steed, the Liath[†] Macha, new risen from the Grey Lake, ere steed and hero in their giant wrestlings and reelings encompassed Banba,[†] and in the quaking night the nations trembled. Here, steeped in Lough Liath's† waters, Finn's golden tresses took on the hue and glitter of radiant snow. From the spilled goblet of the god sprang the hazels whose magic clusters might assuage that hunger of the spirit which knows no other assuagement. The Faed† Fia was shed around them. Here shined and trembled the wisps of druid-grasses, from whose whisperings with the dawn wind pure ears might learn the secrets of life and death. Here beneath those hazels, their immortal green and their scarlet clusters, sprang the well of the waters of all wisdom. Three dreadful queens guarded it. Sometimes they smile seeing afar some youth wandering unconsoled o'er-laden with the burthen of his thoughts, rapt with visions, tormented by the gods, a stranger in his own household, scorned by those he cannot scorn, outcast from the wholesome cheerful life of men—they smile, and smiling dart from rosy immortal fingers one radiant drop upon his pallid lips, and lo the word out of his mouth becomes a sword wherewith he cleaves through mountains; with his right hand he upholds the weak, and with the left prostrates powers, and tyrants tremble before the light of his mild eyes'.[12] The enchanted catalogue is long, much longer than my extract, but I at any rate would not tire were it far longer than it is.

BARDS OF THE GAEL
AND THE GALL

This review of Bards of the Gael and Gall, *an anthology of Irish poetry compiled by George Sigerson, appeared in* The Illustrated London News *of 14 August 1897. The full title of this volume is* Bards of the Gael and Gall, Examples of the Poetric Literature of Erinn Done into English after the Metres and Modes of the Gael *by George Sigerson (London: T. Fisher Unwin, 1897).*

A reprinting of this review appeared in Yeats Annual 5 *(ed. Warwick Gould [London: Macmillan, 1987]). Deirdre Toomey, in her introduction to the article, for which she offered footnotes, argues the case for accepting it as Yeats's work, and she also gives a full account of the background of its publication. In a letter dated about early June 1897, Yeats told John O'Leary that he had been asked to "do Sigerson," and there is supporting evidence of why Yeats should have been asked to "do Sigerson." The editor of* The Illustrated London News, *Clement Shorter, was a friend of Yeats. Shorter was married to Dora Sigerson, also a friend of Yeats, who was the daughter of the compiler and editor Dr. George Sigerson. In Au, 171, Yeats described Sigerson as "learned, artificial, unscholarly, a typical provincial celebrity, but a friendly man." Yeats's friendship with Sigerson was strained when, in 1892, Sigerson had sided with Sir Charles Gavan Duffy in the controversy over who would be the editor of the New Irish Library. This review would appear to be a gesture, however anonymous, of reconciliation.*

Sigerson was of Danish ancestry. The "Galls" of the title are the Norse invaders of Ireland, to whose contribution to Irish culture Sigerson wanted to give due credit.

In her introduction to the review, Toomey speculates whether some of the imagery in the poem "The Song of Wandering Aengus" originated in Yeats's reading of this anthology.

Toomey's footnotes are identified as "D.T.'s note."

I was reading a newspaper a couple of years ago, and coming on some
bad Irish verses, began to read them mechanically. I found that they were
moving me greatly, moving me as dozens of bad Irish verses used to move
me when I was a boy; and I laid the paper down to think why. I lit suddenly upon their secret, and upon the secret of much Irish poetry. Their
emotion was the actual emotion of their writer, and they moved me just
as commonplace, sincere words of grief would move me in life.[1] The
same verses written by a writer of a country where the literary habit is
impersonal, as it is in England, would have wearied me from the first.
The love-poems and the hate-poems of Irish literature are almost all
the utterances of some actual love and hate, and we know whom they
praised and whom they cursed. They are the work of a people who are
intensely personal in all the affairs of life, and who utter in verse the
things that others hide in their hearts. When Feilim M'Carthy's four children were killed by the fall of a house, instead of hiding his sorrow, as
an educated Englishman would do, he poured it out in a long circum-
stantial and most poignant song, and Feilim M'Carthy[2] was no mere
naive peasant-poet. The whole song is as personal as these verses, which
I have taken out of the middle of Dr. Sigerson's translation—

> I'll sing each day until my death
> A lay which never sweetness hath,
> Since I am worn, and weak and drear,
> I'll sing their dirge—my children dear.
>
> My grief! in clay lies Callachan,
> By Cormac's side, my sweet-voiced son:
> Anna and Mary, too, my own
> White loves, beneath the same grey stone.
>
> The Spaniard-kings of sharp blue spears
> To these were kin, and these their peers:
> To them were England's kings allied,
> In other times, when that gave pride.
>
> Sweet their cries whene'er I'd come,
> Gaily running to greet me home—
> Who now shall kiss or welcome me,
> Since they, in one grave, buried be?[3]

If one turns over the leaves of *The Golden Treasury,*[4] one thinks but
seldom of the lives of the men who wrote it, but when one turns over
the leaves of this book of Dr. Sigerson's, one thinks of little else, for it

is all a spray flung up by the waters of a most tumultuous life. Here are hymns made by men famous for their austerities, dirges that wives have sung over their husbands and that bards have sung over their kings, and the lamentations over great men driven into exile sung by men who had fought at their side, and the lamentations sung by exiles over the land they have been driven from, and love-poems made by poets whose love sorrows are still tales by the hearth-side. Even when the poems are impersonal and dramatic—and all the poems attributed to Amergin and Ossian and Finn[15] are certainly impersonal and dramatic—tradition insists on taking them literally. Englishmen will never understand us until they understand that our opinions are often for opinion's sake, but that our emotions are almost always the results or precedents of action; and that sentiment, which is emotion not seeking an utterance in action, is commoner with them than with us.

I know no book so full of what is most characteristic in our fierce and passionate, and, as I believe, very great lyric literature as this book of Dr. Sigerson's. His introduction about the influence of Gaelic metres, through the Latin hymns of the early Irish evangelists, upon the literature of Europe, and about the possible Gaelic origin of rhyme, is of the first importance, and is worthy of the attention of historical students both in this country and upon the Continent.[6]

AGLAVAINE AND SÉLYSETTE[†]

Yeats had a higher regard for Maurice Maeterlinck as a philosopher and prophet than as a dramatist. As with those of John Todhunter, however, he praised the plays of Maeterlinck as symptoms of a change in public taste toward a poetic and away from naturalistic drama. He had been acquainted with Maeterlinck's plays since the early nineties and he had formed his opinion of Maeterlinck much earlier than his review of Aglavaine and Sélysette, which appeared in The Bookman for September 1897.

In a letter to Olivia Shakespeare of 7 April 1895 he had stated his reservations:

> I feel about his things generally however that they differ from really great work in lacking that ceaseless revery about life which we call wisdom . . . I said to Verlaine, when I saw him last year, "Does not Maeterlinck touch the nerves sometimes when he should touch the heart?" "Ah yes," said Verlaine, "he is a dear good fellow and my very good friend, but a little bit of a mountebank." This touching the nerves alone, seems to me to come from a lack of reverie. He is however of immense value as a force helping people to understand a more ideal drama (CL1, 460).

Yeats thought for a time that he had found "that ceaseless reverie about life" in Maeterlinck's Treasure of the Humble (see pp. 340–41 above).

The opening section of this review, contrasting Flaubert with Villiers de L'Isle-Adam and Maeterlinck, was revised for inclusion in the first part of Yeats's essay "The Autumn of the Flesh," which appeared in 1898 (E&I, 189–94, as "The Autumn of the Body").

In Aglavaine and Sélysette (1896), Maeterlinck deals with a love triangle, driven by jealousy. Sélysette is the beautiful but childish wife of Meleander. They live in a somber castle, surrounded by forest, and Sélysette spends much time in her solitary tower. Into this world laden

with symbols comes Aglavaine, who had only once met Meleander, but
they had exchanged many letters. Soon the love of Aglavaine and
Meleander is obvious to Sélysette. At the tragic climax, she slips and
falls from her tower, presumably a suicide who has offered her life as
a sacrifice to her love for Meleander.

The literary movement of our time has been a movement against the
external and heterogeneous, and like all literary movements, its
French expression is more intelligible and obvious than its English
expression, because more extreme. When one compares *La Tentation
de Saint Antoine* of Flaubert, the last great work of the old romantic
movement, with the *Axël* of Villiers de L'Isle-Adam,† the first great work
of the new romantic movement, one understands the completeness of
the change. A movement which never mentions an external thing
except to express a state of the soul, has taken the place of a movement
which delighted in picturesque and bizarre things for their own sakes.
M. Maeterlinck has called himself a disciple of Villiers de L'Isle-
Adam,† who, in the words of a recent French critic, 'opened the doors
of the beyond with a crash that our generation might pass through
them'[1]—I quote from memory—but he has carried his master's revolt
farther than his master, and made his persons shadows and cries. We
do not know in what country they were born, or in what period they
were born, or how old they are, or what they look like, and we do not
always know whether they are brother and sister, or lover and lover,
or husband and wife. They go hither and thither by well-sides, and by
crumbling towers, and among woods, that are repeated again and again,
and are as unemphatic as a faded tapestry; and they speak with low,
caressing voices which one has to hold one's breath to hear. The old
movement was full of the pride of the world, and called to us through
a brazen trumpet; and the persons of *Axël* were lifted above the pride
of the world, by the pride of hidden and august destinies, the pride of
the Magi[2] following the star over many mountains; but these souls are
naked, and can little but tremble and lament. They have not hitherto
needed to do more, for they were made to prolong the sense of terror
Shakespeare put into the line, 'the bay trees in my country are all withered',[3] the terror at we do not know what, mixed with a pity for we do
not know what, that we come to in contemplation when all reasons,
all hopes, all memories have passed, and the Divine ecstasy has not found
us. M. Maeterlinck has, however, made the persons of *Aglavaine and
Sélysette*[4] with a partly different purpose, for he has found a philosophy in his search for the quintessence, the philosophy of his beautiful
Trésor des Humbles,[5] and he would have his persons speak out of its

wisdom. It will make his plays more beautiful in time, for the serious fault of his best plays, even of *Les Aveugles* and *L'Intruse*,[6] is that they have not the crowning glory of great plays, that continual revery about destiny that is, as it were, the perfect raiment of beautiful emotions. Its immediate effect is mischievous, for Meleander and Aglavaine, his most prominent persons, continually say things, which they would say differently or not at all, if their maker were only thinking of them as persons in the play. The first act and part of the second act are a little absurd, because Meleander and Aglavaine explain when they should desire and regret; and because their overmastering sense of certain spiritual realities has blinded them to certain lesser realities, which natures of so high a wisdom could not have been blinded to; and because the art, which should be of a cold wisdom, has shared in their delusions and become a little sentimental. One is not indeed moved until the play begins to eddy about Meligrane, an old grandmother, Yssaline,[†] a child, and Sélysette, a childlike woman, persons whose natures are so narrowed because of forgotten and unknown things, that M. Maeterlinck cannot speak through their lips, but must let them speak as their destinies would have them speak. They speak more movingly than the persons of *Les Aveugles* or *L'Intruse*, for though still hardly more than shadows and cries, they have each, as the persons in Shakespeare have, their portion of wisdom, while all they say is beautiful with the pathos of their little interests and their extreme weakness. I do not think M. Maeterlinck has indeed written anything as beautiful as one thing that is said by old Meligrane to her granddaughter, Sélysette.

'So do I often think of those days, Sélysette. I was not ill, then, and I was able to carry you in my arms or run after you. . . . You wandered to and fro, and your laughter rang through the house, then suddenly you would fling open the door and shriek in terror, "She is coming, she is coming, she is here!" And no one knew whom you meant, or what it was that frightened you; you did not know yourself; but I would pretend to be frightened too, and would go through the long corridors with you till we reached the garden. And it all went for so little, and served no purpose, my child; but we understood each other, you and I, and smiled at each other, night and morning. . . . And[7] thus, thanks to you, have I been a mother a second time, long after my beauty had left me; and some day you will know that women never weary of motherhood, that they would cherish death itself, did it fall asleep on their knee.'

THE TRIBES OF DANU

Yeats's article entitled "The Tribes of Danu" in The New Review *for November 1897 is the first of six long essays on various aspects of Irish folklore and supernatural experience. The other articles in the series are:*

> *"The Prisoners of the Gods"* (Nineteenth Century, *January 1898)*
> *"The Broken Gates of Death"* (Fortnightly Review, *April 1898)*
> *"Ireland Bewitched"* (Contemporary Review, *September 1899)*
> *"Irish Witch Doctors"* (Fortnightly Review, *September 1900)*
> *"Away"* (Fortnightly Review, *April 1902).*
> *(For these last two articles, see LAR, 26–45, 64–81.)*

As with the first result of his friendship and collaboration with Lady Augusta Gregory (1852–1932), this essay represents a milestone in Yeats's career. They had met in the summer of 1896, and during the following year their friendship ripened as Lady Gregory started her endeavor to help the sick, discouraged, and unhappy Yeats. He spent part of the summer of 1897 at Coole, where he accompanied Lady Gregory on her rounds of the peasant cottages. She had been collecting folktales for some time, and Yeats, who had published his collection of folktales from the Sligo region in 1894, happily joined in the project.

Yeats regarded the folklore materials in these articles as much Lady Gregory's as his own. In a letter of 22 December 1898, he described a direct collaboration on a "big book of folklore"—a project not to be completed until 1916 and not to be published until 1920:

> *One hand should not do the actual shaping and writing—apart from peasant talk—and I would wish to do this. In some cases my opinions may be too directly mystical for you to accept. In such cases I can either initial the chapters containing them or make a general statement about them in the preface. If you agree to this, all future essays can either appear over our two signatures or I can add a footnote saying that a friend, whose name I do not give, because it is easier to collect if one is not known to be writing, is*

helping me throughout. Please agree to this arrangement as I dis-like taking credit for what is not mine and it will be a great plea-sure to do this work with you (CL2, 323–24.)

In the 1902 preface to The Celtic Twilight *he told his readers that a more ambitious folklore project was under way: "I shall publish in a little while a big book about the commonwealth of faery, and shall try to make it systematical and learned enough to buy pardon for this hand-ful of dreams"* (The Celtic Twilight and a Selection of Early Poems, introduction by Walter Starkie [New York: Signet Classics, 1962], p. 32). *But the only collection to come from the collaboration was the two volumes of* Visions and Beliefs in the West of Ireland, Collected and Arranged by Lady Gregory; with Two Essays and Notes by W. B. Yeats (London: G. P. Putnam's Sons, 1920). *These two essays, which might have been, as Yeats put it in the letter quote above, "too mystical for you" were "Witches and Wizards and Irish Folklore" and "Sweden-borg, Mediums and the Desolate Places," both dated 1914 (LE, 47–83). Yeats's involvement with Lady Gregory's two volumes can be traced in his letters. On 9 May 1911, he wrote to his father that he was set-tling down to work on the project—"Finding myself unfitted for verse, which is always a strain . . ." (L, 558). On 5 March 1912, he told his father that he was writing a lecture on the supernatural world which would serve as an introduction to the Lady Gregory work—probably the two essays printed above (L, 567–68). And, three years later, on 24 June 1915, he told John Quinn, "I have also nearly finished my Notes for Lady Gregory's book, and that has laid the ghost for me. I am free at last from the obsession of the supernatural, having got my thoughts in order and ranged on paper" (L, 595). With all of A Vision before him, this must be surely the most inconclusive "at last" in Yeats's lifetime.*

The footnotes to these articles indicate some parallels in the Lady Gregory volumes, but the similarities cited are by no means complete. Lady Gregory arranged her material under rather simple headings such as "Biddy Early" and her presentation of this material is direct and without much commentary. Yeats's essays begin and end with his interpretations, but the central portions of these articles are mainly reportage of folklore.

Such an allegation as this article makes—that the peasants of the west of Ireland have a widespread and deep belief in the pagan Irish super-natural—could not fail to arouse clerical reaction, and Yeats tells Lady Gregory in a letter of 17 November 1897 that there was "rather a blow" about it (CL2, 143). For whatever reason, all the other arti-cles appeared in other journals.

The phrase "Tribes of Danu" is a translation of Tuatha dé Danaan,

*the people of the goddess Dana. These are the gods who were wor-
shipped in pre-Christian Ireland before the coming of the Milesians.*

I.—THE LANDS OF THE TRIBES OF DANU

The poet is happy, as Homer was happy, who can see from his door
mountains, where the heroes and beautiful women of old times were
happy or unhappy, and quiet places not yet forsaken by the gods. If a
poet cannot find immortal and mysterious things in his own country,
he must write of far-off countries oftener than of his own country, or
of a vague country that is not far off or near at hand, for even the most
fleeting and intelligible passions of poetry live among immortal and mysterious things; and when he does not write of his own country the waters
and mountains about him, and the lives that are lived amongst them,
are less beautiful than they might be. He will be more solitary too, for
people will find little in their lives to remind them of him, and he will
find little in his writings to remind him of them, and the world and poetry
will forget one another. The more he has of spiritual passion the more
solitary he will be, for who would not think *Prometheus Unbound*[1] better to read and better to remember if its legends and its scenery were
the legends and the scenery they had known from childhood, or that
Shelley had known from childhood and filled with the passion of
many memories? Indeed, I am certain that the writers of a spiritual literature, if it is not a literature of simple prayers and cries, must make
the land about them a Holy Land; and now that literature which is not
spiritual literature is, perhaps, passing away, we must begin making our
lands Holy Lands, as the Jews made Palestine, as the Indians made
Northern India, as the Greeks made the lands about the Ionian[2] Sea. I
think that my own people, the people of a Celtic habit of thought, if
genius which cannot be whistled for blow their way, can best begin, for
they have a passion for their lands, and the waters and mountains of
their lands remind them of old love tales, old battle tales, and the exultant hidden multitudes. There is no place in Ireland where they will not
point to some mountain where Grania slept beside her lover, or where
the misshapen Fomor were routed, or to some waters where the
Sacred Hazel once grew and fattened the Salmon of Wisdom with its
crimson nuts;[3] nor is there, I think, a place outside the big towns
where they do not believe that the Fairies, the Tribes of the goddess
Danu, are stealing their bodies and their souls, or putting unearthly
strength into their bodies, and always hearing all that they say. Nothing shows more how blind educated Ireland—I am not certain that I
should call so unimaginative a thing education—is about peasant Ireland, than that it does not understand how the old religion which made

of the coming and going of the greenness of the woods and of the fruit-fulness of the fields a part of its worship, lives side by side with the new religion which would trample nature as a serpent under its feet; nor is that old religion faded to a meaningless repetition of old customs, for the ecstatic who has seen the red light and white light of God smite them-selves into the bread and wine at the Mass, has seen the exultant hidden multitudes among the winds of May, and if he were philosophical would cry with the painter, Calvert: 'I go inward to God, outward to the gods.'⁴

II.—THE PERSONS OF THE TRIBES OF DANU

The old poets thought that the tribes of the goddess Danu were of a perfect beauty, and the creators of beautiful people and beautiful arts. The hero Fiachna sang when he came from among them:

> They march among blue lances,
> Those troops of white warriors with knotted hair,
> Their strength, great as it is, cannot be less.
> They are sons of queens and kings,
> On the heads of all a comely
> Harvest of hair yellow like gold.
> Their bodies are graceful and majestic,
> Their eyes have looks of power and blue pupils,
> Their teeth shine like glass,
> Their lips are red and thin.⁵

And 'every artist harmonious and musical' is described in an old book by one Duald mac Firbis, of Lecan,† as of the Tribes of the goddess Danu, that is to say, inspired by the Tribes of the goddess Danu.⁶ It took me a long time to find out that they still kept their beauty, for the peasant visionaries have never been from their own countrysides, and can only compare what they have seen to commonplace things and tell you that they have seen rooms 'grander' than some commonplace room 'up at the Lodge,' or marching people, who looked (as a poteen-maker, who had praised their magnificence, said to me) 'for all the world like policemen.' But now I ask careful questions, and am told, as I was told the other day by a woman, who was telling of a sight one Martin Roland saw in a bog, that 'their women had their hair wound round their heads, and had a wild look, and there were wreaths of flowers upon their horses'; or, as I was told when I asked an old man who has seen them, and whose uncle used to be away among them, if their great people had crowns of one shape: 'O no, their crowns have all kinds of shapes, and they have dresses of all kinds of colours'; or, as I was told by the same old man, when the friend who was with me held up a sapphire ring and made it flash, and asked if their dresses were as beautiful: 'O, they are far grander than that'; or, as I was told by a blind piper, when I asked if he had any of their music: 'I have no music like theirs, for there is no music in the world like theirs.'

Many have thought that the Tribes of the goddess Danu have become little, like the fairies in the *Midsummer Night's Dream,* and some have built a theory on their littleness; but they are indeed tall and noble, as many have told me. They have among them monsters and grotesque persons who are now big and now little; but these are their old enemies, the Fomor, the Caetchen, the Laighin, the Gailioin, the Goborchin, the Fir Morca, the Luchorpain, the Firbolg,[7] and the Tribes of Domnu, divinities of darkness and death and ugliness and winter cold and evil passion; and they[8] can take shapes and sizes that are not their true shapes and sizes, as they and the Druids do in the poems, and become 'very small and go into one another, so that all you see might be a sort of a little bundle'; or become 'like a clutch of hens,' or become like 'a flock of wool by the road,' or become like a tar-barrel 'flaming and rolling,' 'or look like a cow and then like a woman'; but all the while 'they are death on handsome people because they are handsome themselves.' The Country of the Young,[9] as the poets call their country, is indeed the country of bodiless beauty that was among the Celtic races, and of which (if D'Arbois de Jubainville[10] has written correctly) the Greek mythology and all that came of it were but the beautiful embodiment; and it still lives, forgotten by proud and learned people, among simple and poor people. When the Irish peasant passes into a sudden trance and, sleeping, is yet awake and awake is yet sleeping, it is still that bough of golden apples, whose rustling cast Cormac, son of Art, into a Druid sleep, whose rustling has overcome him;[11] and its beauty is not the less beautiful because Christianity has forbidden its rustling, and made Eve's apple grow among its golden apples.

III.—THE HOUSES OF THE TRIBES OF DANU

Although a man has told me that 'the Others', as the Galway peasant, like the Greek peasant, has named the gods, can build up 'in ten minutes and in the middle of a field a house ten times more beautiful than any house in the world', and although some have told me that they live everywhere, they are held by most to live in forts or 'forths', the little fields surrounded by clay ditches that were the places of the houses of the ancient people. Every countryside is full of stories of the evils that have fallen upon the reckless or unbelieving people, who have broken down the ditches of the forts, or cut the bushes that are in them. A man, who has a mill and a farm near Gort, in Galway County,[12] showed me where a fort on his farm had been cut through to make a road, and said: 'The engineer must have been a foreigner or an idolater, but he did not live long anyway'; and the people of a neighbouring townland tell how an old man, who is not long dead, cut a bush from one behind his house, and 'next morning he had not a blade of hair on his head—not one blade, and he had to buy a wig and wear it all the rest of his life'. A distant relation of my own bid his labourers cut down some bushes in a fort in Sligo,[13] and the next morning they saw a black lamb among his sheep, and said it was a warning, and would not cut the bushes; and the lamb had gone the morning after that. A great number of the people of every countryside have seen some fort lighted up, with lights which they describe sometimes as like torches, and sometimes as like bonfires; but once, when I questioned a man who described them as like a bonfire, I found that he had seen a long thin flame, going up for thirty feet and whirling about at the top. A man, who lives near the fort where the old man lost his hair, sees a woman lighting a fire under a bush in the fort; but I do not know what the fire is like, as I have not been able to question him; but a girl says the fires come with a sudden blaze 'like a man lighting his pipe'. Somebody in almost every family that lives near a fort has heard or seen lights or shadows, or figures that wail or dance, or fight or play at hurling,[14] which was a game among the Tribes of Danu in old days, or ride upon horseback, or drive in strange carriages that make a muffled sound. I know one fort where they hear the galloping of horses, as if from underground, but 'the Others' are generally supposed to live in the forts, as the ancient people lived in them and are indeed sometimes said to be the ancient people doomed to await the end of the world for their redemption, because they had (as a man said to me) 'Freemasons and all sorts of magicians among them',[15] or, as another said to me, 'because they used to be able to put souls into rocks and to make birds and fishes speak, and everybody who has read about the old times knows that fishes and birds used to speak'.

Certain queerly-shaped bushes, not near forts and often alone in the middle of fields, and certain trees, are also frequented and protected. The people say that you must not hurt these bushes and trees, because 'the Others' have houses near them; but sometimes it seems that, if you hurt one of them, you hurt one of 'the Others', for I have been told of a man who went to cut a bush on the road to Kinvara, in Galway County, 'and at the first blow he heard something like a groan coming from beneath it; but he would not leave off, and his mouth was drawn to one side all of a sudden, and two days after he died.'[16] A man[17] has told me that he and another went in their boyhood to catch a horse in a certain field full of boulders and bushes of hazel and rock roses and creeping juniper that is by Coole Lake;[18] and he said to the boy who was with him: 'I bet a button that if I fling a pebble on to that bush, it will stay on it', meaning that the bush was so matted that the pebble would not be able to pass through it. So he 'took up a pebble of cow-dung, and as soon as it hit the bush, there came out of it the most beautiful music that ever was heard'. They ran away and, when they had gone about two hundred yards, they looked back, and saw a woman dressed in white walking round and round the bush: 'First it had the form of a woman and then of a man, and it going round the bush'. He said that some time afterwards 'the master'[19] sent men to cut down the bushes in that part of the field, and a boy was cutting them near the matted bush, and a thorn ran into his eye and blinded him'. There is an old big elm[20] at the corner of a road a couple of miles from the field; and a boy, who who was passing before daylight with a load of hay, fell from his cart, and was killed just beside it, and people say that the horse was standing quite still by him when he was found, and that a shower of rain, which fell just after he was taken away, wet everything except the dust where he had lain. Many places have bad names, because people have fallen from their carts at them, and 'the Others' are said to have these people among them. The old big elm has not altogether a bad name, because it is said that one day a man was passing by it, who had come from Galway with 'a ton weight in his cart', and 'the lynching of his wheel came out, and the cart fell down, and a little man about two and a half feet high came out of the wall, and lifted up the cart, and held it up until he had the lynching put up again, and never said a word, but went away as he came'. This may be a story come out of old times; but it may not, for simple people live so close to trance that the lynching may never have come off, and the carter may have seen it all awake and yet asleep or asleep and yet awake; or the lynching may have come off, and the carter may have put it on with his own hands, and not have known that he put it on. There is a plantation of younger trees near the big old elm which they protected also; and when a man called Connellan went a while ago to cut trees there, 'he was prevented, and never could get the hand-saw near a tree, nor the man that was with him' (but I have not been able to find out how he was prevented); and there is a whole wood bordering on the field where the matted bush used to be, which Biddy Early, a famous wise woman,[21] used to call a 'very bad place'; and many see sights in it, and many go astray in it, and wander about for hours in a twilight of the senses. Souls are sometimes said to be put into the trees for a penance; for there was a woman who was 'for seven years in a tree at Kinadyfe, and seven years after that in the little bridge beyond Kilcreest,[22] below the arch with the water running under her; and while she was in the tree, whether there was frost or snow or storm, she hadn't so much as the size of a leaf to shelter her.'

A woman has told me that people only see 'the Others' in the forts and by the bushes and trees, because 'they are thinking of them there', but that 'they are everywhere like the blades of the grass'; and she showed me a corner of a road, where there was neither a fort nor a bush nor a tree, and said that they had put her brother 'into a faint' there, and that the young men were afraid to come home at night from card playing till there were a number of them together. She herself has seen something far from a fort or a bush or a tree: 'I was walking with another girl, and I looked up, and saw a tall woman dressed in black, with a mantle of some sort, a wide one, over her head, and the waves of the wind were blowing it off her, so that I could hear the noise of it. All her clothes were black and had the appearance of being new'. She asked the other if she could see the woman, but she could not: 'For two that are together can never see such things, but only one of them'. They ran away then, and the woman followed them until she came to a running stream. They thought the woman was one who had been 'taken', for they were coming from 'a house of the Kearneys, where the father and mother had died, but it was well known they often came back to look after the children'. She is confident, however, that you must not question a dead person till you come to a bush, showing, as indeed everything shows, that half the dead are believed to have gone to the houses of 'the Others', lured thither by sweet music or by the promise of unearthly love, or taken captive by their marching host.

They live also in certain hills like the hill behind Corcamroe Abbey,[23] in which they have 'a town', and they are very plentiful under waters. A woman at Coole, in Galway, says: 'They are in the sea as well as on the land. That is well known by those that are out fishing by the coast. When the weather is calm, they can look down sometimes, and see cattle and pigs and all such things as we have ourselves. And at night their boats come out and they can be seen fishing; but they never last out after one o'clock'.

IV.—THE FRIENDS OF THE TRIBES OF DANU

Though hundreds in every countryside that I know in Ireland have seen them, and think of seeing them as but a common chance, the most are afraid to see them, because they may not wish to be seen. The people about Inchy, at Coole, point out an old blind man, and say that he was not blind when he was a boy; but one day he heard the coach of 'the Others', the coach-a-bower, or deaf coach, as it is called, because it makes a deaf or muffled sound, and stood up to look at them instead of sitting still and looking another way. He had only time to see beautiful ladies, with flowers about them, sitting in the coach before he was smitten blind. Some of the old books call Midir the king of the fairies;[24] and one of the old books says that three herons stand before his door, and when they see anybody coming, the first heron cries: 'Do not come, do not come'; and the second heron cries: 'Go away'; and the third heron cries: 'Go by the house, by the house.' There are, however, people that the gods favour, and permit to look upon them and go among them. A young man in the Burren Hills[25] told me that he remembers an old poet, who made his poems in Irish, and who met, when he was young, one who called herself Maive, and said she was a queen among them, and asked him if he would have money or pleasure. He said he would have pleasure, and she gave him her love for a time, and then went from him, and ever after he was very sad. The young man had often heard him sing the poem of lamentation that he made, but could only remember that it was 'very mournful', and that it called her 'beauty of all beauties'. 'The Others' are often said to be very good to many people, and to make their crops abundant, and to do them many services. I have been told 'there was a family at Tirneevan, and they were having a wedding there; and when it was going on the wine ran short, and the spirits; and they didn't know what to do to get more, Gort being two miles away; and two or three strange people came in, that they never had seen before, but they made them welcome; and when they heard what was wanting they said they would get it, and in a few minutes they were back with the spirits and the wine, and no place to get it nearer than Gort!' But the people they let look upon them often live in poor and tumble-down houses. I asked a man once if a neighbour of his, who could see things, had the cure that is made out of seven common things, and can end 'all the evils that are in the world'; and he answered: 'She has the scenery for it, but I do not know that she has it'—meaning that his neighbour's house was a poor and tumble-down house.

[26]There was an old Martin Roland, who lived near a bog a little out of Gort, who saw them often from his young days, and always towards the end of his life. He told me a few months before his death that 'they' would not let him sleep at night with crying things at him in Irish and with playing their pipes. He had asked a friend of his what he should do, and the friend had told him to buy a flute, and play on it when they began to shout or to play on their pipes, and maybe they would give up annoying him, and he did, and they always went out

into the field when he began to play. He showed me the flute, and blew through it, and made a noise, but he did not know how to play; and then he showed me where he had pulled his chimney down, because one of them used to sit up on it and play on the pipes. A friend of his and mine went to see him a little time ago, for she heard that 'three of them' had told him he was to die. He said they had gone away after warning him, and that the children (children they had 'taken', I suppose) who used to come with them, and play about the house with them, had 'gone to some other place', because 'they found the house too cold for them, maybe'; and he died a week after he said these things. His neighbours were not certain that he really saw anything in his old age, but they were all certain that he saw things when he was a young man. His brother said: 'Old he is, and it's all in his brain the things he sees. If he was a young man we might believe in him'. But he was improvident and never got on with his brothers. A neighbour said: 'The poor man! they say they are mostly in his head now, but sure he was a fine fresh man twenty years ago, the night he saw them linked in two lots, like young slips of girls walking together. It was the night they took away Fallon's little girl'; and she told how Fallon's little girl had met a woman 'with red hair that was as bright as silver' who took her away. Another neighbour, who was herself 'clouted over the ear' by one of them for going into a fort where they were, said: 'I believe it's mostly in his head they are, and when he stood in the door last night I said: "The wind does be always in my ears and the sound of it never stops", to make him think it was the same with him; but he says: "I hear them singing and making music all the time, and one of them is after bringing out a little flute, and it's on it he's playing to them." And this I know, that when he pulled down the chimney where he said the piper used to be sitting and playing, he lifted up stones, and he an old man, that I could not have lifted when I was young and strong'. The people often tell one, as a proof that somebody is in communication with 'the Others', that nobody can do so much work as he does, or that nobody can lift such weights as he does, or that nobody can play so well at the hurling as he does. The Country of the Gods is called 'the Country of the Young', and the strength of their youth is believed to fall about those they love just as it fell about Cuchulain[†] and the other heroes in the poems, and as the strength of Apollo was believed to fall about his priests at Hylae,[27] so that they could leap down steep places and tear up trees by the roots, and carry them upon their backs over narrow and high places. When one has crossed the threshold of trance, it may be that one comes to the secret Waters of Life, where Maeldun[28] saw the dishevelled eagle bathing till it had grown young again, and that their drifting spray can put strength into our bodies.

Those who can see 'the Others' as easily as Martin Roland saw them, look on them very much as we look on people from another townland; and indeed many among those who have seen them but seldom, think of their coming and going as of a simple and natural thing and not a thing to surprise anybody. I have often been told in Galway that the people in the North of Ireland see them easily; and a friend[29] has written for me an account of a talk she had with an old woman in Tyrone,[30] who considers their coming and going a very small and natural thing. It is quite accurate, for my friend, who had heard the old woman's story some time before I heard of it, got her to tell it over again, and wrote it out at once. She began by telling the old woman that she did not like being in the house alone because of the ghosts and fairies; and the old woman said: 'There's nothing to be frightened about in fairies, Miss. Many's the time I talked to a woman myself that was a fairy or something of the sort, and no less and more than mortal anyhow. She used to come about your grandfather's house, your mother's grandfather that is, in my young days. But you'll have heard all about her.' My friend said that she had heard about her, but a long time before, and she wanted to hear about her again; and the old woman went on: 'Well, dear, the very first time ever I heard word of her coming about was when your uncle, that is, your mother's uncle, Joseph, was married, and building a house for his wife, for he brought her first to his father's, up at the house by the Lough. The foundations were marked out, and the building stones lying about, but the masons had not come yet, and one day I was standing with my mother fornent[31] the house, when we sees a smart Wee Woman coming up the field over the burn to us. I was a bit of a girl at the time, playing about the sporting myself, but I mind her as well as if I saw her there now!' My friend asked how the woman was dressed, and the old woman said: 'It was a grey cloak she had on, with a green Cashmere skirt and a black silk handkercher tied round her head, like the countrywomen did use to wear in them times'. My friend asked: 'How wee was she?' And the old woman said: 'Well, now, she wasn't wee at all when I think of it, for all we called her the Wee Woman she was bigger than many a one, and yet not tall as you would say. She was like a woman about thirty, brown-haired, and round in the face. She was like Miss Betty, your grandmother's sister, and Betty was like none of the rest, not like your grandmother nor any of them. She was round and fresh in the face, and she never was married, and she never would take any man, and we used to say that the Wee Woman, her being like Betty, was maybe one of their own people that had been took off before she grew to her full height, and for that she was always following us and warning and foretelling. This time she walks straight over to where my mother was standing: "Go over to the Lough this minute"—ordering her like that!—"go over to the Lough, and tell Joseph that he must change the foundation of this house to where I'll show you forenenst the thorn bush. That is where it is to be built, if he is to have luck and prosperity, so do what I'm telling ye this minute." My mother goes over to the Lough, and brings Joseph down and shows him, and he changes the foundations, the way he was bid, but didn't bring it exactly to where was pointed, and the end of that was, when he came to the house, his own wife lost her life with an accident that come to a horse that hadn't room to turn right with a harrow between the bush and the wall. The Wee Woman was queer and angry when next she come, and says to us: "He didn't do as I bid him, but he'll see what he'll see"'. My friend asked where the woman came from this time, and if she was dressed as before, and the woman said: 'Always the same way, up the field beyant the burn. It was a thin sort of shawl she had about her in summer, and a cloak about her in winter, and many and many a time she came, and always it was good advice she was giving to my mother, and warning her what not to do if she would have good luck. There was none of the other children of us ever seen her unless me, but I used to be glad when I seen her coming up the burn, and would run out and catch her by the hand and the cloak, and call to my mother: "Here's the Wee Woman!" No man body ever seen her. My father used to be wanting to, and was angry with my mother and me, thinking we were telling lies and talking foolish-like. And so one day when she had come, and was sitting by the fireside talking to my mother, I slips out to the field where he was digging, and "Come up," says I, "if ye want to see her. She's sitting at the fireside now talking to mother." So in he comes with me and looks round angry-like and sees nothing, and he up with a broom that was near hand and hits me a crig with it, and "Take that now," says he, "for making a fool of me," and away with him as fast as he could, and queer and angry with me. The Wee Woman says to me then: "Ye got that now for bringing people to see me. No man body ever seen me and none ever will." There was one day, though, she gave him a queer fright anyway, whether he seen her or not. He was in among the cattle when it happened, and he comes up to the house all trembling-like. "Don't let me hear you say another word of your Wee Woman. I have got enough of her this time." Another time all the same he was up Gortin to sell horses, and, before he went off, in steps the Wee Woman, and says she to my mother, holding out a sort of a weed: "Your man is gone up by Gortin, and there's a bad fright waiting him coming home, but take this and sew it in his coat, and he'll get no harm by it." My mother takes the herb but thinks to herself: "Shure there's nothing in it," and throws it on the floor, and lo and behold and sure enough! coming home from Gortin, my father got as bad a fright as ever he got in his life. What it was I don't right mind, but anyway he was badly damaged by it. My mother was in a queer way, frightened by the Wee Woman, after what she done, and sure enough the next time she was angry. "Ye didn't believe me," she said, "and ye threw the herb I gave ye in the fire, and I went far enough for it. Ye'll believe me when I tell ye this now."' She then told them of a time they were in Edinburgh and of a countrywoman that came up and talked to them. They did not remember at first, but when she told them what they had talked about, they remembered.

'There was another time she came and told how William Hearn was dead in America. "Go over", she says, "to the Lough, and say that William is dead, and he died happy, and this was the last Bible chapter ever he read," and with that she gave the verse and chapter. "Go", she says, "and tell them to read them at the next class-meeting, and that I held his head while he died". And sure enough word came after that how William had died on the day she named. And, doing as she bid about the chapter and hymn, they never had such a prayer meeting as that. One day she and me and my mother was standing talking, and she was warning her about something, when she says of a sudden: "Here comes Miss Letty in all her finery, and it's time for me to be off". And with that she gave a swirl round on her feet, and raises up in the air, and round and round she goes, and up and up, as if it was a winding stairs she went up, only far swifter.[32] She went up and up, till she was no bigger nor a bird up against the clouds, singing and singing the whole time the loveliest music I ever heard in my life from that day to this. It wasn't a hymn she was singing, but poetry, lovely poetry, and me and my mother stands gaping up, and all of a tremble. "What is she at all, mother?" says I. "Is it an angel she is or a fairy woman, or what?" With that up come Miss Letty, that was your grandmother, dear, but Miss Letty she was then, and no word of her being anything else, and she wondered to see us gaping up that way, till me and my mother told her of it. She went on gay dressed then, and was lovely looking. She was up the lane where none of us could see her coming forward when the Wee Woman rose up in that queer way, saying: "Here comes Miss Letty in all her finery"'. Who knows to what far country she went or to see who dying?

'It was never after dark she came, but daylight always as far as I mind, but wanst, and that was on a Hallow Eve night.[33] My mother was by the fire, making ready the supper, she had a duck down and some apples. In slips the Wee Woman. "I'm come to pass my Hallow Eve with you", says she. "That's right", says my mother, and thinks to herself: "I can give her supper nicely". Down she sits by the fire awhile. "Now I'll tell you where you'll bring my supper", says she. "In the room beyond there beside the loom, set a chair in and a plate". "When ye're spending the night, mayn't ye as well sit by the table and ate with the rest of us?" "Do what you're bid, and set whatever you give me in the room beyant. I'll eat there and nowhere else." So my mother sets her a plate of duck and some apples, whatever was going, in where she bid, and we got to our supper and she to hers; and when we rose I went in, and there, lo and behold ye, was her supper plate a bit ate of each portion, and she gone!'[34]

The old woman went on to tell how her mother made the Wee Woman angry 'off and on like she did about the herb, and asking questions that way. The Wee Woman said one day: "You're in trouble now, but it is in thicker trouble you will be, and you'll mind this warning, and believe what I tell you". And after this she quit coming.' But the old woman saw her once more, and before the 'thick trouble' came, as it did: 'One night I was over on some errand to your uncle's people's place. Rightly I mind it was a basket of praties we were carrying, me and a girl called Rosanna M'Laren, and coming over the stile by the haggard, I leaped over first, the better to help with the basket, and what do I see across the burn, over by a haystack, but the Wee Woman with all her hair hanging about her, lovely long brown hair, and she combing away at it; and I gives a screech, startled like, and Rosanna drops the basket, and all the praties spilt, but when I turned my head back, she was clean gone, while you would take time to wink, and the two of us took to our heels as hard as we could, and round the end of the house. I don't know what came over me to be scared that way at seeing her, but maybe she was angered, for from that day to this I never seen or heard tell of her, but once that she came to my mother in Belfast. She was always friendly with me, and I was always glad to see her, and I would run out to meet her; but none of the children ever seen her except myself, only my mother and me, and no man body at all at all, as I have told ye.'

'Uncle Joseph's' house had to be moved, one has no doubt, because it was 'on the path'; for there are stories everywhere of houses that had to be pulled down, because they were 'on the path' or 'in the way,' or were pulled down by the whirling winds that are 'the Others' journeying in their ways. There is a house in Gort, for instance, on which, people say, it is impossible to keep a roof, although the roofs keep on the houses beside it. I have no doubt either that the old woman's mother threw the herb away, because she was afraid of it, for the gifts of 'the Others' are often believed to bring ill-luck in the end. The people say: 'O, yes, it is best to be without them anyway.' If the 'Wee Woman' was, as I think she was, one of the dead, she came on Hallow Eve because it was the beginning of the old Celtic winter,[35] and the time when many old nations held a festival of the dead amid the dropping leaves and gathering cold. In Brittany[36] a table covered with food and a warm fire are left for them even now on 'All Souls Night', which is but two days from Hallow Eve. 'The Others', however, are said also to be busier, on Hallow Eve and on the first of November, than at any other time, except the first of May, the beginning of the old Celtic summer.[37] The Wee Woman ate by herself, because 'the Others', and the dead, and even the living, that are among them, may not eat while mortal eyes are looking. The people put potatoes on the doorstep for them, often night after night throughout the year, and these potatoes must not have been 'put on the table', for they would not eat them if they had been 'put before any common person'; and there is a young man near Gort who is believed to go out of our world at night, and it is said, though not correctly, that he will not let anybody see him eating. All ancient people set food for the dead, and believed that they could eat as we do, and about this and about the possibility of them and of 'the Others' bringing and taking away solid things I have much to say, but at present I hold a clean mirror to tradition. They often go away as the Wee Woman did by going up and round and round in the air. A woman who lives by Kiltartan bog says: 'I often saw a light in the wood at Derreen. It would rise high over the trees going round and round. I'd see it maybe for fifteen minutes at a time, and then it would fall like a lamp'; and the whirling winds that are their winds, but were called the dance of the daughters of Herodias[38] in the middle ages, show how much their way is a whirling way.

All of us are said to have a great many friends among them—relations and forbears snatched away, and they are said to come at times like the Wee Woman to warn us and protect us, and lament over us. I have been told that nobody can tell how many have been snatched away, for that two or three years ago 'eighteen or nineteen young men and young girls' were taken out of one village. The Country of 'the Others', 'the Country of the Young', is in truth the heaven of the ancient peoples, and I can discover, and will show[39] in the stories told of it, the ancient thoughts, plausible and complex thoughts, about life and death. It has been the Celt's great charge to remember it with ancient things, among forgetful peoples; and it may be his charge to speak of it and of ancient sanctities to peoples who have only new things. It was perhaps for this that the Roman went by him afar off, and that the Englishman is beating in vain upon his doors and wondering how doors of dreams can be so greatly harder than doors of iron; and that his days pass among grey stones and grey clouds and grey seas, among things too faint and seemingly frail to awaken him from the sleep, in which the ancient peoples dreamed the world and the glory of it, and were content to dream.

THREE IRISH POETS

Yeats's encomium for his friends AE, Lionel Johnson, and Nora Hopper appeared as "Three Irish Poets" in the "A Celtic Christmas" issue of The Irish Homestead *in December 1897. This year was the peak of Yeats's Pan-Celtic propaganda, and in the opening paragraph, envisaging the birth of a Celtic, symbolist, occult Messiah at the turn of the century is one of his most fervent annunciations. Yeats wrote separate articles on all three of these poets during the following year for* The Dublin Daily Express. *Versions of these articles were reprinted in* A Treasury of Irish Poetry in the English Tongue *(see P&I, 111–17). The present article was accompanied by a sketch of Yeats, presumably by AE, who had begun, in November 1897, his association with Horace Plunkett's Irish Agricultural Organisation Society and who was to edit* The Irish Homestead, *the society's journal, from 1905 onward.*

It is hardly an exaggeration to say that the spiritual history of the world has been the history of conquered races. Those learned in the traditions of many lands, understand that it is almost always some defeated or perhaps dwindling tribe hidden among the hills or in the forests, that is most famous for the understanding of charms and the reading of dreams, and the seeing of visions. And has not our Christianity come to us from defeated and captive Judea?[1] The influence of the Celt, too, has been a spiritual influence, and men are beginning to understand how great it has been. The legends of King Arthur and the Holy Grail, which had so great an influence on the whole of Europe in the twelfth century, and so great a part in the foundation of chivalry, were Celtic legends, and some say Irish legends transformed by Welsh and Breton story-tellers.[2] The legends that gave Dante the structure of his poems are believed to have been Irish legends of the visions seen by devout persons in a little island in Lough Derg;[3] and but for the legends and history of the Highlanders, who are in all things of one stock with ourselves, Sir Walter Scott could hardly have begun that great modern

368

mediaeval movement, which has influenced all the literature and art
and much of the religion of the nineteenth century.[4] Until our day the
Celt has dreamed half the dreams of Europe, while others have written them but to-day he is beginning to write his own dreams, and such
great Bretons as Lamennais, Chateaubriand, Renan, and Count Villiers
de L'Isle-Adam,[†] the founder of the present spiritual movement in
French literature, and the great Welshman, William Morris, the
founder of the decorative movement in English art, prove that he can
write persuasively.[5] The bulk of the poets of modern Ireland has been
so exclusively political, or so exclusively national, in a political sense,
that it has hardly busied itself like the poets of Wales and Brittany with
the spiritual part of life, but now we have several poets who are
speaking with what I think is the truest voice of the Celt. I call them
spiritual, not because they are religious, in the dogmatic sense of the
word, but because they touch our deepest and most delicate feelings,
and believe that a beauty, not a wordly beauty, lives in worldly things.
AE,[†] Miss Nora Hopper, and Mr. Lionel Johnson are good types of this
new school. AE[†] takes our ancient legends just as the story-teller of the
twelfth century took the legends of the Holy Grail and shows us their
spiritual meaning. For instance, we read somewhere of a certain well
called 'Connla's well',[6] and how a sacred hazel tree grew over it and
dropped nuts, that were nuts of wisdom to all who eat of them; and
in his dream the well seemed to fill the world, and the thoughts that
came to him from the beauty of nature, seemed but its dropping
berries; and he made this poem about it.

> A cabin on the mountain side hid in a grassy nook,
> With door and windows open wide where friendly stars may
>   look;
> The rabbits shy can patter in; the winds may enter free,
> Who throng around the mountain throne in living ecstasy.
> And when the sun sets dimmed in eve and purple fills the air,
> I think the sacred hazel tree is dropping berries there,
> From starry fruitage waved aloft where Connla's well o'er-
>   flows;
> For sure the enchanted water runs through every wind that
>   blows.
> I think when night towers up aloft and shakes the trembling
>   dew,
> How every high and lonely thought that thrills my being
>   through,
> Is but a shining[7] berry dropped down through the purple air,
> And from the magic tree of life the fruit falls everywhere.

To Irish people accustomed to the eloquent and argumentative poetry of *The Nation*[8] newspaper, this new poetry will sometimes seem strange and difficult, but it is really very like the Celtic legends that influenced the world long ago. Miss Hopper has written of many beautiful legends and read into them many tender and beautiful meanings, but her 'Fairy Fiddler' must be my one example.

> 'Tis I go fiddling, fiddling,
>   By weedy ways forlorn;
> I make the blackbird's music
>   Ere in his breast 'tis born;
> The sleeping larks I waken
>   Twixt the midnight and the morn,
>
> No man alive has seen me
>   But women hear me play
> Sometimes at door or window
>   Fiddling the souls away:
> The child's soul and the colleen's
>   Out of the covering clay.
>
> None of my fairy kinsmen
>   Make music with me now:
> Alone the raths I wander,
>   Or ride the whitethorn bough,
> But the wild swans, they[9] know me,
>   And the horse that draws the plough.

That is a little snatch of song that will not soon pass away. Mr. Lionel Johnson is before all else a Catholic poet,[10] and many of his poems are hymns, many of them written in Latin, like the mediaeval hymns; but he is not the less for that, but rather so much the more for that—an Irish and a Celtic poet. His 'Christmas and Ireland' begins with these passionate verses:

> The golden stars give warmthless fire,
>   As weary Mary goes through night,
> Her feet are torn by stone and briar;
>   She hath no rest, no strength, no light:
> O Mary, weary in the snow,
>   Remember Ireland's woe!

O Joseph, sad for Mary's sake!
    Look on our earthly mother too:
Let not the heart of Ireland break,
    With agony its ages through:
For Mary's love, love also thou
    Ireland, and save her now!

Harsh were the folk, and bitter stern,
    At Bethlehem, that night of nights.
FOR YOU NO CHEERING HEARTH SHALL BURN:
    WE HAVE NO ROOM HERE, YOU NO RIGHTS.
O Mary and Joseph! hath not she,
    Ireland, been even as ye![11]

His political poetry cannot be quoted here, but it is not less exalted and passionate, and would sound well in our ballad books.

This new school cannot fail to influence Irish thought very strongly, for it is full of the dreams that we dream in our most exalted moments. Few who have not read deeply in the history of literary movements, know how strong is the influence of the highest kind of poetry, for it does not directly influence many minds, but it influences the finest minds and through them many minds. This new school, and the ever increasing knowledge of the old poetry in Gaelic, must in time make many strong and delicate minds spend themselves in the service of Ireland that would else have spent themselves in alien causes, and Ireland may become again a spiritual influence in the world.

THE PRISONERS OF THE GODS

The second in the group of six articles which Yeats organized from the folk materials gathered by himself and Lady Gregory was "The Prisoners of the Gods" in The Nineteenth Century *for January 1898.*

None among people visiting Ireland, and few among the people living in Ireland, except peasants, understand that the peasants believe in their ancient gods, and that to them, as to their forbears, everything is inhabited and mysterious. The gods gather in the raths or forts, and about the twisted thorn trees, and appear in many shapes, now little and grotesque, now tall, fair-haired and noble, and seem busy and real in the world, like the people in the markets or at the crossroads. The peasants remember their old name, the *sheagh sidhe,* though they fear mostly to call them by any name lest they be angry, unless it be by some vague words, 'the gentry', or 'the royal gentry', or 'the army', or 'the spirits', or 'the others', as the Greek peasant calls his Nereids,[1] and they believe, after twelve Christian centuries,[2] that the most and the best of their dead are among them.

A man close by the bog of Kiltartan[3] said to the present writer: 'I don't think the old go among them, when they die, but, believe me, it's not many of the young they spare, but bring them away till such time as God sends for them'; and a woman at Spiddal, in northwestern Galway, where the most talk nothing but Gaelic, said: 'There are but few in these days that die right. The priests know all about them, more than we do, but they don't like to be talking of them, because they might be too big in our minds'. Halloran of Inchy,[4] who has told me and told a friend of mine[5] many stories, says: 'All that die are brought away among them, except an odd old person'. And a man at Spiddal says: 'Is it only the young go there? Ah, how do we know what use they may have for the old as well as for the young?' A fisher woman among the Burren Hills says: 'It's the good and the handsome they take, and those that are of use, or whose name is up for some good action. Idlers they

372

don't like; but who would like idlers?' An old man near Gort has no fear of being taken, but says: 'What would they want with the like of me? It's the good and the pious they come for'. And an old woman living on a bog near Tuam says: 'I would hardly believe they'd take the old, but we can't know what they might want of them. And it's well to have a friend among them, and it's always said you have a right not to fret if you lose your children, for it's well to have them there before you. They don't want cross people, and they won't bring you away if you say so much as one cross word. It's only the good and the pious they want; now, isn't that very good of them?'

There are countless stories told of people who meet 'the others' and meet friends and neighbours among them. This old woman tells of 'a man living over at Caramina, Rick Moran was his name, and one night he was walking over the little green hill that's near his house, and when he got to the top of it he found it like a fair green, just like the fair of Abbey with all the people that were in it, and a great many of them were neighbours he used to know when they were alive, and they were all buying and selling just like ourselves. And they did him no harm, but they put a basket of cakes into his hand and kept him selling them all through the night. And when he got home he told the story, and the neighbours, when they heard it, gave him the name of the cakes, and to the day of his death he was called nothing but Richard Crackers'.

A Spiddal man says: 'There was a man told me he was passing the road one night, near Cruach-na-Sheogue, where they are often seen dancing in the moonlight, and the walls on each side of the road were all crowded with people sitting on them, and he walked between, and they said nothing to him. And he knew many among them that were dead before that time'. And a weatherbound boatman from Roundstone had a friend who was 'out visiting one night, and coming home across the fields he came into a great crowd of them. They did him no harm, and among them he saw a great many that he knew that were dead, five or six out of our own village. And he was in his bed for two months after that. He said he couldn't understand their talk, it was like the hissing of geese, and there was one very big man that seemed the master of them, and his talk was like a barrel when it is being rolled'. Halloran of Inchy knew a man that was walking along the road near the corner where Mr. Burke and the soldier who was with him were shot in the time of the land troubles,[6] and he saw 'in the big field that's near the corner a big fire and a lot of people round about it, and among them a girl he used to know that had died'.

The old inhabitants of the forts dug caves under the forts, in which they kept their precious things, one supposes, and these caves, though shallow enough, are often believed to go miles. They are thought pathways into the country of the dead, and I doubt not that many who have gone down into them shaking with fear, have fallen into a sudden trance, and have had visions, and have thought they had walked a great way. The fisher woman among the Burren Hills tells this story, that has doubtless come of such a trance, and would be like the visions of St. Patrick's Purgatory[7] if it were at all Christian:

'There's a forth[8] away in the county Clare, and they say it's so long that it has no end. And there was a pensioner, one Rippingham, came back from the army, and a soldier has more courage than another, and he said he'd go try what was in it, and he got another man to go with him, and they went a long, long way and saw nothing, and then they came to where there was the sound of a woman beetling.[9] And then they began to meet people they knew before, that had died out of the village, and they all told them to go back, but still they went on. And then they met the parish priest of Ballyvaughan, Father Ruane, that was dead, and he told them to go back, and so they turned and went. They were just beginning to come to the grandeur when they were turned away'.

The dead do not merely live among their captors as we might among a strange people, but have the customs and power which they have, and change their shapes and become birds and beasts when they will. A Mrs. Sheridan said to me, 'Never shoot a hare, for you wouldn't know what might be in it. There were two women I knew, mother and daughter, and they died, and one day I was out by the wood and I saw two hares sitting by the wall, and the minute I saw them I knew well who they were. And the mother made as though she'd kill me, but the daughter stopped her. Bad they must have been to be put into that shape, and indeed I knew that they were not too good. I saw the mother another time come up near the door as if to see me, and when she got near she turned herself into a big red hare'. The witches are believed to take the shape of hares, and so the hare's is a bad shape. Another time she saw 'the old Captain standing near the road, she knew well it was him, and while she was looking at him he was changed into the shape of an ass'.

Young children are believed to be in greater danger than anybody else, and the number of those whose cries are heard in the wind shows how much 'the others' have to do with the wind. A man called Martin, who lives by Kiltartan bog, says: 'Flann told me he was by the hedge up there by Mr. Gerald's farm one evening, and a blast came, and as it passed he heard something crying, crying, and he knew by the sound it was a child that they were carrying away'.

All the young are in danger, however, because of the long lives they have before them, and the desire of 'the others' to have their lives devoted to them and to their purposes. When I was staying with a friend in Galway a little time ago, an old woman came from the Burren Hills to ask for help to put a thatch on her cottage, and told us, crying and bemoaning herself, of the snatching away of her five children. One of us asked her about a certain place upon the road where a boy had fallen from his cart and been killed, and she said:

'It's a bad piece of the road. There's forth near it, and it's in that forth my five children are that were swept from me. I went and I told Father Lally I knew they were there, and he said, "Say your prayers, my poor woman, that's all you can do". When they were young they were small and thin enough, and they grew up like a bunch of rushes, but then they got strong and stout and good-looking. Too good-looking they were, so that everybody would remark them and would say, "Oh! look at Ellen Joyce, look at Catherine, look at Martin! So good to work and so handsome and so loyal to their mother!" And they were all taken from me; all gone now but one. Consumption they were said to get, but it never was in my family or in the father's, and how would they get it without some privication?[10] Four of them died with that, and Martin was drowned. One of the little girls was in America and the other at home, and they both got sick at the one time, and at the end of nine months the both of them died.

'Only twice they got a warning. Michael, that was the first to go, was out one morning very early to bring a letter to Mr. Blake. And he met on the road a small little woman, and she came across him again and again, and then again, as if to humbug him. And he got afraid, and he told me about her when he got home. And not long after that he died.

'And Ellen used to be going to milk the cow for the nuns morning and evening, and there was a place she had to pass, a sort of an enchanted place, I forget the name of it. And when she came home one evening she said she would go there no more, for when she was passing that place she saw a small little woman with a little cloak about her, and her face not the size of a doll's face. And with the one look of her she got, she got a fright and ran as fast as she could and sat down to milk the cow. And when she was milking she looked up and there was the small little woman coming along by the wall. And she said she'd never go there again. So to move the thought out of her mind I said, "Sure that's the little woman is stopping up at Shemus Mor's house." "Oh, it's not, mother", says she. "I know well by her look she was no right person". "Then, my poor girl, you're lost", says I, for I knew it was the same woman that Michael saw. And sure enough, it was but a few weeks after that she died.

'And Martin, the last that went, was stout and strong and nothing ailed him, but he was drowned. He'd go down sometimes to bathe in the sea, and one day he said he was going, and I said, "Do not, for you have no swim". But a boy of the neighbour's came after that and called to him, and I was making the little dinner for him, and I didn't see him pass the door. And I never knew he was gone till when I went out of the house the girl from next door looked at me some way strange, and then she told me two boys were drowned, and then she told me one of them was my own. Held down, they said he was, by something underneath. They had him followed there.

'It wasn't long after he died I woke one night, and I felt some one near, and I struck the light, and there I saw his shadow. He was wearing his little cap, but under it I knew his face and the colour of his hair. And he never spoke, and he was going out the door and I called to him and said, 'O Martin, come back to me, and I'll always be watching for you!' And every night after that I'd hear things thrown about the house outside, and noises. So I got afraid to stop in it, and I went to live in another house, and I told the priest I knew Martin was not dead, but that he was still living.

'And about eight weeks after Catherine dying I had what I thought was a dream. I thought I dreamt that I saw her sweeping out the floor of the room. And I said, "Catherine, why are you sweeping? Sure you know I sweep the floor clean and the hearth every night". And I said, "Tell me where are you now?" and she said, "I'm in the forth beyond". And she said, "I have a great deal of things to tell you, but I must look out and see are they watching me". Now, wasn't that very sharp for a dream? And she went to look out the door, but she never came back again.

'And in the morning, when I told it to a few respectable people they said, "Take care but it might have been no dream but herself that came back and talked to you". And I think it was, and that she came back to see me and to keep the place well swept.

'Sure we know there were some in the forth in the old times, for my aunt's husband was brought away into it, and why wouldn't they be there now? He was sent back out of it again, a girl led him back and told him he was brought away because he answered to the first call, and that he had a right only to answer to the third. But he didn't want to come home. He said he saw more people in it than he ever saw at a hurling, and that he'd ask no better place than it in high heaven'.

Mystics believe that sicknesses and the elements do the will of spiritual powers, but Mrs. Joyce had not heard this, and so could only deny that her children had died of consumption or were drowned by the unaided waters. Her aunt's husband was doubtless called by a voice into the fort, and he went at the first call, instead of waiting, as the country people say all should, for the third call, which it seems cannot be called except by the living; and doubtless wandered about there in a dream and a sleep until it seemed in his dream that a girl of 'the others' led him out of the fort and he awoke.

Next to young children women after childbirth are held to be in most danger. I hear often of a year in which many were taken out of South Galway. A man about Tillyra said to me: 'It's about fourteen years since so many young women were brought away after their child being born. Peter Regan's wife of Peterswell, and James Jordan's wife of Derreen, and Loughlin's wife of Lissatunna—hundreds were carried off in that year. They didn't bring so many since then; I suppose they brought enough then to last them a good while'. And a man near Gort says: 'And it's not many years ago that such a lot of fine women were taken from Gort very sudden after childbirth—fine women. I knew them all myself'.

These women are taken, it is believed, to suckle children who have been made captive or have been born from the loves of spirits for mortals. Another man from near Gort says: 'Linsky the slater's mother was taken away, it's always said. The way it's known is, it was not long after her baby was born, but she was doing well. And one morning very early a man and his wife were going in a cart to Loughrea one Thursday for the market, and they met some of those people, and they asked the woman that had her child with her, would she give a drink to their child that was with them. And while she was doing it they said, 'We won't be in want of a nurse to-night; we'll have Mrs. Linsky of Gort'. And when they got back in the evening, Mrs. Linsky was dead before them'.

A fisherman from Aasleagh showed a correspondent, who was sailing along by the Killeries, a spot on the side of Muel Rae where there was a castle 'haunted by evil spirits' who were often heard 'making a noise like screeching and crying and howling and singing', and 'Peter's brother's wife' was there; 'she was taken in her labour. It was an evil spirit that was in her, she couldn't bring it to the birth alive. In the morning when her crying was done they went to see her. There wasn't a bit of her there'. Evil spirits had 'fetched her away, and they took the sack of potatoes to put her in, and the potatoes were running all over the road even down to the water. She's there shut up to nurse the queen's child. A fine creature she was'. The tales of fishermen are full of the evil powers of the world.

The old woman who lives on the bog near Tuam says: 'There are many young women taken by them in childbirth. I lost a sister of my own in that way. There's a place in the river at Newton where there's stones in the middle you can get over by, and one day she was crossing, and there in the middle of the river, and she standing on a stone, she felt a blow on the face. And she looked round to see who gave it, and there was no one there, so then she knew what had happened, and she came to my mother's house, and she carrying at the time. I was but a little slip at that time, with my books in my hand coming from the school, and I ran in and said, "Here's Biddy coming", and my mother said, "What would bring her at this time of the day?" But she came in and sat down on a chair, and she opened the whole story. And my mother, seeing she got a fright, said to quiet her, "It was only a pain you got in the ear, and you thought it was a blow". "Ah", she said, "I never got a blow that hurted me like that did".

'And the next day and every day after that, the ear would swell a little in the afternoon, and then she began to eat nothing, and at the last her baby wasn't born five minutes when she died. And my mother used to watch for her for three or four years after, thinking she'd come back, but she never did'.

Many women are taken, it is believed, on their marriage day, and many before their babies are born, that they may be born among 'the others'. A woman from the shore about Duras says: 'At Aughanish there were two couples came to the shore to be married, and one of the new-married women was in the boat with the priest, and they going back to the island. And a sudden blast of wind came, and the priest said some blessed words that were able to save himself, but the girl was swept'.

This woman was drowned, doubtless. Every woman who dies about her marriage day is believed to die, I think, because a man of 'the others' wants her for himself. Next after a young child and a woman in childbirth, a young, handsome and strong man is thought in most danger. When he dies about his marriage day he is believed to die, I think, because a woman of 'the others' wants him for herself. A man living near Coole says: 'My father? Yes, indeed, he saw many things, and I'll tell you a thing he told me, and there's no doubt in the earthly world about it. It was when they lived in Inchy they came over here one time to settle a marriage for Peter Quin's aunt. And when they had the marriage settled they were going home at dead of night. And a wedding had taken place that day, of one Merrick from beyond Turloughmore, and the drag was after passing the road with him and his party going home. And in a minute the road was filled with men on horses riding along, so that my father had to take shelter in Carthy's big haggard. And the horsemen were calling on Merrick's name. And twenty-one days after he lay dead. There's no doubt at all about the truth of that, and they were no riders belonging to this world that were on those horses'.

The hurling was the game of the gods in old times, and 'the others' are held everywhere to-day to delight in good hurlers and to carry them away. A man by the sea-shore near the Connemara hills in western Galway says: 'There was a man lived about a mile beyond Spiddal, and he was one day at a play, and he was the best at the hurling and the throwing and at every game. And a woman in the crowd called out to him, "You're the strongest man that's in it". And twice after that a man that was beside him and that heard that said, saw him pass by, with his coat on, before sunrise. And on the fifth day after he was dead. He left four or five sons, and some of them went to America, and the eldest of them married and was living in the place with his wife. And he was going to Galway for a fair, and his wife was on a visit to her father and her mother on the road to Galway, and she bid him to come early, that she'd have commands for him. So it was before sunrise when he set out, and he was going up a little side road through the fields to make a short cut, and he came on the biggest fair he ever saw, and the most people in it, and they made a way for him to pass through. And a man with a big coat and a tall hat came out from them and said, "Do you know me?" And he said, "Are you my father?" And he said, "I am, and but for me you'd be sorry for coming here, but I saved you; but don't be coming out so early in the morning again". And he said, "It was a year ago that Jimmy went to America". And that was true enough. And then he said, "And it was you that drove your sister away, and gave her no peace or ease, because you wanted the place for yourself". And he said, "That is true". And he asked the father, "Were you all these years here?" And he said, "I was. But in the next week I'll be moved to the west part of Kerry, and four years after that my time will come to die". It was the son himself told me all this'.

This man was taken according to the traditional philosophy because someone praised him and did not say 'God bless him', for the admiration of a sinner may, it says, become the admiration of 'the others', who do many works through our emotions, and become as a rope to drag us out of the world.

They take the good dancers too, for they love the dance. Old Langan, a witch doctor on the borders of Clare, says: 'There was a boy was a splendid dancer. Well, one night he was going to a house where there was a dance. And when he was about half way to it, he came to another house where there was music and dancing going on. So he turned in, and there was a room all done up with curtains and with screens, and a room inside where the people were sitting, and it was only those that were dancing sets that came to the outside room. So he danced two or three sets and then he saw that it was a house they had built up where there was no house before for him to come into. So he went out, but there was a big flagstone at the door, and he stumbled on it and fell down. And in a fortnight after he was dead'.

I know a doctor who met one day among the Burren Hills the funeral of a young man he had been attending some time before. He stopped and asked the sister why he had not been sent for of late, and she said, 'Sure you could do nothing for him, doctor. It's well known what happened, him such a grand dancer, never home from a wedding or a wake till three o'clock in the morning, and living as he did beside a forth. It's *they* that have him swept'.

All the able-bodied, however, should fear the love of the gods. A man who lives by Derrykeel, on the Clare border, says of a friend and neighbour of fifty years ago: 'We were working together, myself and him, making that trench you see beyond to drain the wood. And it was contract work, and he was doing the work of two men, and was near ready to take another piece. And some of the boys began to say to him, "It's a shame for you to be working like that, and taking the bread out of the mouth of another", and I standing there. And he said he didn't care what they said, and he took the spade and sent the scraws out flying to the right and to the left. And he never put a spade into the ground again, for that night he was taken ill and died shortly after. Watched he was and taken by *them*'.

Even the old and feeble should not feel altogether safe. I have been told at Coole that 'there was a man on this estate, and he sixty years, and he took to his bed and the wife went to Biddy Early,[11] a famous wise woman of whom I have many stories, and said, 'It can't be by *them* he's taken. What use would he be to them, being so old?' And Biddy Early is the one that should know, and she said, 'Wouldn't he be of use to them to drive their cattle?'

But all are not sad to go. I have heard 'there were two men went with poteen to the island of Aran. And when they were on the shore they saw a ship coming as if to land, and they said, "We'll have the bottle ready for those that are coming". But when the ship came close to land it vanished. And presently they got their boat ready and put out to sea. And a sudden blast came and swept one of them off. And the other saw him come up again, and put out the oar across his breast for him to take hold of it. But he would not take it, but said, 'I'm all right now', and sank down again, and was seen no more'.

There is indeed no great cause why any should fear anything except in the parting, for they expect to find there things like the things they have about them in the world, only better and more plentiful. A man at Derrykeel says: 'There was a woman walking in the road that had a young child at home, and she met a very old man having a baby in his arms. And he asked would she give it a drop of breast milk.

So she did, and gave it a drink. And the old man said, "It's well for you did that, for you saved your cow by it; but to-morrow look over the wall into the field of the rich man that lives beyond the boundary, and you'll see that one of his was taken in the place of yours". And so it happened'.

Mrs. Colahan of Kiltartan says: 'There was a woman living on the road that goes to Scahanagh, and one day a carriage stopped at her door and a grand lady came out of it, and asked would she come and give the breast to her child. And she said she wouldn't leave her own children, but the lady said no harm would happen them, and brought her away to a big house, but when she got there she wouldn't stop, but went home again. And in the morning the woman's cow was dead'.

And because it is thought 'the others' and the dead may need the milk for the children that are among them, it is thought wrong to 'begrudge' the cows. An old farmer at Coole says: 'The way the bad luck came to Tommy Glyn was when his cow fell sick and lay for dead. He had a right to leave it or to kill it himself. But his father-in-law was covetous, and he cut a bit of the lug off it, and it rose again, and he sold it for seven pound at the fair of Tubber. But he never had luck since then, and lost four or five bullocks, near all he owned'. To 'cut a bit of the lug[12] off it' is, it seems, a recognised way of breaking the enchantment.

A man at Gortaveha says: 'There was a drunkard in Scariff, and one night he had drink taken he couldn't get home, and fell asleep by the roadside near the bridge. And in the night he woke and heard them at work, with cars and horses, and one said to another, 'This work is too heavy; we'll take the white horse belonging to Whelan' (that was the name of a rich man in the town). So, as soon as it was light, he went to this rich man, and told him what he heard them say. But he would only laugh at him and said, "I'll pay no attention to what a drunkard dreams". But when he went out after to the stable, the white horse was dead'. A woman near Spiddal says: 'We had a mare, the grandest from this to Galway, had a foal there on that floor, and before long both mare and foal died. And I often hear them galloping round the house, both mare and foal, and I not the only one, but many in the village can hear them too'.

Roots and plants are taken too. I have heard of their pulling the nuts in the woods about Coole, and a woman who lives on the side of the road between Gort and Ardrahan says: 'There was a girl used to come with me every year to pick water grass, and one year I couldn't go and she went by herself, And when she looked up from picking it she saw a strange woman standing by her with a red petticoat about her head and a very clean white apron. And she took some of the water in her hand and threw it in the girl's face and gave her a blow and told her never to come there again. Vexed they were the water grass to be taken away; they wanted it left to themselves'.

A Galway lady tells of great noises that she and her household heard coming out of the apple room, and I asked a friend's gardener if he ever heard noises of the kind, and he said, 'For all the twelve nights I slept in the apple house I never say anything, and I never went to bed or stripped off my clothes all the time, but I kept up a good turf fire all the night. But every night I could hear the sound of eating and of knives and forks, I don't know, was it the apples they were eating or some dinner they brought with them. And one night one of them jumped down from the granary over the bed, I could hear him scraping with his hands, and I went out and never came in again that night, and ever since that time I am a bit deaf'. Once he was in the grape house and there came a great wind and shook the house, and when it had gone by one of the bunches had been 'swept'. He has often heard that the pookas, a kind of mischievous spirits that come mostly in the shape of animals and are associated with November, take away the blackberries in the month of November, and he says: 'Anyway, we know that when the potatoes are taken it's by 'the gentry', and surely this year they have put their fancy on them'.

Kirwan, the faery man of a place opposite Aran, under the Connemara hills, who learns many things from his sister who is away among them, says: 'Last year I was digging potatoes, and a boy came by, one of *them,* and one that I knew well before. And he said, "They're yours this year, and the next two years they will be ours". And you know the potatoes were good last year, and you see how bad they are this year, and how they have been made away with. And the sister told me that half the food in Ireland goes to them, but that if they like they can make out of cow dung all they want, and they can come into a house and use what they like, and it will never be missed in the morning'.

The woman on the bog near Tuam says: 'There's a very loughy woman living up that boreen beyond, is married to a man of the Gillanes, and last year she told me that a strange woman came into her house and sat down, and asked her had she good potatoes, and she said she had. And the woman said, "You have them this year, but we'll have them next year". And she said, "When you go out of the house it's your enemy you'll see standing outside". And when she went away the woman went to the door to see what way did she go, she could see her nowhere. And sure enough there was a man standing outside that was a near neighbour and was her most enemy'. A correspondent found a man on the Killeries cutting oats with a scissors, and was told that they had seen his scythe the year before, and to keep him from taking the oats they 'came in the middle of the night and trampled it all down, so he was cutting it quietly this year'.

It is, I think, a plausible inference that, just as people who are taken grow old among them, so unripe grain and fruits and plants that are taken grow ripe among them. Everything, according to this complex faith, seems to have a certain power of life it must wear out, a certain length of life it must live out, in either world, and the worlds war on one another for its possession.

A sound of fighting is often heard about dying persons, and this is thought to come of fighting between their dead friends who would prevent their being taken, and those who would take them. An old man died lately near Coole, and some of the neighbours heard fighting about his house, though one neighbour of his own age will not believe it was for him, because he was 'too cross and too old' to be taken; and last year I met a man on the big island of Aran who heard fighting when two of his children died. I did not write his story down at the time, and so cannot give his very words. One night he heard a sound of fighting in the room. He lit the light, but everything became silent at once and he could see nothing. He put out the light and the room was full of the sound of fighting as before. In the morning he saw blood in a box he had to keep fish in, and his child was very ill. I do not remember if his child died that day, but it died soon. He heard fighting another night, and he tried to throw the quilt on the people who were fighting, but he could not find anybody. In the morning he found blood scattered about and his second child dead. A man he knew was in love with a girl who lived near and used to sleep with her at night, and he was going home that morning and saw a troop of them, and the child in the middle of them. Once, while he was telling this story, he thought I was not believing him, and he got greatly excited and stood up and said he was an old man and might die before he got to his house and he would not tell me a lie, before God he would not tell me a lie.

A man near Cahir-glissane[13] says: 'As to fighting for those that are dying, I'd believe in that. There was a girl died not far from here, and the night of her death there was heard in the air the sound of an army marching and the drums beating, and it stopped over her house where she was lying sick. And they could see no one, but could hear the drums and the marching plain enough, and there was like little flames of lightning playing about it'.

A woman at Kiltartan[14] says: 'There does often be fighting heard when a person is dying. John King's wife that lived in this house before I came to it, the night she died there was a noise heard, that all the village thought that every wall of every garden round about was falling down. But in the morning there was no sign of any of them being fallen'.

A woman at Spiddal[15] says: 'There are more of them in America than what there are here, and more of other sort of spirits. There was a man came from there told me that one night in America he had brought his wife's niece that was sick back from the hospital, and had put her in an upper room. And in the evening they heard a scream from her, and she called out, "The room is full of them, and my father is with them and my aunt". And he drove them away, and used the devil's name and cursed them. And she was left quiet that night, but the next day she said, "I'll be destroyed altogether to-night with them". And he said he'd keep them out, and he locked the door of the house. And towards midnight he heard them coming to the door and trying to get in, but he kept it locked and he called to them by way of the keyhole to keep away out of that. And there was talking among them, and the girl that was upstairs said she could hear the laugh of her father and of her aunt. And they heard the greatest fighting among them that ever was, and after that they went away, and the girl got well. That's what often happens, crying and fighting for one that's sick or going to die'.

A woman at Coole[16] says: 'There was an old woman the other day was telling me of a little girl was put to bake a cake, for her mother was sick in the room. And when she turned away her head for a minute the cake was gone. And that happened the second day and the third, and the mother was vexed when she heard it, thinking some of the neighbours had come in and taken it away. But the next day an old man appeared, and they knew he was the grandfather, and he said, "It's by me the cake was taken, for I was watching the house these three nights, where I knew there was one sick in it. And you never knew such a fight as there was for her last night, and they would have brought her away but for me that had my shoulder to the door". And the woman began to recover from that time.'

The woman on the bog near Tuam says: 'It's said to be a very good place, with coaches and all such things, but a person would sooner be in this world, for all that. And when a man or a woman is dying, the friends and the others among them will often gather about the house and will give a great challenge for him'.

And Langan, the faery man on the borders of Clare and Galway, says: 'Everyone has friends among them, and the friends would try to save when others would be trying to bring you away'.

Sometimes those they are trying to take seem to have a part in the fight, for they tell about Kiltartan of a woman who seemed dying, and suddenly she sat up and said, 'I have had a hard fight for it', and got well after; and they understood her words to mean that she was fighting with the host of 'the others'.

Sometimes, too, the friends and neighbours and relations who are among them are thought to help, instead of hindering, the taking away. The fisher woman from Burren says: 'There was my own uncle that lived on the road between Kinvara and Burren, where the shoe-maker's shop is now, and two of his children were brought away from him. And the third he was determined he would keep, and he put it to sleep between himself and the wife in the bed. And one night a hand came in at the window and tried to take the child, and he knew who the hand belonged to, and he saw it was a woman of the village that was dead. So he drove her away and held the child, and he was never troubled again after that'.

And Kirwin the faery man says: 'One night I was in the bed with the wife beside me, and the child near me, next the fire. And I turned and saw a woman sitting by the fire, and she made a snap at the child, and I was too quick for her and got hold of it, and she was at the door and out of it before I could get hold of her'. The woman was his sister, who is among them and has taught him his unearthly knowledge.

In November 'the others' are said to fight for the harvest, and I may find, when I know more, that this fight is between the friends of the living among the dead, and those among the dead who would carry it away. The shadow of battle was over all Celtic mythology, for the gods established themselves and the fruitfulness of the world, in battle against the Fomor, or powers of darkness and barrenness; and the children of Mile[†17] or the living, and perhaps the friends of the living, established themselves in battle against the gods and made them hide in the green hills and in the barrows of the dead, and they still wage an endless battle against the gods and against the dead.

MR. LIONEL JOHNSON'S
POEMS

Lionel Johnson (1867–1902) was one of Yeats's closest friends of the nineties. He taught Yeats some Latin and Greek, a little of the Church Fathers, and the deportment of a gentleman. Yeats gave in his autobiography some of Johnson's dicta: "One should be quite unnoticeable" and "Life is ritual" (Au, 149 and 234, respectively). A master of some arts such as punctuation, which Yeats had never mastered, he once told his friend, ". . . you need ten years in a library, but I have need of ten years in the wilderness" (Au, 238).

Johnson was not Irish although he claimed that his family had once thought of themselves as Irish. He seems to have acquired at the time of his conversion to Catholicism a passionate devotion to Ireland—his only radicalism, as he called it. His learned orthodoxy enabled Yeats to demonstrate to the Irish clergy that the Irish literary revival was friendly to the church. Yeats, however, never liked those poems inspired by Johnson's patriotism. They reminded him too strongly of Thomas Davis and The Nation school.

Before Johnson's sudden, accidental death in 1902, he and Yeats had drifted apart. His excessive drinking whenever they met caused Yeats to feel himself morally implicated and thus Yeats avoided visiting him. Still, Johnson appears as an exemplar in the "tragic generation" in Yeats's autobiography and in the 1919 poem "In Memory of Major Robert Gregory."

While Yeats does not seem to have reviewed Johnson's 1895 volume of poems, he reviewed Ireland, with Other Poems (London: Elkin Mathews, 1897) in "Mr. Lionel Johnson's Poems" in The Bookman for February 1898. A poem in the 1895 collection had been dedicated to Yeats and several of the poems in the present collection were dedicated to distinguished people, among them Thomas Hardy, Edmund Gosse, George Santayana, E. K. Chambers, Louise Imogen Guiney, Roger Fry, Dr. Birkbeck Hill, and Will Rothenstein.

Arthur Hallam distinguishes in the opening of his essay[1] on Tennyson between what he calls 'the aesthetic school of poetry', founded by Keats and Shelley, and the various popular schools. 'The aesthetic school' is, he says, the work of men whose 'fine organs' have 'trembled with emotion, at colours and sounds and movements unperceived by duller temperaments',[2] 'a poetry of sensation rather than of reflection', 'a sort of magic producing a number of impressions too multiplied, too minute, and too diversified to allow of our tracing them to their causes, because just such was the effect, even so boundless and so bewildering, produced on their imaginations by the real appearance of nature.'[3] Because this school demands the most close attention from readers whose organs are less fine, it will always, he says, be unpopular compared to the schools that 'mix up'[4] with poetry all manner of anecdotes and opinions and moral maxims. This little known and profound essay defines more perfectly than any other criticism in English the issues in that war of schools which is troubling all the arts, and gradually teaching us to rank such 'reflections' of the mind as rhetorical and didactic verse, painted anecdotes, pictures 'complicated with ideas' that are not pictorial ideas, below poetry and painting that mirror the 'multiplied' and 'minute' and 'diversified' 'sensation' of the body and the soul. Mr. Johnson, like Wordsworth and Coleridge, has sometimes written in the manner of the 'popular schools,' and 'mixed up' with poetry religious and political opinions, and though such poetry has its uses everywhere, and in Ireland, for which Mr. Johnson has written many verses, and where opinion is still unformed, its great uses, one must leave it out when one measures the poetical importance of his poetry. I find poetry that is 'a sort of magic', in *Poems*, published in 1895, and in the present book, *Ireland* (Elkin Mathews), and the most unpopular 'sort of magic', for it mirrors a temperament so cold, so austere, so indifferent to our pains and pleasures, so wrapped up in one lonely and monotonous mood that one comes from it wearied and exalted, as though one had posed for some noble action, in a strange *tableau vivant*,[5] that casts its painful stillness upon the mind instead of upon the body. Had I not got Mr. Johnson's first book when I was far from books, I might have laid it down scarcely begun, I found the beginning so hard, and have lost much high pleasure, many fine exaltations; and though I have kept his new book as long as I could before reviewing it, I do not know if I admire the first book more merely because I have had longer to make its sensations my own sensations. In a poem that changes a didactic opinion to a sensation of the soul, Mr. Johnson sings the ideal of his imagination and his verse.

> White clouds embrace the dewy fields
>   Storms lingering mist and breath:
> And hottest heavens to hot earth yield
>   Drops from the fire of death.
>
> *Come!* sigh the shrouding airs of earth:
>   *Be with the burning night;*
> *Learn what her heart of flame is worth,*
>   *And eyes of glowing light.*
>
> I come not. Off, odorous airs!
>   Rose-scented winds, away!
> Let passion garnish her wild lairs,
>   Hold her fierce holiday.[6]
>
> I will not feel her dreamy toils
>   Glide over heart and eyes:
> My thoughts shall never be her spoils,
>   Nor grow sad memories.
>
> Mine be all proud and lonely scorn,
>   Keeping the crystal law
> And pure air of the eternal morn:
>   And passion, but of awe.

Poetry written out of this ideal can never be easy to read, and Mr. Johnson never forgets his ideal. He utters the sensations of souls too ascetic with a Christian asceticism to know strong passions, violent sensations, too stoical with a pagan stoicism to wholly lose themselves in any Christian ecstasy. He has made for himself a twilight world where all the colours are like the colours in the rainbow, that is cast by the moon, and all the people as far from modern tumults as the people upon fading and dropping tapestries. His delight is in 'the courtesy of saints', 'the courtesy of knights', 'the courtesy of love', in 'saints in golden vesture,' in the 'murmuring' of 'holy Latin immemorial', in 'black armour, falling lace, and altar lights at dawn', in 'rosaries blanched in Alban air', in all 'memorial melancholy' things.[7] He is the poet of those peaceful, unhappy souls who, in the symbolism of a living Irish visionary,[8] are compelled to inhabit when they die a shadowy island paradise in the West, where the moon always shines, and a mist is always on the face of the moon, and a music of many sighs always in the air, because they renounced the joy of the world without accepting the joy of God.

The poems, which are not pure poetry according to Arthur Hallam's definition, will, I think, have their uses in Catholic anthologies, and in those Irish papercovered books of more or less political poetry which are the only imaginative reading of so many young men in Ireland. 'Parnell', 'Ways of War', 'Ireland's Dead', 'The Red Wind',' 'Ireland', 'Christmas and Ireland', 'Ninety-Eight', 'To the Dead of '98', and 'Right and Might', even when they are not, as they are sometimes, sensations of the body and the soul, will become part of the ritual of that revolt of Celtic Ireland which is, according to one's point of view, the Celt's futile revolt against the despotism of fact[10] or his necessary revolt against a political and moral materialism. The very ignorance of literature, among their Irish readers, will make the formal nobility of their style seem the more impressive, the more miraculous.

MR. RHYS' *WELSH BALLADS*

As "Fiona Macleod," William Sharp's literary alter ego, proved valuable to Yeats by showing how the Celtic Movement had spread to Scotland, so Ernest Rhys supplied him with a Welsh ally for the movement. In "Four Years: 1887–1891," he remembers Rhys (1859–1946), whose Welsh Ballads *(London: David Nutt, 1898) he reviewed in* The Bookman *for April 1898, as "a writer of Welsh translations and original poems, that have often moved me greatly, though I can think of no one else who has read them." In the same passage he wrote, "Between us we founded* The Rhymers' Club. . . ." *(Au, 147). Aside from his work as a novelist, poet, autobiographer, and translator, Rhys was most famous as the longtime editor of* Everyman's Library. *During the nineties he was an editor of a series called the Camelot Classics and had helped to publish in that series some of Yeats's first anthologies of Irish fairy tales and fiction.*

The movement that found a typical expression in the consolations of *In Memoriam*, in the speculations of 'Locksley Hall', in the dialectics of 'Bishop Blougram's Apology', in the invective of *Les Châtiments*, and found its explanation when Matthew Arnold called art a criticism of life, has been followed by a movement that has found a typical expression in the contentment of *The Well at the World's End*, in the ecstasy of *Parsifal*, in the humility of *Aglavaine and Sélysette*[†], in the pride of *Axël*,[†] and might find its explanation in the saying of William Blake that art is a labour to bring again the golden age.[1] The old movement was scientific and sought to interpret the world, and the new movement is religious, and seeks to bring into the world dreams and passions, which the poet can but believe to have been born before the world, and for a longer day than the world's day. This movement has made painters and poets and musicians go to old legends for their subjects, for legends are the magical beryls in which we see life, not as it is, but as the heroic part of us, the part which desires always dreams and emotions greater than any in the world, and loves beauty and does not hate sorrow, hopes in secret that it may become. Because a great portion of the legends of Europe, and almost all of the legends associated with the scenery of these islands, are Celtic, this movement has given the Celtic countries a sudden importance, and awakened some of them to a sudden activity.

Wales, which gives us so much excellent scholarship, seems alone untouched by a propagandist fire, for since Lady Guest's *Mabinogion*,[1] she has given us little of her old literature, except prose translations from Taliesin and Davyth ap Gwilym and Lywarch Hen[2] and the like, by men so ignorant of any meaning in words finer than the dictionary meaning, that were it not for one or two delicate and musical translations in *The Study of Celtic Literature*,[3] Welsh poetry would not even be a great name to most of us; while unlike Ireland and Celtic Scotland, she has never made a new literature in English. Mr. Ernest Rhys' poems, with the exception of a few poems by Mr. Lionel Johnson,[4] which follow far less closely in the manner of the old Welsh poetry, are, so far as I know, the first Welsh poetry in the English language which is moving and beautiful. Mr. Rhys' book contains ten free translations from the Welsh, some dozen poems inspired by Welsh legends, and some eighteen or nineteen poems more or less inspired by Welsh scenery, and one translation from the Irish. The translations are particularly excellent, and make one look eagerly for the life of Davyth ap Gwilym, the greatest of the mediaeval Welsh poets, illustrated with translations, which he announces as in preparation, in his notes on 'The Poet of the Leaves'.[5] These stanzas from different parts of 'The Song of the Graves', a condensation of a poem of seventy-three (Mr. Rhys says seventy-two) stanzas in *The Black Book of Carmarthen*, are an example of his manner at its best.[6]

> In graves where drips the winter rain,
> Lie those that loved me most of men:
> Cerwyd, Cywrid, Caw, lie slain.
>
> In graves where the grass grows rank and tall,
> Lie, well avenged ere they did fall:
> Gwrien, Morien, Morial.
>
> In graves where drips the rain, the dead
> Lie, that not lightly bowed the head:
> Gwrien, Gwen, and Gwried.

Seithenin's lost mind sleeps by the shore,
'Twixt Cinran and the grey sea's roar;
Where Caer Cenedir starts up before.

In Abererch lies Rhyther' Hael,
Beneath the earth of Llan Morvael;
But Owain ab Urien in lonelier soil.

Mid the dreary moor, by the one oak tree,
The grave of stately Siawn may be;
Stately, treacherous, and bitter was he!

Mid the salt-sea-marsh where the tides have been,
Lie the sweet maid, Sanaw; the warrior Rhyn;
And Henin's daughter, the pale Earwyn.

And this may the grave of Gwythur be;
But who the world's great mystery,—
The grave of Arthur shall ever see?[7]

And so on, for the remembrance of Arthur is not the climax, but only a passing moment of a more unearthly sorrow in a dirge which must fade out with the same impassioned monotony in which it began. 'The Calends of Winter', in which Mr. Rhys has certainly improved his original by giving appropriateness to the moral saying which seems to have been added to each stanza by some mediaeval copyist without thought of the meaning of the stanza, is almost as fine; and 'The Song of the Wind', and 'The Lament of Lywarch Hen',[8] and 'The Lament for Cyndylan', and, indeed, all the translations are beautiful in their different ways. 'The House of Hendre',[†] which is inspired by some legend of a poet who saw in a vision the seven heavens, and Merlin and Arthur there,[9] and the heroes and the poets about them, and his own seat waiting, and so longed for death, the best of the original poems, has a melancholy, like that of curlews crying over some desolate marsh, which is partly in the words and partly in the very singular metre. The poems whose association with Wales is slighter, the mere link of the name of some Welsh village or mountain side at times, are much less successful. It is as though Mr. Rhys' imagination, which, like the imagination of a child, delights in a fanciful prettiness, needs the gravity of some old legend or old model before it can rise to a high argument. This fanciful prettiness, which, like all fanciful prettiness, is sometimes a little conventional, and an occasional indecision in the words and rhythm, is the defect of a temperament, which is shaping itself gradually, and with much labour, for beautiful expression.

THE BROKEN GATES OF DEATH

The third article of the folklore series based on materials collected by Lady Gregory was "The Broken Gates of Death," published in The Fortnightly Review, *April 1898. Most of this article appears to be Yeats's arrangement of Lady Gregory's materials, but the ending sounds distinctly like Yeats's own work. It seems curious that the first three articles of this more or less connected series appeared in three different periodicals. The fourth was to appear in still a fourth periodical—* The Contemporary Review—*but the fifth and sixth also appeared in* The Fortnightly Review.*

This third article aroused a touch of controversy. The magazine Outlook *of 16 April 1898 contained a paragraph which accused Yeats of being unable to separate his "dreams and poetic fancies from the realities" he had witnessed (quoted in CL2, 211). The writer doubted Yeats's facts, and said that Yeats's article was "the dream of a poetical folk-lorist" (CL2, 211). Presuming his adversary was a Catholic, Yeats promised him that if he read the remaining articles, "he will find that the Irish peasant has invented, or that somebody has invented for him, a vague though not altogether unphilosophical reconciliation between his Paganism and his Christianity" (CL2, 213). The article "Irish Witch Doctors" (September 1900) speaks briefly of such a reconciliation at the very beginning of the essay (see LAR, 26–27).*

––––––––––

The most of the Irish country people believe that only people who die of old age go straight to some distant Hell or Heaven or Purgatory. All who are young enough for any use, for begetting or mothering children, for dancing or hurling, or even for driving cattle, are taken, I have been told over and over again, by the 'others', as the country people call the fairies; and live, until they die a second time, in the green 'forts', the remnants of the houses of the old inhabitants of Ireland, or under the roots of hills, or in the woods, or in the deep of lakes. It is not wonderful, when one remembers this nearness of the dead to the living, that the country people should sometimes go on half-hoping for years, that their dead might walk in at the door, as ruddy and warm as ever, and live with them again. They keep their hopes half-living with many stories, but I think only half-living, for these stories begin mostly: 'There was an old man on the road', or 'There was one time a tailor', or in some like way; and not with the confident, 'There was a sister of Mick Morans, that is your own neighbour', or 'It happened to a young brother of my own', of the mere fairy tales. I once heard them called in the partly Elizabethan speech of Galway, 'Maybe all vanities', and have heard many sayings like this of a woman at Inchy,[1] 'Did I know anyone that was taken by them? Well, I never knew one that was brought back again'. Such stories have the pathos of many doubts. Numbers of those said to have been brought back, were children. A fisher woman among the Burren Hills says: 'There was an old man on the road one night near Burren, and he heard a cry in the air over his head, the cry of a child that was being carried away. And he called out some words, and the child was left down into his arms and he brought it home, and when he got there he was told that it was dead. So he brought in the live child, and you may be sure it was some sort of a thing that was good-for-nothing that was put in its place'.

And another woman among the Burren Hills says: 'There was one time a tailor, and was a wild card, always going to sprees. And one night he was passing by a house, and he heard a voice saying, "Who'll take the child". And he saw a little baby held out, and the hands that were holding it, but he could see no more than that. So he took it and he brought it to the next house, and asked the woman there to take it in for the night. Well, in the morning, the woman in the first house found a dead child in the bed beside her. And she was crying and wailing, and called all the people. And when the woman from the neighbouring house came, there in her arms was the child she thought was dead. But if it wasn't for the tailor that chanced to be passing by, and to take it, we may know well what would have happened to it'.

Sometimes a spell, like the spell of fire, even where used by accident, is thought to have brought the dead home, as in this tale, another Burren woman told a friend of mine:

'There was a man lived beyond on the Kinvara road, and his child died and he buried it. But he was passing the place after, and he'd asked a light for his pipe in some house, and after lighting it, he threw the sod, and it glowing, over the wall where he had buried the child. And what do you think, but it came back to him again, and he brought it to its mother. For they can't bear fire'.

Most of the stories are about women who are brought back by their husbands, but almost always against their will, because their will is under enchantment.

An old man at Lisadell, in county Sligo, who told me also a number of traditional[†] tales of the kind that are told generation after generation in the same words and in the same chanting voice, told me one tale, full of that courtesy between 'the others' and the living which endures through all the bitterness of their continuous battles.

His father had told him 'never to refuse a night's lodging to any poor travelling person', and one night 'a travelling woman' or beggar woman, told him that in her place, a woman died, and was taken by 'the gentry', and her husband often saw her after she was dead, and was afraid to speak to her. He told his brother, and his brother said he would come and speak to her, and he came, and at night lay on a settle at the foot of the bed. When she came in, he laid hold of her and would not let her go, although she begged him to let her go because 'she was nursing the child of the King'. Twelve messengers came in one after the other, and begged him to let her go, but he would not; and at last the King came himself, and said that she had been always well treated, and let come and nurse her own child, and that if she might stay until his child was weaned, he would send her home again, and leave, where they could find it, money to pay a debt of some forty pounds that 'was over' her husband. The man said, 'Do you promise this on your honour as a King'? and the King said, 'I do', and so the man let her go, and all happened as the King had promised.

They are brought back more violently in most of the stories, as in this story told to a friend of mine by a man at Coole:[†] 'And I'll tell you a thing I heard of in the country. There was a woman died and left her child. And every night at twelve o'clock she'd come back, and bring it out of the bed to the fire, and she'd comb it and wash it. And at last six men came and watched and stopped her at the door, and she went very near to tear them all asunder. But they got the priest, and he took it off her. Well, the husband had got another wife, and the priest came and asked him, "Would he put her away and take the first wife again"? And so he did, and brought her to the chapel to be married to her again, and the whole congregation saw her there'. When my friend asked if that was not rather hard on the second wife, he said: 'Well, but wasn't it a great thing for the first poor creature to be brought back. Sure there's many of those poor souls wandering about'.

Those who are brought back are sometimes thought to bring with them unholy knowledge. A woman at Kiltartan says: 'There's a man in Kildare that lost his wife. And it was known that she would come back at twelve o'clock every night to look at her baby. And it was told the husband that if he had twelve men with him with forks when she came in, they would be able to keep her from going out again. So the next night he was there and all his friends with forks, and when she came in they shut the door, and when she saw she could not get out, she sat down and was quiet. And one night as she sat by the hearth with them all, she said to her husband: "It's a strange thing that Leuchar would be sitting there so quiet with the bottom after bein' knocked out of his churn". And her husband went to Leuchar's house, and he found it was true as she had said. But after that he left her, and would not go back to her any more'.

Sometimes the women themselves tell how they are to be brought back, but they have sometimes to be seized and held before they will speak, as though a human touch broke the enchantment, as in this story told by a woman at Gort. 'There was a woman beyond at Rua died, and she came back one night, and her husband saw her at the dresser looking for something to eat. And she slipped away from him that time, but the next time she came he got hold of her, and she bid him come for her to the fair at Eserkelly, and watch for her at the Custom Gap, and she'd be on the last horse that would pass through. And then she said: "It's best for you not to come yourself, but send your brother". So the brother came, and she dropped down to him, and he brought her to the house. But in a week after he was dead and buried. And she lived a long time; and she never would speak three words to anyone that would come into the house, but working, working all the day. I wouldn't have liked to live in the house with her after her being away like that'.

I heard a story from a man at Donerail,[†] in county Cork, of a woman who bade a man go and look for her in a certain fort, and told him to hold her, even though she would struggle to escape, and scream out, either because the enchantment would have returned again, or because she would not have 'the others' think her willing to leave them. I have only heard one story of a woman who came back of her own will, and without the help of anybody. A woman at Kiltartan says: 'Mick Foley was here the other day telling us news,[†] and he told the strangest thing ever I heard that happened to his own first cousin. She died and was buried, and a year after, her husband was sitting by the fire, and she came back and walked in. He gave a start, for she said, "have no fear of me, I was never in the coffin and never buried, but I was kept away for the year". So he took her again, and they reared four children after that. She was Mick Foley's own first cousin, and he saw the four children himself'.

The dead body was but an appearance made by the enchantment of 'the others', according to the country faith.

If the country people sometimes doubt that those they have seen die can come and live with them as before, they never doubt that those they have seen die constantly visit them for a little while. A woman at Kiltartan says: 'It's well known that a mother that's taken from her child will come back to it at night, and that's why a light is kept burning all night for a good while after a woman dying that has left young children in the house'. And I have even been told that a mother always comes to her children; and because of the greater power of the dead, a dead mother is sometimes thought better than a living one.

Another woman at Kiltartan[2] says: 'Did the mother come to care them? Sure an' certain she did, an' I'm the one that can tell that. For I slept in the room with my sister's child after she dyin'—and as sure as I stand here talkin' to you, she was back in the room that night. An' a friend o' mine told me the same thing. His wife was taken away in childbirth, an' the five children she left that did be always ailin' an' sickly, from that day there never was a ha'porth ailed them'.

And another woman at Kiltartan[3] says: 'My own sister was taken away, she an' her husband within twenty-four hours, an' not a thing upon them, an' she with a baby a week old. Well, the care of that child fell upon me, an' sick or sorry it never was, but thrivin' always'.

Sometimes nothing but a chance is believed to prevent the dead being kept in the world for good. A woman at Sligo knew a Mayo man who was told to wait for his wife in a certain yard at night, and that she would come riding on a white horse, and would stay with him if he would snatch her from her horse, but the owner of the yard laughed at him and would not give him the key; while the terror of the husband did the mischief in a story told by an old man at Gortavena. 'There was a man and he a cousin of my own, lost his wife. And one night he heard her come into the room where he was in the bed with the child beside him. And he let on to be asleep, and she took the child and brought her out to the kitchen fire, and sat down beside it, and suckled it. And she put it back then into the bed again, and he lay still and said nothing. The second night she came again, and he had more courage and he said, "Why are you without your boots?" for he saw that her feet were bare. And she said, "Because there's nails in them". So he said, "Give them to me", and he got up and drew all the nails out of them, and she brought them away. The third night she came again, and when she was suckling the child, he saw she was still barefoot, and he asked why didn't she wear the boots? "Because", said she, "you left one sprig in them, between the upper and lower sole. But if you have courage", says she, "you can do more than that for me. Come to-morrow night to the gap up there beyond the hill, and you'll see the riders going through, and I'll be the one you'll see on the last horse. And bring with you some fowl droppings and urine, and throw them at me as I pass, and you'll get me again". Well, he got so far as to go to the gap and to bring what she told him, but when they came riding through the gap he saw her on the last horse, but his courage failed him, and he let what he had in his hand drop, and he never got the chance to see her again. Why she wanted the nails out of the boots! Because it's well known they will have nothing to do with iron. And I remember when every child would have an old horse-nail hung round its neck with a bit of string, but I don't see it done now'.

The mother comes sometimes out of hate of the second wife or the second wife's children. A man near Gort says: 'There was a little girl I knew, not five years of age, and whenever the second wife would bid her rock the cradle or do anything for her children, she'd just get as far as the bed, and lie down asleep. It was the mother put that on her, she wouldn't have her attending to the children of the second wife'.

A woman at Kiltartan says: 'There was a man had buried his wife, and she left three children; and when he took a second wife she did away with the children, hurried them off to America and the like. But the first wife used to be seen up in the loft, and she making a plan of revenge against the other wife. The second one had one son and three daughters. And one day the son was out digging in the field, and presently he went into what is called a fairy hole. And there a woman came before him, and says she, "What are you doing here, trespassing on my ground?" And with that she took a stone and hit him in the head, and he died with the blow of the stone she gave him. And all the people said, it was by the fairies he was taken'.

And a woman at Inchy says: 'There was a woman in Ballyderreen died after her baby being born. And the husband took another wife, and she very young, that everybody wondered she'd like to go into the house. And every night the first wife came in the loft, and looked down at her baby, and they couldn't see her, but they knew she was there by the child looking up and smiling at her. So at last someone said that if they'd go up in the loft after the cock crowing three times, they'd see her. And so they did, and there she was, with her own dress on, a plaid shawl she had brought from America, and a cotton skirt with some edging at the bottom. So they went to the priest, and he said Mass† in the house, and they didn't see so much of her after that. But after a year the new wife had a baby, and one day she bid the first child to rock the cradle. But when she sat down to do it, a sort of a sickness came over her, and she could do nothing, and the same thing always happened, for her mother didn't like to see her caring the second wife's baby. And one day the wife herself fell in the fire and got a great many burns, and they said that it was she did it. So they went to the blessed well of Tubber Macduagh; and they were told to go there every Friday for twelve weeks, and they said seven prayers and gathered seven stones every time. And since then she doesn't come to the house, but the little girl goes out and meets her mother at a fairy bush. And sometimes she speaks to her there, and sometimes in her dreams. But no one else but her own little girl has seen her of late'.[4]

People indeed come back for all kinds of purposes. I was told at Sligo about four years ago of a man who was being constantly beaten by a dead person. Sometimes it was said you could hear the blows as he came along the road, and sometimes he would be dragged out of bed at night and his wife would hear the blows, but you could never see anything. He had thought to escape the dead person by going to a distant place, Bundoran I think, but he had been followed there. Nobody seemed to give him any pity, for it was 'an old uncle of his own that was beating him'.

Sometimes people come back out of mere friendliness, though the sight of them is often an unwholesome sight to the living. A man on the coast opposite Aran,[†] in Western Galway, told a friend and me this tale as we were coming from a witch-doctor's. 'There was a boy going to America, and when he was going, he said to the girl next door, "Wherever I am when you're married, I'll come back to the wedding". And not long after he went to America he died. And when the girl was married and all the friends and neighbours in the house, he appeared in the room, but no one saw him but his comrade he used to have here; and the girl's brother saw him too, but no one else. And the comrade followed him and went close to him, and said, "Is it you indeed?" And he said, "It is, and from America I came to-night". And he asked how long did that journey take, and he said "three-quarters of an hour", and then he went away. And the comrade was never the better of it; either he got the touch, or the other called him, being such friends as they were, and soon he died. But the girl is now middle-aged, and is living in that house we're just after passing, and is married to one Bruen'.

Many and many are believed to come back to pay some debt, for, as a woman at Gort says: 'When some one goes that owes money, the weight of the soul is more than the weight of the body, and it can't get away till someone has courage to question it'.

A man who lives close to the witch-doctor says: 'There was a man had come back from Boston, and one day he was out in the bay, going to Aran[†] with £3 worth of cable he was after getting in M'Donough's store, in Galway. And he was steering the boat, and there were two turf boats along with him, and all in a minute the men in them saw he was gone, swept off the boat with a wave, and it a dead calm. And they saw him come up once, straight up as if he was pushed, and then he was brought down again and rose no more. And it was some time after that a friend of his in Boston, and that was coming home to this place, was in a crowd of people out there. And he saw him coming to him, and he said, "I heard you were drowned". And the man said, "I am not dead, but I was brought here, and when you go home bring these three guineas to Michael M'Donough, in Galway, for it's[†] owed him for the cable I got from him".[†] And he put the three guineas in his hand and vanished away'.

Only those the living retake in their continuous battle against 'the others', and those 'the others' permit to return for an hour, are thought to come in their own shape; but all the captives of 'the others', according to some tellers of tales, return in a strange shape at the end of their unearthly lives. I have been told about Gort that nobody is permitted to die among 'the others', but everybody, when the moment of their death is coming, is changed into the shape of some young person, who is taken in their stead, and put into the world to die, and to receive the sacraments.

A woman at Kiltartan says: 'When a person is taken, the body is taken as well as the spirit, and some good-for-nothing thing left in its place. What they take them for is to work for them and to do things they can't do themselves. You might notice it's always the good they take. That's why when we see a child that's good-for-nothing we say "Ah, you little fairy".'

A woman near Gort says: 'There was a woman with her husband passing by Eserkelly, and she had left her child at home. And a man came and called her in, and promised to leave her on the road where she was before. So she went, and there was a baby in the place where she was brought to, and they asked her to suckle it. And when she was come out again, she said, "One question I'll ask, what were those two old women sitting by the fire?" And the man said, "We took the child to-day and we'll have the mother to-night, and one of those will be out in her place, and the other in the place of some other person",[†] and then he left her where she was before. But there's no harm in them, no harm at all.'

She said 'there's no harm in them' because they might be listening to her.

Death among 'the others' seems not less grievous than among us, for another woman near Gort says: 'There was a woman going to Loughrea with a bundle of flannel on her head, was brought into the castle outside Roxborough[5] gate to give the breast to a child, and she saw an old woman beside the fire, and an old man behind the door, who had eyes red with crying. They were going to be put in the place of people who were to be taken that night. "The others" gave her a bottle, and when she'd put a drop of what was in it on her eyes, she'd see them hurling, or whatever they were doing. But they didn't like her to be seeing so much, and after a little time the sight of one of her eyes was taken away from her'.

A man who lives near Gort was coming home from a fair, 'And there were two men with him, and when three persons are together, there's no fear of anything, and they can say what they like'. One of the men pointed out a place they were passing: 'And it was a fairy place, and many strange things had happened there', and the other 'told him how there was a woman lived close by had a baby. And before it was a week old her husband had to leave her because of his brother having died. And no sooner was she left alone than she was taken, and they sent for the priest to say Mass in the house, but she was calling out every sort of thing they couldn't understand, and within a few days she was dead. And after death the body began to change, and first it looked like an old woman and then like an old man, and they had to bury it the next day. And before a week was over, she began to appear. They always appear when they leave a child like that. And surely she was taken to nurse the fairy children, just like poor Mrs. Gleeson was last year'.

And a woman from Kiltartan says: 'My sister told me that near Cloughballymore, there was a man walking home one night late, and he had to pass by a smiths' forge, where one Kenealy used to work. And when he came near he heard the noise of the anvil and he wondered Kenealy would be working so late in the night. But when he went in he saw they were strange men that were in it. So he asked them the time and they told him, and he said, "I won't be home this long time yet". And one of the men said, "You'll be home sooner than what you think", and another said, "There's a man on a grey horse gone the road, you'll get a lift from him". And he wondered that they'd know the road he was going to his own house. But sure enough, as he was walking, he came up with a man on a grey horse and he gave him a lift. But when he got home his wife saw he looked strange-like, and she asked what ailed him, and he told her all that had happened. And when she looked at him, she saw that he was taken. So he went into the bed, and the next evening he was dead. And all the people that came in knew by the appearance of the body that it was an old man that had been put in his place, and that he was taken when he got on the grey horse. For there's something not right about a grey or a white horse, or about a red-haired woman. And as to forges, there's some can hear working and hammering in them all the night'.

Forges and smiths have always been magical in Ireland. S. Patrick[†] prayed against the spells of women and smiths, and the old romances are loud with the doings of Goibniu,† the god of the smiths, who is remembered in folktale as the Mason Goban, for he works in stone as in metal.⁶

Another woman from Kiltartan says: 'Near Tyrone there was a girl went out one day to get nuts near the wood. And she heard music inside the wood, and when she went home she told her mother. But the next day she went again, and the next, and she stopped so long away that her mother sent the other little girl to look for her, but she could see no one. She came in after a while, and she went inside in to the room, but, when the girl came out, she said she heard nothing. But the next day after that she died. The neighbours all came in to the wake, and there was tobacco and snuff there, but not much, for it's the custom not to have so much when a young person dies. But when they looked at the bed, it was no young person in it, but an old woman with long teeth, that you'd be frightened, and the face wrinkled and the hands. So they didn't stop, but went away, and she was buried the next day. And in the night the mother could hear music all about the house, and lights of all colours flashing about the windows. She was never seen again, except by a boy that was working about the place; he met her one evening at the end of the house, dressed in her own clothes. But he couldn't question her where she was, for it's only when you meet them by a bush you can question them there. I'll gather more stories for you, and I'll tell them some time when the old woman isn't in the house, for she's that bigoted, she'd think she'd be carried off there and then'.

Tyrone is a little headland in the south of Galway Bay.

Sometimes the 'old person' lives a good time in the likeness of the person who has been taken, as in this tale, told by a woman at Ardra-han:⁷ 'My mother told me that when she was a young girl, and before the time of side-cars, a man that lived in Duras married a girl from Ardrahan side. And it was the custom then, for a newly-married girl to ride home on a horse behind her next of kin. And she was on the pillion behind her uncle. And when they passed Ardrahan churchyard, he felt her to shiver and nearly to slip off the horse. And he put his hand behind for to support her, and all he could feel was like a piece of tow. And he asked her what ailed her, and she said she thought of her mother when she was passing the churchyard. And a year after her baby was born, and then she died. And everyone said, the night she was taken was her wedding night'.

An old woman in the Burren Hills says: 'Surely there are many taken. My own sister that lived in the house beyond, and her husband and her three children, all in one year. Strong they were, and handsome and good and best, and that's the sort that are taken. They got in the priest when first it came on the husband, and soon after a fine cow died, and a calf. But he didn't begrudge that if he'd get his health, but it didn't save him after. Sure Father Leraghty said, not long ago in the chapel, that no one had gone to heaven for the last ten years.

'But whatever life God has granted them, when it's at an end, go they must, whether they're among them or not. And they'd sooner be among them than go to Purgatory.

'There was a little one of my own taken. Till he was a year old, he was the stoutest and the best, and the finest of all my children, and then he began to pine, till he wasn't thicker than a straw, but he lived for about four years. How did it come on him? I know that well. He was the grandest ever you saw, and I proud of him, and I brought him to a ball in this house, and he was able to drink punch. And soon after I stopped one day at a house beyond, and a neighbouring woman came in with her child, and she says: "If he's not the stoutest, he's the longest". And she took off her apron and the string of it to measure them both. I had no right to let her do that, but I thought no harm of it at the time. But it was that night he began to screech, and from that time he did no good. He'd get stronger through the winter, but about the Pentecost, in the month of May, he'd always fall back again, for at that time they're at the worst. I didn't have the priest in, it does them no good but harm, to have a priest take notice of them when they're like that. It was in the month of May, at the Pentecost,[8] he went at last. He was always pining, but I didn't think he'd go so soon. At the end of the bed he was lying with the other children, and he called to me and put up his arms. But I didn't want to take too much notice of him, or to have him always after me, so I only put down my foot to where he was. And he began to pick straws out of the bed, and to throw them over the little sister that was beside him till he had thrown as much as would thatch a goose. And when I got up, there he was, dead, and the little sister asleep, and all covered with straws'.

She believed him to fall under the power of 'the others,' because of the envy of the woman who measured him, for 'the others' can only take their prey through 'the eye of a sinner'. She dwelt upon his getting worse, and at last dying, in May, because 'the others' are believed to come and go a great deal in May.

Sometimes 'the old person' is recognised by the living, as in this tale told by another woman in the Burren Hills: 'There were three women living at Ballindeereen:[9] Mary Flaherty, the mother, and Mary Grady, the daughter, and Ellen Grady, that was a by-child of hers. And they had a little dog, called Floss, that was like a child to them. And the grandmother went first, and then the little dog, and then Mary Grady, within a half-year. And there was a boy wanted to marry Ellen Grady that was left alone. But his father and mother wouldn't have her, because of her being a by-child. And the priest wouldn't marry them not to give the father and mother offence. So it wasn't long before she was taken too, and those that saw her after death knew it was the mother that was there in place of her. And when the priest was called the day before she died, he said, "She's gone since twelve o'clock this morning, and she'll die between the two masses to-morrow". For he was Father Hynes that had understanding of these things. And so she did'.

Sometimes 'the old person' is said to melt away before burial. A woman near Cork[10] says: 'There were two brothers, Mullallys, in Ballaneen. And when one got home one night and got into the bed, he found the brother cold and dead before him. And not a ha'porth on him when he went out. Taken by them he surely was. And when he was being buried in Kiltartan, the brother looked into the coffin, finding it so light, and there was nothing in it but the clothes that were around him. Sure if he'd been a year in the grave he couldn't have melted away like that'.

A woman from Kiltartan says: 'There was a girl buried in Kiltartan, one of the Joyces, and when she was laid out on the bed, a woman that went in to look at her saw that she opened her eyes, and made a sort of face at her. But she said nothing but sat down by the hearth. But another woman came in after that and the same thing happened, and she told the mother, and she began to cry and roar that they'd say such a thing of her poor little girl. But it wasn't the little girl that was in it at all, but some old person. And the man that nailed down the coffin left the nails loose, and when they came to Kiltartan churchyard he looked in, and not one they saw inside it but the sheet and a bundle of shavings'.

'The others' sometimes it seems take this shape; a woman in the Burren Hills tells of their passing her in the shape of shavings driven by the wind. She knew they were not really shavings, because there was no place for shavings to come from.

Even when cattle are taken, something or someone is put in their place. A man at Donerail[†] told me a story of a man who had a bullock that got sick, and that it might be of some use, he killed it and skinned it, and when it was in a trough being washed it got up and ran away. He ran after it and knocked it down and cut it up, and after he and his family had eaten it, a woman, that was passing by said: 'You don't know what you have eaten. It is your own grandmother that you have eaten'.

A man in the Burren Hills, says: 'When anyone is taken something is put in his place, even when a cow or the like goes. There was one of the Nestors used to be going about the country skinning cattle, and killing them, even for the country people, if they were sick. One day he was skinning a cow that was after dying by the roadside, and another man with him. And Nestor said, "It's a pity we couldn't sell the meat to some butcher, we might get something for it". But the other man made a ring of his fingers, like this, and looked through it, and then bade Nestor to look, and what he saw was an old piper that had died some time before, and when he thought he was skinning the cow, what he was doing was cutting the leather breeches off the piper. So it's very dangerous to eat beef you buy from any of those sort of common butchers. You don't know what might have been put in its place'.

And sometimes cattle are put in the place of men and women, and Mrs. Sheridan, a handsome old woman who believes herself to have been among 'the others', and to have suckled their children, tells many stories of the kind; she says: 'There was a woman, Mrs. Keevan, killed near the big tree at Raheen, and her husband was after that with Biddy Early, and she said it was not the woman that died at all, but a cow that died and was put in her place'.

Biddy Early was a famous wise woman,[11] and the big tree at Raheen is a great elm tree where many mischiefs and some good fortunes have happened to many people. Few know as much as Mrs. Sheridan about 'the others', and if she were minded to tell her knowledge and use the cure they have given her for all the mischiefs they work, she would be a famous wise woman herself, and be sought out, perhaps, by pilgrims from neighbouring counties. She is, however, silent, and it was only when we had won her confidence, that she came of herself, with some fear of the anger of 'the others', and told a friend and myself certain of the marvels she had seen. She had hitherto but told us tales that other people had told her, but now she began:

'One time when I was living at Cloughauish, there were two little boys drowned in the river there. One was eight years and the other eleven years. And I was out in the fields and the people looking in the river for their bodies, and I saw a man coming over the fields and the two little boys with him, he holding a hand of each and leading them away. And he saw me stop and look at them, and he said: "Take care, would you bring them from me (for he knew I had power to do it), for you have only one in your house, and if you take these from me, she'll never go home to you again". And one of the boys broke from his hand and came running to me, but the other cried out to him, "O Pat, will you leave me!" So then he went back, and the man led them away. And then I saw another man, very tall he was, and crooked, and watching me like this, with head down; and he was leading two dogs, and I knew well where he was going and what he was going to do with the dogs. And when I heard the bodies were laid out, I went to the house to have a look at them, and those were never the two boys that were lying there, but the two dogs that were put in their place. I knew them by a sort of stripes on the bodies, such as you'd see on the covering of a mattress. And I knew the boys couldn't be in it, after me seeing them led. And it was at that time I lost my eye, something came on it, and I never got the sight of it again'.

'The others' are often described as having striped clothes like the striped hair of the dogs.

The stories of the country people, about men and women taken by 'the others', throw a clear light on many things in the old Celtic poems and romances, and when more stories have been collected and compared, we shall probably alter certain of our theories about the Celtic mythology. The old Celtic poets and romance writers had beautiful symbols and comparisons that have passed away, but they wrote of the same things that the country men and country women talk of about the fire,— the country man or country woman who falls into a swoon, and sees in a swoon a wiser and stronger people than the people of the world, but goes with less of beautiful circumstance upon the same journey Etain went when she passed with Midher into the enchanted hills; and Oisin when he rode with Niamh[†] on her white horse over the sea; and Conla when he sailed with a divine woman in a ship of glass to "the ever-living, living ones"; and Cuchulain[†] when he sailed in a ship of bronze to a divine woman; and Bran, the son of Feval, when a spirit came through the closed door of his house holding an apple-bough of silver, and called him to 'the white-silver plain'; and Cormac, the son of Art, when his house faded into mist, and a great plain, and a great house, and a tall man, and a crowned woman, and many marvels came in its stead.[12] And when the country men and country women tell of people taken by 'the others', who come into the world again, they tell the same tales the old Celtic poets and romance writers told when they made the companions of Finn[†] compel, with threats, the goddess Miluchra to deliver Finn[†] out of the Grey Lake on the Mountain of Fuad; and when they made Cormac, the son of Art, get his wife and children again from Manannan,[†] the son of Lir; and, perhaps, when they made Oisin sit with Patrick[†] and his clergy and tell of his life among the gods, and of the goddess he had loved.[13]

LE MOUVEMENT CELTIQUE:
FIONA MACLEOD

This article echoes Yeats's earlier sentiments about Fiona Macleod which appeared in his Sketch *review of 28 April 1897. His articles on the Celtic Movement, the kind of term from which he later distanced himself (see "Irish Language and Irish Literature" (LAR, 50) appeared in April 1898 in* L'Irlande Libre, *which, as the* "Organe de la colonie irlandaise à Paris," *was the principal means of propaganda for Maud Gonne's* Association Irlandaise. *Although Yeats joined the organization shortly after its founding in 1896, two essays, "Le Mouvement Celtique: Fiona Macleod" (1 April 1898) and "Le Mouvement Celtique II: M. John O'Leary" (1 June 1898, also included in this collection), translated into French by an unknown hand, were his only contributions to the paper.*

Je base ma foi en l'influence prochaine des races celtiques dans la littérature, principalement sur les innombrables légendes encore enfouies dans de vieux manuscrits irlandais, comme aussi sur les traductions peu connues et les traditions populaires.

La littérature se renouvelle sans cesse au moyen des légendes et par le souvenir que celles-ci conservent de la manière dont ont pensé et imaginé des races plus passionnées que nos races modernes.

De ces antiques races, la mine féconde des légendes slaves et finlandaises est loin d'être aussi riche que le foyer celtique: Wagner, Morris et leur précurseur Ibsen ont fait main base sur les fables scandinaves, qu'ils se sont appropriées; de même, les fables grecques et latines ont été mises au pillage par des centaines de générations.[1]

Les antiques légendes celtiques sont à la fois originales et d'une beauté extraordinaire. Il se peut qu'elles aient encore sur la littérature une influence aussi grande qu'ont eu celles du pays de Galles, aux douzième et treizième siècles.

Leur traduction et leur mise en lumière absorbent la pensée de beaucoup d'érudits, tels que: Herr Windisch,[†] en Allemagne; M. de Jubainville[†] en France; les professeurs Nutt[†] et Rhys, en Angleterre; le docteur Hyde et M. Hayes[†] O'Grady, en Irlande; dans le même temps que, pour fonder la nouvelle littérature romantique, M. Standish O'Grady, Miss Hopper,[†] MM. Hinkson,[2] et enfin Miss Fiona Macleod, ont commencé à utiliser les dites légendes. En d'autres pays encore d'autres écrivains vont, je crois, se mettre aussi à l'oeuvre et alors, peut-être quelque littérateur étranger, quelque Wagner ou Morris, donnera-t-il à ce réveil enivrant sa forme parfaite et définitive.

Miss Fiona Macleod est le nom le plus intimement lié à ce mouvement, à cette renaissance celtique, comme disent les journaux. Ses contes, puisés tantôt dans les écrivains irlandais, tantôt parmi d'autres vieux auteurs qu'on appelle les Irlandais-Ecossais (population des îles à l'ouest de l'Ecosse, au milieu de laquelle elle est née), ses contes, dis-je, renferment l'âme même du peuple.

Je fus grandement désappointé par ses premières oeuvres: *Pharaïs* et le *Vaurien de la Montagne,*[3] il me semblait qu'elle n'y tenait aucunes des promesses qu'on attendait de son jeune talent. On y trouvait une continuelle véhémence, une monotonie de passion, une prolixité de langage qui me déplurent. Il me semblait entendre un de nos incultes paysans politiques irlandais déversant en phrases confuses ses interminables lamentations, et je me dis: 'Voici un esprit qui court à sa perte, faute de mesure'. Je ne fus vraiment conquis qu'après avoir lu quelques-unes de ces courtes nouvelles dénommées: *Contes Spirituels, Contes Barbares* et *Romans Tragiques* que j'emportai avec moi dans l'île méridionale d'Aran,[†4] où vivent les plus primitifs et les plus simples des paysans irlandais.

Alors je jugeai Miss Macleod en pleine possession de son art,—un art où désormais régnait la mesure. Bien plus! je reconnus que les personnages de ses contes étaient ceux-là mêmes qui m'entouraient. Après avoir fermé le livre, il m'arrive de conserver les croyances et les légendes dont parlent ces histoires, la foi en des êtres qui furent des phoques avant de devenir des hommes, des esprits qui se meuvent autour de nous, des grands saints et des héros qui sont plus 'vivants' dans l'esprit de ce peuple que ne le sont les hommes publics dont il est question dans les journaux. Il m'apparut que Miss Macleod avait sur le monde exactement les mêmes instincts que ces graves paysans avec lesquels je m'entretenais; qu'elle était devenue comme leur propre voix, non par une étude plus approfondie de leurs saveurs, mais par suite d'une identité de nature.

Dans ces courtes nouvelles, elle ne reproduit pas littéralement les vieilles légendes; elle compose, d'après les mêmes croyances populaires, des contes nouveaux qu'elle fait ressortir de ce fonds commun, comme d'une forêt fantastique, mystérieusement hantée. Mais son dernier ouvrage 'The Laughter of Peterkin',[†] reproduit assez fidèlement les légendes les plus fameuses de la vieille Irlande, et cette reproduction est la meilleure de toutes celles que notre 'mouvement' a produites.

Ce livre ne peut manquer d'aider à l'union de sentiments que nous souhaitons créer entre les Celtes irlandais et écossais, en leur rappelant tout à la fois leurs origines semblables et ces trésors d'héroïques légendes.

Une communauté de sentiments, non seulement entre ces deux peuples, mais encore avec les Celtes gallois, sera peut-être l'un des résultats décisifs du 'Mouvement Celtique', et bien des événements sociaux, politiques, aussi bien que littéraires, en peuvent dériver.

AE'S[†] POEMS

Yeats's review, in The Sketch *of 6 April 1898, of the book* The Earth
Breath and Other Poems *(London and New York: Lane/The Bodley
Head, 1897) was accompanied by a small self-portrait sketch by AE.
Although Yeats's statement in the review that "... without a convention, there is, perhaps, no perfect spiritual art" was here applied only
to AE's paintings, we know from Yeats's autobiography that he had
much the same statement to make about AE's poetry. Yeats wanted him
to submit his visions to the questions of the intellect and he was impatient that AE seemed unable or unwilling to distinguish between his
visions and reality. AE, in his turn, thought that Yeats's theory of the
masks was the attempt of a style to create a personality and hence a
reversal of the natural order. In a letter to George Moore, AE said of
Yeats's artistically created personality, "The error in his psychology is
that life creates the form, but he seems to think that the form creates
life" (Letters from AE, ed. Alan Denson [London: Abelard-Schuman,
1961], p. 110). Both men admired each other and quarreled with the
special privilege of old friends.* The Earth Breath *was dedicated to Yeats.*

Upon the walls of a certain lecture-room in Dublin,[1] where men who
are themselves visionaries lectured until lately upon Indian and Neoplatonic[2] and Christian visionaries, AE.[†] has painted some very fantastic
pictures: a young man looking at his own image in the scales of a serpent; a vast stone figure sitting on a mountain with a devotee prostrating
his body in adoration before it, while his soul rises up threatening it
with a spear; a man huddled up in darkness while his soul rushes out
and grasps a star; a company of little figures moving among mushrooms
and long grasses: picture everywhere melting into picture. They are the
work of a hand too bewildered by the multitudinous shapes and
colours of visions to narrow its method to a convention, and, without
a convention, there is, perhaps, no perfect spiritual art. It has sought

unavailingly, despite much talent, to make of unmoving and silent paint a mirror for the wandering, exultant processions that haunt those margins of spiritual ecstasy, where colours are sounds, and sounds are shapes, and shapes are fragrances. The poems of AE,[†] the little paper-covered book published by a friend who hired a garret for that purpose, and this larger book, *The Earth Breath,* published by Mr. John Lane,[3] are a more perfect mirror, because poetry changes with the changing of the dream. All things in these elaborate and subtle verses are perpetually changing, and all things are the symbols of things more unsubstantial than themselves. The poet looks at the heavens, and they become a great bird with a blue breast and wings of gold, and at the wood, and it becomes a great sheep shaking its shadowy fleece, and then bird and sheep become, through some vague wisdom floating in the rhythm and in the colour of the words, moments of the divine tenderness. A bird with diamond wings passes through his imagination, and he knows it a soul wandering from its body in a deep sleep;[4] and when he thinks of the girdle of twilight eyes in the moon may see about the earth, where day and night mingle, he thinks of beauty hung between death and life, eternity and time, sleep and waking.[5] He would bring before his eyes the eternal house of the soul, and calls up a burning diamond, and, while he watches it, it has changed, as in the changes of a hashish dream, to islands fringed with flames.[6] All things that have shape and weight change perpetually, being, indeed, but symbols. 'For every star and every deep' filled with stars 'are stars and deeps within'.[7] It is the doctrine of all mystics, the doctrine that awakened Plotinus to his lonely and abstract joy. 'In the particular acts of human life', he wrote, 'it is not the interior soul and the true man, but the exterior shadow of the man alone, which laments and weeps, performing his part on the earth as in a more ample and extended scene, in which many shadows of souls and phantom forms appear'.[8] Even when we are in love, AE.[†] would have us love the invisible beauty before the visible beauty and make our love a dream.

> Let me dream only with my heart,
>   Love first, and after see;
> Know thy diviner counterpart
>   Before I kneel to thee.
>
> So in thy motions all expressed
>   Thy angel I may view;
> I shall not on thy beauty rest,
>   But beauty's ray[9] in you,

he writes in verses that have a Jacobean music, and a nobility of thought that is not Jacobean.[10] He would have our love, too, end as well as begin in the invisible beauty, and in another poem sings to the visible beauty of the woman—

> O beauty, as thy heart o'erflows
> In tender yielding unto me,
> A vast desire awakes and grows
> Unto forgetfulness of thee.[11]

It is this invisible beauty that all life seeks under many names, and that makes the planets 'break in woods and flowers and streams', and 'shake' the winds from them 'as the leaves from off the rose', and that 'kindles' all souls and lures them 'through the gates of birth and death', and in whose heart we will all rest when 'the shepherd of the ages draws his misty hands away through the glimmering deeps to silence' and 'the awful fold'.[12] It kindles evil as well as good, for it awakens 'the fount of shadowy beauty' that pours out those 'things the heart would be' and 'chases' 'in the endless night'.[13] All things are double, for we either choose 'the shadowy beauty', and our soul weeps, or the invisible beauty that is our own 'high ancestral self',[14] and the body weeps. Many verses in this little book have so much high thought and they sing it so sweetly and tenderly that I cannot but think them immortal verses.

LE MOUVEMENT CELTIQUE: II.
M. JOHN O'LEARY

The first section of "Le Mouvement Celtique" (see pp. 407–9 above) was an original essay which borrowed little from an earlier review of Fiona Macleod's prose. The second part, however, "M. John O'Leary," which appeared in L'Irlande Libre *on 1 June 1898, is, with the exception of the two introductory paragraphs, a direct translation of most of the first paragraph of Yeats's review of* Recollections of Fenians and Fenianism, *which had appeared in* The Bookman *for February 1897 (see pp. 329–31 above).*

M. John O'Leary est aujourd'hui président du Conseil central exécutif de l'organisation qui se prépare à célébrer la révolte de 1798, et, il y a dix ou douze ans, il eut une influence prédominante sur les débuts de ce mouvement littéraire irlandais qui, maintenant qu'il a rencontré comme alliés les mouvements écossais et gallois, est devenu le mouvement celtique. De jeunes nationalistes qu'éloignait le mouvement utilitaire de Parnell: M. Rolleston, l'editeur de la *Revue de l'Université*, qui fut de courte durée, et ou furent publiés tant d'écrits de notre nouvelle école; Miss Katharine† Tynan, qui venait à peine de publier son premier volume de poésie lyrique; le docteur Douglas Hyde, lequel n'avait pas encore commencé à publier les ouvrages qui ont fait de lui le plus fameux de nos savants gaéliques,[1] et d'autres, qui ont plus ou moins de notoriété, apprenaient chez lui à se comprendre et à connaître leurs communes aspirations.

Les qualités mêmes qui ont empêché M. O'Leary d'être un véritable homme d'action, l'ont rendu propre à exercer une influence sur ces mouvements de pensée et de sentiment qui sont les sources de l'action.

Je me souviens d'une conversation que j'eus, il y a une couple d'années, avec mon voisin de table, à un souper en l'honneur, je crois de Thomas Davis: 'Nos hommes publics, me disait-il, à l'exception de John O'Leary, ont eu peur de différer du peuple en quoi que ce soit; aussi pas un, à part John O'Leary, ne nous inspire-t-il le moindre respect'.[2] Cet homme était, si nos souvenirs sont exacts, commis dans un grand magasin, et c'était le type de la jeune génération de Dublin. Il avait probablement donné son adhésion pour les choses pratiques à quelque leader qui avait plus d'éloquence ou qui s'attachait avec plus de force aux questions du moment, mais il ne lui avait donné son adhésion que pour les choses pratiques. D'aussi loin qu'il pouvait se souvenir, M. John O'Leary avait dénoncé tel ou tel expédient politique, tel ou tel leader populaire, et affirmé que, l'humanité étant supérieure aux nations, il y a des choses qu'un homme ne doit pas faire, peut-être même pour sauver une nation.

Si cela eût été dit par quelqu'un qui n'eût pas souffert comme M. John O'Leary des années d'emprisonnement et d'exil, mon voisin n'y eût pas prêté l'oreille; mais, les choses étant comme elles étaient, M. John O'Leary représentait à son imagination la conscience nationale. Il y en a quantité d'autres, aurait-il dit peut-être, qui pourraient nous donner un meilleur avis sur la question de savoir si une chose est utile ou ne l'est pas, mais il n'y a que M. John O'Leary pour dire si cela est juste ou injuste, et pour le dire, non seulement à la tranquille lumière de votre foyer, mais, s'il est nécessaire, dehors, sur la voie publique, devant une foule furieuse. Il m'avait toujours semblé que sa passion pour la justice abstraite est la passion celtique pour les idées, intensifiée par la défiance à l'égard des expédients qui viennent aux hommes dont les espérances ont été maintes fois déçues, et que les Irlandais, hommes et femmes, à mesure qu'ils deviennent instruits, doivent hériter d'une pareille passion, sinon à un degré pareil. Certainement, les jeunes gens que j'ai rencontrés dans les sociétés de la 'Jeune Irlande' dans les sociétés littéraires irlandaises et dans les écoles d'art irlandaises, lui ressemblent plus qu'ils ne ressemblent à cet Irlandais aux lèvres mobiles, prompt à l'émotion et à la sympathie, impressionnable, qu'est le seul Irlandais dont quelques Anglais aient jamais entendu parler.

La cruauté même du journalisme irlandais et de la politique irlandaise vient d'une tendance à juger les hommes, non les uns par les autres, non par l'expérience du degré de supériorité qu'on peut espérer rencontrer dans la vie et dans la politique, mais par quelque étalon abstrait.

CELTIC BELIEFS
ABOUT THE SOUL

Yeats's article "Celtic Beliefs About the Soul" in The Bookman *for September 1898 was a review of* The Voyage of Bran *(London: D. Nutt, 1895, 1897), edited by Kuno Meyer and Alfred Nutt. Meyer's translation of the early Irish saga furnished the title for both volumes of this work although it served only as an example for Nutt's long essay. More than half of the first volume was devoted to the first part of the essay, "The Happy Otherworld," and almost all of the second volume to the other part, "The Celtic Doctrine of Rebirth."*

Alfred T. Nutt (1856–1910), editor of the Folk-lore Journal *and manager of his father's, David Nutt's, publishing firm, had been a useful irritant to Yeats on the subject of folklore. In 1888 Yeats did some copying work for the Nutt firm in the Bodleian Library and in the British Museum. Although Nutt specialized in the publication of folklore, none of Yeats's work was published by his company. On the occasion of a bad review of Lady Wilde's* Ancient Cures, Charms and Usages of Ireland *in* The Academy *of 1890, Yeats wrote a letter to this journal defending the more imaginative retelling of folktales in contrast to the scientific approach, typified for Yeats by Nutt's* Folk-lore *Journal (CL1, 229). In his reply, Nutt reminded Yeats that he had borrowed a tale from the* Folk-lore *Journal for his* Fairy and Folk Tales of the Irish Peasantry.*

Nutt had published Douglas Hyde's translation of Gaelic folktales Beside the Fire *in 1890, and in Yeats's review of this book for* The National Observer, *28 February 1891 (see "Irish Folk Tales," pp. 124–27 above), he complained that Hyde was too much a scholar and too little an artist to finish fragmentary folktales. Yeats asked, "Is it the evil communications of that very scientific person, Mr. Alfred Nutt (he contributes learned notes), which have robbed us of the latter page of 'Guleesh na Guss Dhu'?"*

Nutt's assertion in his essay of the striking similarities in Greek and Irish primitive folklore and religion added to Yeats's conviction that

Ireland was entering a literary golden age to match that of Greece. Once out of its epic stage, Ireland would soon enter the next stage according to the tripartite development set forth in 1893 in Yeats's lecture on "Nationality and Literature" (UP1, 266–75) and this stage would be its dramatic age. That Yeats intended Ireland to rival the Attic stage is stated explicitly in two essays gathered in Ideas of Good and Evil: *"Ireland and the Arts" and "The Galway Plains." As Greek drama originated in the cult of Dionysus, so Irish drama would be based upon legends of the Tuatha dé Danaan still current among the peasants.*

Celtic legends are, according to certain scholars, our principal way to an understanding of the beliefs out of which the beliefs of the Greeks and other European races arose. Mr. Nutt has written a masterly book upon the most important of all old beliefs—the beliefs about the destiny of the soul and the light Celtic legends have thrown upon it. His book is indeed so masterly that I have no doubt that D'Arbois de Jubainville's[†] *Mythologie Irlandais,* Professor Rhys' *Celtic Heathendom,*[1] and it are the three books without which there is no understanding of Celtic legends. Mr. Nutt published the first volume in 1895 as a commentary on *The Voyage of Bran,* an old Celtic poem translated and annotated by Kuno Meyer for the purpose; and described with much detail 'the happy other world' in Celtic and Greek and Anglo-Saxon and Jewish and Scandinavian and Indian literature.[2] He showed 'that Greek and Irish alone have preserved the early stages of the happy other world conception with any fulness',[3] and that Ireland has preserved them 'with greater fulness and precision' than the Greeks. He describes in *The Voyage of Bran,* vol. 2, the Celtic and Greek doctrine of the rebirth of the soul, of its coming out of the happy other world of the dead, and living once more, and of its power of changing its shape as it desires. By comparing the Greek cult of Dionysus[†] and the Irish cult of the fairies, he concludes that its rebirth and its many changes are because 'the happy other world' is the country of the powers of life and increase, of the powers that can never lay aside the flame-like variability of life. He describes the old orgiac[†] dances, in which the worshippers of the powers of life and increase believed themselves to take the shapes of gods and divine beasts, and first, he thinks, imagined 'the happy other world', in which their momentary and artificial ecstasy was a continual and natural ecstasy. If the fairy legends of the Irish peasants were better collected, he would have even more copious evidence to prove the association of continual change and of the continual making of new things with the inhabitants of the other world, with the dead as well as with the fairies. I have been often told that 'the fairies' change their shapes and colours every moment, and that they can build their houses in a moment and that they can make the fields fruitful and make the milk abundant, and that they can make food or money out of cow dung, and change apples into eggs, or anything into any other thing; and all that is told of the fairies is told of the dead who are among them. The traditional explanation of the battle fought by the fairies in autumn for the harvest is probably less allegorical and less simple than Mr. Nutt's, who explains it as a battle between the powers of life and increase against the powers of death and decay. The peasants are very positive—I have given their words in the January *Nineteenth Century*[4]— that a bad harvest with us is a good harvest among the fairies, and the analogy of a battle fought about the dying makes one inclined to believe that the battle is between the guardians of the living who would leave the harvest for the living, and the fairies and the dead who would take the harvest for themselves. The main argument of Mr. Nutt's book is the argument of Mr. Frazer's *Golden Bough*[5] applied to Celtic legends and belief, and being itself a deduction from peasant custom and belief, and not, like the solar myth theory,[6] from the mythology of cultivated races, it must look always for the bulk of its proofs and illustrations to peasant custom and belief. Mr. Nutt seems to imply in a footnote[7] that the solar myth mythology is a later development and is based upon the harvest mythology, and this shows an accommodating spirit not to be found in Mr. Lang[8] and Mr. Frazer. Mr. Nutt is indeed so tolerant that I am filled with wonder when I find him writing, like other folklorists, as if you had necessarily discovered the cause of a thing when you had discovered its history. Man may have first perceived 'the happy other world' in the orgiac[†] dance or in some other ecstasy, but to show that he has done so, though important and interesting, is not to make a point in the great argument about the mystery of man's origin and destiny.

JOHN EGLINTON
AND SPIRITUAL ART

In late October 1898, Yeats and his friends undertook a public controversy designed, as Yeats noted in a letter to Lady Gregory, to "keep people awake until we announce The Irish Literary Theatre in December . . ." (CL2, 287). The initial points at issue were John Eglinton's rejection of ancient Irish myth and saga as subjects for an Irish national school of drama and Yeats's affirmation of them. Yeats's hope of expanding the discussion "into a discussion of the spiritual origin of the arts" (287) was realized in a second round of essays in which Eglinton supported a philosophical view of poetry, exemplified by Wordsworth—in opposition to such aesthetic models as Keats, the early Tennyson, and the French symbolists—and Yeats's rejection of Arnold's view of poetry as a criticism of life.

The exchange began with John Eglinton's "What Should Be the Subjects of a National Drama?" in the 18 September 1898 issue of The Dublin Daily Express, *a paper that usually carried a number of literary articles each Saturday. Yeats partially answered Eglinton in "The Poems and Stories of Miss Nora Hopper" on 24 September 1898 (P&I, 116–17). Although only the postscript of this article dealt directly with Eglinton, Yeats probably meant his introductory remarks for him as well. Eglinton's reply in* The Daily Express *of 8 October 1898, "National Drama and Contemporary Life," provoked the present essay, Yeats's "Mr. John Eglinton and Spiritual Art," in* The Daily Express *of 28 October 1898. Eglinton's next salvo was "Mr. Yeats and Popular Poetry," on 19 November 1898. AE joined the controversy on 12 November 1898 with "Literary Ideals in Ireland." William Larminie entered the lists with "Legends as Materials for Literature" on 19 November 1898.*

Yeats's final contribution was "The Autumn of the Flesh," on 3 December 1898, which he reprinted as "The Autumn of the Body" in Ideas of Good and Evil *(London, 1903). The controversy ended with AE's "Nationality and Cosmopolitanism in Literature" on 10 Decem-*

ber 1898, and on 12 January 1899, Yeats published his "Important announcement—Irish Literary Theatre" in The Daily Express.

The above articles in this controversy were collected in Literary Ideals in Ireland, *which was published in May 1899. Yeats revised this article for the later printing and that text is reprinted here. Yeats wrote in John Quinn's copy: "This was a stirring row while it lasted and we were all very angry. W. B. Yeats. New York, 1904" (Wade, 286).*

Mr. John Eglinton wrote recently that though 'the ancient legends of Ireland undoubtedly contain situations and characters as well suited for drama as most of those used in Greek tragedies', yet 'these subjects', meaning old legends in general, 'refuse to be taken up out of their old environment, and be transplanted into the world of modern sympathies. The proper mode of treating them is a secret lost with the subjects themselves.'[1] I might have replied by naming a good part of modern literature; but as he spoke particularly of drama I named Ibsen's *Peer Gynt,* which is admittedly the chief among the national poems of modern Norway; and Wagner's musical dramas, which I compared with the Greek tragedies, not merely because of the mythological substance of *The Ring* and of *Parsifal,*[2] but because of the influence both words and music are beginning to have upon the intellect of Germany and of Europe, which begins to see the German soul in them.

He replied by saying that he preferred Ibsen's dramas, which are 'not ideal', which is nothing to the point, and that 'the crowd of elect persons seated in curiously devised seats at Bayreuth does not seem very like the whole Athenian democracy thronging into their places for a couple of obols supplied by the State, and witnessing in good faith the deeds of their ancestors'.[3] He is mistaken about the facts, for Wagner's musical dramas are not acted only or principally at Bayreuth, but before large crowds of not particularly elect persons at Vienna and at Munich and in many places in Germany and other countries. I do not think the point important, however, for when I spoke of their influence I thought less of the crowds at Vienna or at Munich than of the best intellects of our day, of men like Count Villiers de L'Isle-Adam,[†] the principal founder of the symbolist movement, of whom M. Rémy[†] de Gourmont has written, 'He opened the doors of the unknown with a crash, and a generation has gone through them to the infinite'.[4] The crowds may applaud good art for a time, but they will forget it when vulgarity invents some new thing, for the only permanent influence of any art is an influence that flows down gradually and imperceptibly, as if through orders and hierarchies.

His second article abandons the opinion—an opinion that I thought from the beginning a petulance of rapid writing—that ancient legends 'cannot be transplanted into the world of modern sympathies', and thinks that a poet 'may be inspired by the legends of his country', but goes on to distinguish between 'two conceptions of poetry mutually antagonistic, two ways of treating legends and other things'. I am glad to discuss these distinctions with him, for I think it a misfortune that Mr. John Eglinton, whose influence on Irish opinion may yet be great, should believe, as I understand him to believe, in popular music, popular painting, and popular literature. He describes the 'conception' of poetry, he believes me to prefer, as preferred 'by those who are rather in sympathy with art than with philosophy', as regarding the poet as 'an aristocratic craftsman' as looking for 'the source of inspiration' to 'the forms and images, in which old conceptions have been embodied—old faiths, myths, dreams', and as seeking 'in poetry an escape from the facts of life'; and he describes the 'conception' he himself prefers and calls Wordsworthian as looking 'to man himself as the source of inspiration', and as desiring a poetry that expresses 'its age' and 'the facts of life', and is yet, strange to say, 'a spiritual force' and the work of 'a seer'.[5]

I will restate these distinctions in the words of the younger Hallam, in his essay on Tennyson; one of the most profound criticisms in the English language. Arthur Hallam described Tennyson, who had then written his earlier and greater, but less popular poems, as belonging to 'the aesthetic school', founded by Keats and Shelley—'A poetry of sensation rather than of reflection', 'a sort of magic producing a number of impressions too multiplied, too minute, and too diversified to allow of our tracing them to the causes, because just such was the effect, even so boundless and so bewildering, produced' on the imagination of the poet 'by the real appearance of nature'. This poetry, the work of men whose 'fine organs' 'have trembled with emotion at colours and sounds and movements unperceived by duller temperaments', must always, he thinks, be unpopular because dull temperaments shrink from, or are incapable of the patient sympathy and exaltation of feeling needful for its understanding. He contrasts it with the popular school, the school he thinks Wordsworth belonged to, in all but his highest moments, which 'mixes up' anecdotes and opinions and moral maxims for their own sake—the things dull temperaments can understand—with what is sometimes the poetry of a fine temperament, but is more often an imitation.[6]

This poetry of the popular school is the poetry of those 'who are rather in sympathy' with philosophy than with art, and resembles those paintings one finds in every Royal Academy surrounded by crowds, which 'are rather in sympathy' with anecdotes or pretty faces of babies than with good painting. It is the poetry of the utilitarian and the rhetorician and the sentimentalist and the popular journalist and the popular preacher, but it is not the poetry of 'the seer,' the most 'aristocratic' of men, who tells what he alone has tasted and touched and seen amid the exaltation of his senses; and it is not a 'spiritual force', though it may talk of nothing but spiritual forces, for a spiritual force is as immaterial and as imperceptible as the falling of dew or as the first greyness of dawn. Why, too, should Mr. John Eglinton, who is a profound transcendentalist,[7] prefer a poetry which is, like all the lusts of the market place, 'an expression of its age' and of 'the facts of life', the very phrases of the utilitarian criticism of the middle century—to a poetry which seeks to express great passions that are not in nature, though 'the real appearance of nature' awakens them; 'ideas' that 'lie burningly on the divine hand', as Browning calls them, 'the beauty that is beyond the grave', as Poe calls them?[8]

The Belgian poet, M. Verhaeren,[9] has also discussed these 'two conceptions of poetry', and has described the one as founded on physical science and the other as founded upon transcendental science, and has shown that 'the bias of belles lettres at present', of which Mr. John Eglinton complains, has accompanied a renewed interest in transcendental science. And it may well be that men are only able to fashion into beautiful shapes the most delicate emotions of the soul, spending their days with a patience like the patience of the middle ages in the perfect rounding of a verse, or in the perfect carving of a flower, when they are certain that the soul will not die with the body and that the gates of peace are wide, and that the watchers are at their places upon the wall.

I believe that the renewal of belief, which is the great movement of our time, will more and more liberate the arts from 'their age' and from life, and leave them more and more free to lose themselves in beauty, and to busy themselves, like all the great poetry of the past and like religions of all times, with 'old faiths, myths, dreams', the accumulated beauty of the age. I believe that all men will more and more reject the opinion that poetry is 'a criticism of life',[10] and be more and more convinced that it is a revelation of a hidden life, and that they may even come to think 'painting, poetry, and music' 'the only means of conversing with eternity left to man on earth'.[11] I believe, too, that, though a Homer or a Dante or a Shakespeare may have used all knowledge, whether of life or of philosophy, or of mythology or of history, he did so, not for the sake of the knowledge, but to shape to a familiar and intelligible body something he had seen or experienced in the exaltation of his senses. I believe, too, that the difference between good and bad poetry is not in its preference for legendary, or for unlegendary subjects, or for a modern or for an archaic treatment, but in the volume and intensity of its passion for beauty, and in the perfection of its workmanship; and that all criticism that forgets these things is mischievous, and doubly mischievous in a country of unsettled opinion.

A SYMBOLIC ARTIST AND
THE COMING OF SYMBOLIC ART

Yeats's article "A Symbolic Artist and the Coming of Symbolic Art" first appeared in The Dome *of December 1898, where it was accompanied by three drawings (see pp. 424 to 426). The ideas on symbolism expressed here are a further development of those in his essays "Symbolism in Painting" and "The Symbolism of Poetry," written about the same time and collected in* Ideas of Good and Evil *(London, 1903) (E&I, 146–64).*

The subject of this article, the artist and poet Althea Gyles (1868–1949), came from an old and wealthy family in Kilmurry, Co. Waterford. She had studied art in Dublin around 1890, and in London around the years 1891 and 1892. Rather little was known about Gyles's life until the publication in the first issue of Yeats Studies *(Bealtaine, 1971) of Ian Fletcher's "Poet and Designer: W. B. Yeats and Althea Gyles" (42–79). Since then, Mary E. Holahan has completed a dissertation on Gyles, "Althea Gyles: Visions of the Celtic Twilight" (University of Delaware, 1978), but overall, little work has been done on Gyles (see CL2, 680–83).*

In the early nineties, Gyles lived for a time at the Dublin Theosophical Society's rooms at number 3 Upper Ely Place, and Yeats has given, without naming her, a memorable picture of the "strange, red-haired girl" at that time, starving and neurotically driven (Au, 193–95). During the period of her closest association with Yeats, she designed covers for The Secret Rose *(London: Lawrence & Bullen, 1897), the 1899 edition of* Poems *(London: T. Fisher Unwin, 1899), and the book that bears her most famous design,* The Wind Among the Reeds *(London: John Lane, 1899). During 1899 her friendship with Yeats was strained because of her affair with Leonard Smithers (1861–1907), who was, among other things, a publisher of pornographic books. "A very unpleasant thing has happened," Yeats wrote to Lady Gregory. "Althea Gyles, after despising Symons and Moore for years because of their morals, has ostentatiously taken up with Smithers, a person of so immoral a life that people like Symons and Moore despise him" (CL2, 473). In the same year, she sided with Yeats in a schism in the Order of the Golden Dawn against Aleister Crowley (1875–1947). Crowley published in his magazine* Equinox *in 1909 a story, "At the Fork of the Roads," in which Yeats is called "Will Bute," Althea Gyles bears the name "Hypatia Gay," and Crowley is "Count Swanoff."*

Yeats thought highly enough of Gyles's poetry to write an introduction to the poem "Sympathy" for the 1900 edition of T. W. Rolleston and Stopford Brooke's A Treasury of Irish Poetry *(London, John Murray, 1900). After the present article,* The Dome *magazine printed in the December 1898 issue Yeats's "Aodh Pleads with the Elemental Powers" (238), Miss Gyles's "Sympathy" (239), and a poem by Nora Hopper, "Mary's Carol" (240–41). After 1900 Gyles published poems in various magazines. She died in a London nursing home in 1949.*

The only two powers that trouble the deeps are religion and love, the others make a little trouble upon the surface. When I have written of literature in Ireland, I have had to write again and again about a company of Irish mystics[1] who have taught for some years a religious philosophy which has changed many ordinary people into ecstatics and visionaries. Young men, who were, I think, apprentices or clerks, have told me how they lay awake at night hearing miraculous music, or seeing forms that made the most beautiful painted or marble forms seem dead and shadowy. This philosophy has changed its symbolism from

Althea Gyles: *The Knight upon the Grave of His Lady.* See p. 428 for Yeats's comments.

Althea Gyles:
Noah's Raven.
See p. 428 for
Yeats's comments.

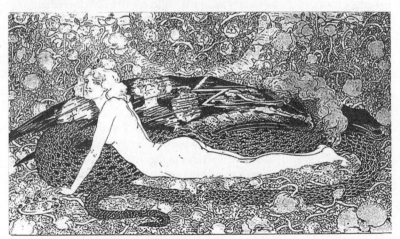

Althea Gyles: *Lilith Regina Tragœdiae*. See p. 429 for both Yeats's comments and Miss Gyles's legend for this drawing.

Althea Gyles: *Deirdre*. The Gaelic phrase above the drawing means "The Tragedy of the Children of Uisneach." See p. 429 for Miss Gyles's legend for this drawing.

time to time, being now a little Christian, now very Indian, now altogether Celtic and mythological; but it has never ceased to take a great part of its colour and character from one lofty imagination. I do not believe I could easily exaggerate the direct and indirect influences which AE[†] (Mr. George Russell), the most subtle and spiritual poet of his generation, and a visionary who may find room beside Swedenborg[2] and Blake, has had in shaping to a definite conviction the vague spirituality of young Irish men and women of letters. I know that Miss Althea Gyles, in whose work I find so visionary a beauty, does not mind my saying that she lived long with this little company, who had once a kind of conventual house; and that she will not think I am taking from her originality when I say that the beautiful lithe figures of her art, quivering with a life half mortal tragedy, half immortal ecstasy, owe something of their inspiration to this little company. I indeed believe that I see in them a beginning of what may become a new manner in the arts of the modern world; for there are tides in the imagination of the world, and a motion in one or two minds may show a change of tide.

Pattern and rhythm are the road to open symbolism, and the arts have already become full of pattern and rhythm. Subject pictures no longer interest us, while pictures with patterns and rhythms of colour, like Mr. Whistler's, and drawings with patterns and rhythms of line, like Mr. Beardsley's[3] in his middle period, interest us extremely. Mr. Whistler and Mr. Beardsley have sometimes thought so greatly of these patterns and rhythms, that the images of human life have faded almost perfectly; and yet we have not lost our interest. The arts have learned the denials, though they have not learned the fervours of the cloister. Men like Sir Edward Burne-Jones and Mr. Ricketts[4] have been too full of the emotion and the pathos of life to let its images fade out of their work, but they have so little interest in the common thoughts and emotions of life, that their images of life have delicate and languid limbs that could lift no burdens, and souls vaguer than a sigh; while men like Mr. Degas,[5] who are still interested in life, and life at its most vivid and vigorous, picture it with a cynicism that reminds one of what ecclesiastics have written in old Latin about women and about the world.

Once or twice an artist has been touched by a visionary energy amid his weariness and bitterness, but it has passed away. Mr. Beardsley created a visionary beauty in *Salome with the Head of John the Baptist,*[6] but because, as he told me, 'beauty is the most difficult of things', he chose in its stead the satirical grotesques of his later period. If one imagine a flame burning in the air, and try to make one's mind dwell on it, that it may continue to burn, one's mind strays immediately to other images; but perhaps, if one believed that it was a divine flame, one's mind would not stray. I think that I would find this visionary beauty also in the work of some of the younger French artists, for I have a dim memory of a little statue in ebony and ivory. Certain recent French writers, like Villiers de L'Isle-Adam,[17] have it, and I cannot separate art and literature in this, for they have gone through the same change, though in different forms. I have certainly found it in the poetry of a young Irish Catholic who was meant for the priesthood, but broke down under the strain of what was to him a visionary ecstasy; in some plays by a new Irish writer[8]; in the poetry of AE;[†] in some stories of Miss Macleod's;[9] and in the drawings of Miss Gyles; and in almost all these a passion for symbol has taken the place of the old interest in life. These persons are of very different degrees and qualities of power, but their work is always energetic, always the contrary of what is called 'decadent'. One feels that they have not only left the smoke of human hearths and come to The Dry Tree, but that they have drunk from The Well at the World's End.[10]

Miss Gyles' images are so full of abundant and passionate life that they remind one of William Blake's cry, 'Exuberance is Beauty', and Samuel Palmer's command to the artist, 'Always seek to make excess more abundantly excessive'.[11] One finds in them what a friend, whose work has no other passion, calls 'the passion for the impossible beauty';[12] for the beauty which cannot be seen with the bodily eyes, or pictured otherwise than by symbols. Her own favourite drawing, which unfortunately cannot be printed here, is *The Rose of God,* a personification of this beauty as a naked woman, whose hands are stretched against the clouds, as upon a cross, in the traditional attitude of the Bride, the symbol of the microcosm in the Kabala;[13] while two winds, two destinies, the one full of white and the other full of red rose petals, personifying all purities and all passions, whirl about her and descend upon a fleet of ships and a walled city, personifying the wavering and the fixed powers, the masters of the world in the alchemical symbolism. Some imperfect but beautiful verses accompany the drawing, and describe her as for 'living man's delight and his eternal revering when dead'.[14]

I have described this drawing because one must understand Miss Gyles' central symbol, the Rose, before one can understand her dreamy and intricate *Noah's Raven.*[15] The ark floats upon a grey sea under a grey sky, and the raven flutters above the sea. A sea nymph, whose slender swaying body drifting among the grey waters is a perfect symbol of a soul untouched by God or by passion, coils the fingers of one hand about his feet and offers him a ring, while her other hand holds a shining rose under the sea. Grotesque shapes of little fishes flit about the rose, and grotesque shapes of larger fishes swim hither and thither. Sea nymphs swim through the windows of a sunken town and reach towards the rose hands covered with rings; and a vague twilight hangs over all. The story is woven out of as many old symbols as if it were a mystical story in 'The Prophetic Books'.[16] The raven, who is, as I understand him, the desire and will of man, has come out of the ark, the personality of man, to find if the Rose is anywhere above the flood, which is here, as always, the flesh, 'the flood of the five senses'.[17] He has found it and is returning with it to the ark, that the soul of man may sink into the ideal and pass away; but the sea nymphs, the spirits of the senses, have bribed him with a ring taken from the treasures of the kings of the world, a ring that gives the mastery of the world, and he has given them the Rose. Henceforth man will seek for the ideal in the flesh, and the flesh will be full of illusive beauty, and the spiritual beauty will be far away.

The Knight upon the Grave of His Lady tells much of its meaning to the first glance; but when one has studied for a time, one discovers that there is a heart in the bulb of every hyacinth, to personify the awakening of the soul and of love out of the grave. It is now winter, and beyond the knight, who lies in the abandonment of his sorrow, the trees spread their leafless boughs against a grey winter sky; but spring will come, and the boughs will be covered with leaves, and the hyacinths will cover the ground with their blossoms, for the moral is not the moral of the Persian poet: 'Here is a secret, do not tell it to anybody. The

hyacinth that blossomed yesterday is dead'.[18] The very richness of the
pattern of the armour, and of the boughs, and of the woven roots, and
of the dry bones, seems to announce that beauty gathers the sorrows
of man into her breast and gives them eternal peace.

It is some time since I saw the original drawing of *Lilith*,[19] and it has
been decided to reproduce it in this number of *The Dome* too late for
me to have a proof of the engraving; but I remember that Lilith, the
ever-changing phantasy of passion, rooted neither in good nor evil, half
crawls upon the ground, like a serpent before the great serpent of the
world, her guardian and her shadow; and Miss Gyles reminds me that
Adam, and things to come, are reflected on the wings of the serpent;
and that beyond, a place shaped like a heart is full of thorns and roses.
I remember thinking that the serpent was a little confused, and that the
composition was a little lacking in rhythm, and upon the whole caring less for this drawing than for others, but it has an energy and a
beauty of its own. I believe that the best of these drawings will live, and
that if Miss Gyles were to draw nothing better, she would still have won
a place among the few artists in black and white whose work is of the
highest intensity. I believe, too, that her inspiration is a wave of a hidden tide that is flowing through many minds in many places, creating
a new religious art and poetry.

NOTE. The following are the legends for two of Miss Gyles' drawings,
as chosen by herself:

DEIRDRE. 'There is but one thing now may comfort my heart, and
that thing thy sword, O Naisi.'

LILITH REGINA TRAGŒDIAE. 'O Lilith, tristissima, cujus in corde
terrae prima magna tragaedia acta est, propter te adhuc amoris
manum tenet invidia.' ('O most sorrowful Lilith, in whose heart was
played Earth's first great tragedy, still for thy sake does Hatred hold
Love's hand.')[20]

HIGH CROSSES OF IRELAND

Yeats's ability to draw together disparate ideas and enthusiasms is everywhere manifest in his work of the late nineties. Despite dissimilarities, the Irish Literary Theatre, as it took shape in his essays, would re-create the theatre of the ancient Greeks on a model given by the French realist Antoine. Similarly, his essay "High Crosses of Ireland," a review of a lecture by Margaret MacNair Stokes (1832–1900) to the National Literary Society on 14 January 1899, welded the research of this archaeologist and artist to Yeats's masters in Celtic studies—John Rhys, Alfred T. Nutt, and H. d'Arbois de Jubainville—as well as to his studies of William Blake and mysticism. Yeats's review, signed "Rosicrux," appeared in The Daily Express *on 28 January 1899. Allan Wade attributes this review to Yeats in* A Bibliography of the Writings of W. B. Yeats, *1958, p. 326.*

Most of us who are writing in Ireland now are dreaming of a literature at once romantic and religious, and as the country housewife rakes among the ashes at dawn for the still glowing embers of yesterday's fire—for the seed of the fire, as she calls it—we search for the religious life of other times among old Irish monuments and legends. The work of Mr. Nutt and Professor Rhys and M. de Jubainville[†1] has made known something of the religious life in the Pagan legends, and the greater part of contemporary Irish and Highland literature has come of the discovery. Until I heard Miss Stokes's lecture to the National Literary Society[2] on 'The High Crosses of Ireland', I did not know how much had been done to make intelligible much of what was most naive and charming in the religious life of the first Christian centuries in Ireland. Though she has only published her drawings and photographs of two crosses, she has drawn and photographed a very great number, and hopes to do all the crosses of Ireland.[3] The four walls of the Leinster Lecture Hall were covered with photographs and drawings, reproducing, on a large scale, the ornaments and scenes sculptured in the panels of the crosses. She has

430

found explanations of many of the panels in *The Byzantine Guide to Painters,* and in other mediaeval works, in which artists found subjects and their traditional treatment.[4] She has found repeated over and over again on different crosses such things as Noah entering the Ark, Daniel in the Lion's Den, the Fall of Man, David playing upon his harp, Jacob wrestling with the Angel, and chariots and hunting scenes to describe Heaven to people who still remembered 'the great plain', 'the land of the ever living', 'the land of the living heart', where the dead heroes lived in the delight of war and of the chase.[5]

One does not find the more profound life of the middle age in these simple things, but I think one finds it in a curious diagram, which Miss Stokes has copied from Mr. Lawlor's edition of *The Book of Mulling,* and, like him, believes to be the ground plan of an Irish Monastery of the 9th or 10th century, and of the high crosses set about it.[6] Two concentric circles, with their edges close together, mark the double foss of the monastery, and outside these circles are marked the places of six [*sic*] crosses—two to the south, two to the west, two to the north, two to the east; inside the circles are marked the places of three more; and the place of another is marked upon the double foss. There are half-obliterated words in Irish at the places of the crosses, to explain that the two southern crosses are dedicated to S. Mark and Jeremiah, and the two western to S. Matthew and Daniel, and the two northern to S. John and Ezekiel, and the two eastern to S. Luke and Isaiah,[7] while the three crosses inside the circle are dedicated to Father, Son, and Holy Spirit. The words explaining the cross between the circles have been obliterated altogether. The whole figure is a mystical symbol. The Evangelists[8] and their anti-types have their crosses in the four quarters of the heavens, because of the lion and man and eagle and ox, which they inherit from the Old Testament and from Paganism, and the attributions of these creatures to the strength of God, to His incarnation, to His revelation in the darkness of the world, and to His sacrifice when the incarnation ended at the crucifixion; and because of the resemblance of these things to the sun in his southern strength, to his setting in the west, to his journey under the earth, and to his rising in the east. I have no doubt that this, or something like it, is the meaning; but I am about to make, with much doubt, a suggestion about the cross between the circles. Miss Stokes suggests that all the crosses were once on the edges of circles, and by supposing that one circle went through all the places of the crosses of the Evangelists and another through all the places of the crosses of the prophets, and by counting the two circles of the double foss, she discovers seven circles, which she compares with the seven heavens and with the seven rings of petals in the mystical rose. In spite of a passion for the symbolism of the mystical rose, which has saddened my friends, I do not believe this, for I think if this were true the double foss would have two crosses. I suggest that the whole diagram represents a paradise, more remote than the seven heavens, containing the Trinity guarded by the Prophets and the Evangelists; and that the double foss and its single cross symbolise its walls.[9] Mediaeval mystics represented this ultimate paradise as a round mirror, and Jacob Boehme,[†] who gathered into himself the dying mysticism of the Middle Ages, made it almost a fourth person of the Trinity.[10] It was almost certainly a familiar symbol in ancient Ireland, for two years ago an old man on the north island of Aran[†] told me of it. Nobody, he said, might look into it but God and this vexed Satan, who was then an angel, and Satan looked in 'and Hell was made in a minute'. Jacob Boehme[†] describes God the Father as seeing Himself in it as God the Son, and meditating about what He saw, and so making God the Holy Spirit. Blake called it 'the looking-glass of Enitharmon', his name for the mother of all, and 'the imagination of God', and many names besides.[11] It is notable, too, that the cross on the double foss is to the south-east, where S. Adamnan—or was it S. Furza?—one of the earliest of Christian missionaries,[12] and William Blake, one of the latest, saw Paradise, perhaps because the sun in the south-east has put off the chill of night without putting on the fierceness of noon, and because of all that was symbolised by this mildness. I have given my explanation doubtfully, for the mystics I have read, wrote either much earlier or much later than the time to which Miss Stokes refers this diagram, and I have read their mysticism for its own sake, and not with any thought of its historical changes. I have met young Catholics of deep piety, and some that have heard voices and seen visions, and I am certain that some day one among them, having become scholar[†] as well as visionary, and having mastered the mysticism of the Middle Ages, will tell us how much of it is reflected in the crosses and illuminated missals of this country.

Rosicrux

NOTES ON TRADITIONS
AND SUPERSTITIONS

Yeats published the folklore materials he and Lady Gregory had collected at regular intervals in the later nineties, and in 1899 he was asked for his comments on the "Traditions and Superstitions collected at Kilcurry, County Louth, Ireland," by Bryan J. Jones. Jones's material, his descriptions of his peasant "authorities," Yeats's notes, and brief rejoinders by Jones appeared in the March 1899 issue of Folk-lore, *the journal of the (London) Folk-lore Society.*

Yeats commented by number on ten of Jones's eleven items:

*1. Sightings of the "Dead Coach," a silent black coach drawn by headless horses and driven by a headless driver over a certain route "[w]henever anyone in the parish is about to die" (*Folk-lore, *vol. 10, 1, 119).*

2. The "Church of Fire" at Faughart which, while under construction on the site of an ancient fort, appeared to be consumed in flames one night, in manifestation of the fairies' displeasure.

3. The appearance, one moonlit night, of several hundred soldiers of the "gentry," the fairies, returning to the fort at Faughart after "some fight between themselves" (120).

4. The ghost of a hired man which returns to his former employers' yard as a big black dog.

6. The fairy transportation "toward daybreaking" of a man, who flew from his doorstep to the top of Faughart Hill and was returned "when the half-past five horn blew" (120–21).

7. A boarded-up cottage, attached to a modern farmhouse, where the ghost of the farmer's father is said to have been trapped because it had "haunted the family so constantly" (121).

8. The story of a woman who was carried away for a time when she crossed a stream to help "what appeared to be a woman sitting on the opposite bank, wailing and 'batting the water with its hands'" (121).

9. The belief that upon death a spirit travels "over all the ground he travelled over while alive," during which time it is visible (121).

10. *"If the first lamb you see in the season be white it is lucky, but if it be black you will die within the year"* (121).

11. The *"death warning"* given a family when a pigeon flew into their house and out again *"while at the same time there was a tap on the window"* (122).

———————

Mr. Clodd[1] having shown the above notes to Mr. W. B. Yeats, the latter gentleman kindly forwarded the following memoranda upon them:

I have stories about most of the things in the slip of folklore you send. I will be dealing with a good many of the subjects in a month or two.[2]

(1.) The coach is very common; Mr. Jones is perhaps wrong in calling it 'the Dead Coach.' The people of Co. Galway usually call it 'the *Deaf* Coach,' because it makes a 'deaf' sound. They describe 'deaf' as muffled or rumbling. I never heard before of its being soundless. Has he mistaken 'deaf' for 'dead'?

(2.) I am always hearing of forts and of certain rooms in houses being seen as if on fire. It is the commonest phenomenon in connection with forts, in all parts of Ireland I know.[3]

(3.) I am collecting material about fairy battles, and am trying to find out when they coincide with May Day, or November Day, or thereabouts, or else with death.

(4.) A Newfoundland dog, according to my uncle's old servant, is 'a very quiet form to do your penance in'. She is a Mayo woman and very much of a saint.[4]

(6.) It is always dangerous to go out late at night. I have a number of Galway and Sligo stories of people being carried to a distance, including one in which I myself am supposed to have been carried four miles in County Sligo. Compare the spiritualistic medium, Mrs. Guppy, being carried across London with a saucepan in one hand and an egg in the other. She weighed about nineteen stone.[5] I have met about four peasants who believe in fairies but not in ghosts. I have never met the converse, though I have met a man in Co. Roscommon who denied both, but believed in water-horses.

(7.) A ghost has to go anywhere it is sent; but if you send it to an unpleasant place, you have to do your own penance there when you die. My uncle's old servant again.

(8.) Am greatly interested in the fairy 'batting the water with her hands.' A man at Ballisodare,† Paddy Flynn, used the same phrase about the Banshee.[6]

(9.) I never heard this about the soul travelling where it had gone in life. It is very interesting.

(10.) I have heard of the fairies putting a black lamb into a flock as a warning to a Sligo relation of my own who had cut a fairy bush. In a couple of days the lamb had vanished. I suppose therefore that black lambs are uncanny.

(11.) I have a friend whose family (an old Kerry family, I think) has this death-warning.

THE IRISH
LITERARY THEATRE

Yeats continued his publicity for the "Irish Literary Theatre" with an article which appeared in Literature *on 6 May 1899, two days before the initial performances. The article repeats many of Yeats's themes as he stated them in his lecture to the Irish Literary Society on 23 April 1899 and in the first issue of* Beltaine *in May 1899, but here these views are directed to a wider audience for whom Yeats's usual direct appeal to national pride must be altered to envisage an audience "touched . . . by a world-wide movement of thought and emotion."*

The last few months have been of an extreme importance to that Irish intellectual movement, which began with the break up of the political movement of Parnell, for they have done more than the preceding ten years to interest the Irish leisured classes in Irish thought and Irish literature. Certain political impulses have helped; but the Irish *Daily Express,* a paper whose policy is under the direction of Mr. Horace Plunkett, has been the chief mover in what had seemed an almost impossible change.[1] The intellectual movement has created a great number of books of all kinds, but most of us thought it would have to find its principal readers for years to come among the Irish in England, who read the English literary papers; for nothing but its Gaelic text books—and fifty thousand of these have been sold in a single year—had a considerable sale in Ireland. Now, however, the sons and daughters of the landlords and officials are beginning to read, and at the same time old rancours are dying down; and that sense of something going to happen, which alone gives creative spirits their opportunity, whether in action or thought, has begun to spread among all classes. A year or two ago Mr. Martyn[2] and myself would have found few helpers for our theatrical experiment; while to-day we have found so many helpers and so few hinderers, and hinderers are usually plentiful in Ireland, that, despite a despondent disposition, which astrologers trace to the moon having risen at my birth among a trouble of hostile stars, I have begun to hope for a measure of success.

And yet we are uncompromising enough. We have called our experiment 'The Irish Literary Theatre,' although we knew that 'literary' sounded ill in playgoers' ears; and we have issued a circular describing the Norwegian theatre, which hatched 'that northern phantom' Dr. Ibsen, as the only theatre at once literary and popular.[3] We have appealed to the imaginative minority and not to the majority which is content with the theatre of commerce; and, if we do not fail too badly, we will make a like appeal next spring, and so from spring to spring, for, though we have engaged good and experienced actors, we have economized sufficiently on our scenery, and on our stage, to be able to wait for a full success.

Our plays will all be about Irish subjects; and, if we can find enough writers, and I have little doubt we will find them, who will write with some depth and simplicity about legends associated with the rivers and mountains of Ireland, or about Irish historic personages and events, or about modern Irish life, an increasing number of persons will desire to hear a message that will so often illustrate the circumstance of their lives. On the 8th of May we give a play of mine, *The Countess Cathleen,* which is founded on old legends, and the next night a play of Mr. Martyn's, *The Heather Field,* a very profound and simple criticism of modern life; and next year, in all likelihood, Calderon's *St. Patrick's Purgatory,* which is about the conversion of Ireland; and a play by either Mr. Standish O'Grady or Miss Fiona Macleod. I think that nearly all our little group of Irish or Celtic writers will try their hands at play-writing, and, as our political disorders and a double share of the mediaeval-man in our blood have given us a dramatic temper, our intellectual movement may begin to speak through the theatre. The first weeks of May, being also the date of our Musical Festival, and in most years (though not in this) of the festival of the Gaelic League,[4] the most vigorous and powerful of our organizations, will perhaps become the season of a great racial gathering, drawing enthusiasts from far scattered towns and hill-sides as by a triple evocation. It may happen that the imaginative minority will spread their interests among the majority, for even the majority becomes imaginative when touched by enthusiasm. Men who are not more intelligent than London theatre-goers listen with sympathy and understanding to quiet and sincere miracle-plays in Brittany; and the crowds who went in procession when Cimabue had the cry, or who chanted the ballad of 'Chevy Chase,'[5] or who filled the play-houses for Shakespeare, only differed from the crowds who think Rossetti's women 'guys,'[6] and poetry of kinds 'a bore,' and Ibsen an 'immoral' and inexpert writer, because they were touched by the fervour of religion, or by the delight of a familiar legend, or by a world-wide movement of thought and emotion.

THE DOMINION OF DREAMS

Yeats's fourth and last article on Fiona Macleod, the review of The Dominion of Dreams *(Westminster: Constable, 1899) in* The Bookman *for July 1899 found Yeats still convinced that hers was a salutary and necessary kind of literature, although he was growing more restless over the deficiencies of her style. It seems likely that in 1899 Yeats was still unaware that Fiona was the feminine alter ego of William Sharp, for two years later he was still addressing letters to her. However, Yeats may have suspected the truth but still have written letters to her to reach that part of Sharp's personality.*

One of Miss Macleod's new stories tells how a certain shepherd, wandering at night over a lonely marshland, sees a piper piping among a flock of sheep. He had a black feather in his bonnet and black streamers from his pipes, and his music was now full of mockery and now full of melancholy, and when the shepherd tried to go towards him he seemed always as far off as ever. The shepherd stood to listen, and suddenly he found that the piper was quite close, and that what he had thought sheep were but shadows of all shapes and sizes. They were, and he did not know how he knew this, the shadows of all the piper had seen that day—the shadows of trees and plants and cattle, and of a dead man in a corrie,[1] and of the shepherd himself, as he had lost it an hour ago at the set of the sun. Being terrified, and angry because he was terrified, he tried to seize the piper with his hands, and fell against a rock, striking his head, and as he fell he saw the shadows change to a flock of curlews and fly away. Presently he awoke out of a swoon and began wandering here and there, looking for the curlew that had been his shadow, until being at last worn out, he lay down and slept, and as he slept the piper came, but looking different, for now he had long black hair, and stood beside him and took up the shadow of a reed and played upon it. A curlew came nearer and nearer, and the piper played it back into a shadow and played the shadow into the mind of the shepherd.

When day had come the shepherd awoke and gave 'three cries of the curlew,'[2] and began to wander back aimlessly in the way he had come. People explained his madness by saying that the Dark Fool, the Amadan Dhu,[3] had 'touched' him.

I give this story, which loses much of its mystery in my bare chronicle, because it is easier to unwind it than to unwind her more complicated stories, and I am anxious to discover the thoughts about which her art is wound. Other writers are busy with the way men and women act in sorrow or in joy, but Miss Macleod has re-discovered the art of the myth-makers, and gives a visible shape to joys and sorrows, and makes them seem realities and men and women illusions. It was minds like hers that created Aphrodite out of love and the foam of the sea, and Prometheus out of human thought and its likeness to leaping fire.[4] We understand in some dim way that her Amadan Dhu is some half-inspired madness such as marked men out in early times for a terrified worship, and that the shadows that gather about him like sheep are but our own memories, the things that make us ourselves and bind us to the world, in some peaceful mood, and that the shadows changed into curlews are our memories in some wilder mood; and because the links of resemblance are subtle and the full meaning beyond our reach, we understand with our emotions rather than with our reason, and the story is not allegory, but symbolism, and not prose, but poetry. Swedenborg and Jacob Boehme[5] have begun to cast off the manners of the schools, and to talk the fairy tales of children, and from this union of the lofty with the simple religious myth has been re-born.

A change in thought in the world makes us understand that we are not walled up within our immediate senses, but bound one to another, and to some greater life, by a secret communion of thought and emotion that can in a moment fling up into the waking mind some dream or vision of a far-off friend, and of his circumstance, or of a hidden and consoling loveliness; and at once a kind of literature, which passed away with the ancient world and its witchcraft, begins to arise in every European country. This literature has a power over strange effects, for it can trust itself to dim emotions of beauty, as no literature can, which believes its revelation comes out of the waking mind. One of these stories tells of Eoan and Finola,[6] whose house is 'on a sun-swept mound in the wood'. 'Long ago he had eaten mistletoe berries[7] in moonshine, and had not waked again. Finola, loving him more than life, had changed herself into the white stillness of sleep, and was a dream in his mind, and lay quiet and glad and at rest'. And in another we are told of Aevgrain the daughter of Deirdre.[8] 'Then her white hands moved like swans through the shadowy flood that was her hair, and she put sleep from her'.

Every kind of inspiration has its besetting faults, and perhaps because those who are at the beginning of movements have no models and no traditional restraints, Miss Macleod has faults enough to ruin an ordinary writer. Her search for dim resemblances sometimes brings her beyond the borders of coherence; and she has a way of using literary words, when the right words are the words of daily speech, that often makes some beautiful invention seem unreal. There is scarcely a story that would not be the better for the crossing out of many words. Before her shepherd sees the Dark Fool he hears the crying of sheep, and it is called a 'lamentable melancholy sound, like children crying in some forlorn place'.[9] How much better this would have been without 'lamentable' and with 'lonely' or the like instead of 'forlorn'! At another place she spoils a beautiful old Gaelic saying, that calls the cry of the wind and the cry of the wave and the cry of the curlew, the three oldest cries in the world, by calling them 'the three lamentable elder voices of the world.'[10] The bent of nature, that makes her turn from circumstance and personalities to symbols and personifications, may perhaps leave her liable to an obsession from certain emotional words, which have for her a kind of symbolic meaning, but her love of old tales should tell her that the great mysteries are best told in the simpler words.

IRELAND BEWITCHED

The fourth of the six articles Yeats assembled from Lady Gregory's folk collections is "Ireland Bewitched," which appeared in The Contemporary Review *for September 1899. (See the introductory note to "The Tribes of Danu" for more information regarding this collaboration.)*

Some of the parallels between stories given in this article and the versions in Visions and Beliefs in the West of Ireland, Collected and Arranged by Lady Gregory; with Two Essays and Notes by W. B. Yeats *(London: G. P. Putnam's Sons, 1920) are indicated in the footnotes. The names of the tale-tellers and of the characters in the stories are usually changed from Yeats's version in Lady Gregory's. While Yeats probably gave false names to his informants to protect them, there is no evidence that Lady Gregory's names are any more authentic.*

When one talks to the people of the West of Ireland, and wins their confidence, one soon finds that they live in a very ancient world, and are surrounded by dreams that make the little round fields that were the foundations of ancient houses (forts or forths as they call them), a great boulder up above on the hillside, the more twisted or matted thorn trees, all unusual things and places, and the common crafts of the country always mysterious and often beautiful. One finds the old witches and wisemen still busy, and even the crafts of the smith and of the miller touched with a shadow of old faiths, that gives them a brotherhood with magic. The principal crafts were once everywhere, it seems, associated with magic, and had their rites and their gods; and smith-craft, of which one hears much from Galway story-tellers, that was once the distinguishing craft of races that had broken many battles upon races whose weapons were of stone, was certainly associated with a very powerful magic. A man on the borders of Clare and Galway tells how his house was enchanted and filled with smoke that was like the smoke of a forge, and a man living by the sea in North Galway says: 'This is a fairy stream we're passing; there were some used to see them by the side of it, and washing themselves in it. And there used to be heard a fairy forge here every night, and the hammering on the iron could be heard and the blast of the furnace'. A man at Kiltartan[1] says: 'Blacksmiths are safe from these things,' meaning fairy mischiefs, 'and if a blacksmith was to turn his anvil upside down and say malicious words he could do you great injury'.[2] A man in the Burren Hills says: 'Yes, they say blacksmiths have something about them. And if there's a seventh blacksmith in succession from seven generations, he can do many strange things, and if he gave you his curse you wouldn't be the better of it. There was one at Belharbour, Jamsie Finucane,[3] but he did no harm to any one, but was as quiet as another. He is dead now and his son's a blacksmith, too'. A woman near Coole says: 'A seventh son has the power to cure the ringworm, and if there is a seventh blacksmith in a family he can do his choice thing'. And an old man near Kiltartan says: 'Blacksmiths have power, and if you could steal the water from the trough in the forge, it would cure all things'. And a woman from Ardrahan says: 'A blacksmith can do all things. When my little boy was sick I was told to go to a forge before sunrise and to collect some of the dust from the anvil. But I didn't after, he was too far gone'. A drunken blacksmith at a village in the county of Clare, when asked by a friend who has collected many of these and other stories for me, if he had ever been to the famous wise woman, Biddy Early, answered: 'I never went to Biddy Early for a cure myself, for you should know that no ill or harm ever comes to a blacksmith'.

Iron is believed to be the great dissolver of all charms, and one hears stories of enchanted people and creatures that take their right shape when you point a gun at them and look along the iron of the barrel. It seems to be this property of iron that makes blacksmiths invulnerable. A woman from near Feakle says: 'There was a man one time that was a blacksmith, and he used to go every night playing cards. And for all his wife could say he wouldn't leave off doing it. So one night she got a boy to go stand in the old churchyard he'd have to pass, and to frighten him.

'So the boy did so, and began to groan and to try to frighten him when he came near. But it's well-known that nothing of that kind can do any harm to a blacksmith. So he went in and got hold of the boy, and told him he had a mind to choke him, and went his way.

'But no sooner was the boy left alone than there came about him something in the shape of a dog, and then a great troop of cats. And they surrounded him, and he tried to get away home, but he had no power to go the way he wanted, but had to go with them. And at last they came to an old forth and a fairy bush, and he knelt down and made the sign of the cross and said a great many Our Fathers. And after a time they went into the fairy bush and left him.

'And he was going away and a woman came out of the bush, and called to him three times to make him look back. And he saw it was a woman he knew before, that was dead, and so he knew she was among the fairies. And she said to him, "It's well for you I was here, and worked hard for you, or you would have been brought in among them, and be like me". So he got home.

'And the blacksmith got home, too, and his wife was surprised to see he was no way frightened. But he said, "You might know that there's nothing of the sort that could harm me".

'For a blacksmith is safe from all, and when he goes out in the night he keeps always in his pocket a small bit of iron, and they know him by that.

'So he went on card playing, and they grew very poor after'.

Millers, too, have knowledge and power. An old man I knew, who believed himself to be haunted, went to the nearest miller for a cure; and a woman among the Slieve Echtge hills says that 'a miller can bring any one he likes to misfortune by working his mill backwards', and adds, 'just as the blacksmith can put his anvil upside down'.

The people who have most knowledge, however, are not thought to have it from a craft, but because it has been told them, revealed to them, as it might be told or revealed to anybody. Once everybody almost had it, for as an old man in Kiltartan says: 'Enchanters and magicians they were in the old times, and could make the birds sing and the stones and the fishes speak'. But now only a few have it. One hears comparatively little of magic of the old wonder-working kind, but one does hear something of it. An old woman from the borders of Sligo and Mayo says that she remembers seeing, when she was a child, 'a wild old man in flannel who came from Erris.' He and the men used to sit up late at night sometimes, playing cards in a big barn. She was not allowed to go into the barn because children kneel down and look up under the cards, and a player has bad luck if anybody kneels when he is playing, but her father often told her that when they had been playing a long time 'the wild old man' would take up the cards and move them about and a hare would leap out of the cards, and then a hound would leap out after the hare and chase it round and round the barn and away.

One hears sometimes of people who can see what is happening at a distance, or what is happening among 'the others' (the fairies), or what is going to happen among us. A woman at Coole says: 'There was a man at Ardrahan used to see many things. But he lost his eyesight after. That often happens, that those who see those things lose their earthly sight'.

A man of the large island of Aran says: 'There was a strange woman came to the island one day and told some of the women down below what would happen them. And they didn't believe, she being a stranger, but since that time it's all been coming true'. And it is sometimes said that if you have the habit of walking straight on the road, and not of wavering a little from side to side, you are more likely to 'see things' than another, which means, I suppose, that you should be in good health and strength if you are 'to see things'. The gift most valued seems to be the power of bringing back people who are in the power of 'the others', or of curing the many illnesses that 'the others' are believed to give us, that they may take us into their world. It is possible that all illness was once believed to come from them, but I am not sure, because a distinction is now made between the illnesses they make and ordinary illnesses. A man on one of the Aran Islands told my friend, with many other stories which I have, how he got a little of the knowledge and the use he made of it. He has not, however, the whole of the knowledge, for the people are at this moment looking out for a 'knowledgeable' man or woman, to use their own words, as at present they have to go to Roundstone in Galway. The man says: 'There are many can do cures because they have something walking with them, what we may call a ghost, from among the Sheogue (the fairies). A few cures I can do myself, and this is how I got them. I told you I was for five quarters in Manchester, and where I lodged were two old women in the house, from the farthest side of Mayo, for they were running from Mayo at that time because of the hunger. And I knew they were likely to have a cure, for St. Patrick blessed the places he was not in more than the places he was in, and with the cure he left, and the fallen angels, there are many in Mayo, can do them.

'Now it's the custom in England never to clear the table but once in the week, and that on a Saturday night. And in that night all is set out clean, and all the crusts of bread and bits of meat and the like are gathered together in a tin can and thrown out in the street. And women that have no other way of living come round with a bag that would hold two stone, and they pick up all that's thrown out, and live on it for a week. But often I didn't eat the half of what was before me, and I wouldn't throw it out, but I'd bring it to the two old women that were in the house, so they grew very fond of me.

'Well, when the time came that I thought I'd draw towards home, I brought them one day to a public-house, and made a drop of punch for them, and then I picked the cure out of them, for I was wise in those days. There was a neighbour's child was sick and I got word of it, and I went to the house, for the woman there had showed me kindness, and I went in to the cradle and I lifted the quilt off the child's face, and you could see by it, and I saw the signs, that there was some of their work there. And I said, "You're not likely to have the child long with you, ma'am." And she said, "Indeed, I know I won't have him long". So I said nothing, but I went out, and whatever I did and whatever I got there, I brought it in again and gave it to the child, and he began to get better. And the next day I brought the same thing again and gave it to the child, and I looked at him and I said to the mother, "He'll live to comb his hair grey". And from that time he got better, and now there's no stronger child in the island, and he the youngest in the house.

'After that the husband got sick, and the woman said to me one day: "If there's anything you can do to cure him, have pity on me and my children, and I'll give you what you'll ask". But I said, "I'll do what I can for you, but I'll take nothing from you, except maybe a grain of tea or a glass of porter, for I wouldn't take money for this, and I refused £2 one time for a cure I did". So I went and brought back the cure, and I mixed it with flour and made it into three little pills that it couldn't be lost, and gave them to him, and from that time he got well.

'There was a woman lived down the road there, and one day I went into the house when she was after coming from Galway town, and I asked charity of her. And it was in the month of August when the bream fishing was going on, and she said, "There's no one need be in want now, with fresh fish in the sea and potatoes in the gardens", and she gave me nothing. But when I was out the door, she said, "Well, come back here". And I said, "If you were to offer me all you brought from Galway I wouldn't take it from you now".

'And from that time she began to pine and to wear away and to lose her health. And at the end of three years she walked outside her house one day, and when she was two yards from her own threshold she fell on the ground, and the neighbours came and lifted her up on a door and brought her into the house, and she died.

'I think I could have saved her then—I *think* I could. But when I saw her lying there I remembered that day, and I didn't stretch out a hand and I spoke no word.

'I'm going to rise out of the cures and not to do much more of them, for *they* have given me a touch here in the right leg, so that it's the same as dead; and a woman in my village that does cures, she is after being struck with a pain in the hand. Down by the path at the top of the slip, from there to the hill, that is the way they go most nights, hundreds and thousands of them some nights; sleeping in that little cabin of mine

I heard them ride past, and I could hear by the feet of the horses that there was a long line of them there.'

Of all who have had this gift in recent years in the south-west of Ireland, the most famous was Biddy Early,[4] who had most other fairy gifts likewise. She is dead some twenty years, but her cottage is pointed out at Feakle in Clare. It is a little rough-built cottage by the roadside, and is always full of turf-smoke, like many others of the cottages, but once it was sought out by the sick and the troubled of all the south-west of Ireland. My friend[5] went to Feakle for me a while back, and found it full of memories of Biddy Early's greatness. Nobody there denies her power, but some of the better off think her power unholy, and one woman says: 'It is against our religion to go to fortune-tellers. She did not get her power from God, so it must have been from demons'. The poor think better of her, and one man[6] says: 'She was as good to the poor as to the rich. Any poor person she'd see passing the road she'd call in and give them a cup of tea or a glass of whisky and bread and all they wanted. She had a big chest within in that room, and it was full of pounds of tea and bottles of wine and of whisky and of claret and all things in the world'. 'I knew her well', says one, 'a nice fresh-looking woman she was. It's to her the people used to be flocking, to the door and even to the window, and if they'd come late in the day they'd have no chance of getting to her, they'd have to take lodgings for the night in the town. She was a great woman. If any of the men that came into the house had a drop too much drink taken, and said an unruly word, she'd turn them out. And if any of them were disputing or fighting or going to law, she'd say, "Be at one and you can rule the world". The priests were against her, and used to be taking the cloaks and the baskets from the country people to keep them from going to her'. An old pensioner[7] at Kiltartan says: 'When I was in the army, whenever a Clare man joined, we were sure to hear of Biddy Early'; and another man[8] says that people came to her 'from the whole country round, and from Limerick and Loughrea, and even from England and Wales. She had four or five husbands, and they all died of drink, one after another. They had the temptation, for maybe twenty or thirty people would be there in the day looking for cures, and every one of them would bring a bottle of whisky. Wild cards they were or they wouldn't have married her'. Everybody tells of her many husbands, though not always of the same number. A man in Burren says: 'She had three husbands; I saw one of them the day I was there, but I knew by the look of him he wouldn't live long'. She is believed to have journeyed all over the country with the fairies, and she seems to have first seen and thrown her enchantment on one of the men she married, when on one of these journeys.

A woman near Roxborough says: 'There was a Clare woman with me when I went there, and she told me there was a boy from a village near her brought tied in a cart to Biddy Early, and she said: "If I cure you, will you be willing to marry me"; and he said he would. So she cured him and married him; I saw him there at her house. It might be that she had the illness put on him first.' One man at Feakle seems to think that she had a lover or a husband among 'the others' also, for he says: 'Surely she was away herself, and as to her son, she brought him with her when she came back, and for eight or nine years he was lying on the bed. And he'd never stir as long as she was in it, but no sooner was she gone away anywhere than he'd be out down the village among the people, and then back again before she'd get to the house'. Some, however, say that this boy was not her son but her brother. Most of the country people think she got her knowledge from this boy, though a witch doctor in Clare, whom I have described elsewhere,[9] says that she told him her knowledge came to her from a child she met when she was at service. A woman at Burren says: 'He was a little chap that was astray. And one day when he was lying sick in the bed, he said: "There's a woman in such a house has a hen down in the pot, and if I had the soup of the hen I think it would cure me". So Biddy Early went to the house, and when she got there, sure enough there was a hen in the pot on the fire. But she was ashamed to tell what she came for, and she let on to have only come for a visit, and so she sat down. But presently in the heat of talking she told what the little chap had said. "Well", says the woman, "take the soup and welcome, and the hen too, if it'll do him any good". So she brought them with her, and when the boy saw the soup, "It can't save me", says he, "for no earthly thing can do that. But since I see how kind and how willing you are, and did your best for me all these years, I'll leave you a way of living". And so he did, and taught her the cure. That's what's said at any rate'.

But others say that after his death she was always crying and lamenting for the loss of him, and that she had no way of earning her bread, till at last he appeared to her and gave her the gift. One man who was cured by her thinks that she got her knowledge through having been among the fairies herself, and says: 'She was away for seven years; she didn't tell it to me, but she told it to others'; and adds, 'any how it is certain that when the case was a bad one, she would go into a stable, and there she would meet her people and consult with them'. An old man near Coole says: 'Biddy Early surely did thousands of cures; out in the stable she used to go, there her friends met her, and they told her all things'. Another says: 'She used to go out into a field and talk with her friends through the holes in the walls'. Many tell, too, of a bottle in which she looked and found out whatever she wanted to know. A young man at Feakle, too young to remember her, says: 'The people do be full of stories of all the cures she did. It was by the bottle she did all. She would shake it, and she'd see everything when she looked at it'. She would say at once whether the sickness she was asked to cure was a common sickness or one of those mysterious sicknesses the people lay at the door of the fairies. A woman at Kiltartan says: 'It's I was with this woman here to Biddy Early. And when she saw me she knew it was for my husband I came, and she looked in her bottle, and said: "It's nothing put upon him by my people that's wrong with him". And she bid me give him cold vinegar and some other things—herbs. He got better after. And sometimes she would see in the bottle that the case was beyond her power, and then she would do nothing'. An old woman near Feakle says: 'I went there but once myself, when my little girl that was married was bad after her second baby being born. I went to the house and told her about it. And she took the bottle and shook it and looked in it, and then she turned and said something to himself (her husband) that I didn't hear, and she just waved her hand to me like that, and bid me go home, and she would take nothing from me. But himself came out and told me that what she was after seeing in the bottle was the face of my little girl and her coffin standing beside her. So I went home, and sure enough on the tenth day after she was dead'. Another woman tells a like story, but does not mention the bottle: 'Often I heard of Biddy Early, and I know of a little girl was sick, and the brother went to Biddy Early to ask would she get well. And she said: "They have a place ready for her, it's room for her they have". So he knew she would die, and so she did'.

A woman at Feakle[10] says: 'I knew a man went to Biddy Early about his wife, and as soon as she saw him she said, "On the fourth day a discarded priest will call in and cure your wife". And so he did, one Father Ford'. A woman at Burren[11] says: 'I went up to Biddy Early one time with another woman. A fine stout woman she was, sitting straight up in her chair. She looked at me, and she told me my son was worse than what I was, and for myself she bid me to take what I was taking before, and that's dandelions. Five leaves she bid me lay out on the table, with three pinches of salt on the three middle ones. As for my son, she gave me a bottle for him, but he wouldn't take it; and he got better without'. One does not know whether this was a common illness, but in most of the stories the illness is from the fairies. Somebody has been 'overlooked'—that is, looked at with envy or with unbridled admiration by some one who would not say, or forgot to say, 'God bless him', or its like; and because this emotion has given the persons looked at into the power of the fairies, who can only take people 'away' 'through the eye of a sinner', he has been given 'the touch' or 'the stroke' that is the definite beginning of their power. I have been told that only those who have been or are themselves 'away'—that is, in the world of fairy, a changeling taking their place upon the earth—can cure those who are 'away', though many can cure 'the touch' or 'the stroke'. There are, however, stories of cures that contradict this. A woman near Gort says: 'There was a boy of the Brennans in Gort was out at Kiltartan thatching Heniff's house. And a woman passed by, and she looked up at him, but she never said, "God bless the work". And Brennan's mother was on the road to Gort, and the woman met her, and said, "Where did your son learn thatching?" And that day he had a great fall, and was brought home hurt. And the mother went to Biddy Early, and she said, "Didn't a red-haired woman meet you one day going into Gort, and ask where did your son learn thatching; and didn't she look up at him as she passed? It was then it was done". And she gave a bottle, and he got well after a time'. 'The touch' or 'the stroke' often show themselves by a fall. A red-haired woman is always unlucky, and a woman near Gort who had told a friend and neighbour about an old man who lost his hair all at once in a fairy fort after he had cut down some bushes, says: 'The old man here that lost his hair went to Biddy Early, but he didn't want to go, and we forced him and persuaded him. And when he got to the house she said, "It wasn't of your own free will you came here", and at the first she wouldn't do anything for him. And then she said, "Why did you go to cut down the phillibine (magpie) bush—that bush you see out of the window?" And she told him an old woman in the village had overlooked him—Daly's sister—and she gave him a bottle to sprinkle about her house. I suppose it was the bush being interfered with she didn't like'. Another woman near Gort says: 'There was a man I knew sick, and he sent to Biddy Early, and she said, "Was Andy in the house?" And they said he was, "Well", says she, "the next time he comes in ask him his name and his Christian name three times". And so they did, and the third time he turned and went out. And the man got better, but Andy's stock all went from him, and he never throve from that time'.

The asking the name is, no doubt, connected with the belief that if you know a person's name you have power over him. I have a story of a Tipperary woman who was tormented by fairies, who were always trying to get her name from her that they might have power over her.

A woman near Coole[12] says: 'It was my son was thatching Heniff's house when he got the touch, and he came back with a pain in his back and his shoulders, and took to the bed. And a few nights after that, I was asleep, and the little girl came and woke me, and said, "There's none of us can sleep with all the cars and carriages rattling round the house". But, though I woke and heard that said, I fell into a sound sleep again, and never woke till morning. And one night there came two taps to the window, one after another, and we all heard it, and no one there. And at last I sent the other boy to Biddy Early, and he found her in the house; she was then married to her fourth man. And she said he came a day too soon, and would do nothing for him; and he had to walk away in the rain. And the next day he went back, and she said, "Three days later and you'd have been too late". And she gave him two bottles; the one he was to bring to boundary water and to fill it up, and that was to be rubbed to the back, and the other was to drink. And the minute he got them he began to get well; and he left the bed, and could walk, but he was always delicate. When he rubbed the back we saw a black mark, like the bite of a dog, and as to his face, it was as white as a sheet. I have the bottle here yet, though it's thirty year ago I got it. She bid the boy to bring whatever was left of it to a river, and to pour it away with the running water. But when he got well I did nothing with it and said nothing about it, and here it is now for you to see, and you the first I ever showed it to. I never let on to Father Curran[13] that I went to her, but one time the bishop came. I knew he was a rough man, and I went to him and made a confession, and I said, "Do what you like with me, but I'd walk the world for my son when he was sick". And all he said was, "I wouldn't have wondered if your messenger had had the two feet cut off from him". And he said no more'.

An old man near Coole says: 'I got cured by her myself one time. Look at this thumb. I got it hurted, and I went out into the field after, and was ploughing all the day, I was that greedy for work. And when I went in, I had to lie on the bed with the pain of it, and it swelled, and the arm with it, to the size of a horse's thigh. I stopped two or three days in the bed, and then my wife went to see Biddy Early; and she came home; and the next day it burst, and you never saw anything like all the stuff that came away from it. A good bit after I went to her myself, where it wasn't quite healed, and she said, "You'd have lost it altogether if your wife hadn't been so quick to come". She brought me into a small room, and said good words and sprinkled water from a bottle, and told me to believe. The priests were against her, but they were wrong. How could that be evil doing that was all charity and kindness and healing? She was a decent-looking woman, no different from any other woman of the country. The boy she was married to at the time was lying on the bed drunk. There were side cars and common cars and gentry and country people at the door, just like Gort market, and dinner for all that came. And every one would bring her something, but she didn't care what it was. Rich farmers would bring her the whole side of a pig. Myself I brought a bottle of whisky and a shilling's worth of bread, and a quarter of sugar, and a quarter pound of tea. She was very rich, for there wasn't a farmer but would give her the grass of a couple of bullocks or a filly—she had the full of a field of fillies if they'd all been gathered together.

'She died a good many years ago. I didn't go to the wake myself, but I heard that her death was natural'.

A well-to-do man near Kilchriest[14] says: 'It was all you could do to get to Biddy Early with your skin whole, the priests were so set against her. I went to her one time myself, and it was hard when you got near to know the way, for all the people were afraid to tell it.

'It was about a little chap of my own I went, that some strange thing had been put upon. When I got to her house there were about fifty to be attended to before me, and when my turn came, she looked in her bottle, a sort of a common greenish one that seemed to have nothing in it, and she told me where I came from, and the shape of the house and the appearance of it, and of the little lake you see there, and everything round about. And she told me of a limekiln that was near, and then she said the harm that came to him came from the forth beyond that. And I never knew of there being a forth there; but after I came home I went to look, and there, sure enough, it was.

'And she told me how it had come on him, and bid me remember a day that a certain gentleman stopped and spoke to me when I was out working in the hayfield, and the child with me playing about. And I remembered it well; it was old John Lydon, of Carrig,[15] that was riding past, and stopped and talked, and was praising the child. And it was close by that forth beyond that John Lydon was born.

'I remembered it was soon after that day that the mother and I went to Loughrea, and when we came back the child had slipped on the threshold of the house and got a fall, and he was screeching and calling out that his knee was hurt, and from that time he did no good, and pined away and had the pain in his knee always.

'And Biddy Early said: "While you're talking to me now the child lies dying". And that was at twelve o'clock in the day. And she made up a bottle for me, herbs, I believe, it was made of, and she said, "Take care of it going home, and whatever may happen, don't drop it", and she wrapped it in all the folds of my handkerchief. So when I was coming home and got near Tillyra, I heard voices, and the man that was with me said, "Did you see all the people beyond the wall?" And I saw nothing, but I kept a tight hold on the bottle. And when we got to the Roxborough gate, there were many people talking and coming to where we were. I could hear them and see them, and so could the man that was with me; but when I heard them I remembered what she had said, and I took the bottle in my two hands and held it, and so I brought it home safely. And when I got home they told me the child was worse, and that at twelve o'clock the day before he lay, as they thought, dying. And when I brought in the bottle to him he pulled the bed-clothes up over his head, and we had the work of the world to make him swallow it. But from the time he took it the pain in his knee left him and he began to get better. And Biddy Early had told me not to let May Day pass without coming to her again when she gave me the bottle. But seeing him so well, I thought it no use to go again, and he got bad again, and it was not on May Day, but was in the month of May he died. He took to the bed before that, and he'd be always calling to me to come inside the bed where he was, and if I went in he'd hardly let me go. But I got afraid, and I didn't like to be too much with him.

'He was not eight years old when he died, but Mark Spelman,[16] that used to live beyond there at that time, told me privately that when I'd be out of the house and he'd come in, the little chap would ask for the pipe and smoke it, but he'd never let me see him doing it. And queer chat he had, and he was old-fashioned in all his ways.' The child was evidently 'away', and a changeling believed to have taken his place. May Day, Midsummer Day, and November Eve,[17] which are old Celtic festivals, are thought times of great activity among the fairies, and that is why he was to bring the child to Biddy Early before May Day. One story tells how she offered to show a mother the child the fairies had taken from her and whom she thought dead. A woman from Kiltartan[18] says: 'My mother got crippled in her bed one night, God save the hearers! And it was a long time before she could walk again with the pain in her back, and my father was always telling her to go to Biddy Early, and so at last she went. But she would do nothing for her, for, she said, "What ails you is nothing to do with my business". And she said, "You have lost three, and one was a grand little fair-haired one, and if you'd like to see her again I'll show her to you". And when she said that, my mother had no courage to look and to see the child she lost, but fainted then and there. And then she said, "There's a field with corn beyond your house, and a field with hay, and it's not long since the little fellow that wears a Lanberis[19] cap fell asleep there on a cock of hay. And before the stooks of corn are in stacks he'll be taken from you, but I'll save him if I can. And it was true enough what she said; my little brother that was wearing a Lanberis cap had gone to the field and fallen asleep on the hay a few days before. But no harm happened him, and he's all the brother I have living now. And it was Bruen from Gort went with my mother where his sister was sick. And she turned to him and she said, "When you get home, the coffin will be level with the door before you". And sure enough when he got home the sister had died, and the coffin had been brought and left at the door'.

The people always believed, I think, that whenever she saved anyone the fairies were trying to take, somebody or something was taken instead. She would sometimes ask people who came to her if they were ready to pay the penalty, and there is a story of one man who refused to lose a cow to save the wife he had come about, and when he got home she was dead before him. A well-to-do farmer near Gort, says, however: 'It was Donovan gave his life for my sister that was his wife. When she fell sick he said he'd go to an old woman, one Biddy Early, that lived in the mountains beyond, and that did a great deal of cures, but the priests didn't like any one to be going to her. So he brought her there and she cured her the first time, but she says, "If you bring her again you'll pay the penalty".

'But when she fell sick again, he brought her the second time, but he stopped a mile from the house himself. But she knew it well and told the wife where he was, but she cured her, and that time the horse died. And the third time she fell sick he went again, knowing full well he'd pay the penalty. And so he did and died. But she married again, one O'Mara, and lives over there towards Kinvara'.

A cow or a horse or a fowl was generally sufficient. A man at Corcomroe says: 'Did I ever hear of Biddy Early? There's not a man in this country side over forty years of age that hasn't been with her some time or other.

'There's a man living in that house over there was sick one time, and he went to her and she cured him, but, says she, "You'll have to lose something, and whatever it is, don't fret after it". So he had a grey mare and she was going to foal, and one morning when he went out he saw that the foal was born and was lying by the side of the wall. So he remembered what she had said to him, and he didn't fret.' Sometimes, however, the people believed that many lives were given instead of one. A man at Burren whom she cured says: 'I didn't lose anything at the time, but sometimes I thought afterwards it came on my family, when I lost so many of my children. A grand stout girl went from me, stout and broad, what else would ail her to go?'

One often hears of the difficulty of bringing the bottle Biddy Early gave safe home, because of the endeavours of the fairies to break it. A man near Gort says: 'Sometimes she'd give a bottle of some cure to people that came, but if she'd say to them, you'll never bring it home, break it they must on the way back with all the care they'd take of it'.

A man near Gort says: 'There was a boy I knew went to Biddy Early and she gave him a bottle, and she told him it would cure him if he did not lose it in the crossing of some road. And when he came to that place, for all he could do, the bottle was broke.'

A woman in Burren says: 'Himself went one time to Biddy Early, for his uncle Donoghue that was sick, and he found her, and her fingers all covered with gold rings, and she gave him a bottle, and she said, "Go into no house on the way home, or stop nowhere, or you'll lose it".

'But going home he had a thirst on him, and he came to a public-house, and he wouldn't go in, but he stopped and bid the boy bring him a drink. But a little farther on the road the horse got a fall and the bottle was broke.'

And one story implies that the bottle was likely to be broken if you went 'too late'. A man from between Gort and Kiltartan says: 'Biddy Early didn't like you to go too late. Brien's sister was sick a long time, and when the brother went to her at the last she gave him a bottle with a cure. But on the way home the bottle broke, and the car and the horse got a fright and ran away. And when Dr. Nolan was sent for to see her, he was led astray, and it's beyond Ballylee he found himself. And surely she was *taken* if ever any one was'.

Her 'second sight' seems to have been even more remarkable than her cures, and every one who ever went to her speaks of it with wonder. A very old woman in Kiltartan[20] says: 'I went to Biddy Early one time myself, about my little boy that's now in America, that was lying sick in the house. But on the way to her I met a sergeant of police, and he asked where I was going, and when I told him, to joke like he said, "Biddy Early's after dying". "Then the devil die with her", said I. Well, when I got to the house, what do you think, if she didn't know that, and what I said. And she was vexed, and at the first she would do nothing for me. I had a pound for her here in my bosom, but when I held it out she wouldn't take it, but she turned the rings on her fingers, for she had a ring for every one, and she said, "A shilling for one, sixpence for another". But all she told me was that the boy was nervous, and so he was, she was right in that, and that he'd get well, and so he did.

'There was a man beyond, one Coen, was walking near the gate the same day, and he turned his foot and hurt it, and she knew that. She told me she slept in Ballylee Mill last night, and that there was a cure for all things in the world between the two wheels there'.

The witch doctor Kerwin says that 'the cure for all ills' was the moss on the stones, but that it cured evils done by the fairies and not common evils. When Biddy Early spoke of sleeping in Ballylee Mill, which is a great many miles from Feakle, she meant that she had been 'away' the night before and journeyed about where she would. A woman near

Derrykeil in the Slieve Echtge hills, says: 'I went to her myself one time to get a cure for myself where I was hurt with a fall I got coming down that hill over there. And she gave me what cured me, and she told me all about the whole place, and that there was a bowl broken in the house, and so there was'. A fall is often believed to be the work of the fairies. A woman at Tillyra says: 'There was a boy of the Saggartons in the house beyond went to Biddy Early, and she told him the name of the girl he would marry, and he did marry her after. And she cured him of a weakness he had and cured many, but it was seldom the bottle she'd give could be brought home without being spilled. I wonder did she go to *them* when she died? She got the cure among them anyway'.

A woman in Gort says: 'There was a man went to Biddy Early, and she told him that the woman he'd marry would have her husband killed by her brother. And it happened, for the woman he married was sitting by the fire with her husband and the brother came in having a drop of drink taken, and threw a pint pot at him that hit him in the head and killed him. It was the man that married her that told me this. One time she called in a man that was passing, and gave him a glass of whisky, and then she said to him, "The road you were going home by, don't go by it". So he asked why not, and she took the bottle, a long shaped bottle it was, and looked at it, holding it up, and then she bid him look through it and he'd see what would happen. But her husband said: "Don't show it to him, it might give him a fright he wouldn't get over". So she only said: "Well, go home by another way", and so he did and got home safe, for in the bottle she had seen a party of men that wouldn't have let him pass alive.

'She got the rites of the Church when she died, but first she was made to break the bottle'.

A man at Corcomroe says: 'There was a man, one Flaherty, came to his brother-in-law's house one day to borrow a horse. And the next day the horse was sent back, but he didn't come himself. And after a few days more they went to ask for him, but he had never come back at all. So the brother-in-law came to Biddy Early's. And she and some others were drinking whisky, and they were sorry that they were at the bottom of the bottle. And she said, "That's no matter; there's a man on his way now, there soon will be more". And sure enough there was; for he brought a bottle with him. So when he came in he told her about Flaherty having disappeared. And she described to him a corner of a garden at the back of a house, and she said, "Go look for him there and you'll find him". And so they did, dead and buried.

'Another time a man's cattle was dying, and he went to her and she said: "Is there such a place as Benburb?" naming a forth up on the hill beyond there, "for it's there they're gone". And sure enough it was toward that forth they were straying before they died.' The cattle were in Benburb 'forth' or rath, for cattle are taken by the fairies as often as are women.

She was consulted about all kinds of things, for she knew all fairy things. A man at Doneraile, Co. Cork, tells how a man asked her to help him to find a buried treasure, but the story is vague, and he did not know the name of the man. He indeed knows much about her, but it is all vague, and he thinks that she is still living. He says: 'A man dreamed there was treasure in a certain "forth", and he went to her and asked what he should do. She said it must not be more than four that would dig for it. He and she and two others went, and they dug until they came to the lid of a big earthen pot, and she killed a black cock. A thing like a big ox came at them, and she said it was no use and that they must go home, because five and not four had come. They found a man watching behind the ditch, and they beat him before they went home. The next day the hole they had dug was filled up.'

The priests tried vainly to keep the people from going to her.

An old man on the beach at Duras says: 'The priests were greatly against Biddy Early, and there's no doubt at all it was from the fairies she got her knowledge. But who wouldn't go to hell for a cure when one of his own is sick?'

An old woman at Feakle[21] says: 'There was a man I knew, living near the sea, and he set out to go to her at one time. And on the way he went into his brother-in-law's house, and a priest came in there and bid him not to go. "Well, Father", says he, "cure me yourself if you won't let me go to her to be cured". And when the priest wouldn't do that, he said: "Go on I will", and he went to her. And the minute he came in: "Well", says she, "you made a great fight for me on the way". For though it's against our creed to believe it, she could hear every earthly thing that was said in every part, miles off. But she had two red eyes, and some used to say, "If she can cure so much, why can't she cure her own eyes?"'

When she spoke of the red eyes, an old man who was listening said: 'She had no red eyes, but was a nice clean-looking woman. Any one might have red eyes at a time they'd have a cold, or the like'; this man had been to see her. A woman at Burren says: 'There was one Casey, in Kinvara, and he went to her one time for a cure. And Father Xavier came to the house and was mad with him for going, and, says he, "You take the cure out of the hand of God". And Mrs. Casey said, "Your reverence, none of us can do that". "Well", says Father Xavier, "then I'll see what the devil can do, and I'll send my horse to-morrow that has a sore on his leg this long time, and try will she be able to cure him".

'So next day he sent a man with his horse, and when he got to Biddy Early's house she came out, and she told him every word Father Xavier had said, and she cured the sore. So after that he left the people alone. But before it he'd be dressed in a frieze coat, and a whip in his hand, driving away the people from going to her'.

A woman near Coole[22] says: 'The priests took the bottle from Biddy Early before she died, and they found some sort of black things in it'. The bottle was of course merely a bottle of some kind of liquid in which she looked as 'crystal gazers' look into their crystals. She was surrounded all her life by a great deal of terror and reverence, but perhaps the terror was the greatest. She seems to have known how greatly she was feared, for a man who lived by the roadside near Tillyra says: 'I was with her myself one time and got a cure from her for my little girl that was sick. A bottle of whisky I brought her, and the first thing she did was to give me a glass out of it, "For", says she, "you'll maybe want it, my poor man". But I had plenty of courage in those days'.

A little while ago I met in Dublin a young man not at all of the people, and he told me that an uncle of his had once been her landlord, but had evicted her because of the scandal of seeing such great crowds drawn to her by what he held superstition, or diabolical power, I am not sure which. She cursed him, and in a very little time a house he was visiting at was burned to the ground and he was burned to death.

The 'knowledgeable' men and women may leave their knowledge to some one before they die, but few believe that Biddy Early left her knowledge to any one. One woman said to my friend, 'It's said that at a hurling the other day, there was a small little man seen, and that he was a friend of hers, and that she had left him the gift'; but the woman's husband said 'No; the bottle was broken, and, anyhow, she had no power to pass it on; it was given to her for the term of her life'.

THE LITERARY MOVEMENT
IN IRELAND

*On 27 April 1899, Yeats wrote to Lady Gregory that he had accepted
a commission of £30 "to do an article . . . on The Intellectual Movement in Ireland for* The North American Review" *(CL2, 404). The
result, "The Literary Movement in Ireland," in the issue for December 1899, is an extended statement of the major sources of inspiration
of the movement. A revised version was included by Lady Gregory—
along with essays by AE, D. P. Moran, George Moore, Douglas Hyde,
and Standish O'Grady—in her* Ideals in Ireland *(1901). The present
text is the revised version; for the earlier version, see* The North
American Review. *Most of Yeats's changes have the effect of qualify-
ing his earlier assertions or placing his ideas in a less immediate and
narrow chronology. Also, the second version quotes less from Douglas
Hyde and more from Lady Gregory, in anticipation, perhaps, of the
appearance of her collection of translations,* Poets and Dreamers.*

Yeats's other contribution to Ideals in Ireland *was "A Postscript to
a Forthcoming Book of Essays by Various Irish Writers," published in
the 1 December 1900 issue of Standish O'Grady's* All Ireland Review
(see LAR, 51–52).

I have just come to a quiet Connacht† house from seeing a little movement, in a great movement of thought which is fashioning the dreams
of the next generation in Ireland, grow to a sudden maturity. Certain
plays, which are an expression of the most characteristic ideals of what
is sometimes called the 'Celtic movement', have been acted in Dublin
before audiences drawn from all classes and all political sections, and
described at great length in every Nationalist newspaper. Whatever be
the merit of these plays, and that must be left to the judgment of time,
their success means, as I think, that the 'Celtic movement', which has
hitherto interested but a few cultivated people, is about to become a
part of the thought of Ireland.

Before 1891, Unionists and Nationalists[1] were too busy keeping one or two simple beliefs at their fullest intensity for any complexity of thought or emotion; and the national imagination uttered itself, with a somewhat broken energy, in a few stories and in many ballads about the need of unity against England, about the martyrs who had died at the hand of England, or about the greatness of Ireland before the coming of England. They built up Ireland's dream of Ireland, of an ideal country weighed down by immemorial sorrows and served by heroes and saints, and they taught generations of young men to love their country with a love that was the deepest emotion they were ever to know; but they built with the virtues and beauties and sorrows and hopes that would move to tears the greatest number of those eyes before whom the modern world is but beginning to unroll itself; and, except when some rare, personal impulse shaped the song according to its will, they built to the formal and conventional rhythm which would give the most immediate pleasure to ears that had forgotten Gaelic poetry and not learned the subtleties of English poetry. The writers who made this literature or who shaped its ideals, in the years before the great famine,[2] lived at the moment when the middle class had brought to perfection its ideal of the good citizen, and of a politics and a philosophy and a literature which would help him upon his way; and they made a literature full of the civic virtues and, in all but its unbounded patriotism, without inconvenient ardours. They took their style from Scott and Campbell and Macaulay, and that 'universally popular' poetry which is really the poetry of the middle class, and from Beranger and that 'peasant poetry' which looks for its models to the Burns of 'Highland Mary' and 'The Cotter's[†] Saturday Night.'[3] Here and there a poet or a story-writer found an older dream among the common people or in his own mind, and made a personality for himself, and was forgotten; for it was the desire of everybody to be moved by the same emotions as everybody else, and certainly one cannot blame a desire which has thrown so great a shadow of self-sacrifice.

The fall of Parnell[4] and the wreck of his party and of the organisations that supported it were the symbols, if not the causes, of a sudden change. They were followed by movements and organisations that brought the ideas and the ideals which are the expression of personalities alike into politics, economics, and literature. Those who looked for the old energies, which were the utterance of the common will and hope, were unable to see that a new kind of Ireland, as full of energy as a boiling pot, was rising up amid the wreck of the old kind, and that the national life was finding a new utterance. This utterance was so necessary that it seems as if the hand that broke the ball of glass, that now lies in fragments full of a new iridescent life, obeyed some impulse from beyond its wild and capricious will. More books about Irish subjects have been published in these last eight years than in the thirty years that went before them, and these books have the care for scholarship and the precision of speech which had been notoriously lacking in books on Irish subjects. An appeal to the will, a habit of thought which measures all beliefs by their intensity, is content with a strenuous rhetoric; but an appeal to the intellect needs an always more perfect knowledge, an always more malleable speech. The new writers and the new organisations they work through—for organisations of various kinds take the place held by the critical press in other countries—have awakened Irish affections among many from whom the old rhetoric could never have got a hearing, but they have been decried for weakening the national faith by lovers of the old rhetoric. I have seen an obscure Irish member of Parliament rise at one of those monthly meetings of the Irish Literary Society,[5] when the members of the society read sometimes their poems to one another, and ask their leave to read a poem. He did not belong to the society, but leave was given him, and he read a poem in the old manner, blaming the new critics and praising the old poems which had made him patriotic and filled his imagination with the images of the martyrs, and, as he numbered over their names, Wolfe Tone, Emmet, Owen Roe, Sarsfield,[6] his voice shook, and many were angry with the new critics.

The organisations that are making this change are the Irish Literary Society in London, the National Literary Society in Dublin, which has founded or rather sheltered with its influence, the Irish Literary Theatre, and the Feis Ceoil Committee in Dublin, at whose annual series of concerts of Irish music, singers and pipers from all parts of Ireland compete; and more important than all, the Gaelic League,[7] which has worked for the revival of the Gaelic language with such success that it has sold fifty thousand of its Gaelic text-books in a year. All these organisations have been founded since the fall of Parnell; and all are busy in preserving, or in moulding anew and without any thought of the politics of the hour, some utterance of the national life, and in opposing the vulgar books and vulgarer songs that come to us from England. We are preparing, as we hope, for a day when Ireland will speak in Gaelic, as much as Wales speaks in Welsh, within her borders, but speak, it may be, in English to other nations of those truths which were committed to her when 'He set the borders of the nations according to His angels;' as Dionysius the Areopagite[8] has written. Already, as I think, a new kind of romance, a new element in thought, is being moulded out of Irish life and traditions, and this element may have an importance for criticism, even should criticism forget the writers who are trying to embody it in their work, while looking each one through his own colour in the dome of many-coloured glass.[9]

Contemporary English literature takes delight in praising England and her Empire, the master-work and dream of the middle class; and, though it may escape from this delight, it must long continue to utter the ideals of the strong and wealthy. Irish intellect has always been pre-occupied with the weak and with the poor, and now it has begun to collect and describe their music and stories, and to utter anew the beliefs and hopes which they alone remember. It may never make a literature preoccupied with the circumstance of their lives, like the 'peasant poetry', whose half deliberate triviality, passionless virtue, and pas-sionless vice has helped so many orderly lives; for a writer who wishes to write with his whole mind must knead the beliefs and hopes, which he has made his own, with the circumstance of his own life. Burns had this preoccupation, and nobody will deny that he was a great poet; but even he had the poverty of emotions and ideas of a peasantry that had lost, like the middle class into which it would have its children absorbed, the imagination that is in tradition without finding the imagination that is in books. Irish literature may prolong its first inspiration without renouncing the complexity of ideas and emotions which is the inheritance of cultivated men, for it will have learned from the discoveries of modern learning that the common people, wherever civilization has not driven its plough too deep, keep a watch over the roots of all religion and all romance. Their poetry trembles upon the verge of incoherence with a passion all but unknown among modern poets, and their sense of beauty exhausts itself in countless legends and in metaphors that seem to mirror the energies of nature.

Dr. Hyde has collected many old Irish peasant love-songs, and, like all primitive poetry, they foreshadow a poetry whose intensity of emo-tion, or strangeness of language, has made it the poetry of little coter-ies. His peasant lover cries—[10]

> It is happy for you, O blind man, who do not see much of
>   women.
> O! if you were to see what I see, you would be sick even as I
>   am.
> It is a pity, O God, that it was not blind I was before I saw her
>   twisted hair.
> I always thought the blind were pitiable, until my calamity
>   grew beyond the grief of all,
> Then though it is a pity I turned my pity into envy.

In a loop of the loops in a loop am I.
It is sorrow for whoever has seen her, and it is sorrow for him
    who does not see her every day.
It is sorrow for him who is tied in the knot of her love, and it
    is sorrow for him who is loosed out of it.
It is sorrow for him who is near her, and it is sorrow for him
    who is not near her.

Or he cries—

O Maurya! you are my love, and the love of my heart is your
    love—
Love that is without littleness, without weakness,
Love from age till death,
Love growing out of folly,
Love that will send me close beneath the clay,
Love without a hope of the world,
Love without envy of fortune,
Love that has left me withered in captivity,
Love of my heart beyond women;
And a love such as that, it is seldom to be got from any man.[11]

And Lady Gregory has translated a lament, that Raftery[12] the wandering fiddler made for a fiddler some sixty years ago, into the simple
English of the country people of to-day—

The swans on the water are nine times blacker than a black-
    berry, since the man died from us that had pleasantness
    on the top of his fingers;
His two grey eyes were like the dew of the morning that lies
    on the grass;
And since he was laid in the grave, the cold is getting the
    upper hand.
There are young women, and not without reason, sorry and
    heartbroken and withered, since he was left at the
    church;
Their hair, thrown down and hanging, turned grey on their
    head.
No flower in any garden, and the leaves of the trees have leave
    to cry, and they falling on the ground;
There are no green flowers on the tops of the tufts since there
    did a boarded coffin go on Daly.

All are not like this, but the most inspired and, as I think, the most characteristic are like this. There is a square stone tower called Ballylee Castle,[13] a couple of miles from where I am writing. A farmer called Hynes, who had a beautiful daughter, Mary Hynes, lived near it some sixty years ago; and all over the countryside old men and old women still talk of her beauty, and the young and old praise her with a song made by Raftery—

O star of light, and O sun in harvest,
O amber hair, O my share of the world;
There is no good to deny it or to try and hide it,
She is the sun in the heavens who wounded my heart.

There was no part of Ireland I did not travel,
From the rivers to the tops of the mountains,
To the edge of Lough Greine,[14] whose mouth is hidden,
And I saw no beauty but was behind hers.

It is Mary Hynes, the calm and easy woman,
Has beauty in her mind and in her face;
If a hundred clerks were gathered together
They could not write down a half of her ways.[15]

This song, though Gaelic poetry has fallen from its old greatness, has come out of the same dreams as the songs and legends, as vague, it may be, as the clouds of evening and of dawn, that became in Homer's mind the memory and the prophecy of all the sorrows that have beset and shall beset the journey of beauty in the world.[16] A very old woman who remembers Mary Hynes said to me, and to a friend who was with me: 'I never saw one so handsome as she was, and I never will until I die. There were people coming from all parts to look at her, and maybe some of them forgot to say, "God bless her".[17] Any way she was young when she died, and my mother was at her funeral, and as to whether she was taken, well, there's others have been taken that were not handsome at all, and so it's likely enough she might have been, for there is no one to be seen at all that is handsome like she was'. The spirit of Helen[18] moves indeed among the legends that are told about turf-fires, and among the legends of the poor and simple everywhere. A friend of mine was told a while ago, in a remote part of Donegal, of a young man who saw a light before him on the road, and found when he came near that it was from a lock of hair in an open box. The hair was so bright that, when he went into the stable where he slept, he put the box into a hole in the wall and had no need of a candle. After many wanderings he found her from whose head it had been taken, and after many adventures married her and reigned over a kingdom.

The peasant remembers such songs and legends, all the more, it may be, because he has thought of little but cows and sheep and the like in his own marriage, for his dream has never been entangled by reality. The beauty of women is mirrored in his mind, as the excitement of the world is mirrored in the minds of children, and like them he thinks nothing but the best worth remembering. The child William Blake said to somebody who had told him of a fine city, that he thought no city fine that had not walls of gold and silver.[19] It may be that poetry is the utterance of desires that we can only satisfy in dreams, and that if all our dreams were satisfied there would be no more poetry. Dreams pass from us with childhood, because we are so often told they can never come true, and because we are taught with so much labour to admire the paler beauty of the world. The children of the poor and simple learn from their unbroken religious faith, and from their traditional beliefs, and from the hardness of their lives, that this world is nothing, and that a spiritual world, where all dreams come true, is everything; and therefore the poor and simple are that imperfection whose perfection is genius.

The most of us think that all things, when imagined in their perfection, that all images which emotion desires in its intensity, are among the things nobody has ever seen or shall ever see; and so we are always reminding one another not to go too far from the moderation of reality. But the Irish peasant believes that the utmost he can dream was once or still is a reality by his own door. He will point to some mountain and tell you that some famous hero or beauty lived and sorrowed there, or he will tell you that Tír na nÓg, the country of the young, the old Celtic paradise,—the Land of the Living Heart, as it used to be called,—is all about him. An old woman close by Ballylee Castle said to a friend of mine the other day, when someone had finished a story of the poet Usheen's return from Tír na nÓg,[20] where he had lived with his fairy mistress: 'Tír na nÓg? That place is not far from us. One time I was in the chapel of Labane, and there was a tall thin man sitting next to me, and he dressed in grey; and after the mass I asked him where he came from. "From Tír na nÓg", he said. "And where is that?" I asked him. "It's not far from you", he said. "It's near the place where you live". I remember well the look of him, and he telling me that. The priest was looking at us while we were talking together'.

There are many grotesque things near at hand, the dead doing their penance in strange shapes, and evil spirits with terrible and ugly shapes, but people of a perfect beauty are never far off; and this beauty is often, I know not how often, that heroic beauty 'which changes least from youth to age', and which has faded from modern painting and poetry before a fleeting voluptuous beauty. One old Mayo woman, who can neither read nor write, described it to me, though with grotesque comparisons. She has been long in service, and her language has not the simplicity of those who live among fields. She was standing in the window of her master's house looking out toward a mountain where Queen Maeve, the Queen of the Western Spirits,[21] is said to have been buried, when she saw 'the finest woman she ever saw' travelling right across from the mountain and straight to her. The woman had a sword by her side and a dagger lifted up in her hand, and was dressed in white, with bare arms and feet. She looked 'very strong and warry and fierce, but not wicked;' that is, not cruel, at all. The old woman had seen the Irish giant, and 'though he was a fine man, he was nothing to this woman, for he was round, and could not have stepped out so soldierly'. She told me that she was like a certain stately lady of the neighbourhood, 'but she had no stomach on her, and was slight and broad in the shoulders, and was handsomer than anyone you ever saw now; she looked about thirty'. The old woman covered her eyes with her hands, and when she uncovered them the apparition had vanished. The neighbours were 'wild' with her for not waiting to see if there was a message, for they are sure it was Queen Maeve, who often shows herself to the pilots. I asked the old woman if she had seen others like Queen Maeve, and she said: 'Some of them have their hair down, but they look quite different, like the sleepy-looking ladies you see in the papers. Those with their hair up are like this one. The others have long white dresses, but those with their hair up have short dresses, so that you can see their legs right up to the calf'. After some careful questioning I found that they wore what appeared to be buskins.[22] She went on: 'They are fine and dashing-looking, like the men one sees riding their horses in twos and threes on the slopes of the mountains, with their swords swinging'. She repeated over and over: 'There is no such race living now, none so fine proportioned', or the like, and then said: 'The present queen is a nice, pleasant-looking woman, but she is not like her. What makes me think so little of the ladies is that I see none as they be', meaning the spirits; 'when I think of her and of the ladies now, they are like little children running about, without being able to put their clothes on right. Is it the ladies? Why, I would not call them women at all!'

There are many old heroical tales about Queen Maeve, and before she was a queen she was a goddess and had her temples, and she is still the most beautiful of the beautiful. A young man among the Burren Hills of Clare told me, a couple of years ago, that he remembered an old poet who had made his poems in Irish, and had met in his youth one who had called herself Queen Maeve, and asked him if he would have money or pleasure. He said he would have pleasure, and she gave him her love for a time, and then went from him and ever after he was very sad. The young man had often heard him sing a lamentation he had made, but could only remember that it was 'very mournful', and called her 'Beauty of all Beauty'. The song may have been but a resinging of a traditional theme, but the young man believed it.

Many, perhaps most, of those that I have talked with of these things have all their earthly senses, but those who have most knowledge of these things, so much indeed that they are permitted, it is thought, to speak but broken words, are those from whom the earthly senses have fallen away. 'In every household' of the spirits even, there is 'a queen and a fool, and, maybe, the fool is the wisest of all'. This fool, who is held to wander in lonely places and to bewitch men out of the world,—for the touch of the queen and of the fool give death,—is the type of that old wisdom from which the good citizen and the new wisdom have led the world away, forgetting that 'the ruins of time build mansions in eternity'.[23] The poetry that comes out of the old wisdom must turn always to religion and to the law of the hidden world, while the poetry of the new wisdom must not forget politics and the law of the visible world; and between these poetries there cannot be any lasting peace. Those that follow the old wisdom must not shrink too greatly from the journey described in some verses Miss Hopper, a poet of our school, has put into the mouth of Daluan,[†] the fairy fool—

The world wears on to sundown, and love is lost or won,
But he recks not of loss or gain, the King of Ireland's son.
He follows on for ever when all your chase is done,
He follows after shadows, the King of Ireland's son.[24]

Alone among nations, Ireland has in her written Gaelic literature, in her old love tales and battle tales, the forms in which the imagination of Europe uttered itself before Greece shaped a tumult of legend into her music of the arts; and she can discover, from the beliefs and emotions of her common people, the habit of mind that created the religion of the muses. The legends of other European countries are less numerous, and not so full of the energies from which the arts and our understanding of their sanctity arose, and the best of them have already been shaped into plays and poems. 'The Celt,' as it seems, created romance, when his stories of Arthur and of the Grail became for a time almost the only inspiration of European literature, and it would not be wonderful if he should remould romance after its oldest image, now that he is recovering his possessions.

*　　*　　*

The movement of thought which has made the good citizen, or has been made by him, has surrounded us with comfort and safety, and with vulgarity and insincerity. One finds alike its energy and its weariness in churches which have substituted a system of morals for spiritual ardour; in pictures which have substituted conventionally pretty faces for the disquieting revelations of sincerity; in poets who have set the praises of those things good citizens think praiseworthy above a dangerous delight in beauty for the sake of beauty. The Romantic movement, from the times of Blake and Shelley and Keats, when it took a new form, has been battling with the thoughts of the good citizen, as moss and ivy and grass battle with some old building, crumbling its dead stone and mortar into the living greenery of earth. The disorders of a Shelley or of a Heine[25] in their art, and in their lives that mirror their art, are but a too impetuous ardour of battle, a too swift leaping of ivy or of grass to window ledge or gable end; and the intensity and strangeness of a picture by Rossetti or of an early picture by Watts are but a sudden falling of stones.[26] Moss and ivy and grass gather against stone and mortar in unceasing enmity, for while the old is crumbling the new is building; and the Romantic movement will never have perfect victory unless, as mystics have thought, the golden age is to come again, and men's hearts and the weather to grow gentle as time fades into eternity. Blake said that all art was a labour to bring that golden age,[27] and we call romantic art romantic because it has made that age's light dwell in the imaginations of a little company of studious persons.

Because the greater number of persons are too busy with the work of the world to forget the light of the sun, romantic art is, as I think, about to change its manner and become more like the art of the old poets, who saw the golden age and their own age side by side like substance and shadow. Ever since Christianity turned men's minds to Judea, and learning turned them to Greece and Rome, the sanctity has dwindled from their own hills and valleys, which the legends and beliefs of fifty centuries had filled so full of it that a man could hardly plough his fields or follow his sheep upon the hillside without remembering some august story, or walking softly lest he had divine companions. When the valleys and the hills had almost become clay and stone, the good citizens plucked up their heart and took possession of the world and filled it with their little compact thoughts; and romance fled to more and more remote fairylands, and forgot that it was ever more than an old tale which nobody believes. But now we are growing interested in our own countries, and discovering that the common people in all countries that have not given themselves up to the improvements and devices of good citizens, which we call civilization, still half understand the sanctity of their hills and valleys; and at the same time a change of thought is making us half ready to believe with Ecclesiasticus, that 'all things are made double one above another',[28] and that the forms of nature may be temporal shadows of realities.

In a little time places may begin to seem the only hieroglyphs that cannot be forgotten, and poets to remember that they will come the nearer the old poets, who had a seat at every hearth, if they mingle their own dream with a story told for centuries of some mountain that casts its shadows upon many doors, and if they understand that the beauty they celebrate is a part of the paradise men's eyes shall look upon when they close upon the world. The paradise of the Christian, as those who think more of the order of communities than of the nature of things have shaped it, is but the fulfilment of one dream; but the paradise that the common people tell of about the fire, and still half understand, is the fulfilment of all dreams, and opens its gates as gladly to the perfect lover as to the perfect saint, and only he who understands it can lift romance into prophecy and make beauty holy. Their paradise, Tirnan-og, the Land of the Living Heart, the Grass Green Island of Apples, call it what you will, created that religion of the muses which gave the arts to the world; and those countries whose traditions are fullest of it, and of the sanctity of places, may yet remould romance till it has become a covenant between intellectual beauty and the beauty of the world. We cannot know how many these countries are until the new science of folklore and the almost new science of mythology have done their work; but Ireland, if she can awake again the but half-forgotten legends of Slieve Gullion, or of Cruachmagh, or of the hill where Maeve is buried,[29] and make them an utterance of that desire to be at rest amid ideal perfection which is becoming conscious in the minds of poets as the good citizen wins the priests over to his side; or if she can make us believe that the beautiful things that move us to awe, white lilies among dim shadows, windy twilights over grey sands, dewy and silent places among hazel trees by still waters, are in truth, and not in phantasy alone, the symbols, or the dwellings, of immortal presences, she will have begun a change that, whether it is begun in our time or not for centuries, will some day make all lands holy lands again.

Ireland has no great wealth, no preoccupation with successful persons to turn her writers' eyes to any lesser destiny. Even the poetry which had its form and much of its matter from alien thought dwelt, as the Gaelic ballads had done before it, on ideas living in the perfection of hope, on visions of unfulfilled desire, and not on the sordid compromise of success. The popular poetry of England celebrates her victories, but the popular poetry of Ireland remembers only defeats and defeated persons. A ballad that is in every little threepenny and sixpenny ballad book asks if Ireland has no pride in her Lawrences and Wellingtons,[30] and answers that these belong to the Empire and not to Ireland, whose 'heart beats high' for men who died in exile or in prison; and this ballad is a type of all. The popular poetry, too, has made love of the earth of Ireland so much a part of her literature that it should not be a hard thing to fill it with the holiness of places. Politics are, indeed, the forge in which nations are made, and the smith has been so long busy making Ireland according to His will that she may well have some important destiny. But whether this is so or not, whether this destiny is to make her in the arts, as she is in politics, a voice of the idealism of the common people, who still remember the dawn of the world, or to give her an unforeseen history, it can but express the accidents and energies of her past, and criticism does its natural work in trying to prophesy this expression; and, even if it is mistaken, a prophecy is not always made all untrue by being unfulfilled. A few years will decide if the writers of Ireland are to shape themselves in our time for the fulfilment of this prophecy, for need and much discussion will bring a new national agreement, and the political tumult awake again.

Copy Texts,
Emendations,
and Notes

COPY TEXTS
USED IN THIS VOLUME

1. The Poetry of Sir Samuel Ferguson—I: *The Irish Fireside* (9 October 1886), 220.
2. The Poetry of Sir Samuel Ferguson—II: *The Dublin University Review* (November 1886), 923–41.
3. The Poetry of R. D. Joyce: *The Irish Fireside* (27 November and 4 December 1886), part 1, 331, and part 2, 347–48.
4. Clarence Mangan (1803–1849): *The Irish Fireside* (12 March 1887), 169–70.
5. A fragment of "Finn MacCool": from John Kelly's essay "Aesthete among the Athletes: Yeats's Contributions to *The Gael*" in *Yeats: An Annual of Critical and Textual Studies,* ed. Richard J. Finneran, 2 (Ithaca, N.Y.: Cornell University Press, 1984), 86–91.
6. The Celtic Romances in Miss Tynan's New Book: from John Kelly's essay "Aesthete among the Athletes: Yeats's Contributions to *The Gael*" in *Yeats: An Annual of Critical and Textual Studies,* ed. Richard J. Finneran, 2 (Ithaca, N.Y.: Cornell University Press, 1984), 98–114.
7. Miss Tynan's New Book: *The Irish Fireside* (9 July 1887), 444.
8. The Prose and Poetry of Wilfred Blunt: *United Ireland* (28 January 1888), 6.
9. Irish Fairies, Ghosts, Witches, etc.: *Lucifer* (15 January 1889), 399–404.
10. *Irish Wonders: The Scots Observer* (30 March 1889), 530–31.
11. John Todhunter: *The Magazine of Poetry* (Buffalo) (April 1889), 143–44.
12. William Carleton: *The Scots Observer* (19 October 1889), 608–9.
13. Popular Ballad Poetry of Ireland: *The Leisure Hour* (November 1889), 32–38.
14. Bardic Ireland: *The Scots Observer* (4 January 1890), 182–83.
15. Tales from the Twilight: *The Scots Observer* (1 March 1890), 408–9.
16. Irish Fairies: *The Leisure Hour* (October 1890), 811–14.
17. Irish Folk Tales: *The National Observer* (28 February 1891), 382–84.
18. *Gypsy Sorcery and Fortune Telling*: from John Kelly's essay "Yeatsian and Rational Magic" in *Yeats Annual* 3, ed. Warwick Gould (London: Macmillan Press, 1985), 186–87.
19. Plays by an Irish Poet: *United Ireland* (11 July 1891), 5.
20. Clarence Mangan's Love Affair: *United Ireland* (22 August 1891), 5–6.
21. A Reckless Century. Irish Rakes and Duellists: *United Ireland* (12 September 1891), 5.
22. Oscar Wilde's Last Book: *United Ireland* (26 September 1891), 5.
23. The Young Ireland League: *United Ireland* (3 October 1891), 5.
24. A Poet We Have Neglected: *United Ireland* (12 December 1891), 5.
25. Poems by Miss Tynan: *Evening Herald* (London) (2 January 1892), 2.
26. The New 'Speranza': *United Ireland* (16 January 1892), 5.
27. Dr. Todhunter's Irish Poems: *United Ireland* (23 January 1892), 5.

69. William Carleton: *The Bookman* (New York) (August 1896), 549–50.
70. Greek Folk Poesy: *The Bookman* 11, no. 61 (October 1896), 16–17.
71. *The Well at the World's End: The Bookman* 11, no. 62 (November 1896), 37–38.
72. Miss Fiona Macleod as a Poet: *The Bookman* 11, no. 63 (December 1896), 92–93.
73. *Young Ireland: The Bookman* 11, no. 64 (January 1897), 120.
74. Mr. John O'Leary: *The Bookman* 11, no. 65 (February 1897), 147.
75. Mr. Arthur Symons' New Book: *The Bookman* 12, no. 67 (April 1897), 15.
76. Miss Fiona Macleod: *The Sketch* (28 April 1897), 20.
77. *The Treasure of the Humble: The Bookman* 12, no. 70 (July 1897), 94.
78. Mr. Standish O'Grady's *Flight of the Eagle: The Bookman* 12, no. 71 (August 1897), 123.
79. Bards of the Gael and the Gall: from Deirdre Toomey's essay "Bards of the Gael and Gall: An Uncollected Review by Yeats in *The Illustrated London News*" in *Yeats Annual 5*, ed. Warwick Gould (London: Macmillan Press, 1987), 208–10.
80. *Aglavaine and Sélysette: The Bookman* 12, no. 72 (September 1897), 155.
81. The Tribes of Danu: *The New Review* (November 1897), 549–63.
82. Three Irish Poets: *The Irish Homestead* (December 1897), 7.
83. The Prisoners of the Gods: *The Nineteenth Century* (January 1898), 91–104.
84. Mr. Lionel Johnson's Poems: *The Bookman* 13, no. 77 (February 1898), 155–56.
85. Mr. Rhys' *Welsh Ballads: The Bookman* 14, no. 79 (April 1898), 14–15.
86. The Broken Gates of Death: *The Fortnightly Review* (April 1898), 524–36.
87. *Le Mouvement Celtique:* Fiona Macleod: *L'Irlande Libre* 2, no. 4 (1 April 1898), 1.
88. AE's Poems: *The Sketch* (6 April 1898), 476.
89. *Le Mouvement Celtique:* II. M. John O'Leary: *L'Irlande Libre* 2, no. 6 (1 June 1898), 2.
90. Celtic Beliefs About the Soul: *The Bookman* 14, no. 84 (September 1898), 159–60.
91. John Eglinton and Spiritual Art: *Literary Ideals in Ireland* (London: T. Fisher Unwin, 1899), 31–37.
92. A Symbolic Artist and the Coming of Symbolic Art: *The Dome* (December 1898), 233–37. Illustrations are found on pp. 227, 229, 231, and 255.
93. High Crosses of Ireland: *The Daily Express* (Dublin) (28 January 1899), 3.
94. Notes on Traditions and Superstitions: *Folk-lore* (March 1899), 119–23.
95. The Irish Literary Theatre: *Literature* (6 May 1899), 474.
96. *The Dominion of Dreams: The Bookman* 16, no. 94 (July 1899), 105.
97. Ireland Bewitched: *The Contemporary Review* (September 1899), 388–404.
98. The Literary Movement in Ireland: *Ideals in Ireland* (London: At the Unicorn, 1901), 87–102.

EMENDATIONS
TO THE COPY TEXTS

The Poetry of Sir Samuel Ferguson—I

Page.Line	Copy Text Reading	Authority for Emendation
4.10	Dierdre	proper name
4.16	books, 'The Fairy Thorn.' Does	misprint
6.3	Dierdre	proper name
6.26	Dierdre	proper name
6.26	Dierdre	proper name
7.2	Knocknurea	proper name
7.37	De Vere	proper name
7.37	Dierdre	proper name
8.17	Dierdre	proper name
8.18	Conar	proper name
8.21	Usnac	proper name
8.21	Naise	proper name
8.30	Albu	proper name
8.33	Usnac	proper name
8.35	Conar	proper name
9.9	Spencer	proper name

The Poetry of Sir Samuel Ferguson—II

12.22	Tian	proper name
13.6	Cuchullin	proper name
14.10	counseller	misspelling
14.15	Cuchullin	proper name
14.39	Naisi	proper name
16.1	Naisi	proper name
17.12	Neesa's	proper name
19.15	Cuchullin	proper name
20.11	Sidhs	proper name
21.33	find	grammatical error
26.38	persistance	misspelling

The Poetry of R. D. Joyce

31.20	In the midst . . . companie!	quotation marks added
33.30	Dierdre	proper name
34.2	Feilemid	proper name
34.16	Lavarcum	proper name

34.26	Cuffin	proper name
35.10	Lavarcum	proper name
35.16	Lavarcum	proper name
36.11	Dierdre	proper name
36.18	Dierdre	proper name
36.18	Manahun	proper name
36.19	Dierdre	proper name
36.22	Naide	proper name
36.23	Dierdre	proper name
37.1	Dierdre	proper name
37.3	Dierdre	proper name
38.4	sunny shore	end punctuation added
38.6	Dierdre	proper name

Clarence Mangan

41.15	Mount Pleasant-square	proper name
43.11	ago	end punctuation added

Finn MacCool

46.41	Fin-eyes	proper name
47.2	Fin	proper name
47.2	Fin	proper name
47.21	Fin	proper name
47.27	Fin	proper name
48.3	Fin	proper name
48.4	Caolte	proper name
48.5	Millitia	misspelling
48.5	Albian	misspelling
48.9	Cuchillin	proper name
48.15	Cuchillin	proper name
48.19	Arthirian	misspelling
48.24	Fin	proper name
48.25	Fin	proper name
48.26	Cullun	proper name
48.37	Fin	proper name
48.39	Fin	proper name
48.41	Fin	proper name
49.9	Fin	proper name
49.9	Caolte	proper name
49.24	Fin	proper name
49.28	Hy-Brazil	proper name
49.29	Fin	proper name
49.35	Caolte	proper name
50.7	De Vere	proper name

The Celtic Romances in Miss Tynan's New Book

53.8	De Vere	proper name
53.10	Ehell	proper name
53.16	biggest. Argosy	punctuation error

53.20	Fionn Mac Cumhaill	proper name
53.22	Fionn	proper name
54.6	*Tir N'an Oge*	proper name
55.21	Fionn	proper name
55.37	Fionn	proper name
56.12	Fionn	proper name
56.13	Fionn, To	compositor's error
56.29	Fionn	proper name
57.17	Fionn	proper name
57.29	Benbulben	proper name
57.30	Fionn	proper name
57.30	Fionn	proper name
58.14	Fionn	proper name
60.17	'Fergussonish'	proper name
61.25	cheerfull	misspelling
62.21	rhiming	misspelling
62.29	*Valeare*	misspelling
62.35	'a child's day'	title
62.37	tears in	"and" added for clarity

Miss Tynan's New Book

65.13	pro-Raphaelite	proper name
65.16	finding her	"of" added for clarification
66.10	dew.	no end punctuation

The Prose and Poetry of Wilfred Blunt

71.27	Soloman	proper name
72.7	succeeding	printer's error

Irish Fairies, Ghosts, Witches, etc.

77.34	Sheoques	misspelling
77.41	*moruada*	misspelling
78.1	[parentheses added]	standardized style
78.40	sheoques	misspelling
79.16	sheoques	misspelling
79.23	sheoques	misspelling
79.26	Lepracaun	standardized spelling
79.27	[period inserted]	punctuation error
79.31	MacNally	proper name
79.39	Lepracaun	standardized spelling
80.34	*Piast-vestea*	misspelling
81.12	Dumaleaque	proper name
81.32	Tuath-de-Danan	proper name
81.37	Tuath-de-Danan	proper name

Irish Wonders

83.10	M'Anally	proper name
83.19	M'Anally	proper name

84.9	M'Anally	proper name
84.13	M'Anally's	proper name
84.15	M'Anally	proper name
84.17	leprechawn	standardized spelling
84.24	leprechawn	standardized spelling
85.6	leprechawn	standardized spelling
85.7	leprechawn	standardized spelling
85.9	M'Anally's	proper name
85.20	M'Anally	proper name

William Carleton

89.34	had	compositor's error
89.34	head	compositor's error

Popular Ballad Poetry of Ireland

94.7	leprechuan	standardized spelling
95.7	Earie	proper name
95.8	Hamborg	proper name
95.9	Fergusson	proper name
96.7	Timoleaque	proper name
96.8	Hefferman	proper name
97.33	(though now forty years since)	quotation marks misplaced
98.4	Mitchell	proper name
98.7	Mitchell	proper name
98.31	Fergusson	proper name
99.40	Mitchell	proper name
100.12	Mitchell	proper name
103.17	Osburne	proper name
103.28	Fergusson	proper name
103.36	'	quotation mark backwards
104.4	'	quotation mark backwards
105.20	Fergusson	proper name
105.27	Fergusson	proper name
105.36	Fergusson	proper name
107.24	Darcy	proper name
108.1	De Vere	proper name

Bardic Ireland

109.14	Fergusson	proper name
109.15	Fergusson	proper name
109.17	*Innisfail*	title
109.21	Fergusson	proper name
110.34	Cuchullin	proper name
110.43	Cuchullin	proper name
111.5	Dananns	proper name
111.7	Joubainville	proper name
111.17	Tuath dé Danann	proper name
111.21	Ma Cool	proper name
112.14	Cuchullin	proper name

Irish Fairies

121.9	Sleive	proper name
122.14	Lepricaun	standardized spelling
122.17	McNally	proper name

Irish Folk Tales

124.23	Paudeen	title
125.26	M'Anally's	proper name
126.12	*Leabhar Sgeulaighteachta*	title
126.33	fadoques	misspelling
126.33	fibeens	misspelling

Gypsy Sorcery and Fortune Telling

129.13	Altsedenberg	proper name

Plays by an Irish Poet

132.18	Mathew's	proper name
132.32	Rappacini's	title
133.6	Rappacini	proper name

Clarence Mangan's Love Affair

134.17	marrying	misspelling
135.42	Mountpleasantsquare	proper name
136.30	He seems	"there" added for clarity
136.40	Michel	proper name

A Reckless Century. Irish Rakes and Duellists

141.10	bragadochio	misspelling

Oscar Wilde's Last Book

143.24	Wainwright	proper name
144.27	Dorian Grey	title
144.32	M'Ilvaine	proper name

The Young Ireland League

147.23	are	grammatical error
147.32	rankerous	misspelling

A Poet We Have Neglected

151.1	Kamskchatka	proper name
151.1	Kate of Ballyshannon	title
151.14	Kate O'Ballyshannon	proper name

| 151.27 | sparkling Irish minstrelsy | proper name/title |
| 151.36 | book | printer's error |

Poems by Miss Tynan

153.22	De Vere	proper name
153.22	Innisfail	title
153.23	Fergusson's	proper name
154.7	tapestery-like	misprint
154.8	Cloudalkin	misprint
155.2	morchandise	misprint
155.7	landscapes	misprint
155.9	Lis	misprint
155.9	subtely	misprint
155.14	of of	printer's error
155.15	*naivette*	misprint
155.17	Fourteenth monk	missing word
156.17	unheed	misprint
156.23	I when	misprint
156.24	when	misprint

The New 'Speranza'

158.10	Nationale	misspelling
158.16	patricien	feminine form
158.17	fore knowledge	misspelling
158.24	Chatre	proper name
158.32	Huges	proper name

Dr. Todhunter's Irish Poems

160.15	De Vere	proper name
160.16	Innisfail	title
160.21	De Vere	proper name
160.22	Conaire	title
162.3	Agadoe	title

Clovis Hugues on Ireland

163.1	Huges	proper name
163.27	Huges	proper name
166.12	Union Mediteranneene	proper name
166.27	decendants	misspelling

Sight and Song

| 168.33 | Gypsey | title |
| 169.32 | Callihroë | title |

Some New Irish Books

171.8	Lyricus	title
171.25	heartly	misspelling
172.15	Moy Tura	proper name
172.16	songs of Arcady	title

Dublin Scholasticism and Trinity College

174.16	delution	misspelling

'Noetry' and Poetry

180.15	Savage Armstrong	proper name
180.19	Longman	proper name
180.24	The Garland of Greece	title
181.6	Lugnaquilia's	proper name
181.10	Lugnaquilia	proper name

Invoking the Irish Fairies

184.3	pentegram	misspelling

Hopes and Fears for Irish Literature

186.4	Decadants	misspelling
186.38	M'Carthy's	proper name
186.38	Fardiah	proper name

The Death of Oenone

190.19	Beckett	proper name
192.16	all	proper name

The Vision of MacConglinne

194.16	Lea	proper name
194.28	Cathar	proper name
194.34	Cathar	proper name
194.34	Pican	proper name
194.37	Pican	proper name
194.39	Cathar	proper name

The Wandering Jew

197.7	Faery Queen	proper name
197.22	De Gama	proper name
198.26	make	printer's error

A Bundle of Poets

202.13	and that our	"that" deleted for clarity

The Writings of William Blake

206.26	Blundel	proper name

The Message of the Folk-lorist

211.3	Thistelton	proper name
212.9	Pascajoula	proper name
212.33	Mid-summer	title
212.34	Puck Peasblossom	punctuation added for coherence

Two Minor Lyrists

214.30	Imogen	proper name
215.8	Imogens	proper name
215.10	Ballishannon	proper name
215.11	Ballishannon	proper name
215.35	dewdroops	misprint
217.8	Guest	title

The Ainu

222.11	Shangalin	proper name
222.15	Corea	proper name
222.25	Shangalin	proper name

Reflections and Refractions

228.21	Khayam	proper name

A Symbolical Drama in Paris

235.3	theatre science having	punctuation error
235.8	Kaladasa	proper name
235.21	Axel	title
235.22	Villiers de l'Isle-Adam	proper name
235.27	Axel	title
236.1	Villiers de l'Isle-Adam	proper name
236.9	Villiers de l'Isle-Adam	proper name
236.14	Axel	proper name
236.33	Axel	proper name
237.3	Axel	title
237.20	Axel	title
237.39	Axel	title

The Evangel of Folk-lore

239.11	Wylde	proper name
239.12	MacAnally	proper name
239.17	tale	misprint
240.2	Wylde	proper name

A New Poet

242.24	A.E.	pseudonym's usual style
242.25	*Homeward:*	title
243.17	Throne's	title
243.31	A.E.	pseudonym's usual style

Some Irish National Books

246.22	De Vere	proper name
246.34	doggrel	misprint
248.4	Tirconnell	proper name

Battles Long Ago

255.16	Cuchullin	proper name
255.25	Cuchullin	proper name
256.2	Mor Rega	proper name
256.9	Cuchullin	proper name
256.9	Cuchullin	proper name

An Excellent Talker

257.19	*no*	title
257.27	Daubeney	proper name
258.23	*Grey*	title

Dublin Mystics

259.28	*Homeward:*	title
260.14	A.E.	pseudonym's usual style
260.19	A.E.	pseudonym's usual style
260.20	Eglington	proper name
260.25	sience	misprint
260.32	hostes	misprint

The Story of Early Gaelic Literature

261.22	*Connaught*	title
261.25	Cuchullain	proper name
261.26	Joubainville	proper name
262.9	Cuchullin	proper name

Irish National Literature, I: From Callanan to Carleton

265.27	Connaught	title
265.29	Bere	proper name
266.7	Cashla Gal Mo Chre	title
266.9	De Vere	proper name
266.10	De Vere	proper name
266.34	Concobar	proper name
267.20	*The Nolans*	title
267.21	*Crohore*	title
267.28	*Fardaroughu*	title

Irish National Literature, II: Contemporary Prose Writers

271.39	MacPherson's	proper name
272.2	Fin	title
272.3	Cuchullin	title
275.21	Connaught	proper name
275.26	Hayse	proper name
275.28	*Silex Godaelica*	title

Irish National Literature, III: Contemporary Irish Poets

280.5	A.E.	pseudonym's usual style
282.2	*Connaught*	title
282.29	though does	"it" added for clarification
283.16	*Louise de Vallière*	title
283.25	*cuckoo songs*	title
283.31	*Legends and Lyrics*	title
284.25	A.E.	pseudonym's usual style
284.33	A.E.'s	pseudonym's usual style
284.33	*Homeward:*	title
285.29	*Homeward:*	title
285.38	De Vere	proper name
286.2	De Vere	proper name
286.12	De Vere	proper name
286.19	De Vere	proper name
286.22	Turaun	proper name
287.2	De Vere	proper name
287.4	A.E.	pseudonym's usual style
287.5	Fin	proper name

Irish National Literature, IV: A List of the Best Irish Books

289.17	Beru	proper name
290.18	Moria	title
290.18	Bourke	title
290.19	A Book of Irish Verse	title
290.25	A.E.	pseudonym's usual style
290.36	*Nolans*	title

290.37	Crohore	title
290.38	hook	title
290.40	*Barny O'Reirdan*	title
290.41	"Tales and Stories"	title
291.1	Griffen	proper name
291.3	Blackwood	title
291.5	Fardorougha	title
291.13	Cuchullin	proper name
291.14	his	title
291.22	Hero Tales	title
291.23	Folklore	title
291.25	Fairy Legends of the South of Ireland	title
291.28	Silva Gadaelica	title
291.28	Hayse	proper name
291.30	Manuscript Materials	title
291.35	Red Hugh	title
291.36	Mitchell	proper name
292.2	Irish Poems	Irish Songs and Poems
292.5	De Vere	proper name
292.7	Legends and Lyrics	title
292.8	Homeward:	title
292.9	Connaught	proper name
292.10	Connaught	title
292.21	Irlandais	title
292.22	Joubainville	proper name

The Chain of Gold

296.12	Cuchullin	proper name
297.1	Cuchullin	proper name
297.3	Usheen	proper name

William Carleton

300.42	O'Donohue	proper name
300.43	O'Donohue	proper name
301.17	Eve	title
301.18	Paddy go Easy	title

William Blake

304.3	Urigen	title
304.10	Urigen	title
304.34	Thell	title

An Irish Patriot

305.26	Montagu	proper name
306.28	Montagu	proper name
307.31	Montagu	proper name

The New Irish Library

310.37   Brown   proper name

William Carleton

313.19   Nolans   title
313.19   Crohore of the Billhook   title
313.26   Fardaroughu   title

Greek Folk Poesy

316.33   Vlachopoulo   proper name

The Well at the World's End

320.33   Behmen   proper name

Young Ireland

327.1   Maddyn   proper name
327.3   Gissipus   title
327.35   Clarance   proper name
327.36   O'Hussy   proper name
327.37   Macguire   title
328.37   Clarance   proper name

Mr. John O'Leary

330.38   Magher   proper name
330.39   Magher   proper name

Mr. Arthur Symons' New Book

333.13   gradaul   misprint
334.14   Mélanite   title
334.27   Mélanite   title

Miss Fiona Macleod

337.19   The Mountain Lover   title
337.28   The Sin-Eater   title
337.31   Arran   proper name
337.32   Arran   proper name
337.34   Arran   proper name
338.7   hear   misspelling
338.25   Lilleth   proper name

The Treasure of the Humble

340.28	Lisle Adam	proper name

Mr. Standish O'Grady's *Flight of the Eagle*

344.36	Sleive Fuad	proper name
344.37	Sleive Fuad	proper name
344.39	Alwain	proper name
344.40	Taru	proper name
344.41	Leath Macha	proper name
344.43	Bunba	proper name
345.1	Lieth's	proper name
345.5	Fead Fia	proper name

Bards of the Gael and the Gall

348.9	Fionn	proper name

Aglavaine and Sélysette

349.1	*Selysette*	title
350.12	de L'Isle Adam	proper name
350.18	de L'Isle Adam	proper name
351.16	Yssalene	proper name

The Tribes of Danu

355.25	Laccan	proper name
361.36	Cuchullin	proper name

Three Irish Poets

368.29	Dearg	proper name
369.6	Lisle Adam	proper name
369.17	A.E.	pseudonym's usual style
369.18	A.E.	pseudonym's usual style

The Prisoners of the Gods

385.23	Mill	proper name

Mr. Rhys' *Welsh Ballads*

390.22	*Selysette*	title
390.23	Axel	title
391.9	Mabenogian	title
392.25	Hendré	title

The Broken Gates of Death

395.4	tradition	misprint
395.26	Cool	proper name
396.27	Doneraill	proper name
396.34	newses	misprint
398.36	mass	usage
399.18	Arran	proper name
399.39	Arran	proper name
400.6	its	punctuation error
400.7	him. And	punctuation error
400.32	person, and	punctuation error
401.42	S. Patric	standardized spelling
402.1	Goibnui	proper name
404.34	Doneraill	proper name
406.20	Niam	proper name
406.22	Cuchuallain	proper name
406.31	Fion	proper name
406.32	Fion	proper name
406.34	Mananan	proper name
406.35	Patric	proper name

Le Mouvement Celtique: Fiona Macleod

408.1	Herr Windron	proper name
408.2	M. de Joubanville	proper name
408.2	Nuts	proper name
408.3	Kayse O'Grady	proper name
408.5	Hoper	proper name
408.26	Arran	proper name
409.2	Petekin	title

AE's Poems

410.1	'A.E.'s'	pseudonym's usual style
410.22	A.E.	pseudonym's usual style
411.4	'A.E.,'	pseudonym's usual style
411.30	'A.E.'	pseudonym's usual style

Le Mouvement Celtique: II. M. John O'Leary

413.18	Catherine	proper name

Celtic Beliefs About the Soul

416.18	De Joubainville	proper name
416.31	Dionysius	proper name
416.35	orgaic	misspelling
417.28	orgaic	misspelling

John Eglinton and Spiritual Art

419.34	L'Isle Adam	proper name
419.35	Remy	proper name

A Symbolic Artist and the Coming of Symbolic Art

426.8	A.E.	proper name
427.24	De l'Isle Adam	proper name
427.29	A.E.	proper name

High Crosses of Ireland

430.20	De Joubainville	proper name
432.7	Boehmen	proper name
432.10	Arran	proper name
432.13	Boehmen	proper name
432.29	scholour	misspelling

Notes on Traditions and Superstitions

434.39	Ballesodare	proper name

The Literary Movement in Ireland

459.20	Connaught	proper name
460.27	Cottar's	title
465.28	Tir-nan-og	proper name
465.32	Tir-nan-og	proper name
465.33	Tir-nan-og	proper name
465.36	Tir-nan-og	proper name
467.23	Dalua	proper name

NOTES

The Poetry of Sir Samuel Ferguson—I

1. Yeats is quoting lines 19–20 of William Wordsworth's poem "The Solitary Reaper," which first appeared in vol. 2 of his *Poems* (London, 1807). Wordsworth reads "For old".

2. Yeats presumably meant by this catalog the following:

   the Indian: Mahabharata, the epic poem which is one of the main sources for Vedic myth. This poem is difficult to date, for it was constantly added to over many centuries, but it had taken on something of its present form by A.D. 350. The other main source of Indian myth is the *Ramayana*, ascribed to the poet Valmiki. Parts of this poem date from 500 B.C.

   the Homeric: The Iliad and *The Odyssey*, the two epic poems attributed to Homer, both dealing with the Trojan War, an event which has been dated in the early thirteenth century B.C. The authorship of these epics has long been a matter of controversy, but "Homer" has been usually dated from the mid-ninth century B.C.

   the Charlemagnic: Charlemagne lived from 740 to 814. *Le Chanson de Roland* dates from the mid-eleventh century. Italian epics on the character of Roland were written by Pulci, Boiardo, and Ariosto.

   the Spanish, circling around the Cid: Poema del Cid was written around 1140 in Castilian, and is based on the exploits of Ruy Díaz de Bivar (ca. 1043–99) in his wars against the Moors.

   the Arthurian: the legends about King Arthur and his Round Table, such as were gathered by Malory into *Morte d'Arthur* (printed by Caxton in 1485).

   the Scandinavian: such as the Icelandic Sagas (the Eddas) and the tales gathered in the *Niebelungenlied*.

   and the Irish: the Red Branch (or Ulster) Cycle gathered into *Táin Bó Cuailgne*, as well as the Fenian legends about Finn MacCool.

3. Ferguson's first and most highly regarded book was *Lays of the Western Gael* (London: Bell and Daldy, 1865).

4. In contrast to Yeats's quotation, Ferguson in *Lays of the Western Gael* reads "mother is"; "highland reel"; "cried,"; "rock" instead of "sock"; "away" with no comma; "ancle" instead of "ankle"; "heavy-sliding"; "hill-side"; "rowan"; and "Fairy Hawthorne" (105–6). Yeats left out two quatrains here.

5. In these stanzas, Ferguson reads "voices in"; "maiden's"; "For,"; "mountain-ashes"; "Whitethorn"; and "Power" (106–7). Yeats omitted a quatrain here.

6. In these stanzas, Ferguson reads "clasp'd"; and "Soft o'er" (108). For the line "No scream can they raise, nor prayer can they say," Ferguson reads "No scream can any raise, nor prayer can any say," (108). Ferguson reads

further, "away,"; "cause:"; "eyes" (no comma); "raise,"; and "away" (no comma) (108–9).

7. Algernon Charles Swinburne (1837–1909), British poet associated with the Pre-Raphaelite movement; his *Poems and Ballads* (London: Edward Moxon and Co., 1866) inaugurated a controversy over this so-called fleshly school of poetry, a phrase coined by Robert Buchanan (1841–1901) in an article of that title published in *The Contemporary Review* for October 1871. During Swinburne's life the allegedly immoral and pagan topics of his poetry gained him notoriety, but he was then and has since been appreciated as a metrical genius.

8. *"the things of the old time before"*: This phrase is from the twelfth quatrain of Ferguson's poem "Adieu to Brittany" (*Poems of Sir Samuel Ferguson* [Dublin: Talbot Press, 1918], p. 79). Yeats quotes this quatrain in the second article on Ferguson, p. 24.

9. Yeats echoes British poet and social critic Matthew Arnold's famous dictum that poetry is ". . . the criticism of life under the conditions fixed for such a criticism by the laws of poetic truth and poetic beauty" ("The Study of Poetry," *The Complete Prose Works of Matthew Arnold*, ed. R. H. Super, 11 vols. [Ann Arbor: University of Michigan Press, 1973], IX, 163). Arnold (1822–88) first used this phrase on 23 November 1863 in an Oxford lecture on French writer Joseph Joubert (1754–1824), entitled "A French Coleridge." "The Study of Poetry" was originally published as the general introduction to *The English Poets*, ed. T. H. Ward (London: Macmillan and Co., 1880).

10. Yeats refers to *Deirdre: A One-Act Drama of Old Irish Story* (Dublin: Roe, 1880).

11. Congal's enemy was King Domnal. The name "Ardrigh" which Yeats gives is a version of the Gaelic *ard rí*, which means "high king."

12. Knocknarea is a mountain, reputed to be the burial place of Queen Maeve, and an important part of what was for Yeats the symbolic landscape of Sligo. It is west of Sligo, overlooking Ballysodare Bay. See "The Hosting of the Sidhe" in *Poems*.

13. Ferguson, in *Congal*, book 3, reads "hands" with no comma; and "gay-dressed," (58).

14. William Morris (1834–96), British poet, artist, and socialist. Yeats retold this anecdote, supplying Morris's name, in the preface to Lady Augusta Gregory's *Cuchulain of Muirthemne* (London: J. Murray, 1902), p. xii. The Battle of Clontarf took place on 23 April 1014, when Scandanavian invaders were routed by the Irish of Munster, Connacht, Ulster, and Meath. The battle took place on the north side of Dublin Bay near the village named Clontarf. Brian Boru, leader of the Irish forces, died in the battle, together with his son. The Norsemen are said to have lost six thousand men.

15. Yeats recounts with greater detail, in the next article in this edition, how poorly Ferguson's *Poems* were reviewed in *The Academy* magazine. See p. 11.

16. *"Can anything good come out of Galilee", they thought:* The phrase "Can there be any good thing come out of Nazareth" comes from John 1:46 in the Bible.

17. *a letter published the other day in the* Irish Monthly: This 21 July 1884 letter was printed with "Sir Samuel Ferguson. In Memoriam," by *The Irish Monthly* of October 1886, pp. 529–36. In the letter, Ferguson does not

himself so overtly "declare" the "true cause of this want of recognition," as Yeats's allusion makes out. The editor of *The Irish Monthly* in the preface explains the letter's context, p. 534:

> In our twelfth volume (1884) 'O' [Justice John O'Hagan] devotes eighteen pages to a minute and loving study of the epic of "Congal," and later, in the same volume, this well qualified critic discusses in a still longer article the miscellaneous poems of his friend. When only the first part of this eloquent étude had been published, Sir Samuel Ferguson wrote the following letter to the Editor of this magazine, who ventures to print it, as another evidence of the courtesy and kindliness of the writer:

> > Gatehouse Hotel, Tenby, South Wales
> > 21st July, 1884.
> > My Dear Sir—Let me thank you for your obliging letter, enclosing Mr. de Vere's note, which reached me while on vacation in the country. I have also heard from JUSTICE O'Hagan, who tells me you contemplate the insertion of a second notice of my poems—It is very grateful to me to find appreciation among my own countrymen. It has hitherto been also totally denied me in the great centres of of [*sic*] criticism in England. Possibly de Vere divines the true cause. My business is, regardless of such discouragements, to do what I can in the formation of a characteristic school of letters for my own country. For the sympathy and encouragement you give me, accept my warmest thanks, and believe me
> > > Yours very faithfully,
> > > Samuel Ferguson

Justice John O'Hagan (1822–90) was an active member of the Young Ireland party, and wrote poetry and criticism for *The Nation* under the pseudonym "Sliabh Cuilinn." As "O," he wrote twenty or so pieces, to be found in *Dublin Acrostics* (Dublin: Hodges, Smith, 1866). His 1884 articles in *The Irish Monthly* on Ferguson were later reprinted in *The Poetry of Sir Samuel Ferguson* (Dublin: M. H. Gill and Son, 1887), just after the death of his friend. For Aubrey de Vere, the Anglo-Irish poet, see note 18 below. His "note" sent to Ferguson by the editor has apparently not survived, but at any rate it, not Ferguson's own letter, overtly explains Ferguson's lack of critical reception as a discrimination against his Irish nationalist subjects. Ferguson's letter only says de Vere might "possibly" be right in so conjecturing.

18. Aubrey de Vere (1814–1902), Anglo-Irish poet, was a member of the Oxford Movement, composed of intellectuals who were drawn to Catholicism under the leadership of John Henry Newman. De Vere became a Catholic in 1851, and in the 1860s and 1870s he produced a series of poems on Irish subjects.

19. This speech of the spy begins with the line "I know not if a king; but one I saw . . ." (*Poems,* 78).

20. In *Poems,* Ferguson reads, "Before him on the floor" with no commas; and "feats:" (78).

21. See the next article in this collection, which first appeared in the November 1886 issue of *The Dublin University Review.*

22. *soul-ward:* "soulward" in *Poems* (113).
23. Untraced. Yeats used this saying again in *If I Were Four-and-Twenty* (1919), end of section iv: "'The passionate minded,' says an Indian saying, 'love bitter food.'"
24. Cf. this phrase and these lines from "Easter, 1916":

> "Being certain that they and I
> But live where motley is worn . . ."

25. *barbarous truth:* These lines are from Edmund Spenser's *The Faerie Queene* (ed. A. C. Hamilton [London and New York: Longman, 1977]), 1. 6. 12.1–4:

> The doubtfull Damzell dare not yet commit
> Her single person to their barbarous truth,
> But still twixt feare and hope amazd does sit,
> Late learned what harme to hastie trust ensu'th. . . .

The Poetry of Sir Samuel Ferguson—II

1. *convenances:* a French word, which might be translated as "proprieties" or "expediences."
2. Edward Dowden (1843–1913) was professor of English at Trinity College, a post he was given four years after his graduation from that same college. His best-known work of criticism is his study of Shakespeare. Because Dowden was a friend of John Butler Yeats, the poet's father, William had met Dowden several years before this article appeared. Yeats said in his autobiography that he first worshipped Dowden, but was soon repelled by the older man's detachment as a scholar (*Au*, 94–96). Dowden admired Ferguson's poems, but he had said so only in private letters. During the nineties, Yeats and Dowden quarreled frequently over literary politics and critical matters, but Dowden always had a high regard for Yeats's poetry. Dowden had written not one but two chapters on the British novelist George Eliot in his *Studies in Literature* (London: C. K. Paul, 1878). George Eliot was the pen name of Mary Ann Evans (1819–80). For Yeats's opinion of George Eliot, see *CL1*, 7–8.
3. Ferguson's poems were reviewed in *The Academy* of 24 July 1880. The anonymous critic made the comment about "low water-mark" in reference to Ferguson's "Hymn of the Fisherman." The critic also said of this "hymn" that "we would suggest that it would be more reverent if persons who have not the gifts necessary for composing poetry would confine themselves entirely to secular subjects."
4. In an obituary in *The Athenaeum* of 14 April 1886, p. 205, John Pentland Mahaffy said of Ferguson that despite the poet's knowledge of the "real grievances of his country . . . yet there was never a more loyal or orderly British citizen, or one who felt more deeply the mistakes that are made, and the crimes that are committed, under the guise of demanding justice for his country. He never lent his poetic talent to increase the volume of Irish discontent."

   Socrates, the Athenian philosopher, was condemned in 399 B.C. to drink the poisonous hemlock on the charge of having corrupted the youth of the city. The story is recounted by Plato in his *Apology of Socrates*. Cf. the version by Xenophon in his *Memorabilia* and *Symposium*.

5. William Morris, according to Yeats's preface to Lady Gregory's *Cuchulain of Muirthemne* (London: J. Murray, 1902), p. xii, where he retells the anecdote, supplying Morris's name.

6. Arthur and his queen Guinevere are the symbolic royal couple in the Arthurian legends recorded by Thomas Malory in *Morte d'Arthur* (1485). These legends, of course, were crucial to British national mythology.

7. In *Congal* (Dublin: Edward Ponsonby/London: Bell and Daldy, 1872), Ferguson recounts the legend of this seventh-century Ulster king's battle with his enemy Domnal, king of all Ireland. See Yeats's summary of and comment on this epic poem in the previous article in this collection. See below for Yeats's summary of the Deirdre story.

8. Thomas Davis (1814–45) was a leading figure of the Young Ireland movement and one of the founders of *The Nation* newspaper with Charles Gavan Duffy and John Blake Dillon. Davis's poems were collected shortly after his death in *The Poems of Thomas Davis* (Dublin: James Duffy, 1846), and he soon became the quintessential nineteenth-century Irish nationalist poet. James Clarence Mangan (1803–49), Dublin-born poet, was famous for the archetypally "Irish" despair of his poetry and the misery of his life, which included alcoholism and opium addiction, poverty, and an eventual death from cholera.

   Homer is the traditional "author" of *The Iliad* and *The Odyssey*, the two great epics of Greek literature. By calling Ferguson "the one Homeric poet of our time," Yeats clearly means to privilege both him and Irish mythology.

9. Ferguson lists this order for his poems in the "Introductory Note" to "Deirdre," in *Poems* (97). Ferguson's spelling, Cuchullin, in the title of his poem is now standardly spelled "Cuchulain."

10. For "who bid this to my board", Ferguson reads "who bade thee to my board,"; for "might know;", Ferguson reads "might know:"; for "man", Ferguson reads "man,"; and for "my mind", Ferguson reads "mind," (*Poems*, 54–55).

11. In his article on "Popular Ballad Poetry of Ireland," pp. 93–108 in this collection, Yeats describes Ferguson as "some old half-savage bard chanting to his companions at a forest fire."

12. These lines are from *Lays of the Western Gael* (33).

13. *said::* "said," in *Lays of the Western Gael* (34).

14. *Uladh:* Irish for Ulster.

15. *king,:* "king" in *Lays of the Western Gael* (34).

16. *blood::* "blood;" in *Lays of the Western Gael* (35). Conor is usually spelled "Conchubar" in Yeats's works.

17. *counseller:* "councillor" in *Lays of the Western Gael* (35).

18. *gained:* "gain'd" in *Lays of the Western Gael* (35).

19. At this point in *The Dublin University Review* printing, the following footnote, signed "Ed. D.U.R.," appeared: "Mr. Gosse is now in so much trouble about other matters than his poetry, that it may seem unkindly at the present juncture to add a stone, or even a pebble, to the cairn of his reputation. It is right then to say that Mr. Yeats' remarks were in type before the appearance of the last Quarterly Review." Edmund Gosse (1849–1928), better known as a literary historian and biographer than as

a poet, later became an acquaintance of Yeats. Yeats considered Gosse, Andrew Lang, and Austin Dobson, taken as a group, to be his immediate predecessors, and rivals, in English poetry. Gosse's *From Shakespeare to Pope* (1885) had been given a devastating review by J. Churton Collins in *The Quarterly Review* of October 1886. Collins collected that review in his *Ephemera Critica* (1901).

20. Aeschylus was a Greek dramatist, whose most famous surviving work is the trilogy consisting of the plays *Agamemnon, The Libation Bearers,* and *The Furies.*

21. Matthew Arnold (1822–1888), English poet and critic, whose short epic "Sohrab and Rustum" appeared in *Poems* (London, 1853). Like Cuchulain, who unwittingly kills his son Conlai, the warrior Rustum in the Persian story unknowingly kills his son, Sohrab.

22. Illan Finn, the younger and more sympathetic son, whom Yeats quotes Deirdre talking to, and Buino Borb, "who afterwards betrays her," as Yeats summarizes.

23. *I would:* The lines in Ferguson, *Poems,* read:

> Deirdre.
> And therefore thou?—
> Illan.
> "Would rather if I might," (120).

24. For "Oh", Ferguson reads "Oh!"; for "us,", Ferguson reads "us" with no comma; and for "methinks", Ferguson reads "methinks," with a comma (*Poems,* 124).

25. the *"Red-Branch" house:* The Red Branch House is also known as Emain Macha and was the headquarters for the Red Branch Knights of Conchubar MacNessa.

26. The game of chess between Naoise and Deirdre is the central episode of Yeats's own play *Deirdre.* Cf. Ferguson in *Poems* (131ff).

27. *gone:* Ferguson reads "gone," in "Deirdre's Lament for the Sons of Usnach," *Lays of the Western Gael* (177).

28. *linkèd:* Ferguson reads "linked" in *Lays of the Western Gael* (178).

29. This seventh stanza is not in the version of the poem reprinted in standard Ferguson editions. Justice O'Hagan, to whom Yeats refers below, included a stanza which is in his reprinting of the poem in his study, *The Poetry of Sir Samuel Ferguson* (Dublin: M. H. Gill and Son, 1887). O'Hagan gives the following as the seventh stanza, p. 178:

> In the falcon's jesses throw,
> Hook and arrow, line and bow;
> Never again by stream or plain
> Shall the gentle woodsmen go.

For more on O'Hagan, see note 39, p. 499.

30. *true-love:* Ferguson reads "true love" in *Lays of the Western Gael* (179).

31. *ringing;:* Ferguson reads "ringing:" in *Lays of the Western Gael* (179).

32. *chorus:* Ferguson reads "chorus," in *Lays of the Western Gael* (179).

33. *Echo, now sleep,:* Ferguson reads "Echo now, sleep," in *Lays of the Western Gael* (179).

34. Ardan was a brother of Naoise, Deirdre's beloved, and one of the sons of Usnach killed by Conor. "Neesa" was Ferguson's early spelling of "Naoise." In the "Introductory Note" to "The Tain Quest" in *Lays of the Western*

Gael, Ferguson mentions "Neesa son of Usnach" as the lover of "Deirdre."
In the *Deirdre* of *Poems,* Ferguson writes "Naisi."

35. Ferguson in *Lays of the Western Gael* reads "Stag,",: "Heron," (179).
36. Ferguson reads "straight!" (179).
37. Ferguson reads "clan" (179).
38. Ferguson reads "Eman," and "clan;" (180).
39. John O'Hagan (1822–90) was a leading member of the Young Ireland Party, and issued *The Poetry of Samuel Ferguson* (Dublin: M. H. Gill and Son, 1887).
40. Alfred, Lord Tennyson (1809–92), British poet laureate, published *Idylls of the King,* a series of poems drawn from Arthurian lore, beginning in 1859.

    Girton was a woman's college, founded in 1869 and moved in 1873 to Cambridge, although it had at that time no official connection with the university. Tennyson does not appear to have been involved in Girton.
41. See Ferguson's own prose summary of this "foiled vengeance" in the "Introductory Note" to "The Tain Quest" in *Lays of the Western Gael,* pp. 3–5. To prosecute this vengeance, Fergus allied himself with Maeve and Ailill, queen and king of Connacht. Maeve was the embittered ex-wife of Conor. Eventually, she attacked Conor, because his chief in the territory of Cuailgne abused a messenger she had sent to buy "a notable dun bull." This war is the subject of the Táin Bó Cuailgne, or "Cattle Raid of Cooley," which Ferguson never rendered, although "The Tain Quest" in *Lays of the Western Gael* recounts how its text, reputedly authored by Fergus himself, was recovered.
42. *full-grey, majestical, of face serene;:* "Full-gray, majestical, of face serene," in *Conary (Poems,* 68).
43. *war,:* "war" in *Poems* (71).
44. In this stanza, Ferguson's *Poems* reads "among" with no comma (72); "enquire" instead of "inquire" (73); "but, as ordered, duteous, slew"; and "casquets" (73).
45. *Fair-haired he is,:* Ferguson reads "Fair-haired he is" with no comma (*Poems,* 76).
46. From the opening of this stanza through the word "companionship," Ferguson has set these lines in quotes as the speech of the spy. The next line ("Then . . . cried") is without quotes, and is inset as a new verse paragraph. The following lines, beginning "Gods!" through the end of the quoted lines, are set in Ferguson (77) as the speech of Ferragon, with the first line inset as a new verse paragraph.
47. *One I saw: Poems,* 78, shows these words as part of this full line: "'I know not if a king; but one I saw'."
48. Ferguson reads "curtain:"; "fresh-ploughed tillage land," with a comma; "he had," with a comma; "hand: like" (*Poems,* 79).
49. Ferguson reads "men," with a comma; "bagpipe"; and "mouth-piece" (*Poems,* 74).
50. *These pipers . . . are.:* Ferguson sets these lines in quotation marks as Ferragon's interpretation of the spy's information (*Poems,* 74).

    To-night their pipes will play: "Tonight their pipes shall play" in Ferguson (74). These lines are set in quotation marks as the speech of Ingcel; the first line is inset as a new verse paragraph.
51. *At once:* "At once—" (*Poems,* 86).
52. Ferguson (88) reads "pipers. I" and "said Conal. 'Trust in me:".

53. These two phrases appear in *Poems* (88).
54. This phrase appears in *Poems* (90).
55. *cup-bearer:* "cupbearer" in *Poems* (90).
56. These lines appear in *Poems* (93).
57. Donnybrook, a southern suburb of Dublin, was famous for its fair, established by King John in 1204; hence the name's association with brawling.
58. *near:* "hard" in *Lays of the Western Gael* (18). Yeats does not quote all of this first line, which in Ferguson reads "Now they've lost their noblest treasure, and in dark days hard at hand."
59. *A mist . . . wafture green.:* In *Lays of the Western Gael* (19), these lines read:

> Fergus rose. A mist ascended with him, and a
> flash was seen
> As of brazen sandals blended with a mantle's
> wafture green;

60. *Cuanna, and sat down,:* Ferguson reads "Cuanna; and sat down;" and "toil," with a comma in *Congal,* book 5 (129).
61. Maldun is the coward's name; the episode occurs in *Congal,* book 5 (129–31).
62. Ferguson's poem on Thomas Davis was first published in *The Dublin University Magazine* in February 1847, p. 198. *The Dublin University Magazine* printing of the poems reads "spring-time.";"broad-cast forth the corn in golden plenty,";"Davis, is";"Oh, brave young men, my love, my pride, and promise,";"set,";"justice" with no comma; "yet:"; and "belong!".
63. Yeats is alluding to a letter that poet William Wordsworth (1770–1850) wrote to the Reverend J. K. Miller, vicar of Walkeringham, dated 17 December 1831, in *The Prose Works of William Wordsworth,* ed. Rev. Alexander B. Grosart (London: E. Moxon/New York: AMS Press, 1967), vol. 3, p. 317. Wordsworth was replying, at the age of sixty-two, in this letter to the plea that he write more in prose, presumably on topics of political controversy:

> There is yet another obstacle: I am no ready master of prose writing, having but little practised in the art. This last consideration will not weigh with you; nor would it have done with myself a few years ago; but the bare mention of it will serve to show that years have deprived me of courage, in the sense the word bears when applied by Chaucer to the animation of birds in spring time.

Wordsworth is alluding to the first stanza of Geoffrey Chaucer's "The General Prologue" of *The Canterbury Tales.*
64. In *The Dublin University Magazine* of November 1886, Yeats gives the following note:

> In her obituary notice of Ferguson in the *Academy,* Miss Stokes gravely errs in asserting that after Davis's death he "severed himself wholly" from the national movement. Her subsequent statement that he "always" cherished the hope—"the fulfillment of which was cut short by his friend's early death"—that Davis would eventually turn into a kind of West Briton, is a still more flagrant violation of biographical truth. Two years after Davis's death, Ferguson was

chairman of the Protestant Repeal Association, and delivered in that capacity a speech so National in tone that Emmet might have owned it. See Sir C. G. Duffy's *Four Hundred Years of Irish History* (London/New York: Cassell, Petter, and Gelpin, 1883), Book III, ch. I. True it is that he afterwards suppressed some of his patriotic *Poems,* "lest, by any means, the Nationalists should claim him for their own." But the suppression was not carried far enough. We claim him through every line. Irish singers, who are genuinely Irish in thought, subject and style, must, whether they will or no, nourish the forces that make for the political liberties of Ireland.

Robert Emmet (1778–1803) was an Irish patriot and journalist who was executed in September 1803 for allegedly trying to start an Irish republic. The Stokes obituary of Ferguson appeared in *The Academy and Literature* (London) of 21 August 1886, pp. 120–22. Yeats's last quotation from Stokes is slightly but significantly inaccurate. Stokes wrote: "lest by any means the so-called 'Nationalists' should claim him as their own" (121).

65. The poem is in *Lays of the Western Gael* (95).
66. Ferguson reads "Mac William's" and "Beheld" (95); and "no:" and "valley:" (96).
67. Brahman is the highest and Sudra the lowest of the four great Hindu castes.
68. Yeats may have been referring to an address given by Ernest Renan at a "Celtic feast" (*Fête celtique*) at Quimper on 17 August 1885. This speech, like many others delivered at these feasts, is in praise of Brittany and the Celtic race in general. The speech may be found in Renan's *Discours et conférences* (Paris, 1887).
69. *Leave to him : . . . Arvôr:* "Adieu to Brittany," in *Lays of the Western Gael* (140).
70. Ferguson's "Introductory Note" to "Aideen's Grave" in *Lays of the Western Gael,* p. 60, begins as follows:

> Aideen, daughter of Angus of Ben-Edar (now the Hill of Howth), died of grief for the loss of her husband, Oscar, son of Ossian, who was slain at the battle of Gavra (Gowra, near Tara in Meath), A.D. 284.

> Ossian, sometimes Oisin, was the son of Finn MacCumhail, and is reputed to have been the bard of the Fenian cycle of Gaelic mythology. The "Fenian" cycle of legends concerns the "fian," or "band of warriors," who followed Finn. Historically, the "fiana" flourished in the third century, under the king Cormac mac Art.

71. *They heaved . . . grave:* p. 61 of "Aideen's Grave" in *Lays of the Western Gael* shows the opening lines as follows:

> They heaved the stone; they heap'd the cairn:
> Said Ossian, "In a queenly grave . . .

72. The Tuatha dé Danaan were the descendants of the goddess Dana. The gods of light and goodness, they defeated the Firbolgs and the Fomorians, and they became rulers of Ireland. They were later defeated by the Mile-

sians, who drove them to the underworld. Popular mythology regards the race of fairies and demons as of Danaan origin.

73. In these stanzas from *Lays of the Western Gael*, Ferguson reads "Queen" (61); "lark's"; "streams" with no comma; and "decline" with no comma (62).

74. *old Green Plain:* "Old Green Plain" (62). Ferguson gives this note to the phrase:

> The plain of Moynalty, Magh-n'ealta, i.e., the plain of (bird) flocks, is said to have been open and cultivable from the beginning; unlike the other plains which had to be freed from their primaeval forests by the early colonists. Hence its appellation of the Old Plain. It extends over the north-eastern part of the county of Dublin, and eastern part of Meath.

75. In these stanzas from *Lays of the Western Gael*, Ferguson reads "again," and "pail," (62); and "chill:" and "Ben Edar" (69).

76. For this episode, see Yeats's earlier summary of Ferguson's "The Naming of Cuchullin" in this article. In Ferguson's "The Welshmen of Tirawley," *Lays of the Western Gael*, the blinded Emon Lynott raises up his son Emon Oge to avenge his father's blindness on the Barrett clan of Tirawley.

77. "West Britonism" is Yeats's scornful term for the betrayal of Irish identity by the Irish who imitated British manners and mores.

The Poetry of R. D. Joyce

1. The British poets William Wordsworth (1770–1850) and Samuel Taylor Coleridge (1772–1834) collaborated in the production of *Lyrical Ballads* (1798). In the preface to the second edition (1800), Wordsworth made his famous call for poetry to imitate the ordinary speech of common men, instead of adhering to the Latinate, poetic diction insisted on by Dryden, Pope, and the "Augustan" poets. The British poet Percy Bysshe Shelley (1792–1822) wrote poetry and poetic drama highly influenced by the "anarchistic" philosophies of William Godwin, and was a close friend of George Gordon, Lord Byron.

2. For Homer, see "The Poetry of Sir Samuel Ferguson—I," note 2; Victor Hugo (1802–1885), the "Father of French Romanticism," wrote, in the preface to his play *Cromwell* (1827) the French counterpart to Wordsworth's preface to *Lyrical Ballads* (1800), repudiating classicism and calling for a more passionate and "populist" literature. While Yeats refers to Hugo the poet, Hugo was also famous for his novels. Robert Burns (1759–96), born in Scotland from a background of peasant farmers, was famous for his *Poems Chiefly in the Scottish Dialect* (1786), which rendered into dialect many traditional songs, lyrics, and ballads, as well as including original compositions. Sir Walter Scott (1771–1832), Scottish poet and novelist, is known for his ballad poetry and for his pioneering of the historical romance.

3. *Limerick:* County in southwestern Ireland.

4. In *Ballads, Romances, and Songs* (Dublin: J. Duffy, 1861), the poem is entitled "Romance of the Black Robber." Joyce gives this note on the title: "Partly from one of the ancient Fenian romances" (22). "Fenian" romances were the tales concerning Finn MacCool and his fian, or band of warriors. Ossian, Finn's son, is the reputed bard of the cycle. It is unclear which "ancient Fen-

ian romance" Joyce thought he was drawing on, but Joyce's ballad loosely resembles the tale of how Finn found Bran, his valiant dog, while Finn and his companions were rescuing the stolen children of a king from a giant. See "How Fion Found Bran," in John Gregorson Campbell, *Waifs and Strays of Celtic Tradition*, Argyllshire series. No. 4: *The Fians; or, Stories, Poems, and Traditions of Fionn and His Warrior Band* (London: D. Nutt, 1891).

5. *By Mumhan's mountain:* "By a Mumhan mountain" in Joyce, *Ballads, Romances, and Songs*, p. 22. In *Ballads of Irish Chivalry* (London: Longmans, Green, and Co./Dublin: Talbot Press, 1908), which was edited and annotated by Patrick Weston Joyce, Robert's brother, the headnote to this poem, p. 62, reads:

> The 'Mumhan mountain'* [note: "Mumhan [pron. Mooan], Munster"] of this ballad is Blackrock, between Ardpatrick and Glenosheen, near Kilfinane, Co. Limerick.

Joyce's headnote continues with much topographical and etymological information.

6. In stanza 2, Joyce reads "foam" for "fount"; "home,—" for home;—"; and "stark,—" for "stark." (*Ballads, Romances, and Songs*, 22). In stanza 4, Joyce reads "sat" for "went" (22).

7. In stanza 7, Joyce reads "there" for "then" (23). In stanza 9, Joyce reads "Robber" for "robber"; "gray" for "grey"; and "spring-tide" for "Springtide" (23). In Stanza 10, Joyce reads "gold," for "gold" without a comma (23).

8. In stanza 12, Joyce reads "For, though wan and worn," (24). In stanza 13, Joyce reads "Prince" and "always" for "away" (24). In stanza 14, Joyce reads "Prince" (24).

9. *"Murgal and Garmon":* "Romance of Meergal and Garmon" in Joyce, *Ballads, Romances, and Songs*.

10. *Hy Brasil* is a legendary phantom island west of the Aran islands. In the "Romance of Meergal and Garmon" in *Ballads, Romances, and Songs*, "Fytte the Third," vi, Joyce writes:

> There a crystal stream danced downward with a wild melodious song,
> And like children of the rainbow flew the warbling birds along (85).

11. *those vulgar ballads . . . London Streets:* so-called blue-books and chapbooks, which were often lurid accounts of murders and thievings with didactic morals tacked on at the end, and were notoriously popular among the urban British working class throughout the nineteenth century. See Leslie Shepard, *A History of Street Literature* (Detroit: Singing Tree Press, 1973). Henry Mayhew's *London Labour and the London Poor* (London, 1851) is the best contemporary source on this street literature in England.

12. In Joyce, *Ballads, Romances, and Songs*, this poem begins thus:

> THE COCK AND THE SPARROW.
> AIR—"The Game Cock".
> I.
> One morn . . . (179).

Yeats omits the last two stanzas of the poem in Joyce's original edition.

13. Joyce reads "morn" with no comma on p. 179. In Joyce's *Ballads of Irish Chivalry* (1872) the following note appears: "Cragnour: Carriganoura, now a grey old castle ruin rising over the north bank of the Funshion, two miles below Mitchelstown, Co. Cork: conspicuous across the river from the main road." The phrase "crop-ears," below, refers to Puritans, and here, specifically, to Oliver Cromwell's army.

14. In stanza 1, Joyce reads "'neath" with an apostrophe; and "smoke—" (179). In stanza 2, Joyce reads "roses:"; "noses;"; "harrow—" and "psalms" (180). In stanza 3, Joyce reads "theirs,"; "sparrow, with voice sad and low:—"; and "But 'I'd rather . . .'" (180).

15. *Puritan triumph:* A reference to Oliver Cromwell's campaign in Ireland beginning in 1649.

16. At this point in *The Irish Fireside* of 27 November 1886 this statement appears:
   (To be concluded next week). Part Two appeared in the 4 December issue.

17. *"The Three Sorrows of Song,"*: More often these related tales are called "The Three Sorrows of Story-telling," as in Douglas Hyde's book of that title (London, 1895); Yeats's review of Hyde's book is on pp. 268–69 in this collection. The three traditional songs in the cycle are: "Deirdre," "The Children of Lir," and "The Fate of the Children of Tuireann."

18. Joyce, *Deirdre* (Boston: Roberts Brothers, 1876), reads "him" with no comma, and "lip," with a comma (10).

19. Joyce reads "And from the door in solemn slow array"; "Paced rustling up the hall in varied hue"; "Great King,"; "sport" with no comma; "loves and plots"; "Court"; and "vellum" with no comma" (14). The line "Smirking and smiling on the baby bright" has no period, but continues as follows:

> That in her arms lay clad in lily white,
> With large blue eyes and downy yellow hair,
> And skin like pink-leaves when the morns are fair.

20. *Caffa, the Druid:* Druids were the pagan priests of the ancient Britons and Gauls, and seem also to have existed in ancient Ireland. See Douglas Hyde, *A Literary History of Ireland* (London: T. Fisher Unwin, 1899), chapter 9, for a summary of Irish Druidism and its effects on Irish literature. In this chapter, Hyde cites Caesar's *Gallic Wars* (book 6, chapters 13 and 14) on the Irish Druids not having an "over-Druid" as Druids of the Britons and Gauls did.

21. *Led by one aged lord:* This line does not appear in Joyce. Evidently it is Yeats's own addition. Joyce reads "Now unto all thing was he callous grown" (*Deirdre*, 18).

22. Joyce reads "thereby;" (24); "and loud cackling in their fear"; "mere,—"; "warrior's words of doom"; "room;"; and "clamor" (25).

23. Joyce reads "Oh come,"; "sun" with no comma; "filled" for "full"; "'What am I?'—for in grove or garden walk"; "creep or walk"; "'What am I?'"; "was churlish too" for "is curlish too"; "'Ugly! Ugly! Ugly!'" (32); and "him," (33).

24. *The great world spread out:* This phrase comes after the lines next quoted by Yeats. The passage quoted by Yeats continues:

> Till from the topmost boughs at length I gazed
> Over the garden wall, and then half-dazed

With wonder saw I the great world spread out
That Levarcam tells all the tales about! (44)

25. Joyce reads "'neath"; "branch," with a comma; "gay" with no comma; "branches green"; "'Come up! come up! come up, and see the world!'"; "Higher," with a comma"; and "limb," with a comma (44).
26. *Alba:* Scotland.
27. Eman: Sometimes "Emain" or "Emania," this is the seat of the ancient kings of Ulster, and the location of the Red Branch House (Emain Macha), where Fergus's minions murdered Deirdre, her lover, Naoise, and the other sons of Usnach. See "The Poetry of Sir Samuel Ferguson—II," note 25.
28. Joyce, *Blanid,* reads "O THOU"; "Poet,"; "fame"; "Hill of Rest"; "makers"; and "minstrelsy," (9).
29. Joyce, *Blanid,* correctly reads "stricken"; "quicken"; and "rays!" (98). In Joyce, pp. 97–98, this quotation ("Where . . . rays.") is inset with quotation marks as the speech of the "FIRST SPIRIT," rather than of any human character in the poem.
30. See "The Poetry of Sir Samuel Ferguson—I," note 7.
31. Joyce, *Blanid,* reads "drew" with no comma (in second stanza quoted); "ear" with no comma; and "horn!" (100). On p. 101, Joyce reads "lakelet and a cry!"; "eyes! No"; "captive;—"; "floor" with no comma; and "stream-bank" with no comma.

Clarence Mangan (1803–1849)

1. These lines are from "The Unrealities," a Mangan translation of Schiller's *Die Ideale.* The translation first appeared as part of "Anthologia Germanica No. I: The Lyrical and Smaller Poems of Schiller" in *The Dublin University Magazine* for January 1835; it was collected in *Poems by James Clarence Mangan,* ed. John Mitchel (New York: P. M. Haverty, 1859). Schiller's lines are:

> Er ist dahin, der süsse Glaube
> An Wesen, die mein Traum gebar,
> Der rauhen Wirklichkeit zum Raube,
> Was einst so schön, so göttlich war.

2. *Poets of Munster:* The third edition of Mangan's *The Poets and Poetry of Munster* (ed. C. P. Meehan [Dublin, 1884]) was the first edition to print Mangan's "Fragment of an Unfinished Autobiography." According to the title page of the first edition (Dublin, 1849), the book is "A Selection of Irish Songs by the Poets of the Last Century, with Poetical Translations by the Late James Clarence Mangan, Now for the First Time Published. With the Original Music, and Biographical Sketches of the Authors. By John O'Daly, Editor of 'Reliques of Irish Jacobite Poetry,' 'Kings of the Race of Eibhear;' Author of 'Self-Instruction in Irish,' and Assistant Secretary to the Celtic Society."
3. *on:* "upon" in *Poets and Poetry of Munster,* p. xlix.
4. For an account of this story, see Appendix 1: Alfred and the Cakes, in *Asser's Life of King Alfred,* trans. Simon Keyes and Michael Lapidge (New York: Viking Penguin, 1983), p. 197: "Without any doubt the best-known story concerning King Alfred is the account of how the king, while snatching a

few days' anonymous refuge at the house of a herdsman during the period
of his greatest misfortunes, was so preoccupied with his troubles that he failed
to notice some loaves of bread burning in the oven: for this he was duly
berated by the herdsman's wife." As Keyes and Lapidge stress, this episode
is not included in Asser's late-ninth-century *Life of King Alfred*. The earliest extant manuscript for the tale is "an anonymous *Vita S. Neoti*, a work
apparently composed not long after the transfer, probably in the late tenth
century, of relics of St. Neot from their original location in Cornwall to a
priory at Eynesbury (soon renamed St. Neot's) in Huntingdonshire" (Keyes
and Lapidge 197). Keyes and Lapidge's Appendix I provides "a translation
based on a fresh collation of the manuscript sources" for Vita S. Neoti.

5. *beautiful and spirituelle, says Mitchel:* "beautiful, spirituelle, and a
coquette" on p. 11 of John Mitchel's "James Clarence Mangan: His Life,
Poetry, and Death," the biographical preface to *Poems by James Clarence
Mangan* (New York, 1859). Yeats's "informant" was apparently John
O'Regan, Archdeacon of County Kildare, though Sir Charles Gavan Duffy
affirmed the story. Yeats later defended his identification of Miss Stackpoole in an 1891 *United Ireland* article, "Clarence Mangan's Love Affair,"
pp. 134–38. For further information, see *CL*1, 46–47. In *James Clarence
Mangan: An Autobiography* (Blackrock: Irish Academic Press, 1996),
Ellen Shannon-Mangan argues that this identification is only misguided
rumor, and that Mitchel was relying on Duffy for his information, but that
Duffy had been "misled, though probably not intentionally, by Mangan himself" (90). Shannon-Mangan points out that Margaret Stackpoole, the
"Frances" Yeats identifies, would only have been about eleven when Mangan was supposed to have been jilted, making her an unlikely candidate for
his affections (90).

6. In "Broken-hearted Lays," *Poems by James Clarence Mangan* (New York,
1859), p. 449, Mangan reads "woman," and "feelings, turning."

7. *one of his strange latter poems:* In the last stanza of "Broken-hearted
Lays," the poem Yeats has just quoted from *Poems by James Clarence Mangan* (New York, 1859), these lines appear, p. 450:

> Oh! in an hour like this, when thousands fix,
> In headlong desperation, on self-slaughter,
> Sit down, you droning, groaning bore! and mix
> A glorious beaker of red rum-and-water!

8. *An acquaintance:* Yeats's quotation begins well into this sentence from
Mitchel's biographical preface in *Poems by James Clarence Mangan* (New
York, 1859), p. 13: "The first time the present biographer saw Clarence
Mangan, it was in this wise—Being in the [Trinity] college library, and
having occasion for a book in that gloomy apartment of the institution
called the 'Fagel Library,' which is the innermost recess of the stately building, an acquaintance. . . ."

9. In Mitchel's biographical preface to *Poems by James Clarence Mangan*
(New York, 1859), p. 13, Mangan reads both "garment;" and "celebrated;" with a semicolon.

10. *that which was so difficult to calm Goethe—distinguish between fact
and illusion:* Johann Wolfgang Goethe (1749–1832), German Romantic
author. See "Miss Tynan's New Book," note 4.

11. *Mrs. Atkinson's 'Biography of Mary Aikenhead':* Mary Aikenhead, Her Life,

Her Work, and Her Friends, by "S. A." (Dublin, 1879). The subsequent quotes are from a passage on pp. 259–60; see the biography for Yeats's debts to "S. A." in this paragraph.

12. *"These poets have nerves in every pore".:* "those poets have nerves at every pore." in "S. A.," *Mary Aikenhead, Her Life, Her Work, and Her Friends* (Dublin, 1879), p. 59–60.
13. In "The One Mystery," *Poems by James Clarence Mangan* (New York, 1859), p. 451, Mangan reads "No more, no more—" and "adore!"
14. In *Poems by James Clarence Mangan* (New York, 1859), p. 460, Mangan reads "blow—"; "anticlimax"; "ago!"
15. *"Nameless,":* "The Nameless One" in *Poems by James Clarence Mangan* (New York, 1859).
16. The text here appears to be corrupt and should probably read "many say" or "one may say."
17. *The White Tzar:* Probably Yeats means Alexander III, who ruled 1881–94.
18. In "Siberia," *Poems by James Clarence Mangan* (New York, 1859), p. 432, Mangan reads "by"; "Funeral-paced,"; "lives,"; and "live—".
19. See Yeats's "Popular Ballad Poetry of Ireland," pp. 93–108, for Yeats's more extended comparison of Davis and Mangan.

Finn MacCool

1. This name appears as "Finn-eges" in *Transactions of the Ossianic Society* 4 (1859), 301. [Kelly's note] See emendation, p. 478, for *Gael* printing, "Fin-eyes."
2. In a note, John Kelly includes John O'Donovan's translation of this poem from *Transactions* 4 (1859), 303, in *Yeats: An Annual of Critical and Textual Studies* 2 (1984), 87. Yeats's translation can be found in P2, 512, poem A12.
3. *Transactions* 4 (1859), 300–301, n. 4. [Kelly's note]
4. Yeats takes many of these details from Nicholas O'Kearney's introduction to *The Battle of Gabhra* in *Transactions* 1 (1854), 41–46. [Kelly's note]
5. *Ardrigh:* High king. Cormac Mac Art was high king of Ireland during the time of Finn MacCool.
6. *Fenian Poems, Second Series,* ed. John O'Daly, *Transactions of the Ossianic Society* 6 (1861), 3–19. "The Chase of Sliabh Guilleann [Cuillin]" tells how Finn is enchanted into a decrepit old man, but is finally restored to vigor, except for his hair, which remains grey. [Kelly's note]
7. The legend provided Yeats with the story for "The Madness of King Goll" (*P,* 16–18). [Kelly's note]
8. This incident occurs near the end of *The Pursuit After Diarmuid O'Duibhne, and Grainne the Daughter of Cormac Mac Art,* ed. Standish Hayes O'Grady, *Transactions of the Ossianic Society* 3 (1857), 1–211. [Kelly's note]. Kelly's note (on p. 90) continues with a quotation from *Transactions.*
9. O'Grady, *History of Ireland: Critical and Philosophical,* 1, 333: "No person dares to take any salmon, fawn, or smaller game, even though he found them dead on his path at the end of every ridge, except a person belonging to the ranks of the Fianna Eireen." O'Grady does not specifically mention a hare. [Kelly's note]
10. The opening stanzas of the poem "Aideen's Grave" by Sir Samuel Ferguson, published in *Lays of the Western Gael and Other Poems* (London: Bell and Daldy, 1865), pp. 60–69. [Kelly's note]

Ferguson reads "the cairn:" with a colon instead of a semicolon; "Ossian, In a queenly"; "leave her, 'mong"; "The cliff" with opening quotation marks; "And bare, above, the heather steep" with no comma (*Poems* [Dublin: Talbot Press, 1918], 6).

11. Frederick Barbarossa was crowned Holy Roman Emperor in 1155; he drowned during the Third Crusade in 1190.
12. See 11.16–18 of "The Secret Rose" (*P,* 67). [Kelly's note]
13. Troy, the city in Asia Minor at which happened the famous siege that is the subject of Homer's *Iliad.* In 480 B.C. Leonidas defended the pass at Thermopylae in Greece against Xerxes and his Persian army.

The Celtic Romances in Miss Tynan's New Book

1. For Ferguson, see 3–27, passim; for de Vere, see "The Poetry of Sir Samuel Ferguson—I," note 18; for Joyce, see 28–38.
2. Untraced.
3. Here and below, we are using the corrections to quotations that Kelly provides in his article. In the first stanza, Tynan reads "King" and "stone," with a comma (p. 1).
4. In this stanza, Tynan reads: "tree the"; "accursed, it"; "fight," with a comma; and "And, as . . . love's" (2).
5. Tynan reads "summer noons" (3).
6. Tynan reads "at her ear" (8).
7. Tynan reads "worlds" (9).
8. Tynan reads "noon-sun's" (9).
9. Tynan reads "knee," (9).
10. Tynan reads "warm flush" and "feast's" (10).
11. In this stanza, Tynan reads "one"; "games I"; and "flower," (13).
12. In this stanza, Tynan reads "thy name"; "night. Now, by"; and "ground" with no comma (13).
13. In this stanza, Tynan reads "her and . . . minute's"; and "gain" (13).
14. In this stanza, Tynan reads "King. But"; "knight!' Like"; and "tears her laughter suddenly" (13). Yeats omits the stanza that follows this, in which Oscar tells Diarmuid that he is under *gesa* and must elope with Grainne (*Shamrocks,* p. 14). [Kelly's note]
15. Tynan reads " 'Sweet, thou . . . death!' " (14).
16. In this stanza, Tynan reads "sleeping." and "King" (21).
17. This line occurs earlier in the poem (*Shamrocks,* 16). The Druid is in fact the god Aengus, Diarmuid's foster-father. [Kelly's note]
18. Tynan reads "fights, shall" (26).
19. Tynan reads "By . . . *thou* keepest watch" (27).
20. In this stanza, Tynan reads "not nor shelter in a single-trunkèd tree"; "channel:"; "feet"; and "wake afar" (29).
21. Although Muadhan is briefly mentioned in part four of Tynan's poem (*Shamrocks,* 29), this incident does not occur. Yeats slightly misquotes O'Grady's translation in *Transactions* 3 (1857), 79–81. [Kelly's note]. The version in *Transactions* differs in the beginning sentences: "He himself went into the next wood to him, and plucked in it a straight long rod of a quicken tree; and he put a hair and a hook upon the rod, and put a holly berry upon the hook, and went [and stood] over the stream, and took a fish that cast. He put up the second berry, and killed the second fish; and he put up the third berry, and killed the third fish. He [then] put the hook and the

hair under his girdle, and the rod into the earth, and took his three fish with him where Diarmuid and Grainne were, and put the fish on spits" (79–81).

22. In this stanza, Tynan reads "eyes"; and "ever." (43).
23. Tynan reads "old,"; "Death . . . morning—" (43); and "ears his warning" (43). The lovers' married life is described in part six of the poem (pp. 40–43). Yeats is quoting the antepenultimate and penultimate stanzas of this part. [Kelly's note]
24. In this stanza, Tynan reads, "valley," and "airs and" (54).
25. In this stanza, Tynan reads, "son,'"; "'But"; "thee" with no comma; and "thee—" (54).
26. In this stanza, Tynan reads, "dusk gloaming . . . bier,"; "hovering lit . . . grey;" and "away;" (54).
27. Since Yeats preferred the alternate ending, he had perhaps written—or meant to write—"and a few, I fear." [Kelly's note]
28. '*We digress all the days of our life*': In his preface to *The History of the World* (1614), paragraph 70, Sir Walter Raleigh (1552–1618) writes, "For seeing we digress in all the ways of our lives: yea, seeing the life of man is nothing else but digression; I may the better be excused, in writing their lives and actions."
29. "The Story of Aibhric" (*Shamrocks*, 71–81). [Kelly's note]
30. In this stanza, Tynan reads "since out in the eastern skies" and "the herd" for "the head" (72).
31. In this stanza, Tynan reads "gone"; "palace hall"; and "alone:" (72).
32. In this stanza, Tynan reads "long, gold . . . west" and "nest," (73).
33. In this stanza, Tynan reads "strange,"; "with the drifts,"; and "wing" (73).
34. In this stanza, Tynan reads "face and"; "cowered and"; and "chill;" (73).
35. These lines have been conflated, probably by the compositor. "While I wandered alone" and "On my father's throne" are separate lines (*Shamrocks*, 78). [Kelly's note]
36. "And laid on each brow" is a separate line (*Shamrocks*, 80). [Kelly's note]
37. In this stanza, Tynan reads "Saint . . . / Where" (80); "overhead and the grasses wave / All for her sake"; and "And shall not" (81). In his article, Kelly notes that the lines in the stanza have been conflated "probably by the compositor. New lines should begin at 'Where she shall' 'And the voices,' and 'And [I] shall not.'"
38. The note was from T. W. Rolleston (1875–1920), poet, scholar, and man of letters (*L*, 35). For Rolleston's criticism of *Shamrocks*, see above (p. 95 in Kelly's article). Tynan was less concerned by his views than was Yeats, and told Father Matthew Russell in an unpublished letter of 12 May 1887 that "Mr. Yeats is suddenly afraid of Rolleston's review: I am not" (*Archivae Provincia Hibernia*). Rolleston was a friend and disciple of O'Leary and contributed a number of poems to *The Gael*. [Kelly's note]
39. "The Fate of King Feargus" (*Shamrocks*, 100–111). [Kelly's note]
40. Ferguson's poem "Fergus Wry-Mouth" first appeared in his *Poems* (Dublin: William McGee; London: George Bell & Sons, 1880), pp. 44–47. [Kelly's note]
41. In this stanza, Tynan reads "his face grew shadowed;" "babe, and"; and "whisperèd—" (p. 104).
42. In this stanza, Tynan reads "on the sea-shore"; "at their" for "on their"; and "babies'" (107).
43. In this stanza, Tynan reads "then, for"; "lakeside, and where no"; and "face, like" (108).

44. In this stanza, Tynan reads "King . . . well"; "From the knowledge"; and "deer, and . . . ball," (108). Kelly notes that "the seven lines just quoted form a single stanza" (110).
45. Tynan reads "she . . . afraid" (*Shamrocks,* 109).
46. Tynan reads "a look of shrinking hate" (109).
47. In this stanza, Tynan reads "forest-paths . . . tangled brake,"; "lake," (110).
48. In this stanza, Tynan reads "daybreak"; "the story, . . . wood-sprite"; "close of day;"; "knew, his . . . drear"; and "Gods . . . King" (111).
49. Ferguson's poem "The Fair Hills of Ireland" first appeared in *Lays of the Western Gael* (pp. 225–26). It has two refrains: "*Uileacan dubh O!*" and "On the fair hills of holy Ireland." Yeats's remarks are of interest given his own use of the refrain.
50. Published by Kegan Paul, London, 1885.
51. From Wordsworth's poem "Laodamia" (l. 74). [Kelly's note]
52. *Shamrocks:* "A Child's Day" (pp. 55–58); "The Heart of a Mother" (pp. 64–66); "St. Francis to the Birds" (pp. 116–19). The last was chosen by Yeats for publication in *A Book of Irish Verse* (1895). [Kelly's note]
53. *Shamrocks:* "Death and the Man" (pp. 126–29); "Sanctuary!" (pp. 82–85). [Kelly's note]
54. This was Christina Rossetti (1830–94), poet and sister of Dante Gabriel Rossetti. Tynan had met her in 1885 and corresponded with her thereafter. On 1 January 1886, Christina Rossetti wrote praising "Sanctuary!", which she said "Has a very touching feeling, and may easily go to the reader's heart because I *think* it comes from the writer's" (unpublished letter, Morris Library, Southern Illinois University, Carbondale). [Kelly's note]
55. "Autumnal" (*Shamrocks,* 112–13). [Kelly's note]
56. In all stanzas Tynan reads "September" with no following comma. In the second line of the first stanza, Tynan reads "wheat:", and the second line of each stanza ends with a colon. At the end of the first stanza, Tynan reads "comes, grey". In the second stanza Tynan reads "heart, dost" as do the third lines of all the following stanzas (*Shamrocks,* 112).
57. In this stanza Tynan reads, "May,", "these we . . . Winter with" (112).
58. In this stanza Tynan reads, "robin with . . . a-fire" (112), "her love-song" (113).
59. Tynan reads "trees like . . . cressets burn" (113).
60. Tynan reads "green young" (113).
61. In this stanza Tynan reads "apples so", "true hearts . . . and danger," (18).
62. The noted poetess is untraced.

Miss Tynan's New Book

1. Tynan's *Louise de la Vallière* (London, 1885) was written before she met Yeats, and hence before he had had the chance to impress on her the need to express her Irish character in her poetry. Louise de la Vallière (1644–1710) was the mistress of Louis XIV, but after losing the affection of the king, she retired to a convent in 1674. Yeats calls Tynan's mannerism in this early volume "Pre-Raphaelite" because the poems obviously imitate the style of Christina Rossetti, who, together with her brother Dante Gabriel Rossetti, pioneered the so-called Pre-Raphaelite school of poetry.
2. *"Dermot and Grania—The Fate of King Fergus and the Story of Aibhric":* The Irish Fireside printing has combined three separate poems in Tynan,

Shamrocks (London, 1887): "The Pursuit of Diarmuid and Grainne," "The Fate of King Feargus," and "The Story of Aibhric."

3. Yeats mentioned these longer poems in his review "The Celtic Romances in Miss Tynan's New Book," which appeared in *The Gael* for 11 June 1887 (see pp. 51–64).

4. *"I now . . . themselves"*: Yeats may have had in mind a description of the young Goethe by August Kestner, one of Goethe's companions of the period, in *Goethe und Werther. Briefe Goethes*, ed. Kestner (Stuttgart and Augsburg, 1855):

> Er hat sehr viel Talente, ist ein wahres Genie, und ein Mensch von Character, besitzt eine ausserordentlich lebhafte Einbildungskraft, daher er sich meistens in Bildern und Gleichnissen ausdrückt. Er pflegt auch selbst zu sagen, dass er sich immer uneigentlich ausdrückte, niemals eigentlich ausdrücken könne: wenn er aber älter werde, hoffe er die Gedanken selbst, wie sie wären, zu denken und zu sagen.

Yeats read no German, but he may have encountered the passage in Lewes's famous *Life and Works of Goethe* (Boston, 1856), where Kestner's remarks were translated by Lewes as follows (p. 173):

> He has a great deal of talent, is a true genius and a man of character; possesses an extraordinarily vivid imagination, and hence generally expresses himself in images and similes. He often says, himself, that he always speaks figuratively, and can never express himself literally; but that when he is older he hopes to think and say the thought itself as it really is.

5. *"The sun and his good knights" riding "Up the eastern field of the cloth of gold"*: These exact lines are not found in *Louise de la Vallière* (London, 1885), although the sun is often figured as a king. The following lines from "The Lark's Waking" most closely approximate Yeats's quotation:

> And the fair sun rides up the Easter skies,
> Clad in bright robes of state kingly worn? (83)

Like Elaine, with small dead hands on her resting heart,: "The Dead Spring," in *Louise de la Vallière* (London, 1885), begins:

> Like Elaine, with small dead hands
> On her resting heart, . . . (19).

6. In *Louise de la Vallière* (London, 1885), p. 130, Tynan reads, "Outside"; "blue—"; "musical;" and "dew" with no comma.

7. *Roman de la Rose:* This title is italicized in *Louise de la Vallière* (London, 1885), p. 131. Later in this passage, p. 131, Tynan reads "neigh;"; "unbound,"; "embroidery;" "are" for "run"; and "strings snap" for "string snaps". *The Romance of the Rose* is a verse allegory begun by Guillaume de Lorris around 1237 and finished by Jean de Meun around 1277.

8. In "The Sick Princess" the heroine runs away in peasant costume and recovers her health. At the ending, which Yeats objected to, the princess and

her lover, also in disguise, meet years later and go off into the enchanted forest to live in a fairy palace.

9. In *Shamrocks* (London, 1887), "Angel of the Annunciation," p. 611,
Tynan reads in the second stanza "by" for "at"; "skies;" with no question
mark. In the third stanza, Tynan reads "Angel passed through" and "tips;"
with a semicolon.

The Prose and Poetry of Wilfred Blunt

1. While serving his sentence in the prison in Galway, Blunt more likely
"asked for pen and paper" to compose the sonnets in his collection *In Vinculis* (London, 1889) than to edit *The Love Sonnets of Proteus*. *The Love
Sonnets of Proteus* was published by Kegan Paul & Co. in 1880, and
Blunt's preface is signed "August 17th, 1880."

2. The Brahman philosopher was Babu Mohini Chatterji (so spelled by Hone
and Madame Blavatsky), an Indian theosophist whose visit to Dublin in 1885
was described by Yeats in "The Way of Wisdom" in *The Speaker* for 14 April
1900. This article was reprinted as "The Pathway" in the eighth volume of
Yeats's *Collected Works in Verse and Prose* (London, 1908). Yeats also wrote
a poem about him, entitled "Mohini Chatterjee" (#259, in *P*).

3. The first three editions did bear the following "Preface," signed only
"August 17th, 1880": "The author of these sonnets, styling himself Proteus, acknowledges thereby a natural mood of change. He here lays bare
what was once his heart, to the public, but what for good or evil is his
heart no longer, thus closing for ever his account with youth. He stands
upon the threshold of middle life, and already his dreams are changed. The
gods of his youth have ceased to be his gods. Yet, while looking back upon
the feelings here portrayed as things now foreign to his life, and recogniz-
ing the many errors and exaggerations of his youth, he finds it impossible
wholly to regret the past, knowing that those only are beyond all hope of
wisdom who have never dared to be fools."

Yeats's version differs slightly from Blunt's. In *The Love Sonnets of
Proteus* (London, 1885), Blunt's "Preface to the Fourth Edition" is printed
as follows:

No life is perfect that has not been lived,—youth in feeling,—manhood in battle,—old age in meditation.
Again, no life is perfect that is not sincere.
For these two reasons I have decided to add my name to the title-
page of this the Fourth Edition of the *Sonnets of Proteus*.
                                        W. S. B.
                                        Crabbet Park, Sussex
                                        March 13th, 1885."

4. In "On the Shortness of Time," in *The Love Sonnets of Proteus*, 4th edition (London, 1885), p. 103, Blunt reads "Forgetful of Time's waste" for
"Forgetful to Time's waste"; "thy soul's decay" for "the soul's decay";
"breath" with no comma; "grow,"; and "grey".

5. In "Laughter and Death," in *The Love Sonnets of Proteus*, 4th edition (London, 1885), Blunt reads "futurity" for "futility"; "voice."; and "die?" (98).

6. *Sidikhaled:* The title of Blunt's poem gives this as two words, "Sidi
Khaled." There is a Sidi Khaled in Algeria, southwest of Biskra.

7. In "The Oasis of Sidi Khaled," in *The Love Sonnets of Proteus,* Blunt reads "underfoot"; "Tis" with no apostrophe; "around"; "What is this"; "eyes."; and "sigh." (118).

8. *'Bedouins of the Euphrates':* Lady Anne Blunt, *Bedouin Tribes of the Euphrates* (London, 1879), "edited, with a preface and some account of the Arabs and their horses, by W. S. B., in two volumes."

9. *"God has made me courageous,"* one will says: "'God has not given me courage,' they will sometimes say, 'and I do not fight,' just as an English hunting man will admit having 'lost his nerve'" (Lady Anne Blunt, *Bedouin Tribes of the Euphrates* [London, 1879], vol. 2, 202–3).

10. Lady Blunt did not claim that the Bedouins are "virtuous without law"; rather, she said that they have a strict respect for their own tribal law, but none for European or Turkish law (vol. 2, 205).

11. *Shem:* "Shem!" in "To the Bedouin Arabs," in *The Love Sonnets of Proteus,* 4th edition (London, 1885), p. 119. Shem is, according to the Old Testament, one of the sons of Noah and the progenitor of the Semitic races. Japhet, mentioned below in line 12, is another of Noah's sons and is traditionally thought to have been the father of the Indo-European races.

12. In "To the Bedouin Arabs," in *The Love Sonnets of Proteus,* 4th edition (London: 1885), Blunt reads "Firstborn"; "forever children"; "loitering on" with no comma; and, in the last line quoted by Yeats, "you. I" (119).

13. *A Pilgrimage to Nejd, The Cradle of the Arab Race* (London, 1881), two volumes.

14. 2 Chron. 8:4 states that Solomon founded Tadmor. The modern spelling, used by Lady Blunt, is "Tudmur." Tudmur is also the modern name for Palmyra.

15. "The Sultan's Heirs in Asia" appeared in *The Fortnightly Review* of 1 July 1880, pp. 16–30. The article "Recent Events in Arabia" was not found in either *The Fortnightly Review* or *The Nineteenth Century.* The first part of "The Future of Islam," entitled "Census of the Mohammedan World. The Haj.", appeared in *The Fortnightly Review* for 1 August 1881, pp. 204–23; part two, "The Modern Question of the Caliphate," appeared in the same journal for 1 September 1881, pp. 315–32; part three, "The True Metropolis-Mecca," in the same journal for 1 October 1881; part four, "A Mohammedan Reformation," appeared in the same journal for 1 November 1881; the conclusion, "England's Interest in Islam," appeared in the same journal for 1 January 1882.

16. Cairo is the capital of modern Egypt; Mecca is in modern Saudi Arabia, and is an Islamic holy city, because it was there that Mohammed (ca. 570–632), the prophet of Islam, grew up, received his visions, and first began preaching.

  The noun Tartar designates an inhabitant of the regions of Central Asia, east of the Caspian Sea. Generally, the Tartars refer to a group of tribes, Mongolian and Turkish in origin, which overran and sacked much of Asia under Ghengis Khan (ca. 1202–27). Yeats seems to attribute to Blunt the opinion that the Arab would be the inheritor of Ghengis Khan's empire.

17. "Mahomedism" is Islam.

18. "The Egyptian Revolution: A Personal Narrative" appeared in *The Nineteenth Century,* September 1882, pp. 324–46.

19. Arabi Pasha (ca. 1839–1910) was an Egyptian soldier-politician who in 1881–82 led a revolt against European rule in Egypt. He was defeated by the British at Tel-el-Kebir in September 1882 and put on trial for rebellion.

Blunt aided his defense, but after pleading guilty Arabi was sentenced to exile in Ceylon for twenty years. He was pardoned and returned to Egypt in 1901.

20. *poet:* "poet," in *The Nineteenth Century,* September 1882, p. 332. George Gordon, Lord Byron (1788–1824), the British Romantic poet, was in 1823 elected a member of the Greek revolutionary committee. Byron died in Missolonghi of rheumatic fever while trying to unify the Greek rebel leaders.

Blunt, in *The Nineteenth Century,* reads "liberty" (lowercase) and "Indeed" with no comma (322).

21. In *The Nineteenth Century,* p. 322, Blunt identifies the following passage as an excerpt from a letter that he wrote to then Prime Minister William Gladstone on December 20, 1881.

In this passage, Blunt reads "God" with no comma; "I have never but once heard"; "He disclaims, and I believe him, all personal ambition;" (322). On p. 333, Blunt reads "doubt that the army"; "the army itself is but"; "its guardian" with no punctuation; "national"; "an assembly"; and "for ourselves" with no comma; and "and for those".

22. Caliph Omar was the second caliph after Mohammed; he succeeded the caliph Abu Bekr and ruled from 634 to 644.

23. *hast, indeed,:* "hast indeed" in *The Nineteenth Century* (333).

24. This poem was published in 1883 in a volume with the same title.

25. Blunt's series, "Ideas in India," was printed in *The Fortnightly Review* for 1884 in five parts: "I. The Agricultural Danger" (August 1884), pp. 164–78; "II. Race Hatred" (October 1884), pp. 445–59; "III. The Mohammedan Question" (November 1884), pp. 624–37; "IV. The Native States" (February 1885), pp. 234–48; "V. The Future of Self-Government" (March 1885), pp. 386–98.

26. Blunt estimates this percentage in "The Agricultural Danger," in *The Fortnightly Review* of August 1884, pp. 169–70. On page 165, Blunt gives this note to "Deccan ryot": "I use the term 'Deccan' in its broader and, I believe, original sense of the [S?]outh Country, not as it is sometimes applied to the dominion of the Nizam only."

The passage Yeats quotes from *The Fortnightly Review* reads "India" with no comma; "tempt night after night"; "Asia" with no comma (175).

27. George Frederick Samuel Robinson, first marquess of Ripon (1827–1909), served as viceroy of India from 1880 to 1884. What Yeats calls his "Irish action" was Ripon's contribution as Lord President of the Council during the first Gladstone ministry (1868–74) to the disestablishment of the Anglican Church of Ireland and the enactment of an Irish land bill.

28. "Race Hatred," *The Fortnightly Review,* 1884, XLII, N.S. XXXI, 454–55. Yeats changed this passage considerably and it should read as follows: "I am glad to be able to bear testimony to the fact that no Viceroy, Lord Canning possibly excepted, ever enjoyed such popularity as Lord Ripon did in the early part of last winter. Wherever I went in India I heard the same story; from the poor peasants of the south who for the first time had learned the individual name of the ruler, from the high caste Brahmins of Madras and Bombay; from the Calcutta students; from the Mohammedan divines of Lucknow; from the noblemen of Delhi and Hyderabad, everywhere his praise was in all men's mouths, and moved the people to surprise and gratitude. 'He is an honest man,' men said, 'and one who fears God.'"

29. This passage is from "The Native States," *The Fortnightly Review,* 1885, XLIII, N.S. XXXVII, 247. The text should read "raised, and the Viceroy".

At the end of the passage here quoted, the sentence continues "and to the last moment all the world believed that the Residency had triumphed."

Nizam is the title of the ruler of Hyderabad from the early eighteenth century to 1950.

Irish Fairies, Ghosts, Witches, etc.

1. Paraclesus (1493–1541), born Theoprastus Bombast von Hohenheim, was a Swiss-born physician who lectured on medicine in Basle from 1527 to 1528. Because Paracelsus contradicted the traditional methods of Galen, he quarreled with the medical faculty and left the university to wander. Paracelsus believed in "the Divine Alchemy of Creation," wherein God separated by (al)chemical process the elements from the primal matter, the Mysterium Magnum. To the Aristotelean notion of four elements, Paracelsus added the three "principles" of sulphur, mercury, and salt. According to Paracelsus, the elements were inhabited by spirits: air by sylphs, water by nymphs or undines, earth by gnomes, and fire by salamanders. Paracelsus believed that the elements were also inhabited by other supernatural or spiritual beings; such notions led the Rosicrucians to champion Paracelsus.

   Adolphe d'Assier was the author of *Essai sur l'humanité et le spiritisme, par un positiviste* (Paris, 1883). The English translation was by H. S. Olcott, *Posthumous Humanity, A Study of Phantoms* (London, 1887).

2. Yeats wrote an article on the contrast between Irish and Scots treatment of witches that he reprinted in *The Celtic Twilight* as "A Remonstrance with Scotsmen for having Soured the disposition of their Ghosts and Faeries." There he echoes the present passage thus: "In Ireland we have left them alone. To be sure, the 'loyal minority' knocked out the eye of one with a cabbage-stump on the 31st of March, 1711, in the town of Carrickfergus. But then the 'loyal minority' is half Scottish. You have discovered the faeries to be pagan and wicked. . . . In Scotland you have denounced them from the pulpit. In Ireland they have been permitted by the priests to consult them on the state of their souls. Unhappily the priests have decided that they have no souls, that they will dry up like so much bright vapour at the last day; but more in sadness than in anger they have said it. The Catholic religion likes to keep on good terms with its neighbours" (*Myth*, 107–8).

3. Thomas Crofton Croker (1798–1854) compiled *Fairy Legends and Traditions of the South of Ireland* (London, 1826–28). At the beginning of "The Confessions of Tom Bourke," which appears in that compilation, Croker writes that Bourke "is of a class of persons who are a sort of black swans in Ireland: he is a wealthy farmer. Tom's father had, in the good old times, when a hundred pounds were no inconsiderable treasure, either to lend or to spend, accommodated his landlord with that sum, at interest; and obtained as a return for the civility, a long lease, about half a dozen times more valuable than the loan which procured it. The old man died worth several hundred pounds, the greater part of which, with his farm, he bequeathed to his son Tom. But besides all this, Tom received from his father, upon his death-bed, another gift, far more valuable than worldly riches, greatly as he prized, and is still known to prize, them. He was invested with the privilege, enjoyed by few of the sons of men, of communicating with those mysterious beings, called 'the good people'" (Croker, vol. 1, pp. 51–52).

4. Thomas Keightly (1789–1872) helped Croker edit *Fairy Legends*. Keightly published his own *Fairy Mythology* anonymously in 1828. In the first note

in his chapter "Ireland," in vol. 2, Keightly writes, "In real worth, as a display of character and modes of thinking, there is, in our opinion, nothing in the Fairy Legends equal to 'The Confessions of Tom Bourke.' They who sneer at popular legends, and those who present them to the public, would perhaps abate their censure if they were acquainted with the cultivated and philosophical mind of the amiable writer of that tale, and knew the rapid progress he is making towards eminence in an arduous and honourable profession. His Macarthy [*sic*] Banshee and Crookened Back are also both admirable. The latter, in the manner in which character, incident, and scenery are blended, comes up to our ideal of legendary writing" (177).

5. Jane Francesca, Lady Wilde (1826–96), was the mother of Oscar Wilde and an author of note in her own right. Her *Ancient Legends, Mystic Charms, and Superstitions of Ireland* (London, 1887) was followed by *Ancient Cures, Charms and Usages of Ireland* (London, 1890). Yeats's favorable review of this second book is included in the present edition, pp. 113–16.

6. This passage from "An Irish Adept of the Islands," *Ancient Legends, Mystic Charms, and Superstitions of Ireland* (vol. 1), reads "heart,"; "spirits, or meat,"; "him—'Winter"; "grave, and" (191); "usages, such"; "Monday;" and "suicides as accursed" (192).

7. This passage in Lady Wilde reads "off"; "dead—so"; "devoted" for "given"; and "charity.'" (192).

To this point Yeats has cited Wilde's quotation of "A man who knew him" [the "Irish Adept" of the title]. At this point Wilde stops quoting this oral source and resumes her own voice, although the punctuation in *Lucifer* would lead one to assume that the following paragraph is from the same speaker as the previous quotations.

8. Wilde's sentence reads "Though now an old man, he has never had a day's sickness. No one has ever seen him in a rage, nor heard an angry word from his lips but once; and then being under great irritation, he recited the Lord's Prayer backwards, as an imprecation on his enemy" (192).

9. The *Lucifer* printing reads *moruada*. Yeats corrected it in a clipping in MS 12147 (National Library of Ireland).

10. Bantry is a town at the head of Bantry Bay in southwest Ireland.

11. Turlogh Carolan (1670–1738), blind musician remembered as "The Last of the Bards." James Hardiman, in his "Memoir of Carolan" in *Irish Minstrelsy, or Bardic Remains of Ireland* (London, 1831), tells the story of Carolan and the rath at some length (1, xlix).

12. May Eve is Beltaine, the first day of summer. Yeats mentions the other principal Celtic festival days in the text that follows. Midsummer Eve is 24 June, now celebrated as Bonfire Day. November Eve is Samhain, which marks the change from the old year to the new. According to fairy lore, the fairies were more active on these holidays that marked the change of seasons, especially on Samhain, when the Otherworld was at its most accessible. The fourth holiday, which Yeats doesn't mention here, is Lughnasa, celebrated on 1 August.

13. "The Butter Mystery," *Ancient Legends, Mystic Charms, and Superstitions of Ireland* (London, 1887), vol. 2.

14. Patrick Kennedy (1801–73) was a folklorist and Dublin bookseller. His folklore appeared in *The Dublin University Magazine* and his published works include *Fictions of Our Forefathers* (Dublin and London: M'Glashen and Gill, 1859) and *Legendary Fictions of the Irish Celts* (London: Macmillan and Co., 1866).

15. *claimed in one of his works to know spells for making the fairies visible:* On p. 103 of *Legendary Fictions of the Irish Celts,* Patrick Kennedy writes, "We could name the receipt for rendering the 'Good People' visible, when a small whirlwind is at work with dust and dry leaves; but as much as we wish to diffuse a knowledge of the social economy Fairy Land, we are not anxious that any of our readers should make personal acquaintance with individuals of that country, or practise any magic rites whatsoever. You set dangerous machinery in motion, without knowing how to put it at rest again, or whether it may not tear your own person to pieces."

16. For David Rice McAnally, see Yeats's review of *Irish Wonders: The Ghosts, Giants, Pookas, Demons, Leprechawns, Banshees, Fairies, Witches, Widows, Old Maids and Other Marvels of the Emerald Isle* (Boston and New York: Houghton Mifflin, 1888), the next item in this collection.

17. *robbing wine-cellars:* McAnally mentions the Cluricaun in his section on leprechauns in *Irish Wonders* (pp. 139–42), but a reference to robbing wine cellars is not found there.

18. Yeats's short novel *John Sherman* was published in 1891 under the pseudonym "Ganconagh."

19. Yeats corrected the spelling of *Piast bestea* in a clipping in MS 12147 (National Library of Ireland).

20. John O'Donovan (1809–61) was, as Yeats mentions, an eminent Irish antiquarian. In 1840 O'Donovan and his brother-in-law Eugene O'Curry (1796–1862) founded the Irish Archaeological Society; in 1850 he assumed the chair of Celtic studies at the University of Belfast. His publications were many, typically dealing with Irish lore from archaeological or linguistic perspectives. Probably his most famous work was his seven-volume compilation *Annala Rioghacta Eireann, Annals of the Kingdom of Ireland by the Four Masters* (Dublin, 1848–51).

21. In "Irish Popular Superstitions: Chapter III.—Fairy Lore and Enchantment," *The Dublin University Magazine,* June 1849, this article, like the two preceding chapters and the introduction, are unsigned.

22. *The Book of Armagh,* while once supposed to be in the handwriting of St. Patrick, is now attributed to the scribe Feardomhnach and was compiled around 807. It contains lives of St. Patrick as well as Latin versions of his *Confessions.*

23. Yeats's authorities for this parallel between Greek and Celtic mythology were John Rhys, in his *Lectures on the Origin and Growth of Religion as Illustrated by Celtic Heathendom* (London and Edinburgh: Williams and Norgate, 1888); and Henri d'Arbois de Jubainville's *Le Cycle mythologique irlandais et la mythologie celtique* (Paris: E. Thorin, 1884).

24. "Domnian" comes from "Domnu," whom Rhys in *Lectures on the Origin and Growth of Religion as Illustrated by Celtic Heathendom* (London, 1888) identified as the goddess of the deep. Her sons, the "Fir Domnaan," along with other Titans—the Firbolgs, the Formorians—war with the Tuatha dé Danaan, the gods of light.

25. The sequel to this article never appeared.

Irish Wonders

1. William Carleton (1794–1869), Irish novelist and storyteller, whose *Traits and Stories of the Irish Peasantry* served Yeats well as a source for his folklore compilation. Yeats published in 1889 a collection of stories from Car-

leton, and in October 1889, he reviewed Carleton's *Red-Haired Man's Wife* for *The Scots Observer* (see pp. 88–92).

2. This description of a fairy ball can be found on page 99 of a reprint of the 1888 version of *Irish Wonders* (Detroit: Grand Rivers, 1971). In it, "Fairy Glen" is not capitalized.

3. *daoine sí* in Irish.

4. Yeats was told this by Biddy Hart (*P&I*, 58). Yeats also used the "beautiful parlours" information in "Drumcliff and Rosses" in *The Celtic Twilight* (*Myth*, 88).

5. Yeats gave some of McAnally's information on leprechauns as authoritative in his notes to *Fairy and Folk Tales of the Irish Peasantry*.

6. Lough Erne is in Co. Fermanagh in the northwest of Ireland; the lough flows west out to Donegal Bay.

7. *"to circumvent her,"*: "to sarcumvint her" in *Irish Wonders*, p. 106.

8. *"Divil take the stick,"*: "Divil take the shtick" (107).

9. *"a little atomy . . . leprechawn"*: McAnally reads ". . . a little attomy av a man alang wid her, that was a Leprechawn" (108).

10. *houses of their ancestors: all waiting*: It is "homes of their ancestors, all waiting" in McAnally, p. 111. This quotation comes from McAnally's chapter "The Banshee."

11. *Mahabharata and Divine Comedy*: the *Mahabharata*, an Indian epic poem of great length, is one of the chief sources for Vedic myth. It is best known in one of its parts, the *Bhagavad-Gita*. Yeats was probably referring generally to the Hindu doctrine of reincarnation. The Dante reference is to canto 13 of the *Inferno*, where the souls of suicides are imprisoned within trees.

12. "Another name for the God of Flies" is Beelzebub, which is literally translated from the Hebrew as "lord of the flies."

John Todhunter

1. The Religious Society of Friends, or Quakers, as they are more commonly called, are a Christian sect that was founded by George Fox (1624–91). They stress the guidance of the Holy Spirit and spurn the use of religious rites and services. They are most well known for their long-standing tradition of pacificism. The silence Yeats refers to here stems from their particular form of worship, which might pass in silence or vocal prayer, depending on how members felt themselves moved by the Spirit.

2. Sir Walter Scott (1771–1832), Thomas Moore (1779–1852), and George Gordon, Lord Byron (1788–1824), famous poets as are those in the list Yeats gives in the next sentence.

3. Edmund Spenser (1552–99), John Milton (1608–74), Alfred, Lord Tennyson (1809–92), Robert Browning (1812–89), Samuel Taylor Coleridge (1772–1834), John Keats (1795–1821), and Percy Bysshe Shelley (1792–1822).

4. Richard Whatley (1787–1863), archbishop of Dublin. Whatley was active in Irish cultural and political life, particularly where educational reform was concerned.

5. The composer George Frederic Handel (1685–1759) lived briefly in Dublin from 1741 to 1742; his oratorio *Messiah* premiered in Dublin on 13 April 1742.

6. Edmund John Armstrong (1841–65), prolific, though short-lived poet. His

works were collected in *Poetical Works* (1877). His brother George Francis Savage-Armstrong (1845–1906) was also a poet and a professor of English at Queen's College, Cork. In 1900 he would attack the Literary Revival and be accused by Yeats of being obsolete. In 1892 Yeats twice reviewed Savage-Armstrong's work, in "Some New Irish Books," pp. 170–72, and "'Noetry' and Poetry," pp. 180–81 in this volume.

7. For Edward Dowden, see "The Poetry of Sir Samuel Ferguson—II," note 2.

8. Dr. Hudson is untraced. Sir William Stokes (1839–1900) was a professor in the Royal College of Surgeons in Ireland.

9. *Cornhill Magazine* was a literary periodical that ran from 1860 to 1875; its specialty was the serialization of novels. Its first editor was novelist William Makepeace Thackeray (1811–63). Because Thackeray died in 1863, Yeats's statement is inaccurate.

10. Todhunter married Katharine Ball in 1870. Her brother, Sir Robert Stawell Ball (1840–1913), was a professor of astronomy at Trinity College, Dublin, and did much to popularize the field during his lifetime. He was the Royal Astronomer from 1874 to 1892.

11. John Kells Ingram (1823–1907) was a poet and scholar; he was professor of Greek at Trinity College, Dublin, and had a hand in the founding of Alexandra College. He is the author of "Who fears to speak of Ninety-eight," published in *The Nation* in April 1843 under the title "The Memory of the Dead."

12. Dora Louise Digby (1853–1935) had been a student of Todhunter's at Alexandra College.

13. *A Study of Shelley* appeared in 1880; *The True Tragedy of Rienzi, Tribune of Rome* in 1881; *Forest Songs* also in 1881; *Helena in Troas* in 1885; and *The Banshee and Other Poems* in 1888.

14. Edward William Godwin (1833–86), Fellow of the Society of Arts, was an architect and designer of art furniture, as well as of theatrical costumes and sets.

William Carleton

1. *The Carlow College Magazine* ran from May 1869 to April 1870. Father Kavanagh is untraced.

2. The "Publisher's Preface" to *The Red-Haired Man's Wife* (Dublin: Sealy, Bryers & Walker/London: Simpkin, Marshall & Co., 1889) reads as follows: "THE MSS. of the present work was placed in our hands many years ago, but owing to a serious mishap (which, by the aid of a literary friend we have, fortunately, been able to remedy), its introduction to the public has been delayed. We entertain no doubt, however, that even now this last work of WILLIAM CARLETON will be hailed with welcome." D. J. O'Donoghue, in his *Life of Carleton* (1896), says that the "literary friend" was a Mr. MacDermott. See *CL1*, 172.

3. *"Sthagan Varagy"*: Carleton reads "Sthagan Varagy ('the Market Lounger')," p. 2.

4. *the town*: *The Red-Haired Man's Wife* (1889) reads "this town" (2).

5. *Varagy, the beloved of the girls,*: Carleton reads "Varagy—the beloved of the girls—" (2).

6. *well.*: Carleton reads "well!" (2).

7. Carleton converted to Protestantism around 1828. His first story, "A Pilgrimage to Patrick's Purgatory," appeared in *The Christian Examiner* in

April and May of 1828. Its title was changed to *The Lough Dearg Pilgrim* when it was published with *Father Butler* in 1829 (Dublin: William Curry). *Traits and Stories of the Irish Peasantry* (first series) was first published in 1830; the second series was published in 1833. *Fardorougha the Miser; or the Convicts of Lisnamona* (Dublin: William Curry) was first published in 1839. *The Black Prophet* appeared in 1847. The other work Yeats mentions, *Irish Life and Character, or Traits and Stories of the Irish Peasantry*, most likely does not fit the time line Yeats has set up here. Though published without a date on the title page, it includes *Valentine M'Clutchy*, which was first published in 1845. For a comprehensive and instructive bibliography of Carleton's works, see Barbara Hayley's *A Bibliography of the Writings of William Carleton* (Gerrards Cross: Colin Smythe, 1985).

8. *Fardorougha the Miser; or the Convicts of Lisnamona* was serialized in *The Dublin University Magazine* in 1837–38, and *The Black Prophet, a Tale of the Famine* in the same magazine in 1846.

9. Yeats expressed the same idea, perhaps more beautifully, in his introduction to *Stories from Carleton*, p. xvii: "When I read any portion of the 'Black Prophet,' or the scenes with Raymond the Madman in 'Valentine M'Clutchy,' I seem to be looking out at the wild, torn storm-clouds that lie in heaps at sundown along the western seas of Ireland; all nature, and not merely man's nature, seems to pour out for me its inbred fatalism" (*P&I*, 28).

10. Yeats means the Library of Ireland series sponsored by *The Nation* and published by James Duffy. The "humorous tales" Yeats here refers to are probably Carleton's *Tales and Sketches*, published by Duffy in 1845.

11. The Church of Ireland, the Irish branch of the Church of England.

12. "The Scarlet Woman" is a derogatory epithet for the Roman Catholic Church. *The Christian Examiner* was edited by the exceedingly anti-Catholic Rev. Caesar Otway (?1779–1842). Otway also edited *The Dublin Penny Journal* and *The Dublin University Magazine*.

13. Carleton was born in Co. Tyrone in Ulster.

14. The "Hero of the Boyne" is William of Orange (1650–1702), who defeated James II at the Battle of the Boyne in 1690.

15. Yeats erred somewhat; Carleton died in January 1869.

16. The Fenian Brotherhood was a secret society dedicated to ending British rule in Ireland. It was organized in the late 1850s by John O'Mahony in the United States and by James Stephens in Ireland. Their uprisings were unsuccessful but the movement did much to spur the nationalist movement in Ireland.

17. Yeats told the same story (*Au*, 270–71), with names supplied, and apparently under the impression that he had never told it before: "O'Leary had told me the story, not I think hitherto published. A prominent Irish American, not long released from the prison where Fenianism had sent him, cabled to Parnell: 'Take up Land Reform side by side with the National Question and we will support you. See Kickham'. What had Parnell, a landowner and a haughty man, to do with the peasant or the peasant's grievance? And he was indeed so ignorant of both that he asked Kickham, novelist and Fenian leader, if he thought the people would take up land agitation, and Kickham answered: 'I am only afraid they would go the Gates of Hell for it'; and O'Leary's comment was, 'and so they have'."

Popular Ballad Poetry of Ireland

1. *little blue-paper-poem books:* Yeats refers in his article "William Carleton" (see p. 91) to "the 'National Library'—that series of blue-covered
   sixpennies which has done so much for Ireland." He means the Library of
   Ireland series sponsored by *The Nation* and published by James Duffy.
2. *Anglo-Saxon households:* used in the sense of "non-Celtic," hence English.
3. For information on the leprechaun and the pooka, see Yeats's article "Irish
   Fairies, Ghosts, Witches, etc.," above, pp. 75–81.
4. Elizabeth Tudor reigned as queen of England from 1558 to 1603.
5. It is not clear how Yeats arrived at his number of twenty-six such poets.
   Yeats may be taking his cue from Mangan's *Poets and Poetry of Munster*
   (Dublin: John O'Daly, 1850), one of Yeats's sources for this article, which
   lists twenty-five Irish-language poets in its table of contents.
6. *lord upon the hill;:* Yeats is apparently quoting from Sir Charles Gavan
   Duffy's *Ballad Poetry of Ireland*. The thirty-ninth edition (Dublin: James
   Duffy, 1866) reads "Lord upon the hill:" (p. 112). The poem is "The
   County of Mayo," which is given as "Translated from The Irish, By George
   Fox" (110). Duffy misattributes the poem to Thomas Lavelle; its author is
   Thomas Flavell. Thomas Hardiman included an untranslated version of the
   poem in his *Irish Minstrelsy* (I, 337–38); he noted that the poem is known
   "sometimes as 'The lament of Thomas Flavell,' having been composed by
   a bard of that name, a native of the island of Bophin, on the western coast"
   (I, 337). The persons named in the poem are untraced.
7. *Colonel Hugh McGrady:* Duffy reads "Colonel Hugh Mac Grady" (112).
8. John O'Tuomy or Sean O Tuama (1706–75) kept for a time a public house
   in Limerick, where poets in the area would congregate. He was known as
   "An Ghrinn," or "The Gay," because of his hospitality, which Mangan
   notes in *The Poets and Poetry of Munster* (John O'Daly's edition) "must
   have inevitably led to bankruptcy" (8).
9. *Gael—:* The original differs from Yeats's version as follows: "Gael,";
   "cheer,"; and "He is" (9).
10. Yeats has created two identities, but the biographical information belongs
    to just one man, Donnchadh Ruadh Mac Conmara (1715–1810). He trav-
    eled widely, going first to Rome to study for the priesthood, and after aban-
    doning that idea, he returned to Ireland and set up as a schoolmaster. He
    later traveled to Newfoundland and Europe and is said to have composed
    one of his more famous poems, "The Fair Hills of Ireland" (Bán Chnoic Éire-
    ann Óigh), in Hamburg. This poem was adapted by James Clarence Man-
    gan under the title "The Fair Hills of Eire, O." Ferguson published a
    version, titled "The Fair Hills of Holy Ireland," in his review of Hardiman
    in the October 1834 issue of *Dublin University Magazine*. The translation
    Yeats gives here is from Duffy's *Ballad Poetry of Ireland*, which gives the
    title as "The Fair Hills of Ireland."
11. This Gaelic phrase is usually translated as "O sad lament!"
12. The original differs from Yeats in this stanza as follows: "ear;" "fanned,"
    (185).
13. *ringleted,:* Duffy's edition reads "ringletted," (185).
14. *ground,:* Duffy's edition reads "ground;" (186).
15. John O'Daly gave biographical sketches of some of these men in *The Poets
    and Poetry of Munster*. The full names and dates are: Andrew MacGrath/
    Andrais Mac Craith (ca. 1708–95); Owen Roe O'Sullivan/Eoghan Rua

Ó Súilleabháin (ca. 1748–84) seems not to have deserved the word "profligate" but does not seem to have been particularly pious; John MacDonnell/Sean "Clarach" Mac Domhnaill (1691–1754). Mac Domhnaill and Mac Craith were friends of Sean O Tuama, mentioned above. Sean Ó Coileain/ John O'Cullen, also given sometimes as John Collins (1754–1817), a Cork poet whom Cleeve, vol. 3, p. 90, *Dictionary of Irish Writers* (Cork: Mercier, 1971), has described as "except for Raftery, the last of the poets of the old tradition." Ferguson's translation was entitled "Lament over the Ruins of the Abbey of Timoleague," *Lays of the Western Gael* (London: Bell and Daldy, 1865). William Dall (Blind) Heffernan (ca. 1700–60) was a Tipperary poet. Yeats wanted to write an entry on him for the *Dictionary of National Biography*, but no such article ever appeared (*CL*1, 116). Heffernan wrote "Caitlin ni Uallachain," which James Clarence Mangan translated as "Kathaleen Ny-Houlahan."

16. Yeats is speaking of the tradition of "aisling" poetry.
17. *Kathleen, Ny-Houlahan:* literally, Kathleen, the daughter of Houlahan: allegorical figure for Ireland, especially as a long-suffering woman. The origin of this figure appears to be the Heffernan poem cited above. Yeats used this character in "Red Hanrahan's Song about Ireland." His patriotic one-act play, *Cathleen ni Houlihan,* was first performed in Dublin on 2 April 1902. "Roisin Dubh" is Irish for "the little black rose," or, as Mangan entitled his translation of the poem, "Dark Rosaleen."
18. Yeats is quoting from the last stanza of Mangan's poem "Dark Rosaleen." The quotation begins "O!" in *The Poems by James Clarence Mangan; with a Biographical Introduction by John Mitchel* (New York: P. M. Haverty, 1859). The original differs from Yeats's version as follows: 'slogan cry,; "serene."; and in Mangan, all instances of the phrase read "My Dark Rosaleen" (344).
19. Edward Walsh (1805–50) was a hedge school teacher. He contributed poems regularly to national magazines like *The Nation* and *The Irish Penny Journal* and published two collections of poetry, *Reliques of Irish Jacobite Poetry* (with John Daly; Dublin: S. Machen, 1844) and *Irish Popular Songs* (Dublin: James McGlashan, 1847). James (Jeremiah) Joseph Callanan (1795–1829) was for a short time a schoolteacher before turning his attention to ballad collecting and his own poetry. His works were published in *The Recluse of Inchidony and Other Poems* (London: Hurst, Chance, 1839) and *The Poems of J. J. Callanan* (Cork: Bolster, 1847).
20. Lisbon is the capital of Portugal.
21. Malta is an island in the Mediterranean south of Sicily.
22. Poems by Callanan that are frequently anthologized include "Dirge of O'Sullivan Beare" and "The Outlaw of Loch Lene."
23. Londonderry, also known as Derry, is a city in Ulster, on the north coast of Ireland; Spike Island is in the bay outside Cork, near Cobh.
24. *"We remember . . . House.":* Yeats is quoting from the preface by "J.S.S." to the second edition of Walsh's *Irish Popular Songs* (1883), where this sentence begins "Well we remember" (iv).
25. This parenthetical phrase was left outside the quotation marks in *The Leisure Hour* printing.
26. The 1883 edition of Walsh reads as follows: "Jonses's-road" (iv); "at that time"; and "Clonliffe House" (v).
27. John Mitchel (1815–75) was the assistant editor of *The Nation* newspaper, and in 1848 he founded *The United Irishman*. For his articles in that jour-

nal he was tried and convicted on a charge of "treason-felony." During his five years of penal servitude he kept his famous *Jail Journal,* which was published in New York in 1854 after his escape from Van Diemen's Land, now Tasmania.

28. Yeats is quoting from Mitchel's *Jail Journal.* The original 1854 (New York: Office of the "Citizen") edition, p. 35, reads: "He stooped down and kissed my hand. 'Ah!' he said, 'you are the man in Ireland most *to be envied'*."

29. The punctuation in Mitchel's version differs slightly: "Poor Walsh! He has a family of young children; he seems broken in health and spirit; ruin has been on his traces for years, and I think has him in the wind at last. There are more contented galley-slaves moiling at Spike than the school-master" (35).

30. Sir Charles Gavan Duffy (1816–1903) helped to found *The Nation* newspaper. In 1855 he emigrated to Australia, where he had a distinguished political career, becoming prime minister of Victoria in 1871. In his retirement in the south of France in 1880, he wrote his memoirs about the Nation movement. In the mid-1890s, Yeats became involved with Duffy in a struggle over the editorship of a publishing venture called "The New Irish Library." Duffy became the editor.

31. In "Plans and Methods" (*Uncollected Prose,* 1975 ed., vol. 2, p. 202), Yeats identifies William Allingham as the poet, but the volume of poems is untraced.

32. *no cattle, "to drive through the long twilight.":* This quotation is from Samuel Ferguson's poem "Cashel of Munster" in *The Oxford Book of English Verse* (Oxford: Oxford University Press, 1958).

33. Yeats seems to be placing these earliest poems about 1200, although there is a tradition of Irish poetry that goes back much further.

34. Yeats adapted a translation by Edward Walsh (p. 18 of the 1883 edition of *Irish Popular Songs*) of a stanza from the song "Edmund of the Hill" by Edmund O'Ryan. Walsh's version is as follows:

> My hope, my love, we will proceed
> Into the woods, scattering the dews,
> Where we will behold the salmon, and the ousel in its nest,
> The deer and the roe-buck calling,
> The sweetest bird on the branches warbling,
> The cuckoo on the summit of the green hill;
> And death shall never approach us
> In the bosom of the fragrant wood!

Yeats published his version in *Poems and Ballads of Young Ireland* (1888). This poem, entitled "Love Song" (from the Gaelic), is reprinted as additional poem A14 in *P,* with some punctuational changes.

35. For James Clarence Mangan, see the article "Clarence Mangan" above, pp. 39–44.

36. These lines are from Mangan's translation of Friedrich von Schiller's poem "Die Ideale"; the lines in Mangan (*The Poems by James Clarence Mangan; with a Biographical Introduction by John Mitchel* [New York: P. M. Haverty, 1859]) read:

> All my Divinities have died of grief,
> And left me wedded to the Rude and Real.

37. Mitchel, in his "Biographical Introduction" to Mangan's *Poems,* p. 11, identifies Mangan's love as "a certain fair and false 'Frances'." Yeats identified Mangan's love as Miss Stackpoole in his article "Clarence Mangan," pp. 39–44 in this volume. See "Clarence Mangan," note 5.

38. This sentence in Mitchel's "Biographical Introduction," p. 13, reads as follows: "It was an unearthly and ghostly figure, in a brown garment; the same garment (to all appearance) which lasted till the day of his death."

39. In this sentence, Mitchel's version differs as follows: "celebrated;" ; "murderer;" ; "a table"; "reading" with no comma; and "gaze on" (13).

40. Mangan was forty-six when he died.

41. In Shannon-Mangan's book, pp. 423–24, she notes that Sir Frederick Burton drew Mangan in the morgue after his death and later presented the drawing to the National Gallery of Ireland.

42. The poem Yeats quotes here is Mangan's "Siberia," pp. 432–33 in Mitchel's edition of his *Poems.* There are changes in Yeats's version. Mangan's original reads as follows:

> In Siberia's wastes
>   The Ice-wind's breath
> Woundeth like the toothed steel
> Lost Siberia doth reveal
>   Only blight and death.
>
> Blight and death alone.
>   No Summer shines.
> Night is interblent with Day.
> In Siberia's wastes alway
>   The blood blackens, the heart pines.
>
> In Siberia's wastes
>   No tears are shed,
> For they freeze within the brain.
> Nought is felt but dullest pain.
>   Pain acute, yet dead;
>
> Pain as in a dream,
>   When years go by
> Funeral-paced, yet fugitive,
> When man lives, and doth not live,
>   Doth not live—nor die.
>
> In Siberia's wastes
>   Are sands and rocks.
> Nothing blooms of green or soft,
> But the snowpeaks rise aloft
>   And the gaunt ice-blocks.
>
> And the exile there
>   Is one with those;
> They are part, and he is part,
> For the sands are in his heart,
>   And the killing snows.

> Therefore, in those wastes
>   None curse the Czar.
> Each man's tongue is cloven by
> The North Blast, who heweth nigh
>   With sharp scymitar.
>
> And such doom each drees,
>   Till, hunger-gnawn,
> And cold-slain, he at length sinks there,
> Yet scarce more a corpse then ere
>   His last breath was drawn.

43. *The north blast, who:* Mangan, p. 433, reads "The North Blast, who". Editions by Louise Imogen Guiney (1897) and D. J. O'Donoghue (1903) read "that" for "who."
44. Yeats quotes the fifth of nine stanzas. The first line of Duffy's version of this poem in his *Ballad Poetry of Ireland* (39th edition), p. 45, reads "O, think on Donnell of the Ships, the Chief whom nothing daunted—" (45). Donnell is Red O'Donnell (1571–1602), the earl of Tyrconnell.
45. The original differs from Yeats's quotation as follows: "sleeps,"; "rouse—"; and "good Woman of the Three Cows" (45).
46. Mangan's version was entitled "Prince Aldfrid's Itinerary through Ireland." According to D. J. O'Donoghue in his *Poems of James Clarence Mangan* (1903), the prose translation from which Mangan worked was by John O'Donovan from the 15 September 1832 *Dublin Penny Journal.* Mangan's original (from Mitchel's 1859 edition) of the quoted stanzas reads as follows:

> I found in Innisfail the fair,
> In Ireland, while in exile there,
> Women of worth, both grave and gay men,
> Many clerics and many laymen.
>   * * * *
> Gold and silver I found, and money,
> Plenty of wheat and plenty of honey;
> I found God's people rich in pity,
> Found many a feast and many a city.
>   * * * *
> I found the good lay monks and brothers
> Ever beseeching help for others,
> And in their keeping the holy word
> Pure as it came from Jesus the Lord.
>   * * * *
> I found in Munster unfettered of any,
> Kings, and queens, and poets a many—
> Poets well skilled in music and measure,
> Prosperous doings, mirth and pleasure.
>   * * * *
> I found in Ulster, from hill to glen,
> Hardy warriors, resolute men;
> Beauty that bloomed when youth was gone,
> And strength transmitted from sire to son.

* * * *

I found in Leinster the smooth and sleek,
From Dublin to Slewmargy's peak;
Flourishing pastures, valor, health,
Long-living worthies, commerce, wealth.

* * * *

I found strict morals in age and youth,
I found historians recording truth;
The things I sing of in verse unsmooth,
I found them all—I have written sooth.

47. *Slewmargy's peak:* Mitchel, p. 381, gives this note: "Slewmargy, a mountain in the Queen's county, near the river Barrow." County Leix is the former Queen's County, which was named after Mary I.
48. *he:* The context suggests that Yeats means Mangan, not Alfred.
49. Thomas Davis (1814–45) was one of the founders of *The Nation* newspaper in 1842, and he was the most famous poet of the Young Ireland movement.
50. *rebel party:* Young Ireland.
51. *O'Connellites:* followers of Daniel O'Connell, who sought reform through constitutional means.
52. This poem, "Lament for Thomas Davis," appeared in *The Dublin University Magazine* (February 1847), pp. 198–99. Each stanza opened with quotation marks; only the last closed with quotation marks as well.
53. *Ballinderry:* river in Co. Armagh, flowing into Lough Neagh from the west shore.
54. *broadcast . . . plenty:* Ferguson reads "broad-cast forth the corn in golden plenty,".
55. *'Even such . . . toil![']:* Ferguson shows no quotation marks on these lines, nor at the end of the following stanza.
56. *Ballyshannon:* town on the northwest coast of Ireland, in Co. Donegal. The end of this line in Ferguson reads "Summer."
57. *calm clear:* Ferguson, p. 198, reads "calm, clear".
58. *Young . . . now?:* Before this half stanza Yeats omits two stanzas; four more follow it in *The Dublin University Magazine,* the last of which he quotes on p. 23, in "The Poetry of Sir Samuel Ferguson."
59. Davis's poem "The Sack of Baltimore" appears in Duffy's *Ballad Poetry of Ireland* (1866), pp. 213–15, and in Davis's *National and Other Poems* (Dublin: M. H. Gill & Sons, 1907), pp. 53–54, for example. Baltimore is a small town (and not the source for the name of the American city) on the south Irish coast, southwest of Cork and near Cape Clear. Algerian pirates attacked the town in 1631, carrying off many of the people as slaves. The poem "OH! For a Steed," pp. 16–17 in Davis, begins "OH! For a steed, a rushing steed, and a blazing scimitar. . . ."
60. In Davis's edition, this poem, "OH! The Marriage," is given as an air with the musical title listed as "The Swaggering Jig," p. 21. Davis's first line reads "OH! the marriage, the marriage," (21).
61. *mo bhuachaill for me;:* Davis's edition reads "me,". Here and in the last stanza, the italics were provided by Yeats or *The Leisure Hour* editor. *Mo bhuachaill* means "my bridegroom" in Irish.
62. Two lines up, Davis reads "to me;", in this line, "true".

63. *away.:* Davis reads "away;".
64. Davis's poem has the following line endings in this stanza: "fair—"; "night—"; "skim,"; "can see,"; "marriage,".
65. For more information on Sir Samuel Ferguson, see the first two articles in this volume.
66. The title of this poem is "The Welshmen of Tirawley." It first appeared in *The Dublin University Magazine* in September 1845, pp. 308–14. It was later included in *Lays of the Western Gael*. While this poem is mentioned only in passing in Yeats's two articles on Ferguson in this collection (pp. 3–27), Ferguson's *Conary* is discussed at length in these articles.
67. Gerald Griffin (1803–40), best known as a novelist. Yeats in his article "Irish National Literature, IV: A List of the Best Irish Books" listed Griffin's novel *The Collegians*. "Gille Machree" translates as "Brightener of My Heart." Writing as the O'Hara brothers, John Banim (1798–1842) collaborated with his brother Michael on many novels dealing with Irish life. In the article mentioned above, Yeats noted John Banim's *The Nowlans* (volumes 1 and 2 of *Tales of the O'Hara Family,* 2nd series [London: Colburn, 1826]) and two of their collaborations, *John Doe* (London: Simpkin and Marshall, 1825) and *Father Connell* (London: Newby and Boone, 1842). Banim's poem was included in Duffy's *Ballad Poetry of Ireland,* which appears to be Yeats's source for this version of the poem. "Soggarth" is an anglicized form of the Irish word *sagart,* for "priest."
68. This line, in Duffy's version, p. 56, reads "Nor, out of fear to you,".
69. The beginning of this stanza reads "Who, in", and in the present line, "cabin-floor".
70. Banim's first line of this stanza begins, "Who,—on the marriage-day,". On the fourth line, Banim reads, "Soggarth aroon,—", and in the present line "christening,".
71. *Who as:* Duffy's version reads "Who, as".
72. Banim's line reads "And when my heart was dim,".
73. *aroon.:* Duffy's version reads "aroon," and in the following line "shake,".
74. The full names and dates of the poets in this list are as follows: John Keegan (1809–49); John Frazer (1804–52); Denis Florence McCarthy (1817–82); Thomas D'Arcy McGee (1825–68); McGee was assassinated in the city of Ottawa, Canada, after visiting Ireland, where he was highly critical of the Fenian movement; Michael Doheny (1805–63), whose one famous song was "A Cushla Gal Mo Chree" (Bright Vein of My Heart); Sir Charles Gavan Duffy (1816–1903); John Kells Ingram (1823–1907); John Keegan Casey (1846–70); Charles Joseph Kickham (1826–82); Robert Dwyer Joyce (1830–83), whose national epic *Deirdre* Yeats comments upon earlier in this collection (pp. 28–38); Alfred Percival Graves (1846–1931); the lines of his that Yeats quotes here are lines four and five of the poem "The Little Red Lark," the opening poem of Graves's *Irish Songs and Ballads* (Manchester: Alexander Ireland and Co., 1880); Yeats is referring to Graves's collection *Father O'Flynn and Other Irish Lyrics* (London: Swan Sonnenschein, 1889); William Allingham (1824–89); Aubrey Thomas de Vere (1814–1902).
75. Thomas Moore (1779–1852), the author of the best-known book of Irish songs, *Irish Melodies* (1808–34). Charles James Lever (1806–72), Samuel Lover (1797–1868), both primarily known as novelists.

Bardic Ireland

1. *Senchus Mor:* the *Law of Distress,* a compilation of ancient Gaelic law; *The Book of the Dun Cow: Lebor na hUidre,* a codex, dating from the early twelfth century, which contains an important compilation of bardic tales.
2. Standish James O'Grady (1846–1928), novelist and historian, considered by Yeats to have begun the Irish Literary Revival; O'Grady is often referred to as the "Father of the Irish Renaissance." The histories Yeats is referring to include O'Grady's *History of Ireland: The Heroic Period* (Dublin: E. Ponsonby/London: Sampson Low, Searle, Marston, & Rivington, 1878) and a second volume, *History of Ireland: Cuculain and His Contemporaries* (Dublin: E. Ponsonby/London: Sampson Low, Searle, Marston, & Rivington, 1880). This Standish O'Grady should not be confused with the Gaelic scholar and author of *Silva Gadelica* (London: Williams and Norgate, 1892), Standish Hayes O'Grady (1832–1915).

   Lady Ferguson (née Mary Catherine Guinness), married to Sir Samuel Ferguson, published *The Story of the Irish Before the Conquest;* the complete title is *The Irish Before the Conquest. From the Mythical Period to the Invasion under Strongbow.* (Dublin: Bell and Daldy, 1868; a second edition, Dublin: Sealy, Bryers, and Walker, 1890).
3. For Ferguson's ballads, see the first two articles in this collection. *Legends of St. Patrick* (London: Henry S. King and Co., 1872).

   Inisfail: this poem is included in de Vere's collection entitled *The Sisters, Inisfail and Other Poems* (Dublin: McGlashan & Gill, 1861).
4. *the landing of Strongbow:* Richard de Clare, known as "Strongbow," landed near Waterford in 1169; he had been promised Leinster by Diarmuid Mac Murrough, who had sought help from Henry II of England to become high king of Ireland. This landing marks the beginning of the Anglo-Norman invasion and of the eventual conquering of Ireland by England.
5. St. Patrick (?390–461); patron saint of Ireland. Patrick traveled Ireland converting Irish kings and clans to Christianity; he introduced Latin, the Christian creed, and the laws of the church to the pagan Irish.
6. The *ard-reigh* (*ard rí*), or high king, who met his death crossing the Alps was King Daithi.
7. *Táin Bó Cuailgne: The Cattle Raid of Cooley.*
8. The incident of the hen's egg plays an important part in Yeats's late play *The Herne's Egg* (1938), in which Congal, King of Connacht, kills Aedh, King of Tara, because he is served a hen's egg instead of a herne's.
9. *Fenian militia:* the Fianna Eireann, or the warriors of Finn MacCool, a legendary Irish hero. See "Bardic Ireland," note 13.
10. *Chiefs of the Red Branch:* the court of King Conchobar of Ulster; their name comes from the hall where they feasted (see "The Poetry of Sir Samuel Ferguson—II," note 25); Cuchulain is the greatest of these chiefs.
11. Battle of Gabra or Gavra, ca. A.D. 284, at which Oscar, son of Oisin, was supposedly killed by King Cairbre.
12. Yeats changes the wording of this phrase in a clipping contained in MS 12147 (National Library of Ireland). *The Scots Observer* printing read "unless, indeed, her whole history . . .".
13. *Cuchulain, Finn, Oisin:* legendary heroes of Ireland; Cuchulain was a hero of Ulster; his exploits are recorded in the *Táin Bó Cuailgne.* Finn MacCool

was the leader of the Fianna Eireann, a group of hunter warriors and poets who lived in the forests; Oisin is Finn's son, a poet, who gives his name to the Ossianic (or Fenian) cycle of stories, which recounts the exploits of Finn and his men.

14. *Fomorians, Tuatha dé Danaan, Milesians:* the Fomorians are a mythic race from the sea, invaders who repeatedly attacked Ireland until they were driven out by the Tuatha dé Danaan (people of the goddess Dana); the Tuatha dé Danaan form the pantheon of the Celtic gods. The Milesians are descendants of the nine sons of Mil, who ultimately conquered Ireland and the Tuatha dé Danaan. *The Book of Invasions (Leabhar Gabhála)* was transcribed from a twelfth-century manuscript and describes five early mythic conquests of Ireland and is the source of the mythology surrounding the Tuatha dé Danaan. Sir John Rhys (1840–1915) was the author of *Lectures on the Origin and Growth of Religion as Illustrated by Celtic Heathendom* (London, 1888). H. d'Arbois de Jubainville (1827–1910) was the author of a twelve-volume series, *Cours de littérature celtique.* The second volume, *Le Cycle mythologique irlandais, et la mythologie celtique* (1884), was translated into English by Richard Irvine Best and published in Dublin in 1903.

15. In the Old Testament (Gen. 5–9) of the Bible, Noah builds an ark which saves himself, his family, and all species of animals from the destruction of a flood which God causes to engulf the earth.

16. *Holy Virgin, when will brother Edmund come home from the meeting?:* Yeats used a version of this quotation in his article on Finn MacCool for the 23 April 1887 issue of *The Gael.* John Kelly has identified it as from *Fenian Poems,* ed. John O'Daly, *Transactions of the Ossianic Society* 4 (1859), 300–301, note 4. The version of the quotation used earlier reads "Oh, Virgin Mary, what a long time till brother Edmund comes home from the meeting." See the Finn MacCool article, pp. 45–50.

17. *Iberian, Ugrian, Belgae:* the Iberians are the people who once lived in what is now Spain and Portugal and who are the ancestors of the Basques; the Ugrians are members of the Finno-Ugric peoples of western Siberia and Hungary; the Belgae are the ancient Gallic people who lived in what is now Belgium and northern France.

18. *Brehon Laws:* a complex body of common law which grew out of custom, habit, and public opinion and which governed daily life in early Ireland.

19. *Nibelungenlieds, Eddas:* the *Nibelungenlied* is an epic poem in Middle High German that was written about A.D. 1200 (the correct German plural would be *Nibelungenlieder*); the Eddas are a series of Old Norse poems that were collected in the early thirteenth century.

20. *the Danes expelled:* Brian Boru ended the dominance of the Danes in Ireland at the Battle of Clontarf in 1014.

21. *the landing of the Norman:* the Norman is Richard "Strongbow" de Clare, who, as noted in note 4 to this chapter, led the Anglo-Norman incursion into Ireland in 1169.

22. Conchobar (alternate spelling of Conchubar) was a legendary king of Ulster; his exploits are recounted in the Red Branch Cycle. He raised Cuchulain as a foster son.

23. Edgar Quinet (1803–75) in his *Génie des religions* (1842), book 5, "La Religion hébraïque," section one, "Jéhovah—La Révélation par le désert." Quinet contrasted the effect of the unchanging desert on Judaic monotheism with the effects of the ever-changing sea upon the polytheism of

Greece and India. Yeats repeated this idea in "Earth, Fire and Water," a short piece printed in *The Speaker,* 15 March 1902, and reprinted in *The Celtic Twilight* (1902). By that time, he had become considerably more vague in his memories: "Some French writer that I read when I was a boy said that the desert went into the heart of the Jews in their wanderings and made them what they are" (*Myth,* 80).

24. *Parsees:* members of a Zoroastrian religious community in India. Parsis see fire as a symbol of their supreme god, Ahura Mazda.

Tales from the Twilight

1. The western islands are the Aran Islands, located off the coast of Co. Galway.
2. Howth is now a suburb of Dublin on the northeastern edge of Dublin Bay.
3. *Innismurray:* a tiny island off the coast of Co. Sligo.
4. Sir William Wilde (1815–76), antiquarian, writer, and doctor, married Jane Francesca Elgee in 1851.
5. Douglas Hyde (1860–1949) collected and translated much folklore and poetry from the Irish in books such as *Beside the Fire* (London: D. Nutt, 1890) and *Love Songs of Connacht* (London: T. Fisher Unwin, 1893). See Yeats's review, pp. 218–21.
6. Lady Wilde, *Ancient Cures, Charms and Usages of Ireland,* (London: Ward and Downey, 1890), p. 34.
7. For Lady Wilde on madness, see p. 39; for the "falling sickness," see p. 42; and for "any minor evil," see p. 12 or 27, respectively.
8. Lady Wilde ("Love Charms"), p. 32; young girls do this to their beloved men.
9. *weird:* probably in the sense *Oxford English Dictionary* gives as "an evil fate inflicted by supernatural power, especially by way of retribution."
10. Lady Wilde ("Malific Charms"), p. 47.
11. According to Yeats's piece "A Remonstance with Scotsmen for having Soured the Disposition of Their Ghosts and Faeries," the place was Carrickfergus and the year 1711 (*Myth,* 107).
12. Lady Wilde ("The Western Isles"), pp. 149–51.
13. This tale does not appear in Lady Wilde, though on p. 116 she tells of English settlers corrupting *La-mas-abhal,* a spirit's name, into "lamb's wool."
14. Lady Wilde ("The Western Isles"), p. 151.
15. Lady Wilde, pp. 151–52, has both husband and wife attacked by the cats.
16. *Hollantide:* All Hallow's Eve, 1 November. This superstition, however, resembles most the one Lady Wilde tells about Whitsuntide, pp. 109–10.
17. The following paragraph is essentially the same as a passage in "Concerning the Nearness Together of Heaven, Earth, and Purgatory" (*Myth,* 98–99).
18. Lady Wilde, p. 122, tells of a son haunting his mother with this complaint.
19. Lady Wilde, p. 250, reads "Even contention is better than loneliness."
20. Lady Wilde, p. 250, reads "God is nigher to us even than the door. God stays long, but He strikes at last."
21. In Lady Wilde, the first and second proverbs are found on p. 250; the third proverb is from p. 248 and it reads "Every nursling as it is nursed; every web as it is woven."
22. William Shakespeare (1564–1616), English playwright and poet. The witches Yeats refers to are presumably the weird sisters in his play *Macbeth.*

When Yeats refers to "Teuton gloom," he is referring to the belief that the Germanic peoples of northern Europe depicted the preternatural in a way different from Greco-Roman civilization. Yeats was doubtless familiar with Goethe's *Faust*.

23. Untraced.
24. *Brockens:* Brocken is the name of the highest mountain in the Harz Mountains of Saxony and, according to German folklore, is where witches celebrate Walpurgis Night on 30 April.

Irish Fairies

1. A place for quarantining those ill with cholera.
2. Yeats's source for this tale is untraced.
3. One of the four provinces of Ireland, which are Ulster in the north, Connacht in the west, Leinster in the east, and Munster in the south.
4. Sligo is the county in the west of Ireland that Yeats considered home.
5. Grange is a village in Sligo north of Sligo town. This story of the girl who disappeared was told in *The Celtic Twilight* in the chapter entitled "Belief and Unbelief." In *The Celtic Twilight,* Yeats said that the girl "was" at service, and he placed the story "about three years ago" (*Myth,* 7–8).
6. Ben Bulben is the headland on the Atlantic coast of Ireland north of Sligo town. Some of the material in this paragraph appeared in altered form in the "Kidnappers" chapter of *The Celtic Twilight* (*Myth,* 70).
7. Ballisodare, also spelled Ballysodare, is a village in Co. Sligo south of Sligo town.
8. *old Gaelic poem:* Untraced.
9. Edward Walsh (1805–50), the compiler and translator of *Irish Popular Songs* (Dublin, 1847). The song is "The Fairy Nurse." For comparison, see Yeats's "The Unappeasable Host." Another version of "The Fairy Nurse" appears in *1000 Years of Irish Poetry* (ed. Kathleen Hoagland [New York: Grosset & Dunlap, 1947], p. 439). For more on Walsh, see "Popular Ballad Poetry of Ireland," note 19.
10. The keeners are those who raise the funeral cry over the dead. [Yeats's note]
11. *A sluagh shee* means "fairy host," and "airy" is the peasant's way of saying "aery." [Yeats's note]
12. *koel shee,* fairy music. [Yeats's note]
13. *When:* Hoagland's printing reads "Where," p. 439.
14. In the introduction to *Irish Fairy Tales* (1892), Yeats attributes this statement to Old Biddy Hart and "an old man" (*P&I,* 59).
15. This tale was included in *The Celtic Twilight* as "The Three O'Byrnes and the Evil Faeries" (*Myth,* 86–87).
16. Slieve League is in Co. Donegal in the north of Ireland. Its cliffs are north of Donegal Bay to the west of Carrigan Head.
17. Cashel Nore is an anglicized form of Casleain Oir, Irish for "castles of gold."
18. *The Celtic Twilight* version in the collected edition of Yeats's works (1908) has "coffin" changed to "coffer." *Myth* reads "coffin" (86).
19. Cork is the main city (in the county of the same name) on the south coast of Ireland. The name of the henwife is Mrs. Quinn.
20. John O'Tuomy (1706–75) ran a public house in Limerick, where he reputedly dispensed free drinks to sessions of the bards, who revered his memory.
21. David Rice McAnally Jr., the author of *Irish Wonders: The Ghosts,*

Giants, Pookas . . . and Other Marvels of the Emerald Isle (1888). Yeats reviewed this book twice, unfavorably (see pp. 82–85), but often quoted McAnally as an authority.

22. *Fir Darrig:* In his review of McAnally's *Irish Wonders,* p. 135, Yeats calls this fairy the "Far Darrig."

23. Yeats used this story four times. It first appeared under the title "Columkille and Rosses" in *The Scots Observer,* 5 October 1889. Aside from the present article, Yeats also included it in *Irish Fairy Tales* (London, 1892) and, under the title "Drumcliffe and Rosses," in *The Celtic Twilight.* In its *Celtic Twilight* form, the teller is referred to as "Michael H—" and no mention is made of his having only one arm.

24. The Royal Canal runs from the River Shannon (north of Lough Ree in Co. Longford) to Dublin Bay.

25. Mullingar is a cattle-trading town in Co. Westmeath, about fifty miles west of Dublin.

26. In a clipping of this article, contained in MS 12147 (National Library of Ireland), Yeats added commas before and after the phrase "as he ploughs and digs."

27. This proverb is one Lady Wilde collected in her *Ancient Cures, Charms and Usages of Ireland:* "The lake is not encumbered by the swan; nor the steed by the bridle; nor the sheep by the wool; nor the man by the soul that is in him" (250).

Irish Folk Tales

1. Hyde had heard the story of the Indian juggler from Colonel Henry Olcott, one of the founders of the Theosophical Society of America, who had visited Ireland at that time to examine Irish fairy lore from a theosophic standpoint. In the 1910 edition, p. 190, the note wherein Hyde makes this contrast is the sixth to "The Well of D'Yerree-na-Dowan."

2. *through:* Hyde (1910 ed.) reads "throughout," (p. 77).

3. See "The Poetry of Sir Samuel Ferguson—I," note 9.

4. *"the improving book":* Untraced.

5. Henrik Ibsen (1828–1906), Norwegian dramatist. Among the Ibsen plays that Yeats may have been referring to are *A Doll's House* (1879), *Ghosts* (1881), and *Hedda Gabler* (1890). Yeats reviewed F. E. Garrett's translation of Ibsen's *Brand* in *The Bookman,* October 1894. See pp. 252–54 in this collection.

6. Thomas Crofton Croker (1798–1854) was the author of *Fairy Legends and Traditions of the South of Ireland* (London: Murray, 1825). Croker and the other folklorists mentioned in this review were Yeats's sources for his compilation *Fairy and Folk Tales of the Irish Peasantry* (1888). Patrick Kennedy (1801–73) was the author of *Legendary Fictions of the Irish Celts* (London: Macmillan, 1866) and *The Fireside Stories of Ireland* (Dublin: M'Glashan and Gill, and Patrick Kennedy, 1870). The anonymous writer remains unidentified; Yeats lists this source in his *Irish Fairy and Folk Tales* (Gerrards Cross: Colin Smyth, 1988).

7. Gerald Griffin (1803–40), a novelist, poet, and playwright; Yeats considered him a source for Irish folklore. William Carleton (1794–1869) was a novelist and short story writer whom Yeats praised for his authentic depiction of Irish subjects; Samuel Lover (1797–1868) was a novelist, dramatist, and painter. Lover also founded *The Dublin University Magazine* in 1833.

8. . . . *for fear of putting his readers up to mischief:* Kennedy (1891 ed.), p. 103, explains, "we are not anxious that any of our readers should make personal acquaintance with individuals of that country, or practise any magic rites whatever. You set dangerous machinery in motion, without knowing how to put it at rest again, or whether it may not tear your own person to pieces."

9. *Ancient Legends, Mystic Charms, and Superstitions of Ireland,* 2 vols. (London: Ward and Downey, 1887) and *Ancient Cures, Charms and Usages of Ireland* (London: Ward and Downey, 1890). Yeats wrote a notice of the second volume for *Boston Pilot* (22 February 1890) (*LNI,* 27), and his review of this same volume for *The Scots Observer* is reprinted in this collection, pp. 113–16. David Rice McAnally Jr.'s book *Irish Wonders: The Ghosts, Giants, Pookas . . . and Other Marvels of the Emerald Isle* (London: Ward, Lock, 1888) was reviewed by Yeats in *The Scots Observer* for 30 March 1889. Jeremiah Curtin (1835–1906), collector of *Hero-tales of Ireland* (Boston: Little, Brown, 1894) and *Myths and Folk-lore of Ireland* (Boston: Little, Brown, 1889), was also known as a translator of Polish and Russian literature.

10. *Campbell of Islay:* John Francis Campbell (1822–85), whose researches were published in four volumes as *Popular Tales of the West Highlands Orally Collected* (1860–62).

11. *sennachie:* Irish word for "chronicler" or "bard."

12. *Teig O'Kane:* Yeats included Hyde's English translation of this tale in his *Fairy and Folk Tales of the Irish Peasantry.*

13. Alfred Nutt (1856–1910) was a publisher and folklorist. For more information, see Yeats's review of Nutt's *Voyage of Bran* (*The Bookman,* September 1898), pp. 415–16.

14. *Guleesh na Guss Dhu:* the title of one of Hyde's tales; Guleesh na Guss Dhu (Guleesh Black Foot) is a character in the story so named because he refuses to wash his feet.

15. This passage in Hyde reads ". . . and there he saw the loveliest woman that was, he thought, upon the ridge of the world. The rose and the lily were fighting together in her face, and one could not tell which of them got the victory" (112).

16. *the cronawn:* italicized in Hyde (122). In Hyde this passage reads ". . . the sharp whistle of the fadogues and flibeens (golden and green plover), rising and lying, lying and rising, as they do on a calm night" (122).

17. *rest:* Hyde (1910 ed.) reads "rest," (171).

18. *gentlemen of the sun-myth:* Yeats is probably referring to the theory of Friedrich Max Müller (1823–1900).

19. *that:* Hyde reads "That," with this capitalized word beginning a new line.

20. Emanuel Swedenborg (1688–1772), a Swedish religious and scientific writer.

21. *"man of ten centuries":* Coleridge had much to say of Swedenborg, both complimentary and critical, but this remark has not been traced.

22. Yeats learned this in *The Spiritual Diary of Emanuel Swedenborg . . . ,* Translated from the original by J. H. Smithson, vol. 1, London, 1846. Diary entry no. 1161 reads:

> That the spiritual angels, or such as constitute the spiritual class dislike butter, was made evident from this circumstance:—that although at other times I relished butter, yet [when in their society]

I did not for a long while, even for some months, desire it; and when I tasted it, it wanted its agreeable flavour, and consequently its relish, such as I had before enjoyed (354).

23. *a friend of mine:* Untraced.
24. See "Irish Fairies," note 27.

Gypsy Sorcery and Fortune Telling

1. In his article, Kelly recounts how Samuel Taylor Coleridge told this story about his son Hartley at the house of Charles Lamb; this tale appears in *Diary, Reminiscences, and Correspondence of Henry Crabb Robinson,* ed. Thomas Sadler (London, 1872), vol. 1, 177–78.
2. *sweetness and light:* an oft-quoted phrase from Matthew Arnold's book *Culture and Anarchy* from a section entitled "Sweetness and Light" where Arnold says, "In thus making sweetness and light to be characters of perfection, culture is of like spirit with poetry, follows one law with poetry" (Cambridge: Cambridge University Press, 1954, p. 54). Arnold himself took the phrase from Jonathan Swift's "Battle of the Books," where Aesop closes his speech on the dispute between the "Antients" and the Moderns by arguing that the Antients furnish "Mankind with the two Noblest of Things, which are Sweetness and Light" (*A Tale of a Tub, To which is added The Battle of the Books and the Mechanical Operation of the Spirit* [Oxford: Oxford University Press, 1958], pp. 234–35).
3. Kelly, p. 188, notes that this quote is from Charles Leland, pp. 169–70 ("Gypsy Witchcraft").
4. *Hermes Trismegistus,* or "thrice greatest Hermes," is the Egyptian god Thoth, to whom are ascribed numerous books on alchemy, philosophy, theology, medicine, and geography. Helena Petrovna Blavatsky (1831–91) was a Russian spiritualist; along with Henry Steel Olcott (1832–1907), she was the founder of the Theosophical Society in 1875. Yeats's article "Irish Fairies, Ghosts, Witches, etc.," pp. 75–81, was written for the theosophical magazine *Lucifer.* Yeats wrote about Mme. Blavatsky and his experiences with the Theosophical Society in his autobiography.
5. Kelly notes that these quotations are from Leland, pp. 170–71 (188). In the passages quoted here and in the preceding sentence, Leland reads "occult literature,"; "MME. Blavatsky,"; "Outside of us always Somebody Else"; "met in visions"; and "in spiritual unity".
6. *The Rosicrucian Fratres of Germany:* The Rosicrucians were a secret religious society said to have been founded in 1484 by Christian Rosenkreuz; members were thought to have knowledge of alchemy and power over the elements.
7. *"Murriker":* Untraced.
8. The shoemaker is Jacob Boehme (1575–1624); Kelly recounts that in 1600, Boehme was "filled . . . with the illumination of God" after he saw the "sunlight reflected from a dish" (188).
9. Kelly notes that Yeats is quoting from Leland, p. 191.
10. Kelly notes that Yeats is quoting from Leland, p. 171.
11. Leland was most well known for his "Hans Breitmann" ballads, published in *Graham's Magazine,* in 1857. These ballads were later collected and published in 1871 as *The Breitmann Ballads* (Kelly 183, 187).
12. According to Kelly, Yeats refers to Leland, 11, p. 21.

13. Kelly records that "these lines, not entirely accurate in Yeats's transcription, occur on p. 31 and are recited by Transylvanian gipsies as they 'wind a barley-straw round a stone, which is thrown into a running stream'" (189). Leland reads "thy house.";"not all,"; "from me;"; and "into the water!"

14. *faëry lands forlorn:* This phrase is from John Keats's "Ode to a Nightingale," l. 70.

15. Leland, p. 46, notes that certain magicians among Hungarian Gypsies obtain their power from spirits of water and earth, known respectively as the *Nivasi* and *Pchuvusi* (Kelly 189).

16. According to Kelly, the scientist is "perhaps Karl Vogt, a German chemist . . . who 'argued that the brain secreted thought like bile'" (189). The quotation in Yeats's text is untraced.

17. Merlin is the wizard of the Arthurian legends. Faustus (Latin form of the German Faust) is a legendary figure who seems to have been based on an historical Georg Faust of the late fifteenth and early sixteenth centuries; the central event of the legend is Faust selling his soul to the Devil. The centaur Chiron was renowned for his knowledge of music, medicine, and hunting; he taught Heracles and Achilles and other heroes. Kelly cites the Mage Zoroaster as the man who "met his own image" and suggests that Yeats is referring to ll. 192–93 from act I of Shelley's *Prometheus Unbound:*

> The Mage Zoroaster, my dead child,
> Met his own image walking in the garden
> (Kelly 189).

Plays by an Irish Poet

1. The title of this collection had no definite article. *Poems and Ballads of Young Ireland* (Dublin: M. H. Gill) appeared in 1888. Aside from pieces by Todhunter, it contained contributions by Yeats, Katharine Tynan, Douglas Hyde, and T. W. Rolleston.

2. *Vaudeville:* a theater in London's Leicester Square. The production of *Helena in Troas* described below was given at Hengler's Circus in April 1886 with Beerbohm Tree in the cast.

3. *Bedford Park:* The Yeats family and Todhunter were living in this suburb of London. Yeats had encouraged Todhunter to write a pastoral drama for the clubhouse theater in Bedford Park. For Yeats's description of Bedford Park and Todhunter, see *Au,* 113–23.

4. *One of the performers:* Florence Farr (1860–1917).

5. The phrase "pale passion lover" may be a paraphrase of John Fletcher's lines:

> Fountain heads, and pathless groves,
> Places which pale passion loves.
> (The Nice Valour, Song, 3, 3).

Yeats may have been referring to Fletcher's other play *The Faithful Shepherdess* (ca. 1609).

6. Yeats refers to English poet Robert Browning (1812–89), who not only lived in Italy but wrote many poems with Italian settings, notably *The Ring and the Book* (1868).

7. Nathaniel Hawthorne (1804–64), American novelist and short story writer. "Rappaccini's Daughter" first appeared in *Mosses From an Old*

Manse (1846). Hawthorne visited Italy, but after he wrote "Rappaccini's Daughter."

8. Yeats had been working on his play *The Countess Kathleen* for two years. He changed the spelling of the title to "Cathleen" in 1895.

9. *"Oh, Lord, confine my wrinkles to my heels":* Untraced.

10. *Kabalist:* adherent to a system of Jewish theosophy, which, by interpreting the Scriptures through mysticism, claims to arrive at an understanding of sacred mysteries. The word "kabala" or "cabala" is from the Hebrew word *qabbalah,* meaning tradition.

11. Yeats may have been alluding to evidence of sorcery in Dublin which he found in the memoirs of Dr. Adam Clarke (ca. 1762–1832). He mentions this evidence in a letter to the editor of *United Ireland,* printed on 30 December 1893. The editors of *CL1* have not been able to find any such evidence in the memoirs of Dr. Adam Clarke. (See *CL1,* 374.)

12. In the summer of 1891, Yeats and many another Irishman expected the quick passage of Home Rule. In his autobiography, he said that the fall of Parnell and the failure of Home Rule turned Ireland's attention to things other than politics, such as literature and the theater. See Book II of *Au,* "Ireland After Parnell," 169ff.

13. Richard Brinsley Sheridan (1751–1816) was born in Dublin. His most famous plays are *The Rivals* (1775) and *The School for Scandal* (1777). Oliver Goldsmith (1728–74) was born in Co. Longford. Goldsmith's most famous play was *She Stoops to Conquer* (1773). Goldsmith's most famous poem is "The Deserted Village," probably based on his memories of Lissoy in Westmeath, where he grew up.

14. *"a real locomotive engine"* or *"a real fire engine":* Such phrases as these were used to attract audiences to many of the spectacular stage melodramas of the second half of the nineteenth century.

15. *"the union of hearts":* Yeats is repeating a political slogan of his day. In *The Politics of Irish Literature* (Seattle: University of Washington Press, 1972), Malcolm Brown notes that the phrase was coined to counter the effects of the Tory slogan "Unionism" (312).

Clarence Mangan's Love Affair

1. *Fishamble-street:* a Dublin street near the quays south of the River Liffey and bordering the east side of Christchurch Cathedral.

2. *the Wandering Jew:* a legendary figure who was condemned to wander the earth without rest until Judgment Day after he insulted Jesus Christ when Christ was on his way to be crucified.

3. *"more than any understood":* Untraced.

4. The passages cited above can be found on p. 26 of Mangan's *Autobiography,* ed. James Kilroy (Dublin: Dolmen Press, 1968).

5. King Alfred (848–899) was king of the West Saxons (891–899) and is remembered for his revival of letters during his reign; he is thought to have begun the tradition of English prose translations from Latin. For the story of letting the cakes burn, see "Clarence Mangan," note 4 (p. 505).

6. Percy Bysshe Shelley (1792–1822), British Romantic poet.

7. William Blake (1757–1827), English mystic, poet, and artist. Yeats's high number of references to Blake derive from his work as co-editor with Edwin J. Ellis on *The Works of William Blake: Poetic, Symbolic, and Critical,* 2 vols. (London: Quaritch, 1893).

8. *"whistled him down the wind"*: this expression was used by John Mitchel on page 11 of his "Biographical Introduction" to his collection of Mangan's poems which he published in 1859.
9. For John Mitchel, see "Popular Ballad Poetry of Ireland," note 27. The Reverend C. P. Meehan (1812–90) was a close friend of Mangan's, collected his poems, and officiated at his funeral.
10. Yeats named her in his article for *The Irish Fireside*, 12 March 1888.
11. This quotation is from Mangan's translation of a poem by Friedrich Rückert (1789–1866) entitled "Und dann nicht mehr." Mitchel quoted some stanzas of it in his biographical introduction to Mangan's poems. The following is a sample:

> I saw her once, one little while, and then no more.
> Earth looked like heaven a little while, and then no more.
> Her presence thrilled and lighted to its inner core
> My desert breast a little while, and then no more.

12. In "The Nameless One: A Ballad," the following stanza would seem to support Yeats's reference:

> And he fell far through that pit abysmal,
> The gulf and grave of Maginn and Burns,
> And pawned his soul for the devil's dismal
> Stock of returns.
> (Poems, ed. Mitchel, 453)

13. This title is usually given as *Anthologia Germanica*.
14. *The Dublin University Review* did not begin until the late 1880s. Yeats meant *The Dublin University Magazine*, which ran from 1833 until 1877. Mangan contributed to *The Dublin University Magazine* from 1834 to 1849.
15. In Mitchel's edition of Mangan's poems this passage reads as follows: ". . . in a brown garment; the same garment (to all appearance) which lasted . . ." (13).
16. Clarence Mangan, *Poems* (1859), p. 13.
17. *one whom some have called a seer*: The phrase is from the last line of Mangan's poem "Irish National Hymn": "And these words come from one whom some have called a Seer" (Mitchel, *Mangan's Poems*, p. 448).
18. *and see men as trees walking*: In the Bible, Mark 8:24, a blind man says, "I see men as trees walking," after which Jesus cures him.
19. *Mary Aikenhead, Her Life, Her Work, and Her Friends*, by Sarah Atkinson (Dublin, 1879), pp. 259–60.
20. Untraced.

A Reckless Century. Irish Rakes and Duellists

1. Mount Pelier is south of Dublin, on the way into the Wicklow Mountains. The Hell-Fire Club wasn't particular to Dublin; there were several around London and one in Limerick. Walsh reads "Hell-fire Club" (8).
2. *these eighteenth-century worshippers of his*: perhaps members of the Hell-Fire Club, though Walsh doesn't recount this anecdote.
3. John Edwards Walsh (1816–69), *Ireland Sixty Years Ago* (Dublin: McGlashan, 1847).

4. Sir Jonah Barrington (1760–1834), author of *Personal Sketches of His Own Time*, 3 vols. (London: Colburn, 1827–32).
5. *whose iniquitous rules and regulations have been preserved by a contemporary writer:* Untraced.
6. *"Hawkabites," the "Sweaters," and "Pinkindindies":* Walsh mentions all three of these groups, though he focuses his attention on recounting the activities of the Pinkindindies (18).
7. The Battle of the Boyne took place on 12 July 1690; William of Orange defeated King James II of England, ensuring a British, and largely Protestant, rule over Ireland until the twentieth century.
8. *"the infamous invader had been impoverishing Mr. Maguire for centuries":* Untraced.
9. *the last bardic college came to an end in 1680:* Although no specific reference could be found which gives this date for the end of the bardic colleges, Douglas Hyde in his *A Literary History of Ireland: From Earliest Times to the Present* (1899) notes that all the bardic colleges had disappeared by 1700.
10. The Volunteers were a force, raised in part by Henry Flood, to repel a possible French invasion during the American Revolution. Their number grew to forty thousand and they were able to demand, with success, such concessions as the opening of the British colonies to Irish trade. Jonathan Swift (1667–1745), poet, prose satirist, novelist, and dean of St. Patrick's Cathedral in Dublin from 1726 until his death.
11. *the Parliament House:* now the Bank of Ireland on College Green in Dublin.
12. Yeats's name within the secret Order of the Golden Dawn was "Demon est Deus Inversus" (a demon is an inverted god).
13. Isaiah 2:4 in the Bible reads "They shall beat their swords into ploughshares and their spears into pruning hooks; one nation shall not raise the sword against another, nor shall they learn war any more."

Oscar Wilde's Last Book

1. See the previous article in this collection.
2. Thomas Griffiths Wainewright (1794–1847) wrote art criticism for *The London Magazine* and exhibited paintings at the Royal Academy. He committed forgery in 1822 and 1824, and he was thought to have poisoned several of his relatives. Convicted of forgery, he was exiled to Tasmania, where he died. Wilde's memoir of Wainewright is contained in "Pen, Pencil, and Poison," printed in *Intentions*, London, 1891.
3. *"Beer, bible, and the seven deadly virtues have made England what she is":* In Wilde's *The Picture of Dorian Gray* (1891), chapter 17, Lord Henry Wotton says to Gladys, Duchess of Monmouth, "Beer, the Bible, and the seven deadly virtues have made our England what she is."
4. *"I labour under a perpetual fear of not being misunderstood":* Untraced.
5. John Bull is the name of a character who represents England in an eighteenth-century satire by John Arbuthnot; John Bull has been widely known as the personification of the English nation.
6. Walter Besant (1836–1901), voluminous romancer and writer of novels advocating social reform. Wilde's famous epigram on Besant is from part two of "The Critic as Artist," reprinted in *Intentions*.
   coldblooded Socialist: George Bernard Shaw (1856–1950). Yeats met Shaw at one of William Morris's gatherings. Their dislike was mutual.

"he had no enemies, but is intensely disliked by all his friends": Shaw in his *Sixteen Self Sketches* (1949) recounts this quip thus: "he hasn't an enemy in the world, and none of his friends like him."

7. *Cheapside*: a district and street in London.
8. *cheiromantist*: someone who can predict the future by looking at one's palm.
9. *the Dean of Chichester*: Chichester is a cathedral city in southern England.
10. *Lord Arthur Savile's Crime* reads " 'Have you dropped anything, sir?' said a voice behind him suddenly" (67).
11. *His account*: in "The Economic Basis of Socialism" from *Fabian Essays* (London, 1889).

Adam Smith (1723–90) revolutionized economic theories with his work *An Inquiry into the Nature and Causes of the Wealth of Nations*, published in 1776.
12. James Abbott McNeill Whistler (1834–1903), the American painter, was descended on his father's side from an old British family with an Irish branch. His mother was of Scots origin.

The Young Ireland League

1. Charles Stewart Parnell (1846–91) was the leader of the Irish members in the House of Commons from 1880 to 1890; he tried to establish Home Rule for Ireland.
2. In the general election of July 1892, Gladstone's Liberal Party won a majority. In 1893 a Home Rule bill was passed by the House of Commons, but it was rejected by the House of Lords.
3. *Leinster*, the eastern province of Ireland; *Rathmines*, a suburb of Dublin; *Arran-quay*, a quay on Dublin's River Liffey; *Passage West*, a town in Ireland just east of Cork; *Maryborough*, a town in Co. Leix, southwest of Dublin; *Thurles*, a city in Co. Tipperary.
4. Among these Irish towns, large and small, one notes the mention of Glasgow, in Scotland.
5. After the split in the Irish Home Rule faction, those men who rejected Parnell's leadership were led by Justin McCarthy (1830–1912).
6. Patrick Weston Joyce (1827–1914), compiler and translator of *Old Celtic Romances* (London: C. Kegan, Paul and Co., 1879). In this roll call of Irish literature are to be found the names of authors whom Yeats discusses in other articles in this collection: those not identified by their full names are William Carleton, John and/or Michael Banim, Gerald Griffin, Charles Lever, Maria Edgeworth, Douglas Hyde, Thomas Crofton Croker, Jane Francesca (Lady Wilde), and Thomas Moore, the compiler of *Irish Melodies* (1808–34).
7. Yeats is referring to *The Best Hundred Irish Books*, originally published in *The Freeman's Journal* and reprinted as a separate pamphlet in Dublin in 1886.
8. *The National Press* had been bought by Tim Healy, Parnell's opponent, as a rival newspaper to *The Freeman's Journal*. See CL1, 259–60, for Yeats's speculations about the authorship of a hostile review of Katharine Tynan's *A Nun: Her Friends and her Order* in *The National Press*. The "hand" in this article which Yeats recognized has not been traced.

A Poet We Have Neglected

1. Dante Gabriel Rossetti (1828–82), an English Pre-Raphaelite poet and painter; Sir John Everett Millais (1829–96), an English painter.
2. For information on Thomas Davis and James Clarence Mangan, see "The Poetry of Sir Samuel Ferguson—II," note 8. For Samuel Ferguson, see the first article in this collection.
3. Ballyshannon is a port town in Co. Donegal to the northeast of Sligo.
4. *United Ireland,* in which this article appeared, was then a Parnellite journal. The "now" Yeats refers to was only two months after Parnell's death and was a time of continued political wrangling between Parnell's followers and those Irishmen who had voted him out as leader of the Home Rule faction.
5. *small Western seaboard town:* Sligo town.
6. These lines are the opening section of "A Stormy Night. A Story of the Donegal Coast" from *Irish Songs and Poems* (London: Turner and Reeves, 1887). Yeats reversed the fourth and fifth lines as well as making one verbal change—on line five, Yeats wrote "Human wile" for "Human Will." The first five lines of Allingham (1890 ed.), p. 136, read:

> A Wild west Coast, a little Town,
> Where little Folk go up and down,
> Tides flow and winds blow:
> Night and Tempest and the Sea,
> Human Will and Human Fate: . . .

On line 7, Allingham reads "be,".
7. In 1864.
8. Kamchatka is a peninsula on the far eastern edge of Russia bordering the Bering Sea.
9. *Erne:* Lough Erne in Northern Ireland.
10. In this stanza, Allingham, p. 37, reads "One summer day"; "my Joy"; "swam close,"; and "girl of any, O,—". "Ochone" is a cry of lamentation.
11. In this stanza, Allingham, p. 37, reads "and salmon, now"; "my life,—"; and "my wife,".
12. H. Halliday Sparling's collection of Irish ballads, *Irish Minstrelsy,* 1887.
13. George Herbert (1593–1633), Richard Crashaw (1612–49), and Robert Herrick (1591–1674) are all seventeenth-century English poets.
14. Yeats contributed a letter on "The Young Ireland League" to *United Ireland,* 3 October 1891. In the letter Yeats had referred generally to "poems of William Allingham."
15. *Flower Fancies:* Reeves & Turner's third volume of Allingham is entitled *Flower Pieces and Other Poems* (London, 1888).
16. "Twilight Voices" was included in Yeats's *A Book of Irish Verse* (London, 1895). Allingham reads "Out of the dimness vague and vast?—" (93).
17. *Laurence Bloomfield:* volume 2 (1890) of Reeves & Turner's *Collected Works.*
18. *sound of a clarionet:* this and the succeeding phrase about salmon are almost identical with Yeats's 1888 *Providence Sunday Journal* article (2 September 1888). See *LNI,* 71ff.

Poems by Miss Tynan

1. The Young Ireland movement.
2. Michael Doheny (1805–63) was chiefly famous for his song "Bright Vein of My Heart."
3. For Thomas Davis, see "The Poetry of Sir Samuel Ferguson—II," note 8. William Allingham (1824–89) was a prolific poet, of whose works Yeats liked best the Irish songs and ballads of Allingham's native Ballyshannon. *The Spirit of the Nation* (1843) was a collection of patriotic songs by contributors to *The Nation* magazine. See Yeats's review of Allingham's work in "A Poet We Have Neglected," pp. 149–52. For de Vere, see "The Poetry of Sir Samuel Ferguson—I," note 18. For Sir Samuel Ferguson, see the introduction to "The Poetry of Sir Samuel Ferguson—I," p. 3.
4. The title of the book was *Ballads and Lyrics,* by which name Yeats refers to it below.
5. See pp. 51–64 and 65–67 for Yeats's reviews of *Shamrocks.*
6. For Rossetti, see "A Poet We Have Neglected," note 1.
7. Clondalkin is a town outside Dublin where Katharine Tynan grew up.
8. This stanza from "Apologia" in *Ballads and Lyrics* reads "low hills with" with no comma and "bough and", also with no comma (vii). Yeats omitted the two following stanzas.
9. This stanza in Tynan reads "white,"; "southern-wood"; "bee,"; "fur" with no comma; and "roses, old and sweet," (viii). Yeats omitted the following stanza.
10. This stanza in Tynan reads "ground." (ix).
11. Yeats omitted the first stanza of this poem, "Sheep and Lambs."
12. This line in "Sheep and Lambs" reads "me by" (6).
13. This line in Tynan ends with a period (6).
14. This stanza in Tynan reads "sweet" with no semicolon and "feet" with no period (6).
15. Tynan's poem reads "Cross" (7).
16. This line in Tynan reads "abroad," (7).
17. Tynan's title is "To Rose in Heaven." Rose Kavanagh (1859–91), a native of Co. Tyrone, was a poet and journalist. According to D. J. O'Donoghue, her poems appeared widely in Irish newspapers and magazines, often attributed to the pen-name "Ruby." As a journalist, she wrote for the *Dublin Weekly Freeman,* and there her work appeared under the name "Uncle Remus" (*The Poets of Ireland* [Dublin: Hodges, Figgis, and Co., 1912], p. 222).
18. Tynan reads "singing-bird" (34).
19. Tynan's poem reads "cloister" and "child to him" (35).
20. This stanza in Tynan's poem reads "and were wise" and "dusts" (35).

The New 'Speranza'

1. An interview with Gonne appeared in *Le Figaro,* Tuesday, 29 December 1981, entitled "Au Jour le Jour."
2. *"Pathetic and persuasive . . . elite of Paris so moved."*: printed in the 3 January 1892 edition of *L'Etendard national.* The members of Maud Gonne's audience mentioned in the text are untraced.
3. *L'Etendard national* is the newspaper that printed Gonne's speech on Sunday, 3 January 1892. That speech is reprinted below:

'Vous me faites le grand honneur de m'inviter à prendre la parole.

'Je suis étrangère, je n'ai pas l'habitude de parler votre belle langue, et je vous prie d'avance d'être indulgents.

'J'ai donné à l'Irlande tout mon coeur et je lui donnerais avec joie ma vie, si les événements le permettaient.

'Aujourd'hui, je veux raconter à la France, la grande patrie des idées nobles et généreuses, ce que j'ai vu en Irlande, d'héroïsme, de patriotisme, de misère fièrement supportées, de foi nationale invincible et, si je réussis à faire passer dans les consciences et dans les coeurs l'indignation qui m'anime contre les oppresseurs de mon pays, je pourrai dire que j'ai rempli ma modeste mission de femme et de patriote. Voilà mon devoir et voilà mon but!

'Ah! que je voudrais avoir la force de vous faire connaître l'art, la littérature, l'histoire de mon pays, tout ce merveilleux passé que vit éternellement dans le coeur et dans la mémoire de ma race!

'Nos morts illustres, nos héros, nos martyrs, tout ce monde de souvenirs, d'exemples, de gloires, d'actions immortelles que l'Angleterre n'a pas pu ensevelir et qui se dressera un jour contre elle!

'Messieurs, la tyrannie anglaise en Irlande, depuis deux siècles, est à la fois un défi à Dieu et un attentat contre l'humanité tout entière. L'Irlande que l'Angleterre appelait hypocritement l'Ile soeur, a été traitée par elle en vassale, puis en esclave. Nous ne pouvons faire un pas sur le sol de notre patrie sans y fouler la trace d'un crime. 'La faim, a érit votre grand poète Victor Hugo, la faim c'est le crime public'. Ce crime, l'Angleterre l'a accompli contre l'Irlande avec les circonstances aggravantes de préméditation froide et calculée. Pendant deux siècles, elle a raidi ses bras de fer pour serrer l'Irlande à la gorge et pour l'étouffer. Elle oubliait que le sang des martyrs est la semence éternelle de la liberté.

'A ceux qui nous demandent: Qui êtes-vous et que voulez-vous être? nous repondons: Nous sommes trois choses: premier une race; deuxième une patrie; troisième une démocratie; et nous voulons faire de ces trois choses *une nation*!

'Notre civilisation est l'une des plus vieilles de l'Europe. Lorsque le monde subissait la domination romaine, l'Irlande celtique restée libre, developpait les tendances de son génie; Montalembert lui a rendu cet homage, L'Irlande s'était donné une langue, une poesie, un culte, en un mot, une civilisation égale ou même superieure à celle de la plupart des peuples païens.

'Patrick y apporta le christianisme, mais la religion nouvelle, loin d'affaiblir l'énergie ou d'atrophier le caractère des Celtes s'y appropria, devint l'âme et la foi de notre race.

'L'esperance de la race irlandaise est indestructible. Des deux rivages de l'Atlantique elle pousse le cri gaëlique: liberté! En Amerique, sept millions d'Irlandais attendent et veillent.

'Ceux qui, depuis la conquête, se croient nos maîtres, n'ont enchaînent que le corps de l'Irlande, son âme n'a jamais été en leur pouvoir, et des profondeurs mêmes des prisons, elle s'est élancée jusqu'au Ciel.

'Et c'est parce que nous sommes une race fidèle aux grandeurs de son histoire que nous sommes demeurés une patrie invincible. Les

Anglais ne sont en Irlande qu'une *colonie*! Ils y sont campés, ils y vivent les *armes à la main*. L'Irlande, ses traditions, son culte, sa poesie, ses oeuvres, son génie, ses vivants et ses morts, tout ce noble patrimoine d'honneur et de gloire n'appartient qu'aux Irlandais.

'Ah, il y a longtemps que l'aristocratie anglaise essaie de briser notre nationalité. Mais ni les confiscations violentes ordonnées par Jacques, ni le hache des bourreaux à la solde de Cromwell, ni les lois pénales édictées par la maison d'Orange n'ont eu raison de la ténacité des Celtes. Nous sommes aujourd'hui ce que nous étions il y a 7 siècles; rien n'a fléchi; rien n'a tremblé, rien n'a capitulé! Et un mot magique, pieusement transmis de génération en génération, a accompli ce miracle:—Patrie! Combien cette lutte a été féroce, impitoyable, acharnée, ces chiffres seuls le prouvent. Au siècle dernier, l'Irlande comptait 12 millions d'habitants; au commencement de ce siècle, nous étions encore 9 millions; aujourd'hui nous ne sommes plus que 4 millions et demi!!!

'L'Angleterre ne pouvant vaincre, essaie d'exterminer!

'L'Irlande ne peut être qu'une démocratie puisque c'est contre la feodalité que nous luttons.

'La conquête a fait de l'Irlande la terre des privilèges; l'émanicipation en fera la terre de l'égalité et de la justice.

'Jadis, de puissants réformateurs ébranlèrent toute l'Allemagne avec le cri 'guerre aux châteaux, paix aux chaumières'. En Irlande, le château s'est déclaré lui-même l'ennemi de la chaumière; il en a fait le réduit de la misère et du désespoir, il l'a dépeuplés et souvent il l'a détruite!

'Nous rendrons la vie aux chaumières, nous y ferons rentrer les véritables principes de l'Evangile, et la fraternité cessera d'être une ironie des hommes.

'Opprimés, nous tournons nos regards vers cette terre française où toute souffrance trouve un asile ou une espérance; vers votre patrie; patrie de tous les peuples.

'Nous vous demandons trois choses; Votre souvenir; votre enseignement et votre appui.

'Nous somme frères par le sang et par les larmes; frères des deuils et des gloires héroïques. Nous pouvons inscrire sur notre étendard les noms les plus beaux de vos annales: Fleurus, Denain, Fontenoy, l'Irlande y était; le brigade irlandais toujours décimé et toujours vivant, a pris sa part de vos victoires comme de vos malheurs. Votre incomparable grandeur, nous en portons le reflet. Pour séparer l'Irlande et la France, il faudrait arracher vingt pages de notre commune histoire, il faudrait renier nos morts immortels.

'Vous venez d'entendre et d'applaudir le langage autorisé de nos plus fermes, de nos plus vaillants patriotes, Gill, Kenny, Harrington, James O'Kelly. Ils exprimaient les sentiments de 10 millions d'Irlandais d'Irlande et d'Amérique, et quand ils parlaient ainsi dans leurs lettres, c'est le coeur de l'Irlande tout entière que vibrait en eux.

'L'Egypte, le Méditerranée, le Droit public européen, toutes ces causes sacrées qui ont trouvé ici même, dans ce banquet, de si éloquents interprètes, ne sont pas seulement les notres.

'Permettez à l'Irlande de garder l'espoir qu'elle pourra un jour, à côte de vous, les defendre. Et surtout, oh! surtout, si nous pouvions

d'un seul coup payer à la France toute notre dette de reconnais-
sance, que ce soit pour vous aider à rentrer dans votre patrimoine à
ramener dans la maison de la mère désolée les deux filles volées: la
Lorraine et l'Alsace!

'Et si nous ne pouvons pas mourir pour vous, Français, dont les
pères sont morts pour l'indépendance des peuples, nous vous
apprendons du moins comme L'Irlande sait mourir!

'Je bois au jour où la lutte éclatera entre le Droit et L'Oppression . . .

'A la revanche des nobles vaincus!

'A la délivrance de l'Irlande et de l'Alsace-Lorraine!

'A la victoire ou à la mort!'

4. For more information on this man, see the article "Clovis Hugues on Ireland," pp. 163–66.
5. An aeolian harp is a stringed box that makes music when currents of air
pass through it.
6. Maud Gonne, in her speech, mentions "the brigade," meaning the Irish
Brigade. Its members were also known as "The Wild Geese." After King
James lost to King William at the Battle of the Boyne in 1690 and the
treaty of Limerick was signed in 1691, many Irish soldiers accompanied
General Patrick Sarsfield to France instead of offering their allegiance to
the British crown. Eventually retained by the French crown, the Irish
Brigade's most significant contribution to France was at the battle of
Fontenoy in 1745.

Dr. Todhunter's Irish Poems

1. This movement, better known as the "Young Ireland movement," was
organized by Thomas Davis; its members included Sir Charles Gavan
Duffy, John Mitchel, John Blake Dillon, and Thomas Francis Meagher. It
disseminated its ideas through *The Nation* magazine.
2. For Allingham, see "The New 'Speranza'," note 3. For de Vere, see "The
Poetry of Sir Samuel Ferguson—I," note 18.
3. *Conary* was published in Ferguson's *Poems* (Dublin: William McGee,
1880). *Deirdre: A One-Act Drama of Old Irish Story* (Dublin: Roe, 1880).
4. The Library of Ireland was published by James Duffy around 1845–46.
Works by nationalists and Young Irelanders such as Charles Gavan Duffy
and Thomas Davis appeared in this series.
5. The "Scotch Ossian" Yeats refers to is James MacPherson (1736–96), who
supposedly discovered and translated poems written by Ossian in the third
century A.D. Walt Whitman (1819–92) was the author of *Leaves of Grass*.
6. The River Shannon, Ireland's principal river, flows southwest from Northern Ireland to the Atlantic.
7. In Todhunter, each stanza is numbered with Arabic numerals. This stanza
is "1." and the next is "2."; the next two are "8." and "9." Todhunter
reads "Green,"; "there" (for "thou"); and "spectre-thin," (3).
8. *How the nation:* Todhunter reads "And the nation . . ." (3).
9. In this last stanza, Todhunter reads "exiles" and "wrongs," (7).
10. *The Sons of Turann:* Todhunter's title is "The Lamentation for the Three
Sons of Turann." Yeats and his friends Katharine Tynan, T. W. Rolleston,
and John O'Leary arranged for the publication of this volume in 1888.

11. *Methinks . . . storm:* "Three Witches" opens with this line: "Methought I saw three sexless things of storm" (138).
12. *racy of the soil:* This was the heading of *The Nation,* the Young Ireland newspaper. In *A Final Edition of Young Ireland* (vol. 1, 40), Duffy attributes this phrase to Stephen Woulfe:
    "When Municipal Reform was before Parliament, Peel asked contemptuously what good corporations would do a country so poor as Ireland. 'I will tell the right honourable gentleman,' said Stephen Woulfe, afterwards Chief Baron, 'they will go far to create and foster public opinion, and make it racy of the soil.' This was the aim of the *Nation,* and we took for motto 'To create and foster public opinion in Ireland, and make it racy of the soil'".
    It is interesting that in the original the phrase was applied to public opinion, but Yeats here applies it to literature.
13. *Poems and Lyrics: Ballads and Lyrics* (London: Kegan Paul, 1891) is the correct title. F. J. Allan wrote *Aids to Sanitary Science* (1891). It is more likely that Yeats meant F. M. Allen, the pen-name of Edmund Downey (1856–1937), an author of many humorous works.
14. This series was called the "New Irish Library." Yeats later thought that his fears here expressed were realized. See "New Irish Library Controversy" in *UP*1, 239–45.

Clovis Hugues on Ireland

1. *The Review of Reviews* (New York edition) had a paragraph on Maud Gonne on page 6 of its February 1892 issue. The magazine was edited by W. T. Stead.
2. Separatists were those who wished to sever both Ireland's political and cultural ties with England.
3. Hubert Clovis Hugues (1851–1907) was a French poet and radical politician. He was imprisoned for his support of the Paris Commune of 1871, and he killed a rival journalist in a duel in 1877. His wife shot and killed a court official in the Palais de Justice in 1884 and was acquitted after a sensational trial. Hugues, like Lucien Millevoye, was a follower of General Boulanger.
4. Edwin J. Ellis (1848–1916) was co-editor with Yeats of the works of William Blake, a project then nearing completion. Yeats reviewed Ellis's *Fate in Arcadia* in the September 1892 *Bookman* (see pp. 176–79).
5. The French original of this poem is on pp. 281–84 of Hugues's *Les Roses du laurier* (2nd ed., 1903). The poem is in book 3, "Pour l'idée."
6. Daniel O'Connell (1775–1847), an Irish nationalist leader and orator; he worked for the Repeal of the Act of Union of 1800 and helped to achieve Catholic Emancipation. He was known as "The Liberator."
7. *Union Méditerranéenne:* The Union Méditerranéenne is described by Yeats in an earlier article, "The New 'Speranza',", as a group of "French sympathizers with the cause of Ireland."
8. *the old brigade:* the Wild Geese. See "The New 'Speranza',", note 6.

Sight and Song

1. *The aim . . . incarnate:* page v of *Sight and Song.*
2. Bradley and Cooper also wrote under the names Arran and Isla Leigh.

3. Benozzo Gozzoli (1420–1497) was an early Italian Renaissance painter.
4. *Purple deep:* Field reads "Purple-deep" (20).
5. Yeats's dislike for George Eliot was persistent. An early letter of Yeats outlines his reasons for this dislike (*CL1*, 7–8).
6. *St. Jerome:* Michael Field's title is "Saint Jerome in the Desert."
7. The original of this line reads: "And grey his beard that, formal . . ." Yeats, or *The Bookman*'s compositors, ignored the elaborate indentation scheme of the original.
8. *Callirrhoë* (1884), *Brutus Ultor* (1886), and *The Tragic Mary* (1890) are early verse plays by Michael Field.

Some New Irish Books

1. Wicklow is the county just south of Dublin.
2. *Lugnaquilla:* mountain in the Wicklow Mountain range south of Dublin.
3. William Larminie (1849–1900), born in Castlebar, Co. Mayo, was better known as a folklorist than as a poet; Yeats gave high praise to Larminie's *West Irish Folk Tales* (London, 1894) in a review in *The Bookman* of June 1894.
4. Larminie's "Ghosts," p. 41, in *Fand and Other Poems* (Dublin, 1892) reads "hideous, and vile:", "our waking;—". For Yeats's reading of "most sweet—", Larminie ends the line without a dash. Larminie reads "Or evil-odorous, poison-laden" and "Therefore if" and "Let the".
5. *"Fand"* and *"Moytura"*: Fand is the wife of Manannán Mac Lir, the god of the sea; Yeats discusses her in his note to the poem "The Secret Rose." Her relationship with Cuchulain figures prominently in Yeats's play *The Only Jealousy of Emer*, based on the eighth-century legend "The Wasting Sickness of Cuchulain." There are two places named Moytura; the southern Moytura in Co. Mayo was the location of the first defeat of the Fir Bolg by the Tuatha dé Danaan. Legend has it that seven years later the second defeat of the Fir Bolg took place in northern Moytura in Co. Sligo.
6. The name of the author of *Songs of Arcady* given in *United Ireland*, W. O'Reilly, is inaccurate. This volume was the work of Robert James Reilly (1862–95), doctor and poetaster who occasionally contributed poems to *The Irish Monthly, Irish Fireside,* and *United Ireland*. For the identification of Reilly, see D. J. O'Donoghue's *The Poets of Ireland*, (Dublin, 1912).

Dublin Scholasticism and Trinity College

1. Ireland's National Library, located in central Dublin, was opened in 1890; almost every book ever published in Ireland is kept there.
2. As is obvious from the context, Yeats meant by "scholasticism" all formalized higher education, not the philosophy of Scotus or Aquinas.
3. Yeats attended the Godolphin School, Hammersmith, London, from 1877 to 1880. He attended the Erasmus Smith High School in Dublin from 1881 to 1883. After graduation he did not go to Trinity College, from which his father had graduated, and went instead to the Metropolitan School of Art in Dublin.
4. Dublin Castle was the administrative center for the British government in Ireland from the early thirteenth century to 1922. Trinity College in Dublin was founded in 1591 by Elizabeth I; a stronghold of Protestantism in Yeats's day, it would have opposed nationalism.

5. *Dagon of the Philistines:* Dagon is the Phoenician and Philistine god of agriculture and the earth and the national god of the Philistines.
   She . . . Oxford: In *Essays in Criticism,* 1st and 2nd series, p. 6, Matthew Arnold writes: "Adorable dreamer [Oxford], whose heart has been so romantic! who hast given thyself so prodigally, given thyself to sides and to heroes not mine, only never to the Philistines."
6. *Tercentenary uproar:* Trinity would have celebrated its three hundredth anniversary the year before this article appeared.
7. Tractarianism was the principles set forth in a series of pamphlets issued at Oxford (1833–41) by members of what came to be known as the Oxford Movement. It was generally a movement within the Church of England toward older and more traditional doctrines and liturgical forms. Its most famous member, John Henry Newman, eventually became a Catholic. Arthur Hugh Clough (1819–61), English poet.
8. Duffy had made a speech to the Irish Literary Society, London, in which he had suggested the publication of books on Irish subjects at popular prices. The speech was printed in the same issue of *United Ireland* as this article. Yeats quotes from *Jerusalem,* plate 9, p. 176, lines 29–31 (*The Complete Writings of William Blake,* ed. Geoffrey Keynes [London: Nonesuch Press, 1925]):

> That he who will not defend Truth may be compell'd to defend
> A Lie: that he may be snared and caught and snared and taken:
> That Enthusiasm and Life may not cease; arise Spectre, arise!

9. The Orangemen were members of a secret society formed in the north of Ireland in 1795; their object was to uphold the political power of Protestants; in Yeats's day, Orangemen were those Protestants who opposed Home Rule. West Briton was an epithet used to describe those Irish who adopted English or European attitudes and mores in lieu of those considered by nationalists to be Irish.

A New Poet

1. Arcadia, an area of ancient Greece, which became during the Renaissance the embodiment of a pastoral ideal, noted for the idyllic life of its shepherds.
2. The Whitman quotation is from "So Long!" in *Leaves of Grass:*

> Camerado, this is no book,
> Who touches this touches a man. . . .

3. Ellis's book contains no poem entitled "The Maid Well Loved." Ellis's title is "The Outcast."
4. *Eli, Eli, . . . me.:* Ellis reads "Eli, thou hast forsaken me!" (p. 161). Ellis and Yeats are both referring to Jesus' Crucifixion (see the Bible, Matt. 27:46).
5. The first seven stanzas of this poem in Ellis begin with quotation marks signaling them as the speech of the ghost of Jesus. On p. 162, Ellis reads "devils and"; "selves and clave to this:—"; "here where"; "Oh you"; "Eli! Eli! call my soul;" ; "but if he"; "That thou shouldst"; and "life, and be,". On p. 163, Ellis reads "flesh of thine,"; "Thou too shalt know what came

to me,"; "self-hood fine"; "his sake"; "him, my light,"; "shade to rave"; "he cannot save!" and "Joseph's son".

6. This poem, entitled "The Outcast" in Ellis, on p. 85, reads "God the Ever-living makes"; "deathly Winter frost,"; "God the Ever-loving wakes"; "moves a wraith;"; "fires that shrink,"; and "in wandering by:—".

7. Ellis reads "lost him"; "accost him"; "no showing:"; "missed him:"; "kissed him:"; and "serve them;" (69). On p. 70, Ellis reads "nor break;"; "For outgrowing"; and "like a child" with no comma.

8. Francis Bacon, in his essay "Of Beauty," writes: "There is no Excellent *Beauty* that hath not some Strangeness in the Proportion" (Sir Francis Bacon, *The Essayes of Counsels, Civill and Morall*, ed. Michael Kiernan [Oxford: Clarendon Press, 2000], p. 132).

'Noetry' and Poetry

1. Yeats's friend is untraced. *nous:* a word from Greek philosophy meaning "mind" or "intellect."

2. Yeats had reviewed Savage-Armstrong's collection for *United Ireland*, 23 July 1892. See "Some New Irish Books," pp. 170–72.

3. The phrase "neither gods nor men nor booksellers can tolerate" is a translation of lines 372–73 of the Roman poet Horace's *Ars Poetica* (the Art of Poetry).

4. Yeats is quoting from the poem "Lugnaquillia" in Savage-Armstrong's *Stories of Wicklow* (London, 1886). In this passage, Savage-Armstrong reads "heart,"; "'T is a dream" with a space after the "T"; "godlike"; "cause" with no comma; "innumerable" with no comma; "motion" with no comma; and "Law;" (174–75). "Lugnaquilla" is the standard spelling for this mountain.

Invoking the Irish Fairies

1. The zodiac is one way of representing the relationship between the sun, earth, planets, and stars. It is divided into twelve constellations; each has a sign to represent it: Capricorn, Aquarius, Pisces, Aries, Taurus, Gemini, Cancer, Leo, Virgo, Libra, Scorpio, and Sagittarius. Astrologers have used the zodiac since ancient times as a means of determining an individual's fate.

2. *Isis and Osiris:* Isis was an Egyptian goddess of fertility and the wife and sister of Osiris; Osiris was the Egyptian god who, when he died and was resurrected annually, symbolized the vitality and fertility of nature.

3. Yeats is surely referring to *Tabula Bembina sive Mensa Isiaca. The Isiac Tablet of Cardinal Bembo. Its History and Occult Significance* by William Wynn Wescott (Bath: Robt. H. Fryar, 1887). On p. 2, Wescott traces the history of the tablets, and there mentions how they came into the possession of Pietro, Cardinal Bembo (1460–1547), Italian Renaissance historian and man of letters.

4. *Klippoth* is the Hebrew word for demons. Literally, "the world of shells," in Kabalistic cosmology, it is formed from emanations of the Yetzirah or world of the gods.

5. While a pentagram is a five-pointed star with one point pointing straight up, an inverted pentagram is a five-pointed star with two points pointing straight up. An inverted pentagram is considered to be a sign of Satan.

6. By 1895 this doctrine of the moods as spiritual emanations of the world

soul was to become an essential part of Yeats's aesthetic. See "Irish National Literature. II," pp. 270–76.

Hopes and Fears for Irish Literature

1. French poet Paul Verlaine (1844–96) served a two-year prison sentence at Mons for having wounded the poet Arthur Rimbaud in a quarrel at Brussels in July 1873. Yeats met Verlaine in 1894; his sketch of Verlaine appeared in *The Savoy* (April 1896); see *UP1*, 397–99.
2. *Decadents:* a group of French and English writers of the late nineteenth century whose works are characterized by extreme aestheticism and a penchant for the abnormal or perverse. Noted Decadents are Charles Baudelaire and Oscar Wilde. Where Verlaine called it "a school of the sunset" is untraced. Also, the quotation "As a reproach, and caught up as a battle cry" is untraced.
3. The Rhymers' Club.
4. Yeats refers to "Ferdiah: an episode from the Táin Bó Chuailgne" by Denis Florence MacCarthy, the two epics *Blanid* and *Deirdre* by R. D. Joyce (see "The Poetry of R. D. Joyce," pp. 28–38), and Sir Samuel Ferguson's epic *Congal* (see "The Poetry of Sir Samuel Ferguson—II," pp. 10–27). Yeats comments on *Conary* in "The Poetry of Sir Samuel Ferguson—II." A poem by the title of "The Welshmen of Tirawley" can be found in *Lays of the Western Gael* (Dublin: Sealy, Bryers, and Walker, 1892). Yeats discusses it briefly in "Popular Ballad Poetry of Ireland," pp. 93–108.
5. John Francis O'Donnell (1837–74), Irish poet and journalist. Yeats gave a bad review to O'Donnell's collected poems in an article for *The Boston Pilot*, 18 April 1891 (collected in *LNI*, 45–49).
6. Oscar Wilde.
7. "Know thyself" was inscribed at the oracle at Delphi; Yeats would have known the phrase, also, from epistle 2 of Alexander Pope's *An Essay on Man*:

> Know then thyself, presume not God to scan;
> The proper study of mankind is Man. (ll. 1–2)

8. Yeats developed at great length the metaphor of the growing tree, which he compared to the growth of a national literature in his lecture "Nationality and Literature," reprinted in *United Ireland* on 27 May 1893 (*UP1*, 266–75).

The Death of Oenone

1. *The Divine Comedy*, written in the fourteenth century by Dante Alighieri, describes the journey of Dante through Hell, Purgatory, and Paradise; Homer's *Iliad* is a Greek epic which recounts the war of the Greeks against Troy to recover Helen, the wife of Menelaus.
2. The drama *Queen Mary* was published in 1875 and the drama *Harold* in 1877. The drama *Becket* was published in 1884, following a trial edition in 1879.
3. *Tiresias, and Other Poems* was published in 1885.
4. For William Morris, see "The Poetry of Sir Samuel Ferguson—I," note 13. *The Earthly Paradise* appeared between 1868 and 1870.

5. The correct titles of these poems are "The Church-Warden and the Curate," "St. Telemachus," and "The Silent Voices."
6. . . . *pilots of purple twilight:* "Locksley Hall," l. 122.
7. *suns,:* Tennyson reads "Suns," p. 108, in *The Death of Oenone, Akbar's Dreams, and Other Poems* (London, 1892).
8. The anecdote about Blake and the astronomer is from Alexander Gilchrist's *Life of William Blake,* 2nd ed., 2 vols. (London: Macmillan, 1880):

> Some persons of a scientific turn were once discoursing pompously and, to him, distastefully, about the incredible distance of the planets, the length of time light takes to travel to the earth, etc., when he burst out, 'Tis false! I was walking down a lane the other day, and at the end of it I touched the sky with my stick!" (vol. 2, 371).

9. *the stuff that dreams are made of:* a quotation from William Shakespeare's *The Tempest,* 4.1.148. Shakespeare reads "We are such stuff / As dreams are made on."
10. *the clearest of the clear, the surest of the sure:* in a letter to B. P. Blood, Tennyson describes a state of "waking trance" he experienced frequently where "individuality itself seemed to dissolve and fade away into boundless being, and this not a confused state but the clearest, the surest of the surest, utterly beyond words—where death was an almost laughable impossibility—the loss of personality (if so it were) seeming no extinction, but the only true life" (*Memoirs of Alfred Tennyson,* vol. 2, p. 473).
11. William T. Stead recounts this story in his article "Tennyson the Man: A Character Sketch," in *Review of Reviews,* December 1892 (American edition, pp. 568–69).
12. For Shelley, see "The Poetry of R. D. Joyce," note 1. Tennyson's title is "God and the Universe."
13. For Hugo, see "The Poetry of R. D. Joyce," note 2. Thomas Carlyle (1795–1881) was a Scottish writer and historian. The source of this anecdote is untraced.
14. Tennyson reads "Cry to the lotus . . ." and "Call to the cypress . . ." (28).

The Vision of MacConglinne

1. *treasure . . . in poetry:* Meyer reads "for my own treasure is only in Heaven, or on earth, in wisdom, or in poetry" (56).
2. *Ye curs, . . . Cork:* Meyer reads ". . . ye curs and robbers and dung-hounds and unlettered brutes, ye shifting, blundering, hang-head monks of Cork" (28). Cork, Ireland's second most populous city, is located on the southern coast.
3. *numerous . . . heaven:* Meyer reads ". . . numerous as the sand of the sea, or sparks of fire, or dew on a May morning, or the stars of heaven," (102).
   In Yeats's version, "The Crucifixion of the Outcast," this sentence becomes, in part, ". . . and are not the fleas in the blanket as many as the waves of the sea and as lively?"
4. *little . . . them:* p. 16, ll. 17–19.
5. The Lee is the river running through Cork city.
6. *Hell:* Meyer reads "hell" (106).
7. *a cow . . . Cork.:* Meyer reads "a cow out of every close, an ounce for every

householder, a cloak for every church, a ring of gold, a Welsh steed, a white sheep out of every house from Carn to Cork" (110).

The Wandering Jew

1. Friedrich Heinrich Karl, Baron de la Motte-Fouqué (1777–1843) was a German cavalry officer and a voluminous writer of prose, poetry, and drama. Yeats may have read the F. E. Burnett translation (Leipzig: Bernhard Tauchnitz, 1867) of Fouqué's *Sintram and His Companions,* which reads "At last he mentioned his own name; it sounded Greek and noble, but none of us could retain it" (272–73).
2. In *The Daily Chronicle* for 12 January 1893, Buchanan said of *The Wandering Jew,* "As to the literary quality of the poem: "I am indifferent. I have no respect whatever for mere art or mere literature. . . ."
3. *Wandering Jew:* a legendary man who was condemned to wander the earth without rest until Judgment Day because he had insulted Jesus Christ when Christ was on his way to the Cross.
4. Golgotha is a hill near Jerusalem where Jesus Christ was crucified. Buchanan's phrase for what Yeats calls here "the Spirit of Humanity" is "the Spirit of Man" (2nd ed., 1893, 46).
5. Gautama Buddha (?563–?483 B.C.), an Indian philosopher and founder of Buddhism; Nero (A.D. 37–68), a Roman emperor; Galileo Galilei (1564–1642), an Italian astronomer and physicist; Giordano Bruno (?1548–1600), an Italian philosopher, executed by the Inquisition; Montezuma (?1480–1520), the last Aztec emperor in Mexico; Francesco Petrarch (1304–74), an Italian poet, famous for the development of the sonnet; Vasco da Gama (?1469–1524), a Portuguese explorer who sailed around Africa to Calcutta in 1498; Christopher Columbus (?1451–1506), an Italian navigator in the service of Spain, whose voyage to the West Indies in 1492 opened the Americas to exploration and exploitation.
6. *National Reformer:* a serial published in London from 1860 to 1893. Yeats's reference to "the publication of a certain Fleet Street house" is untraced.
7. *"is played out":* Yeats misrepresents this as Buchanan's sentiments. In his "Notes to the Second Edition," p. 155, Buchanan writes: "For the past fortnight a wild warfare, awakened by the Poem, has been waged in the columns of a London daily newspaper, by antagonists who have spared neither me nor each other; this warfare has spread to the London Churches, which are wildly discussing the work and shrieking angry negatives to the editorial question 'Is Christianity played out?'"
   On p. 156, Buchanan further explains: "I wished to appeal to those with whom Religion, real Religion is an eternal verity. . . . It [his poem] is not a polemic against Jesus of Nazareth; it is an expression of love for his personality, and of sympathy with his unrealized Dream."
8. *"grand valley":* this phrase and geography do not appear to be Buchanan's, though sections 3–5 (pp. 22–43) develop a vision of judgment on a plain outside a city.
9. For Blake, see "Clarence Mangan's Love Affair," note 7. In Geoffrey Keynes's edition of *The Complete Writings of William Blake* (London: Nonesuch Press, 1925), vol. 3, Blake reads as follows:

I intreat, then, that the Spectator will attend to the Hands & Feet, to the Lineaments of the Countenances; they are all descriptive of

Character, & not a line is drawn without intention, & that most discriminate & particular. As Poetry admits not a Letter that is Insignificant, so Painting admits not a Grain of Sand or a Blade of Grass Insignificant—much less an Insignificant Blur or Mark (154).

10. Buchanan reads "in Judgment there" (40) and "sockets of a Skeleton," (45). At the end of this sentence in Buchanan, the line and sentence continue.

11. Buchanan reads "shadows of the Throne"; "shrouded Skeleton"; and "Human yet" (47).

12. Dante Alighieri (1265–1321), Italian poet; William Shakespeare (1564–1616), English playwright and poet.

13. *like him who fell into pride of old time:* Yeats is making an allusion here to Satan, who was expelled from heaven for the sin of pride he committed in setting himself up as an equal to God.

A Bundle of Poets

1. Arthur Hallam (1811–33) is perhaps best known for his friendship with and encouragement of Alfred, Lord Tennyson. The two met at Cambridge, where both were involved with the group known as "The Apostles." Later, Hallam became engaged to Tennyson's sister Emily. Tennyson was much affected by Hallam's early death; his poem *In Memoriam A. H. H.* (1850) is, in part, a reflection on this friendship. Richard Le Gallienne (1866–1947), English author.

2. *the most famous friendship of the century:* a reference to the friendship between Hallam and Tennyson.

3. Legend has it that King Arthur was king of the Britons around the sixth century A.D. Lancelot was the greatest and most romantic of King Arthur's Knights of the Round Table, as well as the lover of King Arthur's queen, Guinevere.

4. Shelley's "A Defence of Poetry." Browning's "Essay on Shelley" was prepared to be printed in 1852 with a collection of Shelley's letters. Since the letters proved to be forgeries, the essay did not appear at that time but was published by the Shelley Society, London, 1888.

5. *"On some . . . Tennyson":* Hallam equally capitalizes all words in the title, and his title reads ". . . Poetry, And. . . ."

6. Dante Gabriel Rossetti (1828–82) and Algernon Charles Swinburne (1837–1909) are both nineteenth-century English poets whom Yeats here associates with the aesthetic movement. For more on Swinburne, see "The Poetry of Sir Samuel Ferguson—I," note 8.

7. *the aesthetic movement:* a movement in the late 1880s which was influenced by the writings of John Ruskin and Walter Pater; one of its more notable adherents was Oscar Wilde.

8. Hallam reads "popular, whose"; "understand," and "pain," (97).

9. The phrase "And yet" is not Hallam's but Yeats's. Hallam reads "Every bosom"; "this demand" (99); "bile,"; and "popular," (100).

10. *other of those essays:* see p. xxxiii of Le Gallienne's introduction.

11. Henry VIII (1491–1547) was king of England from 1509 to 1547; Anne Boleyn (1507–36) was his second wife. Thomas Cranmer (1489–1556) was archbishop of Canterbury; he supported Henry VIII's claim to be the head of the Church of England after Henry severed his ties with the Roman Catholic Church.

12. Paul Verlaine (1844–96), French poet. See Yeats's 1896 article on Verlaine in *UP1*, 397–99.
13. "To Modern Rhymers" was dedicated to Arthur Symons, p. 11.
14. Yeats is alluding to Matthew 5:45: "He maketh his sun to rise on the evil and the good, and sendeth rain on the just and the unjust."
15. The subtitle of Sarah Piatt's book was *Pictures, Portraits, and People in Ireland.*
16. The "certain Boston gentleman" is untraced.
17. *"In . . . Cloyne": An Enchanted Castle, and Other Poems,* 1893, p. 72, prefaces the poem with this line, which suggests that the poem was written "in memoriam": "[C. L. P., OB. JULY 18, 1884.]". Cloyne is a city in Ireland, located southwest of Cork.
18. Piatt reads "way,"; "what is there!"; and "Lost, in the dark somewhere" (72).
19. The original poem reads "hands" instead of "heads" (72).
20. *ivy that:* Piatt reads "ivy, that" (72).

The Writings of William Blake

1. For Dante Gabriel Rossetti (1828–82), see "A Poet We Have Neglected," note 1 (p. 540). William Michael Rossetti (1829–1919) was a brother of Dante Gabriel and an art critic and editor.
2. Dante Gabriel Rossetti edited a selection of Blake's poems in the second volume of Gilchrist's *Life and Works of William Blake* (London: Macmillan, 1880). The remarks Yeats quotes are from the introductory note to *Ideas of Good and Evil,* vol. 2 of Gilchrist, 1880, p. 85.
3. This is the edition prepared by Yeats and Edwin J. Ellis in 1893.
4. This quotation and the one above, "The tigers of wrath . . .", are both "Proverbs of Hell" from Blake's *Marriage of Heaven and Hell,* pp. 35–37, in David V. Erdman, *The Poetry and Prose of William Blake* (New York: Doubleday, 1965).
5. *the Peckham Rye vision:* On p. x of his introduction, Housman recounts the following as the first of Blake's visions: "The first of these visions took place when, as a small boy, he was rambling through Peckham Rye. On his return he told how he had seen a tree full of angels, and gave his evidence so circumstantially that his father, taking the matter seriously, prepared to give him a thrashing, from which only his mother's entreaty saved him."
6. Housman's sentence began: "The prophetic books have seemed, therefore, too large" (xxvii).
7. *unlovely and:* Housman reads "unlovely, and" (xxvii).
8. *The Bookman* printing had originally read "clear Fury." In a clipping in MS 12148 (National Library of Ireland), Yeats changed it back to Housman's own phrase—"clean fury."
9. *thought, when:* Housman reads "though, where" (xxvii).
10. Emanuel Swedenborg (1688–1772), Swedish philosopher, scientist, and mystic. Swedenborg had a great influence on Blake, who was, for a time, a member of his New Church. Jacob Boehme (1575–1624), German theosophist and mystic.
11. Yeats refers to Jacob Boehme's *Mysterium Magnum, oder Erklärung über das Erste Buch Mosis* (1623) and his *Aurora, oder Morgenröthe im Aufgang* (1612).
12. In John Bunyan's allegory *The Pilgrim's Progress* (1678), the protagonist,

Christian, passes through numerous places on his journey, including House Beautiful, where he meets Prudence, Piety, and Charity. William Blake did watercolor illustrations for *The Pilgrim's Progress* that included a portrait of House Beautiful, though they were published for the first time only in a 1941 edition of Bunyan's work (New York: The Limited Editions Club).

The Message of the Folk-lorist

1. *Young's Night Thoughts:* Edward Young (1683–1765), an English clergyman, published *The Complaint; or Night Thoughts* in nine books between 1742 and 1745.
2. Yeats added "naught but" to a page proof of this article in MS 12148 (National Library of Ireland).
3. The Thirty-nine Articles contain the doctrines of the Church of England. *The Book of Common Prayer* is a collection of prayers and services used in the Church of England.
4. Yeats's parade of worthies includes the Greek epic poet Homer; the Greek tragedians Aeschylus and Sophocles; the medieval Italian poet Dante Alighieri; and Johann Wolfgang von Goethe, author of *Faust.*
5. Donegal is a county in the north of the Republic of Ireland.
6. Slavonia is a region in southeastern Europe. The adjective "Slavonian" could include any of those people of Bulgaria, the Czech Republic, Slovakia, Ukraine, the former Yugoslavia, and Belarus.
7. In canto 13 of Dante's *Divine Comedy,* Virgil tells Dante of a tree that will bleed if he breaks off a branch. The damned soul within the tree is Piero delle Vigne, adviser and chancellor of Holy Roman Emperor Frederick II. Edmund Spenser (1552–99) was an English poet; his *Faerie Queene* (book 1, canto 2, stanza 30) also includes an incident where a tree branch is broken off and bleeds. Here, the soul in the tree is Fradubio, made into a tree by the false Duessa.
8. In a German legend, Faust is a magician who sells his soul to the Devil in exchange for power and knowledge of the world. Martyred in A.D. 303, Saint Agnes is considered the patron saint of virgins; her feast day is 21 January. The phrase "upon the honeyed middle of the night" is from John Keats's *Eve of St. Agnes,* stanza 6, line 4: "Upon the honey'd middle of the night."
9. The phrase "up to a great" was added by Yeats in page proof.
10. *Olympus:* Mount Olympus is the dwelling place of the gods in Greek mythology.
11. Yeats added "And" in page proof.
12. *for lack of those great . . . serpents in their hair:* Here, Yeats refers respectively to the god Zeus and to one of the Gorgons, Medusa.
13. *The Speaker* printed "scolds", which Yeats changed in page proof to "scalds". In this sentence, *The Speaker* printing read "whole army", which Yeats changed to "multitude" in page proof.
14. Thomas Firminger Thiselton-Dyer (1848–1928) was an English clergyman and folklorist. He published widely on topics in folklore.
15. *these folktales . . . current:* Thiselton-Dyer reads "These folk-tales are interesting, as embodying the superstitions of the people among whom they are current" (357). This remark by Thiselton-Dyer follows the Swedish ballad about the shroud and the rose leaves quoted afterward by Yeats.
16. In Greek mythology, Dis is a god of the underworld and Hades is the underworld where Dis rules.

17. The editors have not located such an assertion in the works of Jacob Boehme. Here, as elsewhere, Yeats may have confused Boehme's words with William Law's interpretation of Boehme. In Law's explanations of his symbolic drawings, which illustrate Boehme's principles, he had this to say of a peacock representing man: "On the Right Side is a Peacock, as a Signature and Character of Man, in the State represented here, even in his most glittering Appearance. But if everyone should set down his own peculiar Signature and Character, there would appear as many Figures, as there are Beasts and other Animals in the World; nay truly many more. Because the manifold Combinations and Mixtures whereby three or four or more of those Beasts, which in outward Nature have all but one single Body, jointly concurring, and entering as it were into one compound Body, make up but one Bestial Nature or Property, in one Person after this, and in another after another Manner. For no one that ever came from Adam and Eve can here except himself" ("An Illustration of the Deep Principles of Jacob Behmen, the Teutonic Theosopher, in Figures, Left by the Reverend William Law, M. A." In *The Works of Jacob Behmen*, 4 vols., London, for G. Robinson, 1772, vol. 2, p. 28).

18. *moths: The Speaker* printing read "horses". Yeats changed it in page proof.

19. The Zulus are part of the Bantu nation in southeastern Africa. On p. 40, Dyer quotes lines from Sir Edward Tylor's *Primitive Culture* (New York, 1883) with neither of the commas Yeats inserts here.

20. The Algonquin Indians can be any of several North American Indian tribes who once lived near the Ottawa River and tributaries of the St. Lawrence River in Canada. The statement about the Algonquin Indians is not Thiselton-Dyer's but is quoted by him (p. 40) from Tylor's *Primitive Culture*, vol. 1, p. 452. The Zulu passage quoted above is a paraphrase of Tylor, vol. 1, pp. 452–53.

21. *In Denmark . . . rest:* Dyer writes "In Denmark the night-raven is considered an exorcised spirit. . . . This ominous bird is ever flying towards the east, in the hope of reaching the Holy Sepulchre, for when it arrives there it will find rest" (88–89). To the latter sentence Dyer gives this note: "Henderson's *Folk-lore of Northern Countries*, p. 126; Thorpe's *Northern Mythology*, ii, p. 211."

22. *Saemund Edda:* "'Saemund Edda'" in Dyer's sentence (96).

23. *Maeldune: The Speaker* printing read "Maclunds." Yeats changed this in page proof to "Maeldune," the hero of a romance translated by P. W. Joyce in his *Old Celtic Romances.* Tennyson's poem on this subject, "The Voyage of the Maeldune," served Yeats and other early Celtic revivalists as an example of what a great poet could do with Celtic materials. *The Speaker* printing read "this great saint"; Yeats changed it to "that great saint" in page proof.

24. *often:* Yeats added this word in page proof.

25. Thiselton-Dyer reads "from thine eyes my" and "rose-leaves" (357).

26. *the Indians . . . "Phantom Music":* On pages 414–15, Thiselton-Dyer tells this story in quotes as taken from "Gayarre, in his 'Louisiana.'" The Pascagoula River runs through southern Mississippi into the Gulf of Mexico at the town of Pascagoula.

27. *The Speaker* printing read "adequate knowledge of folk-lore".

28. From this point until the end of the article, Yeats revised his galley proofs extensively. Printed here is the result of Yeats's revisions. The printed version in *The Speaker* was as follows:

Could he have been as full of folk-lore as was Shakespeare, or even Keats, he might have delivered his message and yet kept as close to our hearthstone as did the one in *The Tempest* and *Midsummer Night's Dream,* or as did the others in "The Eve of St. Agnes;" but as it is, there is a world of difference between Puck and Peasblossom and the lady who waited for 'The honeyed middle of the night' upon the one hand and the spirits of the hour and the evil voices of Prometheus upon the other. Shakespeare and Keats had the folk-lore of their own day, while Shelley had but mythology; and a mythology which has been passing for long through literary minds without any new influx from living tradition loses all the incalculable instructive and convincing quality of the popular traditions. No conscious invention can take the place of tradition, for he who would write a folk tale, and thereby bring a new life into literature, must have the fatigue of the spade in his hands and the stupors of the fields in his heart. Let us listen humbly to the old people telling their stories, and perhaps God will send the primitive excellent imagination into the midst of us again. Why should we be either 'naturalists' or 'realists'? Are not those little right hands lifted everywhere in affirmation?

29. *The Speaker* printing read "Puck and Peasblossom"; Yeats crossed out the "and" but added nothing. We have added the comma that is clearly indicated. Puck and Peasblossom are fairies in Shakespeare's *A Midsummer Night's Dream.*
30. Yeats's remarks about Shelley's poem "Prometheus Unbound: A Lyrical Drama in Four Acts" (1820) are a summary of his essay "The Philosophy of Shelley's Poetry," part 1 of which ("His Ruling Ideas") was originally published in *The Dome* (July 1900) and an expanded version, parts 1 and 2 ("His Ruling Symbols"), appeared in *Ideas of Good and Evil* (1903).

Two Minor Lyrists

1. "Q" was Arthur Quiller-Couch (1863–1944), novelist, poet, and editor of the *Oxford Book of English Verse.* He was then the principal literary critic of *The Speaker.*
    "Q" reads "Extra Outdoor Officer" and "way, at one time or another," on pp. x–xi of his introduction to *Verses by the Way.*
    The Albert Docks are located on the south side of the Thames River in London, near the Albert Bridge. Cornwall is the southwesternmost county in England; the town Yeats refers to is Helston.
2. *"The indolent reviewer":* untraced.
3. Robert Burns (1759–96), Scottish poet. The lines

In vain my teardrops flow
For thee, dead Imogene

occur in "Song," p. 42, and not in *Via Amoris,* the sonnet sequence in the collection.
4. The phrases "wild adventures" and "floating wickedness" are from Quiller-Couch's introduction, p. xi.
5. William Allingham (1824–89), Irish poet. See "Poems by Miss Tynan," note 3.

6. Ralph Waldo Emerson (1803–82), American author associated with the Transcendental movement. These are ll. 147–48 of Emerson's poem "Saadi."
7. William Blake, *Milton,* book 1, section 27, vol. 2, p. 343 in *The Writings of William Blake,* ed. George Keynes (London, 1925).

> For in every Nation & every Family the Three
> Classes [the Elect, the Reprobate, and the
> Redeemed] are born,
> And in every Species of Earth, Metal, Tree, Fish,
> Bird, & Beast.
> We [Los and the Laborers of the Vintage] form the
> Mundane Egg, that Spectres coming by fury or
> amity,
> All is the same, & every one remains in his own
> energy. . . .

8. Edward Capern (1819–94) was known as "the rural postman of Bideford." His works include *Wayside Warbles* and *Sungleams and Shadows.* Joseph Skipsey (1832–1903) was a coal miner turned poet. For most of his later life he was caretaker of Shakespeare's house at Stratford-on-Avon.
9. *"A Lytell . . . Hode":* Hosken reads "A lytell gest of Robyn Hode" (p. 55). Quiller-Couch quotes almost the entire poem in his introduction to *Verses by the Way,* pp. xxiii–xxiv. "A Lytell Geste of Robyn Hode" is a well-known ballad poem, first printed by Wynkyn de Worde; it contained the first biography of Robin Hood. In the ballad, Robin Hood is a noble robber who steals from the rich to give to the poor; loved by Maid Marian, he lives in Sherwood Forest with his band of outlaws, who include Little John, Friar Tuck, Scarlet, and Much.
10. Hosken reads "withdrawn:—"; "day—"; "spray,"; and "world, that" (55).
11. Hosken reads "free," (55) and "song," (56).
12. Hosken reads "I:—Robin," and "sylvan scene." (56). Lincoln green is an olive color; it is named for a fabric that originated in Lincoln, England.
13. In MS 12148, National Library of Ireland, Yeats changed "few new books" to "few first books".
14. *The best of his longer poems:* This poem, on pp. 13–23, is entitled "The Story of Simon Pierreauford."
15. The Gare du Nord is a train station in Paris serving the channel ports. Haig reads "Pierreauford"; "wife Lisette"; and "Cafe, he and she." (23).
16. Haig reads "portly rest"; "door"; "four"; and "guest." (23).
17. The last poem in the book, p. 69.
18. Haig reads "Oh, where shall I find rest?—"; "vale o'er"; ". . . find—"; "Wind,"; "great, grey sea"; and "Eternity" (69).
19. The phrase Cloud-Cuckoo-Land is from fourth-century B.C. Athenian playwright Aristophanes' play *The Birds,* in which the birds build an imaginary city in the sky. In Greek, the word is *nephelococcygia.*

Old Gaelic Love Songs

1. *Eternal Adversary:* the Devil; and "Him" above refers to God.
2. The girl in the poem "The Tailoreen of the Cloth" (p. 37) praises her lover thus:

> I do not think it prettier how you cut (your cloth)
> Than how you shape the lies; . . .

The passage paraphrased is from "Ringleted Youth of My Love" (p. 43):

> You promised me high-heeled shoes,
> And satin and silk, my storeen,
> And to follow me, never to lose,
> Though the ocean were round us, roaring;

3. This poem is "My Grief on the Sea" (p. 29). The passage paraphrased by Yeats is as follows:

> On a green bed of rushes
> All last night I lay,
> And I flung it abroad
> With the heat of the day.

4. The three preceding chapters of "The Songs of Connacht" began to appear in *The Nation* in 1890. What became *The Love Songs of Connacht* was published in *The Weekly Freeman* in 1892 and early 1893. Hyde later published three more chapters of "Songs of Connacht" consisting of "Songs Ascribed to Anthony Raftery" in 1903. In 1906 Hyde published two volumes of *Religious Songs of Connacht*.

5. In this passage, Hyde reads "drinking-songs,"; "chapter entirely contrary to them should follow . . ."; "to-day"; "life of the Gaels"; "foolish mirth, or"; "more grief, and"; "same class of men who"; "We cannot prove"; "say against (*i.e.* contradict)" (Hyde ended the sentence with a period rather than a question mark); "composed all" (this last sentence also begins a new paragraph); and "love songs" with no hyphen (3).

6. This poem, "If I Were to Go West," was printed by Hyde in stanzaic form (pp. 5–7), even though Hyde's translation was not what Yeats considered a translation into English verse. In this review, Yeats omits the opening stanza. Here is the poem as it appeared in Hyde's text:

> If I were to go west, it is from the west I would not come,
> On the hill that was highest, 'tis on it I would stand,
> It is the fragrant branch I would soonest pluck,
> And it is my own love I would quickest follow.
>
> My heart is as black as a sloe,
> Or as a black coal that would be burnt in a forge,
> As the sole of a shoe upon white halls,
> And there is great melancholy over my laugh.
>
> My heart is bruised, broken,
> Like ice upon the top of water,
> As it were a cluster of nuts after their breaking,
> Or a young maiden after her marrying.
>
> My love is of the colour of the blackberries,
> And the colour of the raspberry on a fine sunny day.

Of the colour of the darkest heath-berries of the mountain,
And often has there been a black head upon a bright body.

Time it is for me to leave this town,
The stone is sharp in it, and the mould is cold;
It was in it I got a voice (blame), without riches
And a heavy word from the band who back-bite.

I denounce love; woe is she who gave it
To the son of yon woman, who never understood it.
My heart in my middle, sure he has left it black,
And I do not see him on the street or in any place.

7. Gustave Flaubert (1821–80), French writer. Yeats most likely found the expression "thrusts of power" in Walter Pater's review of the second volume of Flaubert's correspondence, "Correspondance de Gustave Flaubert," which appeared in the 3 August 1889 issue of *The Athenaeum.* Pater quotes Flaubert as saying, "Yet still it is saddening to think how many great men arrive easily at the desired effect, by means beyond the limits of conscious art. What could be worse built than many things in Rabelais, Cervantes, Molière, Hugo? But, then, what sudden thrusts of power! What power in a single word!" (ed. B. F. Bart, *Madame Bovary and the Critics: A Collection of Essays,* p. 36). The excerpt is from a letter to Louise Colet, dated 27 March 1853: "Néamoins il y a une chose triste, c'est de voir combien des grands hommes arrivent aisément à l'effet en dehors de l'Art même. Quoi de plus mal bâti que bien des choses de Rabelais, Cervantès, Molière et d'Hugo? Mais quels coups de poing subits! Quelle puissance dans un seul mot!" (*Oeuvres complètes de Gustave Flaubert: Correspondance,* troisième série [1852–54] [Paris: Louis Conard, 1927], p. 143).
8. Yeats is mistaken in saying that Hyde gives prose versions of all the poems. While Hyde gives prose versions of many poems, most appear in verse form.
9. Yeats changed each appearance of Hyde's "oh, . . ." to "O, . . ." (135). Hyde reads "tell." (135).
10. *here,:* Hyde reads "here." (135).
11. Edward Walsh, translator of *Reliques of Irish Jacobite Poetry* (1844) and *Irish Popular Songs* (1847). See "Popular Ballad Poetry of Ireland," note 19. James Clarence Mangan's collection was *Poets and Poetry of Munster* (1850).
12. Yeats is using a famous proverb: "When Adam delved and Eve span, / Where was then the gentleman?" This version appears in John Ray's *English Proverbs* (1678), and its use is famously associated with Wat Tyler's insurrection in 1381.
13. *types and symbols:* Yeats is referring to Wordsworth's *Prelude,* where in book 6 Wordsworth describes his feelings upon crossing the Simplon Pass: "The unfettered clouds and region of the Heavens, / Tumult and peace, the darkness and the light— / Were all like workings of one mind, the features / Of the same face, blossoms upon one tree, / Characters of the great Apocalypse, / The types and symbols of Eternity, / Of first and last, and midst, and without end" (ll. 634–40).
14. *song of the birds,:* The proverb appears in Hyde's book, but there the first line reads "A tune is more lasting than the voice of the birds" (5).

The Ainu

1. *Sakhalin:* This island is off the Pacific coast of Russia, north of Japan.
2. *"leisurely meanderings":* Howard includes China in his list of where he meandered (1).
3. The Ainu are an aboriginal people of the islands of northern Japan with features described as Caucasoid or Australoid and with light skin, not black, as Yeats paraphrases Howard, and more body hair than the average Japanese.
4. Isabella L. Bird (Mrs. J. F. Bishop), author of *Unbeaten Tracks in Japan* (New York: G. P. Putnam, 1880).
5. *affirm . . . flame.:* See pp. 172, 176–77, in Howard for Yeats's source for this paraphrase.
6. In Yeats's second article on "Irish National Literature" (*The Bookman,* August 1895), he identifies this statement as "words put into the mouth of St. Dionysius." Yeats here means the mystical theologian Dionysius, the Pseudo-Areopagite (c. 500). The sentence Yeats quotes can be found in *The Mystical Theology and the Celestial Hierarchies of Dionysius the Areopagite* (trans. and ed. by the Shrine of Wisdom [Surrey, England: Shrine of Wisdom, 1965]) in chapter 9 of "The Celestial Hierarchies": "For the Most High established the boundaries of the nations according to the number of the Angels of God" (47). This statement occurs in the context of the following two paragraphs: "Accordingly the Word of God has given our hierarchy into the care of Angels, for Michael is called Lord of the people of Judah, and other Angels are assigned to other peoples. For the Most High established the boundaries of the nations according to the number of the Angels of God.
   "If someone should ask why the Hebrews alone were guided to the divine Illuminations, we should answer that the turning away of the nations to false gods ought not to be attributed to the direct guidance of Angels, but to their own refusal of the true path which leads to God, and the falling away through self-love and perversity, and similarly, the worship of things which they regarded as divine."
7. *there are . . . us.:* As occurs quite often in this review, Yeats here liberally embellishes Howard. On p. 177, for example, Howard reads "there are three heavens—'the high vaulty skies,' 'the star-bearing skies,' and 'the foggy heavens.'"
8. In the National Library of Ireland, MS 12148, Yeats changed this sentence. *The Speaker* printing begins "The good, whether they be men or animals."
9. *The Ainu . . . stick.:* On pp. 170–71, Howard describes the appearance and function of these "Inao." See also p. 179 on the lack of priests.
10. *The women . . . men.:* Howard, p. 195, uses much the same phrase, but Yeats minimizes the misogyny Howard describes on p. 194: "They seem to think that in the view of the 'Highest,' all good Ainus are equal, except in the case of women—that a woman is not an Ainu, and therefore she does not count."
11. *concluding appeal:* Nowhere does Howard make such a "concluding appeal." For example, on pp. 200–201, 203, and 209, Howard admires the "natural religion" of the Ainu fully as much as Yeats does. On p. 189, Howard observes that the Russian administration had done nothing to try to Christianize the Ainus; and on p. 190, in response to his question

"Would the Ainu probably be susceptible to Christian teaching?" he quotes the experience of a Reverend Mr. Batchelor with the Yezo Ainus which suggests that the Sakhalin Ainus might be more susceptible to Christian missionary work. This speculation on Howard's part hardly matches Yeats's characterization of it.

12. The Women's Liberal Federation was formed in 1887 as an umbrella organization for various Women's Liberal Associations in England. While this group worked to support the Liberal Party in England, most of the women in the Federation did so because the Liberal Party was more sympathetic to women's suffrage, their ultimate goal. The Salvation Army was founded by William Booth in 1865. Organized along semi-military lines, the Salvation Army is an international charity designed to promote evangelical Christianity.

Reflections and Refractions

1. Alfred Tennyson (1809–92), English poet; see Yeats's review of Tennyson, "The Death of Oenone," pp. 189–92. Algernon Charles Swinburne (1837–1909), English poet and critic; Robert Browning (1812–89), English poet; often known as "Mr. Barrett Browning" because of his wife Elizabeth Barrett Browning's success, Browning himself had to wait for twenty or more years before his own work began to claim attention in the 1860s. Walt Whitman (1819–92), American poet; it was not until 1860, five years after the first edition of *Leaves of Grass* was printed, that Whitman had a regular publisher. Because his early work was ignored, Whitman anonymously published favorable reviews of his own work.

2. *Refractions and Reflections:* Yeats reverses Weekes's title.

3. Weekes reads "First, the" in stanza 2; and "—Gave me woundrous ease." in stanza 3 (20); "haste," in stanza 5; "crowed:"; and "Eternal heart" without a period in stanza 6 (21).

4. Weekes reads "time"; "stars:"; "chime"; and "smiled" (4).

5. *"Art"*: This epigram precedes the poem: "By pardon of the Master" (107).

6. *hence,:* Weekes reads "hence" (107).

7. *"That"*: This poem begins with this epigraph:

. . . alone
From all eternity (98).

8. *this:* Weekes's poem reads "thy" (98).

9. The *Rubáiyát of Omar Khayyám* was translated by Edward Fitzgerald (1809–83) and published in 1859. Omar Khayyám (d. 1122) was a Persian poet, mathematician, and scholar.

Seen in Three Days

1. *the great Persian poet: Selections from the Rubaiyat and Odes of Hafiz* (London: J. M. Watkins, 1920), p. 5, reads as follows: "Hafiz has been nicknamed by the Persian poet Jami, Lisanul-Ghaib, i.e. the tongue of the hidden or invisible; and also Tarjumanul-Israr, i.e. the interpreter of mysteries." This book was in Yeats's library (*YL*, 115).

2. Ellis reads "Sun"; "Earth still"; "rain,—"; "bubblet of the soft sea-foam" (1); "Angel"; and "Earth" (2).

3. Ellis reads "darkness to her eyes." with a period at the end of the line (4).
4. *A chain . . . learning,:* This phrase is untraced, though on page 4, the angel says to the seer, "You do not see the winding chain of unforgotten learning in strange lands that coils me round and wants to wind on you."
5. *Death:* Ellis reads "death" (12).
6. *Who . . . maid?:* This quotation is from Ellis (12).
7. William Blake illustrated an 1808 edition of "The Grave," a widely circulated eighteenth-century poem by Robert Blair (1699–1746). Ellis reads "Love's . . . error," (16). The upas tree is a poisonous tree in Java.
8. *"chills the blood," but "warms the wondering, exultant soul.":* Ellis reads:

> . . . the sweet unheard 'Farewell'
> That chills the warm red blood, yet under blood,
> Makes glad the wondering exultant soul (22).

9. *"the first . . . loose,":* This phrase is from Ellis (31); *"silently . . . lovers,":* Ellis reads:

> Fate dreams she sits upon a throne alone
> Silently parting lovers . . . (10).

Beauty broods . . . give the stone.: Yeats here paraphrases Ellis (50).
10. *"Mother Night . . . high":* Ellis reads:

> . . . Mother Night
> Put off old age and raised her
> love-lamp high, (45).

11. For the Wandering Jew, see *"The Wandering Jew,"* note 3. Pythagoras (ca. 582–500 B.C.), a Greek philosopher and mathematician.
12. Yeats's review in *The Bookman* was accompanied by the reproduction of one of Ellis's engraved pages (to be seen on the facing page).
13. Ellis reads "Laughing Stars" (44); "age and"; and "& slept" (45).

A Symbolical Drama in Paris

1. *Ibsenism:* a reference to the vogue of imitating the Norwegian dramatist Henrik Ibsen (1828–1906).
2. Kalidasa (ca. 400) was an Indian dramatist; he is best known for his play *Sakuntala.* Sophocles (?496–406 B.C.), Greek dramatist; William Shakespeare (1564–1616), English playwright and poet. For Goethe, see "Clarence Mangan," note 10.
3. Emile Zola (1840–1902), French novelist.
4. Sir Arthur Wing Pinero (1855–1934) and Henry Arthur Jones (1851–1929), English playwrights.
5. The Théâtre Libre of Paris was founded by André Antoine in 1887. The Independent Theatre was founded in London in 1891 by J. T. Grein; its aim was to produce original plays first and commercial successes second. Some of the playwrights produced included Yeats, George Bernard Shaw, George Moore, and Ibsen.
6. This passage in brackets was quoted by Yeats in his preface to Finberg's translation of *Axel.* See *P&I,* pp. 157–58.

7. According to W. H. O'Donnell, the puppet plays (written for marionettes) of Maeterlinck are *Alladine et Palomides, Intérieurs,* and *La Mort de Tintagiles;* they were written during the 1880s and 1890s (*P&I,* 291). Maurice Maeterlinck (1862–1949) was a Belgian poet and playwright. See Yeats's review of Maeterlinck's *The Treasure of the Humble,* pp. 340–41 in this collection.

8. This passage in brackets is quoted by Yeats in Finberg, p. 10; see *P&I,* p. 158.

9. *Magician of the Rosy-Cross:* Here, "Rosy-Cross" is a corruption of "Rosicrucian." The Rosicrucians were a fraternal religious and mystic order of the seventeenth and eighteenth centuries. The magician is the character Master Janus.

10. The Verlaine quotation is an English translation of a passage from the article on Villiers in Verlaine's book *Les Poètes maudites* (1884). The passage reads as follows: "Et comment nous retenir de mettre encore sous vos yeux cette fois une pièce tout entière? Comme dans *Isis,* comme dans *Morgane,* comme dans le *Nouveau Monde,* comme dans *Claire Lenoir,* comme dans toutes ses oeuvres, Villiers évoque ici le spectre d'une femme mysteriéuse, reine d'orgueil, sombre et fière comme la nuit encore et déjà crépusculaire avec des reflets de sang de l'or sur son âme et sur sa beauté" (Paul Verlaine, *Oeuvres en prose complètes* [Paris, Editions Gallimard, 1972], p. 683).

11. Medusa is a woman, the only mortal of the three Gorgons; she has snakes rather than hair growing from her head; anyone who looked into the Gorgons' eyes would be turned to stone.

    The Black Forest is in southwestern Germany.

    In Roman mythology, Janus is the god of doorways. He is depicted with two faces looking in opposite directions, toward the past and future.

12. *knowledge that she is in the world will never let him rest:* On p. 250 of Finberg, Axël says, "I see that henceforth to know of your existence in the world would hinder me from living."

13. *"Do not kill me; . . . the spirit of dead roses.":* Yeats is using a translation which later appeared in Arthur Symons's *The Symbolist Movement in Literature* ([London: William Heinemann, 1899], p. 56). On p. 260 of Finberg, Sara says, "What is the use of killing me? That will not help you to forget. Do you know what you are refusing? All the favours of all other women are as nothing, set in the scale against my cruelties! I am the most sombre of maidens. I seem to remember that I have made angels fall! Alas! children and flowers have perished of my shadow. Yield yourself up to my enchantment! I will teach you marvelous words, heady as eastern wines. I can lull you to sleep with mortal caresses. I know the secret of infinite joys, of delicious cries, of pleasures that surpass all hope. Bury yourself in my whiteness and leave your soul there as a flower lies hidden under snow! Cover yourself with my hair and inhale the ghosts of perished roses!"

14. *". . . when I heard the wind blowing in a bed of reeds. . .":* This recollection by Yeats sounds like the inspiration for his 1899 volume of poems, *The Wind Among the Reeds.*

15. Ecclesiastes is a book of wisdom in the Old Testament of the Bible.

16. In his preface to the Finberg edition, Yeats writes, "On my return to London I tried to arrange a performance there, and Miss Florence Farr, who was producing *Arms and the Man* and my *Land of Heart's Desire,* offered her theatre for nothing, but the London public was thought unprepared,

being in its first enthusiasm for Jones and Pinero" (quoted in *P&I*, p. 158).
17. This passage in brackets is quoted by Yeats in Finberg, p. 11; see *P&I*, p. 158.
18. George Chapman (?1559–1634), an English author, dramatist, and translator.

The Evangel of Folk-lore

1. Yeats meant primarily the Young Ireland movement of the 1840s.
2. Jane Barlow (1857–1917) wrote *Bog-land Studies* (London: T. Fisher Unwin, 1892) and *Irish Idylls* (London: Hodder and Stoughton, 1892). Emily Lawless (1845–1913) wrote the novels *Grania* (London: Smith, Elder, and Co., 1892) and *Maelcho* (London: Smith, Elder, and Co., 1894). For Standish O'Grady, see "Bardic Ireland," note 2. Mrs. Hinkson was the married name of Katharine Tynan; see the introduction to "The Celtic Romances in Miss Tynan's New Book," pp. 51–53.
3. Jeremiah Curtin (1835–1906), author of *Myths and Folk-lore of Ireland* (Boston: Little, Brown, and Co., 1890) and *Hero Tales of Ireland* (Boston: Little, Brown, and Co., 1894); Lady Francesca Wilde, author of *Ancient Legends, Mystic Charms, and Superstitions of Ireland* (London: Ward and Downey, 1887), and *Ancient Cures, Charms and Usages of Ireland* (London: Ward and Downey, 1890); Douglas Hyde, author of *Beside the Fire: A Collection of Irish Gaelic Folk Stories* (London: Alfred Nutt, 1890); David Rice McAnally Jr., author of *Irish Wonders: The Ghosts, Giants, Pookas, Demons, Leprechawns, Banshees, Fairies, Witches, Old Maids, and Other Marvels of the Emerald Isle* (London: Ward, Lock, 1888); and David Fitzgerald, folklorist, and author of "Popular Tales in Ireland" in *Revue Celtique* 4 (185–92).
4. *Nebuchadnezzar ate grass,:* Nebuchadnezzar's madness is recounted in the book of Daniel 4:33 in the Bible: "The same hour the word was fulfilled upon Nabuchodonosor, and he was driven away from among men, and did eat grass like an ox, and his body was wet with the dew of heaven: till his hairs grew like the feathers of eagles, and his nails like birds' claws" (Douay-Rheims version, New York: 1914).
5. The tale Yeats describes here is "The Red Pony," pp. 211–18 in Larminie.
6. This tale is entitled "The Woman Who Went to Hell," pp. 188–195.
7. This passage from "The Story of Bioultach" reads in Larminie, p. 50, as follows: ". . . in the place where there were seals, whales, crawling, creeping things, little beasts of the sea with red mouths, rising on the sole and the palm of the oar, making fairy music and melody for themselves, till the sea arose in strong waves, hushed with magic, hushed with wondrous voices."
8. "The Story of Bioultach," pp. 55–56.
9. "Wandering Willie" is a blind fiddler named Willie Steenson in Sir Walter Scott's novel *Redgauntlet*.
10. Donegal is a county in the north of the Republic of Ireland; Roscommon and Galway are counties in the west of the Republic of Ireland.

A New Poet

1. *fate, free will, foreknowledge absolute,:* Yeats paraphrases *Paradise Lost*, book 2, ll. 559–60.

2. The term "transcendental" is usually associated with a movement in American literature in the first half of the nineteenth century. Its leaders were the writers Ralph Waldo Emerson (1803–82) and Henry David Thoreau (1817–62).
3. William Blake writes in *The Marriage of Heaven and Hell* that "to create a little flower is the labour of ages," p. 152, *The Complete Writings of William Blake*, ed. Geoffrey Keynes (New York: Random House, 1957).
4. Among these seven were Yeats, Charles Johnston, Charles Weekes, and Claude Wright (the last on the authority of Richard Ellmann in *Yeats: The Man and the Masks*, New York, 1958, p. 41). About the membership of this Hermetic society Yeats told Ernest Boyd, "George Russell was not a member. He was then very young" (*L*, 592). AE probably first joined the Dublin lodge of the Theosophical Society, founded about 1886. According to *The Dublin University Review* issue of July 1885, p. 155, the first meeting of the Dublin Hermetic Society was held on June 16 at Trinity College. Papers were delivered by Yeats, Charles Johnston, and a Mr. Smeeth.
5. Yeats knew the proverb from Lady Wilde's *Ancient Cures, Charms and Usages of Ireland* (1890), p. 250; see "Tales from the Twilight," pp. 113–16.
6. *final consummation of the world when two halcyons might sit upon a bough:* Yeats is alluding to Percy Bysshe Shelley's *Prometheus Unbound,* act 3, scene 4:

> I cannot tell my joy, when o'er a lake,
> Upon a drooping bough with nightshade twined,
> I saw two azure halcyons clinging downward
> And thinning one bright bunch of amber berries,
> With quick long beaks, and in the deep there lay
> Those lovely forms imaged as in a sky (ll. 78–83).

Yeats refers to this passage in his essay "The Philosophy of Shelley's Poetry," printed in *Ideas of Good and Evil* (London: Macmillan, 1902):

> I have re-read *Prometheus Unbound*, which I had hoped my fellow-students would have studied as a sacred book, and it seems to me to have an even more certain place than I had thought among the sacred books of the world. I remember going to a learned scholar to ask about its deep meanings, which I felt more than understood, and his telling me that it was Godwin's *Political Justice* put into rhyme, and that Shelley was a crude revolutionist, and believed that the overturning of kings and priests would regenerate mankind. I quoted the lines which tell how the halcyons ceased to prey on fish, and how poisonous leaves became good for food, to show that he foresaw more than any political regeneration, but was too timid to push the argument (65–66).

7. *alcahest:* Yeats in his review of Ibsen's *Brand* (*The Bookman,* October 1894), pp. 252–54, defines *alcahest* as follows: "Certain alchemical writers say that the substance left over in the retort is the philosopher's stone, and the liquid distilled over, the elixir or alkahest; and all are agreed that the stone transmutes everything into gold, while the elixir dissolves everything into nothing, and not a few call them the fixed and the volatile."
8. Charles Weekes, whose book *Reflections and Refractions* was reviewed by

Yeats in *The Academy,* 4 November 1893. AE dedicated *Homeward, Songs by the Way* to Weekes.

9. *"places and":* In the second edition of *Homeward, Songs by the Way* (Dublin: Whaley/London: Simpkin, Marshall and Co., 1895), AE reads "places, and"; "went forth in old time from . . ."; "Self-ancestral"; "but filled"; and "homesickness I" (vii).

10. *"the multitudinous meditation":* p. xiii.

11. *Love has found itself the whole.:* The poem here quoted in its entirety is "Sung on a By-Way" (23).

12. AE reads "apart:"; "mine" instead of "my"; "knew" instead of "know"; "sublime;—"; and "but love," (24).

13. In this poem, "Truth," AE reads "thought it,"; "deed:"; "kindled," and "night," (44).

14. In "The Dawn of Darkness," AE reads "children pit-pat"; and "burrows on" (25).

   The line "White for Thy whiteness all desires burn" is from the poem "Desire" (3).

   In "The Great Breath," AE reads "Withers once more the old blue flower of day:" (12).

   In "The Dawn of Darkness," AE reads "evening, shaken" (25).

   "We are but embers wrapped in clay": This line is from AE's poem "Dust" (37).

   "Make of thy gentleness thy might": This line is from "Three Counsellors" (41).

   Be thou thyself that goal in which the wars of time shall cease: This final couplet from "Three Counsellors" reads

   > Only be thou thyself that goal
   > In which the wars of time shall cease.

   "No image of the proud and morning stars looks at us from their faces": This line is from "Day" (16).

15. The publishing house Yeats mentions here, C. Whaley, was located in Dublin.

Some Irish National Books

1. Benjamin Disraeli, first earl of Beaconsfield (1804–81), British statesman (prime minister, 1868, 1874–80) and novelist.

2. Thomas Davis, *The Patriot Parliament of 1689,* edited by Sir C. G. Duffy (London and Dublin: T. Fisher Unwin, 1893).

3. For Sir Charles Gavan Duffy (1816–1903), see "Popular Ballad Poetry of Ireland," note 30; for Thomas Davis (1814–45), see "The Poetry of Sir Samuel Ferguson—II," note 8.

4. *The Bog of Stars and Other Stories and Sketches* (London and Dublin: T. Fisher Unwin, 1893), in the New Irish Library.

5. *The Spirit of the Nation* (Dublin: J. Duffy, 1893), edited by Thomas Davis.

6. Thomas D'Arcy McGee (1825–68), poet of the Young Ireland movement. He emigrated to Canada, where he was assassinated by the Fenians in 1868.

7. *"The Dark Rosaleen", or "O'Donovan's Daughter":* "Dark Rosaleen" is by Clarence Mangan; the other poem is by Edward Walsh.

8. Herbert Halliday Sparling (1860–1924), son-in-law of William Morris. Yeats knew Sparling in the later eighties in London, and he is frequently mentioned in Yeats's correspondence of that period. *Irish Minstrelsy* appeared in 1887.

9. For Jeremiah James Callanan (1795–1829) and Edmund Walsh (1805–50), see "Popular Ballad Poetry of Ireland," note 19.

10. Sir Samuel Ferguson (1810–86) was a poet and antiquarian who greatly influenced Yeats. See Yeats's assessment of Ferguson in "The Poetry of Sir Samuel Ferguson—I" and "The Poetry of Sir Samuel Ferguson—II," the first two items in this collection. For James Clarence Mangan (1803–49), see "The Poetry of Sir Samuel Ferguson—II," note 8; for William Allingham, see "The New 'Speranza'," note 3; for Aubrey de Vere (1814–1902), see "The Poetry of Sir Samuel Ferguson—I," note 18.

11. For Thomas Moore, see "Popular Ballad Poetry of Ireland," note 75.

12. "Come, Liberty, Come!" is by Dennis Florence MacCarthy. McCarthy's poem reads "Come, freshen" (85).

13. *fairest,:* MacCarthy reads "fairest!" (85).

14. *Cameron and Ferguson's little Irish song-books:* Untraced.

15. William Wordsworth (1770–1850) published a collection of poems entitled *Ecclesiastical Sketches* (London, 1822). In his *Poetical Works* (London) of 1837, he changed the title from *Ecclesiastical Sketches* to *Ecclesiastical Sonnets*.

16. Honoré de Balzac (1799–1850); the novel is *Le Médecin de campagne* (Paris, 1833).

17. William Carleton (1794–1869), Irish novelist. See "Irish National Literature, IV," note 4.

18. *Father of Lies:* Satan.

19. William III (1650–1702) was invited to invade England to dethrone James II; he was crowned king of England in 1689. He successfully defended himself against James's attempt to regain the crown at the Battle of the Boyne in Ireland in 1690. James II (1633–1701) was the last Roman Catholic king of England, ruling from 1685 to 1688. After fleeing England in 1688 and unsuccessfully attempting to regain his crown by fighting William III in Ireland, James returned to exile in France.

20. Patrick Sarsfield (?–1693), a major general in the Jacobite War against William; he helped negotiate the treaty at Limerick in 1691. Friedrich Hermann, duke of Schomberg (1615–90), the commander-in-chief against James; he was killed at the Battle of the Boyne. Richard Talbot, earl of Tyrconnell (1630–90), was a lieutenant general for James in the war against William.

21. Charles O'Kelly (1621–95) was a colonel in King James's army during the Jacobite War.

22. Father Edmund Hogan, S.J. (1831–1917) was a Celtic language scholar and an Irish historian; he published a range of books on both subjects. George Noble Count Plunkett (1851–1948) was at various times a poet, politician, and nationalist.

23. For Emily Lawless and Jane Barlow, see "The Evangel of Folk-lore," note 2; for John Todhunter, see "John Todhunter," pp. 86–87; for Mrs. Bryant, see the review of *Celtic Ireland*, pp. 109–12; for Mrs. (Katharine Tynan) Hinkson, see the introduction, pp. 51–53, to "The Celtic Romances in Miss Tynan's New Book."

An Imaged World

1. The poet Henry Vaughan (1621–95) called himself "The Silurist" after the Latin name for the part of Wales in which he was born.
   attend him: Untraced.
2. *the alchemist, Dr. Rudd:* Yeats's source would appear to be the account that appears in Harlean manuscript #6481. This account is in the general collection entitled "From the Learned Works in MSS of the late famous Dr. Rudd, Collected and Methodized by Peter Smart, MA, 1714." The specific work quoted was "Dr. Rudds Treatise of the miraculous Descensions and Ascensions of Spirits—verified by a Practical Examination of Principles in the Great World." On p. 9, the relevant passage begins, ". . . another more admirable Object interposed, I could see—between me and the Light, a most exquisite diving Beauty, black and lovely, her frame neither long nor short, but a mean decent stature; Attired she was (according to the most curious mode of the Country at Sydmouth in the County of Devon now [near?] Exeter) in a habit best pleased her own nature. . . ."
   "half smiling and half sad" . . . elements again: On the verso of p. 27, the account of Rudd's encounter concludes as follows: "here Beata [Nature] stopt me in a mute Ceremony, for I was to be left alone, she lookt upon me in silent smiles, mixt with a pretty kind of sadness, for we were unwilling to part, but her hour of translation was come, and taking her leave she past before my eyes into the Aether of Nature, and this was my Mistress, it is nature, for I have no other."
3. *"glass of imagination":* Garnett, *The Imaged World*, "Acquiescence," p. 93: "And thus it is with the reflections cast by the actual bread-getting world in the glass of imagination."
4. This passage is altered in Yeats's quotation. Garnett's original reads as follows: "O Hyld, down there in the woods my feet have bruised a tiny path amid the autumn grass, as I went, thinking of thee, a little path amid nut bushes winding. It has not led me to an end; O Girl, have pity on that poor bruised path, which cannot speak its heart, and come and pass by it" (from Part I. The Lover in Autumn. "A Little Pathway in the Woods. The Lover beseeches his Mistress," p. 27).
5. This passage is altered in Yeats's quotation. Garnett's original reads as follows: "Tear the swart twilight, oh rushing white rain-storm, tear the edge of the fast-traveling night, and let my love through to me! Yea, all the sombre horizon is ravelling with a foam edge of light in the dying west—ah, if I could get there, if I could get there, thou and my fate would meet me! Art thou jeering at me, O storm-wind? Ah, wait a little, O lone night, and thou shalt hear us whispering our secrets together! O streaming leaves, when the wind has flung ye dying on earth's cold bosoms I shall be lying only lovers' warm breasts' (from Part I. The Lover in Autumn. "The Flowering Earth. The Lover would conquer Fate," 16).
6. This passage is altered in Yeats's quotation. Garnett's original reads as follows: "Faces. Faces, everywhere I saw fresh faces, yet I could not see her gentle face. Faces, faces, fixed and serious faces, all keep passing in a long procession, yet I could not find her frightened face. It is you, you, thousand secret-hiding faces that she feared, your curious eyes and sneering looks if you had guessed her secret" (from Part II. In Grey Crowds. "To Lucile, Who Did Her Duty. Broad Cloth," 62).
7. This passage is altered in Yeats's quotation. Garnett's original reads as fol-

lows: "O young Earth, fresh Earth, Earth of ecstasy, would that we the grey multitudes with our pale pleasures had ne'er been born in thy green lap! Oh grant that memory of us be lost when to the strong young clear-eyed race shall pass thy mountains, plains, and forests. Grant then that our cities lie buried deep, and thy heart, O Earth, betrays us not, when the surf waves break athwart the dance of the twining laughing girls, at purple eve, on the great sea's windy shore" (from Part III. The Lover in Spring. "Bright Green Leaves. Beauty shall Conquer," 119).

8. *precision:* Yeats says elsewhere (*The Bookman,* April 1896) that Blake's great word was "precision." See *"William Blake,"* pp. 302–4.

9. Walt Whitman (1819–82), American poet; Richard Jeffries (1848–87), English writer whose works are infused with his knowledge of the natural world.

   peasant poets of Roumania: Yeats meant *The Bard of the Dimbovitza, Roumanian Folk-Songs* (London: J. R. Osgood, McIlvaine and Co., 1894), a collection of Roumanian folk poems gathered by Elena Vacarescu and translated into English by Carmen Sylva (Elizabeth, queen of Roumania) and Alma Strettell, first series in 1892, second series in 1894. Yeats quoted passages from the second volume in his review of Lucy Garnett's collection *Greek Folk Poesy* (*The Bookman,* October 1896), see pp. 314–18 in this collection.

10. The closest William Blake comes to this phrase is in these sentences from "NUMBER XV. Ruth.—A Drawing," in "A Descriptive Catalogue of Pictures . . ." in *The Writings of William Blake,* ed. Keynes (1925), vol. 3, p. 119: "What is it that distinguishes honesty from knavery, but the hard and wiry line of rectitude and certainty in the actions and intentions? Leave out this line, and you leave out life itself; all is chaos again, and the line of the almighty must be drawn out upon it before man or beast can exist."

11. William Hyde illustrated Yeats's article "Popular Ballad Poetry of Ireland," *The Leisure Hour,* November 1889.

The Stone and the Elixir

1. Garrett's translation reads "the world" instead of "the earth" (217).

2. The passage Yeats quotes does not match Garrett. Garrett reads as follows:

> Grant you are slaves to pleasure: well,
> Be so from curfew-bell to bell:
> Don't be some special thing one minute
> And something else the next, by fits!
> Whate'er you are, be whole-souled in it,
> Not only piecemeal and in bits!
> There's beauty in a true Bacchante:
> Your maudlin toper's charm is scanty.
> Silenus still is picturesque:
> A tippler is the faun's grotesque.
> Go round the country, do but fling
> A watchful glance at folk: you'll see
> That every one has learnt to be
> A little bit of everything.

A little smug (on holy days);
A little true to old-time ways;
A little sensual when he sups—
(His fathers were so in their cups;) (25).

3. Timon, a citizen of Athens and a misanthrope, is the subject of William Shakespeare's play *Timon of Athens;* in Shakespeare's tragedy *King Lear,* Lear foolishly divides his kingdom among his daughters at the cost of his, and their, lives.
4. Henrik Bernhard Jaeger (1854–95) was a biographer of Ibsen. An English translation of his life of Ibsen appeared in 1890. Hjalmar Hjorth Boyesen (1848–95) was a critic of German and Scandinavian literatures.
5. Shaw discusses Brand as an "idealist of heroic earnestness, strength, and courage" on pp. 46–48 of his *The Quintessence of Ibsenism* (London: Walter Scott, 1891). Section 2 of this work is entitled "Ideals and Idealists."
6. *the one amid overwhelming and lifeless snow:* Yeats refers to the end of the character Brand. Yeats refers to Peer Gynt's encounter with the button maker.
7. Dr. Charles Harold Herford's translation of *Brand* also appeared in 1894; William Wilson's prose translation of *Brand* was published in 1891.

Battles Long Ago

1. Richard Wagner (1813–83), a German composer who created, over many years, *Der Ring des Nibelungen,* a tetralogy of operas first produced in its entirety in 1876 at Bayreuth. Wagner's work was based on *Das Nibelungenlied,* a German epic poem of the thirteenth century; William Morris (1834–96) wrote *Sigurd the Volsung* (1876) based on the same epic.

    Alfred Tennyson (1809–92) published *The Idylls of the King* in 1859; it tells the story of King Arthur and his knights.

    Swinburne's poem on this subject, published in 1882, was titled *Tristram of Lyonesse.* Matthew Arnold's poem "Tristram and Iseult" was published in 1852.

    Dr. Dryasdust was "a fictitious character to whom Sir Walter Scott dedicated novels. A laborious dull antiquarian or historian; a scholar occupied with uninteresting details" (*The New Shorter Oxford Dictionary,* 1993, 758).

    The title of this review is taken from William Wordsworth's poem "The Solitary Reaper" (l. 20).
2. Standish O'Grady translated and published the old Irish myths in his *History of Ireland: Heroic Period* (London: Sampson Low, Searly, Marston, & Rivington/Dublin: E. Ponsonby, 1878). His version of these myths had such a great influence on Yeats and AE that he has been called the "Father of the Irish Revival."
3. O'Grady reads "Lu the"; "the maker and decorator of the Firmament, whose hound was the sun"; "Mananan mac"; "with a roar of far-off innumerable waters"; and "the Mor Reega stood in the midst with a foot on either side of the plain, and shouted with the shout of a host . . ." (127).
4. *horns and hoofs are of iron:* In O'Grady, Cuchulain says, ". . . what is this herd of monstrous deer, sad-coloured and livid, as with horns and hoofs of iron?" (155).

An Excellent Talker

1. Walter Pater (1839–94) said this in his review of *The Picture of Dorian Gray*, printed in the November 1891 issue of *The Bookman*.
2. *The soul . . . comedy of life.*: Near the end of act 1 (1907 ed., p. 47), Lord Illingworth says these lines to Mrs. Allonby, but without the comma Yeats inserts in the first sentence after "old." Mrs. Allonby responds to Illingworth with the next two lines.
3. *worship . . . baldness:* Near the end of act 1, Lord Illingworth says the first phrase, to which Mrs. Allonby replies with the second, her "their" referring to "successes," figuratively men, of course (1907 ed., p. 47).
4. *Rarely . . . do:* Near the end of act 2, Lord Illingworth's sentence begins "Rarely, if ever do," (1907 ed., p. 95).
5. *"the impure passion of remorse":* Robert Louis Stevenson, in chapter 3, "Old Mortality," of *Memories and Portraits* (London: Chatto & Windus, 1887), writes:

   The tale of this great failure is, to those who remained true to him, the tale of a success. In his youth he took thought for no one but himself; when he came ashore again, his whole armada lost, he seemed to think of none but others. Such was his tenderness for others, such his instinct of fine courtesy and pride, that of that impure passion of remorse he never breathed a syllable; even regret was rare with him, and pointed with a jest (1912 ed., p. 26).

6. Wilde's "The Decay of Lying" was first published in his *Intentions* (London: Osgood, McIlvaine, 1891).

Dublin Mystics

1. AE's book was published by Whaley and Co. in Dublin.
2. This poem, "A Vision of Beauty," is one of fourteen poems included only in the American edition (Portland, Maine: T. B. Mosher, 1895). His edition reads "Shepherd"; "hordes," (68); "Fold"; and "told," (69).
3. On p. 33, Eglinton's essay "The Chosen People at Work" reads "idealists inevitably divide into two classes—those who content themselves with maintaining a decadent literature, art and science, and those who feel prompted to perpetuate the onward impulse in their own individual lives."
   "idealists" . . . Egypt.: In his second essay, Eglinton repeatedly identifies "The Chosen People" of his title as "that curiously situated class of Idealists, who, as Israel took over the brick-manufacture of Egypt, have in this country been taking over the manufacture of literature" (31–32). The most overt "lofty appeal" to the "Chosen People" to "come out" is the long apostrophe (35–36).
4. *"and the countless . . .":* The first of Eglinton's essays, "Vox Clamantis," reads "and of the countless" (23). The quotation in the previous line occurs earlier in the same sentence.

The Story of Early Gaelic Literature

1. The Gaelic League was founded by Douglas Hyde, Eoin MacNeill, and Father Eugene O'Growney in 1893 for the purpose of reviving Irish culture, especially through the revival of the Irish language.
2. These titles are in *The Love Songs of Connacht* (London: T. Fisher Unwin/ Dublin: Gill and Son, 1893), a collection of folk poetry translated by Douglas Hyde, and *Beside the Fire* (Dublin: David Nutt, 1890), a translation of Gaelic folktales by Douglas Hyde.
3. The mythological cycles take up the different invasions of Ireland and generally concern the Tuatha dé Danaan and their various foes. An account of this phase of Irish history can be found in *The Book of Invasions* (*Leabhar Gabhála*). The other cycles include the Ulster Cycle, also known as the tales of the Red Branch, which include the stories of Cuchulain; the Fenian (or Ossianic) Cycle, which recounts the exploits of Finn MacCool; and the Cycle of the Kings, which includes tales of Ireland's mythical rulers.
   Alfred Nutt (1856–1910) was a writer and publisher of folklore and editor of *Folk-lore Journal*. H. d'Arbois de Jubainville (1827–1910) was professor of Celtic at the Collège de France. The second volume of his series *Cours de littérature celtique* was *Le Cycle mythologique, et la mythologie irlandaise* (Paris, 1884); the work was a touchstone for Yeats as he wrote about Irish folklore. Translated into English as *The Irish Mythological Cycle and Celtic Mythology,* the work was published in Dublin in 1903. John Rhys (1840–1915) wrote *Lectures on the Origin and Growth of Religion as Illustrated by Celtic Heathendom* (London, 1888).
4. Hyde does take up Cuchulain in chapter 7, "The Red Branch or Heroic Cycle," pp. 68–81, which recounts and analyzes the *Táin Bó Cuailgne,* wherein Cuchulain figures prominently. The section of the *Táin* which is discussed in greatest detail is "The Fight at the Ford" between Cuchulain and Ferdiad.
   "The Feast of Brian": The correct title of this tale is "The Feast of Bricriu" or "Fled Bricriu"; the entire chapter, "The Importance of Old Irish Literature," is not devoted to it.
   Cicero,: Hyde reads "Cicero" (42).
   Hyde reads "that there was a custom at the time in Gaul," (42). The passage from Hyde continues ". . . of fighting at a feast for the best bit which was to be given to the most valiant warrior." Hyde notes that in Irish this custom is called *curadh-mir,* or "heroes-bit" (43). Hyde then goes into a discussion of "The Feast of Bricriu," which goes from page 42 to page 46. Posidonius lived and taught at Rhodes at the beginning of the first century B.C. He wrote voluminously, mainly histories. After he went to Rome, he had as pupils the soldier Pompey and the famous orator Cicero.

Irish National Literature, I: From Callanan to Carleton

1. Edward Dowden (1843–1913), professor of English at Trinity College, in a controversy the previous winter, had claimed a place in Irish literature for Archbishop Ussher, Laurence Sterne, Jonathan Swift, and George Berkeley.
2. Thomas Carlyle (1795–1881); Yeats is referring to his *History of the French Revolution* (1837) and his *History of Frederick the Great* (1858–65).
3. For Thomas Moore, see "Popular Ballad Poetry of Ireland," note 75; for

Thomas Davis, see "The Poetry of Sir Samuel Ferguson—II," note 8. Thomas Babington Macaulay (1800–59), a historian; Sir Walter Scott (1771–1832), Scottish novelist; John Gibson Lockhart (1794–1854), Scottish writer. For John Mitchel, see "Popular Ballad Poetry of Ireland," note 27.

4. Yeats explained this doctrine of the "Immortal Moods" in the second of this series of articles. See "Irish National Literature, II: Contemporary Prose Writers," pp. 270–76.

5. See "Popular Ballad Poetry of Ireland," note 27. Mitchel wrote his *Jail Journal* in British convict hulks to which he was sentenced in 1848 for sedition. In 1853 he escaped to America, where the journal was published in 1854.

6. The source of these four lines of verse is John Greenleaf Whittier's "The Tent on the Beach" from *The Tent on the Beach and Other Poems*, (Boston: Ticknor and Fields, 1867). The whole stanza reads as follows:

> And one there was, a dreamer born,
> Who, with a mission to fulfil,
> Had left the Muses' haunts to turn
> The crank of an opinion mill,
> Making his rustic reed of song
> A weapon in the war with wrong,
> Taking his fancy to the breaking-plough
> That beam-deep turned the soil for truth
> to spring and grow (13).

7. For Callanan, see "Popular Ballad Poetry of Ireland," note 19.

8. For Walsh, see "Popular Ballad Poetry of Ireland," note 19.

9. "The Memory of the Dead," also known as "Who Fears to Speak of '98?" was written by John Kells Ingram; "The Marriage" by Thomas Davis; "A Cushla Gal Mo Chree" (Bright Vein of My Heart) by Michael Doheny (1805–63).

   Aubrey Thomas de Vere (1814–1902); William Allingham (1824–89); James Clarence Mangan (1803–49); Sir Samuel Ferguson (1810–86).

10. William Wordsworth (1770–1850) was one of the leaders of the English Romantic movement.

11. Ballyshannon is a town in Donegal. The poem Yeats is referring to is "A Stormy Night. A Story of the Donegal Coast," *Irish Songs and Poems* (London: Reeves and Turner, 1887).

12. *A wild . . . I know*: stanza 1 of Allingham's poem "A Stormy Night. A Story of the Donegal Coast," from his *Irish Songs and Poems* (1887), p. 136, reads:

> A WILD west Coast, a little Town,
> Where little Folk go up and down,
> Tides flow and winds blow:
> Night and Tempest and the Sea,
> Human Will and Human Fate:
> What is little, what is great?
> Howsoe'er the answer be,
> Let me sing of what I know.

Yeats had omitted two lines.

13. *Táin Bó Cuailgne:* The Cattle Raid of Cooley, an Irish epic of the seventh or eighth century.
14. The refrain means "O sad lament!" The poem is a translation of Donnchadh Ruadh MacConmara's "The Fair Hills of Eire," or "Ban Chnoic Eireann Oigh." Mangan's translation was entitled "The Fair Hills of Eire, O," and Samuel Ferguson published a version of the poem, entitled "The Fair Hills of Holy Ireland," in a review of Hardiman's *Irish Minstrelsy* in the October 1834 issue of *The Dublin University Magazine,* and he reprinted his translation in *Lays of the Western Gael* (1865), p. 225.

    Further below in the stanza, Ferguson reads "where her misty" for "when her misty" both in *Lays of the Western Gael,* p. 225, and in the version published in Duffy's *Ballad Poetry of Ireland,* p. 185.
15. Thady Quirk is the old family servant who is Maria Edgeworth's narrator in *Castle Rackrent* (1800).

    John Banim (1798–1842) and Michael Banim (1796–1874) both collaborated on and wrote separately novels of Irish life; William Carleton (1794–1869) wrote novels and stories of Irish peasants.
16. The passage from the beginning of the sentence down to the end of the article is essentially identical to the last two-thirds of the final paragraph of Yeats's review "William Carleton," printed in *The Bookman* in August 1896. *Father Connell* appeared in 1842; *The Nowlans* in 1826; and *Crohoore of the Billhook* in 1825.
17. *Paradise Lost,* 7, 463–65.
18. Charles James Lever (1806–72), prolific Irish novelist. He wrote both novels centered on the military and novels of Irish life.
19. Geoffrey Chaucer (ca. 1343–1400), most famous Middle English poet, author of *Troilus and Criseide* (ca. 1385) and *The Canterbury Tales,* begun around 1386.

The Three Sorrows of Story-telling

1. Robert Dwyer Joyce (1830–83). Yeats wrote a two-part article on this Joyce for *The Irish Fireside* (27 November and 4 December 1886). In it, he reviews Joyce's version of *Deirdre* (Boston: Roberts Brothers, 1876); see "The Poetry of R. D. Joyce," pp. 28–38. Patrick Weston Joyce's version of *Deirdre* is in his *Old Celtic Romances* (London: C. K. Paul and Co., 1879).
2. *Celtic Fairy Tales* (London: David Nutt, 1891), selected and edited by Joseph Jacobs (1854–1916).
3. *The Love Songs of Connacht,* which Yeats reviewed in *The Bookman* (October 1893). See "Old Gaelic Love Songs," pp. 218–21.
4. An *eric* was a fine paid by the ancient Irish as compensation for a homicide. Brian and the other sons of Tuireann perform heroic tasks as payment to Lugh for the slaying of his father, Cian.
5. Ben Edar is the Hill of Howth, northeast of Dublin.
6. In Hyde, this passage is in quotation marks as the speech of Deirdre, and it begins with the line "I am the lonely apple on the tree, . . ." (38). Her speech ends with the lines Yeats quotes here.

Irish National Literature, II:
Contemporary Prose Writers

1. *"little devils . . . themselves"*: The lines "And the little devils who fight for themselves / Rememb'ring the Verses that Hayley sung" appear as ll. 6–7 in a poem included in a letter to Thomas Butts of 22 November 1802 (Keynes, ed., *The Writings of William Blake* [1925], 206).
2. The Divine Brotherhood is untraced.
3. For Standish O'Grady, see "Bardic Ireland," note 2.
4. Yeats means the mystical writer Dionysius the Pseudo-Areopagite (c. 500). *"The Most High . . . God"*: See "The Ainu," note 6.
5. Boötes is the constellation known as the Herdsman; Arcturus is the brightest star in the constellation Boötes; Orion, or the Hunter, is another constellation.
   For James MacPherson, see "Dr. Todhunter's Irish Poems," note 5. For more on Dr. Dryasdust, see "Battles Long Ago," note 1.
6. *Finn and His Companions* (London: T. Fisher Unwin, 1892) and *The Coming of Cuculain* (London: Methuen, 1894). Yeats reviewed the latter in *The Bookman*, February 1895 (see "Battles Long Ago," pp. 255–56).
7. Standish O'Grady, *The Bog of Stars* (London/Dublin: T. Fisher Unwin, 1893); *Red Hugh's Captivity; a picture of Ireland, social and political, in the reign of Queen Elizabeth* (London: Ward and Downey, 1889). This last book was reissued in 1897 as *The Flight of the Eagle* (London: Lawrence & Bullen), and Yeats reviewed it in *The Bookman*, August 1897; see pp. 342–45. *The Story of Ireland* (London: Methuen, 1894).
8. For Charles Stewart Parnell, see "The Young Ireland League," note 1. Oliver Cromwell (1599–1658) was an English general and Puritan statesman; Cromwell was Lord Protector of England, Scotland, and Ireland (1653–58); after the death of Charles I, Cromwell invaded Ireland, where he is remembered for having led massacres at Drogheda and Wexford in 1649.
9. *"the sky was alight . . . flames"*: O'Grady writes, "while his followers were committing Charles Parnell's remains to the earth, the sky was bright with strange lights and flames" (211). He continues, "those strange flames recalled to my memory what is told of similar phenomenon said to have been witnessed when tiding of the death of the great Christian Saint, Columba, overran the North-West of Europe, as perhaps truer than I had imagined" (212). Columba (521–97) is an Irish saint.
10. John Stuart Mill (1806–73) reviewed Jules Michelet's (1798–1874) *History of France* in *The Edinburgh Review,* January 1844. The review was reprinted in volume 2 of *Dissertations and Discussions* (London, 1859). Mill said, "Michelet's are not books to save a reader the trouble of thinking, but to make him boil over with thought. Their effect on the mind is not acquiescence, but stir and ferment" (133).
11. *"of the servile tribes of ignoble countenance"*: On "the people" of Ireland, O'Grady says: "In the days of the bards, they are hardly referred to at all, save in language of swift passing contempt. 'The servile tribes of ignoble countenance,' sings one bard" (185). O'Grady never names this "bard."
12. Emily Lawless (1845–1913) was a writer of poetry, novels, and historical studies. The two novels Yeats mentions here, *Grania* and *Maelcho*, were published in 1892 and 1894, respectively, by the London firm Smith, Elder & Co. This essay contains Yeats's only extended comment on her.

13. *Essex in Ireland* (London: Smith, Elder & Co., 1890) is subtitled "being extracts from a diary kept in Ireland during the year 1599 by Mr. Henry Harvey, sometime secretary to Robert Devereux, earl of Essex." Sir Walter Raleigh (?1552–1618), Elizabethan explorer and statesman; he was in Ireland from 1580 to 1581 and engaged in fighting there.
14. Jane Barlow (1857–1917). The works named here are *Irish Idylls* (London: Hodder and Stoughton, 1892); *Kerrigan's Quality* (London: Hodder and Stoughton, 1894); and *Maureen's Fairing, and Other Stories* (London: Dent, 1895).
15. William Carleton (1794–1869), Irish novelist. See "William Carleton," pp. 298–301.
16. *Potheen* (also spelled *poteen*) is illegally distilled whiskey.
17. Yeats contributed a piece on Nora Hopper (1871–1906) to S. A. Brooke and T. W. Rolleston's *A Treasury of Irish Poetry* (London, 1900). Born in England, Hopper was a folklore enthusiast; she worked as a freelance journalist for both Irish and English papers and periodicals. She later married Wilfred Hugh Chesson.
18. *Ballads in Prose* (London: J. Lane, 1894).
19. Aodh was a son of Finn; the Fianna, or Fenians, were the warriors of the high king of Ireland, ca. 300 B.C. Their most famous member was Finn MacCool.
20. In this passage, Hopper reads as follows:

> The door clanged to behind him, and he went up the aisle walking ankle-deep in the fine dust, and straining his eyes to see through the darkness if indeed figures paced beside him, and ghostly groups gave way before him, as he could not help but fancy. At last his outstretched hands touched a twisted horn of some smooth cold substance, and he knew that he had reached the end of his journey. With his left hand clinging to the horn he turned towards the dark temple, saying aloud, 'Here I stand, Aodh, with gifts to give the Fianna and their gods. In the name of my mother's God, let them who desire my gifts, come to me.' 'Aodh, son of Eochaidh,' a shivering voice cried out, 'give my thy youth.' 'I give,' Aodh said quietly. 'Aodh! Said another voice, reedy and thin, but sweet, 'give me thy knowledge: I, Grania, loved much and knew little.' There was a gray figure at his side, and without a word Aodh turned and laid his forehead on the ghost's cold breast. As he rested thus, another voice said, 'I am Oisin: give me thy death, O Aodh!' Aodh drew a deep breath, then he lifted his head, and clasped a ghostly figure in his arms, and holding it there, felt it stiffen and grow rigid and colder yet. 'Give me thy hope, Aodh!' 'Give me thy faith, Aodh!' 'Give me thy courage, Aodh!' 'Give me thy dreams, Aodh!' So the voices called and cried, and to each Aodh answered and gave the desired gift. 'Give me thine heart, Aodh,' cried another. 'I am Maive, who knew much and loved little.' And with a sickening sense of pain Aodh felt slender cold fingers scratching and tearing their way through flesh and sinew till they grasped his heart, and tore the fluttering thing away. 'Give me thy love, Aodh!' another voice implored. 'I am Angus, Master of Love, and I have loved none.'
> 'Take it,' Aodh said faintly: and there was a pause (139–40).

21. The authors mentioned in the following sentence are Erminda Esler (ca.

1860–1924); Frank Mathew (1865–1924); William O'Brien (1852–1928), author of *When We Were Boys* (1890); Edmund Downey (1856–1937), author of *Anchor-Watch Yarns* (1893), *Merchant of Killogue* (1894), and many other books. *The Real Charlotte* (1894) was by Edith Œ. Somerville (1858–1949) and Martin Ross (pseudonym of Violet F. Martin, 1865–1915). Mrs. Hinkson (1861–1931) was better known by her maiden name, Katharine Tynan. See the introductory note to "The Celtic Romances in Miss Tynan's New Book," pp. 51–53.

22. William Edward Hartpole Lecky (1838–1903), Irish historian; his eight-volume *A History of England in the Eighteenth Century* (London: Longmans Green, 1878–90) dealt extensively with Ireland. He also published a five-volume *History of Ireland in the Eighteenth Century* (London: Longmans Green, 1892).

  Patrick Weston Joyce (1827–1914), brother of Robert Dwyer Joyce (1830–83), the poet, and no relation of James Joyce. P. W. Joyce wrote several histories of Ireland, both for the general public and for schoolchildren; Yeats is most likely referring to *A concise history of Ireland from the earliest times to 1837* (Dublin: M. H. Gill, 1893) and *A short history of Ireland from the earliest times to 1608* (London: Longmans, Green, and Co., 1893). Joyce's *Old Celtic Romances* (London: C. K. Paul & Co.) was published in 1879.

23. Yeats reviewed *Beside the Fire* in "Irish Folk Tales," pp. 124–27. Yeats included "Teig O'Kane" in his *Fairy and Folk Tales of the Irish Peasantry* (1888). "Wandering Willie's Tale" is from Sir Walter Scott's romance *Redgauntlet* (1824). Douglas Hyde's title is *Love Songs of Connacht* (1893).

24. Lady (Jane Francesca Elgee) Wilde's book is *Ancient Legends, Mystic Charms, and Superstitions of Ireland* (1887). For William Larminie, see "Some New Irish Books," note 3; for Jeremiah Curtin, see "Irish Folk Tales," note 9. John Francis Campbell (1822–85), Scottish folklorist. His most well-known collection of folklore is *Popular Tales of the West Highlands* (Edinburgh, 1860–62). Standish Hayes O'Grady (1832–1915)—not to be confused with Standish James O'Grady, mentioned above—was a scholar who published and translated Old Irish manuscripts. See "Bardic Ireland," note 2.

25. Dr. George Sigerson (1836–1925), historian and translator; Richard Ashe King (1839–1932) was a popular novelist as well as author of works on Jonathan Swift and Oliver Goldsmith. He had denounced how partisan politics had squelched literature in Ireland in a speech entitled "The Silenced Sister." Yeats took part in the ensuing controversy (see *UP1*, 305–10). Yeats reviewed his book on Swift in an essay in *The Bookman* in 1896. See "The New Irish Library," pp. 309–11.

That Subtle Shade

1. *famous Hindu philosopher:* probably Mohini Chatterjee, whom Yeats met in Dublin in 1885 and who served as a source for many of Yeats's Indian anecdotes.

2. "Leves Amores" is a poem in Symons's *London Nights,* p. 44; the title can be translated as "light loves" or "frivolous loves." Algernon Charles Swinburne (1837–1909); his *Poems and Ballads* appeared in 1866; its publication caused a literary scandal.

3. Yeats is expounding his doctrine of "The Moods" here; this same senti-

ment appears early in Yeats's article "Irish National Literature, III," pp. 280–87.
4. The following quotation is the first three stanzas of Symons's "Rosa Mundi" (39).
5. Symons reads "a fire:"; "love that is here!"; "Love's, to infinity"; and "eat, and live" (39).
6. Both the Scottish poet John Davidson (1857–1909) of *Fleet Street Eclogues* (London, 1893) fame and Arthur Symons were associated with the Rhymers' Club. The title of Davidson's book of poems is *In a Music-Hall, and Other Poems* (London: Ward and Downey, 1891). Yeats's wording "music-hall" probably comes from the first poem, "Prologue," in Symons's book: "My life is like a music-hall" (p. 3, line 1).
7. These stanzas are from "La Mélinite: Moulin Rouge." In this second stanza, for "Alone apart," Symons reads "Alone, apart," and "mirror, face to face," (24). Yeats described this same lyric in his 1897 review of Symons's *Amoris Victima* (see "Mr. Arthur Symons' New Book," pp. 332–35) as "one of the most perfect lyrics of our time."
8. Percy Bysshe Shelley (1792–1822), English Romantic poet. Shelley writes, "But a poet considers the vices of his contemporaries as the temporary dress in which his creations must be arrayed, and which cover without concealing the eternal proportions of their beauty" (*The Complete Works of Percy Bysshe Shelley*, 10 vols., ed. Roger Ingpen and Walter E. Peck [London: Ernest Benn Ltd., 1930], vol. 7, 117).
9. *"that subtle shade"*: untraced.

Irish National Literature, III: Contemporary Irish Poets

1. Christian Rosencreutz (pseudonym of Johann Valentin Andreae, 1586–1654) was the modern founder of Rosicrucianism. Among his works were *Fama fraternitatis* (1614), *Confessio rosae* (1615), and *Chymische Hockzeit* (1616).
2. For King Arthur, see "A Bundle of Poets," note 3; Arthur's court was known as Camelot.
   For Robert Browning (1812–89) see "Plays by an Irish Poet," note 6; Pompilia and Guido Franceschini are characters in his *The Ring and the Book* (1868). The poem is based on a real murder trial in seventeenth-century Rome. In the poem, Guido murders his wife, Pompilia, and the tale is recounted from several perspectives. The pope's monologue is in book 10.
3. *watcher of the skies*: An allusion to John Keats's "On First Looking into Chapman's Homer": "Then felt I like some watcher of the skies / When a new planet swims into his ken" (ll. 9–10).
4. *"phantoms of the earth and water"*: Blake reads "man is either the ark of God or a phantom of the earth & of the water . . ." ("Annotations of Lavater's Aphorisms on Man," *The Complete Writings of William Blake*, 3 vols., ed. Geoffrey Keynes [London: Nonesuch Press, 1925], vol. 1, 108).
5. *"uncurbed in their eternal glory"*: William Blake, in "A Vision of the Last Judgment" (*The Complete Writings of William Blake*, 3 vols., ed. Geoffrey Keynes [London: Nonesuch Press, 1925]), writes: "the Treasures of Heaven are not Negations of Passions, but Realities of Intellect, From which all Passions Emanate Uncurbed in their Eternal Glory" (vol. 3, 160).
6. John 3:8 in the Bible.

7. While the specific writers to whom Yeats refers are untraced, for the phrase "to weep Irish" see the *Oxford English Dictionary*.
8. Douglas Hyde, *The Love Songs of Connacht* (London, 1893) reads "The same man who will to-day"; "drinking and shouting, will"; and "lost life" (3).
9. Hyde gives verse translations of the two following poems, but Yeats quotes from the prose versions.

Yeats quotes first from the prose version of "Happy it is" (131–33). The irregularly punctuated text of Hyde reads as follows: "It is happy for thee, O blind man, who dost not see much of women. Uch, if you were to see what we see, thou would'st be sick even as I am. It is a pity, O God, that it was not blind I was before I saw her twisted cool. Her snowy body (of) race bright and free, Uch, I think my life a misery. I always thought the blind pitiable until my calamity waxed beyond the grief of all, Then, though it is a pity, my pity I turned into envy, In a loop of the loops in a loop am I. It is woe for whoever saw her, And it is woe for him who sees her not each day. It is woe for him on whom the know of her love is (tied), And it is woe for him who is loosed out of it. It is woe for him who goes to her, and it is woe for him who is not with her constantly. It is woe for a person to be near her, And it is a woe for him that is not near her" (131–32).
10. The passage quoted is a prose translation of "My Love, Oh, She is My Love" (134–36). In Hyde, the text reads (irregularly) as follows: "My love, oh! she is my love, The woman who is most for destroying me; Dearer is she from making me ill Than the woman who would be for making me well. She is my treasure, Oh, she is my treasure, The woman of the grey (?) eye (she) like the rose, A woman who would not place a hand beneath my head, A woman who would not be with me for gold. She is my affection, OH! she is my affection, The woman who left no strength in me; A woman who would not breathe a sigh after me, A woman who would not raise a stone at my tomb" (134–35).
11. "The Dead at Clonmacnois" is translated from the Irish of Angus O'Gillan. While the poem was published in Rolleston's *Sea Spray: Verses and Translations* (Dublin: Maunsel, 1909) for this article, Yeats may have used the version of the poem which appeared in his *Book of Irish Verse* (London: Methuen and Co., 1895), pp. 197–98. If this is so, he quotes the poem correctly, except as noted below.

Rolleston's source for the poem was very likely *Christian Inscriptions in the Irish Language,* "Chiefly Collected and Drawn by George Petrie, and Edited by M. Stokes" (Dublin: The University Press for the Royal Historical and Archaeological Association, 1872), vol. 1, pp. 5–7. The Irish text and English translation are introduced there as follows: "In the Rev. Dr. Todd's list of Irish manuscripts preserved in the Bodleian Library (Rawlinson, B. 486. fol. 29), the following poem, on the tribes and persons interred at Clonmacnois, written by Enoch O'Gillain, who lived on the borders of the River Suck, in the county of Galway, is mentioned. The Editor has to offer her best thanks to Mr. W.D. Macray for his kindness in procuring a tracing of the original MS. for her, and to Mr. Wm. M. Hennessy for the translation and notes with which he has enriched it." A note to the last stanza of the poem, in which Enoch O'Gillain speaks of himself, says, "The name of O'Gillain is not found in the general list of Irish poets" (7). For a translation of this poem into modern Gaelic, see *An Sagart* 7.3–4 (Autumn 1964): 37–39. The translation is by Caitlín Ní Mhaol-Chróin.

Rolleston's version is a translation of the first five stanzas. The version given in Stokes is nineteen stanzas long.

12. In this stanza, Rolleston reads "quiet-water'd"; "fair;" and "Erinn" (47). Saint Kieran, or Ciaran (ca. 516–56), was the abbot and founder of the monastery at Clonmacnoise in Ireland.
    Erin is an Irish name for Ireland.

13. In this stanza, Rolleston reads "stone: his name," (47).
    Conn's title in Irish is "Conn Ced-cathach," or Conn of the Hundred Fights. He was high king of Ireland around A.D. 200. In Curtis's *History of Ireland,* it is claimed that the province of Connacht is named after this Conn, and that he started a line of kings which lasted until 1022.
    Ogham is an ancient form of Irish writing that dates from at least the third century A.D., and perhaps earlier.
    Petrie and Stokes identify the "knot" as "the ornamental designs on the crosses and slabs" (5).

14. *seven Kings of Tara:* Rolleston reads "Seven Kings" (47). Tara is the seat of the high kings of ancient Ireland. According to Peter Berresford Ellis, there were one hundred and eighty-eight high kings of Ireland, with Slaigne the Firbolg being the first and Ruaraidh Ó Conchobar being the last when he accepted Henry II as ruler of Ireland after the Treaty of Windsor in 1175 (*A Dictionary of Irish Mythology,* 35). The number of "Seven Kings" may be a parallel to the fame of the Seven Churches of Clonmacnoise.
    Cairbre: Rolleston reads "Cairbré" (47); in the Stokes edition, he is identified as "Apparently Cairbre Lifechair, son of Cormac Mac Airt" (5).
    there: Rolleston reads "their" (47).

15. *Teffia:* The Stokes edition identifies Teffia as "The ancient name of a district, comprising portions of the present counties of Longford and Westmeath" (5).
    Breagh: of this name *The Field Day Anthology* says "the kings of Bregha (Breagh) resided on the banks of the river Boyne."
    Creide: Creidé. In the Stokes edition, Creide is explained as follows: "The O'Conors of Connacht were sometimes called Sil-Creide, or race of Creide." The Stokes edition explains Clann Conaill as follows: "Not the Cinel-Conaill, or septs descended from Conall Gulban, son of Niall; but the descendants of his brother, Conall Cremthann, of whom were the Clann-Colman, or O'Melachlainns" (5).

16. *Conn the Hundred Fighter:* Rolleston reads "Conn the Hundred-Fighter" (47). See "Irish National Literature, III: Contemporary Irish Poets," note 13.
    Clan Colman: one of the builders of the Great Church of Clonmacnoise, dating from 904, was Abbot Colman Conailleach. See note 15 above.

17. Katharine Tynan (1861–1931). For more information on Katharine Tynan, see the introductory note to "The Celtic Romances in Miss Tynan's New Book," earlier in this collection.

18. *Louise de la Vallière and Other Poems* (London: Kegan Paul, Trench and Co., 1885). See Yeats's review of *Shamrocks* (London: Kegan Paul, Trench and Co., 1887), pp. 65–67.

19. The Ladies' Land League was founded in 1881 by Anna Parnell. When Michael Davitt (founder of the Land League in 1879) and Charles Stewart Parnell were in jail during 1881–82 for activities associated with the Land League, the Ladies' Land League ran the organization and its newspaper, *United Ireland.*

20. For Edward Walsh (1805–50), see "Popular Ballad Poetry of Ireland," note 19.
21. Yeats describes "The Red-Haired Man's Wife" as a popular song, "Sthagan Varagy" or "The Market Stroller," in his review of William Carleton's novel *The Red-Haired Man's Wife*, pp. 88–92. Those songs bear no similarity to Tynan's poem. Both "The Red-Haired Man's Wife" and "Gramachree" are in *Cuckoo Songs*, pp. 35–37 and p. 76, respectively. Both poems are given as variations, but Tynan doesn't identify her sources.
22. In stanza 4, Tynan reads "blue mountains"; and "sweet" and "feet" with no commas (6). In stanza 5, Tynan reads "Cross of shame" (7); and in stanza 6, Tynan reads "on" instead of "of" (7).
23. *Miracle Plays: Our Lord's Coming and Childhood* (London: J. Lane) appeared in 1895.
24. For Nora Hopper, see "Irish National Literature, II," note 17. For a note on AE and on the title of his volume of poems, see the introductory note to Yeats's review "A New Poet," pp. 176–79.
25. *Upanishads:* There is no poem by the title of "Upanishads" in AE's *Homeward, Songs by the Way*, though the poem "Magic" contains a subtitle, "After Reading the Upanishads" (50). Upanishads are the speculative and mystical texts of Hinduism. They were composed beginning around 900 B.C.
26. *Irish Theosophist.* Yeats is probably referring to AE's essay "Yes, and Hope" in the previous 15 August 1895 (3.11 189–92) issue of the journal.
27. *The spirit . . . "report.":* In *Imaginations and Reveries* (New York: Macmillan, 1915), a collection of AE's articles and stories, AE writes the following in an essay entitled "The Renewal of Youth": "Yet these are mysteries, and they cannot be reasoned out or argued over. We cannot speak truly of them from report, or description, or from what another has written" (134).
28. *fire:* AE writes "Fire. And, as it" (135).
29. AE writes "Golden Age" (131).
     AE writes "Let no one bring to this task the mood of the martyr or of one who thinks he sacrifices something. Yet let all who will come. Let them enter the path, facing all things in life and death with a mood at once gay and reverent, as beseems those who are immortal" (136).
     For the phrase "criticism of life," see "The Poetry of Sir Samuel Ferguson—I," note 10.
30. *"which is eternal delight":* William Blake in "The Marriage of Heaven and Hell" (*The Complete Writings of William Blake*, 3 vols., ed. Geoffrey Keynes [London: Nonesuch Press, 1925]) writes "Energy is Eternal Delight" (vol. 1, 182).
31. John Todhunter (1839–1916), poet and dramatist; for Aubrey Thomas de Vere (1814–1902), see "The Poetry of Sir Samuel Ferguson—I," note 18.
32. The editors can find no poem entitled "Red Branch Heroes," though the Red Branch Knights appear and wear armor in de Vere's "The Sons of Usnach" in *The Foray of Queen Maeve and Other Legends of Ireland's Heroic Age* (London: Kegan Paul, Trench and Co., 1882); also, the editors can find no poem "Naisi's Wooing" though the story is retold in "The Sons of Usnach"; "The Children of Lir" can be found in *The Foray of Queen Maeve . . .;* "The Bard Ethell," "The Wedding of the Clans; a Girl's Babble," and "The little Black Rose shall be red at last" can all be found in *The Sister, Inisfail, and Other Poems* (London: Longman, Green, Longman and

Roberts/Dublin: McGlashan and Gill, 1861), pp. 139–51, pp. 177–78, and p. 293, respectively.

33. "The doom of the children of Lir," "The fate of the sons of Usna," and "The lamentations for the three sons of Turann" were retold by Todhunter in his *Three Irish Bardic Tales* (London: J. M. Dent, 1896).

34. Yeats begins with stanza 2; the poem quoted is from *The Banshee and Other Poems* (London: Kegan Paul, Trench and Co., 1888).

35. The River Shannon flows southwest from Northern Ireland to the Atlantic, near Limerick; it is the longest river in Ireland.
   In this stanza, Todhunter reads "dead," (3).

36. In this stanza, Todhunter reads "night wind" (4).

37. During the 1890s, Lionel Pigot Johnson (1867–1902) was a member of both the Rhymers' Club and the Irish Literary Society in London. He was both a literary critic and a poet; his works include *The Art of Thomas Hardy* (London: E. Mathews, 1894), *Poems* (London: E. Mathews, 1895), and *Ireland and Other Poems* (London: E. Mathews, 1897).

38. Finn MacCool was a warrior-hero of the Fianna; his exploits are recorded in the Fenian Cycle of Irish myth; Oisin was the son of Finn MacCool and reputed to be a great poet; Amergin was a son of Milesius and, like Oisin, a warrior and poet.

Irish National Literature, IV: A List of the Best Irish Books

1. Yeats is probably referring to *The Best Hundred Irish Books,* originally printed in *The Freeman's Journal* and reprinted as a separate pamphlet in Dublin, 1886.

2. *"the same law for the lion and the ox is oppression":* William Blake at the end of "The Marriage of Heaven and Hell" (*The Complete Writings of William Blake,* 3 vols., ed. Geoffrey Keynes [London: Nonesuch Press, 1925]), writes: "One Law for the Lion & Ox is Oppression" (vol. 1, 195).

3. For William Allingham, see "Poems by Miss Tynan," note 3.

4. William Carleton (1794–1869) wrote novels and stories of Irish peasant life; early in his career, Yeats greatly admired Carleton. See his articles on William Carleton, pp. 298–301, 312–13.

5. Yeats refers to the introduction to Edward Dowden's *New Studies in Literature* (London, 1895). The twelve-year-old version of this introduction has not been traced. The 1895 version does not read as Yeats quotes. In it Dowden said, "Let the Irish prose writer show that he can be patient, exact, just, enlightened, and he will have done better service for Ireland, whether he treats of Irish themes or not, than if he wore shamrocks in all his buttonholes and had his mouth for ever filled with the glories of Brian the Brave." Brian Boru defeated the Danes at the Battle of Clontarf in 1014.

6. Thomas William Rolleston (1857–1920), poet and translator of Irish verse; Alfred Percival Graves (1846–1931), poet; Douglas Hyde (1860–1949), poet, folklorist, translator of Irish poetry and legend; William Larminie, (1849–1920), folklorist and poet; Lionel Johnson (1867–1902), poet and member, with Yeats, of the Rhymers' Club; Richard Ashe King (1839–1932), novelist and critic; Standish O'Grady (1846–1928) translated Irish myths and published them in prose form; Katharine Tynan Hinkson (1861–1931), prolific novelist and poet; Jane Barlow (1857–1917), poet and novelist; Emily Lawless (1845–1913), novelist and poet.

7. *Dublin Verses. By Members of Trinity College* (London, 1895), edited by Henry Hinkson, Katharine Tynan's husband.
8. Founded in 1866 in Dublin, Alexandra College was a school for women.
9. William Edward Hartpole Lecky (1838–1903) published his *History of England in the 18th Century* (8 vols., 1878–90). Five of the volumes concern Ireland.
10. Robert Burns (1759–96), Scottish poet; Sir Walter Scott (1771–1832), Scottish novelist.
11. See Yeats's *A Book of Irish Verse* (London: Methuen, 1895), pp. 242–45, for this anonymous poem. It is described as "from an Irish keen" (242).
12. *United Ireland* did so on 17 August 1895.
13. Yeats and AE were fellow students at the Metropolitan School of Art in Dublin.
14. D. F. Hannigan, a critic of Yeats's previous list of the best Irish books, had complained that six out of thirty books on the list were by Standish O'Grady.
15. *John Doe* was the result of a collaboration between John and Michael Banim.
16. *Tales of the Irish Fairies:* Yeats probably meant *Tales of the Fairies and of the Ghost World, Collected from Oral Tradition in Southwest Munster,* 1895.
17. This is Yeats's own compilation.
18. *Red Hugh's Captivity* was reprinted in 1897 as *The Flight of the Eagle.* Yeats reviewed it in *The Bookman* of August 1897 (see "Mr. Standish O'Grady's *The Flight of the Eagle,*" pp. 342–45).
19. George Edward Woodberry (1855–1930), American professor, poet, and critic.
20. This volume appeared in 1900 as *A Treasury of Irish Poetry in the English Tongue,* edited by S. A. Brooke and T. W. Rolleston. Yeats contributed several biographical introductions to it.
21. This book appeared in an English translation by Richard Irvine Best as *The Irish Mythological Cycle and Celtic Mythology* (Dublin: Hodges, Figgis, & Co., 1903). The author's name should read "de Jubainville."

The Life of Patrick Sarsfield

1. For Standish James O'Grady, see "Bardic Ireland," note 2. Yeats is here referring to O'Grady's *History of Ireland* (2 vols., 1878, 1880).
2. For Cromwell, see "Irish National Literature, II," note 8.
3. Thomas Carlyle (1795–1881), *Oliver Cromwell's Letters and Speeches with Elucidations* (4 vols., 1845). Carlyle writes:

> There goes a wild story, which owes its first place in History to Clarendon, I think, who is the author of many such: How the Parliament at one time had decided to "exterminate" all the Irish population; and then, finding this would not quite answer, had contented itself with packing them all off into the Province of Connaught, there to live upon the moorlands; and so had pacified the Sister Ireland (*Oliver Cromwell's Letters and Speeches with Elucidations* [London: Chapman and Hall, 1897], vol. 2, p. 165).

Carlyle calls this the "Curse of Cromwell" and notes that it "is the only Gospel of that kind that I can yet discover to have ever been fairly afoot

there" (vol. 2, 168). Colloquially, the "Curse of Cromwell" is known as the phrase "to hell or Connacht."
4. "Fenians" was a popular name for members of the Irish Republican Brotherhood. See "An Irish Patriot," note 1.
5. Thomas Babington Macaulay (1800–59) in his *History of England;* James Anthony Froude (1818–94) in his *The English in Ireland in the Eighteenth Century.*
6. *half armed:* "half-armed" in Todhunter (61).
7. Todhunter wrote "outnumbered by about three to one" (63).
8. *"in civil affairs" by giving out "many orders":* the "friend" Yeats cites as Todhunter's source is identified as Colonel O'Kelly (author of *Macariae Excidum*) (42). Todhunter writes, "Sarsfield also, he [O'Kelly] says, 'gave out many orders' interfering with civil affairs" (121).
9. *so . . . him.:* Todhunter cites O'Kelly, writing "For he was so easy that he would not deny signing any paper that was laid before him" (121).
10. Sarsfield was involved in the abduction of Ann Siderfin by Robert Clifford in May 1682. In March of 1682, Sarsfield himself abducted Elizabeth Herbert, the widow of Lord Herbert of Cherbury. See Piers Wauchope, *Patrick Sarsfield and the Williamite War* (Dublin: Irish Academic Press, 1992), pp. 22–27.

The Chain of Gold

1. For Cuchulain, see "Bardic Ireland," note 13.
2. O'Grady's full title was *Lost on Du Corrig or 'Twixt earth and ocean* (London: Cassel and Company, 1894).
3. *Crusoe:* Robinson Crusoe is the main character of Daniel Defoe's novel of the same title, published in 1719.
4. For Finn MacCool and Oisin, see "Bardic Ireland," note 13.

William Carleton

1. *Milton,* book 2, plate 40, vol. 1, p. 512, in *The Poetical Works of William Blake,* edited by Edwin J. Ellis, London, 1906:

> When on the highest lift of his [the lark's] light pinions he arrives
> At that bright Gate, another Lark meets him, and back to back
> They touch their pinions, tip tip, and each descend
> To their respective Earths, and there all night consult with Angels . . .

2. For Percy Bysshe Shelley and William Wordsworth, see "The Poetry of R. D. Joyce," note 1.
3. For Standish James O'Grady (1846–1928), see "Bardic Ireland," note 2.
4. Carleton's most famous collection was *Traits and Stories of the Irish Peasantry,* first series in 1830, second series in 1833.
5. Maria Edgeworth (1767–1849) titled her novel *Castle Rackrent* (1800). The peasant narrator Yeats is referring to is Thady Quirk, who ends up in possession of the Anglo-Irish Big House by the end of the story.
6. Gaelic scholones were educated Irish bards, scholars who schooled their pupils in a body of classical learning as well as Irish history, law, and the complicated craft of bardic poetry.
7. *"was unrivaled" . . . inexhaustible:* Carleton writes "As a narrator of old

tales, legends, and historical anecdotes he was unrivalled, and his stock of them inexhaustible" (vol. 1, 6).

8. *ranns:* Irish for a verse or stanza.

9. *"round . . . horsewhip":* See Carleton, vol. 1, p. 62.

10. In Carleton, this passage reads "most exquisite of human voices. In her early life, I have often been told by those who had heard her sing . . ." (vol. 1, 7).

11. *family had:* Carleton reads "family, however, had"; "friend, and others"; and "reason, she had" (vol. 1, 8).

    For Turlogh Carolan, see "Irish Fairies, Ghosts, Witches, etc.," note 11.

12. *"I think . . . songs":* In Carleton, only a phrase intervenes between this and the previous quote.

13. *keen:* from the Irish *caoine:* a cry or lament for the dead. In this passage, Carleton reads "exquisite effect, or" and "sympathy, when I assure them, that" (vol. 1, 9).

14. *the great famine:* Several successive failures of the potato crops between 1845 and 1847 caused over a million people to die of starvation or fever, and caused as many to emigrate.

15. *chapel green:* This exact phrase has not been located in Carleton (or O'Donoghue), but Yeats was no doubt thinking of the "Forth" (*fort,* or *rath*) on which local church services were held in Carleton's neighborhood, Tulnavert. See vol. 1, pp. 37–38, for a general description of these outdoor altars, and p. 51 for a specific account of Carleton falling speechlessly in love with Anne Duffy during Easter festivities.

16. In this passage, Carleton reads "fasting, and"; "slipped" instead of "stepped"; and "I am really ashamed even while writing this, of the confidence . . ." (vol. 1, 99).

17. In this passage, Carleton reads: ". . . after having stimulated myself by a fresh *pater* and *ave* [respectively, the prayers known as the "Our Father" and the "Hail Mary"], I advanced—my eyes turned up enthusiastically to heaven . . . my whole soul strong in confidence . . . I made a tremendous stride, planting my right foot exactly in the middle of the treacherous water-lily leaf, and the next moment was up to my neck in water."

18. Frances (née Johnson) Cashel Hoey (1830–1908) was the author of many novels in serial form. She is said to have collaborated on novels that appeared under the name of Edmund Yates (1831–94), who was editor of *The World* magazine, a society newspaper.

19. *The Evil Eye* (1860), *Willy Reilly and His Dear Colleen Bawn* (1854), *Parra Sastha; or, The History of Paddy-Go-Easy and His Wife Nancy* (1845).

William Blake

1. For Shelley, see "The Poetry of R. D. Joyce," note 1.

2. For Swedenborg and Boehme, see "*The Writings of William Blake,*" note 10.

3. The passage quoted here is by William Law, the commentator on *The Way to Christ Discovered and Described in the following Treatises . . .* by Jacob Behmen, Bath, Printed by S. Hazard, for T. Mills . . . Bristol, 1775, pp. 417–18. Yeats elides some of the passage; the complete version is as follows:

    The Word *Image* meaneth not only a *Creaturely Resemblance;* in which Sense *Man* is said to be the *Image* of GOD: But it signifieth also *Spiritual Substance, Birth* or *Effect* of a *Will,* wrought in and

by a *Spiritual Being* in *Power*. And *Imagination*, which we are apt erroneously to consider as only an *airy, idle*, and *impotent Faculty* of the human Mind, dealing in Fiction, and roving in Fancy or Idea, without producing any powerful or permanent Effects, is the *Magia*, or *Power* of raising and forming such *Images* or *Spiritual Substances*. Now this *Magia*, or *Imaginative Property*, which hath *Desire* for its *Root* or *Mother*, is the greatest *Power* in *Nature*; its Works cannot be hindered, for it *creates* and *substantiates* as it goes, and all things are possible to it.

This passage and more were inscribed in Yeats's handwriting in the back of Yeats's 1893 edition of *The Poems of William Blake* (YL, 30–31).

4. Boehme's *The Way to Christ* reads "These [our desires] communicate with eternity and kindle a *life* which always reaches either *Heaven* or *Hell* . . . and here lies the ground of the great efficacy of Prayer, which when it is the *Prayer* of the Heart, the prayer of faith, has a kindling and creating Power and forms or transforms the soul into everything that its desires reach after" (418).

5. From notes to "The Laocoön" (engraved about 1820). In *The Complete Writings of William Blake* (3 vols., ed. Geoffrey Keynes [London: Nonesuch Press, 1925]) Blake said, "Jesus & his apostles & Disciples were all artists . . . The Whole Business of Man is The Arts, & All Things Common . . . Christianity is Art & not Money" (vol. 3, 359–60).

6. Quoted from the introduction to the fourth chapter of Blake's *Jerusalem*:

> . . . Imagination, the real & eternal World of which this Vegetable Universe is but a faint shadow. . . . is the Holy Ghost any other than an Intellectual Fountain? (Keynes ed., III 284).

7. 1 Cor. 3:19, "The wisdom of this world is foolishness with God."

8. William Blake, *Jerusalem*, plate 91, l. 55: "I care not whether a man is Good or Evil, all that I care / Is whether he is a Wise man or a Fool. Go! Put off / Holiness / And put on Intellect."

9. Walter Pater (1839–94), critic and prose writer. Yeats is referring to Pater's *The Renaissance* (London: Macmillan, 1873). In a chapter entitled "Two Early French Stories," Pater writes the following of the Italian and French poetry of what he terms the "medieval Renaissance": "In that poetry, earthly passion, with its intimacy, its freedom, its variety—the liberty of the heart—makes itself felt" (1912 ed., 4).

10. Note on Discourse III of *The Discourses of Sir Joshua Reynolds*. Quoted on p. 328, vol. 2, of the Yeats-Ellis edition of Blake's works (see also *The Poetry and Prose of William Blake*, ed. David V. Erdman [New York: Doubleday, 1965], p. 636).

11. Samuel Palmer (1805–81) was a student of Blake. In a letter to Mrs. Alexander Gilchrist, dated 2 July 1862, Palmer writes about "taking pains": "Emerson says Genius is Patience. I should be inclined to say, Genius is Accuracy. *Talent* thinks, Genius *sees*; and what organ so accurate as sight. Blake held this strongly. His word was 'precision.' Believe me, dear Mrs. Gilchrist, Yours ever truly, S. PALMER" (*The Life and Letters of Samuel Palmer, Painter and Etcher*. Written and Edited by A. H. Palmer [London: 1892], p. 246).

12. *student of mystical*: Garnett reads "student of his mystical" (24).

13. William Hayley (1745–1820), prolific poet; his book *Ballads. Founded on . . . Animals* (1885) was illustrated by Blake.
14. Alexander Gilchrist (1828–61). Gilchrist died before his life of Blake was finished; his wife, Anne Gilchrist, finished it and it was published in 1863 as *Life of William Blake "Pictor Ignotus"* (London: Macmillan, 1863). William Michael Rossetti (see *"The Writings of William Blake,"* note 1) and his brother, Dante Gabriel Rossetti (see "A Poet We Have Neglected," note 1), helped Anne Gilchrist finish the biography.
15. *"Sampson" as a blank verse poem:* Garnett writes of "'Samson' and other short pieces in blank verse" (13).
16. *"may . . . Ossian":* Garnett writes "Blake may not improbably have been influenced by Ossian" (31). In this passage Garnett mentions only that *Thel,* and not the "Prophetic Books," as Yeats paraphrases him, "would have been a very fine poem" if written in "such blank verse as he had already produced in *Edward the Third* and *Samson.*"

An Irish Patriot

1. John O'Leary (1830–1907) was a member of the Irish Republican Brotherhood and editor of their newspaper *The Irish People.* He was sent to prison in 1885 for treasonable writing in this paper. Early in Yeats's career, it was John O'Leary who encouraged Yeats to turn his attention to Ireland.
   Fenianism (a popular name for the Irish Republican Brotherhood) grew out of the failed Young Ireland uprising of 1848 and the unrest brought about by the Great Famine. It was a secret militant movement led by James Stephens in Ireland and John Devoy in America which sought the armed overthrow of British rule in Ireland; like the Young Irelanders' insurrection of 1848, the Fenians' 1867 uprising was a failure.
2. Unionists were those who wished to maintain Ireland's legislative union with Britain (begun with the Act of Union in 1800); nationalists were those who desired that Ireland be separate from Britain both politically and culturally.
3. The Montagues and Capulets are the feuding families of William Shakespeare's tragedy *Romeo and Juliet.*
4. For Thomas Davis, see "The Poetry of Sir Samuel Ferguson—II," note 8; for Thomas Moore, see "Popular Ballad Poetry of Ireland," note 75.
5. For Clarence Mangan, see "The Poetry of Sir Samuel Ferguson—II," note 8; for William Allingham, see "The New 'Speranza'," note 3; "The Welshmen of Tirawley" is a poem by Ferguson; see "Popular Ballad Poetry of Ireland," note 66.
6. For Thomas D'Arcy McGee (1825–68), see "Some Irish National Books," note 6; Charles Kickham (1828–82) was a member of the Irish Republican Brotherhood and a main contributor to its paper, *The Irish People;* he wrote several novels, of which *Knocknagow; or, the Homes of Tipperary* (Dublin, 1873), is the most famous. For William Carleton, see "Irish Wonders," note 1, and Yeats's articles on Carleton included in this volume. For John and Michael Banim, see "Irish National Literature, I," note 15.
7. Yeats is alluding to Petra, an ancient city of southwest Jordan.
   The quote from Milton comes from *Paradise Lost,* book 3, ll. 489–91:
   . . . then might ye see
   Cowls, hoods, and habits, with their wearers, tossed
   And fluttered into rags, . . .

8. This poem is "A Patriot's Rebuke," by Lord Plunkett, archbishop of Dublin. Lady Ferguson quotes it on p. 140, vol. 2.
   Killarney is a town in southwest Ireland.
   The phrase "Kevin's bed" refers to Glendalough in Co. Wicklow. The Gap of Dunloe is a mountain pass to the west of Killarney. Blarney is a small town with a castle of the same name to the northwest of Cork in Ireland.
   Antrim is a county on the northern coast of Northern Ireland.
   The River Shannon flows southwest from Northern Ireland to the Atlantic near Limerick; it is the longest river in Ireland.
9. Ferguson's statement reads "hope and pleasure more than. . . ."; and in Lady Ferguson, this sentence ends as follows: "that I have seen for many years" (vol. 2, 141).
10. The Gaelic refrain means "O black lament."
    Ferguson reads "paths, in summer,"; "fann'd,"; and "yellow sand," (*Lays of the Western Gael*, 1865, p. 225).
11. Ferguson reads "Curl'd" and "ringletted," (*Lays*, 225).

The New Irish Library

1. See Yeats's earlier article from *The Bookman*, August 1894, "Some Irish National Books."
2. These books, in the order of mention, were as follows: *The Patriot Parliament*, edited by Thomas Davis, a collection of historical documents from 1689; *The New Spirit of the Nation* (1894), edited by Martin McDermott; and *A Parish Providence* (1894) by "E. M. Lynch," actually a translation of Balzac's *Le Médecin de campagne*. The Davis volume had been the first in the New Irish Library series. Yeats had given a bad review to both the Balzac translation and the McDermott volume in "Some Irish National Books," pp. 245–48.
3. There is no record of Yeats reviewing *The Irish Song Book,* but such a review may very well exist. See the reviews of "The Story of Early Gaelic Literature" and "The Life of Patrick Sarsfield."
4. For Jonathan Swift, see "A Reckless Century," note 10.
5. *"to bring again the golden age":* This exact phrase has not been found in Blake, but in "A Vision of the Last Judgment," *Writings of William Blake* (edited by Geoffrey Keynes, 1925), Blake writes, "The Nature of my Work is Visionary or imaginative; it is an Endeavor to Restore what the Ancients call'd the Golden Age" (vol. 3, 146).
6. *"the century of philosophers":* Yeats is referring to the eighteenth century. By "the century of poets," Yeats presumably meant the seventeenth century.
7. Sir Thomas Browne (1605–82) wrote widely on philosophy and natural history. His most famous book was *Religio Medici* (1642).
8. Max Simon Nordau (1849–1923) had attempted to prove in *Entartung* (1892; English translation, *Degeneration*, 1895) a relationship between genius and degeneracy.
9. *"the literary consciousness":* Untraced.
10. *persists . . . Macaulay:* On pp. 96–100, Duffy apologizes for Davis as a poet, and does quote "Fontenoy" (100), but praises "his singular fertility" (100) and his "spontaneous gush of natural feeling in unstudied words"

(98) rather than his "greatness" as a poet. Thomas Babington Macaulay (1800–59) was a politician, historian, and author of *The History of England from the Accession of James II* (5 vols., 1849–61). In the comparison of Thomas Davis and Macaulay, Yeats is probably referring to the poems in *The Lays of Ancient Rome* (1842).

William Carleton

1. *William Blake.... symbols of her art:* This passage copies verbatim half of the first paragraph of an earlier review of *The Life of William Carleton,* published in *The Bookman,* March 1896. See the earlier article on Carleton, "William Carleton," pp. 298–301, for the relevant notes on this passage.
2. *William Carleton ... anew:* This continues the passage noted above that Yeats copied from his first review. While here Yeats begins a new paragraph, the earlier review did not, and it read "Carleton, on the other hand, ..." ("William Carleton," p. 299). See "William Carleton," pp. 298–301, for the relevant notes on this passage.
3. *Miss Edgeworth ... the quarryman:* This passage is copied verbatim from the last paragraph of an article on Irish literature that Yeats had done for *The Bookman,* July 1895. See "Irish National Literature, I: From Callanan to Carleton," pp. 263–67, for the relevant notes to this passage.

Greek Folk Poesy

1. *"recordations":* Glennie reads "the Recordations, or Historiography" (23).
2. *"the general conflict theory,":* Glennie, "The Science of Folk-lore": "this Conflict Theory of the Origins of Civilisation" (11).
3. *"civilised" ... leisure to make:* Yeats is summarizing "The Science of Folk-lore," which includes the phrase "progressive Societies, or, in a word, of Civilisation" (8); and connects "wealth and leisure" to "intellectual work" and "the institution of regularly recurring Religious Festivals—the discovery of the Year" (10–11).
4. *"at the very ... evidence":* Glennie, "The Science of Folk-lore," reads: "in the very earliest ages to which anthropological evidence goes back we find ..." (5).
   "at least two different or ... Primitive Man": Glennie reads: "at least two different, or intellectually unequal Species, or Races of Primitive Man" (5).
   "whites differ from blacks.": Glennie reads "Whites now differ from Blacks" (5).
5. Max Müller (1823–1900) was a German philologist and Orientalist. His major work was his edition of *Sacred Books of the East* (Oxford: Clarendon Press, 1879), a fifty-one-volume collection of Oriental non-Christian religious writings.
   Andrew Lang (1844–1912), Scottish scholar and author known for his folklore studies, translations of Homer (see below, note 8), collections of fairy tales, and his poetry.
6. *definition of religion ... matter of conduct:* On p. 31 (section 2, paragraph 5c of "The Science of Folk-lore"), Glennie defines "RELIGION, as, in its

individual reference, *The Ideal of Conduct derived from some general conception of the Environments of Existence;* and, in its social reference, *the Observances in which Environments—conceptions, determined in their forms by the conditions of the interaction between Higher and Lower Social Elements, are authoritatively expressed."*

7. *"Zoonist" is not English . . . moral ideas"*: On pp. 24–25 (section 2, paragraph 3c of "The Science of Folk-lore"), Glennie "would suggest that such technical limitations be given to the terms *Idylls* and *Tales, Songs* and *Stories,* and *Ballads* and *Legends,* that they should be understood as signifying respectively Verser—and Prose—expressions of predominantly Kosmical Ideas, predominantly Moral Notions, and predominantly Historical Memories." In the chart that follows this quote, Glennie includes as his first subspecies of *"Idylls* and *Tales"* expressing "Kosmical Ideas" those that are "Zoonist."

8. Charles Marie René Leconte de Lisle (1818–94), *Homère. L'Iliade; traduction nouvelle par Leconte de Lisle* (Paris: A. Lemerre, 1867); *Homère. L'Odyssée. traduction nouvelle par Leconte de Lisle* (Paris: A. Lemerre, 1867); *Eschyle; traduction nouvelle* (Paris: A. Lemerre, 1872). Pierre Flottes, in his *Leconte de Lisle, l'homme et l'oeuvre* (Paris: Hatier-Boivin, 1954), does not list a translation of Virgil in his bibliography of Leconte de Lisle's translations (155). Samuel Henry Butcher (1850–1910) and Andrew Lang (1844–1912), *The Odyssey of Homer* (London: Macmillan, 1879); Andrew Lang and Walter Leaf (1852–1927) and Ernest Myers (1844–1921), *The Iliad of Homer Done into English Prose* (London: Macmillan, 1882); Andrew Lang, *Theocritus, Bion, and Moschus, Rendered into English Prose: with an Introductory Essay* (8 vols., London: Macmillan, 1880).

   The Bard of the Dimbovitza, Roumanian Folk-Songs, second series (1894), gathered by Elena Vacarescu and translated by Carmen Sylva and Alma Strettel (London: J. R. Osgood, McIvaine and Co., 1894). Carmen Sylva was the pseudonym for Elizabeth, queen of Romania (1843–1916).

9. In "DISTICHS.," number IV, Garnett reads "answer: 'Have . . .'" and "'dear Heart!'" (129).

10. *thee and me,:* Glennie, p. 255, in "The HEGOUMENOS AND THE VLACH GIRL" reads "me." as the final line of the poem.

11. Douglas Hyde, *Beside the Fire: A Collection of Irish Gaelic Folk Stories* (London: David Nutt, 1910) reads "And why did you bring away my gold that I was for five hundred years gathering throughout the hills and hollows of the world" (77).

12. Douglas Hyde, *Love Songs of Connacht* (London: T. Fisher Unwin, 1893/Dublin: Gill and Son, 1893); this passage, from the prose translation of "My Love, Oh, She is My Love" should read: "She is my treasure, Oh, she is my treasure, The woman of the grey (?) eye (she) like the rose, A woman who would not place a hand beneath my head, A woman who would not be with me for gold. She is my affection, Oh! she is my affection, The woman who left no strength in me; A woman who would not breathe a sigh after me, A woman who would not raise a stone at my tomb. She is my secret love, Oh! she is my secret love, A woman who tells us (*i.e.,* me) nothing; . . . A woman who does not remember me to be out, A woman who would not cry at the hour of my death . . ." (135–36).

13. *"Take which . . . watch"*: P. 15 of "AT THE HOUSE" in *The Bard of Dimbovitza* reads:

Take which soever way thou wilt, for ways are all alike;
But do thou only come—I bade my threshold wait the coming.
From out my window one can see the graves—and on my life
The graves, too, keep a watch.

14. For Edward Walsh and Jeremiah (or James) Joseph Callanan, see "Popular Ballad Poetry of Ireland," note 19. See also this same article for Yeats's evaluation of other Young Ireland writers.

The Well at the World's End

1. For Shelley, see "The Poetry of R. D. Joyce," note 1.
2. In Greek legend, Phryxus and his sister Helle, with the help of the sea goddess Ino, flee their father on a flying ram with a golden fleece. Jason and the Argonauts (with the help of Medea) later recover the golden fleece from King Ates in Colchis, at the eastern end of the Black Sea, so Jason can recover his kingdom from his uncle Pelias.

   The happy islands, known also as the Islands of the Blessed and as the Hesperides, were at the end of the world in the west. The great dead heroes of Greek mythology resided here, having been made immortal by the gods.
3. *and said,:* Morris reads "and said:" (vol. 1, 40).
4. *smiled and said,:* Morris reads "smiled, and said" (vol. 1, 40).
5. In this sentence, "if ye" and "blessing but" (vol. 2, 43). The Sage of Swevenham tells this to Ralph, the hero, and Ursula, his companion.
6. Sigurd is the hero who, in the Germanic saga of the Volsungs, slays the dragon, Fafnir; William Morris's translation of the Old Norse saga *Sigurd the Volsung* was published in 1876. Gudrun is the daughter of the king of the Nibelungens and the wife of Sigurd. In Arthurian legend, Guinevere is the wife of King Arthur and the mistress of the knight Lancelot.
7. Jan van Ruysbroeck (1293–1381), Flemish mystic. Maurice Maeterlinck translated his *Die Geestelike Brulocht* into French (*L'Ornement des noces spirituelles,* 1891), and a translation of selections of this work appeared in London, 1894, as *The Adornment of the Spiritual Marriage.*

   "I must rejoice . . . at my joy": Yeats's source for this quotation was the epigraph on the title page of Joris Karl Huysmans's *A Rebours* (Paris, 1884): "Il faut que je me réjouisse au-dessus du temps . . . , quoique le monde ait horreur de ma joie, et que sa grossièreté, ne sache pas ce que je veux dire."
8. Hammersmith is a borough of Greater London in England. Morris's home, Kelmscott House, was in the borough of Hammersmith. See *Au,* 130ff.
9. The statements of Morris refer to John Keats (1795–1821), English Romantic poet; Geoffrey Chaucer (ca. 1340–1400), Middle English poet and author of *The Canterbury Tales* (1386–1400); Italian poet Dante Alighieri (1265–1321); and John Milton (1608–74), author of the epic poem *Paradise Lost* (1667).

Miss Fiona Macleod as a Poet

1. By "nature poets," perhaps Yeats means those among the Romantics who focused on the spiritual connections between man and nature. The "realists" were those writers who attempted to document accurately the various aspects of ordinary life in their novels without exaggeration or idealism.

make our work a mirror: Percy Bysshe Shelley (1792–1822) in the peroration of his "Defence of Poetry" called poets "the mirrors of the gigantic shadows which futurity casts upon the present" (*The Complete Works of Percy Bysshe Shelley,* ed. Roger Ingpen and Walter E. Peck. [London: Ernest and Benn Ltd., 1930], vol. 2, p. 140).

2. *". . . criticism upon life":* A phrase from Matthew Arnold; see "The Poetry of Sir Samuel Ferguson—I," note 10.

3. *"Prayer of Women":* Yeats shortened this poem by twenty-three lines.

4. In this stanza, Sharp reads "hills" and "eyes," (75), followed by lines which Yeats omits.

5. In this stanza, Sharp reads "lips straightened"; "as a barren hill"; and "condemneth him—" (75), followed by lines which Yeats omits.

6. In this stanza, Sharp reads "O Spirit, and the Nine Angels"; "Son, and"; "milk,"; and "Compassionate!" (76).

7. Yeats here quotes phrases out of context, and, by doing so, distorts the poem "The White Peace":

It lies not on the sunlit hill
Nor on the sunlit plain:
Nor ever on any running stream
Nor on the unclouded main—
But sometimes, through the Soul of Man,
Slow moving o'er his pain,
The moonlight of a perfect peace
Floods heart and brain.

8. These passages from "The Rune of the Four Winds" are as follows in Sharp:

By the four white winds of the world,
Whose father the golden Sun is,
Whose mother the wheeling Moon is,
The North and the South and the East and the West: . . . (88)

and,

By the three dark winds of the world;
The chill dull [Yeats omitted "dull"] breath of the Grave,
The breath from the depths ["depth" in Yeats] of the Sea,
The breath of To-morrow: . . . (89).

9. *The Sin-Eater* (Edinburgh: P. Geddes, 1895) and *The Washer of the Ford* (Edinburgh: P. Geddes, 1896) are two of Sharp's collections of Celtic legends.

10. In this stanza from "In the Shadow," Sharp reads "She has"; "hand:"; "sand:"; 'foam." (followed by a stanza break); "rises there"; "outer dark"; and "fair:" (12).

Young Ireland

1. *Rebellion of 1848:* The Young Ireland leaders staged an uprising in the summer of 1848. It was a failure and by autumn of the same year, most of the leaders—William Smith O'Brien, Gavan Duffy, John Blake Dillon,

Thomas Francis Meagher, and John Mitchel—were in prison or in exile.
2. *Young Ireland* (London: Casell, Petter, Galpin & Co) appeared in two volumes (1880–83). An "Irish People's Edition" (Dublin: Gill) appeared in 1884–87. *A Final Edition of Young Ireland* (London: T. Fisher Unwin) was published in 1896.
3. *"racy of the soil"*: See "Dr. Todhunter's Irish Poems," note 12.
4. Daniel Owen Madden (1815–59)—Duffy spelled it "Maddyn" in *Young Ireland*—was the author of *The Age of Pitt and Fox* (London: T. C. Newby, 1846) and *Ireland and Her Rulers; since 1829* (London: T. C. Newby, 1843).

   In the chapter "Young Ireland at Work," Duffy writes: "To the positive teaching of facts and principles Davis constantly longed to add the subtler teaching of the dramatic poet and the painter of the past in fiction. Irish history is full of picturesque incidents and strong characters: it blends with the career of Spain, Austria, and France, at great epochs, and in later times of America and Asia, and he believed it contained inspiration certain to move an artist who came in contact with it. To Madden he wrote:

   'Have you ever tried dramatic writing? Do you know Taylor's "Philip Van Artevelde", and Griffin's "Gisippus"? I think them the two best serious dramas written in English since Shakespeare's time. A drama equal to either of them on an Irish subject would be useful and popular to an extent you can hardly suppose. . . . Ireland is really ripening, that is my chief pleasure. I have too many pursuits to enjoy any of them very keenly, save for an hour of exultation now and then" (131).
5. Sir Henry Taylor (1800–86) published *Philip van Artevelde, a Dramatic Romance in two parts* (London: E. Moxon) in 1834. *Gisippus,* by Gerald Griffin (1803–40), was produced at Drury Lane in 1842.
6. *with an Irish subject:* Duffy reads "on an Irish subject" (vol. 1, 131).
7. The Library of Ireland was a series of books written mainly by the Young Irelanders and published by James Duffy (1809–71) in the later 1840s. The series included collections of poetry and songs, biographical sketches of writers and historical figures, and essays. William Carleton was one of the better known novelists published in the series. The series was cheaply produced and sold for about a shilling; eventually over twenty volumes were issued.
8. In his introduction to *The Treasure of the Humble* (London: George Allen, 1897), A. B. Walkley quotes Maeterlinck as saying, "mystic truths have over ordinary truths a strange privilege; they can neither age nor die" (11). This quote, however, does not appear in the text of the book.
9. In 1893 Yeats had reviewed *The Poems of Arthur Henry Hallam, together with His Essay on the Lyrical Poems of Alfred Tennyson* (London: Elkin Mathews and John Lane, 1893). (See "A Bundle of Poets," pp. 200–204.) Hallam's essay on the early poems of Tennyson became for Yeats a major critical text, and he often quoted Hallam throughout the nineties.

   those heterogeneous . . . immoral of lives: In his essay on Tennyson in *Poems of Arthur Henry Hallam,* Hallam writes: "Minds of this description are especially liable to moral temptations. . . . But it is obvious that, critically speaking, such temptations are of slight moment. Not the gross and evident passions of our nature, but the elevated and less separable desires are the dangerous enemies which misguide the poetic spirit in its attempts at self-cultivation. That delicate sense of fitness, which grows with the growth of artistic feelings, and strengthens with their strength, until it acquires a celerity and weight of decision hardly inferior to the correspondent judgements of conscience, is weakened by every indulgence of heterogeneous aspirations, however pure they may be, however lofty, however suitable to human nature" (96).

10. *The Spirit of the Nation* (Dublin: James Duffy) was the collection of patriotic poetry edited by Thomas Davis (1814–45) and first published in 1843. Yeats had written an appreciation of James Clarence Mangan (1803–49) in 1887 (see "Clarence Mangan," pp. 39–44). See his letter to John Quinn in 1905 (in *L,* 447) for his later reassessment of the poet.

Mangan's titles are "Dark Rosaleen" and "O'Hussey's Ode to the Maguire." The latter poem was not written for *The Nation* but for *The Dublin University Magazine.* It did not appear in that periodical but appeared instead in *Specimens of the Early Native Poetry of Ireland,* ed. Henry R. Montgomery (Dublin: James McGlashan, 1846). O'Hussey (Eochaidh Ó hEódhasa) (ca. 1570–ca. 1617) was chief poet to the Maguire clan. His "Ode to the Maguire" describes Maguire's participation in Hugh O'Neill's march to Kinsale in the winter 1599–1600, where Maguire was killed.

Mr. John O'Leary

1. For Thomas Davis, see "The Poetry of Sir Samuel Ferguson—II," note 8.
2. Yeats recounts this same anecdote, translated into French, in *"Le Mouvement Celtique:* II. M. John O'Leary," pp. 413–14.
3. Yeats quotes this saying of O'Leary's in his *Autobiographies* as an example of O'Leary's gift for saying "things that would have sounded well in some heroic Elizabethan play. 'There are things that a man must not do to save a nation.' He would speak a sentence like that in ignorance of its passionate value, and would forget it the moment after" (*Au,* 101).
4. Young Ireland societies were those that continued to carry on the cultural nationalist goals of the Young Ireland movement of the 1840s; they were still active in 1890s Ireland.
5. In his *Recollections,* O'Leary writes: "Sometime in the year 1846, while recovering from a fever, I came across the poems and essays of Thomas Davis, then recently died. . . . What he was then to me I feel as if I can only faintly shadow forth at this distance of time. Perhaps it may give some notion of the effect produced on me to say that I then went through a process analogous to what certain classes of Christians call 'conversion.' I can but vaguely remember my unregenerate state" (2–3).
6. Thomas Francis Meagher (1823–67) was a Young Irelander tried for revolutionary activities in 1848, sentenced to death, reprieved, and transported to Van Diemen's Land; he escaped to America, where he became a brigadier general in the Civil War. He was drowned in the Missouri River while on his way to become temporary governor in the territory of Montana.

In *Recollections of Fenians and Fenianism* (New York: Barnes and Noble, 1969), O'Leary writes "And here came in, if not the comic, what I have called the untragic side of things. Somehow people did not believe that the capital sentences were at all likely to be carried out, and so when Meagher, in an otherwise effective and even eloquent speech, went on to speak of his young life, his early death, and the rest of it, I could not help

feeling, despite my strong sympathy, as if a certain air of unreality were creeping in upon the scene" (20). O'Leary begins his description of the thwarted rescue on p. 20.
7. The Fenians were members of the Irish Republican Brotherhood, an organization founded principally by James Stephens (1825–1901) in Dublin in 1858. The movement advocated violence in its aim to make Ireland an independent republic.

Mr. Arthur Symons' New Book

1. This quotation is from Symons's foreword to this book (p. vii) and echoes the subtitle of W. H. Pater's *Marius the Epicurean, His Sensations and Ideas* (London: Macmillan, 1885).
2. The four sections can be translated as follows: "Love's Victim," "Love's Exile," "Triumphant Love," and "Victim of the World."
3. The sentence in Symons's foreword reads "Each poem is, I hope, able to stand alone, but no poem has been included without reference to the general scheme of the book, the general psychology of the imaginary hero" (vii).
4. Alfred Tennyson (1809–92) and Robert Browning (1812–89), two of the most famous poets of the Victorian era. See Yeats's review of Tennyson's poems in "The Death of Oenone," pp. 189–92.
5. For Andrew Lang, see "Greek Folk Poesy," note 5. His works of poetry include *Border Ballads* (London, 1895). Henry Austin Dobson (1840–1921), English author, was known for his light verse and imitation of French forms like the rondeau; titles of his collections include *Vignettes in Rhyme* (1873) and *Proverbs in Porcelain* (1897). Sir Edmund William Gosse (1849–1928), English poet and critic, was known for his ties to the Pre-Raphaelites. Robert Seymour Bridges (1844–1930), English poet and playwright known for his metrical experimentation and use of simple diction. Francis Thompson (1859–1907), English poet who is remembered for his popular religious poems such as "The Hound of Heaven" and "The Kingdom of God." William Ernest Henley (1849–1903), English author and editor. As a poet, he wrote ballads and impressionistic verse; some of his poems strike a decidedly patriotic note. As editor of *The Scots Observer,* later *The National Observer,* he published, among others, Yeats, Thomas Hardy, Rudyard Kipling, and H. G. Wells. For Lionel Pigot Johnson, see the introduction to "Mr. Lionel Johnson's Poems" in this collection. Yeats had mentioned the Scottish poet John Davidson in an earlier review of Symons's work; see "That Subtle Shade," note 6. Richard Le Gallienne (1866–1947), English author and critic, was a member of the Rhymers' Club with Yeats and Lionel Johnson. His verse includes *A Jongleur Strayed, Verses on Love and Other Matters Sacred and Profane;* William Watson (1858–1935), English poet; his poems include *Lyric Love* (London: 1892).
6. *Silhouettes* (London: Leonard Smithers, 1892) and *London Nights* (London: Leonard Smithers, 1895) are two of Symons's earlier volumes of poetry.
7. The Luxembourg Gardens are in Paris, on the Left Bank.
8. "The Wanderers," pp. 34–35, is a poem in the collection Yeats is reviewing.
9. This poem appears on p. 24 under the heading "Décor de Théâtre" in Symons's previous collection *London Nights.*
10. In these lines from "The Wanderers," Symons reads "world, and all"; and

"Theirs, because," (34). Yeats begins the quotations at the poem's eighteenth line.

11. The poem "Javanese Dancers" is from *Silhouettes* (London: Leonard Smithers, 1896).
12. The last section and last poem of the collection, "Mundi Victima," appear on pp. 55–72 of *Amoris Victima*.
13. *Even in our love . . . slackening:* This excerpt starts at the twelfth line of the seventh stanza of "Mundi Victima" (65).

Miss Fiona Macleod

1. By "the last age of the world," Yeats is referring to the Victorian age. For a note on the phrase "criticism of life," see "The Poetry of Sir Samuel Ferguson—I," note 10.
2. Robert Louis Stevenson (1850–94), Scottish author; Yeats may be referring to the work that made Stevenson famous, *Treasure Island* (1883). Rudyard Kipling (1865–1936), English author. The "barbarous life" to which Yeats refers is from Kipling's accounts and stories of life in colonial India.
3. The Highlands are the mountainous northern area of Scotland.
4. Macleod's titles are *Pharais, a Romance of the Isles* (1894) and *The Mountain Lovers* (1895).
5. Yeats had visited the Aran Islands (three islands located off the west coast of Ireland) the previous year in search of material for his unfinished novel, *The Speckled Bird*.
6. One commonly held theory is that the Gaelic-speaking people of Scotland emigrated there from Ireland in prehistoric times. At one point, Ireland and Scotland are divided by only twelve miles of sea.
7. St. Colum, also known as St. Columba (521–97), was an Irish missionary. The tale Yeats is referring to is "The Dark Nameless One."
8. Sharp reads "aloud, the"; "seal, lying"; "rock, with"; "'O Ròn,' he said with the good kind courteousness that was his"; and "seal, 'A bad . . .'" instead of "sea. 'A bad . . .'" (124). As Sharp here translates, the phrase "Droch spadadh ort" means "a bad end to you."
9. In this paragraph, Sharp reads "Gown."; "evil pagan faith of the North" is most likely a reference to the pagan Norsemen and Norse mythology; "north"; "known ever"; "Saint, and": Sharp reads "'Saint; and'" (124).
   Picts and wanton Normen: Sharp reads "Picts and the wanton Normen" (124). The Picts are one of the early groups of settlers of North Britain; they were absorbed by the Scots between the sixth and ninth centuries. The Normen are the Norsemen, one of the ancient Scandinavian peoples.
10. In this paragraph, Sharp reads "God knows it"; "you, I, or"; "'Well, well,'" (124).
    Druid here appears to be used synonymously with "Priest." The seal is asking whether Colum is a pagan or Christian; legend has it that St. Columba was originally taught by Druids before converting to Christianity.
11. In this paragraph, Sharp reads "At this, Colum"; "while. Then"; "it, will"; "north"; "Now I" (125).
    Odrum the Pagan: The paragraph immediately following in Sharp explains this name: "Well, I am not denying it, Colum. And what is more, I am Angus MacOdrum, Aonghas mac Torcall mhic Odrum, and the name

I am known by is Black Angus" (*The Sin-Eater and The Washer of the Ford*, New York, 1910, p. 268).

Later in the story the name is given more clearly to Colum: "His body is the body of Angus the son of Torcall of the race of Odrum, for all that a seal he is the seeming; but the soul of him is Judas" (271).

12. She is not called Lilith by name but "Adam's first wife" (127), who in Jewish folklore is known as Lilith.

13. *"The Dan-nan-Ròn"*: Song of the Seal. Sharp's collection *The Dominion of Dreams* (New York: Duffield and Co., 1910) contains the tale "The Dan-nan-Ròn," pp. 299–344, which as Yeats says, tells the story of a man "descended from the seals."

14. Actually, *The Treasure of the Humble* (London: George Allen and Unwin, 1897), which Yeats reviewed in *The Bookman* issue of July 1897 (see "The Treasure of the Humble," the following piece in this collection).

The Treasure of the Humble

1. Yeats may be referring to such nineteenth-century philosophers as Auguste Comte (1798–1857), whose philosophy of Positivism proposed that positive knowledge was that which was derived from empirical experience, or John Stuart Mill (1806–73), who applied the methodology of physical science to the social sciences.

2. Yeats is once again quoting Matthew Arnold's phrase "criticism of life." See "The Poetry of Sir Samuel Ferguson—I," note 10.

3. Yeats greatly admired *Axël*, the play by Jean Marie Mathias Philippe Auguste, comte de Villiers de L'Isle-Adam (1838–1889), French novelist and dramatist. See his review of it, "A Symbolical Drama in Paris," pp. 233–37.

4. Yeats is quoting from "The Awakening of the Soul" (30–32, 33). Maeterlinck reads "verified. And truly . . ."; "in the work-a-day"; "the very humblest"; "men, spiritual"; "mysterious, direct working," (33).

5. Yeats is quoting here from "The Star" (136–37). Maeterlinck reads "Of what avail" and "ego" with no italics (136).

6. Alfred Sutro (1863–1933) was a well-known translator of his day; he also translated Maeterlinck's *Aglavaine and Selysette*, which Yeats reviewed in the September 1897 *Bookman* (see pp. 349–51). Despite his scolding here of Arthur Bingham Walkley (1855–1926), the influential drama critic for *The Star* and *The Times*, Yeats came eventually to value him among his converts to his ideas about drama. In 1902 Walkley again aroused Yeats, when in a review of Gordon Bottomely's *The Crier by Night*, he attributed the production's "completely stupid insolence towards the playhouse and its audience" to the influence of Yeats "and his foolish friends." "The insolence . . . is our wicked defiance," Yeats wrote to Lady Gregory. "I sent him a copy of 'Samhain'" (*CL3*, 271).

Walkley's enthusiastic and sympathetic article about the Irish National Theatre Society's performance in May 1903 (reprinted in *Drama and Life*, New York, 1908) pleased Yeats greatly. In *Samhain* for September 1903, he cited Walkley's "subtle and eloquent words," and he alluded to them in speaking before American audiences in 1904 and later in his letter on the Irish National Theatre to *The Times* of 16 June 1910.

7. *story . . . windows*: On p. ix, Walkley writes "Reversing the course presented by Mr. Squeers for his pupils, M. Maeterlinck, having cleaned w-i-n-d-e-r, winder, now goes and spells it. He began by visualizing and synthesizing his

ideas of like; here you shall find him trying to analyse these ideas and consumed with anxiety to tell us the truth that is in him." The "course" Walkley accuses Maeterlinck of reversing is described in Charles Dickens's *Nicholas Nickleby*, chapter 8, by Mr. Squeers: "We go upon the practical mode of teaching, Nickleby; the regular education system. . . . W-i-n, win, d-e-r, der, winder, a casement. When the boy knows this out of the book, he goes and does it."

8. Samuel Johnson (1709–84). Walkely also uses a quote from Johnson in his introduction (15). Yeats is thus drawing an implicit comparison between Maeterlinck's work and Thomas à Kempis's (1380–1471) spiritual masterpiece, *The Imitation of Christ*.

Mr. Standish O'Grady's *Flight of the Eagle*

1. For W. E. H. Lecky, see "Irish National Literature, II," note 22.
2. *"something other than human life":* In his "Public Address," Blake writes: "Houses of Commons & Houses of Lords appear to me to be fools; they seem to me to be something Else besides Human Life" (*Writings,* ed. Keynes, 1925, vol. 3, p. 134).
3. Sir John Perrot (?1527–92) was president of Munster from 1570 to 1573, and lord deputy of Ireland from 1584 to 1588. He was found guilty of high treason and died in the Tower of London in 1592.
4. *"not less true than proud":* Says O'Grady, "It was a proud speech, and not less true than proud" (4).
5. *one, Feagh MacHugh . . . world:* O'Grady is less absolute than Yeats, saying, on one hand, that Feagh's "Irish captaincy, with its unique privileges and powers, lean against the law too, no Government, not even Perrot's, had been able to cut off" (150). On the other hand, he writes, "He came to Dublin in Court attire, and with the Lady Rose and his sons, mingled from time to time in such society as then surrounded Irish viceroys."

   O'Grady describes Feagh MacHugh as "the chief of South Wicklow and North Wexford. He was a man grown old in wars against the Government, and all the friends of the Government; a wild Ishmael of that wild region, who made war or peace at his pleasure" (128).

   The son Yeats refers to was probably "the Brown Geraldine," Feagh MacHugh's son-in-law. O'Grady explains the confusion: "The two are famous Elizabethan men—Turlough, eldest of Feagh's sons, a man of heroic qualities, and Walker of Ballygloran, Feagh's son-in-law, commonly called the Brown Geraldine, the chieftain's right hand for all great enterprises in the lowlands" (163). In a note to p. 288, O'Grady does tell how Turlough's mother betrayed him, after "the authorities endeavoured to persuade him to betray his father. Turlough refused, and went cheerfully to his death." For Yeats, perhaps this act constitutes not budging.

   "passionately sought him": O'Grady writes, "During Perrot's Viceroyalty there had been at least two eruptions of hostages from the Castle. In one of them was brave Turlough, Feagh's eldest son. He was never retaken, though Perrot passionately sought him" (169).
6. *Pacata Hibernica* by Thomas Stafford (fl. 1633) was, according to the subtitle, "a history of the wars in Ireland during the reign of Queen Elizabeth." O'Grady's edition appeared in 1896.
7. *The Bog of Stars* (London, 1893), a book of stories and sketches of Elizabethan Ireland, appeared in the New Irish Library series in 1893.

8. Sir Felim O'Toole is Feagh MacHugh's brother-in-law and O'Grady further describes him as "Lord of Castle Kevin and Powerscourt Castle on the Dargle; lord generally of North Wicklow" (*Flight of the Eagle*, 138). O'Grady also notes that O'Toole was a friend of Red Hugh O'Donnell (see below) and was in captivity with him in Dublin (138). According to O'Grady, Art O'Toole was the "unserviceable and dissipated cousin of Felim whom the Viceroy, Sir John Perrot, 'had expelled . . . out of Powerscourt Castle, on the Dargle, and had given it to Felim'" (142).

O'Grady calls Lady O'Donnell the "Ineen-Du MacDonald, that is to say, Dark-Daughter MacDonald" (19) and he notes that she was "Scotch, scion of one of the greatest Highland families, the MacDonalds, Lords of the Isles" (18).

Sir William Fitzwilliam (1526–99) was lord deputy of Ireland from 1572 to 1575 and from 1588 to 1599.

Red Hugh O'Donnell (?1571–1602), lord of Tyrconnel, fought sometimes victoriously against the English in the 1590s, and died of poison in Spain. Red Hugh was taken hostage first in 1587 and again in 1590.

Dublin Castle was the seat of the British colonial administration of Ireland from the thirteenth century until 1922, when the Free State was formed. It is still used for government offices.
9. Herodotus (fifth century B.C.) is often called the "Father of History" because the first narrative history of the ancient world, a history of the Greco-Persian Wars, is attributed to him.
10. *too—such:* O'Grady reads "too, such" (254).
11. According to P. W. Joyce in *Old Celtic Romances,* "Slieve Fuad was the ancient name of the highest of the Fews mountains, near Newtown Hamilton, in Armagh; but the name is now lost." On pages 296–97, O'Grady gives this note: "The celebrated Slieve Fuad and Slieve Gullion are the same mountain. . . . Gullion is another form of Culain, foster-father of Cuculain. . . . Culain is Lir by another name, the Gaelic Poseidon, very probably Shakspeare's [*sic*] King Lear. . . . If I am right, then the roots of King Lear may be traced into the very depths of our mythology, and, through Culain, alias Lir of Slieve Fuad, followed far into the wonder-world of the Tuatha De Danan [*sic*] races and the theogony of the ethnic Irish."
12. In this passage, O'Grady reads "once every year"; "hazels, whose"; "wisp"; "dawn-wind" (255); "smile, seeing"; "those whom he"; "and, smiling"; "and, lo!"; "shears" instead of "cleaves"; and "hand, he" (256). Banba, being one of the triune goddesses of Ireland with Fotla and Eire, and hence synonymous with Ireland.

Bards of the Gael and the Gall

1. Yeats gave another account of this experience in *Au,* 105.
2. Sigerson singles out this lament, "The Caoiné of the Children," in his introduction: "a bard, Feilim M'Carthy . . . discovered, one fatal morning, that all his four children had been killed. I know of nothing which depicts, with such intense feeling, the anguish of a parent's heart" (84). M'Carthy was a member of the M'Carthy Mór clan, the first clan of Irish genealogy. As M'Carthy's poem indicates, he was of royal Spanish descent. His lands had been confiscated and he lived as an outlaw in the mountains. A hut, which he had built to shelter his four children, was destroyed in a storm, killing the children. [D. T.'s note]

3. Yeats here quotes the sixth, seventh, tenth, and eleventh stanzas of the poem. Sigerson's version of this poem reads "death,"; "White Loves,"; "gray"; "peers;" with a semicolon instead of a colon, and "home,—" (314).
4. Francis Palgrave's *The Golden Treasury of the Best Songs and Lyrical Poems in the English Language* (London: Macmillan, 1861) was revised again in 1896, and the controversial 'Second Series' dealing with Victorian poetry was to appear in October 1897. Sigerson frequently directs attention to the lives of the poets represented in this collection: in an appendix he offers the tragic life of Queen Gormlai. [D. T.'s note]
5. In Irish mythology, Amergin was one of the Druids who led the Milesians to Ireland. His words upon their arrival form *The Song of Amergin.* For Oisin and Finn, see "Bardic Ireland," note 13.
6. Deirdre Toomey describes Sigerson's claims on pp. 204–5 of her introduction to this review in *Yeats Annual 5* (ed. Warwick Gould [London: Macmillan, 1987]).

Aglavaine and Sélysette

1. The French critic was Rémy de Gourmont (1858–1915). In *Le Livre des masques* (1895), de Gourmont said of Villiers de L'Isle-Adam, ". . . c'est qu'il a rouvert les portes de l'au-delà closes avec quel fracas, on s'en souvient, et par ces portes toute une génération s'est ruée ver l'infini" (*Pages choisies*, Paris, 1922, 240). Yeats quotes this passage more accurately in his essay "John Eglinton and Spiritual Art" (see pp. 418–22).
2. The Magi were three wise men from the East who traveled to Bethlehem by following a star in order to see and pay tribute to the infant Jesus.
3. *Richard II,* 2.4.8.
4. In the English translation of this play, Alfred Sutro dropped the accent from Sélysette, but Yeats retains it throughout the review.
5. See Yeats's review of *The Treasure of the Humble* in *The Bookman* for July 1897, pp. 340–41.
6. Yeats is referring to *Les Aveugles* (1897) or *The Sightless* and *L'Intruse* (1890) or *The Intruder.*
7. In this passage from act 4, scene 5 of *Aglavaine and Selysette* (London: G. Richards, 1897), Maeterlinck reads "you . . . you"; "fro and"; "shriek, in terror:"; "too and"; "And it all went for very little and"; "morning . . . And" (113).

The Tribes of Danu

1. *Prometheus Unbound* was an epic verse drama published by Percy Bysshe Shelley in 1820. See "The Philosophy of Shelley's Poetry" in *Essays and Introductions* for Yeats's early admiration of this work (*E&I,* 65–95).
2. The Ionian Sea is an arm of the Mediterranean between western Greece and southern Italy. Yeats may have been referring to "Ionia," the western part of Asia Minor, where Homer is said to have come from.
3. Yeats refers to the famous legend of Grania, who was pursued with her lover Diarmuid by her original betrothed, Finn MacCool. The "misshapen Formor" were a race of monsters who battled with the Firbolg in Ireland before the coming of the Tuatha dé Danaan. They are, according to a note that Yeats wrote for the 1895 edition of his poems, the ancestors of evil faeries, giants, and leprechauns. (*VP,* 795).

Irish legend has it that the well of Connla, a spring in the otherworld and the source of the rivers of Ireland, is associated with trees that dropped hazelnuts into the water, where they were eaten by salmon. Anyone who could catch and eat the salmon gained wisdom. Legend has it that one seer caught the salmon of wisdom and gave it to Finn MacCool, who, while cooking it, burned his thumb; he sucked his thumb to ease the pain and thus gained wisdom.

4. Edward Calvert (1799–1883), an artist who was a disciple of William Blake, is mentioned in "Under Ben Bulben" in the company of "Wilson, Blake and Claude." The quotation is untraced.

5. This quotation is from Fiachna's song describing the "Plain of the Two Mists" (the land of the dead), which he sings to Loegaire Liban. The passage is from "The Legend of Loegaire Liban" and is translated in *The Irish Mythological Cycle and Celtic Mythology* by H. d'Arbois de Jubainville, translated by Richard Irvine Best (Dublin, 1903, pp. 202–3). Yeats omits a quatrain after the second line of his quotation. The original tale is in the *Book of Leinster*. Lady Gregory's version, "Laegaire in the Happy Plain," is in *Gods and Fighting Men* (London, 1910, 136–39). Yeats's translator could not be discovered, but his version differs substantially from Best's translation of de Jubainville.

6. Yeats refers not to the MacFirbis who compiled the Book of Lecan but to Duald Mac Firbis (1585–1670), compiler of *The Book of Genealogies*. Douglas Hyde quotes the passage Yeats refers to:

> Everyone who is fair-haired, vengeful, large, and every plunderer, every musical person, the professors of musical and entertaining performances, who are adepts in all druidical and magical arts, they are the descendants of the Tuatha De Danaan in Erin (Douglas Hyde, *A Literary History of Ireland*, new edition with introduction by Brian O Cuív, London: Benn, 1967, p. 563).

Hyde notes wryly that no Irish family can trace ancestry to those wonderful people.

7. These pre-Danaan gods of Ireland are discussed in detail in Best's translation of de Jubainville's *Irish Mythological Cycle* (pp. 51–78). The Fomorians were a race of giants and monsters, analogous in de Jubainville's estimation to the Titans who warred with Zeus in Greek mythology. The Fir-Domnann inhabited Munster and Connacht, the Gailoin and the Laighin lived in Leinster, and the Firbolg in Ulster. The "Gorborchin" are Formorians with goats' heads (Jubainville-Best, 54). The Fir Morcha may be followers of More, a Formorian being (Jubainville-Best, 57). "Luchorpains" are dwarfs which Jubainville claimed were rare in Irish mythology (Jubainville-Best, 55).

8. The sequence here is unclear, but "they" probably refers to the Tuatha dé Danaan.

9. Tír na nÓg in Irish. It is the otherworld or afterlife in Irish mythology.

10. De Jubainville drew extended parallels between Greek and Celtic mythology, but also noted important differences. Yeats's statement here is unclear. He may be suggesting a common source of inspiration for both Greek and Celtic mythology, or he may be claiming a primacy of Celtic mythology over the Greek. The latter possibility is not suggested by de Jubainville.

11. Cormac, son of Art, trades his wife and children to Manannan Mac Lir (in

disguise) in exchange for a magic branch with nine golden apples, "And whoever heard it forgot forth with sorrow and care; and men, women, and children would be lulled to sleep by it" (Jubainville-Best, p. 185). Yeats refers to it in this poem "The Dedication to a Book of Stories Selected from the Irish Novelists"—the earlier version of this poem opens:

> There was a green branch hung with many a bell
> When her own people rule in wave-worn Eire;
> And from its murmuring greeness, calm of faery,
> A Druid kindness, on all hearers fell.

12. Gort is a town in southern Galway, near the border with Co. Clare. Galway is a county on the central west coast of Ireland.
13. Sligo is a county in the west of Ireland, north of Galway.
14. Hurling is an Irish sport; it is similar to lacrosse but is played with a wider, netless stick.
15. Freemasons, or the Free and Accepted Masons, form the world's largest secret fraternal society.
16. Lady Gregory tells the same story in *Visions and Beliefs*, vol. 2, p. 233.
17. In Lady Gregory, *Visions and Beliefs*, vol. 2, p. 229, the man's name is "John Mangan," and her version differs in some details.
18. Coole Lake is in Coole Park, outside the town of Gort in Co. Galway.
19. In Lady Gregory, "the master" is "Sir William."
20. The elm was "outside Raheen" according to Lady Gregory, *Visions and Beliefs*, vol. 2, p. 234.
21. Biddy Early is mentioned in other articles in this folklore series, and much space is given to tales about her in the fourth article, "Ireland Bewitched." In Lady Gregory, a Mrs. Scanlon identifies Biddy Early as "Mrs. Tobin," and says, "She has done a good many cures. Her brother was *away* for awhile [i.e., with the fairies] and it was from him she got the knowledge" (*Visions and Beliefs*, vol. 1, 154–55).
22. The majority of place names given in the remainder of this piece and in the later articles in this volume, "The Prisoners of the Gods," "The Broken Gates of Death," and "Ireland Bewitched," are in the west of Ireland, primarily counties Galway and Clare, where Lady Gregory collected her stories. As Lady Gregory says in her collection, "It was on the coast I began to gather these stories, and I went after a while to the islands Inishmor, Inishmaan, and Inisheer . . ." (*Visions and Beliefs*, vol. 1, 5).
23. Corcamroe Abbey, founded in 1194, is on the western coast of Co. Clare.
24. Midir, son of the Dagda, was an important god of the Tuatha dé Danaan.
25. The Burren Hills are in the far west of Co. Clare.
26. Here begins the section reprinted by Yeats as "The Friends of the People of Faery" in *The Celtic Twilight* (London, 1902) and reprinted in *Mythologies* (New York, 1959), pp. 117–24.
27. Cuchulain is the Irish hero whose story is told in the Ulster Cycle of Irish mythology. He figures largely in the *Táin Bó Cuailgne*, or "Cattle Raid of Cooley." Hylae or Hylé is a city in Cyprus that was sacred to Apollo. From it comes his name, Apollo Hylatus.
28. Maeldun is the hero of an ancient Irish saga which Alfred Tennyson used as a subject for "The Voyage of Maeldun." The episode involving the Waters of Life is one of Maeldun's later adventures on one of the series of islands that he encounters. His story is often called the "Irish Odyssey"

because of the similarities of his adventures to those of the hero of Homer's epic.

29. Probably the friend was Lady Gregory.
30. Tyrone is a western county in Northern Ireland, bordering the Republic.
31. *fornent:* in front of, facing.
32. In 1929 Yeats published a group of poems to which he gave the collective name *The Winding Stair* (New York: The Fountain Press). He was probably referring to the winding stair in his tower, Thoor Ballylee. On this important matter of winding stairs, Yeats added the following note to the *Celtic Twilight* reprinting: "A countryman near Coole told me of a spirit so ascending. Swedenborg, in his *Spiritual Diary,* speaks of gyres of spirits, and Blake painted Jacob's Ladder as an ascending gyre" (*Mythologies* 123). The note is dated 1924. It was added to the version printed in *Early Poems and Stories* (London: Macmillan, 1925).
33. Hallow Eve night is the eve of All Saints' Day, 31 October. It is associated with Samhain in Irish theology. See "The Tribes of Danu," note 35.
34. The section excerpted as "The Friends of the People of Faery" ends here.
35. Samhain is 1 November and the beginning of the Celtic New Year and also the first day of winter, when livestock were brought in for the winter; it was accompanied by feasts from the slaughter of cattle that could not be kept. According to de Jubainville, it is the "day on which . . . the descendants of Nemed had to pay to the Formorians the heavy tribute of two-thirds of their children and two-thirds of the corn and milk which the year had produced" (*Irish Mythological Cycle* [Dublin, 1903], p. 63). In Celtic mythology, Samhain is also associated with visits to and from the underworld.
36. Brittany is a region in northwestern France between the English Channel and the Bay of Biscay.
37. Beltaine, or 1 May, is the first day of summer. In ancient Ireland, no Beltaine fires could be lit until the high king of Ireland, the *ard rí,* had lit a fire at Tara.
38. Herodias was the second wife of King Herod in the Old Testament of the Bible. She encouraged her daughter, Salome, to ask Herod for the head of John the Baptist in return for dancing for him.
39. Presumably in the following articles, although this article did not promise a sequel.

Three Irish Poets

1. Judea is today known as southern Israel; Yeats's phrase "defeated and captive" presumably refers to its incorporation into the Roman Empire.
2. The legend of King Arthur may stem from a mention of him in a poem in the *Black Book of Carmarthen,* a twelfth-century manuscript of ancient Welsh poetry. Arthur first appears at length in Geoffrey of Monmouth's *Historia Regum Britaniae* (ca. 1136), which purported to account for the kings of Britain for the previous two thousand years. Writing at the end of the twelfth century, Chrétien de Troyes included an account of Arthur's life in a series of legends that also include *Merlin and Lancelot, Le Chevalier de la Charrette* (ca. 1180), and *Le Conte du Graal* (ca. 1185). After the twelfth century, writers such as Sir Thomas Malory (d. 1471) continued to popularize the legend. His *Le Morte d'Arthur* gives an account of the legend of the Holy Grail.
3. Dante Alighieri (1265–1321), a Florentine poet whose masterpiece *The*

Divine Comedy helped make the dialect of Florence the literary language
of Italy. One presumes that the "structure of his poems" which Yeats refers
to is the tripartite organization of the *Comedy* into *Inferno, Purgatorio,*
and *Paradiso.*

    C. S. Boswell's *An Irish Precursor to Dante* (London: David Nutt,
1908), which discusses the vision of the eighth-century Irish saint Adamnan, mentions visions seen at Saint Patrick's Purgatory on Lough Derg by
the knight Owen in 1153 and written down by Henry of Saltery (Boswell,
234).

4. Sir Walter Scott (1771–1832), a Scottish author who established the form
   of the historical novel; several of his were set in medieval times. Of these,
   Ivanhoe (1819) is the best known. Scott was also the author of historical
   and antiquarian works, including *Provincial Antiquities of Scotland*
   (1819–26). *The Highlanders* to whom Yeats refers are the inhabitants of
   the northern half of Scotland.

5. Bretons are those who come from Brittany, a northwest province of
   France; it was an early stronghold of the Celts. Breton is also the name of
   the Celtic language spoken in this province.

       Felicité Robert de Lamennais (1782–1854), born at St. Malo, was a
   French priest, writer, and philosopher. He was an ardent supporter of the
   ultra-montanist party, which held that the pope had absolute authority
   over the Catholic Church in France; this was in opposition to the Galli-
   canist position, which held that in certain cases the French church could
   act independently or in opposition to papal authority. Lamennais's extreme
   views, however, ultimately led him into conflict with the church because,
   while he allowed the church complete spiritual authority, he left temporal
   authority to the people, advocating that they discard the monarchy in
   favor of democracy. Lamennais refused to abandon his views and eventually left the church because of them. His writings influenced French
   Romantic writers such as Alphonse Lamartine (1790–1869) and Victor
   Hugo (1802–1885).

       François René, vicomte de Chateaubriand (1768–1848), was a writer
   of both prose and fiction works, and in later life, a politician. Author of *Le
   Génie du christianisme* (1802), Chateaubriand was an apologist for Christianity in France after the Revolution and part of the Christian revival of
   that era. His writings made him an important figure in French Romanticism. Joseph Ernest Renan (1823–1892) was a French historian, philosopher, and philologist. He promoted the use of scientific and historical
   methodology to analyze the life of Christ and the spread of Christianity
   and was the author of *La Vie de Jésus* (1863), the first volume of his *Histoires des origines du christianisme* (1863–83). The work caused a public
   controversy because of its unorthodox rationalization of the divinity of
   Christ. For Comte Villiers de L'Isle-Adam, see "*The Treasure of the Humble,*" note 3.

       William Morris (1834–1896), English poet and artist, was co-founder
   and designer for a company that produced furniture, textiles, and wall-
   paper as a reaction against an industrialization which he felt resulted in
   goods of inferior quality. There is no evidence that Morris came from
   Welsh origins.

6. The well of Connla was a spring in the Celtic otherworld and a source
   of the rivers in Ireland. For the sacred hazel, see "The Tribes of Danu,"
   note 3.

7. This version of "The Nuts of Knowledge" differs in a number of details from the version printed in AE's *The Divine Vision and Other Poems* (London: Macmillan, 1904), pp. 28–29. In the passage quoted here, AE reads "grassy nook" with no comma; "Where door and windows open wide that friendly stars may look,"; "rabbit,"; "patter in," (28); "Hazel Tree"; "berries there"; "Connla's Well"; "waters run"; "being through"; and "ruddy" instead of "shining" (29).

8. *The Nation*, a newspaper edited by Thomas Davis, was the mouthpiece of the Young Ireland movement of the 1840s. See Yeats's articles "Popular Ballad Poetry in Ireland," "The Young Ireland League," "Irish National Literature, I: From Callanan to Carleton," and "Young Ireland" included in this collection.

9. In this passage from *Ballads in Prose* (1894), Hopper reads "ways forlorn:"; "'tis born:"; "door or window,"; "souls away,—"; "wander"; "whitethorn bough"; and "swans they" (91).

10. Lionel Johnson converted to Catholicism in 1891.

11. In this passage from *Ireland, with Other Poems* (London, 1897), Johnson reads "through night:" (52); "earthly Mother"; "Ireland break"; and "agony, the ages" (52). In Johnson's version, the line beginning "FOR YOU NO CHEERING . . ." and the following line are italicized, not capitalized. In the final line cited here, Johnson reads "even as ye?" (53).

The Prisoners of the Gods

1. The Nereids were sea nymphs, the daughters of Nereus in Greek mythology.

2. Yeats seems to be suggesting that Ireland had only been Christian for twelve centuries (roughly since A.D. 700), though Saint Patrick had begun converting the island before his death (ca. A.D. 432).

3. Kiltartan is in Co. Galway; it is also the name of the dialect Lady Gregory used in many of her plays; this dialect purported to be a faithful rendering of Gaelic English as spoken by those in Kiltartan and its environs. See "The Tribes of Danu," note 22, for more information on the place-names Yeats refers to throughout this article.

4. These names are not, of course, the real names. It seems better to use a name of some kind for every one who has told more than one story, that the reader may recognize the great number of strange things many a countryman and woman sees and hears. I keep the real names carefully, but I cannot print them. [Yeats's note]

5. This friend is surely Lady Gregory.

6. The land troubles, brought on by disputes between peasants and landlords over rents (and in some cases, rack-rents) and evictions, formed the basis for the creation of the Land League, which agitated for tenant ownership of farms. In 1881 a Land Act was passed which gave tenants more equitable rents and a certain degree of tenure. Subsequent Land Acts further secured their rights and ability to own land.

7. St. Patrick's Purgatory is on Station Island in Lough Derg, Co. Donegal. There St. Patrick is supposed to have seen a vision of Purgatory. It had been a famous place of pilgrimage since the Middle Ages.

8. *forth:* alternative form of "fort."

9. *beetling:* "any of various wooden instruments for beating linen, mashing potatoes, etc." (*Random House Dictionary of the English Language*, 2nd ed., unabridged, 1987).

10. *privication:* provocation? The context indicates that the speaker sees consumption as an inherited weakness rather than a virus.
11. For Biddy Early, see "The Tribes of Danu," note 21.
12. *lug:* ear.
13. This story appears in Lady Gregory, vol. 2, p. 83, *Visions and Beliefs in the West of Ireland, Collected and Arranged by Lady Gregory; with Two Essays and Notes by W. B. Yeats* (London: G. P. Putnam's Sons, 1920).
14. In Lady Gregory, *Visions and Beliefs,* vol. 2, p. 82, this story is attributed to "Tom Smith," and in her version "John King's wife" is "John Madden's wife."
15. This story is attributed to "An Islander" in Lady Gregory's *Visions and Beliefs,* vol. 2, p. 81.
16. In Lady Gregory, *Visions and Beliefs,* vol. 2, p. 82, this story is attributed to Mrs. Meagher.
17. In Irish mythology, the Formorians were a violent race of monsters who were eventually subdued by the Firbolgs, who in turn were vanquished by the Tuatha dé Danaan. Míle was the legendary progenitor of the human inhabitants of Ireland called Milesians.

Mr. Lionel Johnson's Poems

1. For Yeats's devotion to Arthur Henry Hallam's essay "On Some of the Characteristics of Modern Poetry, and on the Lyrical Poems of Alfred Tennyson," in *The Poems of Arthur Henry Hallam, together with His Essay on the Lyrical Poems of Alfred Lord Tennyson,* ed. R. Le Gallienne (London: Elkin Mathews and John Lane, 1893), see "Young Ireland," note 9.
2. This passage reads in Hallam, ". . . their fine organs trembled into emotions at colours, and sounds, and movements, unperceived or unregarded by duller temperaments" (*The Poems of Arthur Henry Hallam* . . . , pp. 93–94).
3. In this passage, Hallam reads "They [Keats and Shelley] are both poets of sensation rather than reflection," (93); "magic, producing"; "so boundless, and so bewildering"; and "Nature" (97).
4. *mix up:* Hallam reads "Hence, whatever is mixed up with art, and appears under its semblances, is always more favorably regarded than art free and unalloyed" (100).
5. Literally, a living picture. A *tableau vivant* is a representation of a painting, statue, historical scene, etc., presented in silence by a costumed person or group of persons. A precursor of the contemporary game "charades," the creation of tableaux vivants was a popular nineteenth-century entertainment.
6. *dewy fields:* The poem is "An Ideal" from *Ireland, with Other Poems.* Johnson reads "dewy Field,"; "Storm's"; "Heavens"; "burning night:" (81); and "fierce holiday:" (82). The poem was dated 1888 and dedicated to Standish O'Grady.
7. *"rosaries blanched . . .":* Johnson reads "Ivories blaunched" in "Glories" (*P,* 44). This pastiche of quotations is from "The Age of a Dream," p. 85; "The Church of a Dream," pp. 84–85; and "Glories," p. 44—all poems from Johnson's *Poems* (London: Elkin Mathews, 1895).
8. Yeats is most likely referring to AE. In his review of AE's *Homeward, Songs by the Way* ("A New Poet"), Yeats called AE an "arch-visionary" (p. 242).
9. "Parnell," "Ways of War," "Ireland's Dead," and "The Red Wind" are from *Poems.*

10. In his *The Study of Celtic Literature* (London: Smith, Elder and Co, 1867), Arnold says, "Sentimental,—*always ready to react against the despotism of fact;* that is the description a great friend of the Celt gives of him" (102), and footnotes that the "friend" is Henri Martin (1810–83), whose work *Histoire de France* contained several chapters on the Celts.

Mr. Rhys' *Welsh Ballads*

1. *In Memoriam* and "Locksley Hall" are both poems of Alfred, Lord Tennyson. Robert Browning's dramatic monologue "Bishop Blougram's Apology" was first published in *Men and Women* (London: Chapman Hall, 1855).

    Victor Hugo (1802–85), while in exile on the island of Jersey, arranged to have published *Les Châtiments* (1853) in Brussels. The book contains versified invectives against Napoleon III.

    For Matthew Arnold and "the criticism of life," see "The Poetry of Sir Samuel Ferguson—I," note 10.

    Except for Wagner's music drama *Parsifal* (1877), Yeats's examples are all works he reviewed in *The Bookman:* William Morris's romance *The Well at the World's End* (see pp. 319–21), Maurice Maeterlinck's play *Aglavaine and Sélysette* (see pp. 349–51), and Villiers de L'Isle-Adam's *Axël* (pp. 233–37).

    art is a labour . . . golden age: In "A Vision of the Last Judgement," vol. 3, p. 146, *Writings of William Blake* (Keynes ed., 1925), Blake writes "The Nature of my Work is Visionary or Imaginative; it is an Endeavor to Restore what the Ancients call'd the Golden Age." Yeats seems to have been fond of his version of the Blake phrase, also using it on p. 310, in "The New Irish Library," also in this volume.

2. Lady Charlotte Elizabeth Guest (1812–95) was the translator of a famous collection of Welsh romances called *The Mabinogion* (3 vols., London, 1838–49).

    Songs of Urien's victories, attributed to Taliesin, the Welsh bard of the sixth century, were collected in *The Book of Taliesin.* Dafydd ap Gwilym, a Welsh bard of the fourteenth century, is chiefly famous for his poem to the woman with whom he eloped, Morvydd of Angelsey. Llywarch Hën was also a sixth-century Welsh bard.

3. Matthew Arnold's study, first published in London in 1867 by Smith, Elder and Co.

4. In Johnson's volume *Ireland, with Other Poems* (London: Elkin Mathews, 1897) were included such poems as "Cyhiraeth" and "To Morfydd Dead."

5. *life of Davyth ap Gwilym . . . "The Poet of the Leaves.":* On p. 170 of *Welsh Ballads and Other Poems* (1898), Rhys writes in his note that "Davyth ap Gwilym was an immediate contemporary of Chaucer, and may claim to be the fine flower of Welsh mediaeval poetry" and that "we are awaiting now the Oxford text promised by Mr. Gwenogvryn Evans, which will finally set at rest many disputed points."

6. Rhys's note reads as follows:

    > Englynion y Betev (Bedden). The original text in *The Black Book of Carmarthen* consists of seventy-two primitive three-lined englynion or stanzas (which are not properly and metrically englynion at all), whose long-drawn monotony adds to the dirge-like effect of the metre. Of these, less than a fourth are here reproduced (173–74).

A *Facsimile of the Black Book of Carmarthen* (Oxford, 1888) dates the work as ca. 1148, but notes, "The melancholy truth is that the MS. is more or less fragmentary; how fragmentary we have no means of judging" (ix). This statement rather qualifies Yeats's and Rhys's disagreement over whether the original is seventy-two or seventy-three stanzas.

Identifying names from Rhys's translation (86–89) is difficult; as Rhys states in his note, "The whole poem is a memorial of the burial places of some two hundred warriors, maidens, bards, and others, and in some places serves as the sole record of place-names and names of slain heroes, of great importance in early British history" (174).

7. Yeats omits many stanzas from the passage he quotes here. In these stanzas, Rhys reads "Llan Morvael:" (87); "oak-tree,"; "Siawn may be:"; "salt sea-marsh,"; "warrior, Rhyn;"; and "Hennin's daughter".
8. The full title of this poem is "The Lament of Llywarch Hën in his Old Age," pp. 65–66 in Rhys.
9. Merlin is a wizard who figures largely in Arthurian legend. For information on Arthur, see "A Bundle of Poets," note 3, and "Three Irish Poets," note 2. Legend has it that Arthur is carried away to the island of Avalon, where he may have been buried or where he may have recovered from his wounds and from whence he may return.

The Broken Gates of Death

1. See "The Tribes of Danu," note 22.
2. Lady Gregory tells this story in *Visions and Beliefs in the West of Ireland, Collected and Arranged by Lady Gregory; with Two Essays and Notes by W. B. Yeats* (London: G. P. Putnam's Sons, 1920), vol. 1, pp. 181–82.
3. Lady Gregory, in the same passage cited above in "The Broken Gates of Death," note 2, attributes this story to "Martin Rabbit."
4. This story appears in vol. 1, pp. 190–91, of Lady Gregory's *Visions and Beliefs.* The well of Tubber Macduagh appears again later in the book when a Mrs. Feeney tells that it is "a great place to bring children to, to get them back when they've been changed by the faeries," p. 220.
5. Loughrea is a town in Co. Galway. Roxborough is the ancestral home of Lady Gregory.
6. Saint Patrick (389–461), the patron saint of Ireland. See "Bardic Ireland," note 5.

   The skill of the smith Goibhniu in making and repairing weapons quickly enabled the Tuatha dé Danaan to defeat the Formorians at the second battle of Moytura.
7. In Lady Gregory, *Visions and Beliefs*, vol. 1, p. 176, the story is attributed to "Mrs. Donnely."
8. Pentecost is a festival of the Christian church which falls on the seventh Sunday after Easter; it celebrates the descent of the Holy Spirit upon the disciples of Jesus Christ and marks the beginning of their mission to the world.
9. In Lady Gregory, the place is Ballinakill, and the women are Mary Grady, Mary Flanagan, and Ellen Lydon, respectively. The priest is called Father Hubert (*Visions and Beliefs,* vol. 1, 238–39).
10. Cork is probably a misprint for Gort since the brother is being buried in Kiltartan.
11. For Biddy Early, see "The Tribes of Danu," note 21.

12. The god Midher carries off Etain, who was his wife in a previous incarnation, from the palace of Eochaid, her husband. Midher and Etain fly off as swans (de Jubainville, *The Irish Mythological Cycle and Celtic Mythology,* trans. R. I. Best, pp. 176–82). The episode with Oisin and Niamh figures in Yeats's "The Wanderings of Oisin."

The "divine woman in a ship of glass" is the messenger of the god of death, Tethra, and she comes to summon Conla, son of Conn, the high king, to the land of the dead (Jubainville-Best, 108).

The woman Cuchulain sails to is Fand, wife of Manannan mac Lir.

Bran is summoned by a goddess with a silver branch to make a journey, during which he encounters Manannan mac Lir. Bran arrives with his band of thirty comrades at an island peopled only by women, whose queen is the goddess who had given him the silver branch (Jubainville-Best, 183).

These wonders take place during the story of how Cormac traded his wife and children to Manannan mac Lir for a magic branch with golden apples, and how Cormac eventually regained them (Jubainville-Best, 185–88).

13. For Slieve Fuad, see "Mr. Standish O'Grady's *Flight of the Eagle,*" note 11. The legend can be found in the poem "The Chase of Sliabh Fuaid. In which is related how Ailne, the wife of Meargach, came to be avenged on the Fianna; and how she assumed the form of a deer, until she lodged Fionn in a dungeon, and the Fianna of Erinn also; and how they were finally released by Conan" in *Fenian Poems,* second series, ed. John O'Daly (Dublin, 1861), in *Transactions of the Ossianic Society for the Year 1858,* vol. 6, pp. 21–75.

In the dialogue of Oisin and St. Patrick, Yeats is referring to the subject matter of his early poem "The Wanderings of Oisin."

Le Mouvement Celtique: Fiona Macleod

1. Richard Wagner's *Der Ring des Niebelungen,* a series of music dramas first performed together in 1876, and William Morris's *Sigurd the Volsung* (1876) are both based on the thirteenth-century German epics, which are themselves variations of the Old Norse *Eddas.* Henrik Ibsen's *Peer Gynt* (1867) drew on Scandanavian folklore.

Yeats made much the same comment later in the year when in *The Dublin Daily Express* of 24 September 1898 he said,

> Modern poetry grows weary of using over and over again the personages and stories and metaphors that have come to us through Greece and Rome, or from Wales and Brittany through the middle ages, and has found new life in those Norse and German legends. William Morris's "Sigurd", if it is as fine as it seemed to me some years ago, may yet influence the imagination of Europe, and Henrik Ibsen's "Peer Gynt" and "The Heroes of Heligoland" are already great influences, while Richard Wagner's dramas of "The Ring", are, together with his mainly Celtic "Parsival" and "Lohengrin", and "Tristan and Iseult", the most passionate influence in the arts of Europe (*UP2,* 125).

2. Yeats's list here contains several figures whom Yeats cites frequently as his authorities on Celtic matters, but whose identities were somewhat

obscured by the rather odd spellings provided by the translator or typesetter. See the textual notes for these spellings. W. O. Ernst Windisch (1844–1918) was a German philologist; Marie Henri d'Arbois de Jubainville was professor of Celtic at the Collège de France. J. M. Synge was to attend his courses in 1898 and 1902. For more information on de Jubainville, see "The Story of Early Gaelic Literature," note 3. For Alfred T. Nutt and John Rhys, see note 3 to this same article and the introductory note to "Celtic Beliefs About the Soul" included in this collection. Standish Hayes O'Grady (1832–1915) was a Gaelic scholar and author of *Silva Gadelica* (London: Williams and Norgate, 1892). For Nora Hopper, see "Irish National Literature, II," note 17, and for Yeats's friend and confidante Katharine Tynan Hinkson, see the introductory note to "The Celtic Romances in Miss Tynan's New Book," pp. 51–53.

3. *Pharaïs* was first published in 1894. The French translation of *The Mountain Lovers* (1895) was *Vaurien de la Montagne*.

4. The stories in "Fiona Macleod's" *The Sin-Eater* (Edinburgh: P. Geddes, 1895) and *The Washer of the Ford* (P. Geddes, 1896) were reissued, slightly augmented, as a three-volume set called *Barbaric Tales, Dramatic Tales,* and *Spiritual Tales* in March 1897. Yeats's review of the tales in *The Sketch* for April 1897, however, suggests that he read the stories in their original format during his first trip to the Aran Islands in August 1896 (see pp. 336–39).

AE's Poems

1. These paintings were on the walls of a room at the Dublin lodge of the Theosophical Society at 3 Upper Ely Place (Ella Young, *Flowering Dusk, Things Remembered Accurately and Inaccurately* [New York: Longmans, Green, and Co., 1945], p. 30).

2. Neoplatonism was developed as a philosophical system by Plotinus in the third century. It combined Platonic doctrine and Oriental mysticism, and in its later history, was influenced by Christianity. A major tenet of the doctrine propounds that existence derives from emanations from the One and the goal of life is to be reunited with the One. It is appropriate that Yeats mentions Neoplatonism since George William Russell's pen name, "AE," consists of the first two letters of the Greek word and Neoplatonic term *aeon,* which in Platonic philosophy is "an emanation, generation, or phase of the supreme deity, taking part in the creation and government of the universe" (*Oxford English Dictionary*).

3. Charles Weekes is the friend of Yeats who started the publishing firm Whaley; the book of poems they worked on together was *Homeward, Songs by the Way.* The authors John Lane (1854–1935) published include Richard Le Gallienne, Oscar Wilde, and Arthur Symons. Lane established the Bodley Head in 1887 and was also publisher of *The Yellow Book,* an arts journal that ran from 1894 to 1897 and whose literary contributors included Henry James, Max Beerbohm, and George Moore, and whose art contributors included Aubrey Beardsley and John Singer Sargent.

4. In this passage, Yeats discusses images from several different poems. The image of the "great bird with a blue breast" is from "The Robing of the King":

On the bird of air blue-breasted glint the rays of gold,
And its shadowy fleece above us waves the forest old . . . (66).

The image of the "bird with diamond wings" is a reference to the third stanza of the poem "The Hour of the King," p. 80:

> On the Bird of Diamond Glory
> Floats in mystic floods of song:
> As he lists Time's triple story
> Seems but as a day is long.

5. Yeats is probably referring here to "The Face of Faces," p. 64, or to "A Vision of Beauty," p. 14.
6. These images are in "Glory and Shadow," pp. 61–62.
7. *"are stars and deeps within"*: This quotation is from AE's "Star Teachers," p. 89 of *The Earth Breath*. In the poem, this phrase starts with an upper-case A, as a new line.
8. Yeats had probably read some Plotinus in the 1895 *Selected Works* edited by Thomas Taylor (1758–1835). The quote is from Plotinus's *Enneads*, 3.2.15, 1.48: "For really here in the events of our life it is not the soul within but the outside shadow of man which cries and moans and carries on in every sort of way on a stage which is the whole earth where men have in many places set up their stages" (*Five Books of Plotinus . . .*, trans. Thomas Taylor [London: Printed for Edward Jeffrey, Pall Mall, 1794], pp. 174–75). Yeats refers to this same quotation of Plotinus again in another article on AE, "The Poetry of A.E." (*UP2*, 122). The nearly life-long discontent with the "lonely and abstract joy" of Plotinus of which this remark is the first evidence culminates in "The Tower" (1925) with Yeats's refusal to "Choose Plato and Plotinus for a friend / Until imagina-tion, ear and eye, / Can be content with argument and deal / in abstract things . . ." (*VP*, 409). The defiant decision in that poem to ". . . mock Plot-inus' thought / And cry in Plato's teeth, / Death and life were not / Till man made up the whole . . ." (415) is softened by a note dated 1928 which reflects Yeats's enthusiastic study of the new translation of Plotinus by Stephen McKenna (1871–1934). "When I wrote the lines about Plato and Plotinus I forgot that it is something in our own eyes that makes us see them as all transcendence" (*VP*, 826).
9. *I may view;:* This poem, "Dream Love," reads "I may view:" (28).
   beauty's ray: AE reads "Beauty's ray" (28).
10. *Jacobean music:* Yeats is probably thinking of the courtly love poetry asso-ciated with Ben Jonson and the cavalier poets.
11. These lines are the last stanza of "Illusion" on p. 49 of *The Earth Breath*.
12. In this passage, Yeats is quoting from AE's "A Vision of Beauty" (15–16). AE reads "the winds are shaken" and "the souls of earth are kindled" (15). In the final part of the poem quoted here, AE's lines read:

> When the shepherd of the Ages draws his misty hordes away
> Through the glimmering deeps to silence, and within the awful fold
> (15–16).

13. *"in the endless night"*: in AE, this phrase reads "in endless flight" (39). Found in "The Fountain of Shadowy Beauty," these phrases are from the lines:

> The Fount of Shadowy Beauty throws
> Its magic rounds us all the night;

What things the heart would be, it sees
And chases them in endless flight. . . .

14. *"high ancestral self,"*: AE reads "high Ancestral Self" ("The Fountain of
Shadowy Beauty," 39).

Le Mouvement Celtique: II. M. John O'Leary

1. Thomas W. Rolleston (1857–1920) was editor of *The Dublin University
Review* from 1885 to 1886. Katharine Tynan's first volume of poems was
Louise de la Vallière (London: Kegan Paul, 1885).
2. Yeats recounts this same anecdote in "Mr. John O'Leary," p. 329.

Celtic Beliefs About the Soul

1. The second volume of de Jubainville's series, *Cours de littérature celtique,*
was *Le Cycle mythologique, et la mythologie irlandaise* (Paris, 1884).
    John Rhys's *Lectures on the Origin and Growth of Religion as Illus-
trated by Celtic Heathendom* (The Hibbert Lectures, 1886) (London:
Williams and Norgate, 1888).
2. Kuno Meyer (1858–1919) was a Celtic philologist well known and well
regarded for his translations. See Yeats's review of his translation of *The
Vision of MacConglinne,* pp. 193–95. On page 241 of volume 2 (*The Voyage of Bran*), Nutt says ". . . that Greeks and Irish alone have preserved the
early stage of the Happy Otherworld conception in any fulness."
3. On page 241 of *The Voyage of Bran,* Nutt says, "Ireland has preserved
with greater fulness and precision, a conception out of which Homeric
Greece had already emerged."
4. The January 1898 issue of *The Nineteenth Century* contained "The Prisoners of the Gods," the second of Yeats's long quarterly articles on Irish
fairy lore which he had collected with Lady Gregory (see pp. 372–85).
5. Sir James George Frazer's *The Golden Bough* had been first published in a
two-volume edition in 1890.
6. The solar myth theory posited that all religions, including Christianity,
were derived from solar worship, and the stories surrounding solar deities
contain similar tropes of birth, death, and rebirth that correspond to the
movement of the sun through the zodiac. See Charles François Dupuis
(1742–1809), *Origine de toutes les cultes* (Paris, 1794).
7. Untraced.
8. For Andrew Lang, see "Greek Folk Poesy," note 5; his work on mythology
includes *Custom and Myth* (London: Longmans, Green, and Co., 1883),
Myth, Ritual, and Religion (London: Longmans, Green, and Co., 1887),
and *Modern Mythology* (London: Longmans, Green, and Co., 1897).

John Eglinton and Spiritual Art

1. These statements are quoted from Eglinton's first essay in this controversy,
"What Should Be the Subjects of National Drama?" published in *The
Daily Express* of 18 September 1898.
2. See *"Le Mouvement Celtique: Fiona Macleod,"* note 1.
3. A city in southwest Germany, Bayreuth is where Wagner chose to build his
Festspielhaus, the opera house that premiered his Ring cycle in 1876.

Yeats is quoting here from Eglinton's second article, "National Drama and Contemporary Life," published in *The Daily Express,* 8 October 1898.

4. For the origin of this statement, see *"Aglavaine and Sélysette,"* note 1.
5. Yeats is quoting again from Eglinton's second article, "National Drama and Contemporary Life," *The Daily Express,* 8 October 1898.

   In his preface to the *Lyrical Ballads,* William Wordsworth states that the subject of his poems comes from "low and rustic life . . . because in that condition, the essential passions of the heart find a better soil in which they can attain their maturity" and that "in that condition the passions of men are incorporated with the beautiful and permanent forms of nature."
6. See Yeats's review of *Young Ireland,* pp. 326–28, for Yeats's lifelong enthusiasm for A. H. Hallam's essay on Tennyson's lyric poetry. In this passage, Yeats is quoting from *The Poems of Arthur Henry Hallam, together with His Essay on the Lyrical Poems of Alfred Lord Tennyson,* ed. R. Le Gallienne (London: Elkin Mathews and John Lane, 1893). Hallam reads "They [Keats and Shelley] are both poets of sensation rather than of reflection", (93); "a sort of magic, producing" (97); "so boundless, and so" (97); ". . . their fine organs trembled into emotions at colours, and sounds, and movements, unperceived or unregarded by duller temperaments" (93–94); and "Hence, whatever is mixed up with art, and appears under its semblance, is always more favorably regarded than art free and unalloyed" (100).
7. Transcendentalism was a nineteenth-century movement which, in part, proposed that a knowledge of reality came from intuitive sources instead of from objective experience.
8. In his "Essay on Shelley" (edited by Donald Smalley) in *The Complete Works of Robert Browning* (ed. Roma A. King Jr. [Athens: Ohio University Press and Baylor University Press, 1981]), Browning is contrasting the "objective poet" and the "subjective poet." The passage which Yeats quotes is a description of the subjective poet: "Not what man sees, but what God sees—the Ideas of Plato, seeds of creation lying burningly on the Divine Hand—it is toward these that he struggles" (vol. 5, 138).

   The Edgar Allen Poe quotation can be found in his essay "The Poetic Principle": "Inspired by an ecstatic prescience of the glories beyond the grave, we struggle, by multiform combinations among the things and thoughts of Time, to attain a portion of that Loveliness whose very elements, perhaps, attain to eternity alone" (p. 98 in *The Poems of Edgar Allen Poe with a Selection of Essays,* Everyman's Library, 1927).
9. Emile Verhaeren (1855–1916), Belgian poet and dramatist, wrote almost no criticism. Verhaeren expressed ideas like these in a speech, "French Poetry of Today," delivered at the Taylorian Institute, Oxford, March 1901. It was reprinted, translated by C. H. Heywood, in *The Fortnightly Review,* vol. 69, April 1901, pp. 723–38. Where Yeats had encountered these ideas by 1898 is unknown.
10. A phrase from Matthew Arnold. See "The Poetry of Sir Samuel Ferguson—I," note 10.
11. In this paragraph, Yeats is quoting, in some cases for the second time, fragments by John Eglinton.

A Symbolic Artist and the Coming of Symbolic Art

1. The Dublin Theosophical Society. See *Au*, 193ff.
2. For George Russell (AE), see *Au*, 195–203. For Emanuel Swedenborg, see "Irish Folk Tales," note 20.
3. James Abbot McNeill Whistler (1834–1903) was an American artist who lived in London. Famous for his colorful personality and trenchant wit, he was involved in famous public disputes, such as one with art critic John Ruskin.

   Aubrey Vincent Beardsley (1872–98) was an English illustrator. Inspired by the Pre-Raphaelites and often linked to the decadents, Beardsley moved beyond both these movements. His work is characterized by its suggestion of both the sinister and the erotic, and his illustrations include those for Oscar Wilde's *Salomé*. He was also art editor for the journal *The Yellow Book*.
4. Charles Ricketts (1866–1931) was an artist and stage designer. Sir Edward Burne-Jones (1833–98) was one of the major artists of the Pre-Raphaelite movement. He did many of the windows at Oxford; his best-known early works there are the east windows of Christ Church Cathedral, done in 1859, which depict the story of St. Frideswide.
5. Edgar Degas (1834–1917) was a French artist known for his painting, bronze sculptures, and drawings of ballerinas; while he is associated with Impressionism, he is also noted for his portrayal of the human body in motion.
6. The publication of the drawing entitled "J'ai baisé ta bouche, Iokanaan," in *The Studio* for April 1893, brought Beardsley the commission to illustrate Lord Alfred Douglas's translation of Oscar Wilde's *Salomé* (London 1894). This drawing, which was also known as "Salome with John the Baptist's Head," is a more ornate version of "The Climax" in the Wilde volume.
7. For Count Villiers de L'Isle-Adam, see "The Treasure of the Humble," note 3.
8. Both the "young Irish Catholic meant for the priesthood" and the "plays by a new Irish writer" are untraced.
9. See Yeats's reviews of Fiona Macleod's work in this collection: "Miss Fiona Macleod as a Poet," pp. 322–25; "Miss Fiona Macleod," pp. 336–39; and "*Le Mouvement Celtique:* Fiona Macleod," pp. 407–9.
10. "The Dry Tree" is a symbol of decadence in *The Well at the World's End*, a romance by William Morris (London: Longmans, Green, and Co., 1896), which Yeats had reviewed for *The Bookman* in November 1896, pp. 319–21 in this collection.
11. One of the proverbs of Hell in Blake's *The Marriage of Heaven and Hell* (ed. Geoffrey Keynes, *The Writings of William Blake* [London: Nonesuch Press, 1925], vol. 1, p. 186).

    Palmer's (1805–81) "command" comes from one of his sketchbooks in which he explains Blake's figures: "There are many mediums in the means—none, O! not a jot, not a shadow of a jot, in the end of great art. . . . We must not begin with medium, but think always to excess, and only use medium to make excess more abundantly excessive. . . ." (A. H. Palmer, *The Life and Letters of Samuel Palmer, Painter and Etcher* [London: Seeley and Co., 1892], p. 16).
12. The friend is untraced, although Lionel Johnson is a likely candidate.
13. For Kabala, see "Plays by an Irish Poet," note 10.

14. Fletcher reprints the verses in *Yeats Studies* (52–53). The phrase Yeats quotes is a distortion of the two lines:

> Wrapt Thee round him for living men's delight
> And his eternal reverie when dead.

15. See accompanying illustration. Althea Gyles coached Yeats in interpreting "Noah's Raven" in a letter to him dated ca. 1895. It is reprinted in *Letters to W. B. Yeats* (ed. Richard J. Finneran, George Mills Harper, and William M. Murphy [New York: Columbia University Press, 1977], pp. 9–11).
16. Yeats refers to Blake. "The Prophetic Books" was not Blake's title but was added later by his editors.
17. *"the flood of the five senses"*: The quotation is from Blake's "Europe" and reads "Plac'd in the order of the stars, when the five senses whelm'd / In deluge o'er the earth-born man . . ." (ed. Keynes, *The Writings of William Blake* [London: Nonesuch Press, 1925], vol. 1, p. 299).
18. The Persian poet is Omar Khayyám. The translation is not Fitzgerald's, but corresponds to part of quatrain 63 in Fitzgerald's version.
19. In Jewish folklore, Lilith is Adam's first wife before Eve; in different legends, she is presented variously as a child kidnapper and murderer and a symbol of lust.
20. This note appeared at the end of the article in *The Dome* printing.

High Crosses of Ireland

1. See "The Story of Early Gaelic Literature," note 3.
2. The National Literary Society was founded in Dublin on 24 May 1892 by John T. Kelly and W. B. Yeats shortly after the London Irish Literary Society had been formed in December 1891 by Yeats and T. W. Rolleston. The formation of the latter had been the cause of debate in Ireland because its implication was that the center for Irish intellectual activity was London, not Ireland. The National Literary Society was formed to promote the appreciation and production of Irish literature in English; its center was in Dublin, but it grew to have many branches in different cities around Ireland.
3. Yeats here refers to Stokes's *The High Crosses of Castledermot and Durrow* (Dublin: The Academy, 1898). Prior to this folio volume, however, Stokes had published drawings of two crosses in her *Early Christian Architecture in Ireland* (London: G. Bell and Sons, 1878).
4. Stokes had translated the latter half of the *Byzantine Guide to Painting,* a manual for artists which dates to the Byzantine school of the twelfth century, from a French version and included it as an appendix to the second volume of Adolphe Napoléon Didron's *Christian Iconography* (London: G. Bell and Sons, 1886), which she helped compile. That portion of the manual prescribes in elaborate detail how biblical scenes such as Yeats names here were to be painted.
5. Genesis 6–8 of the Bible recounts how Noah, an Old Testament patriarch, is chosen by God to build an ark in which he, his family, and a male and female of every species of animal lives during the time of a flood God sends to destroy all other life on earth. The Book of Daniel in the Old Testament recounts how Daniel, a Hebrew prophet, is miraculously saved from being eaten by lions when he is thrown into their den. The disobedience of Adam

and Eve, the first two humans created by God, in the Garden of Eden is known as the Fall of Man; it resulted in Adam and Eve's expulsion from the Garden of Eden and is recounted in the first book of Genesis. David, the second king of Israel (ca. 1010–970 B.C.), was first a lyre player at the court of King Saul (1 Sam. 16:16), the king whom he succeeded. Genesis 32 recounts how Jacob meets a man, wrestles him, and refuses to release him until the man blesses him. The man reveals himself as God, gives Jacob a new name, Israel, and promises that a new nation will come from him.

In "The Wooing of Etain," a story in the Irish mythological cycle, the god Midher courts Etain and desires to take her to "the great plain," Mag Mar, which is variously interpreted as Bregleith, Midher's home and an afterworld (H. d'Arbois de Jubainville, *The Irish Mythological Cycle and Celtic Mythology* [Dublin: Hodges, Figgis, and Co., 1903], pp. 5, 185). Other names for the afterworld were Tire Beo, "the Land of the Living"; Tir n-Aill, "the Other World"; Man Meld, "the Pleasant Plain" (Jubainville, 5); and Tir na nOg, "the Land of Youth." The spellings are those of de Jubainville.

6. *Chapters on the Book of [St.] Mulling* (Edinburgh: D. Douglas) by Hugh J. Lawlor (1860–1938), dean of St. Patrick's, was published in 1897. St. Mulling (sometimes spelled Moling, Mullins, or Mullen) was an Irish saint of the seventh century (d. 697) who founded the monastery (now in ruins) of St. Mullins, Co. Carlow. A slip sheet which prefaces Lawlor's eighth chapter, "The Last Page—II. The Circular Device," notes that "Miss Stokes . . . has discovered near the Cross of Christ and His Apostles what seems to be an indication of the entrance to the cashel, reminding us, as she remarks, of the words, 'I am the door,'" (167). Stokes's reproduction and explanation of "the circular device" taken from Lawlor is on pp. x–xiv of her *High Crosses*.

7. Saint Mark is one the four evangelists and the writer of the Bible's second Gospel, the Book of Mark, in the New Testament. Although the second Gospel in the order in which it is placed in the Bible, it was the first written. Jeremiah was a sixth century B.C. prophet. His teachings form an eponymous book of the Old Testament. Matthew was one of the original twelve disciples of Jesus. Tradition attributes the Book of Matthew to his authorship. Daniel is an Old Testament Hebrew prophet. The Book of Daniel tells of his skill in interpreting dreams and his miraculous survival of a lion's den. John is also one of the twelve original disciples of Jesus; he is author of the fourth Gospel of the New Testament. Ezekiel is a prophet (sixth century B.C.); his prophecies can be found in the Book of Ezekiel in the Old Testament. Luke is author of the third Gospel in the New Testament (the Book of Luke) and the Book of Acts. Isaiah was an eighth-century B.C. prophet; his teachings can be found in the Book of Isaiah in the Old Testament.

8. The Four Evangelists are Matthew, Mark, Luke, and John, the authors of the first four Gospels in the New Testament of the Bible.

9. Yet Stokes likewise proposes, as Yeats does here, that the diagram represents not only the plans for a monastery, but the plans for a paradise as well, St. Mulling's ideal "City of Life" (*High Crosses*, xiv).

10. Yeats's use of the writings of "the greatest of the Christian mystics" (*L*, 262), Jacob Boehme (1575–1624), dates back to the early nineties.

11. In Franz Hartmann's *The Life and Doctrines of Jacob Boehme* (New York: Macoy Publishing, 1929), Boehme is quoted as writing: "By this eternal mir-

roring, or God seeing Himself within Himself, divine self-consciousness—
that is to say, the self-knowledge of God, or, in other words, divine wisdom
exists. The eternal Will, in its aspect as the Father, eternally conceives of itself
as the Son, and, so to say, re-expands as the Holy Spirit" (73).

Yeats draws here on the discussion in his and Edwin J. Ellis's *The
Works of William Blake* of the similar conception of paradise as mirror for
Boehme and Blake (London, 1893, vol. 1, pp. 246–47). Blake's "Looking
Glass of Enitharmon" appears only in *Jerusalem* (63: 21, 38), and "the
imagination of God" is not Blake's phrase but Yeats's own (see Yeats and
Ellis, *Blake*, vol. 1, 246). Yeats comments further on Boehme, Blake, and
imagination in "William Blake and the Imagination" (*Essays and Intro-
ductions* [New York, 1961], p. 112). The description of Enitharmon as
Blake's Great Mother symbol occurs on pp. 329–30 and 339 of the first
volume of the Yeats-Ellis *Blake*.

Yeats owned, and heavily annotated, a copy of Franz Hartmann's *The
Life and Doctrines of Jacob Boehme, The God-Taught Philosopher* (London: K. Paul, Trench, Trübner, 1891); see *YL*, 73. On p. 73 of Hartmann
there is a discussion of "eternal mirroring, of God seeing Himself within
Himself." This discussion continues on p. 75 and ff.

12. St. Adamnan or Eunan (624–704), abbot of Iona (an island in the Heb-
rides off the west coast of Scotland), founded a number of churches in Ireland and Scotland; his most well-known work is *Vita Sancti Columbae*. St.
Fursa or Fursey (d. 648/50) was an early Irish missionary who founded
monasteries in Europe which became scholastic centers affecting the development of the entire Continent.

Notes on Traditions and Superstitions

1. Edward Clodd (1840–1930) was an amateur folklorist and at this time
   vice president of the Folk-lore Society.
2. Yeats published "Ireland Bewitched" in September 1899 (see pp. 442–58).
   However, the "deaf coach," as well as accounts of fairy troops and of people who are taken "away," appears in "Irish Witch Doctors," which was
   published in *The Fortnightly Review* in September 1900 (*LAR*, 26–45).
3. Yeats uses this idea of the rooms in old houses seen in flames in one of his
   last plays, *Purgatory* (1939). In that play, the windows in a ruined house
   light up, revealing figures from the past.
4. In his *Autobiographies*, Yeats declares that "much" of *The Celtic Twilight*
   (London, 1893) is "but [the] daily speech" of Mary Battle, George
   Pollexfen's second-sighted servant (*Au*, 84).
5. Yeats refers to Agnes Nichol (1838–1917), second wife of Samuel Guppy,
   whom she married in 1867. Much information on her is available in *Ency-
   clopedia of Occultism and Parapsychology* (Detroit: Gale Research,
   1996). See also Catherine Berry, *Experiences in Spiritualism* (London:
   J. Burns, 1876). Yeats refers to the famous "transit of Mrs. Guppy" on
   3 June 1871, when the English medium appeared in the center of a spiritualist's table during a seance. Mrs. Samuel Guppy's career, which had
   begun in the late sixties with the materialization of flowers, fruit, and live
   eels at her seances, culminated in "spirit photography," the practice of sitting for photographic portraits so that a spirit's image would also appear,
   a practice which Yeats was much later to undertake. The "transit" was
   widely reported, but Yeats's egg and saucepan are confusing. Contempo-

rary accounts of Mrs. Guppy's feat reported that, having been doing her accounts at the time, she appeared with pen and paper, on which she had just written the word *onions*.

6. Yeats includes this description of the Banshee in his sketch of Paddy Flynn, "A Teller of Tales," in *The Celtic Twilight* (London, 1893), p. 33.

The Irish Literary Theatre

1. Charles Stewart Parnell (1846–91) was an Irish nationalist leader. He was president of the Irish National Land League for which he was imprisoned in 1878; as chair of the Home Rule party in the British Parliament, he convinced Gladstone and the Liberal Party of the rightness of Home Rule. His ability to achieve Home Rule for Ireland was destroyed when a Captain Patrick O'Shea brought a divorce suit against his wife, Katherine, and named Parnell as her lover. The publicity surrounding this affair divided Parnell's party and Gladstone's and effectively shelved the issue of Home Rule. Parnell married Kitty O'Shea but died five months after. His parliamentary candidates were subsequently unsuccessful when they ran for reelection.

   Yeats's reference should be to *The Dublin Daily Express*, owned during the nineties by Horace C. Plunkett (1854–1932), the agricultural reformer and statesman, who bought the paper to publicize his farm policies. During the later nineties, his paper gave much space to contemporary Irish literature, and figures such as AE, John Eglinton, William Larminie, and Yeats all contributed articles.

2. Edward Martyn (1859–1923) was one of the founders, with Yeats and Lady Gregory, of the Irish Literary Theatre. His play *The Heather Field* (1899), along with Yeats's *The Countess Cathleen* (first published in 1892), was one of the first plays to be performed by the theater.

3. For more on Ibsen, see "Irish Folk Tales," note 5. In referring to a "circular," Yeats probably meant the "Plans and Methods" section of the May 1899 issue of *Beltaine,* in which he outlined the guiding principles of the Irish Literary Theatre.

4. Yeats gives more information about these projects and about the "Musical Festival" in his article "Plans and Methods," which appeared in the May 1899 issue of *Beltaine.* There Yeats writes:

   > The Committee thinks of producing in 1900 Denis Florence Macarthy's translation of Calderon's *St. Patrick's Purgatory,* a play about the conversion of Ireland. Miss Fiona Macleod has written, or is writing, three plays, *The House of Beauty, Fand and Cuchullain,* and *The Tanist,* an Irish historical play. Others, too, have written or are writing plays, so that there will be no lack of work to select from. In all or almost all cases the plays must be published before they are acted, and no play will be produced which could not hope to succeed as a book (*UP2,* 160).

   Macleod (William Sharp) completed two plays, *The Immortal Hour* and *The House of Usna;* a third, *The Enchanted Valley,* was never finished. Neither these plays, nor any by Standish O'Grady, were ever produced by the Irish Literary Theatre.

   The Gaelic League was founded in 1893 by Douglas Hyde (the league's

first president) and Eoin MacNeill. Its purpose was to revive Irish language and culture.
5. The Italian artist Giovanni Cimabue (1240–1301/2) was so popular that his Madonna was carried through the streets of Florence during religious processions. "The Ballad of Chevy Chase," one of the oldest English ballads, has been traced back as far as the fifteenth century.
6. *"guys"*: The *Oxford English Dictionary* (2nd ed., 1989) offers the following as one definition of "guy": "a person of grotesque appearance, esp. with reference to dress; a 'fright.'"

The Dominion of Dreams

1. *corrie:* A word derived from Scottish Gaelic meaning "a more or less circular hollow on a mountain side, surrounded by steep slopes or precipices" (*Oxford English Dictionary,* 2nd ed., 1989).
2. *"three cries of the curlew":* This passage, from the tale "Dalua" in *The Dominion of Dreams* (New York: Frederick A. Stokes and Co., 1900), reads "three wails of the wailing cry of the curlew" (9).
3. *Amadan Dhu:* It is "Amadan-Dhu" in Sharp (9).
4. Aphrodite (her name means "foam-born") is the Greek goddess of love and beauty; according to Hesiod, Aphrodite arose out of the foam of the sea in the place where Uranus's genitals had fallen off after he was mutilated by Cronus; it is to her that Paris awarded the Apple of Discord, an act that ultimately led to the Trojan War.
     In Greek mythology, Prometheus, whose name means forethought, is the son of Iapetus; he created man out of clay and water. Prometheus also provided man with fire.
5. For Swedenborg and Boehme, see "The Writings of William Blake," note 10.
6. Eoan and Finola appear in "The Birds of Emar," pp. 260–74.
7. *mistletoe berries:* Sharp reads "mistletoe-berries" with a comma (269).
8. The story of Aevgrain is told in "Honey of the Wild Bees" (247–59). The sentence quoted here continues beyond Yeats's quote and is found on p. 257.
9. *". . . some forlorn place":* Sharp reads "a forlorn place" (4).
10. On p. 10, in "Dalua," Dalua says, "I'm always hearing the three old ancientest cries: the cry of the curlew on the hill, the wail of the wind, and the sighing of the wave."

Ireland Bewitched

1. See "The Tribes of Danu," note 22.
2. The stories told about blacksmiths from this point on to p. 169 were given by Lady Gregory in *Visions and Beliefs,* vol. 2, pp. 239–41, in chapter 11, "Blacksmiths."
3. In Lady Gregory, his name is given as "Pat Doherty."
4. Biddy Early is mentioned in other articles in this folklore series, though much more space is given to her here. Under the heading "Seers and Healers," a whole chapter is devoted to her in *Visions and Beliefs,* vol. 1, pp. 35–69. See "The Tribes of Danu," note 21.
5. Yeats's friend is Lady Gregory. This visit is described in the foreword to the "Seers and Healers" section of *Visions and Beliefs,* vol. 1, pp. 35–37.

6. In Lady Gregory's version, this statement is attributed to "The Little Girl of Biddy Early's House" (vol. 1, 46–47).
7. In Lady Gregory, the pensioner is "A Blacksmith I met near Tulla" (vol. 1, 7–8).
8. The man's name in Lady Gregory's account is "Daniel Curtin" (vol. 1, 41).
9. Yeats relates a story by a witch doctor above in "The Prisoners of the Gods," p. 379.
10. In Lady Gregory, the woman's name is "Mrs. McDonagh" (vol. 1, 53).
11. This story is attributed to "An Old Woman" in Lady Gregory (vol. 1, 55).
12. In Lady Gregory, the woman's name is "Mrs. Locke" (vol. 1, 60–61).
13. In Lady Gregory, the priest's name is "Folan" (vol. 1, 61).
14. In Lady Gregory, the following two stories are attributed to Daniel Shea (vol. 1, 55–58).
15. In Lady Gregory, he is "old James Hill of Creen" (vol. 1, 56).
16. In Lady Gregory, Mark Spelman is "Ned Cahel" (vol. 1, 58).
17. May Day is 1 May and is associated with the Celtic festival Beltaine; Midsummer Day is 24 June; the corresponding Celtic festival Yeats is thinking of may be Lughnasa, which is traditionally celebrated on 1 August. November Eve, usually known as Halloween, falls on 31 October; Samhain is its Celtic counterpart and marks the beginning of the Celtic New Year.
18. The following story is attributed to "Mrs. Dillon" in Lady Gregory (vol. 1, 59–60).
19. *Lanberis:* "Llanberis" in Lady Gregory. This story appears on p. 60.
20. In Lady Gregory, the following story is attributed to "The Spinning Woman" (vol. 1, 51–52).
21. This story is attributed to "Bartley Coen" in Lady Gregory (vol. 1, 44). Coen is also mentioned above on p. 455 of this article.
22. In Lady Gregory, the woman is "Mrs. McDonagh" (vol. 1, 53).

The Literary Movement in Ireland

1. Unionists were those who opposed Home Rule for Ireland; Nationalists were those who not only sought Home Rule (a separate parliament) for Ireland but also wanted to make Ireland a separate nation-state.
2. Yeats is referring to the Young Ireland movement of the 1840s.
3. Sir Walter Scott (1771–1832), Scottish novelist; Thomas Campbell (1777–1844), Scottish poet; Thomas Babington Macaulay (1800–59), Scottish historian and statesman; Pierre-Jean Béranger (1780–1857), French poet; Robert Burns (1759–96), Scottish poet. For more on Yeats's opinion of these writers, see p. 39 of "Twilight Propaganda" in the introduction to *UP*1.
4. See "The Irish Literary Theatre," note 1.
5. The Irish Literary Society was founded by Yeats and T. W. Rolleston in December of 1891 in London to promote the appreciation and production of a national Irish literature in English.
6. Wolfe Tone (1763–98) was a leader of the 1798 uprising. Robert Emmet (1778–1803) led a rebellion in 1803. Owen Roe O'Neill (ca. 1590–1649) commanded the Ulster forces that fought Cromwell. Patrick Sarsfield (?–1693), an Irish Jacobite nobleman and soldier, left Ireland after the defeat of King James at the Battle of the Boyne in 1690 and died in the service of the king of France.

7. The Feis Ceoil or annual Musical Festival was begun in 1897 in Dublin. The Gaelic League was founded in 1893 with Douglas Hyde as its president.
8. See "The Ainu," note 6.
9. *dome of many-coloured glass:* This phrase is from stanza 52 of Percy Bysshe Shelley's poem "Adonais."
10. This poem, "Happy It Is," was translated in Hyde's *Love Songs of Connacht* (London/Dublin, 1893) in a version in the original meter. The text quoted by Yeats is an adaptation of the literal translation given in Hyde's footnote to his verse version (pp. 131–32 of the 1893 edition of *Love Songs*).
11. This poem, "O Maurya," is also an adaptation of the version given by Hyde in a footnote to his verse version (p. 83 of *Love Songs*). Yeats reviewed *Love Songs of Connacht* in *The Bookman*, October 1893 (see "Old Gaelic Love Songs," pp. 218–21).
12. Anthony Raftery (ca. 1784–1835), the blind Gaelic poet, was Yeats's continual example of the popular poet. After hearing the poet's verses on Mary Hynes, Yeats began, in "Dust Hath Closed Helen's Eye," his identification of Raftery and Hynes with Homer and Helen and also the creation of the tower at Ballylee, near which Hynes lived and died, as his personal symbol. The translation by Lady Gregory which follows is given in another version in her *Poets and Dreamers* (Dublin, 1903), pp. 32–33.
13. Ballylee Castle is near Gort in Co. Galway. Yeats bought and restored its Norman keep and sometimes lived there in the summer. He called it Thoor Ballylee.
14. *Lough Greine:* This may be the same body of water as Lough Gráinne, which *A Dictionary of Irish Mythology* notes was home to a monster which appeared every seven years (p. 172).
15. A different version of this poem appears in *Poets and Dreamers* (25).
16. It is probable that no specific passage in Homer is intended.
17. "They should have said, 'God bless her,' so that their admiration might not give the fairies power over her." [Yeats's note]
18. In Greek mythology, Helen was the daughter of Zeus and Leda; reputed to be the most beautiful woman in the world, her kidnapping by Paris from her husband, Menelaus, resulted in the war between Greece and Troy.
19. Alexander Gilchrist in his *Life of William Blake* (London, 1863) recounts "One day, a traveller was telling bright wonders of some foreign city. 'Do you call *that* splendid?' broke in young Blake; 'I should call a city splendid in which the houses were of gold, the pavement of silver, the gates ornamented with precious stones!'" (vol. 1, 7).
20. The story Yeats recounts here forms the subject of his early poem "The Wanderings of Oisin." "Usheen" is also spelled "Oisin" and "Ossian."
21. Queen Maeve, or Medbh, was queen of the western province of Connacht. A formidable warrior, she was an opponent of Cuchulain and eventually brought about his downfall. She figures largely in the *Táin Bó Cuailgne* (The Cattle Raid of Cooley). The mountain where Maeve is said to be buried is Knocknarea in Co. Sligo.
22. *buskins:* boots associated with those worn by Greek or Roman actors.
23. William Blake wrote in a letter to William Hayley, 6 May 1800, "The ruins of Time builds [*sic*] Mansions in Eternity" (*Life of William Blake,* ed. Geoffrey Keynes [London: Nonesuch Press, 1925], p. 797).
24. The poem is from the story "Daluan" in Nora (Hopper) Chesson's *Ballads*

in Prose (London, 1894). Hopper reads "lost and won"; "gain—the King of Ireland's son—"; and "shadows—the King" (97).
25. Heinrich Heine (1797–1856); a German poet, whose *Buch der Lieder* (1827) is known for its romanticism tinged with irony.
26. Dante Gabriel Rossetti (1828–82); an English poet and painter, he is often called the founder of the Pre-Raphaelite movement in England. George Frederick Watts (1817–1904), whose work Yeats admired "when least a moralist" (*Au*, 403–4), is the subject of a lecture by Yeats in 1906 (see "The Watts Pictures" in *UP2*, 342–45).
27. In his notebook to "A Vision of the Last Judgment," Blake said, "The Nature of My Work is Visionary or Imaginative; it is an Endeavour to Restore what the Ancients call'd the Golden Age" (*The Writings of William Blake*, ed. Geoffrey Keynes [London: Nonesuch Press, 1925], vol. 3, p. 146).
28. Ecclesiasticus 42:25. The 1888 edition of *The Apocrypha*, edited by Henry Wace (London, 1888), reads "All things are double one against another" (vol. 2, p. 205).
29. Slieve Gullion, a mountain near Newry in Co. Armagh, has a cairn on its top that is reputed to be the cairn of the chieftain Cuailgne.

   In "The Galway Palins," Yeats speaks of "Cruachmaa of the Sidhe" as a home of the sidhe, or fairies (*E&I*, 211). James McGarry identifies Cruachmaa as the "alleged . . . underworld dwelling of Finnvarra, King of the Fairies of Connacht" (*Place Names in the Writings of William Butler Yeats* [Toronto: Macmillan Company of Canada, 1976], p. 39).

   There is a cairn on top of the hill known as Knocknarea in Co. Sligo which, if not the burial place of Queen Maeve, is at least reputed to have been built in her honor.
30. Alexander Lawrence (1764–1835) led the attack on Seringapatam, India, in 1799. Arthur Wellesley, first duke of Wellington (1769–1852), a British general, famous for his victory over Napoleon at Waterloo, also had a career as governor of Seringapatam in India and then as prime minister of Britain from 1828 to 1830.

INDEX

Page numbers in *italics* refer to illustrations.